II

People and Production

FERNAND BRAUDEL always insisted on the necessity of world history and was rewarded with a worldwide reputation. In his native France he was, until his death in 1985, the acknowledged head of his profession. 'For us he is a prince,' wrote Georges Duby of the Collège de France on the publication of *Civilization and Capitalism*.

Born in a village in Lorraine in 1902, Braudel graduated in history in 1923 and subsequently taught in Algeria, Paris and São Paulo. During the five years he spent as a prisoner-of-war in Germany he wrote the thesis that was to be published in 1949 under the title *La Méditerranée et le monde Méditerranéen à l'époque de Philippe II*. In 1946 he became one of the editorial board of *Annales*, the famous journal founded by Marc Bloch and Lucien Febvre, whom he succeeded at the Collège de France in 1949. In 1956 he became head of the VIème section de L'Ecole des Hautes Etudes, a new department formed to promote the relations betwen history and other social studies. From 1962 until his death he was the chief administrator of the Maison des Sciences de l'Homme.

from the reviews of this volume of *The Identity of France*:

'Braudel was a connoisseur of the varieties of time. His mind was ingenious, capacious and littered with strange objects. It is never a waste of time to enter it.' Eric Christiansen, *Independent*

'History and geography were never so sophisticatedly bonded as in Braudel's insatiable reading of his beloved France.' Frederic Raphael, *Sunday Times*

'Siân Reynolds can now be seen to have done for Braudel what C.K. Scott Moncrieff once did for Proust.' Keith Thomas, *Observer*

'This book should be read by anyone who finds historical writing dull or irrelevant to contemporary society.' *Glasgow Herald*

Books by Fernand Braudel also published by Collins

FERNAND BRAUDEL

THE IDENTITY
OF FRANCE

Volume II
People and Production

Translated from the French
by Siân Reynolds

FontanaPress
An Imprint of HarperCollinsPublishers

First published in Great Britain in 1990
by Collins

This edition first issued in 1991 by Fontana Press,
an imprint of HarperCollins Publishers,
77–85 Fulham Palace Road,
Hammersmith, London W6 8JB

9 8 7 6 5 4 3 2 1

First published in France under the title *L'Identité de la France*, 1986
The contents of this single volume were published in France as volumes II and III

Diagrams and maps in this translation by Leslie Robinson

The Author asserts the moral right to be
identified as the author of this work

Printed and bound in Great Britain by
HarperCollins Book Manufacturing, Glasgow

CONTENTS

When there was world enough and time, 23 – Bodies and
tools, 28 – The great change: from the Stone Age to
agriculture, 34 – Heterogeneity and diversity, 37 – The age
of metals, 46 – Celts or Gauls? A civilization or a history?, 54
– Force of numbers, 66.

The Roman conquest of Gaul: can it be explained?, 73 – The
apogee of Roman Gaul: the reign of Commodus, 82 – Roman
Gaul in trouble: internal division and barbarian invasion, 86
– An ever-kindled fire of protest, 89 – The barbarian
invasions: not to be underestimated, 95 – Rome, a world-
economy, 99 – Merovingian Gaul, 107 – Did Charlemagne's
Empire ever exist?, 114 – The beginnings of Europe: the
birth and establishment of feudalism, 116 – The last
barbarian invasions, 119 – Population and the economy, 120
– Cycles going into reverse, 126.

The tenth century: the end of Rome, 131 – The rise of
Europe in its earliest form, 137 – A stroke of luck for

BOOK TWO   PRODUCTION: A 'PEASANT ECONOMY' UNTIL THE TWENTIETH CENTURY

PART III   THE RURAL INFRASTRUCTURES

CONTENTS

CONTENTS

LIST OF FIGURES

LIST OF FIGURES

TRANSLATOR'S NOTE

Like its predecessor, Volume II of *The Identity of France* carries a glossary at the end of the book of terms left in French in the text and mainly referring to institutions or geographical features peculiar to France.

Once more, I am very grateful to Madame Paule Braudel for her expert and patient help with queries. On completing this volume, I should also particularly like to record my heartfelt thanks to Richard Ollard, whose stern eye, scholarly knowledge and elegance of style have been brought to bear on all my translations of Fernand Braudel's books, for which he has been chief consultant; and to his successor at Collins, Stuart Proffitt, who has steered *The Identity of France* safely to port with the greatest of professional care and cordiality. With all this help, there shouldn't be any mistakes, but if there are, they are mine.

S.R.

VOLUME II

PEOPLE AND PRODUCTION

Foreword

'The difficulty is to find the assumptions that
are relevant to reality.'
Joan Robinson[1]

In Volume I of this book, I set out to relocate the history of France
within its geographical context – a context both too vast and too
rich in contrasts, with the result that several 'Frances' had to co-
exist side by side. If the same history is now considered within its
major *chronological* context, we shall this time discover a series of
consecutive Frances, similar yet dissimilar, alternately expanding
and contracting, united and divided, serene and tormented, privileged and underprivileged. It is this sequence of realities and transformations, or as I prefer to call them *all-inclusive cycles*, that I
should like to map here, for they can be viewed as so many landmarks in time, perhaps even as explanations. In their ebb and flow,
these cycles have stirred up the living mass of our history, as the
tides stir the waters of the sea.

I originally entitled the first part of this volume *Long-term Cycles
in French History*. Then I was afraid this might lead to ambiguity,
since the word *cycle* is as a rule used only by economists. In their
parlance, every cycle tells a two-part story, a journey up and a
journey down, with a peak in the middle. First comes the ascendant
phase, the upturn; then the downward phase, the recession; with
the peak marking the watershed. The ascent starts from a low
point, the downturn ends with another low point. I do indeed
intend to follow oscillations of this general pattern, but to do so
over the long term, something not habitually attempted by economists or indeed by historians. Yet I sincerely believe that history
needs this concept and the somewhat adventurous conceptual
framework it implies.

Let us be clear what we are talking about: these long cycles,
covering several centuries, are not of purely economic origin.
They do not correspond to a historical materialism which assumes

15

the economy to be the basic cause and motive force of all human existence. As always, causes and consequences are mingled and connected in an interactive system where each may by turns become cause, driving force, or consequence. Any period of prolonged decline, any long-term rise in living standards, any economic depression that does not right itself in the short term necessarily implies a combination of factors which may include anything: politics, society, culture, technology, war, et cetera. It is the complex *as a whole* that either stops working properly and begins to destroy itself, or else regains its capacities and stimulates recovery. In other words, a general decline or revival is plain to see, although its true causes may be virtually impossible to identify.

In the end, I am confident that the general reader will be sufficiently familiar with the language of economics (if only from his or her daily paper) to accept the extension of meaning I have given to the word *cycle*. Historians may be more reluctant. We are professionally conditioned after all to consider one at a time the various 'Frances' that have succeeded each other: our ranks include specialists on prehistory, on independent Gaul or the Gallo-Roman period, medievalists, modernists and so on. And that is right and proper. But all these different Frances must somehow be brought into relation with each other. Is it going too far to suggest that their history is persistently cyclical? Each comes into being, flourishes and declines. Each succeeds its predecessor, but without any interruption.

If in this second volume I have chosen to speak the language of demography and economics in order to sketch in the main lines of the past, that is because they present us with the most obvious and easily appreciated signs of these deep-seated movements. How many people were there in the past? And how did they manage to survive, to keep going, as material factors sometimes forced them to move forward or back from the position they had reached? Population (or as André Piatier puts it 'human capital') can be a vital indicator: it is, says Guy Bois,[2] 'the least arbitrary of criteria'. The first two parts of this volume are therefore devoted to population; the last two to economics.

BOOK ONE

———————✤———————

PEOPLE

Numbers and Variations

PART I

The Population of France from Prehistoric Times until the Year 1000

It has been calculated – a little wildly perhaps but graphically – that the total number of people who have lived on earth since the species became established as *Homo sapiens sapiens*, is somewhere between 70 and 100 thousand million. An awesome statistic. 'Will there be room for all these people on the Day of Judgment?' as Alfred Sauvy once half-seriously wrote to me.[1] By these calculations, a total of some 1,000 million people might conceivably have once lived on 'French' soil, breathing, working, leaving a legacy, however slight, to be incorporated into our immense inheritance. There are about 50 million people living in France today; the dead would add up to about twenty times that figure. And we should not forget that they are still present 'under the feet of the living'. The soil of a vineyard in Champagne, Médoc or Burgundy, 'is an artificial soil, fashioned by two thousand years or so of labour'.[2]

So it is not surprising if the territory we call France has for thousands of years been cultivated, if it has gradually become covered with roads and paths, huts, houses, hamlets, villages and towns – 'planted with peasants', as someone once dared to write. The sheer number of people made a difference from the start, influencing the course of events, consecrating the successes of history and indeed prehistory, whether one thinks of the splendours of Lascaux, the great age of dolmens and menhirs, or the glories of Romanesque or Gothic architecture. The size of the population, a multiplier of everything, played its part in the spread of religion, the progress of the state, the new capitalism of the Italian city-states from the twelfth century and so on. Sometimes it worked in the other direction, during those breakdowns or relapses of which Malthus was the gloomy prophet.

No one can fail to be aware today that size of population weighs heavily on the destiny of the world: there were 4.4 thousand million people living on the earth in 1980. 'There will be at least 6 thousand million by the year 2000 and realistically, the number is unlikely to stabilize at less than 10 or 11 thousand million' in the next century, according to the experts who can hardly (alas) be completely mistaken.[3] In the seventeenth century, it used to be thought that power lay in numbers. The 'most widely accepted maxim in politics', noted the French economist Ange Goudar in the eighteenth century, 'is that only a large population can create a mighty state'. What are 'the true interests of our kings?' he asked: 'their power lies in the number of their subjects'.[4] But numbers have their drawbacks as well: who would now dare to apply Goudar's formulas to the present day, when we are all aware of the problems faced by India or China in their need to achieve a drastic reduction in the birth-rate?

Such was not the case in the past. Comparative overpopulation did occur from time to time. But famine and epidemic invariably corrected the balance. It is only in modern times that we have seen a constant, if irregular, expansion of the world population.

CHAPTER ONE

The Prehistoric Population

> 'The attitude that accepts the primacy of History over everything that preceded it is dishonest, and what is more, lacking in scientific rigour.'
> *Jean Markale*[5]

Never say that prehistory is not history. Never say that there was 'no such thing' as Gaul before Gaul, or France before France, or seek to deny that many features of both Gaul and France can be explained by the millennia dating from before the Roman conquest. Think rather of 'all the labour of prehistoric times, during the longest age of the human race' – as Nietzsche once reflected.[6] Unimaginable stretches of lived time, piled one on top of another, reach down to the present day, unaware of them though we may be. How then can the link, the continuity between history and prehistory be denied? At one time, historians used to stake their reputations on exploring from both sides the artificial frontiers erected between antiquity and the Middle Ages,[7] or between the Middle Ages and the modern period. The great challenge of our own time must surely be the divide between prehistory and history.

Unfortunately, the study of prehistory dates from barely a century and a half ago. It was in 1837 that Boucher de Perthes first discovered, embedded in the alluvial terraces of the Somme, flint tools carved by prehistoric men and recognized to be such – recognized by their discoverer that is, for Boucher de Perthes had great difficulty in persuading anyone else of his conclusions until at least 1860. The early volumes of his work *Antiquités celtiques et antédiluviennes*, published in 1847 and successive years, were greeted with the same scepticism and scorn as Darwin's *Origin of Species* in 1859. It was in the same year, 1859, that two leading English scholars crossed the Channel to investigate Boucher de Perthes's discoveries and granted him their approval.[8] Such approval was a revolutionary step, since to recognize as human the traces of beings who had lived at the same time as animal species now extinct, in rock layers agreed by geologists to be of extreme antiquity, necessarily meant relocating the origins of mankind in a far-distant past and this in turn implied the overthrow of long-held assumptions, a revolution in the mind which it is hard for us to imagine today. Hitherto, even scholars had accepted traditional interpretations of the Bible, according to which man had been created merely four millennia before the birth of Christ. Isaac Newton, who was interested in other things besides mathematics and astronomy, had poured scorn on chronologies drawn up by Egyptian scribes vain enough to claim that their ancient monarchy was 'some thousands of years older than the world'.[9]

Thus within a few decades, thanks to the work of Boucher de Perthes and more particularly to that of his contemporary Charles Darwin (both of whom were regarded as scandalous in their own day), the scope of human history had been extended breathtakingly far back in time, whether in terms of the origins of mankind or of the earliest forms of farming, the first villages, the first towns. Extended along with the rest, of course, was our present subject, the history of what is now France.

As tends to happen, not surprisingly perhaps, since they demanded a leap from one intellectual realm to another, the startling new perspectives of prehistory did not immediately disturb the historians of the day: to them the new perspectives remained a matter of little or no concern, lost in the mists of time. At best they amounted to a sort of preface, to be mentioned in an aside, or a few preliminary pages, before embarking on the usual historical narratives, as if nothing had happened.

But as prehistory began to come up with more and more evidence, calculations and hypotheses, it was in fact digging a bottomless pit, chronologically preceding the centuries of recorded history. Bear in mind that history as we generally reckon it represents less than a thousandth part of the total span of human evolution. And for that evolution even to become imaginable required the coming together of various sciences all drawn on by prehistorians: palynology (the study of ancient pollen deposits), palaeontology, comparative anatomy, retrospective haematology, geology, zoology, botany and also, more recently, the study of present-day primitive peoples and finally ethology (animal behaviour) – since mankind, originally thrown upon its modest resources in the natural world, was for millennia on end one animal species among others, surviving only by virtue of social bonds similar to those of animal societies.

All these scientific contributions do not simplify our task: they have after all to be reinterpreted. As Colin Renfrew has pointed out, we cannot expect related disciplines to provide 'a ready-made answer' to our own questions.[10] What is more, the very recent development of new methods of dating (carbon 14, potassium-argon, dendrochronology – reading tree-rings – or other even more sophisticated methods) has led to a profound and disturbing reappraisal of the chronological frameworks and patterns of cultural influence established by two or three previous generations of eminent prehistorians. The prehistory of Europe in particular has to be reinterpreted from the beginning.[11]

All these circumstances make prehistory an exciting and fascinating science but also treacherous terrain: it allows us to approach the truth only by painful sequences of errors, corrections, and provisional hypotheses. It is a science subject to constant revision.

When there was world enough and time

On the really fundamental question, the origins of mankind, nothing can be said with certainty. The discoveries made in one continent after another are continually modifying the overall picture to which they all contribute.

In the present state of knowledge, seeking to trace the human tree back to its primate and hominid branches via the australopithecines of East Africa (and depending on the definition we accept of the earliest hominids),[12] takes us back five, fifteen or even 40 million years BC. As Gabriel Camps has remarked resignedly, with every fresh discovery 'our origins move further and further back into the past'.[13]

If however we confine our inquiries to *Homo* proper, present-day thinking dates mankind's appearance from the moment when the species stood upright – about two million years ago, or perhaps a little earlier. This first biped, *Homo habilis*, was not the first creature to have shaped stones for use as tools. Certain of the australopithecines had already done so. But the upright posture freed his hands, and it was from this time too that his brain capacity would steadily increase, from an initial 600 to 700 cubic centimetres.[14] It was the combination of this over-developed brain, the organ of command, and its servant the hand, 'that enabled man to develop his astonishing powers of all kinds' – conscience, memory, language.[15] After *Homo habilis*, who seems to have appeared first in Africa, came *Homo erectus*, who peopled the temperate zones, then *Homo sapiens* and finally *Homo sapiens sapiens* – the last-named being the latest stage of evolution – you and me.

As far as we can tell, *Homo erectus* may have been present on 'French' territory by about 1,800,000 BC. At Chilhac (Haute-Loire) in the Massif Central, there recently came to light some 'quartz [fragments] undoubtedly carved [by human hands] associated with fauna from the older Quaternary period (Villefranchian)'.[16] These are thought to be the most ancient human traces so far found in Europe. But remains discovered at Solilhac in the same region, dating from about a million years ago, take us on to firmer ground chronologically.[17] Another landmark is provided by the remains, about 950,000 years old, discovered during the excavation in 1958–63 of the cave known as the Trou des Renards (the Foxes' Lair) beside the Vallonet, a small stream in the commune of Roquebrune (Alpes-Maritimes). Here the remains of various ancient fauna – macaque monkeys, *Elephas meridionalis*, horses and cats – were found in association with roughly hewn bones and pebbles. There were no human remains, alas (stones survive longer than fossil skeletons) but it was clear that the cave had been lived in by humans. This is so far the oldest known inhabited site located in Europe.[18]

When one remembers that prehistory, on French soil, covers the period up to the later Iron Age, about 500 BC, one realizes what a breathtaking period of time we are dealing with: almost two million years, 2,000 millennia, 20,000 centuries! To find our bearings on a time-scale like this that defies understanding and imagination, we must turn first to the geologists for help. They have measured the successive ages of the earth and assigned to the historical development of the human race – 'hominization' – the entire Quaternary (or Pleistocene) era, adding for good measure the Villefranchian period (from the end of the Tertiary era) and stopping short at the end of the Quaternary era, the period in which we now live (the Holocene).

Within this vast time-span, geology distinguishes four long ice ages, named by Albrecht Penck after the streams in the Bavarian Alps where he first detected evidence of very ancient, major glaciations: in chronological order, they are known as Günz, Mindel, Riss and Würm. The Günz glaciation begins about two million years BC, while Würm ends in 10,000 BC. Between these glacial episodes, each of which came on very gradually, there were of course interglacial intervals when the temperature rose, and they too were very long and irregular. Hence the sub-periods (Riss I, II, III; Würm I, II, III, IV, V) corresponding to a series of slow changes in the climate almost imperceptible at the time, but cumulatively amounting to immense upheavals.[19] Humans, animals and plants were driven north or south depending on whether warmth or cold dominated: species accustomed to a mild climate were driven south by the cold, while hunters used to living off herds of reindeer or wild horses were drawn northwards in pursuit of them during warmer periods. The whole environment was transformed each time.

To have some idea of what this meant (and since what once happened in the distant past could *theoretically* recur in the far-distant future) imagine what a new ice age might be like, several thousand or million years from now, assuming the continents to remain in their present relative positions.[20] In Europe, a thick layer

of ice would cover the entire Scandinavian peninsula, the Netherlands, Germany, Poland, northern Russia, and the British Isles as
far south as London. France would escape the major glaciers, as it
did in the past, except in mountainous areas, the Alps in particular.
But the Paris basin, including Paris itself, and most of France,
would be covered once more by a Siberian type of tundra, steppe
or forest. There would be an invasion of ice, of different vegetation and trees, with infinite consequences for people, animals and
the whole natural world. Frozen into mighty glaciers, water would
retreat at sea level, exposing once more immense stretches of the
seabed, which would thus link islands like Britain to the Continent. At the foot of the glaciers, moraines would amass great heaps
of debris created by glacial erosion, while the lighter surface matter would be blown away by the wind to form beds of loess, as happened in the past in China and across Europe. The loess of the
Danube basin or the plain of Alsace, the silt of the plateaux round
Paris are of precisely such origin, and these light soils, easy to
plough, were the chosen sites for the first land cultivation both in
France and in the rest of Europe.

In order to date any prehistoric site, the first thing to establish,
therefore, is which ice age or interglacial period one is dealing
with, by identifying animal and vegetable remains, or the type of
diet suggested by the contents of middens. The inhabitants of the
cave on the Vallonet mentioned earlier, the earliest known European site, lived about a million years ago, during the period known
as the Villefranchian, when the Mediterranean south was subject to
the rigours of the Günz ice age. Stones split by frost have been
found there alongside hewn flints and the remains of a cold climate
fauna.[21]

In about 10,000 BC, when the last ice age (Würm) came to an
end, and a temperate climate became established – broadly similar
to that of today – the reindeer moved back north; the mammoths,
unable to adapt, died out. Some of these mastodons, preserved
intact in the permafrost of Siberia, have been found in quite recent
times by scientific expeditions. But they had long figured in the
legends of the tribes of northern Siberia. The Yakuts and
Tunguzes, who sometimes found them frozen upright, as if

FIGURE 1
Distribution of the mammoth between 15,000 and 10,000 BC

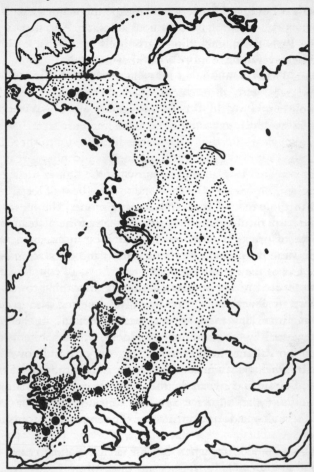

During this period, when glaciers covered much of Europe and Asia, there was a large zone of steppe and tundra, stretching from Northern Spain to Siberia, in which men and wild beasts (reindeer and mammoth in particular) moved about. Almost the whole of France was covered by this inhabitable zone.

After L.-R. Nougier, *Naissance de la civilisation*, 1986.

they had just died (and whose dogs immediately devoured them) imagined them as enormous moles, living underground, or as aquatic creatures who died immediately they came up into the air and the light.[22]

The temperate climate was also variable – so there followed a succession of different prevailing climates: pre-boreal, boreal, Atlantic, sub-boreal and sub-Atlantic.[23] Each one tended to favour certain species – as it might be cattle, horses, ash, oak, beech, chestnut or hazel – and this in turn had automatic repercussions on the diet and habits of mankind.

Bodies and tools

For many thousands of years, mankind wandered among the wild beasts, across the frozen tundra or through forests that became waterlogged whenever the earth warmed up again. Signs of his passage still however survive: bone fragments or entire skeletons, traces of hearths and encampments, and above all countless tools, of which there must be millions, although many of them have by now been broken, lost in earthworks or draining operations, or diverted from museums by amateur collectors of prehistoric artefacts.

Bodies, or what remain of them, constitute the bulk of the evidence. But the most ancient skeletons have disappeared, dissolved away by acid soils. In France, the earliest known tools date from over a million years before the earliest human fossils so far discovered – a jawbone found in 1949 in a cave near Montmaurin (Pyrénées-Orientales). Similar to the famous Mauer jawbone (600,000 BC) it is of uncertain date but certainly more recent (perhaps 450,000 or 400,000 BC)[24] and probably predates by some 100,000 or 150,000 years Tautavel man, whose discovery near the village of that name in the Pyrénées-Orientales caused a great stir on two occasions: first in 1971, when the left parietal of a skull belonging to a young male adult aged about twenty was found: then in 1979, when about three metres away the corresponding right parietal was found, making it possible to reconstitute the

FIGURE 2
Evidence of more sophisticated tools

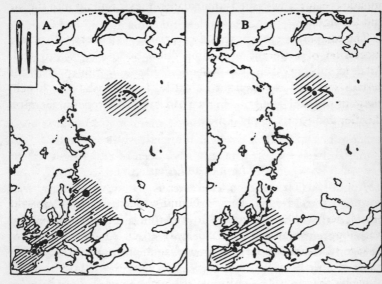

A. Finds of eyed needles (pre-20,000 BC).
B. Finds of composite tools, consisting of blades or points made of
either flint or bone, which were inserted into grooves in wooden or
bone handles.

---

entire skull of a *Homo erectus* with a cranial capacity of almost 1,100
cubic centimetres; what was more, the internal surface of the
frontal bone incorporated a Broca convolution as developed as that
of present-day human beings. Hence the dramatic conclusion that
this prehistoric being could speak, whatever his language may have
been.[25]

On the other hand, he ate raw the meat he had hunted. In the
cave of La Caune de l'Arago where these remains were found,
overlooking the narrow valley of the Verdouble (a tributary of the
Agly) there were no traces of a hearth,[26] although the use of fire
goes back about 500,000 years and many hearths have been found
in the hut-dwellings of Terra Amata near Nice (circa 400,000

BC).[27] The Verdouble valley, enclosed between two cliff-faces, provided a natural shelter, particularly valuable no doubt to Tautavel man, who lived at the time of the Mindel glaciation; and it must also have favoured the plentiful fauna identifiable from the bones piled up at different levels inside the cave by generations of hunters: horses, elephants, aurochs, mouflons, musk-oxen, deer, reindeer, cave lions, Arctic foxes, bears, lynx, panthers and hares. Mingled with the animal bones are human remains which have been crushed in order to extract the bone marrow or brains – apparently evidence of cannibalism,[28] which is also found in many other prehistoric sites, even in the sixth millennium BC. Such cannibalism seems sometimes to have been of ritual significance, obviously so when it is found in association with burials.[29]

About 100,000 years ago, *Homo erectus* gave way to *Homo sapiens*, so-called Neanderthal man.[30] The Neanderthalers undoubtedly peopled the entire Middle East and Europe including France. Their presence outside this large area is still a matter of controversy at least in their European form, which has pronounced characteristics and is easily recognizable. Neanderthal man, so long considered to have been a thickset, brutish species, has now been rehabilitated: endowed with a 'large' brain, larger even than that of present-day man (1600 cubic centimetres as compared to 1400), he was a skilled tool-handler, with an articulated language.[31] One conclusive detail is that Neanderthal man was the first of the species to bury his dead. In this respect, he represents 'a fully-evolved human', 'a whole man' as Pierre Chaunu would put it. The many specimens that have been unearthed (about a hundred in France alone) present the same features throughout Europe, whether in terms of lifestyle and stone tools or in strictly morphological respects. What we have here then is a species with clearly-defined characteristics which remained essentially the same over a mere matter of 60 millennia, or 600 centuries!

Then suddenly, and for no demonstrable reason, this species was wiped out, over a period of five millennia (a short time in evolutionary terms) giving way to *Homo sapiens sapiens*, a completely different species morphologically, already virtually identical with present-day man. How did this transformation take place?

FIGURE 3
Geographical distribution of traces of Neanderthal man (75,000 to 35,000 BC)

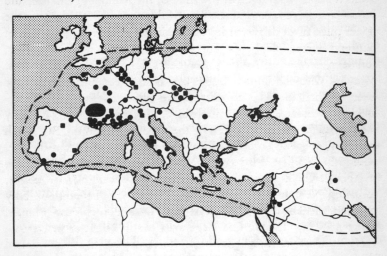

The largest concentration of remains is in France, west of the Massif Central (black patch).

Prehistorians have no ready-made solution to propose, whether in terms of climate or anything else, particularly since no significant human remains have been found dating from the crucial transition period. A general evolution of the entire species can be ruled out: such a vast and stable population, with free genetic interchange, could only have evolved very slowly. In theory then, the Neanderthalers were confronted – peacefully or otherwise – by a new population, one so favoured by circumstances (though we do not know why or how) that it eliminated the original inhabitants in a fairly short space of time. Hence the hypothesis, which remains entirely speculative, that there was some kind of foreign 'invasion', though where the newcomers came from nobody knows, since before their appearance in Europe these 'modern' men were already present at various points of the globe, from Australia to Iraq, from the Sahara to Norway. It is possible that they arrived in

Europe from Palestine where they were already present in about 50,000 BC, alongside authentic Neanderthalers, who did not die out in this region until much later.[32]

By about 35,000 years ago at any rate, *Homo sapiens sapiens* was present almost everywhere on the globe and certainly occupied all of what is now France. This was already 'modern' man, with anatomical characteristics recognizable by medicine today, though with regional differences which prefigure the various physiques found in present-day France: Mediterranean, Alpine, Nordic.[33] The newcomers' evident religious preoccupations probably point to a psychology not unlike our own. And it is with this species that there appears, as if by some miracle, a sense of art and form. It is from the end of the Old Stone Age (the Upper Palaeolithic) that there first appear the extraordinary statuettes apparently representing goddesses of fertility, and above all the wealth of paintings, sculptures and carvings that decorate the walls of the caves, as well as many everyday objects fashioned out of stone, bone, ivory or from the antlers of stag and reindeer. The magnificent cave-paintings, discovered only comparatively recently, are as baffling as they are beautiful.

This multi-faceted art developed slowly, from crude drawings to the extraordinary realism of Lascaux, before being eventually pared down to geometrical signs, no doubt with symbolic significance.[34] But this development was spread over 200 centuries (between about 30,000 and 10,000 BC) which seems an eternity to the modern historian. Think how short by comparison is the age of Romanesque or Gothic architecture, not to mention schools like Impressionism or Cubism, which were the work of no more than a single generation.

Of this early art, France and Northern Spain possess the lion's share. In the lower Vézère valley in the Périgord, where the river forms deep meanders, 'ancient sites are plentiful around and above Les Eyzies: Cro-Magnon, La Mouthe, Les Combarelles, Font de Gaume, Le Cap Blanc, Laussel, La Laugerie, Les Marseilles, La Madeleine, Le Moustier and Lascaux' – so many 'holy places of humanity', writes Pierre Gaxotte, 'with the same claims as Egypt, Nineveh, Athens and Rome'.[35]

FIGURE 4
Distribution of cave paintings of animals, 15,000 to 10,000 BC

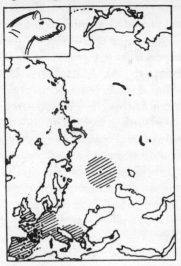

These are concentrated in France and northern Spain.
After L.-R. Nougier, *Naissance de la civilisation*, 1986.

There has been much debate about the significance of this first artistic explosion; no one is willing to see it as gratuitous, as art for art's sake. Did the avid hunters who painted and carved on their cave walls the herds of wild animals among which and off which they lived – mammoths, aurochs, bison, horses, ibex, bears – seek to cast a spell on their prey? Are the masked men, capering in front of the animals in the Trois-Frères cave at the Mas d'Azil and elsewhere, shamans, gods, or the participants in rituals we do not understand? What is the symbolic meaning of this 'writing' which we find so fascinating and mysterious? The force with which it is expressed impels more than respect. Franck Bourdier has even claimed that it is evidence of the cultural superiority of these French and Spanish valleys of south-east Europe over the rest of the world, a superiority which Europe then lost, recovering it, once more for several centuries, only in the twelfth and thirteenth centuries of our era.

Materially, *Homo sapiens sapiens* lived tolerably well and even in some comfort, during the later millennia of the Würm glaciation, sometimes known as the Reindeer Age. Herds of reindeer, which were easy to hunt, provided meat, hides, bones and antlers – in other words food, clothing, tent coverings and the raw material for many small tools. Indeed during what is known as the Magdalenian period, from about 15,000 BC, there was definitely some demographic expansion, with settlement spreading to the mountains and to northern Europe.[36] A general improvement in toolmaking was also a sign both of prosperity and of technical progress. Stone-working had reached remarkable levels of perfection.

Although we find differences of technique from place to place, and evidence of breaks and discontinuities, the general trend everywhere was towards inventive creativity. The Neanderthalers had perfected the bi-facial axe, hide-scraper and borer. There now appear a series of very small tools, sometimes with handles, all specialized, some still made of stone, others using new techniques for carving bone. Thus we find refined types of flint scrapers, smooth and serrated, burins, stone knives, points, eyed needles, fish-hooks and harpoons with carefully chiselled barbs. The curious Solutrean culture,[37] which lasted only 3000 years and had no descendants, has even left behind magnificent bi-facially flaked stone blades, less than a centimetre thick and sometimes 30 or 35 centimetres long. Hunting and fishing techniques (for salmon in particular) were perfected. Spears and arrows launched through the air were already making it possible to kill from a distance. But the truly revolutionary weapon – the bow – only appeared very late, in the last hours of the paleolithic age, just before everything changed, in about 10,000 BC, with the warm period that followed the last ice age and ushered in the temperate climate that is still ours today.

The great change: from the Stone Age to agriculture

Contrary to what one might expect, the warming up of the earth did not immediately lead to an improvement in the human condition. In fact it seriously disturbed the existing cultures, so dependent on hunting. Dense woodlands sprang up, while water released from glaciers formed rivers and lakes everywhere, and the sea level rose, flooding coastal areas. There were no more herds of reindeer or horses to pursue over the frozen tundra. Stag and boar had to be ambushed in the thick forests, and humans had to grow accustomed to the new flora, which forced many changes in their former habits. Diet altered, consisting now less of big game and more of small animals which were easier to trap; it included more vegetable matter – grains, herbs, hazelnuts, acorns, chestnuts, blackberries; lastly it depended heavily on fish from seas, lakes and rivers, and in particular on shellfish and snails, as we know from their countless shells piled up in huge middens, mingled with other remains of food.

From such evidence, the conclusion has often been drawn that there was some kind of 'regression' or 'decadence' among the descendants of *Homo sapiens sapiens*, during the difficult transitional period known as the mesolithic age.[38] Nowadays we are more inclined to view this as a period of adaptation, requiring ingenuity and invention. While the cave paintings disappear before the end of the last ice age, toolmaking techniques do not decline in sophistication. On the contrary: we find increased specialization in very fine tools, carved with precision and ingeniously incorporated into composite implements with handles or hafts made of wood.[39] Hunting had become more difficult, but the hunter now had a bow and arrow, and could take aim at his prey and hit it from a distance. It is true that arrows could kill humans as well as animals. 'The invention of the bow and arrow was as important to prehistoric man as the invention of nuclear arms was to modern mankind,' Robert Ardrey has claimed, exaggerating no doubt to make a point.[40]

Finally, from the seventh millennium BC, there begin to appear in France the first signs of the agricultural revolution which would, within two or three thousand years, have transformed the prehistoric hunters into farmers. The earliest evidence is increased gathering of graminaceae, vesces (vetch) in particular (in what is now the Var), and sometimes even of pulses like lentils and peas (in the Hérault). If agriculture as such did not yet exist, plant-foods were at least being systematically gathered and stored.[41]

The second, even clearer sign is the appearance of sheep-herding, which seems to have come to France from the distant Middle East, where sheep had been domesticated by the tenth or ninth millennium BC. This was the period too of the earliest navigation in the Aegean. It is not surprising then that the sheep (none of whose ancestors are present among the European fauna) appears in the seventh millennium in Eastern Europe, and by about 6000 BC on the shores of the western Mediterranean (including those of southern France). A thousand years later, sheep were being bred in Aquitaine, and by 4500 BC they had reached the coast of Brittany.[42]

So in the western Mediterranean, sheep-farming preceded the great transformation we call the creation of the neolithic economy, in other words that revolutionary apprenticeship in agriculture which marked the birth of Gaul, of what would one day be France, and indeed the whole of Europe, with its ploughed fields and pastures, houses, villages and settled populations of peasants.

This agricultural revolution – as important as the agricultural revolution in eighteenth-century England in modern times – came from the Middle East, the home of wild cereals. The practice of soil cultivation, which was the crucial innovation, accompanied or followed others: settlement in a fixed place, domestic animal breeding, the invention of farm implements such as sickles and millstones (stones that were now polished not hewn) and lastly the creation of pottery. This series of cultural acquisitions took several millennia to become widespread: they reached Europe by two clearly defined routes: westward up the valley of the Danube, and by sea across the Mediterranean. Radio-carbon dating has made it possible to plot the different stages of this diffusion with some accuracy. And now we can already see the two halves of France taking shape: one in the south and one in the north.

Heterogeneity and diversity

The area that is now France, singled out from the start to be a cross-roads, was the destination of two distinct waves of neolithic agriculture. Southern France was affected first, in about 5000 BC, by way of the Mediterranean. Northern and eastern France were affected about 500 years later, from the direction of the Danube. What we have here are two separate cultural contexts, each distinctly located in a particular zone (see Figure 5).

FIGURE 5
The first peasant communities in France, VIth to Vth millennium BC

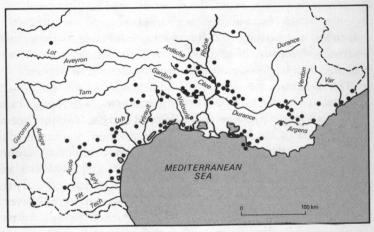

These were scattered along the Mediterranean side of present-day Alpes-Maritimes and Roussillon. Penetration of the hinterland was slow.

In the south, the new ways, although they came earlier, are harder to trace. They were certainly brought by sea, since they spread inland from the coast. But they did not take the form of colonization, bringing enlightenment to new territories. Such anthropological analysis as has so far been possible (on a limited number of skeletons it is true) has led Raymond Riquet to conclude that the changes were 'not accompanied by any migration'.[43] There was, in any case, no sudden break, rather a series of 'contacts, a transfer of ideas and techniques, giving rise to original creations within the indigenous societies'.[44] Moreover, Jean Guilaine thinks, the initial model – agriculture as it had developed in the Levant – was transmitted haphazardly, and in forms altered by its many halts in one or another of the Mediterranean basins which acted as 'so many filters'. On French soil, the result was a slow process of acculturation by the local populations, which gradually (though without abandoning all their previous traditions) came to adopt sheep-farming, a sedentary life, agriculture and the kind of pottery found throughout the western Mediterranean at the time – often decorated by impressions of seashells (in particular the *cardium* or cockle, hence the name of cardial pottery assigned to the neolithic culture in this southern zone), Already well-established, the herding of sheep and goats developed to the point of creating deforestation and soil erosion. During the fifth millennium BC, the first villages began to appear: they were still rudimentary in design, but already on the slopes of the Corbières, for instance, small-scale transhumance of flocks can be detected, with two habitats, the villages down in the plain for winter, and summer encampments on the hills.[45]

This Mediterranean culture, confined to the coastal strip at first, slowly spread to about half the Massif Central and into the Alps, before moving further north again.

In the northern half of France, the situation was very different. Here there really was a break. Agriculture was implanted here from scratch by colonists originally from the Danube valley, at the time a centre of peasant communities which had fully mastered agricultural techniques. They were indeed anthropologically distinct from the previous local population.[46] From about 5000 BC, these Danubians had been moving westwards, in search of new silt soils similar to those they were used to working. By about the middle of the millennium they crossed the Rhine, but did not reach the outskirts of the Paris basin until five centuries later. Here they were confronted by a number of small groups of people still hunting and gathering their food. But since the newcomers only cultivated the fertile alluvial soils of the valleys, they had little difficulty in forcing the mesolithic populations either to retreat to poor soil or to adapt their ways. The new arrivals built large houses in the Danube style, of wood and clay, each big enough to shelter a large family (about ten individuals) and their villages sometimes contained as many as 200 inhabitants. These people were true peasants, much more so than their Mediterranean equivalents, and they brought with them tried and tested farming methods from their country of origin. Indefatigable clearers of forests, they grew wheat and barley on burnt land, bred cattle and pigs (though rarely sheep) and if they continued to hunt wild game, it had only a secondary place in their meat diet. These are the people whose pottery is sometimes known as 'ribbon ware' because of its scrolled patterns.[47]

So neolithic culture was by no means unified in the area that is now France: the cardial culture of the south and the ribbon culture of the north developed independently. Nor was that all. In the west, towards the Atlantic, neolithic culture, of whatever origin (possible seaborne) is found in an original context, with its own pottery, neither cardial nor ribbon, and above all with the extraordinary megalithic architecture whose monuments survive to the present day.[48] Prehistorians long refused to believe that these imposing constructions could be attributed to the local 'barbarians': they could only be the creations of a 'true' civilization, one therefore from the East. On the basis of certain similarities (in particular with the domed burial chambers of Minoan Crete) they imagined some race of experienced navigators from the Aegean, bearing a 'megalithic religion' which they were thought to have introduced to the Atlantic seaboard, beginning in Spain (where megaliths are also to be found) in the middle of the third millennium BC. It was at this late stage that our backward ancestors on the Atlantic coast were deemed to have learnt the techniques of the neolithic age.

Carbon dating has demolished all such theories. The oldest known megalithic monuments are in Brittany and Portugal (not in Spain) and they pre-date any stone architecture in the eastern Mediterranean, including Egypt. For reasons that remain a mystery,

FIGURE 6
Areas of silt and loess in Europe

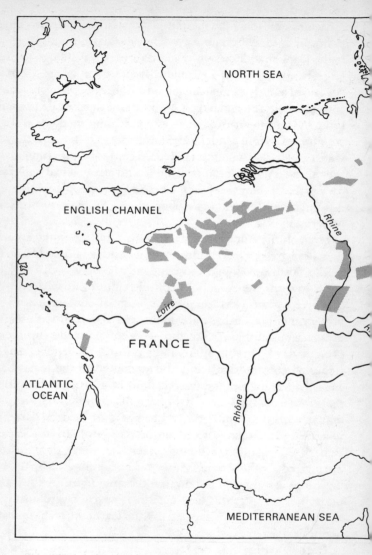

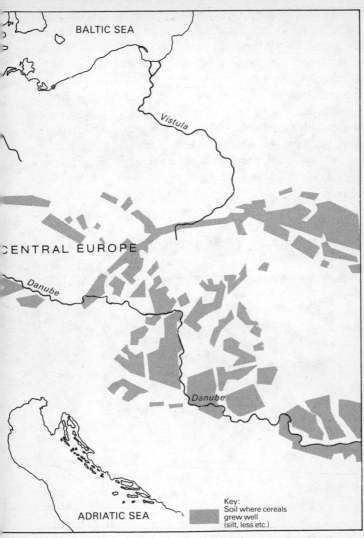

BALTIC SEA

Vistula

CENTRAL EUROPE

Danube

Danube

ADRIATIC SEA

Key:
Soil where cereals
grew well
(silt, less etc.)

Sought after by the peasant farmers of Central Europe, these soils indicate the route taken by the spread of agriculture, up the Danube towards the Rhine and into the Paris basin, during the Vth millennium BC.

this new culture, a largely indigenous one, sprang up in the fifth millennium BC, when the first great dolmens were erected – that of Barnenez, near Morlaix for instance, a fine chambered cairn, 70 metres long with eleven collective tombs as well as another chamber which seems to be some kind of sanctuary.[49] The burial artefacts include smooth pottery without decoration. These first megalithic societies, in all likelihood already peasant societies, were to remain faithful to their style of building, which is found (with some notable variations, of course) along the whole Atlantic seaboard of Europe. In western France, megalithic structures continued for two millennia, and later seem to have reached the south of France, where dolmens are widespread, in the third millennium BC.

FIGURE 7

Geographical distribution of dolmens in France from the Vth to the IIIrd millennium BC

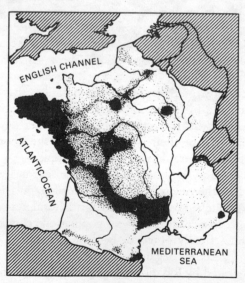

This map shows the spread, in the course of two millennia, of megalithic burial chambers from Brittany, their first site in France, to the south of the country.

By about 4000 BC then, three cultural zones can already be distinguished, separated by the Massif Central which was no doubt somewhat influenced by all of them. In the latter part of this millennium, some links were nevertheless established, with the result that a single culture, or rather elements of a single culture, were tending to cover all of what is now France, apart from the eastern provinces. This original culture, to which the name Chassean (*chasséen*) has been given, after a site at Chassey near Mâcon, seems to have begun in the south in about 3600 BC, 'with its origins in the pre-existing population, and assimilating initiatives of Mediterranean origin'.[50] With its accomplished pottery, smooth, perfectly fired and decorated with geometrical designs, and its sophisticated tools, among them a high proportion of cutting blades, knives and sickles, a variety of arrowheads, several kinds of polished axeheads and all the materials needed by cereal-eaters (pestles, grinders, millstones) this culture seems to have been characterized by abundance.

Apparently under the impulsion of major population growth, this culture rapidly conquered neighbouring areas, advancing northwards up the Rhône valley and westwards to Aquitaine via the Causses and the Naurouze Gap. The result, concludes Jean Guilaine, was a kind of 'national neolithic civilization'.[51] That is not to say that it wiped out all regional variations, but that it placed its own recognizable stamp on the existing collection of regional cultures. Under this forceful impetus, the latter developed what would eventually be their own versions of the 'mother culture', though with considerable individual differences.

I am inclined to think that the Chassean expansion may in fact correspond to the belated acculturation of populations who had remained untouched by the earliest agricultural innovations of the neolithic age. In a context of rapid population growth, the hunters and herdsmen finally opted to become peasants. They emerged from their forests, or began to cut them down. This at any rate is what is suggested by Raymond Riquet's analysis of the civilization which settled quite abruptly in the Paris basin towards the end of the fourth millennium BC.[52] Anthropologists have found here human remains very different from those of the neighbouring

FIGURE 8
Major early Neolithic sites in France, from the VIth to IVth millennium BC

They are distributed among three cultural zones, each of which developed independently, separated by the unoccupied barrier of the Massif Central.

---

ribbon-culture farmers, but very similar to the ancient mesolithic populations. If it is further recalled that the Paris basin, although linked to the rapid spread of Chassean culture throughout what is now France, developed its own tools, of a particularly sturdy nature apparently well-suited for tree-felling, the picture seems complete of a population engaged in land clearance and the search for fresh territory. Is it not possible that the strength of the Chassean expansion derived precisely from its having enabled the neolithic revolution to permeate the whole country, proportionally increasing the resources available to a growing population?[53]

At the same time goods were increasingly beginning to be exchanged. So, among the artefacts found with the dolmens of

FIGURE 9
Sites of the IVth and IIIrd millennia BC

These provide the first signs of a 'national' civilization, in the sense that the Chassean culture spread, through active trading, to cover almost all of France, except the east.

After J. Guilaine, *La France d'avant la France*, 1980.

---

western France we find the new Chassean pottery. In the other direction, the 'button axes', produced by craftsmen in Plussulien (Côtes-du-Nord) out of the very hard rock known as dolerite, were circulating not only throughout Brittany, and north-west and western France, but also along the Rhine, in the Alps and the Pyrenees. The same was true of the polished axes made of hornblende, which came originally from Finistère.[54]

Such movements benefited from a more general expansion, as villages multiplied and prospered. Agriculture became well established. The cult of the earth mother, the goddess of fertility, common to all neolithic societies, acquired a new place, as is attested by the appearance of small figurines, generally modelled out of clay – much fewer in number and less impressive, it must be said, than the countless statuettes of the earth mother, many of them very fine, to be found in the Far East, or in central Europe. There is one exception; the impressive stone statue in Capdenac-le-Haut (Lot) discovered in a Chassean encampment inhabited in about 3000 BC. Indeed this has puzzled the experts, since it resembles no other known object, except possibly some carved pebbles in Yugoslavia, dating from the fifth millennium BC! With the exception of a few 'Venuses', and the fair face of the 'lady of Brassempouy',[55] which date from the upper paleolithic age, the strange 'goddess of Capdenac' can claim to be the oldest prehistoric statue in France.[56]

The age of metals

Prehistory comes to an end with the arrival of metal-working techniques – all of which first appeared either in the Far East or in the Balkans, the cradle of European metallurgy. The first metal to be used was copper, towards the end of the fifth millennium BC, followed by bronze alloys and finally iron – hence the familiar divisions into the Copper, Bronze and Iron Ages. With a considerable time-lag, metallurgic techniques were introduced, one after another, to what is now France: copper between 2500 and 1800 BC; bronze between 1800 and 700 BC; and finally iron, after 700 BC. On each occasion, the phenomenon was linked to the penetration of the region by foreign peoples.

The Copper Age was in fact one of coexistence, since stone tools continued to predominate; it is therefore often described as the Chalcolithic Age, characterized by both copper and stone. This civilization penetrated French territory by way of northern Italy and the Iberian Peninsula, where copper-working had appeared from about 3000 BC. Towards the middle of the third millennium BC, several metal-working centres appeared in southern France, linked to the mineral ore deposits in the Cévennes, the Aveyron, the Quercy, Lozère and Languedoc.[57]

Such production remained local, however, until about 2200 BC, when it was absorbed into and flourished in the cultural orbit of the so-called Beaker culture.[58] This was an imported culture, recognizable throughout Europe by its characteristic pottery (sometimes known as Bell-Beaker, from its shape like that of an upturned bell) and by the many copper objects found associated with it. Foreign immigration seems to have been responsible for this, although so far no satisfactory place of origin has been identified (the Tagus Basin and central Europe have both been suggested). What kind of people were these? Warlike fighters and skilled archers who dominated the land, according to some experts; active merchants and traders according to others, selling their magnificent pottery and copper wares which attracted buyers by their novelty: daggers, blacksmiths' shears, awls, needles. They must have been great travellers at any rate, since they are found in the Iberian peninsula, the Po valley, Sardinia, Sicily, the Rhône valley as high up as its source, the Low Countries, Scotland, England, Bohemia, Moravia, and almost everywhere in France, with the curious exception of the Paris basin, which seems to have been an island of resistance. With these ubiquitous people, one can for the first time begin thinking in terms of 'a certain notion of European unity'. Were they the first to propagate the Indo-European languages in the west? This has been suggested 'with a fair degree of probability'.[59]

Nowhere on French soil, however, did the settlements of the Bell-Beaker culture form compact and homogenous groups, capable of ousting or absorbing the indigenous peoples. Rather the contrary seems to have happened: in France, their traces are entangled with those of the local populations in traditional collective tombs (whereas the newcomers, wherever they did form compact groups, practised individual burial). Evidently there was some kind of intermingling of the two.

However, whereas copper-working was in full swing in France in about 2000 BC, the Middle East and central Europe had abandoned it a thousand years earlier for bronze, an alloy of copper and tin, stronger and less brittle than pure copper. This major technical advance spread to the west only after about 1800 BC.

When it did, it had several consequences: in the first place trade circuits were set in motion by the search for the necessary tin; secondly, the new tools were of such high quality as to oust the last remaining stone implements; even more significantly, it led to an accentuated division of labour (farmers, miners, craftsmen, smiths, traders, warriors) and thus to class distinctions and hierarchies. The people who introduced bronze-working to France were therefore also bringing a new model of society, dominated by a warrior aristocracy, and possibly also a caste of craftsmen smiths.[60] The rites of individual burial reveal the beginnings of social hierarchy: in tombs covered with barrows, important individuals were buried with their personal belongings, magnificent weapons, jewels, ornaments.[61] The importance of the warrior hero is also visible from the new gods, now male and armed (who drive back into the shadows the earth mother or goddess of fertility dear to the neolithic farmers), as well as from the new cults that sprang up, cults of fire and the sun.

This culture spread widely. Between 1800 and 1200 BC, it succeeded in ousting collective burials almost everywhere. The old Breton dolmens, where they were still being used, contained only one body. There was one exception: the Mediterranean south and south-west, from the Pyrenees to Aquitaine, remained faithful to its old collective burial traditions.[62] Nowhere, however, were the local populations physically eliminated. We may imagine them perhaps as the servants and farm-workers of the new masters.

By 1800 BC, bronze metallurgy was becoming very well organized. It was originally confined to the Rhône region in the broad sense (the Swiss Valais, the Rhône valley itself, the Jura and the Alps) but its artefacts – magnificent daggers, strong axes, beads, bracelets, ornamental brooches, awls and needles – were being actively traded in Burgundy, the Massif Central, Aquitaine and even Languedoc-Roussillon. The Rhône valley thus began to play its role as link between the Mediterranean and the Germanic countries.

Three hundred years later, a new series of metal-working centres sprang up along the Atlantic seaboard. It was now that there appeared that essential innovation – serial production of bronze tools (which would oust stone implements for good). Every centre specialized in a particular type of axe, dagger, spearhead or sword. Produced in the plains of Médoc or in Brittany, in Normandy or between the Loire and the Garonne, these artefacts were all exported from province to province and ended up side by side in the same market-places.[63]

Independently of these two zones – Atlantic and Rhône-Alpine – a third production zone can be distinguished in a slightly different cultural context, this time brought by peoples from beyond the Rhine who settled first in Alsace, then in the Paris basin and the central west. Their heavy axes and knives found customers in the south, along the Saône, in the Jura, and even in the Massif Central, while their characteristic pottery is found as far afield as the Charente region.[64]

In about 1200–1100 BC, there was an important cultural upheaval. In the wake of turbulent events in the Aegean, new peoples moved into central Europe and eventually, as was so often to be the case, they crossed the Rhine. Their civilization was a completely original one, since the newcomers cremated their dead – and we know how significant funeral rites were. The urns containing ashes were buried side by side in graveyards known as the 'urnfields'. Three-quarters of France was affected by the 'urn-burial culture' which took root in an economically favourable context. The notable expansion of lowland villages, the use of the plough, the colonization of hill country, the clearing of forests, the use of the cart and of the domestic horse as a draught animal[65] – all these point to a time of major population growth. The only area to remain untouched by this movement was the Atlantic west, an area reaching inland as far as the Paris basin, which thus became a centre for busy markets where the Atlantic and 'Continental' influences competed with each other.

Even in the zones where the newcomers had settled, however, the presence of the local culture remains visible. In Burgundy and elsewhere, over the space of two centuries, burials and cremations were practised side by side, sometimes in the same burial grounds. Local differences remained pronounced, so much so that some archaeologists, believing cultural practices to be identified with different peoples, have talked of five successive waves of invaders. Jean Guilaine thinks rather that we should see such differences as the product of different development processes and indeed has

FIGURE 10
Bronze age sites in France

There were two main areas of production: along the Atlantic seaboard in the west, and in the region between the Alps and Alsace in the east.

After J. Guilaine, *La France d'avant la France, op. cit.*

---

queried whether 'there really were any invasions' at all. Why not think in terms simply of acculturation, he asks, spreading from place to place thanks to contacts between 'travelling traders or small but dynamic groups'?[66]

It is at any rate clear that the Bronze Age was, increasingly as time went on, an era of active exchange (ingots of copper and tin often travelled considerable distances, from Brittany to the Alps or Spain for instance), an era of multiplicity and interpenetration of different cultures.

The Iron Age (from 700 BC to the Roman conquest) was also a period of many upheavals. Its beginning coincided with a deterioration in the climate, which became colder and wetter: lakes overflowed their banks and the foothills of the mountains were

FIGURE 11
Early Iron Age sites in France (700 to 500 BC)

These are concentrated in the zone occupied by the invaders whose civilization is known as Hallstatt: south and east of the Loire.

After J. Guilaine, *La France d'avant la France, op. cit.*

---

invaded by trees – beech, alder, fir and spruce. The expansion of the forests would of course eventually benefit the new iron metal-lurgy, a technology more demanding than that of bronze: it required high temperatures and a massive consumption of wood. After long remaining a secret in its land of origin, the Hittite king-dom, iron-working had spread only slowly and haphazardly, and we do not know when or how it first reached western Europe, either via the Mediterranean, with the Phoenicians, or over the land-routes of Europe in the wake of various waves of immigration which, as usual, crossed the Rhine.[67]

Within the Iron Age, two major periods can be distinguished: the Hallstatt culture,[68] starting in the eighth and seventh centuries BC; and the La Tène culture, from about 500 BC. We know these periods little better than what went before: with the result that many problems face us, and all too often (the reader will not be surprised to learn!) we have no solution.

This is certainly true of the Hallstatt period. We know little about the newcomers, except that they were the first horsemen to appear in the west. (The horse had already been established there for some centuries but only as a draught animal.) They were also the first to bring with them iron-working technology, and possessed a range of new tools and weapons, including the broadsword which gave them unbeatable superiority over any adversary still armed with the old bronze dagger. It was in similar manner that the Dorians, who were also horsemen from north of the Balkans, had destroyed the brilliant Mycenaean civilization in Greece in about 1110 BC, long before Hallstatt.

Such devastation did not occur in 'Gaul' which was the scene rather of infiltration, superimposition and foreign rule. The entire area 'south of a line from Lorraine and Champagne to the mouth of the Loire' was occupied by the invaders. We can trace them by their burial mounds[69] in which dead warriors whether cremated (as in the days of urn-burial) or buried, were always accompanied by their armour, their swords, and sometimes their chariots or their horses' trappings. A crucial feature of these burials is that the tombs of chieftains can always be recognized by their sumptuousness. This society of horsemen was evidently strongly stratified – something which would be one of the chief characteristics of Gaul, and would persist until the Roman conquest and beyond.

But who were these people who prefigured Gaul? Proto-Celts, some maintain. Indo-Europeans but not Celts at all, according to others, who argue that the 'true' Celts, of the so-called La Tène period, destroyed the fortified sites of their predecessors when they arrived. This does not seem altogether conclusive as an argument: after all, the Celtic tribes often warred amongst themselves. The only acceptable criterion for identifying Celtic groups ought of course to be their language. But we know nothing about the language of the Hallstatt people. They came at any rate from central Europe, as the Celts would later do, and their influence spread far and wide, from the Oder to Spain.

Simultaneously with their coming, however, a number of other influences helped to transform the landscape and the society of what would one day be Gaul. The seventh, sixth and fifth centuries BC witnessed the growth and expansion of various Mediterranean civilizations, with the creation of rival colonies by the Greek city-states, the Phoenicians and the Etruscans. In southern Gaul the Phocaeans founded their city Massilia (Marseilles) in 600 BC: ideally situated, it became a thriving centre, attracting towards it down the Rhône-Saône corridor the resources of the 'market' of Gaul (including tin from England); and keeping open trade links with the Mediterranean, despite frequest attacks by the Carthaginians and Etruscans. The latter, coming up from northern Italy, reached Gaul by crossing the Alpine passes, which were already inhabited. The Carthaginians originally came via Spain and before long were using the Atlantic sea-passage.[70]

Was this opening up of Gaul to southern trade the major feature of the later Hallstatt period? It was now that citadel-towns, or at any rate fortified hill-villages first appeared, and in the princely tombs where important persons were buried under barrows with their chariots and all their possessions archaeologists have found precious imported objects of Greek or Etruscan origin. It was at the lower end of one of these hill 'towns', the *oppidum* of Vix in Burgundy, that the discovery was made in 1953 of the magnificent tomb of a young woman lying in a chariot adorned with all her jewels.[71] Beside her were three bronze bowls of Etruscan origin, a silver bowl, two Attic cups, a bronze *oenochoe*, and the famous Vix krater, a huge vessel made of bronze, 1.65 metres high and decorated with a frieze representing warriors and chariots.[72] It is remarkable not only for its splendour but also because it must have been brought a great distance to reach Vix from its place of origin: either Corinth or a workshop in Greater Greece, possibly Phocaea in Asia Minor.

The Vix tomb has been dated from the very end of the sixth century BC. By this time, the invaders of the so-called La Tène civilization, who are generally accepted as being Celts,[73] had already begun to arrive in eastern Gaul. Vix was brutally destroyed in the early years of the fifth century BC, as was the fortress of Le Pègue in the Drôme. Soon afterwards, the fortress of La Camp du Château in the Jura would in turn be abandoned.[74] Hallstatt society was disintegrating as a new foreign conquest – swift, violent and explosive – was taking place on 'French' soil, and would soon cover most of the entire territory. The newcomers were certainly intrepid warriors, determined horsemen, experienced metal-workers, craftsmen of unparalleled skill and, what was more, the purveyors of a dazzling mythology, of an original religion and culture, and of an Indo-European language which was all their own. These were 'our ancestors the Gauls'.

Celts or Gauls? A civilization or a history?

With the La Tène Celts, we are really leaving prehistory and entering the twilight zone of proto-history. But we are not yet in the broad daylight of history, which dates at earliest from the Roman conquest of Gaul (58 to 51 BC). Precise information about the long preamble to 'French history' is therefore sparse.

The Gauls were Celts. But who were the Celts? Indo-Europeans – but that takes us no further forward, since the Indo-Europeans, whose origins go back to the third millennium BC, included a variety of peoples all over the ancient world, from the Atlantic to the Ganges. Only one feature united them: they spoke inter-related languages, making it possible for linguistic experts almost to work one out from another. Not so very long ago, a perfectly simple explanation of the Celtic phenomenon was accepted: the Indo-Europeans had originally been a single people, living south of Jutland on the edge of the Baltic and the North Sea. This people had then scattered, each of its fragments going its own way and developing its own language. Unfortunately this reassuring explanation has been jettisoned and no other has yet replaced it.

The Celts, who belonged to a western branch of the Indo-Europeans (as had the Hallstatt and urn-burial peoples before them and probably even the Bell-Beaker people of the late third millennium), have therefore to be located in an obscure and indeterminate past. By about the seventh century BC, they were probably living in the area corresponding to Bohemia in central Europe, a meeting place and crossroads for many influences. So the Celts cannot be described as a race: anthropologists have discovered both brachycephalic and dolicocephalic strains among them. By the fifth century BC, 'they were almost as heterogeneous as the population of today', and they would become even more so as they occupied new territories.[75] Nor can we really speak of a people – even this vague word is too strong – and certainly not a state. Perhaps they originated from one clan which imposed its leadership, a tribe that later subjugated others; their culture was then exported widely until in the end a coherent whole had been constituted.

FIGURE 12
Celtic Gaul in the second century BC

The map shows the different tribes of Gaul before Provence was conquered by the Romans in 121 BC.

FIGURE 13
Celtic conquests between the fifth and third century BC

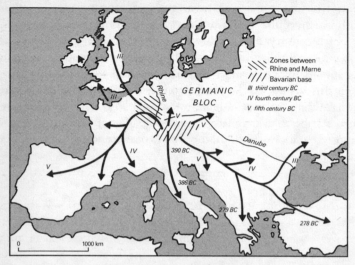

From their original base in Bavaria and the zone between the Rhine and the Marne (occupied as early as the sixth century BC), they spread widely in every direction except north where their progress was halted by the Germanic bloc.

What is so surprising is that such a coherent group should have been formed at all: it must have been the product of many forces operating together, many coincidences, developments and successes. Barry Cunliffe's explanation is very tempting, since it is the only one which gives some meaning to the finished process.[76] According to him, a distant upheaval far back in the past was responsible for everything: in about 1200 BC, the Dorian invasions and the mysterious deeds of the 'peoples of the sea' brought about the sudden collapse of the influential Aegean civilization which had made the eastern Mediterranean, from Egypt to Greece and the Hittite kingdom in Asia Minor, such an extraordinary centre for commercial and cultural exchange, with ramifications reaching far and wide.[77] We can imagine it as like the poacher's lantern, drawing the game from all around. When the lantern went out, central Europe, deprived of its glow, had to manufacture its own light and draw on its own resources (rather as, two thousand years later, after the barbarian invasions of the fifth century, northern Europe, centred on the Low Countries, had to build itself up from scratch to become one of the active centres of medieval Europe). This process, he argues, operated to the advantage of those areas acquainted with the most modern techniques of iron-working. Long kept secret by the Hittites, then transmitted westwards via Illyria and the Balkans, metallurgy was an enabling factor, encouraging the rise of a people of metalworkers and fierce warriors. It was as the descendants of such people that the Celts were to emerge several centuries later – descendants sufficiently numerous and prosperous to have launched a long series of expeditions of conquest.

Celtic expansion, consisting of a series of lightning raids and advances, lasted three or four hundred years and extended over a very wide area. On the diagram (Figure 13) which I have taken from Jacques Harmand,[78] the sheer distance covered is immediately obvious. For centuries on end, Celtic aggression was the only alternative to encroachment by the city-states of the Mediterranean – Greeks, Romans, or Etruscans – the only combative force capable of standing up to them for any length of time and inspiring fear in them.

The first Celtic moves out of the Bavarian region took them westwards. After colonizing the upper and lower Rhineland, they had, by the sixth century BC, settled between the Rhine and the Marne. And it was from this firmly established base that they later launched victorious expeditions throughout Gaul and across the Pyrenees, into the western half of the Iberian Peninsula (the Celtiberians). By the third century BC, they had probably reached the islands of Britain and Ireland.

Meanwhile further raids were launched from Bavaria, in the fifth century BC, over the Brenner and St Gotthard passes. The Celts thus conquered Italy, captured Rome in 386 BC and settled in the Po valley (Cisalpine Gaul), between the Veneti, the Etruscans and the Ligurians. Their advance into southern Italy was however blocked by the Romans and Etruscans[79] and in the end they occupied only a rather narrow strip of territory between the Alps and the Adriatic.

Finally, looking eastwards, the Celts penetrated deeply into the Balkans and Asia Minor, along the Danube valley. They sacked Delphi in 279 BC, crossed the Bosphorus in 278 BC, and in the same year founded a Galatian state which survived until 230 BC. But here, as in Spain, far from home, at the utmost limits of their expansion, the Celts encountered the problem of dwindling numbers. They had to come to terms with the resident peoples, and their influence, although traceable, led to 'mixed settlements, of varying degrees of Celtishness'.[80]

This chronological scenario, reconstructed by Jacques Harmand and necessarily hypothetical (the surviving texts from antiquity lend themselves to various interpretations), seems reasonable to me. We may imagine these victorious raids as being similar to the invasions in 102–101 BC by the Cimbri and the Teutons (Germanic tribes, but with elements of Celtic culture), or more probably like the migration of the Helvetii which Caesar blocked in 58 BC at the beginning of the Gallic wars: long convoys of men, women and children, carts, riders on horseback – a whole people on the move, in disorderly processions which were nevertheless to affect the entire destiny of Europe and the Mediterranean for centuries on end. They brought a confrontation between inland Europe and Mediterranean Europe, between the tribes and the city-states,[81] between barbarians and civilizations, between a primitive economy and one based on money. In their long reign, the Celts never had any real cities, nor a state with developed structures, nor, *a fortiori*, an empire. They had no long-term political aims, no cunningly planned conquests. It was the spirit of adventure, the thirst for booty and sometimes too no doubt the extra mouths to feed that sent them on their travels. They were capable of quarrelling among themselves, or of hiring themselves as mercenaries to the Greeks in Sicily or Asia Minor, or to the Egyptians or Carthaginians. 'Anyone seeking blind courage and readily spilt blood', Michelet tells us, 'hired Gauls'.[82]

*   *   *

Gauls, Celts – these were the same people. Known as *Keltoi* by the Greeks, the Celts who settled in Gaul were christened *Galli* – Gauls – by the Romans. For convenience, I shall call them Celts when referring to the group as a whole and Gauls when speaking of the inhabitants of what would later be France. But when Caesar at the beginning of the *Commentaries* sets out the divisions of Gaul, he describes as 'Celtic' the central section of the country under attack – from the Garonne to the Seine – as distinct from Aquitania to the south (between the Pyrenees and the Garonne) and Belgica to the north (from the Seine to the Rhine).

Having invaded Gaul from the east, the Celts settled in large numbers in Alsace, Lorraine, Champagne and Burgundy,[83] where they made use of the forests and iron ores. Elsewhere, they were less densely concentrated – scarcely touching either the Morvan or the Massif Central. To the south, they encountered resistance from the Iberians in the west and the Ligurians in the east: on either side of the lower Rhône valley, their progress was barred. But in any case, the local populations, although more or less subjugated and repressed, were nowhere wiped out. Henri Hubert,[84] whose works on the Celts are still classics, stresses the very large numbers of invaders: in other words the linguistic, cultural and social extensions of Celtic Gaul must be regarded as the product of a substantial ethnic transfusion. In fact, these Celts – already a mixture of races at their point of departure in central Europe, and having like all migrating peoples picked up on the way a mass of other foreign groups – had had plenty of time in Gaul, where they behaved like lords of creation, to mingle with the conquered population. A process of colonization and acculturation took place over several centuries.

The achievement of the Celts was that they extended and imposed their language and way of life everywhere in Gaul, except the south. Their cultural success can partly be explained by the economy: it flourished and encouraged exchange. We should note that the Celts had brought neither cereal-farming nor craft skills to Gaul: well before their arrival, crops were being grown wherever the forests, marshes or floodwaters of rivers allowed it (the forests were, it is true, more widespread than today, especially north of the Loire: they covered the Beauce, the Orléanais, the Gâtinais, the Blaisois and the Perche).[85] Barley and wheat had been cultivated for centuries already, as had millet. Not yet present were hops, oats, chestnuts and above all vines; but the last-named, having been brought to Provence shortly after its conquest by Rome in 121 BC, would not take long to reach Celtic territory. Similarly, the Gauls were adopting a tradition far older than their own when they sent to graze (usually in the forests) herds of sheep, goats, oxen and pigs in sufficient numbers to be exporting salt meat and wool to Rome, even before the conquest. On the other hand, the Celts may have been responsible for the widespread adoption of the horse – one of their major passions[86] – and they were certainly innovators in the technology of iron-working in many provinces which were still ignorant of this in the early La Tène period. What was more, they were responsible for the large-scale development of iron implements in *agriculture*, still relatively uncommon in the Hallstatt period.

The countryside travelled through by Caesar during his Gallic Wars was by then at any rate inhabited by experienced farmers, certainly in advance of the Romans. It is unlikely (despite the claims of some enthusiasts) that they invented the heavy plough: the many iron ploughshares that have been found could have fitted only a hand-plough, or ard, and not the true wheeled plough which turned over the soil at the same time as it dug a furrow. But the Gauls certainly perfected ploughing techniques, since by the eve of the conquest they were cultivating heavy soils for which the simple hand-plough would have been inadequate,[87] and the Aedui, near Bibracte, had adopted the practice of liming the land.[88] Moreover, the Gauls had the use of excellent farm implements – large scythes for mowing, sickles, axes and even a curiosity which was not found everywhere, a sort of combine-harvester, 'a machine', Pliny the Elder explains, 'consisting of a container with a serrated edge, mounted on two wheels and pushed by a team, so that the ears of corn fell into the box'. Gaul was rich in cereals – a two-edged blessing, since its invaders had no difficulty in living off the land as they made their way north.

In Gaul, the Romans would also find craftsmen of extraordinary skill. Unrivalled ironworkers, who had mastered the technology both of wrought iron and tinplating (indeed Pliny credits the Bituriges with the invention of tinplating), they were also proficient smiths in lead, silver and gold. In response to the Gauls' passion for ornament, their craftsmen created fine jewels, remarkable enamels (one of their specialities), magnificent armour and highly ornamented bridle-pieces for horses. They mined iron and gold in places such as Brassempouy on the edge of the Luz-de-France in the Cévennes: it was here that in 1850 the local miller, who was also an amateur geologist, 'found coins dating from pre-Roman Gaul'.[89] Celtic swords, from the fourth to the first century BC, are also evidence of growing mastery of the techniques of forging and carburizing iron, while at about the same time there appeared an extraordinary variety of specialized implements for leather-working, wood-carving and metal-engraving – virtually the entire range of modern tools.[90]

The Gauls were also weavers of both linen and wool, dyeing them in the bright colours they favoured. They were adept at wood and leather work, using techniques unknown to the Romans: the wine-cask, a convenient substitute for the amphora, was a Celtic invention. They were the first people in Europe to manufacture soap, and they were not only competent shoemakers (producing the heavy clogs with thick soles known as *gallicae*), but also good ceramists and potters.

Pre-conquest Gaul also witnessed the rise of the towns, creating what can fairly be called an urban craft industry. Without wishing to stretch the comparison too far, the appearance of craft guilds in the towns of France in the twelfth century AD seems similarly to have marked a turning point in urban and economic life – as we shall later see.[91] Should we also take particular note of this in Gaul? And since in Bibracte the lower part of town contained a whole district set aside for artisans, should we see this as a sign of the increasing division of labour, the inevitable accompaniment to economic progress?

This economy based on agriculture and crafts was stimulated by quite a brisk flow of traffic. Pre-Roman Gaul offered various means of transport. Its overland tracks were not yet fully fledged roads perhaps, though some were not far off, but they existed, and there were also sea and river routes. Rome would inherit them. The roads cannot have been as rough as has been claimed, since they carried wheeled traffic: not only the luxury vehicles, the *essedum* and *carpentum* – swift, light chariots like those used in war – but also heavy four-wheeled carts, the *carruca*, *reda* and *petorritum* (all Celtic vehicles, copied by the Romans in the third and second centuries BC) which were drawn by teams of animals.[92] What was more, running across Gaul from north to south lay the great amber routes and even more importantly the tin route from Brittany and England, which went via Rouen then down the Seine, Saône and Rhône to Marseilles. The last section of this route can be described as the property of the Arverni, who controlled the stretch along the Rhône.

There were sea-passages too. The Celts were not a sea-going people, for obvious reasons. But in Armorica they found local boat-builders and sailors, in particular on the inland sea of the Gulf of Morbihan, with its islands and islets. This was the famed homeland of the Veneti, whose sea-faring destiny (if we are to believe Alain Guillerm[93]) was either stimulated or confirmed by the appearance off the Breton coast in the fifth century of a Phoenician ship (the voyage of Himilco). This, it seems, marked the start of the famous Veneti fleet: their large and medium-sized vessels, built in Gaul, made regular trips between the Atlantic and Channel coasts, sailing to England and the Scilly Isles where there were rich supplies of tin. By arrangement with Carthage, these ships carried tin ore from Cornwall to the great harbour of Vigo, and as long as Carthage held Spain, shipping from Morbihan continued to expand both north and south, as did that of the Osismi (in what is now Finistère). For the Veneti fleet, although the largest, was not the only one in the region. It cooperated, for instance, with the ships plying between Finistère and the Scheldt. And the vessels of the Pictones and Santones, between the Loire and the Gironde, would one day be requisitioned by Caesar in his campaign against Armorica.[94]

In his *Commentaries*, Caesar uses two terms to describe the towns of Gaul: either *oppidum*, that is, a fortified position, or *urbs*. But was he simply using the latter word (in theory denoting a fully-developed town) as a synonym to avoid repetition? Alesia for example is described by turns as an *oppidum* and an *urbs*. In fact, the town-village networks in pre-conquest Gaul are really bourg-village-hamlet networks. The hamlets were simply huddles of huts built of cob, with thatched roofs and no windows. (The smoke escaped through the roof.) The bourgs may have had some urban functions, but only of a rudimentary kind. The only towns of note were the *oppida* – so it is usually reckoned that every town was a fortress and every fortress a town. Apart from some strongholds protected by water – such as Bourges (Avaricum), the capital of the Bituriges – *oppida* were usually built on hills (Bibracte, Gergovia). They were generally protected by a deep moat and a wall some four metres thick, the famous *murus gallicus* (a combination of timber supports, earth and stones) which ran round the outside, enclosing a large unoccupied space (135 hectares at Bibracte, 97 at Alesia).[95] In times of danger, these could provide refuge for the people from round about and their flocks. But this space was partly taken up by houses, sometimes by an aristocratic compound, a temple or artisans' workshops – an important detail, as has already been remarked. The problem is whether or not to count these fortresses as towns in the regular sense of the word, that is as political, religious and economic centres – whatever their importance or efficiency in this last respect. Venceslas Kruta, one of the most knowledgeable specialists on Celtic history, insists that they were true towns; many other historians deny it.

It seems to me however that evidence for their urban role is provided by the visible transformations which took place in the second and first centuries BC. It was during these two hundred years that the *oppida* first appeared. Until then, the Celts had not built fortresses: their unchallenged power had probably provided security – a sort of *pax celtica*. The same would be true of the early days of the *pax romana* in Gaul. Should we therefore see the sprouting of hill-towns and fortress refuges simply as the result of a decline in the power of the Celtic tribes, as difficulties and dangers multiplied around them? One thinks of the occupation of the *Provincia* by the Romans in 121 BC, or the dramatic migrations by the Cimbri and Teutons in 102–101 BC. These people of uncertain stock, Germanic probably, but living on the northern frontiers of the original Celtic territory, on the Baltic and North Seas, south of Jutland, were affected by the spread of Celtic civilization (their chieftains even had Celtic names). But whether Celticized or not, they came as invaders, pillaging town and countryside. And although Venceslas Kruta tends to minimize the threat they posed (claiming that Roman fears exaggerated it),[96] war was certainly

FIGURE 14
Gaul before the Roman conquest

endemic between the Gallic tribes. The *oppida* must therefore have fulfilled a defensive function, sheltering local populations. These hill-towns would moreover soon prove to be the only way of resisting the Romans, both within Gaul and without it. They were conquered only by long sieges: Numantia in Spain (134–133 BC), and Alesia in Gaul (52 BC).

This much is agreed, but is there any reason why the defensive role of these towns (much like our medieval walled towns after all) should have excluded them from an economic role? On the contrary, argues Venceslas Kruta, the appearance of the *oppida* was a sign of the social change brought about by the end of Celtic expansion, a change that had become irreversible by 225 BC. Until then, there were no towns: 'armed peasants', a sort of 'rural militia', lived as free men in hamlets of a few houses, ever ready to follow a chieftain on some mercenary adventure or new conquest. Once expansion finally came to an end, the population collected at certain points of the territory, a development which brought about the greater dependency of the poor, a more marked hierarchy and the general economic progress of which the *oppida* were precisely a result.[97] How can one fail to agree with Kruta here? Not only would an active peasant society have spontaneously created the urban functions fulfilled by the bourg, but the existence of regular trade routes across Gaul would itself have called for a series of regular staging-posts, and the exchange of goods and services which would tend to favour permanent human settlement. Did not Caesar after all, during his Gallic wars, come across Roman traders living in Cenabum (Orléans), Noviodunum (Nevers) and Cabillonum (Châlon-sur-Saône)?[98] When Vercingetorix adopted the tactic of burning towns ahead of the advancing Romans who had been in the habit of obtaining supplies from them, the Bituriges refused to allow their capital Avaricum to be subjected to this fate, on account of its 'splendour'. We should not of course imagine this as splendour of a monumental kind: no stone buildings have been found on the sites of the Gallic towns. The houses were mostly built of wattle and daub. 'Is there anything more ugly than the *oppida* of Gaul?' asked Cicero.[99] We must think rather in terms of economic 'splendour'. In the event, the Bituriges defended their town at heavy cost. When it fell, Caesar found vast quantities of grain stored inside.[100] And the craft district of Bibracte surely provides even stronger evidence in the same direction. This was certainly the view of Albert Grenier in an article written long ago, about the excavations there.[101] Is Alain Guillerm right then to interpret Paul-Marie Duval's prudent hesitations on this question as support of his own view – that the Gauls had no such things as towns or states?[102] Pierre Bonnaud is surely more correct when he says that 'while the Gauls did not really have proper towns, all the viable elements of towns certainly existed among them . . . and it was from these that so many western and central European towns were born, some modest, many very large'.[103]

This extremely rapid survey of the establishment of the Celts in France has deliberately left on one side the essential problem they pose: how can we ever know the truth about their civilization as a whole? Did it have any overall coherence, transcending the fragmentation of the Celts into various tribes and indeed autonomous states, all mortally jealous of each other? In considering the possibility of such unity, the problem of social organization and religious belief is central, and the role of the Druids is anything but anecdotal, as we shall see in a later chapter.

Force of numbers

Can we derive any significant conclusions from this rapid overview – at once too short and too long to serve as a summary of French prehistory? Too short when one thinks of the mass of information – fragmentary and scattered, it is true – that we possess; but too long for the reader unfamiliar with such matters to be able to retain the account in detail.

In particular perhaps, it should be concluded that the area covered by France was from very earliest times unusually populous. The large number of inhabitants can partly be explained by geographical location: this was a crossroads, a meeting point, a site of confluences. Emmanuel de Martonne[104] once described Europe as a funnel from east to west, its area narrowing as one approaches the Atlantic. France was thus the bottle-neck into which everything was channelled before being brought up short on reaching the ocean seaboard. It thus became a net, or a trap, in which populations were obliged to mingle with each other. According to Colin Renfrew, the concentration of people on the sea coast, already discernible in mesolithic times, explains the appearance of the megaliths in Brittany – the most extraordinary phenomenon in French prehistory. After the introduction of agriculture by the new immigrants, he argues, rapid population growth would have caused land to become scarce. Each community would therefore have been anxious to concentrate around its monuments, which were at once a collective burial site and a symbol of territorial possession.[105]

Various populations, it is claimed, collected and intermingled here: intermarriage took on such proportions in France, says the anthropologist Raymond Riquet,[106] that by neolithic times the population 'had become quite simply modern', taking on 'a more recognizably French appearance in the present sense of the term', that is to say with the racial diversities characteristic of French people today – Alpine, northern, Mediterranean and Lorrainer groups. This lends support to Ferdinand Lot's provocative remark: 'If a contemporary Frenchman wants to know what his ancestors were like, he need only look around him or in the mirror.'[107]

Most important of all for our summing up is of course the matter of numbers. How numerous were our ancestors? No matter that we cannot give a definite answer to this question. For at least twenty years, prehistorians have been showing increasing interest in the habitat of prehistoric populations, in their size, density and expansion. In this debate, we need some orders of magnitude. When population density increases (as Colin Renfrew has reminded us[108]) everything else is unquestionably affected: settlement, intensity of cultivation, social hierarchies, land division. After countless millennia of wandering, hunting and gathering, 'man the hunter' became 'man the farmer'.[109] Agriculture was gradually established, while the prehistoric population steadily increased, perhaps in a ratio of 10 to 1 or even 100 to 1. 'France' gradually saw

its surface covered with villages, hamlets, forest clearings, farmland and people, in particular in the third millenium, until about
1800 BC. At about this high point, if we accept Louis-René
Nougier's helpful calculations,[110] the area later known as Gaul
may have contained as many as 5 million people, 2,500,000 at least.
Useful comparisons can be made between maps showing the neolithic farming areas and those of today. There are even regions
where the population sites in the time of the Chassean expansion
were more numerous than they are now. Prehistorians will rightly
remind us that these sites are not all necessarily contemporary with
one another, and that they cannot simply be added together without risk of error. But there are other signs of a population surplus:
villages surrounding themselves with protective walls and moats,
building up large stocks of food, preparing for war. In collective
burial sites, excavators have found piles of skeletons riddled with
arrowheads.[111]

Can we not also regard as a sign of population surplus the long
and deep recession which set in during the second millennium BC?
There are clear signs of distress during this downturn, for which
convincing reasons have yet to be found.[112] Was this perhaps an
age of epidemics, comparable to the Black Death, which more or
less ushered in the interminable Hundred Years' War in Europe?
Such epidemics, which have been suggested for want of any better
explanation, might have resulted from a deterioration in the climate. But other hypotheses are possible: famine for instance,
which might have resulted precisely from excessive population
increase (as was the case shortly before the Black Death); or wars of
a devastating kind, occasioned either by a shortage of new land, or
as seems to have been the case at the end of the first Iron Age, in the
first millennium BC, by foreign invasion. For whatever reason,
there was a clear revival during the second Iron Age, and the rise
continued until the eve of the Roman conquest.

It is unlikely that Gaul by then contained the 20 million or more
inhabitants enthusiastically claimed for it by Henri Hubert,
Alexandre Moreau de Jonnès, Ferdinand Lot, Albert Grenier and
Camille Jullian. But the Celtic occupation, here as elsewhere in
Europe, undoubtedly corresponded to an age of intensive agricul-

FIGURE 15
Settlement in the Loing Basin in Neolithic times and today

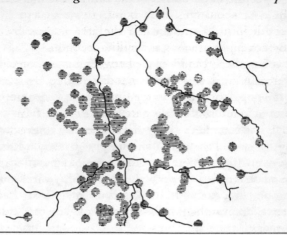

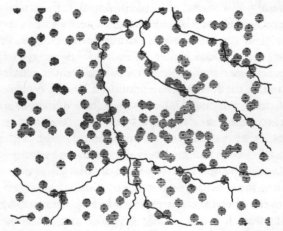

The difference is that there were no neolithic settlements in the alluvial valleys of the Loing and Fay, no doubt because they were marshy, whereas today the plateaux are deserted in favour of the valleys. According to L.-R. Nougier, density of settlement in Neolithic times in this region (with more sites than today, but much smaller ones) was about 10 to 20 to the square kilometre.

After L.-R. Nougier, *Le Peuplement préhistorique*.

ture, in a land both prosperous and populous (even over-populated according to the Latin authors who saw this as the cause for the emigration of so many Gauls). It is possible that the population reached the 10 million estimated by Julius Caesar himself. Karl Julius Beloch suggests a maximum of 5.7 million,[113] Gustave Bloch puts it at 5 million,[114] and Eugène Cavaignac at 8 or 9 million,[115] after critically analysing the censuses reported by Caesar in his *Gallic Wars*, in particular the estimates for the reinforcements called up by the Gauls at the siege of Alesia (52 BC).

May I say that these latter figures seem rather low to me – particularly since Provincia Narbonensis, already a Roman province for over 70 years, was as densely populated as Italy itself? Karl Ferdinand Werner, accepting the figure of 'over 7 million' for Gaul proper, argues for '10 to 12 million inhabitants' in the whole complex, Gaul plus the Roman Provincia.[116] Be that as it may, we can at any rate calculate from these orders of magnitude that 'Gaul before Gaul' – from the third millennium BC down to the Christian era or thereabouts – was the scene of various long-term population shifts, first upwards, then down, then up again. What we have here are *multisecular* cycles as I have already suggested, similar, though much more long-drawn-out in time, to the classic cycle, if such it can be called, which began in the eleventh century AD and reached a peak in about 1350, only to decline swiftly over the century corresponding precisely to the Hundred Years' War (1350 to 1450). Prehistory witnessed no such 'rapid' cycles in the area occupied by Gaul, but the alternation of these cyclic movements was comparable in depth to those which operated at a different pace in medieval France.

Such cycles, even when very slow and seemingly endless, do nevertheless imply a certain cohesiveness: not an absolute fragmentation of settlement, but an appreciable degree of exchanges of goods, culture, technology and people – in other words something that already looks rather like *history*, which can only be the product or consequence of a certain degree of density, a certain level of population.

So there was a 'Gaul before Gaul', in other words a real continuity between what preceded Gaul and Gaul itself. I am inclined to accept (despite the reservations which have been expressed about his basic argument: the number of villages and settlements) Nougier's figure of about five million for the prehistoric population in about 1800 BC. If this was the case, the biological combination was already *in situ* by the end of the neolithic era, the ethnic mix was already accomplished and now became established for good. Later invasions – particularly that of the Celts – however violent and overwhelming, and however powerful in cultural impact would gradually be absorbed into the mass of the pre-existing populations, who would be conquered and sometimes expelled from their land, but who revived to increase and prosper once more. There is safety in numbers of course. Would the same not be true in the face of the Roman conquest, the barbarian invasions of the fifth century AD, or indeed the many immigrants who have caused some anxiety in present-day France? What mattered in the end was the mass, the established majority. In the long run, everyone else would be absorbed into it.

But we need not yet embark on these problems. For the moment, our task is to establish the place of the vast living legacy of prehistory. France and the French are its unwitting heirs and transmitters. Historical haematology is still in its infancy.[117] But is it so surprising if its findings have already indicated that the blood running in the veins of French people today is recognizably the same as in prehistory? This should persuade us to heed a history rooted in the depths of time.

CHAPTER TWO

From Independent Gaul to Carolingian Gaul

Following on from prehistoric Gaul, we find a sequence of four images: first the so-called 'independent' Gaul of the Celts (proto-historic); to be followed in succession by Roman, Merovingian and Carolingian Gaul. These long-drawn out episodes seem, one after another, to have taken similar courses: each in turn prospered, and as regularly declined, as if each was from the start doomed to failure and oblivion, whatever the particular circumstances of its eclipse.

Was there some system at work here, some underlying recurrent process? Perhaps these changes, visible over the long term, are related to the slow ebb and flow of cyclical fluctuations extending over several centuries? Explanations for such trends remain, alas, largely hidden from us for lack of historical evidence. Are we even sure they occurred? Only one or two historians have concerned themselves with these questions.

My aim is to do no more than introduce some economic language to these distant problems, to show that while economic factors were by no means the only ones at work in these far-off centuries, they may nevertheless have played their part. (The reader will no doubt have suspected as much.)

From this point of view, the important thing to note is that during these four long episodes, covering roughly a thousand years between them, whatever the political or economic peaks and troughs, no revolutionary process occurred such as to transform the deep-seated structures and patterns of life: nothing, that is, comparable to the establishment of agriculture several millennia earlier, or to the energy revolution of the Middle Ages, which will presently be discussed. As Robert Fossier has rightly remarked, 'no sudden transformation took place between Roman times and the ninth century'. One might even go further, with Michel Roblin who argues that 'steady evolution ruled out any sudden or far-reaching upheaval between the first century AD and the eleventh'.[118]

The Roman conquest of Gaul: can it be explained?

Independent Gaul was smashed by the swift and bloody Roman conquest. The events (the sieges of Gergovia and Alesia) and the heroes of the story (Ariovistus, Julius Caesar and Vercingetorix) are well-known. It is not my intention to repeat a story imprinted on the memory of every French schoolchild. Not that I am opposed to story-telling: history can tell a tale and be all the more exciting for it. I hope in later volumes of this book to take the opportunity of telling the tale of French history down the ages. But for the moment, I am engaged upon a different 'experiment'. This chapter aims, as I have said, to shed some light on the major stages in French history, paying special attention to the evidence about population, in the hope of identifying the rhythms of an underlying history. So for the moment I am obliged to confine myself to one sector of the historical landscape. While considering independent Gaul, I shall not even try to paint a general picture of its people, institutions, events, societies, economy, or of its secret and in many ways miraculous civilization. This would run counter to the logic of an attempt at explanation. Other approaches and other explanations will follow. I shall eventually return to consider in a different light the landscape we shall now be crossing so rapidly. The reader who bears with me till then will find himself returning to the stern and rebarbative society of Celtic Gaul, to the druids who cut boughs of mistletoe with golden sickles, and to the early Gallo-Roman towns with their combinations of different cultures.

The question I want to ask for now is how the violent episode of the conquest fits into the historical perspective of independent Gaul. Unfortunately, the explanations advanced by historians are not wholly satisfactory or unbiased, obscured as they are by partisan sentiments: inevitably perhaps, given the subject.

The first surprise is that Gaul was conquered within a few years (58 to 52 BC) whereas it took Rome two centuries to subdue Spain. Strabo (the Greek geographer born about the time of the conquest of Gaul) was one of the first to point out this difference.[119]

FIGURE 16
Caesar's Gallic wars (58 to 52 BC)

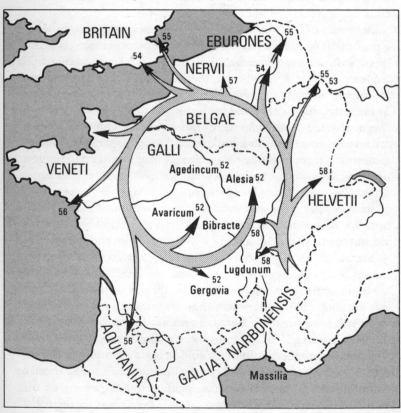

The Roman army's rapid advance across such a vast territory proves that Gaul must have had a fairly developed road network and sufficient agricultural resources to feed men and horses.

And yet *Gallia comata*, 'long-haired' Gaul, had the wherewithal to resist: a large population, *possibly* ten million inhabitants or more; higher density of settlement than the Mediterranean regions under Roman rule; a degree of vitality, indeed a certain prosperity, although the word may seem inappropriate – some historians think Gaul was actually going through a fairly serious economic crisis just before Caesar's arrival. But this crisis, if such there was, did not wipe out evidence of economic coherence and good health. Such evidence should warn us against any simple or one-dimensional explanation of the collapse.

We should beware for instance of laying everything at the door of the superior Roman legions, or the military genius of Julius Caesar (who almost immediately isolated Gaul by repulsing first the Helvetii then the German tribes, finally landing in England and crushing the Veneti fleet). We should not of course underestimate Caesar's role, his lucidity and his prompt actions. But is it enough to argue that the Gauls, who were after all brave fighters, equipped with excellent swords and backed up by an impressive cavalry force, simply gave up at the first setback? That would be to suggest that they displayed the qualities and defects people sometimes attribute to present-day Frenchmen.

The defeat of the Gauls calls for not one but several explanations. We should remember that the conquest of Gaul was not the first, but the third and final act in a sequence. After the bad scare of the Second Punic War, and before the defeat of Carthage, the Romans had fought three fierce campaigns (in 197, 194 and 191 BC) in an attempt to subdue Cisalpine Gaul, which had so defiantly resisted them – its warriors had gone as far as Rome and fought naked against the Romans to make mock of their heavy armour. Then in 121 BC, the Romans had occupied the Provincia (Narbonensis), the most populous area of Transalpine Gaul. By this decisive victory, Rome not only opened up the road to the Iberian peninsula but also struck a mortal blow at the hegemony of the Arverni, and occupied the territory of the Allobroges from the Rhône to Lake Geneva. The Provincia provided a forward base for the advance on the north.

So Caesar's conquest of Gaul was preceded by preliminaries of some moment, which, as Alain Guillerm says, 'destabilized Celtic territory'.[120] It is true that the last of these events had taken place sixty years before Caesar's campaigns. But that does not rule out a connection between these episodes and the rapid collapse of independent Gaul. A comparison might be the way colonial France occupied first Algeria (1830) then Tunisia (1881–3) before forcing its way much later into Morocco (1911–12).

Is it not – all too obviously – the case that Gaul brought about its own defeat by its divisions, its lack of political unity, its 'chaos' as Michelet put it?[121] If Gaul had been a 'nation' or even a coherent political unit, one could quite justifiably speak of treason: on the part of the Aedui, the Remi and many other 'collaborators' – all those Gallic cavalrymen for instance who rode alongside Caesar, or the Lingones, a powerful tribe in the Langres region who more than once lent money to the invader. Gaul was in reality a mosaic of perpetually warring 'tribes', some 60 to 80 *civitates* as the Romans called them; and each of these divisions was itself fragmented. In short, Gaul was hopelessly divided: it was a country where 'rivalries were stronger than the brotherhood of race or identity of language, creed and culture'.[122] Even the druids were unable to unite the Gauls against the invader, try as they might. The country was thus easy prey. Caesar was able to play off one group against another, dividing to conquer. And it is always possible to think that a Gaul united enough to form a strong state might have stood up better to the Romans.

Well, that is one point of view. But one could argue the opposite without falling into a paradox. Coming back to the striking contrast between the rapid conquest of Gaul and the long-drawn-out subjugation of Spain, let us note that geography may have played its part. Gaul, north of the Pyrenees, was a land wide open, rich, relatively populous, with a network of usable roads: it posed no problems of forage or supply. Spain, south of the Pyrenees, was hostile behind its natural barricades, and barren, offering few resources.[123] Strabo notes a further contrast, probably a decisive one: whereas the Spanish resistance was widely scattered, and devoted to what we would call guerrilla warfare, resistance in Gaul quickly became concentrated, which rendered it no less energetic, but much more vulnerable, liable to be overcome in a single campaign. In short, it could be argued that it was Gaul's very coherence, making it possible to mobilize an immense relief army, which enabled it to be crushed in a single major encounter, the siege of Alesia in 52 BC. A guerrilla war on the other hand might have harassed the enemy and seriously delayed him. Strabo's remarks are supported by the experience of other colonial conquests in history. Take the Muslim conquests in the seventh century AD for example: they rapidly overcame Syria (634); Egypt (636) and even Persia (641) which only a few years earlier had singlehandedly defied and inflicted damage on Justinian's Rome. On the other hand it would take Islam fifty years (650–700) to assert its control, and then only in part, over the less organized Maghreb. But Visigoth Spain, a coherent unit, fell to the Muslims at a blow in 711.

Nevertheless, it is not easy to explain Caesar's success. Perhaps this is because of divided opinion amongst historians. Certain writers, especially in the past, have hailed Rome's triumph as having propelled France into a Latinate culture, one of the major components of our present civilization. This was the view taken by Gustave Bloch in the valuable volume he contributed in 1911 to Ernest Lavisse's *Histoire de France*.[124] Others, such as Ferdinand Lot,[125] have considered the Roman conquest as the major disaster in our national history, stifling indigenous development, and putting an end to what France might have been. Camille Jullian, whose nationalism is worn even more obviously on his sleeve, goes so far as to suggest that Gaul, without Rome, might have become assimilated to the Greek civilization of Marseilles (founded 600 BC)[126] – a thesis rather difficult to substantiate. It is true that the Gauls did use the Greek alphabet and that it was not confined to a cultivated elite. According to Strabo, 'the Gauls drew up business contracts in Greek'.[127]

The truth is that the question lies wide open to any counterfactual hypothesis – that perpetual temptation to rewrite the course of history. Alain Guillerm for instance is convinced that Gaul left to herself could have assimilated and neutralized the Germanic tribes under Ariovistus,[128] whereas Roman Gaul was not strong enough in later centuries to withstand the barbarian invasions which finally toppled it. While we are at it, why not invent another scenario: what if Caesar had lost the siege of Alesia, and Rome had then given up trying to conquer Gaul, just as after the failure of Varus (in AD 9) it gave up trying to subdue a Germany which was a hundred times less advanced than Gaul, and for that very reason (among others) harder to overcome? But then why not imagine the opposite? If Rome had been able to establish its frontier along the Elbe instead of the Rhine, perhaps the whole destiny of Europe would have been different.

The fact remains that, once conquered, Gaul quickly succumbed to the victor, opening its doors to the civilization of Italy and the Mediterranean; whether this was done willingly, in full knowledge of the consequences or not, it would profoundly change the country's destiny. It is true that the Gallic nobility began collaborating at an early stage and contributed to the cultural assimilation of Gaul by Rome. And Roman rule, although harsh immediately after the conquest, became more liberal under those 'two great emperors Tiberius (AD 14–37) and Claudius (AD 41–54) who, although much maligned by ancient historiography were the true founders of the stability and survival of the Roman Empire'. The historian Siegfried Jan de Laet has even dared suggest that they replaced 'the colonialism of the Republic with a sort of commonwealth'.[129] We may note in passing that Claudius was responsible for the construction of most of the road network of northern Gaul – a magnificent offering.[130] In AD 48, disregarding the protests of the political aristocracy in Rome, he opened the Senate to Gallo-Roman 'senators'.

But one should beware of categorical judgements. Claudius, whose nickname in Rome was 'the Gaul' (because he had been born in Lyon) certainly wanted to create a peaceable Gaul reconciled with the Empire, but that did not stop him from persecuting the druids who had to take refuge in England. What we have here then is not so much liberalism as an intelligent attempt at assimilation, something which Augustus had already set in train. Julius Caesar's heir had made four visits to Gaul, the longest of them (from 16 to 15 BC) to Lyon, a city founded in 43 BC; and the last in 10 BC, in order to put down unrest on the Rhine frontier. He had also after all divided Gaul into four provinces (Narbonensis, Aquitania, Lugudunensis and Belgica) and continued, as Julius Caesar had before him, to levy soldiers there. He also founded many towns and in order to embellish them did not hesitate to spend part of the treasures of Antony and Cleopatra, as well as his own personal fortune: it is to him that we owe the Maison Carrée in Nîmes, the Pont du Gard viaduct and the Roman theatres in Orange, Arles, Vienne and Lyon. 'Gaul under Augustus was a vast building site' covered with public works.[131] The new towns, in which the Gallic aristocracy would gradually come to reside, were effective centres for Romanization as well as a stimulus to economic progress. Nowadays we tend to say that if the building trade is healthy, everything else is too; it may have been true more than once during our history.

A further factor favouring cultural assimilation was that Gaul was bordered to the south by Spain and the Narbonensis, a province Romanized well ahead of the 'three parts of Gaul'.

What was more, it was protected from incursions across the Rhine by a strong army: the frontier was manned by a hundred thousand soldiers. Vespasian and Domitian would further strengthen these defences by building along the west bank of the Rhine the *limes*, a fortified frontier which ran from opposite Koblenz down the Neckar and on to the Danube. Behind the *limes*, as far as the Rhine, stretched the 'decuman' fields, colonized by settlers.

Eventually in AD 43, on the prompting of Claudius, the legions conquered England, which had to be administered thereafter. Consequently Gaul was guaranteed from attack from the north. Boulogne became a town and the port, with its huge lighthouse, for many years harboured a Roman fleet with orders to patrol the Channel and the North Sea. Security and the *pax romana* were certainly powerful influences on a population which had not known peace and security for years. Rome gave Gaul and the Gauls Latin names (*Gallia*, *Galli*); the terms 'Celt' and 'Celtic' died out. Rome also provided Gaul with a civilization, after a colonial takeover which was in this respect a success. Moreover with the Rhine frontier, fixed by Julius Caesar, Rome gave Gaul its north-west boundary, cutting it off from central Europe whether Celtic (and long-forgotten) or Germanic.

Protected, encircled, endowed with roads, towns, schools and an army whose ranks were open to it, Gaul nevertheless took some time to accept its new destiny wholeheartedly. Despite Tiberius, despite Claudius, despite the advantages of a superior civilization, the first century of Roman rule was troubled, marked by unrest and by rebellions, some of them spectacular and all of them bloody. Certain French historians have indulged in a sort of retrospective nationalism over this resistance, over-exaggerating its importance.[132] I prefer the more measured judgement of Gustave Bloch (1911) and most other historians. These rebellions were really the expression of the humiliation more or less consciously felt by a conquered people; of the various discontents of different regions; the disgruntlement of peasants groaning under taxes and worried by the cadastral land-surveys; the irritation of aristocrats won over to Latin civilization but angered by malpractice within the imperial administration; and the exasperation of artisans who were sometimes forced to flee across the Rhine to escape harassment by the tax authorities.

The unrest reached a peak during the crisis which seriously unsettled the Empire at the end of Nero's reign and after his death in AD 68. A rash of rebellions broke out in several areas of Gaul, sometimes inspired by noblemen who had hitherto been loyal servants of Rome. No sooner was a revolt put down in one place, than it resurfaced somewhere else. Matters were made worse by the mutiny of several legions, taking advantage of political divisions in Rome. The Rhine army, which included many Belgian and German auxiliaries, marched against Gaul in 69. The country barely escaped wholesale pillage. But Caius Julius Civilis, a Batavian or rather German, exploited the situation, put himself at the head of the disbanded legions and offered the towns of Gaul the chance to recover their freedom, and to constitute a Gallic Empire for this purpose. Such an Empire was even briefly proclaimed, in the euphoric moments when there was no Roman army in Gaul.

At this point, two factors intervened to calm matters down. Firstly, there was the distrust felt by Gaul for its ancient German enemy. Such distrust was not without reason: Civilis was probably preparing his own Gallic Wars – was he not systematically destroying the fortifications along the *limes*? Secondly, news came from Rome of the end of the civil war, the triumph of Vespasian, 'the common-sense emperor', and a return to strong government. Orders had been issued to send into Gaul all the troops from the neighbouring countries – Italy, Spain, England. Amid general confusion, the tribe of the Remi summoned all the cities of Gaul to send representatives to Durocortorum (Reims). The deliberations of this assembly led to the triumph of the peace party, and a proclamation was sent to the Treveri requesting them, in the name of all Gaul, to abandon the struggle. The Treveri refused, but were quickly overwhelmed and dispersed by a powerful Roman army under Q. Petilius Cerealis. There was still Civilis to be dealt with. But this was now a matter between Romans and Germans, and following defeat upon defeat, Civilis chose to fall back across the Rhine.[133]

This bloody episode represented the last serious resistance to the conquest in Gaul. Thus from 52 BC to AD 70, a century of Roman rule had finally succeeded in making the Roman writ run more or less everywhere.

Time was already at work: and time would be at work even longer. We should not forget that over five hundred years elapsed between the siege of Alesia (52 BC) and the collapse (in theory at least) of the Western Empire in 476. What would have happened in Algeria if France had occupied the newly formed Regency of Algiers in 1516 and stayed there until 1962? History moved more slowly in those days than it does today. Unlike a river which flows swiftly at its source but more slowly towards its mouth, the tide of history flows slowly at first and only speeds up as it reaches us and our time. An accumulation of experience and circumstances made Gaul Roman – for better or worse, who shall say?

I do not at any rate think we can agree with Michelet that 'Gaul was lost like Atlantis'.[134] Gaul did not sink with all hands after Alesia. In Pierre Lance's view, Gaul remains the underground current, the living source of the history of France.[135] So whether or not one prefers it to our Latin heritage, our Celtic heritage cannot

81

be gainsaid: like it or not, we French share a double heredity. All the same, in cultural terms the Celtic world lost two major battles in Gaul: its language, although still spoken for a long time in certain rural areas, sometimes as late as the twelfth century,[136] has left no more than residual traces in modern French (Breton was a language re-imported from the British Isles in the sixth century or a little earlier). And the Celtic religion, which had flourished for so long, being perpetuated without difficulty during the polytheistic Roman period, was finally overtaken by Christianity with its single God. It would survive only in the store of pagan folklore and popular belief. Can one therefore truly speak of the 'cultural genocide' of Gaul?[137]

The apogee of Roman Gaul: the reign of Commodus

Roman Gaul reached its apogee two centuries after the conquest, with the reign of Commodus, the less than worthy son of Marcus Aurelius. The country's fate was tied to the fortunes of the Empire: when the Empire flourished, Gaul prospered; when the Empire declined, Gaul's fortunes followed suit. Gaul was in fact contained within a kind of world-economy, within that complex of regions centred on the Mediterranean, their pulses beating to the same rhythm: a complex prolonged eastward, in economic respects, as far as Persia, India and the Indian Ocean. At its northern edge, it bordered on the void, looking out on the Baltic and the North Sea, patrolled by the Roman fleet based at Boulogne. To the south, it was blocked by the immensity of the Sahara – but received gold carried from the Sudan by routes across what is now Morocco. In short, the dependent existence of Gaul was governed by the changing fortunes and circumstances of this mighty complex.

The Empire remained in good shape until the death of Marcus Aurelius in AD 161, and Gaul enjoyed the benefits of the *pax romana* until that time. Its economy was expanding: roads, towns and trade were transforming it. Its population was increasing again, more than compensating for the bloody losses of the conquest, the massacres and deportations into slavery which had cut swathes

.traordinary achieve-
At first sight of these
ne's eyes. Of course
48 The future would
ure often betrays the

he form it took, were
1 depth from place to
ice of a differential
diversities. Thus the
terways of the Rhône
e and the Moselle to
culties became seri-
1 Lyon, became the
red the Narbonensis:
across Provence and
rs earlier than the rest
lated and more influ-
vilege, later on in the
otection until 415–43
dians.

erences and contrasts
he Ile-de-France also
ile in the face of the
e nature of an enclave

invasion

nding to break down
D 170–80. The Rhine
nanic marauders were
reached Alsace. One
was restored quickly
Gaul peace and tran-

---

through the people of Gaul. No words can do justice to the atrocities of the conquest: whole tribes, like the Aduatici and the Eburones, between the Rhine and the Scheldt, had been wiped out or sold into slavery,[138] and Caesar had literally 'flooded all the slave markets in Italy with human merchandise'.[139]

Ferdinand Lot[140] was exaggerating when he estimated the population of Gaul before Caesar at 20 million, but Karl Julius Beloch in turn was surely guilty of an underestimate when he calculated that in AD 14 Gaul could have had no more than 4,900,000 inhabitants altogether (1,500,000 and a density of 15 in the Narbonensis, and 3,400,000 in the rest of Gaul, with a density of 6.3).[141] It seems odd to me that he attributes to prosperous Gaul such low densities of settlement within an Empire whose population he sets at about 54 million for an area of 3,340,000 square kilometres, that is 16 inhabitants per square kilometre. If that is the average, Gaul with its 638,000 square kilometres should have had rather more than 10 million inhabitants. Perhaps we can accept as a minimum the 8 or 9 million estimated by Cavaignac, which a recent history of the population thinks 'fairly well established'.[142] But what was the figure a hundred and fifty years later, in the days of Marcus Aurelius and Commodus, when Gaul was at the peak of its prosperity?

This time, Karl Julius Beloch does not hesitate to suggest a much higher figure. Never had the Roman Empire been as populous, he says, as in the early third century: the population had doubled since the death of Caesar. So the five million Gauls he allowed for in AD 14 (a figure which he revised upwards in fact to six or seven million) would have become at least ten million, if not twelve or fourteen, with a density of some 20 inhabitants to the square kilometre.[143] I think these figures may be more reliable than Josiah C. Russell's. But let us agree a minimum of about 10 million. And let us assume that the urban population accounted for 10% of them (not 20% as Robert Fossier[144] suggests: 'four Gauls out of five were country dwellers'). If so, about one million Gauls would have been living in the towns, and supposing there to be about a thousand urban settlements worthy of the name, that would work out at about 1,000 inhabitants per town.

The reader should not protest at the modesty of this figure: it is

FIGURE 17
The road network in Roman Gaul

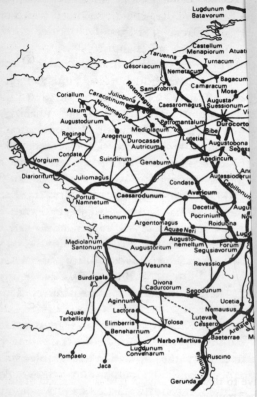

The density of the road network throughout the t
that both population and production were increas

baths, were an impressive sight. What an e
ment it was to bring water to Lyon, or Vienne
mighty aqueducts, one can hardly believe
they were in a way showpieces, 'stage sets'.
show how fragile they were – but then the fu
past.

The urbanization of Gaul at any rate, and
a striking sign of its Romanization. Varying
place, Roman influence now offers evide
history, adding new features to pre-existing
Romans concentrated their efforts on the w
and Saône, leading northwards via the Meu
the ever-troubled Rhine frontier. When di
ous in this area, Trèves/Trier, rather tha
country's real capital. The Romans also favo
the Via Domitia and the Via Aurelia led
Languedoc to Spain. Conquered seventy ye
of Gaul, the Narbonensis, more densely pop
enced by Roman culture, would have the pr
Dark Ages, of remaining under 'Roman' pr
and the arrival of the Visigoths and Burgur

All this contributed further to the diff
between the north and the south of France.
preserved its Roman culture for a long wl
Franks, but the Ile-de-France was more in tl
in an all-encompassing barbarian world.

Roman Gaul in troub
internal division and barbariar

The *pax romana* was already disturbed and t
by the end of the second century, in about
frontier was by now up in arms: in 162, Ger
getting into northern Belgica; in 174, other
should not exaggerate these incidents – ord
and easily.[149] The frontier which afforded

still probably too high. Similar calculations for
the prosperous fifteenth century work out at an
of 500 per town! Our figure may be too hig
Gallo-Roman towns measuring about 200 to 3
there were many more small bourgs, their h
with straw; here the forum was simply the mai
peasants from the nearby countryside brougl
townspeople. But towns they were, just the sai

FIGURE 19
Roman aqueducts into Lyon

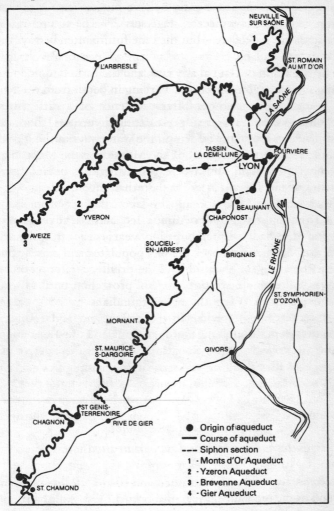

The four aqueducts which provided Lyon's water supply are evidence in themselves of the importance of the Gallo-Roman settlement there. When the barbarian invasions irretrievably damaged this water system, Lyon had partially to abandon its former site.

quillity would not seriously be breached until much later, in 253, by the Franks and the Alemanni. Figure 20 shows that the eastern half of Gaul was subject to raids reaching as far south as the lower Rhône valley and even across to Spain. The panic and disorder were such that in 260 a Gallic officer, Postumus, was proclaimed emperor of Gaul by his troops, not in a spirit of revolt against Rome, but in order to repel the invader. He succeeded in doing so for eight years, even chasing the barbarians back across the Rhine, and restoring order and confidence to Gaul. But in 268, his own troops assassinated him outside Mainz (Moguntiacum), because he had forbidden looting. The 'empire' of Gaul did not long outlive him: in 273, Tetricus, the last of his successors, was vanquished by the emperor Aurelian, and two years later, in 275, several yawning breaches opened up again in the eastern frontier.

This time, the whole of Gaul was affected: overwhelmed, it was put to fire and the sword. It became clear that order could not now be restored, as had still been hoped some years earlier. It was at this point that the towns fell back on their own resources, hastily building fortifications for themselves. We should note, however, that this was still over a century before the 'real' barbarian invasions. For it was only on 31 December 406 that the so-called 'great invasion' took place, led by Radagaisus. Crossing the frozen Rhine, his followers swept through the whole of Gaul, in a tumult of mingled peoples; an invasion that was, paradoxically, less destructive in the end perhaps than the breakthrough of 275.[150]

These dates: 253, 275, 406, should be borne in mind; they prove that Gaul's decline had begun well before the great invasions of the fifth century. The decline of Gaul is synonymous with the decline of the Roman Empire – the sick man who took so long to die. Historians have long debated whether the Empire died from within, bearing its own responsibility for what happened, or whether it succumbed to the hammer-blows of the barbarians, being 'done to death', as André Piganiol[151] maintains. Such questions call for an answer, though we are unlikely to settle the debate, especially since I have chosen to approach it from a particular angle. But can anyone be confident of coming up with the right answer in an area like this?

An ever-rekindled fire of protest

Like the Empire, Gaul too was attacked from within. It witnessed simultaneously a political crisis challenging the authority of the state, that is, the Empire; a social crisis that threatened the stability of its hierarchies; and lastly a damaging deterioration in the economy, of uncertain origin but perceptible effect – there was a fall in the population, in itself a sign that things were not going too well.

FIGURE 20
The invasions of the third century AD

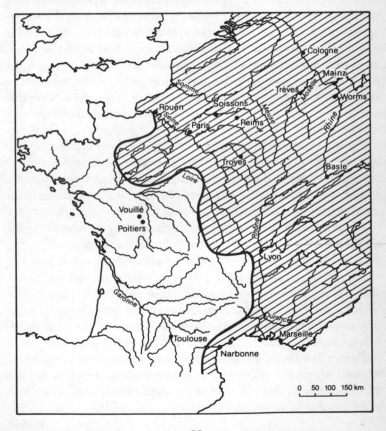

The most important feature of the crisis – consequence as much as cause perhaps – was the unrest spreading among the rural masses (that is, the bulk of the population): a grumbling 'peasant's revolt', almost impossible to quell, and difficult for historians to pin down to any one place. Beyond the *ager* or *laboratorium* cultivated land, lay the vast forests, swamps, hills and scrubland which covered such huge areas and into which any outlaw could quickly disappear. Terms in familiar use, *tractus* or *saltus*,[152] denoted these outlying lands, only partly touched by human settlement – 'wildernesses' forming a third category as it were, alongside town and country-side.[153] Woodlands, huge tracts of which still covered Gaul, contrasted not only with the 'clearings' of the towns, but also with 'civilized' farmland. They held terrors and fantasies: riding through a forest at night sent men mad it was said, and anyone who did so risked being taken for a criminal, according to Anglo-Saxon law, unless he announced his presence by sounding a horn.[154] No doubt few people apart from outlaws or men on the run would have sought refuge there anyway: rather as in colonial America, where runaway slaves from the plantations could find shelter only in virgin forests.

The situation of the peasants of Gaul, whether slaves or small landowners (theoretically free but in practice extremely depen-dent) had progressively declined. As labour became scarce, power-ful landowners, the *potentes*, strove to keep it by force on their large and magnificent estates, the villas, which we now know from exca-vation and particularly from aerial photography to have been far more numerous than was once thought. In the Somme valley for instance, long assumed to have been cultivated only round the towns, with the rest of the country lying waste, systematic aerial observations made by Roger Agache have brought to light on the contrary 'a region covered with huge farms' (680 have so far been plotted with certainty) interspersed with a few tiny settlements.[155] A similar aerial survey is being carried out in Brittany.

The Gallo-Roman villas probably accounted for the bulk of cul-tivated farmland. Generally consisting of about a thousand hec-tares, sometimes more, of arable land, pasture and woodland, these farms were very large, and had extensive buildings: one Gallo-

Roman villa in Montmaurin in Haute-Garonne had 1,500 hectares of farmland and 18 hectares of buildings.[156] Another in the *département* of the Somme, Warfusée Abancourt, had buildings extending over 330 metres.[157] One at Canet near Béziers was more modest: its buildings covered an area of 100 by 62 metres.[158] Near Bordeaux was a fortified villa, already developing into a castle, Burgus Leontii, later to become Bourg-sur-Gironde. Wherever excavations are undertaken today, at Creil on the Oise, for instance, new villas are discovered with their thick walls, heaps of pottery tiles, and ruined leaden conduits for carrying water. Some windows or rather remains of windows have even been found, still roughly embedded in lead surrounds.[159]

Each villa consisted of at least two sections: on one hand there was the *urbana* where the masters lived, surrounded with all the comforts they could wish for, after the Roman fashion: courtyard, peristyle, heating, baths and so on. Apollinaris Sidonius (430–87) who lived in his villa at Avitacus in the Auvergne, about twenty kilometres from Clermont (Avitacus has been firmly identified with the present-day village of Aydat), wrote in June 465 to one of his friends who had remained in town during the hot weather, boasting of the charms of his rural retreat, and the beauty of his baths 'which stand comparison' with the baths contained in public buildings.[160] The master's lodging was a delightful place no doubt. But alongside it there would have been the buildings of the *rusticana*, housing both the farm's cellars and granaries and the quarters of the slaves: the huge kitchen where they ate, the rooms where they slept. Standing apart would be the *ergastulae*, where offenders were locked up, and the house of the *villacus* and his wife who oversaw the labour of the slave gangs and were responsible for managing the farm. Around the villa ran a boundary wall; sometimes, though identification is not certain, there would be a sanctuary.

The usual building plan seems to follow the directions of the Roman agronomists, Varro or Columella – in the choice of site, the design of the buildings and the orientation (facing south and east) of the master's house. This plan is found elsewhere throughout the Roman Empire. Many of these villas ceased to exist as such – and the word 'villa' itself changed in meaning, as villages took over the farming of the estates,[161] which long survived as viable undertakings. It is certainly the case that 'monasteries under St Benedict's rule adopted the layout of the Roman villa'.[162]

But we are less interested in the fabric of the dwellings and the walls surrounding the villa than in its human occupants. The Gallo-Roman villa was a monstrous concentration, 'a veritable rural factory . . . much worse . . . than the urban factories of the nineteenth century in England and France'.[163] It was a machine for enslaving and crushing human beings. In about 451, a monk, distressed at the lot of these victims, wrote:

> When small landowners have lost their houses and plots of land to brigands, or have been expelled by the tax officials, they take refuge on some rich man's estate and become settlers . . . All these people who go to live on the lands of the rich are changed as if they had drunk Circe's potion and been turned into slaves.[164]

Even beggars, itinerants, outlaws and deserters from the army would be forcibly enrolled, then 'fettered to the land and subject to the master'.[165] So we should not be misled by the terms 'small farmer' or 'settler'. The Roman Empire had this dialectical ambiguity between a slave and a settler: the settler was at best a serf, to borrow a term used later.

This trauma was the more acute and hard felt[166] since slavery, which had soon spread everywhere, seems to have been less practised among the Celts than among Mediterranean peoples.[167] What was more, by the efficiency of their production methods, the large estates had grown even larger, annexing as if absent-mindedly the lands of small farmers round about. A slave-owning regime was thus in constant expansion: slaves represented perhaps a third of the population. The system depended on a steady supply of men, maintained by innumerable raids to take captives, even after the end of the Roman presence in Gaul. In the reign of Dagobert for instance (629–39), the royal army returned from an expedition to Aquitaine, bringing long columns of prisoners attached two by two 'like dogs'.[168] But then slaves wore out quickly: on the American plantations of the seventeenth and eighteenth centuries, a slave lasted seven years on average.

To keep up numbers and prevent escapes, a strong state was necessary, providing an ever-present threat of repression. Had not the move in Rome itself from Republic to Empire, that is, to a strong regime supported by the propertied classes, been the consequence of rebellions by slaves? But in Gaul, governmental authority had declined during the reign of Commodus: protests, uprisings and 'peasant revolts' quickly followed. Under Diocletian and Maximianus by contrast (284–305) the imperial regime reasserted its authority and slavery returned in force. But not for long: peasant uprisings soon broke out again.

The first known incidence of revolt was a kind of mass banditry led by one Maternus[169] in about 186–8, a movement like so many others directed at the villages, farms and villas. Its numbers swelled after early success, then scattered after their first encounters with the forces of order, which they could not withstand: in every age, peasant uprisings have proved unable to resist organized soldiery. But defeat did not prevent them surviving in clandestine form. Maximianus put down all the uprisings between the Alps and the Rhine; but guerrilla warfare nonetheless continued.

In the third century, on account of the weight of taxation and currency inflation which brought price rises, the peasant threat grew more insistent, to the point where a new word was coined to refer to the rebels: *Bagaudae* (possibly from *baga*, a Celtic word for combat).[170] In about 440, Salvian[171] wrote justifying the Bagaudae:

I shall now speak [he writes] of the Bagaudae, stripped of their possessions by evil or bloodthirsty men, injured and killed, having lost even the honour of a Roman name. And it is they who are blamed for this misfortune, it is to them that we give this cursed name, we who are responsible for it. We call them outlaws, these men we have turned into criminals. For is it not our own iniquity, the dishonesty of our magistrates, our sentences of banishment and our dispossession that has created the Bagaudae?[172]

Most serious of all perhaps, the rebellious peasant welcomed the barbarians, negotiated with them and took advantage of the trouble they caused to launch his own actions, making matters worse. And besides the barbarians who went to battle and pillaged, there were also barbarians attached to the land. Whether they had deserted from the army of their own accord, or been reduced to slavery by great landowners, they became the companions in misfortune of the Gallo-Roman peasants.

Peasant revolts, essentially mobile affairs, sometimes travelled great distances. Perhaps they were most prevalent in western Gaul with its innumerable forest refuges, where Roman authority, never very strong, had quickly evaporated. This would explain an exchange in a fifth-century comedy 'Querulus' ('Groucho') by an unknown author. One of the characters asks his household god 'to give him the strength to fight and dispossess those who are foreigners'. The god replies 'go and live on the Loire'.[173] In these regions, he explains, people live 'under the law of the jungle', and 'everything is permitted'. The author was probably thinking of the Bagaudae.

In a recent book,[174] Pierre Dockès has defended the rebels and magnified their role. 'The massacred Bagaudae were victorious after all,' he even writes. Their tenacity forced the slave-owning regime to shift towards the less harsh system of serfdom – easier to live under since the serf unlike the slave had a house, a family, a plot of ground, and social constraint had been transferred from his shoulders to the land. The serf had more liberty than the slave and his labour was thus more productive. The transformation was not yet complete however, indeed far from it, by the end of Roman Gaul. That would have to wait until at least the Carolingian era, if then. And many factors – economic, political and social – would intervene to an extent that does not quite fit into the over-simple logic of this quasi-Marxist explanation. I think too that the growing decadence of the towns enabled the countryside to achieve a certain freedom. Under the Carolingians, free peasants were apparently still very numerous, although from now on small landowning was 'in sharp decline'.[175]

For the moment, at any rate, I am not so concerned with a general perspective on the Bagaudae as in showing how seriously rural Gaul was shaken and weakened by this unrest. It was a society already in poor shape that the barbarian invasions fell upon and tore apart.

One might also wonder whether it was because of these troubles and misfortunes in the third century that Christianity began to infiltrate Gaul like a ray of hope? The answer is probably no. The first Christian communities appeared in about the 170s in a few towns: Marseille, Lyon, Autun. But even at the time of the Lyon martyrs in 177, they were still only tiny groups, largely composed of Greeks, or easterners who spoke Greek. It was not until the end of the fourth century AD – long after the Edict of Milan (313) establishing complete freedom of worship in the Empire – that Christianity began to take hold in Gaul: it would still be a long time before the masses would really open their arms to it.

The barbarian invasions: not to be underestimated

In the old days, historians laid the blame for the disintegration both of the Roman Empire and of Gaul entirely on the barbarian invasions. Traditional explanations used to lay great stress on their exploits, from the 'great invasion' by Radagaisus in 406 to the arrival in Gaul of the Visigoths in 412 and the Burgundians in 443. The episode was deemed to have been brought to an end when the Romans and their 'barbarian' allies, at the decisive encounter on the Catalaunian Fields in 451, triumphed over Attila and his hordes of Mongol horsemen, who had appeared from the depths of Asia, driving before them the peoples of central Europe and Germany. A mortal threat had been averted. Did the wave of barbarian invasions really change the course of history? Or are modern historians right to assign less significance to them? The answer is both yes and no.

The initial argument advanced by historians seeking to discount the role of the barbarians is the small number of invaders, demonstrated as long ago as 1900 by Hans Delbrück's classic study.[176]

The Franks may have numbered about 80,000, the Burgundians 100,000, the Vandals some 20,000 (compared to about 80,000 when they crossed the Strait of Gibraltar) and the others something similar. Inevitably they would have been outnumbered by a population of several million. Henri Pirenne[177] used to say that the barbarians may have 'barbarized' the Empire, but they were then themselves swallowed up into its population, their language being ousted by Latin and the Romance tongues, and their religion by Christianity.

But then historians have rarely failed to pour varying degrees of scorn on the 'greedy, loud-mouthed, evil-smelling adventurers', as Lucien Romier called them.[178] For one eminent historian, the Franks represented 'a hotbed of vice, fertile ground for debauchery, betrayal and cruelty'[179] – as if the history of the later Roman Empire had been one of virtue, gentleness and loyalty! The old image of savage horsemen pouring into the west was replaced by that of oafs, 'men who gaped to see the collapsing walls of the Empire on whose gates they had been pounding and which they now entered on tiptoe'.[180] (The *limes* after all was described by the Germans as the *Teufelmauer*, the Devil's Wall.) As for their chiefs, they were described by François Guizot, an early writer in this vein, as 'clinging obstinately to the tatters of Roman pomp, like a Negro king wearing European uniform'.[181]

Does all this really make sense? Or did the historians swing from one exaggerated version to another? Robert Fossier[182] was, if I am not mistaken, the first to put forward an equitable description of both sides, of those who came into Gaul and of those who willingly or otherwise received them. Let us recapitulate the argument.

To take the number of invaders first: it is correct to point out the modest size of the westward-moving populations. But independently of the 'invasions', Gaul was already receiving steady transfusions of 'barbarian' blood. A total of about a million people has been suggested. This would still not be very significant if the population of Roman Gaul really was of the order of 20 to 30 million (a figure which has been suggested but which I do not believe). The proportions of the mixture change of course if that figure was nearer 10 million. Paul Dufournet[183] nevertheless maintains that

in Savoy the Burgundian occupation was so insignificant as to
have little effect: the Gallo-Romans living there, he concludes,
probably had as little chance of seeing the Burgundians as French
peasants did of seeing the Germans during the last war. Similarly in
Provence and Languedoc, tensions were far less pronounced than
they were north of Lyon, west of the Massif Central, or in the Paris
basin.[184]

But even if the newcomers were patently in the minority,
minorities are often the active ingredient within societies, altering
the shape and texture of the whole. Moreover infiltration by
barbarians from across the Rhine had begun very early. It had
happened in a variety of ways – via the Roman armies for instance,
as a matter of long-standing practice: the *limes* along the Rhine was
as much filter as protection, one way of recruiting troops and manual labour without danger. Whether placed as slaves on large
estates, or mingling with the local population after having been
billeted in its midst as soldiers, the barbarians, 'their small numbers
swallowed up by the peasant masses . . . contributed to the birth of
the rural but warlike society of the early Middle Ages', the emergence of which would be hard to explain were it not for 'that long
slow penetration of a military element into the lowest stratum of
society'.[185] They must have modified the agricultural landscape in
places, since on the sites of villas – many of which were burned
down – there grew up villages or scattered hamlets echoing the
former settlement patterns of Germany. The development of grazing also changed the face of farming in a number of ways. Lastly,
the Germanic invaders were no longer, despite all the
unfavourable comment, the same people Tacitus had described.
Independently or through contact with the Romans, they had
achieved real progress. Not a few Germans are recorded as serving
in the Roman army as officers on the staff of the legions or auxil-
iary troops, and as such they had been promoted to the rank of
Roman citizens. In short, we find peasants and nobles intermingling at their own levels, not through invasion and pillage but
by peaceful forms of integration which caused no trouble.

Without wishing to revive the now discredited theory of
Augustin Thierry – that the Franks were the ancestors of the nobles

of the *ancien régime*, and the Gauls the ancestors of the serfs and proletarians – I would nevertheless point out that the Frankish aristocracy joined the considerably more numerous ranks of the established Gallo-Roman aristocracy, which survived by 'collaborating' and also by taking refuge in the higher reaches of the Church. The crucial fact, in my view, was that the Frankish aristocracy strengthened and confirmed a social hierarchy which was to last, despite all the inevitable changes and modifications, as long as the *ancien régime* itself, if not longer.

Gaul was all the same terribly wounded by the many barbarian raids, the looting, murder, rape, fire, manhunts, troop movements, and eventually by the permanent expropriation and occupation by the invaders. The result, though impossible to measure, must have been economic disruption and large-scale population loss. 'We may venture to suggest,' writes one historian,[186] 'that a quarter or a third of the population were victims of the invasions, while remembering of course that in some regions, notably in the north and east, it is no exaggeration to say that over half the population was wiped out, if one bears in mind the famine and epidemics that followed', as well as 'the bands of brigands roaming the country'.

The towns suffered enormously and very soon retreated inside their walls. Within their boundaries, they built fortified strongholds in which to take refuge. The ramparts of these improvised constructions were strengthened with stones taken from monuments. Not that this necessarily saved towns from falling to sudden or prolonged sieges by the barbarians: treachery, fear, hunger or lack of water delivered them up to the enemy. The emperor Julian (361–363) who enjoyed his stay in Lutetia (Paris) during a brief visit to Gaul, wrote to the Athenians that 'the number of towns [in Gaul] whose walls have been destroyed is now about forty-five'.[187]

Some regions survived unscathed, it is true: the south 'saw nothing comparable to what happened north of Lyon or west of the Massif Central'.[188] In fourth-century Toulouse, according to Ausonius, 'life went on just as it had before, the same as in centuries past'.[189] But on the whole, the towns began to shrink: their territory was reclaimed by fields and gardens. Former towns became (or reverted to being) little more than villages, their narrow streets lined with low thatched cottages. The wealthier landowners had left town and retired to their villas, to defend them or to defend themselves inside them, to be closer to their property, and to escape the heavy taxes levied on town-dwellers. Deprived of the thriving markets of the past, scraping a living from their reduced means, the towns tended towards self-sufficiency, as Alexander Rustow[190] has written, eating only the produce of their immediate neighbourhood, from the fields round about. Lyon, its aqueducts broken, slid down from its original site. The countryside too became depopulated. Many villas met tragic ends, as we know from plentiful archaeological evidence. *Agri deserti* spread everywhere. And yet, despite the disaster that had befallen them, despite all that has been said, the collapse of the ancient world 'did not bring about *ipso facto* the complete death of the towns'.[191] They did not overnight become 'corpses of towns' as St Anthony eloquently but excessively put it. The barbarian kings chose certain towns in which to set up their *palatium*, and these were to be peaks of achievement within the limits of the level of trade and civilization of the time. They would survive. Indeed it is somewhat surprising that while the downward economic trend continued for so long to exert its harmful pressure, and Roman Gaul continued inexorably to decline, it did nevertheless withstand these blows. Was it, as I am inclined to think, because Gaul had had a reasonably high standard of living in the first place; because it had a fundamentally healthy constitution? Or was it because the prevailing economic trends did not always affect Gaul deeply, because the Empire was a complex entity – in decline to be sure, but at a slow pace?

Rome: a world-economy

The decline of the Roman Empire unarguably dominated and dictated the destiny of Gaul, but that does not make matters more straightforward – far from it. No serious historian feels qualified to resolve the question categorically, so we all try to surround ourselves with reasonable precautions. I am thinking in particular of the circumstantial conclusion of Marie-Bernadette Bruguière's fine study, which attempts to reconcile all sides of the question.[192]

But if we want to see a little more clearly, we have no choice but to begin with some plausible if not verifiable hypotheses.

The decline of the Empire can be traced on a number of levels – political, economic, social and cultural. We can all agree that it was slow, that it was observable over a long period, and also that it was uneven, that is to say it took the form of deterioration at different times and in different places.

The first signs of weakness were political – the decline of the Empire, its institutions and its army. Their final collapse is conventionally identified with the fall of the Western Empire: in 476, Romulus Augustulus was landed at Ravenna by Odoacer the leader of the Heruli, and the imperial insignia were transferred to Constantinople. It was but a formality, the belated death certificate being no more than official recognition of what had long since occurred. As Fustel de Coulanges put it, 'the Roman Empire had died but nobody noticed'.[193]

The Empire was an economic reality however, as well as a political one: an area within which trading could take place, centred on the Mediterranean Sea and prolonged inland by routes penetrating the countries that bordered it on all sides. The area controlled and stimulated by Rome was a world-economy, a coherent unit covering a large fragment of the planet. And this coherent unit, of which Gaul was a dependent sector, would last until at least the eighth or ninth century, that is until the reign of Charlemagne. Rome seems to have had an indefinite lease of life.

In this historical debate, the work of Henri Pirenne, especially his book *Mahomet et Charlemagne* (1937) is remarkable for having perceived the importance of this world-economy: he suspected that its rhythms were significant, and introduced the perspective of political economy into these obscure centuries, sandwiched between the barbarian invasions of the fifth century and the Muslim invasions of the seventh, eighth and ninth. Pirenne's arguments are now well known. Fifty years ago, they amazed historians: he maintained that the Islamic conquest was significant above

FIGURE 21
The Roman world-economy

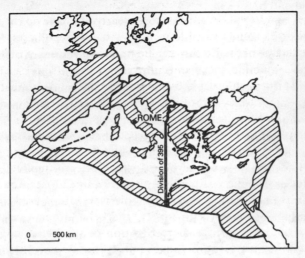

The division of the Roman Empire in 395 into an eastern part and a
western part did not destroy the unity of the Roman world-economy,
which was prolonged beyond the frontiers of the Empire towards the
Danube, the Red Sea and the Indian Ocean.

all for the capture of the Mediterranean, which the infidels com-
mandeered, closing it to Christian shipping and thus sealing the
irremediable fate of the West.

If the reader will bear with me a little, he or she will see how
much I accept or reject of Pirenne's now contested thesis. The crit-
icisms and reservations made of it in the past by historians such as
Marc Bloch,[194] Etienne Sabbe[195] or François-Louis Ganshof[196] –
who believed that they had effectively demolished Pirenne's
'theory' – merely prove that the Mediterranean was not completely closed during these centuries, and that some trading links
were even maintained between Gaul and the Levant. What they do
not clearly enough say is whether Mediterranean trade *slowed down*
or not, and if so between what dates.

In my view traffic did indeed slow down, and in the end that is what matters.

What one finds is in fact a slow decline, over several centuries, and it was this decline that was principally to blame for the ruin and progressive collapse of the Roman Empire. Without entirely absolving the barbarians, I do not regard them as primarily responsible, any more than I do the rulers of the Empire. The latter were often men of mediocre talent, it is true, but among them were several figures of astonishing stature – Diocletian or Constantine for example. Nor do I blame the men of war, such as Stilicho (359–408) or Aetius (390–454), who played an admirable and unexpected part in the defence of the integrity of Gaul. The efforts of all, the best and the worst, were after all to some extent doomed from the start.

Taking as my starting point the year AD 150, which *broadly* represents the high point of Roman Gaul, and as my destination the year 950, which *broadly* represents the low point of the Carolingian era, I propose to take some liberties and imagine a steadily downward general trend, from 150 to 950, without being unduly surprised that this decline lasted some eight centuries without intermission – certainly the eight most obscure centuries in the history of both France and the western world.

I make no claim that this trend exactly corresponds to a slow and steady deterioration of the economic area covered by Gaul or indeed of the world-economy on which the life of the Roman Empire was based – a base which somehow held firm through all the ups and downs of history. At most I see it as indicating an overall tendency, within which the economy of Gaul, our chief concern, may have varied, sometimes improving against the trend, sometimes plunging faster than the norm, its ups and downs now relieving, now aggravating the effects of the general depression. Although the available evidence is insufficient, as we shall see, I believe that there may have been some improvement from the reign of Clovis (d. 511) to that of Dagobert (d. 639) and then again during the age that saw the rise of the Carolingians from the late seventh to the mid-ninth century, interspersed of course with corresponding downturns in the intervening periods. All this is of necessity hypothetical, schematic, intended simply as an explanatory framework with some claim to plausibility.

What we have here then, I think, in spite of momentary upturns, if such occurred, is a long decline probably lasting until about 950. So without accepting all Henri Pirenne's theories, which I invariably find stimulating, I can nevertheless come halfway to meet him.

I do not, for instance, share his view that the entire situation was the result of the Muslim conquests which, from the seventh century on, seized control of all shipping throughout the Mediterranean, especially after the capture of Sicily with its commanding position over east–west sea routes (the island was attacked in 831, Palermo was occupied in 831 and Syracuse in 878). This string of conquests – Syria in 634, Egypt in 636, North Africa in 650–700, Spain in 711 and finally Sicily – did not lead simply to the Mediterranean being closed to Christian shipping. Much later, Ibn Khaldun (1332–1406) was to write that in those far-off days the Christians dared not launch a plank on the waters of the Mediterranean, but this retrospective praise of the glories of Islam sounds very much like boasting. What could the Muslims possibly have *done* with the Mediterranean if they had not exploited the Christian countries on its shores? Truth to tell, they needed them.

Fresh light is shed on precise aspects of this debate by the work of Elyas Ashtor,[197] based on previously unused Arabic documents. When the Muslims took over the Mediterranean, it was not, it seems, thriving at all, but already half-deserted and stagnating as far as all its coastal populations were concerned. So it was not the closure of the Mediterranean to shipping as such, but the general deterioration of its economic life which was the key factor. Only in the ninth or tenth century was this long-term trend reversed, only then was there a revival of activity throughout the Mediterranean, affecting all the countries round its shores, whether Latin, Greek or Muslim. By about 970–85, Arab gold was pouring into Barcelona.[198] Its arrival did not of course change the economic climate. It was merely a sign of the reversal of a long secular trend which now began to move upwards and to provide powerful stimulus to the entire life of the Mediterranean and of Europe.

FIGURE 22
Frankish expansion

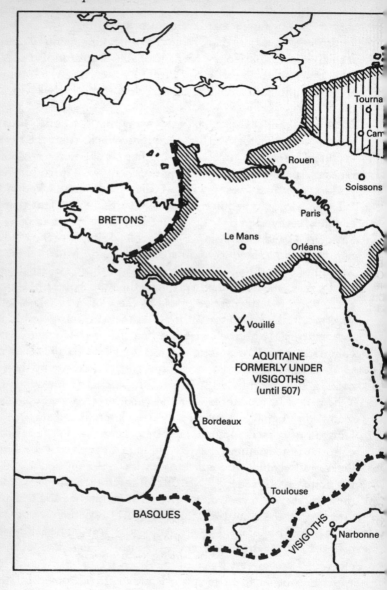

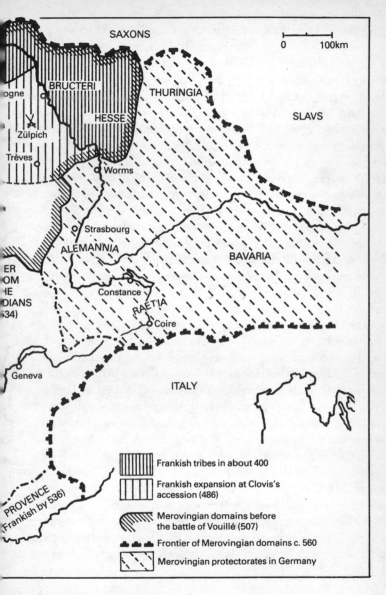

SAXONS

BRUCTERI

THURINGIA

SLAVS

ogne

HESSE

Zülpich

Trèves

Worms

Strasbourg

ALEMANNIA

BAVARIA

ER
OM
HE
DIANS
34)

Constance

RAETIA

Coire

Geneva

ITALY

PROVENCE
(Frankish by 536)

|‖‖‖| Frankish tribes in about 400

|‖‖‖| Frankish expansion at Clovis's accession (486)

Merovingian domains before the battle of Vouillé (507)

Frontier of Merovingian domains c. 560

Merovingian protectorates in Germany

After L. Musset, *Les Invasions, les vagues germaniques*.

We still have not suggested the reasons for this multisecular depression, which provides such a convenient explanation of a process otherwise hard to comprehend.[199] This must one day be the task of a *general history*, if we ever have one, on the model of *general geography*. The trouble is that in the social sciences as in the physical sciences, every hypothesis, even if well established, which it is not in this case, has in turn to be explained and so on. To say that the recession of the early Middle Ages merely reflects the slow deterioration of the world-economy underlying the material wealth of Rome, means acknowledging that Rome as an *economic* reality, a world-economy, survived long after the political collapse of the Empire. Survival poses great problems for the historian! The economic infrastructure of Rome was not, in fact, its only aspect that survived to amaze us. Roman society left a legacy for many centuries of hierarchical division, combined with the dark world of slavery. And what about Latin culture which has persisted down to our own times? Both Europe as a whole and France, a country in the heart of Europe, are still grappling with the legacy of Rome.

In bringing to an end a section which I realize is controversial, I must confess to being attracted by a recent hypothesis, in my view an illuminating one, since if it is true or even half true, it would solve all our problems at a stroke. François Sigaut, the historian and agronomist, has attributed the rise and fortunes of Rome to the conquests that made it possible to extend the system of *latifundia* and slave labour. Slavery, he argues, provided the force that drove the engine, gradually gaining strength and proving durable, an explosive energy source – until that is, the wars of conquest came to an end, and the system entered upon an extremely long-drawn-out crisis. If this really is the key to the answer, all Rome's economic problems become simpler to explain: it is a matter of seeing how trade, business, banking and merchants fitted into a social system that long remained solid before finally disintegrating during the slow decay of the Roman Empire. Was the revival, when it came, the result of instituting serfdom? The debate is still wide open.

Merovingian Gaul

All things considered, Merovingian Gaul, which came into being a little unexpectedly, as a result of Clovis's victories (over Syragrius at Soissons in 486; over the Alemanni at Tolbiac in 496; and over the Visigoths at Vouillé in 507) did not represent a start *ex nihilo*. The troubled centuries that had preceded it had never, despite visible decline, seen the population fall below the minimum density that would enable human life to go on. The population of Gaul at the end of the fifth century may have been as much as five or six million: yielding a density, if its area is taken to be the same as Roman Gaul, of just under 10 inhabitants to the square kilometre. If it had fallen as low as three million, as Russell has calculated, however could it have borne the shocks still in store, in particular the terrible epidemic of bubonic plague from the east, which struck several times during the latter half of the sixth century and then again at the end of the seventh?[200]

All the same, there certainly was a marked fall in the density of settlement, which may explain the relative ease and swiftness of the Frankish conquest. The latter moreover spread beyond the area between the Somme and the Rhine, that is, an area where the Franks, now mingled with other Germanic peoples, had enjoyed the double advantage not only of continuous reinforcements from beyond the Rhine, but also, since the Romans more or less agreed to let them hold the frontier, of having gradually absorbed Gallo-Roman civilization. The conversion and baptism of Clovis by St Rémy (Remigius), possibly on Christmas Day 496, though the date is not certain, was a stroke of luck for them. Whereas other barbarians in Gaul had converted to Arianism, Clovis and the Franks chose the prevailing orthodoxy in Gaul, and the ruling military aristocracy quickly began to collaborate with the civil and ecclesiastical Gallo-Roman elite.[201]

This opened many doors to them, and Gaul helped the newcomers to victory, particularly since the Frankish conquest, last of the invasions, was not uniformly catastrophic, even in the north where Frankish presence was much greater than south of the Loire. In

FIGURE 23
Gaul under Dagobert

After G. Duby, *Histoire de France.*

practice, neither Burgundy nor Provence, neither the Massif Central nor Aquitaine, though attached, not always continuously, to the *Regnum Francorum*, was ever thoroughly colonized.

A further favourable circumstance was that the Merovingians had also seized Bavaria and Thuringia on the German side: in a letter to the emperor in Constantinople in about 631,[202] Dagobert consequently claimed that his rule extended from the Atlantic to the Danube. The result at any rate was that the Rhine frontier was no longer threatened. So despite the incessant feuds of the princes of the blood, who never seem to have had any conception of the state, or of the public good – for them the *Regnum Francorum* was simply, as in Germanic tradition, private property to be divided among the male heirs – despite these major drawbacks and the impossibility of cooperative rule, the conditions were present for the country to be able to breathe again and for life to begin once more in comparative peace. Goods and people began to move around again; the towns, bourgs (*vici*), countryside and villas – in other words all the ancient fabric of Roman Gaul – still remained in place. The *vici* even seemed to multiply in places where roads and trade met. Markets made it possible for farm produce to circulate through the towns and bourgs surrounding the large estates and abbeys.[203] Fairs provided a stimulus to trade: the St Denis fair near Paris was created in 627 by Dagobert.[204] And lastly, money returned to circulation; both royal and private workshops were minting gold coin. This was indeed true of all the barbarian rulers in the west, whether the Vandals, the Burgundians, the Ostrogoths in Italy or the Visigoths in Spain – and they even stamped their coins with the profiles of the emperors of Byzantium.

If proof is needed of the survival of the Mediterranean economy, this is surely it. What is more, Marseille, Narbonne and even Bordeaux remained in touch with the Levant, which continued to send pepper and spices, papyrus, medicinal drugs, silks and even Byzantine gold coins. A recently discovered wreck in the bay of Fos has turned out to be a ship bound for the east with a cargo of loose grain, amphorae of pitch, and stamped pottery.[205] Marble from the Pyrenees was sent not only to northern Gaul, for the building of churches, but also to Spain and Constantinople. And the *Syri*, Syrian and Jewish merchants who spoke Greek, would meet up in the towns and along the trade routes: these were the active promoters of long-distance trade, the men who obtained precious silks, spices and drugs for princes, or who bought gold ingots and slaves. In 585, King Guntram, on entering Orléans, received an official welcome from the colony of Syrian merchants who greeted him in their own language. It is true that Orléans had a special position: with Paris, which became the capital in 502, it lay at the heart of Gaul. But Syrian merchants were also to be found in Narbonne in 589.[206]

We are therefore entitled to speak of an economy open to the outside world, one that had not turned its back on the attractions of Mediterranean trade. But other pressures, both internal and external, were drawing it northwards.

Merovingian Gaul had been fragmented from the start, as a result of dividing the inheritance between the sons of rulers, but these fracture lines often corresponded to pre-existing realities. Thus the vital line along the Loire, or rather the broad frontier formed by the Loire valley, became even more marked. This dividing line dating from earliest times (the internal *limes* charted by Robert Specklin's historical and geographical studies) bisected what would one day be France more firmly than ever (see Figure 9, in Volume I). Nothing was the same north and south of the Loire. Until the mid-eighth century, the Franks described the people of Aquitaine as *Romani*.[207] And that was not all. To the north lay the territories of Austrasia (describable with some exaggeration as a sort of extension of Germany); Neustria (corresponding to a large part of the Paris basin); and finally Armorica, or as we call it Brittany, colonized in the sixth and seventh centuries by Celts from Britain, in particular from Wales. This was a genuine invasion which 're-Celticized' the Breton peninsula so to speak, linguistically, ethnically and religiously: from now on, the Merovingians would have a western frontier even more firmly fixed and which would have to be watched and guarded perpetually. To the south, four areas could be distinguished: Burgundy; Provence; Septimania, occupied by the Visigoths from Spain; and Aquitaine. The latter plus Burgundy, which the Merovingians could reach more easily, were very careful to preserve their autonomy at all costs, to remain spectators of a troubled history which, fortunately for them, mostly took place in the north.

But I will spare you a detailed account of the fratricidal princely battles, or the savage feuds between Fredegond and Brunhilda, the rival queens who went to war with each other – the former in Neustria, the latter, probably a person of high degree ruling Austrasia. For our purposes, the important point is that at first the tempestuous north was the least prosperous, the most barbaric and the least civilized section of Gaul. Both Neustria and Austrasia were obliged to recruit clerics and literate men from the south. Yet it was the north which would eventually impose its way of life on the rest.

A slow but effective pendulum movement, with beginnings it is hard to date, tipped Gaul towards the north, partly removing it from Mediterranean influence. It is true that the latter was already waning. Marseilles and Arles fell into decline in the seventh century, while the regions of the lower Meuse and Rhine – the Low Countries – were expanding, thanks to trade links between the Atlantic, Britain, the North Sea, Scandinavia and the Baltic. While Boulogne's activity dwindled, the rise of Quentovicus, at the mouth of the Canche, was a telling sign, as was the spread of silver coin, specific to northern trade, at the expense of southern gold coin which was tending to die out and would eventually disappear. (This process is clearly explained in Léopold Génicot's still authoritative article of 1947.)[208]

Economic expansion went hand in hand with other developments. Evangelization in the north accompanied economic progress: more churches were built there and more dioceses and abbeys were founded – Luxeuil Abbey for instance, founded in 590 by St Columbanus and converted to Benedictine rule in 620. In short, 'it is not rash to say that northern Gaul was, by the seventh century, the scene of quite active trading, and that by the eighth century, it was economically the most thriving part'[209] of the Frankish kingdoms.

All the same, one should not paint too glowing a picture of Merovingian Gaul. The towns had come back to life, it is true: they were building churches inside their walls and seeing monasteries appear on their outskirts, but they remained modest both in size and activity. The countryside meanwhile was still under the harsh yoke of the great estates. But by now – a clear sign of demographic decline – these domains were suffering from chronic shortages of manpower.[210] And we know for sure that immense forests covered much of the land, running almost continuously from the Alps, via the Jura and the Vosges, to the vast wooded expanses of the

Ardennes. While it was possible for men and their flocks to live by exploiting these wildernesses, it was also true that the forest only regained the land if the peasant had abandoned it. Some historians have argued that agriculture had shrunk overall, by comparison with the Gallo-Roman era, that what was left was a 'discontinuous countryside', with 'villages which were so many enclaves in forest clearings. Trees dominated the landscape.'[211] Gaul was full of wastelands.[212]

So if Merovingian Gaul seems comfortably off, it is only by comparison with the terrible centuries that had gone before. And one should be a little wary of Henri Pirenne's description of it: he tended to depict Merovingian Gaul in a rather rosy light, the better to depreciate the Carolingian era, since the latter was supposed to demonstrate in its decline the closure of the Mediterranean and the resulting economic depression. One of the most entertaining of his arguments, and it is not without substance, was to compare the handwriting of manuscripts in the Merovingian era – cursive and lively, not very beautiful perhaps, but certainly thrusting and energetic – with Carolingian script: orderly, well-shaped, painstaking and lacking in any dynamism. 'The former was made for business and administration,' he concluded, 'the latter for study', and leisurely writing.[213]

No historian now believes that the comparative euphoria of Merovingian Gaul lasted longer than the middle of the seventh century. After the reign of Dagobert (629–39), who had by a succession of dynastic accidents united all Gaul under his rule, things got worse, or as Pierre Riché puts it, there was a 'progressive reversal of the prevailing trend'.[214] The recession would last until the end of the century. If I had to choose a date it would be the battle of Tertry (687) which marked the victory of Austrasia and the Pippin dynasty, and virtually put an end to the reign of the *rois fainéants*, the 'do-nothing' kings, or to be fair, the powerless kings, the last of the Merovingians.[215] It is a date with political but also, I would say, economic significance, marking what was probably a temporary and comparative revival with the coming of the Carolingians.

Perhaps the most significant aspect of the Merovingian era – two centuries of French history after all – was in the end the slow, unspectacular process of fusion between two societies, the Gallo-Roman and the Frankish. These societies mingled 'at court, at the seats of the counts and bishops and throughout the countryside'.[216] In the graveyards, their tombs were no longer distinguished one

FIGURE 24
The Carolingian empire

from the other. This gradual merging of two cultures and two populations was an unmistakable element of progress. Christianity, which took time to penetrate the mass of people, but did so in the end, was no doubt the other major feature of these centuries, which were on the whole uneventful ones.

In that favourite game of historians, selecting what was or was not important, I would confidently vote for the abbeys in their forest clearings, rather than the palaces or villas of the kings.

Did Charlemagne's Empire ever exist?

I hope the reader will forgive me for this provocative title – which will be explained in a moment. I merely want to draw attention to an initial problem (though not to my mind the *main* problem) concerning the fortunes of Carolingian Gaul.

Gaul under the Carolingians is traditionally identified with a sequence of events regarded as important: the Austrasian victory at the battle of Tertry, in 687, brought a new dispensation; in 732 or 733, at the battle of Poitiers, Charles Martel (c.688–741) the true founder of the new Carolingian dynasty, forced back the light cavalry of the Muslim invaders; in 751 his son, Pippin the Short, had himself elected and crowned king; 768 to 814 saw the brilliant reign of Charlemagne, which still impresses us today: on Christmas Day 800, he had himself crowned emperor of the western world. But all the power and the glory, which are no myth, melted away during the calamitous reign of his son, Louis the Pious (814–40) – an attractive figure in some ways, as he was to Michelet who saw him as a sort of forerunner of St Louis – but whose weakness and misplaced piety brought down terrible misfortunes on an Empire still in its infancy and already difficult to defend, still less consolidate. The quarrel for the succession among his sons, even before his death, brought irreparable ruin and disaster, which the division of the Empire at Verdun certainly did not remedy.[217] Meanwhile for some twenty years, the Vikings had already been raiding the coasts and estuaries of the Empire, with increasing vigour from year to year.

The Empire nevertheless continued to exist, at least in the sense that emperors went on succeeding each other. Thus Charles the Bald (838–77) who lacked neither energy nor intelligence, went to Italy in 875, crossing the Alps to have himself crowned emperor in Rome. The trouble was that by leaving 'France' he had failed to notice the real threat, and had to hasten back across the Alps: by the capitulary of Quierzy-sur-Oise (877) he was obliged to make concessions to the grandees of his realm. But then, as Jan Dhondt reminds us, he had been born 'at a time and in a milieu where the imperial Utopia was still alive and well'.[218] So the Empire continued somehow to survive, for a long while to come: as Jacques Madaule[219] has said, even if the 'reality was vanishing the myth was a long time a-dying'. That only happened the day that Otto the Great seized the golden crown in 962, creating the Holy Germanic Roman Empire, which would last until 1805. Twenty-five years after this transfer of imperial dignity to Germany, Hugh Capet in 987 became King of France, founding the Capet dynasty. This event, insignificant in itself, was the first link in a very long chain – meeting the definition of a 'long-term event'.[220]

Of these three centuries, the most important period is without question the age dominated by the strong personality of Charlemagne, and his most spectacular achievement was undoubtedly the foundation of the western Empire. I think we may disregard Ernst Curtius's unsubstantiated remark that Charlemagne was 'the first representative of the modern world':[221] he is really more like a man from the past, *mutatis mutandis* a latter-day Diocletian, trying to establish or re-establish peace and security in the West. Nowadays – is this quite fair? – he seems to have fallen from favour with the historians. And it is precisely because of these negative views that I queried whether there ever really was a Carolingian Empire. Let us clear up this point if possible.

The first witness for the prosecution should by rights be Neculai Iorga, since for once he does not hesitate to engage in polemic and paradox. The Empire, he writes, 'never existed, either from a territorial or an administrative point of view . . . we should not be misled by the towns with their garrisons. There was an emperor but no Empire; and while an Empire without an emperor cannot be envisaged, it is perfectly feasible to have an emperor without an Empire'.[222] This is sticking his neck out with a vengeance, but Iorga is not the only historian to refuse to be impressed by the Carolingian legend. Pierre Bonnassié[223] has dismissed Charlemagne's Empire as 'an anachronism from the start'; Robert Fossier has described it as 'stillborn'. And of the Empire's decline he says, 'pieced together by the Carolingians, the rags and tatters of Rome once more fell apart'.[224] Jan Dhondt, in the most forceful book I know on the early Middle Ages in western Europe, is hardly less pessimistic.[225] We should not imagine, he says, 'a vast and coherent Empire, dwelling in serenity and safety'. Rather it was 'a constellation, with a solid nucleus, its authority increasingly fragile on the outer edges', while on 'every frontier, its enemies were massing'.

Agreed, Charlemagne's Empire was besieged on every side, by the furious sea of 'barbarians'. Agreed, it was far from coherent, being composed of various fragments, of various peoples, some loyal, others indifferent or openly hostile. But was France not already, under the Merovingians, as in every age, an assembly of different peoples? And Europe too, which the Carolingian emperor tried to unite under his reign, had always been irreducibly diverse. The trouble was that attacks and disturbances from both inside and outside the frontiers followed close on each other's heels. The Empire only gave a certain impression of strength between about 800 and 840 (if then). By the time of Charlemagne's death, his realm was already in distress. All in all, if what we are looking for is the establishment of imperial authority, it might be more proper to speak of a Carolingian episode – lasting less than half a century.

The beginnings of Europe: the birth and establishment of feudalism

But are we to consider only this short period of political history? And is it to be dismissed in a few brief sentences? The views quoted above touch a raw nerve it is true, but are they quite fair? So-called

Carolingian France from the battle of Tertry (687) to the election of Hugh Capet (987) witnessed three centuries of history: did nothing of significance take place in that time?

The answer is of course that the Carolingian experience was the creator – or if you prefer, confirmed the creation – of both Christendom and Europe, two terms which were then co-terminous, like two congruent geometrical figures.

The sharp shock of Poitiers was decisive, more than fundamental, a symbolic event. To take liberties we would discourage in a sixth-former, could it not really be called the First Crusade, the first really significant confrontation between Christendom and Islam? Christianity, after being partly eliminated from the Mediterranean by Islam, spread into the north and east of Europe: St Boniface and Charlemagne's armies converted Germany to Christianity, bringing it under Europe's wing. In Merovingian times, Germany had never been so closely attached to Gaul, never so intimately associated with it. Perhaps it is true that Gaul was biting off more than it could chew with the Carolingian conquests – the *dilatatio regni* – while allowing the enemy to creep in at the gate. It certainly found itself encircled, flanked by a sort of Third World to the east. But few would deny the importance of this first coming together – however imperfectly – of the different fragments making up Europe.

The Carolingians brought about not only the birth of Europe but that of feudalism, that is to say all the diversity, division, fragmentation and *plurality* the term implies. Since Merovingian times, it is true, the state had been obliged, whenever it was short of money, to reward the services it needed by grants of land, an unwieldy and inconvenient currency, which had to be subtracted from former 'fiscal' lands[226] or found by amputating large slices of the royal domains. Where the Merovingians had made their mistake was in allowing these land concessions to become hereditary, thus ruining themselves in the process. But soon after the battle of Tertry, the future Carolingians, in order to consolidate their position, further encouraged this development, while bringing it more firmly under control. They did not do things by halves, but changed their counts (*comites*) as often as present-day French governments change their prefects.[227] They packed the Church hierarchy with their allies. Charles Martel distributed the immense wealth of the Church as he saw fit, with the pretext (or sometimes without it) of the struggle against Islam. Church lands were confiscated and then handed over to beneficiaries who – as somewhat paltry compensation – became vassals of the Church.

The three first Carolingian rulers, Charles Martel, Pippin the Short and Charlemagne, were undoubtedly remarkable men of great energy. They did not hesitate to take land back: from now on, land was granted only in the user's lifetime (as a 'living', to use a term from a later period), and not in perpetuity. The counts, who were the essential agents of royal authority, were supervised by the *missi dominici*; from time to time they would be moved to another county to avoid extending their property in a particular area and becoming entrenched there. Such 'honours'[228] as they had been accorded might also be withdrawn. Going further, the Carolingians also devised and put into practice a social hierarchy: liegemen and vassals were directly bound to the sovereign by an oath of loyalty. These bonds reached down as far as free men, who all had to serve at their own expense in the king's armies: wealthy men provided light cavalry, while the wealthiest of all provided the two or three thousand heavy cavalry, equipped with saddles and stirrups, technical novelties which 'made [them] the most formidable fighting force in Europe'.[229]

But the structure was fragile: from top to bottom the entire edifice depended on the sovereign's authority. On the death of Charlemagne, cracks began to appear. Under Louis the Pious, serious trouble began, and after his reign matters went from bad to worse. Thus in 843 at the judicial assembly of Coulaines in 'France', it was decided that 'the king cannot take back a living on a mere whim, or while under treacherous influence or out of base cupidity'.[230] There was a return to the dangerous Merovingian practice whereby sovereigns began giving out fiscal and royal estates 'with both hands'. 'By 880 practically nothing was left.'[231]

But there is no need to dwell at length on the well-known deterioration of the Carolingian state. By the time it came to an end, feudalism was firmly installed. We shall soon have occasion to meet it again.

The last barbarian invasions

This 'endogenous' decay from within of the Carolingian edifice seems to be far more responsible for its collapse after 840 or 850 than the last barbarian invasions – 'exogenous' phenomena which affected the whole of western Europe and which I consider more as consequences or signs of the times than as contributory causes. We should not place too much importance on the part played by invasions, whether of Vikings, Avars, Magyars or Saracens.

The term 'Saracens' denoted all Muslims and Arabs, including those of Ifriquya, present-day Tunisia, the point of departure for the conquest of Sicily and for raids on Christian coasts in the western Mediterranean. The Saracens brought calamity to Italy of quite different proportions from that experienced in Gaul. Nor should we exaggerate the depredations of the Saracen pirates and adventurers who had a stronghold at La Garde-Freinet on the coast of Provence, not far from the bay of Saint-Tropez.

The Avars and Magyars were horsemen from central Asia. The first were wiped out in 779 by Charlemagne, and need not concern us here. The latter for many years came on pillaging expeditions deep into the heart of France where they left chilling memories. They were driven back, eventually but definitively, into what is now Hungary, as a result of the major victory won over them by Otto the Great on 10 August 955 at the battle of Lechfeld.

The Vikings posed a much more serious danger both to Europe and to France. Swooping down in their longships they struck at vulnerable points on the long coastline of mainland Europe, and sailed up river estuaries to attack inland towns like Rouen and Nantes which were both looted. Paris, which was besieged in 885–887, was only saved by the brave resistance of Eudes (Odo), *dux Francorum*, son of Robert the Strong, an ancestor of the Capet line. Burgundy too was raided, and even Clermont, in the heart of the

Auvergne, was sacked, demolished and burnt down three times,[232] the attackers having reached it via the Loire and the Allier.

Are these devastating raids the real explanation for the decline of the Carolingians? Historians no longer think so, just as 'we have jettisoned the legend relating to the "split" in the ancient world following the barbarian occupations in the fifth century', as Paul Rolland puts it.[233] Anne Lombard-Jourdan shares this view, pointing out that the raids and devastation 'never put a stop to trade'.[234] Jakob van Klaveren even maintains that Viking looting actually put back into circulation the precious metals hoarded by churches and monasteries and thus revived the western economy.[235] The Vikings had in any case already acquired precious metals before they came west, thanks to trade with what would later be Russia.

This kind of argument corresponds to Maurice Lombard's theory[236] about the Muslim conquest, namely that it put into circulation the 'treasure' of the Middle East, breathing new life and vigour into the Mediterranean economy. But is this really convincing? Neither silver nor gold ever revived an economy; rather it was the return of growth and activity within the economy that attracted money and put it into circulation. It was the overall economic climate that truly called the tune, creating, finding and using its currency as necessary.

Population and the economy

To return to the longer-term perspective, I should like to view Carolingian Gaul much as I did Merovingian Gaul. I see it as affected by a long-term movement, an upward and beneficial one from the late seventh century until roughly 840–50 when it turned into a downward trend, as usual faster than the upward one, from 850 to roughly 950. In this decline, Michel Rouche recognizes 'a series of multi-faceted crises; a fresh *cycle* [his word, my italics] of decay seems to begin'.[237]

This is the kind of debate, it may be objected, that can only proceed by hypothesis. But this time we do have better documentation than was the case for the Merovingians. Jan Dhondt has gone ahead of us to test the ground, so we can venture on to it without major risk. And the arguments he has assembled will lead us almost – if not quite – to the conclusions he reached himself.

Let us examine the arguments in order:

1. In the first place, one should dismiss the image often suggested in the past of Gaul under the Carolingians as made up essentially of tiny territorial units, self-contained islands imprisoned within 'the massively expanding forests, all-invading wastelands, heaths and moors',[238] – doomed therefore to self-sufficiency. It is true that the Carolingian administration urged those in charge of royal villas to 'see as far as possible that it does not become necessary to request or buy anything from outside'.[239] But that does not mean that the villas did not produce surpluses, nor that they did not sell such surpluses in the market-place. In fact the whole country – towns, fortresses, bourgs and even villages – was buzzing with markets, as the documents abundantly testify.[240] In one document[241] dated 864, we read: *Similiter per civitates et vicos atque per mercata, ministri reipublicae provideant ne illi, qui panem coctum aut carnem . . . aut vinum . . . vendunt, adulterare aut minuere possint* ('in towns and villages, the authorities will watch the people who sell cooked bread or meat or wine at market, lest they should adulterate them or cheat the buyer').

These local markets, which were to be found everywhere, did not rule out longer-distance trade based on the towns, fairs and ports, the most active of which were in the north, from Quentovicus on the Canche to Duurstede in Friesia. It was very short-lived activity in some cases: certain ports sprang up in the eighth century only to die so completely in the tenth 'that we are now not sure where they were'.[242] But their visible prosperity was a sign that Gaul's economy was still thriving, and it furthered the northward shift of trade that had begun under the Merovingians, including some exchanges linked to the Viking incursions, which were not always exclusively devoted to pillage. Throughout Gaul, grain, salt, wood and luxury goods including spices were transported over long distances. It must be understood once and for all that no economy of any size could have survived under the mortal regime of autarky. It is frankly absurd to speak of Carolingian Gaul as stagnant, made up of tiny self-contained units, whereas it was actually thronged with itinerants, wandering preachers, monks whom the poorer abbeys had had to send away, rebellious serfs – for the peasant revolt was still rumbling – pilgrims, soldiers and traders. 'Carolingian society [was] literally based on a shifting population.'[243]

Let us add, to complete the picture, that gold coin disappeared by about 700, but that silver coin took its place from then on, and circulated, as Dhondt has shown, in much greater quantities than was once thought: it has to be 'reckoned in millions rather than in tens of thousands of coins'.[244] Finally there were the merchants: the Syri had no doubt vanished, but there remained the Jews who had active colonies in Arles, Nîmes, Mainz (the centre of the grain trade) or Verdun which specialized in the trade in slaves from Slavonic countries who were exported to Muslim Spain. The Byzantine Empire was more or less closed to these Jewish merchants but they by-passed it via Egypt and Syria and were to be found as far afield as India and China. Alongside them there appeared new traders: Italians, Friesians, Scandinavians.[245] Was it so surprising to find Viking merchants in Paris after the siege of 885–887?

2. Gaul under Charlemagne was, on the whole, as populous as it had been under the Merovingians. The population may even have expanded between the eighth and the mid-ninth centuries: mountain dwellers came down to the plains, more land was being cleared as we know from the documents,[246] and there was the arrival in the south-west of the Mozarabs[247] driven from Spain by the sudden Muslim conquest in 711. The polyptics[248] of the abbeys of Saint-Germain-des-Prés. Saint-Bertin and Saint-Rémy record densities the equivalent of 50 persons per square kilometre – on what was of course fertile land. It is equally true that there were still many poor regions, and *salti* – uninhabited wildernesses.

As to the size of the population, historians have speculated on the basis of documents which are few in number but suggestive. I am inclined to reject the figures advanced by J. C. Russell[249] (five million in the mid-ninth century) as clearly too low: the density must have been fairly low to have left the way open to invaders, but it must also have been fairly high to allow the kind of activity already briefly mentioned. With all the usual precautions, let us suggest that Charlemagne's Empire (some 1,200,000 square kilometres) may have contained between 15 and 18 million inhabitants; the population of Gaul (about half the area of the empire, if reckoned within its old frontiers) might therefore work out at between 7.5 and 9 million inhabitants. This is the figure long ago suggested by Karl Julius Beloch: rather more than 8 million, or a little less than Roman Gaul at the height of its prosperity.[250]

One thing alone is certain: historians are today unanimous – and this is the essential point – that 'there was a halt in demographic increase after 840, probably lasting until 950',[251] because of the shrinking size of the peasant population, which was being propelled more forcibly than ever towards serfdom. Something that represented freedom and betterment for slaves meant an intolerable worsening of conditions for free men, who still probably formed the majority of the rural population.

3. The most spectacular debate concerns the history of money. Jan Dhondt set about explaining this at great length: I shall abridge his argument, transposing it into the language of world-economies used today,[252] which was not available to our guide (who died in 1972). I do not think this simplification of his thought unduly distorts it.

So let us imagine a circle, with inside it the Byzantine Empire, plus Syria, Egypt and Arabia. In the ninth century this was a zone where gold currencies were the norm. Outside the circle we must put Persia, Russia under the Varangians, Scandinavia, Carolingian Gaul, plus Muslim Spain and North Africa – all countries where the normal currency was silver. This classification tells us three things:

a) Islam was divided, something people often forget.

b) at the centre of the world-economy, economic power was divided between two zones, the Byzantine Empire on one hand, and eastern Islam, around the Mediterranean, on the other, since Byzantium, which owned little gold of its own, depended on Islam for the production of precious metals. This situation was not unlike what would later be the case in modern Europe, when Spain supplied the world with gold and silver from the Americas, channelled through the ports of Seville and Cadiz.

c) in the ninth century, this dualism at the centre was a source of weakness both for Islam and for Byzantium.

In the interests of clear exposition, this schematic presentation of course leaves aside or neglects many known facts. So I have not for instance mentioned that Islam, with gold dinars and silver dirhams, was bi-metallic; nor have I pointed out that in the area dominated by gold, silver still circulated, but in the form of ingots or even small change; that the Carolingians were by the end of the ninth century paying the Vikings tribute in gold to fend off their raids; in short that there was constant interchange between gold and silver, the ratio being (especially in later times) of 1 part gold to 12 of silver, at equal weight.

That said, I should like to employ a criterion which is crude but reliable. In whichever part of a world-economy (that is, a group of interlinked economies affecting one another) gold was dominant, there would also be found the centre, the beating heart of the whole complex. We are amazed by the raids of the Varangians – or Norsemen – across the huge heart of Russia, where they founded Kiev en route to the Black Sea, Constantinople and Islam. But traffic went the other way too. The thousands of Muslim coins (over 200,000) found by archaeologists in Russia and Scandinavia trace a path revealing the most curious (because the most heroic) connection of this distant age, crossing the entire Russian isthmus from the Black Sea to Sweden. If thousands of these coins were preserved in their original form in the north it was because, unlike the west, these countries had no workshops for melting down and reminting coin.[253] Note though that this 'money trail' mentioned by Pirenne does not consist of gold. The Muslims exported silver coin to pay for their purchases abroad from still backward regions. If gold points to domination, silver points to a marginal or dominated economy. Proof of this proposition, if it is needed, is the case of Spain under the Ummayads – a sort of Islamic Far West: no sooner had it acquired the gold dust of the Sudan in the tenth century, and changed from silver to gold currency, than it became overnight the dominant power within Islam. Or, an even better example, when the minting of gold coins resumed in the west (in Genoa in 1250 and in Florence a year later) it marked the dramatic moment when Christendom asserted its material superiority over the surrounding world-economy of which it became the centre.

The reader will have guessed where these remarks are leading. If Carolingian Gaul moved, in about 700, out of the gold zone to which Merovingian Gaul had been attached, it was because it had become more marginal. Indeed was it not paying for its contact with the dominant economies by exporting foodstuffs, timber and slaves? The last-mentioned is a really tell-tale sign – a feature of under-development rather than of civilization, compared to Byzantium or Islam.

We may also note that Muslim gold coins are not found in Gaul after 870, that 'the few Arabic gold goins recently found in excavation were apparently buried in about 840'.[254] Not a very strong argument perhaps, but an argument all the same in support of the reversal, in the mid-ninth century, of the prevailing trend. Jan Dhondt draws our attention to the silver *denarius*, which increased slightly in weight in the ninth century (a sign that silver was devalued) and particularly to the fact that half and quarter *denarii* were minted, but he may be deceived in his view that this fragmentation of the currency brought the market economy closer to popular production and consumption:

> The true economic revolution lies here and nowhere else [he writes]: major trade and long-distance links are important, yes, but a thousand times more important is the introduction of millions of consumers and producers to the market circuit. This was the great irreversible feature, the major economic revolution that sets the Carolingian era firmly at the start of the modern economic world! From now on, both large and small producers were selling, and both large and small consumers were buying.[255]

But had this not always been the case from the start, once *markets* existed at all? If such progress was made, it must have been during a period when the economic 'superstructure' was deficient in some way – something theoretically not impossible, and even plausible. Labour shortages would begin to be felt – so we would have to redesign our explanations to some extent. Trouble at the top of the economy would be transformed if not exactly into a blessing for the base, at any rate into better conditions. To find out if this was so, one would have to know how fast money circulated, which way prices moved, and many other things we are unlikely ever to discover. But it is at least something to be able to ask these questions.

Cycles going into reverse

To sum up, a very long cycle was going into reverse after the peak of 850. The trend would continue downwards until the broad-based revival after the year 1000. The cycle which I am somewhat rashly identifying has of course to be explained itself. Round about 1100, give or take a few years, the western economy began to pick up – another reversal of the trend which lasted several centuries. And every lasting change of direction poses many problems as to its causes and consequences – I say causes *and* consequences since we cannot classify the processes at work firmly in either one of these categories.

The upturn of around 1100 was marked by revival and general economic growth, by a deterioration of the state, and by the collapse of the old society which had lost its structures. Was this revival identifiable with a more determined move towards serfdom, something which had taken a long time to develop but which provided new impetus for an economy that had long been in the doldrums? Did this bring innovation and a stimulus to production? It may not be excessive to end with such a hypothesis.

PART II

The Population from the Tenth Century to Our Own Time

Some things we know,
some things we have to guess.
Jan Dhondt[1]

This section sets out to explain, to render intelligible if that is at all possible, the long story of France's history over some ten centuries. Even when we adopt the accommodating and selective perspective of the long term, *la longue durée*, the enterprise is still something of a gamble, full of risks. But they are risks well worth taking.

Over this entire stretch of time, there is only one exceptional trough in the population figures, and that is visible at first sight, a 'Hiroshima' as Guy Bois has called it:[2] the traumatic collapse of not only the French but the entire European population between 1350 and 1450, under the triple onslaught of famine, the Black Death and the Hundred Years' War. In France, as throughout western Europe, it would take at least a century (1450–1550) if not two (1450–1650) for this deep and gaping wound to heal: a quarter, a third, half and in some places as many as 70% of the population had perished.[3]

Between 1450 and the present day, however, there would be no further catastrophe on this scale. The difference this makes is incalculable, and provides the true key to any overall explanation. 1450 was a watershed of which no remotely comparable example exists throughout the rest of French history.

The millennium we are about to observe falls sharply, indeed starkly, into two more or less equal halves. The years from 950 to 1450 represent one long, self-contained 'biological' cycle, lasting several hundred years, the most clearly visible one of its kind in our history. Its characteristic lack of symmetry in a way validates it and will surprise no one: first a slow rise, the product of various favourable circumstances, between 950 and 1350, followed by a comparatively rapid fall, punctuated by a series of stages[4] between 1350 and 1450. The downward movement was roughly four times faster than the upward one. Such dissymmetries are quite usual: losses always happen faster than gains.

The long second half of the millennium however, from 1450 to our day, has been characterized by uninterrupted population growth, varying in speed or regularity, with bursts of expansion and even momentary setbacks, but never disrupted seriously enough to open the door to real disaster. So if, as I believe, there is a secular cycle at work from 1450 to the present age, we have so far only seen its upward curve; and the predictions of present-day demographers (who foresee a world population of 10,000 million by mid-twenty-first century) suggest that the trend will continue. It is impossible at this stage to forecast a demographic downturn which would give this long period of growth the cyclical character it does not yet possess – and far be it from me to regret it, whether on behalf of the real world, present or to come, or for the sake of theoretical neatness. Theory can only summarize events, it cannot dictate them.

These preliminary remarks have stressed the essential contrast between the first five centuries of our huge field of observation and the last five. It is a contrast accompanied of course by others, which it helps to explain. And we are free to explore what they have to tell us, in all their multiple forms. What have still to be explained – if at all possible – are the slow but in the end decisive mechanisms that run through history and make it intelligible.

CHAPTER THREE

A Near-perfect Multi-secular Cycle; or the Early Modern Age of France and Europe (950–1450)

The age between the tenth century and the Hundred Years' War is described by German historians as the 'High', by French historians as the 'Low' Middle Ages. I prefer simply to call it the first modern period, an age which would bring about a fantastic transformation in western Europe. This was the time when both France and Europe began to take a certain shape. This *first* modern age can be distinguished both from what preceded it and from what followed. It issued from a Carolingian Europe still deeply marked by Rome, and it was succeeded by the *truly* modern period – urban, capitalist, and monarchical – which would come into its own only after the hardships of the Hundred Years' War. For this first modern age could not handle its own growth: its terrible fall was in a sense the price it paid for success.

The tenth century: the end of Rome

We have before us then a multisecular cycle, visible both in its entirety and in its continuity: in its entirety, since we can observe both its upward and its downward phases; in its continuity, since we can trace it without interruption from mid-tenth to mid-fifteenth century. There is no question about its terminal date, in about 1450. On the other hand, there is more doubt about its beginnings.

I was tempted, I confess, to plump for the round figure and have the rise of Europe beginning in the year 1000, when, as we have often enough been told, people waited in horror for the end of the world: an ideal starting point if we are looking for a *low-water mark*, with no shortage of sinister omens. But for one thing it is no longer clear that panic about the millennium (strongly condemned by the Church incidentally) really affected the great mass of people. Today's historians[5] think that their predecessors may have exaggerated its importance, yielding to that fascination with the dramatic which may tempt the historian to turn stage director. And secondly, the tenth century was not really 'the dark age of iron and lead' described by certain chroniclers.[6]

There are in fact signs that the tenth century had some positive aspects, that it witnessed a degree of equilibrium and revival, with improved economic health and spurts of growth or at any rate the basic conditions conducive to such growth. For one thing, the last of the invasions – by Vikings, Magyars and Saracens – came to an end. This was no small advantage. At the same time, the towns came back to life, grew larger, extended their fortifications, developed suburbs and erected many churches. Huge cathedrals were built at Châlons-sur-Marne, Sens, Beauvais, Senlis and Troyes – destined to disappear during the Gothic wave of the twelfth and thirteenth centuries.[7] Coin was being minted in various centres. Markets were created and fairs appeared or re-appeared.[8] Long-distance trade expanded and became more organized. Friesian cloth[9] was being sold throughout Christendom. These are all reasons for placing the beginning of European population growth somewhere around 950, give or take a few years, and bearing in mind that the initial and terminal dates of any long-term movement are bound to be approximate.

The implication of moving the date back fifty years is that the visible growth of the eleventh century had the way paved for it by a longer period of accumulation than one might have thought. The end of the barbarian invasions no doubt explains a great deal: Viking pirates became more or less confined to the banks of the lower Seine valley in 911; the Magyar advance was successfully halted by the Germans at Merseburg (933) and Lechfeld, near Augsburg (955); Saracen incursions were kept in check as the general level of activity in the Mediterranean dropped. One might be inclined to see all this as a stroke of luck for Europe and for France, one that might alter the course of their destinies, a blessing apparently from heaven. I say apparently, since if the West had for centuries lain open to the invader, it was precisely because it had been insufficiently populated and inadequately defended. But now its population had gradually increased, its towns had built fortifications. Experience had taught how to resist Magyar horsemen, or the Viking longships that ranged up and down French rivers. In short something which is usually – and rightly – presented as a cause could just as well be described as a consequence. Part of the reason for the halting of the barbarian invasions was the newly discovered strength of the West.

We should not however imagine France bathed in the golden glow of new-found peace. Internal wars were forever being waged, whether they took the form of quarrels between rival warriors, the quelling of rebels or robber barons, the efforts of the king to extend his authority to new provinces, or the long war which had already begun, on French soil in 1109, between France and England – sometimes known as 'the first Hundred Years' War'.[10] Pillage, murder, banditry and insecurity were part of everyday life. That is what explains repeated intervention by the Church and sometimes by the state as well, to promote what was known as 'God's peace' or 'God's truce', through the creation of associations whose members bound themselves by oath for so many years, or seasons of the year, or even on certain days of the week, to deal peacefully with their neighbours:

> Henceforth in the bishoprics and counties, let no man break into the churches; let no man carry off horses, foals, oxen, cattle, asses or she-asses with their burden, sheep, goats or swine. Let no man lead others to build or besiege a castle except people dwelling on [his] own land, freehold[11] or beneficium;[12] . . . let no man harm monks or their companions who travel without arms; . . . or stop any peasant, man or woman, and compel them to pay ransom.[13]

Such was the wording of the first pact of this kind, devised in about 990 by Guy d'Anjou, bishop of Le Puy. It should be added that neither knights nor peasants agreed to observe this first 'God's truce' until they had been rounded up by armed bands led by the bishop's nephews! So we should not be too ready to assume that peace reigned in France after the year 1000. Peace, that jewel without price, did not become widespread until 1250.[14] War was after all an economic activity like any other: it thrived on general prosperity as other activities did.

So the expansion of the tenth and subsequent centuries co-existed with circumstances that often contradicted it. But it provided a powerful underlying thrust, a force for life, capable of healing if not every wound and injury, at least a good number of them.

An essential aspect of this extraordinary transformation, but one rarely given prominence, must have been the gradual disappearance of the context and material structures of the Roman world. The Roman Empire at its most extensive had been a powerful world-economy, a coherent whole based essentially on the Mediterranean, that privileged zone of communications. The shores and coastlines of the inland sea were annexed and drawn into an all-encompassing economic life centred on Rome and Italy. When the capital of the Empire was transferred from Rome to Constantinople in 324, the centre of the world-economy moved east, benefiting the *Pars Orientis*, the Eastern Empire created in 395 by the division of Theodosius's inheritance. But neither this break nor the suppression in 476 of the Western Empire destroyed the economic infrastructure of the Roman world: the world-economy that provided its material foundations was maintained, though in reduced form. Byzantium with its gold coinage, its sumptuous silks, its fleets, its capacity for quick economic recovery, its many free peasants, continued to dominate the western world still under barbarian rule and, with less success, the countries conquered by Islam. The West, whether Gaul under Clovis or France under Hugh Capet, continued to look to the Mediterranean. These were marginal economies, held in thrall and fascination.

The other lasting legacy of Rome was slavery. François Sigaut's recent thesis[15] is our reference here: under the Republic, he argues, the Italian and Roman peasantry had colonized the area which was to be the Roman Empire. But slavery was the mechanism that both accompanied and promoted the rise of Italy, creating large estates, the *latifundia*, with their surplus production.

FIGURE 25
France under the Capets

Royal domains on accession of Philip Augustus	Acquired under Saint Louis
Acquired under Philip Augustus	Acquired under Philip III ('The Bold')
Acquired under Louis VIII	Acquired under Philip IV ('The Fair')
English possessions in France, 1328	

When the supply of slaves began to run out (no more conquests meant no more slaves) the *latifundia* system declined in Italy, but was extended into new regions – North Africa, Spain and Gaul. This meant continuity, if not exactly a new lease of life. Roman Gaul was gradually drawn, not entirely, but very largely, into the slave-owning regime of the Gallo-Roman villa. Here too, however, time eventually wrought change and decay. For such a regime to survive required both a strong government and the wars that provide slaves. The wars continued all right, inside Gaul or on its frontiers, but the strong command at the centre melted away. Did it create feudalism, or did feudalism destroy it? It hardly matters, for the outcome was the same.

Meanwhile the free peasantry, which had never ceased to exist, continued to survive. It was upon this stratum after all that the Carolingian conquest depended and drew in considerable measure.[16]

Consequently while the land was still being worked in places by slaves, as it had been under the later Empire,[17] the general situation had already changed by the tenth century. Serfdom gradually became established – sometimes at the expense of free peasant proprietors no doubt. But by replacing slavery, it would also be the instrument of a kind of progress and, in a way, of liberation for the peasant. The serf, in most ways that mattered, owned the land to which he was bound. Ownership stimulated him to work and produce the surpluses without which the superstructures of society – economy, politics and culture – would have been unthinkable. Is it time to suggest apropos of serfdom – the instrument of increased productivity – a thesis similar to François Sigaut's argument about slavery in the ancient world?

The really big change, however, brought about during the tenth and subsequent centuries, was that a *new* world-economy was taking the place of the Roman context. Now it was no longer the Mediterranean that was central, but the landmass of western Europe. The revival of Italy and the striking advance of the Low Countries provided the twin poles of its activity; between the two lay the attraction of the fairs of Champagne and Brie.[18] A renaissance was about to take place – the 'true' renaissance if we are to believe certain eminent medievalists like Armando Sapori and Gino Luzzatto.[19] But is the word 'renaissance' really suitable, implying the rebirth of something from the past? My feeling is rather that something new was being created, an unquestionable innovation: nothing less than the birth of Europe.

The rise of Europe in its earliest form

1. *Population*. The primary factor in the rise of Europe was population growth. The increasing number of people acted as a kind of cement: hamlets, villages and towns expanded, goods were more freely exchanged, and a certain coherence was the result. But in seeking to measure this demographic exuberance, we usually have the choice only between local case-studies and overall estimates, in other words approximations. Josiah Russell has estimated the population of France in about 1100 as 6,200,000, or almost five times that of England (1,300,000 in 1086,[20] according fairly reliably to the Domesday Book). But in 1328, the *État des paroisses et des feux* (Parish and household register) reported the French population as about 20 million.[21] If the figure of 6,200,000 was accurate for 1100 (it seems rather low to me), that would mean the population had more than tripled. England's population of 1,300,000 in 1086 had by about 1346 become 3,700,000, that is, it too had almost tripled.[22] Wilhelm Abel, taking these figures and others relating to Italy and Denmark, has concluded that the population multiplied roughly by three throughout Europe.[23]

Certainly there had been substantial progress. In about 1300, life expectancy 'was between thirty and thirty-five years in England. So it was considerably better than in ancient Rome (about twenty-five), about equal to that of China in 1946, and scarcely inferior to that of England in the years 1838–54'.[24] This increase was in fact spread over three centuries, at an annual rate of perhaps 0.4% – a long-term movement, not always perceived by the people who lived through it. So we should not think immediately in terms of a tidal wave or a massive upheaval. Population change could take the form of accumulation, distortion or transformation.

Change did not happen overnight, nor did the movement occur at the same pace everywhere: there were times of rapid advance in wealthy areas, and of slowdown, stagnation and even decline in poor regions.

The essential point is that this movement was everywhere rooted in the peasantry. Everything began in the countryside, though not in uniform fashion. France was a land of variety, and feudalism produced fragmentation and a mass of local particularities. But everywhere, it was from the peasant world that the towns were populated or repopulated. The origins of the demographic explosion lay in the countryside. The word 'feudalism' is trying to enter this debate: it carries many problems for Marxist historians once one tries to define it. The crucial feature – too often neglected – is the role played by ordinary people, by the uncontrolled, uncoordinated actions of the peasant: dominated and held in check though he might be, he was also becoming firmly attached to the land and determined to produce goods for himself and his masters. The word *serfdom*, which cannot be avoided, puts the accent too exclusively on the personal status of the peasant, whereas that status was less important than his calling, his level of prosperity, the extent and value of his land. 'There was virtually no relation between juridical status and standard of living: independent peasants (for some still existed) were poor, serfs were rich.'[25] The peasant movement underlying the creation of Europe in its earliest form was a move toward rural freedom and independence, towards an emancipation by no means complete but already becoming visible.

2. *Land clearances*. The Europe which was taking shape was therefore the result of land clearance, crop cultivation and animal grazing. It began with the land which had to be broken and brought under the plough, rescued from the hostile forces of nature, and turned into productive farmland. Whether the miracle was achieved by serfdom or by peasant determination, farmland increased its area at the expense of heath, forest, riverbank and marsh, even in some places of reclaimed seashore or land cultivated in the distant past. It amounted to a massive operation of internal colonization, launched from ancient villages now recovering

formerly abandoned territory, and even moving beyond their old boundaries, 'putting out shoots', as Marc Bloch describes it, or else as the result, possibly at a later date, of systematic projects on the part of landlords (sometimes in partnership), of abbeys, or of the king himself.

Such development of large tracts of virgin soil called for an endless supply of 'hands' to wield pick and hoe. If all else failed, these 'colonists' would often be recruited by campaigns to the sound of the trumpet and with many promises: in 1065, the abbey of Saint-Denis undertook to welcome and protect any newcomer on to the land being cleared at Chapelle d'Aude in the Bourbonnais, 'be he thief or runaway serf'. Labourers flooded in.[26]

As a rule, the new fields began by taking over wildernesses where 'there was no man nor woman', 'untilled areas hitherto the home of scrub and weeds. The chronicle of [the monks of] Morigny . . . depicts the peasants battling fiercely with plough and hoe against brushwood, caltrop and bracken, and all those "tiresome plants attached to the bowels of the earth".'[27]

Most important of all was the struggle against the forest, the greatest challenge. Only a few forests remained intact – in the Sologne for instance; almost everywhere else, they were in retreat, or had entirely disappeared as at Ponthieu or Vimieu. To the south of Paris the wooded expanses of the Bièvre, the Iveline, the Laye, the Cruye and the Loge valleys were relentlessly attacked by the clearers of land. It was along the central corridor known as the Val Crison, which cut across the compact mass of the forest of Cruye, between Rueil and the Sèvres valley, that Abbé Suger of Saint-Denis settled sixty families, the first inhabitants of the village of Vaucresson.[28] In Dauphiné, once the valleys had been cleared, the clearance gangs moved higher up, in their hunger for land, 'to tackle the Alpine forests'.[29]

Deforestation – *essarter* was the word in the north, *artiguer* in the south – cutting down trees, then uprooting their stumps, was the backbreaking work which in the end gave France the rural landscape that would be preserved for centuries, sometimes down to the present day. Such labour was dictated by unavoidable necessity: more land had to go under the plough to feed the expanding population. This extension of arable land may have destroyed as much as half of all the forest cover in France – by a rough estimate about 13 million of the 26 million hectares the country measured in the year 1000.[30]

The venture was not without risk, for it was important to maintain a balance between forest and arable land, the two resources of peasant life. Care had to be taken not to destroy too much of the forest, which provided grazing for animals as well as supplies of wood for building and heating. Medieval civilization was after all founded on wood, a state of affairs prolonged well into the modern period. We even find it surviving into our own day in places like the little *pays* of Der (Haute Marne) in *la Champagne humide*: here all the houses and even the churches are built of oak.[31] Think too of those wild men of every forest, the charcoal-burners and woodcutters, not to mention carpenters, shipbuilders, coopers, wheelwrights, clog-makers, all the industries that needed wood for fuel, and last but not least the towns – which were not only made of wood (Troyes was still being rebuilt in wood after the great fire of 1524) but also burned wood to keep warm.[32]

This great wave of colonization was not accomplished at one blow; what is more, the patterns of settlement and exploitation of the newly claimed land were extremely diverse. For instance on the tertiary plateaux with a topsoil of silt separating the Oise from the Seine valley – the *pays* of Valois, Soissonnais, Multien,[33] Orxois[34] and Brie – we know from Pierre Brunet's magnificent book[35] that a whole range of determinedly different patterns were to be found: some villages were arranged on the fishbone or spider-web model, others were linear; crop rotation was sometimes extended to take in extra fields or *quartiers* formerly the property of deserted villages; some hamlets might be based on a former Gallo-Roman villa which they had eventually absorbed,[36] while others clustered round a large farm for which they provided the necessary labour; and a whole series of *villeneuves* appeared, in no way identical with each other, each with its own shape. There are more documents available about the Brie, probably because this comparatively high ground, well-watered and extensively forested, was cleared at a later date. We can learn from them who the landowners were: nobles, clerics, rich commoners – from Paris in particular but also from Coulommiers or Meaux (soon to be a major centre of the grain trade).[37] And to change region, a study is surely waiting to be made of the cultivated terraces of Provence or the Pyrenees.

The conditions of colonization could vary depending on whether it was undertaken by the aristocracy, the Church or the peasants. Examples of the latter are of course the most difficult to identify. And yet among historians a theory is emerging which puts greater stress on the pump-priming action of village communities. That is not to suggest that no land clearance was carried out between the Seine and Oise by noble landowners, no deforestation by Cistercians, Premonstratensians or, at a later date, Templars and Hospitallers. But while St Norbert founded his abbey at Prémontré in 1120, 'in a terrible wilderness in the forest of Saint-Gobain, a foetid marsh, a sterile and uncultivated land, the haunt of fever and wild beasts', the new order also owned property on the fertile land of the Soissonnais, already under cultivation and which had only to be taken over, extended and planned, consisting of no fewer than five 'granges' of impressive size – respectively 275, 195, 235, 180 and 143 hectares.[38] This was because religious orders often obtained existing farmland in the shape of donations, or by purchase. It is true that they brought to it improved organization, especially such latecomers as the Templars and Hospitallers – in other words they harnessed and disciplined the efforts of the local peasants which probably went back to Carolingian times.

This is the interpretation suggested by François Julien-Labruyère's vigorous book[39] on the Aunis and Saintonge regions, where he mentions ecclesiastical establishments resulting from the legacies of the faithful in the eleventh and twelfth centuries, leading, he argues, 'to a *second hierarchy* . . . alongside that of the seigneurial fiefdoms'.

The same thing has been noticed and commented on by Guy Bois apropos the monks of Cluny. 'A proper estimate of their role', he writes, 'should start from the following observation: in the establishment of the agrarian system and the cultivation of the countryside round Cluny, the greater part had already been accomplished before the monastery was built. It was the work of the local communities of free peasants whose vigorous actions can be traced in the documents of the turn of the tenth century.'[40] If, as I believe, this observation holds for other places, a general explanation to which Guy Bois briefly alludes might gain credence: might this early activity in the countryside be directly related to the diminished role of the towns? If so, we might have to revise downward yet again our image of the decadence of the late Carolingian era.

All the same, in fairness to the monks, one should recognize the importance of the 'leadership function' they fulfilled, with their policy of consolidating landholdings and their efficient direct farming methods, as well as their concern to improve communications, roads, bridges and commercial activity within a wide radius.

Lastly, in this progressive re-ordering of cultivated land, we should note the part played by improved equipment. Under this heading one could put iron, which did not replace wood but was added to it; the new kind of plough, with mobile front-axle and before long with metal ploughshare and mould-board, which spread throughout northern France (but when? in Carolingian times or later? opinion is divided);[41] the growing number of draught animals, oxen or horses; the newly devised horse-collar; better understanding and increased frequency of ploughing; and the practice here and there of marling the land.

3. *The towns*. The re-ordering of the countryside was accompanied by a spectacular growth of the towns. At no other period were so many new towns founded. They sprang up everywhere, alongside older towns which survived and often played a leading role – such as the episcopal seats of Reims, Châlons, Soissons, Noyon, Tours, Lyon, Vienne, Narbonne, Bordeaux, Bourges.[42] Depending on whether one is more impressed by the revival of the old towns or the birth of the new, resulting from growth in the countryside, one will be in favour of one or other argument: that the urban renewal preceded the rural revival or, on the contrary, that it came in its wake. Henri Pirenne and Maurice Lombard[43] come down in favour of the towns; Guy Fourquin, Georges Duby and Lynn White[44] argue that the rural economies were the first to take off –

as does Jean Favier in decisive fashion: 'Urban development [in France]', he writes, 'is not to be thought of as accompanying agricultural expansion, still less as competing with it. It proceeded from it.'[45]

What is certain is that the towns only truly began to live and to develop thanks to the surplus production of the countryside, which came to town in the form of dues paid to landlords, or tithes received by the Church. To say so means accepting in broad outline a thesis passionately defended by Werner Sombart, namely that the birth of the town depended on the presence within it of privileged people – nobles, churchmen, courtiers and before long wealthy commoners, all owners of land and thus in receipt of dues payable in kind. Perhaps one should see this priority of the rural over the urban as a characteristic feature of this 'first' model of Europe, as compared to the second, the Europe of the true Renaissance in the fifteenth and sixteenth centuries, which also witnessed a return to sound economic health with the consequences that all such developments bring. But on that occasion it was unquestionably the towns – with their superior civilization – that led the way. They had been less affected than the countryside by the troubles and devastation of the Hundred Years' War. With their burgeoning capitalism and their already sophisticated economy, they towered above the surrounding countryside. The sixteenth-century take-off was initiated from the top down rather than, as in the days of the Capets, from the bottom up. Guy Bois has noted, apropos of Normandy, 'the extent to which industrial and commercial activity [now] suddenly expanding, had strong repercussions on the farming sector'.[46]

Even so, we should beware of over-simplifying. For it will easily be appreciated that even in the eleventh and twelfth centuries, the large towns where fairs were held, the major commercial centres and the key ports owed most of their growth not to developing the immediate countryside, but rather to large-scale and long-distance trade. The latter, under royal patronage, was already thriving under the Carolingians, and trading partners included England, Spain and the eastern markets via Strasbourg.[47]

Whatever the mode of their development, the towns of this

'first' Renaissance certainly played a full part in the take-off, attracting inhabitants from the surrounding area and stimulating traffic within both a broad and a narrow radius. Certain urban centres, favoured by the road network perhaps, or by a river, a coastal site, a ford or a well-sited port, were the scene of accelerated expansion. Around these privileged towns grew up the suburbs where merchants chose to live. As they increased in size, such towns might sub-divide into a number of urban nuclei to handle the different tasks that fell to them. 'Toulouse had three centres: the bishop's city; the Bourg Saint-Sernin under the abbot, and the Château Narbonnais belonging to the count.' Poitiers – was this a record? – was divided into six urban districts.[48]

In short, the towns grew up surrounded by and under the aegis of various institutions, often jealous rivals. When a town succeeded in liberating itself, after patient or sometimes violent effort, it was by playing off such institutions against each other. To acquire guarantees and 'liberties', to reduce the taxes levied on them, and to obtain the right to govern themselves (*se muer en seigneurie* as it was called), such were the aims of the so-called communal movement by the towns. (The earliest concerted effort to become a *seigneurie* was at Le Mans in 1070.)[49] But I do not intend for the moment to tackle this immense and much-discussed problem, which will crop up again when we come to consider the state.

What matters for the moment is to show that it was implicit in the very logic of the towns – whether or not they were created by the agricultural revolution – that they should take the lead, provide the superstructure. For a town, merely to exist was to dominate. So sooner or later, with greater or lesser display of force or splendour, they came to tower over the countryside, providing it with a 'model', subjecting it to their needs; and the bigger they grew, the more heavily they weighed on the bourgs and villages round about. The three major features of the urbanizing process were: the absorption by the town of most of the craftsmen from the workshops of the châteaux; the appearance of urban tradesmen who set up shop, then, as the urban market developed, began to specialize and sub-divide their wares (becoming microcapitalists or monopolists inside the town); and lastly the presence of merchants who would soon be taking an interest in long-distance trade.

The town was thus responsible for the spread of a new way of life, a superior form of economy for which it was the centre. The fuel on which this fast-growing economy ran was money. That is tackled in another chapter of the book, to which the reader may refer. At this stage in my argument, I would merely like to point out that this was a decisive turning-point.

4. *The industrial revolution.* The overall expansion of the economy was accompanied by a number of technical innovations: ships now had stern-mounted rudders and several masts,[50] carts were 'pulled by iron-shod horses and their wheels were protected by iron rims', various tools and implements were made of iron. By the services he rendered, the blacksmith established his curious and persistent pre-eminence: 'Horses and other draught animals which had to be shod at intervals would regularly bring the peasant to the smithy, where iron farm implements could also be mended.'[51]

But such details are of relatively minor importance in what is known as the 'first industrial revolution', which spread thanks to the extraordinary proliferation first of water-mills, invented by the Romans, and later of windmills. At first, and for a long time to come, these mills, made of wood, 'contained a costly mechanism [the millstone with its iron shafts], which would be taken apart in time of war to be hidden away'.[52] As important and valuable as the mechanism was the operator in charge, the miller, a specialist at his trade. 'The income he . . . derived [from the mill] was sometimes graced with the title of fief, and it even happened that he might be received in liege-homage by the local seigneur.'[53]

The mills were mechanical slaves, robots, serving their masters: there were no fewer than 20,000 water-mills in France by the early twelfth century. It has been calculated that this was the equivalent of 600,000 human workers – an immense asset.[54]

By the late thirteenth century the number of water-mills had risen to 40,000, and by the end of the fifteenth there were 70,000, as against 20,000 windmills, which were a later arrival: the water-mill has been described as 'feudal' and the windmill as already in a sense 'capitalist'.[55] Many of these mills were still working in the early twentieth century.[56] We can add another detail to our collection of contrasts between north and south: 'there were two ways of building windmills [in France], on a pivot in the north-east and on a cylinder in the south-east. The boundary between them is roughly the same as for round and flat roof tiles.'[57]

It is not so easy to weigh up the relative role of these mechanical slaves in the overall economy.[58] But one can certainly imagine the difference made to everyday life by this invention which was after all quite elementary. Indirect but I think telling evidence is the story told by a twentieth-century Italian, who arrived at Gondar in 1936 during the conquest of Ethiopia, and was astonished to find grain still being crushed by hand. He got hold of an old motor to make one millstone turn on top of another, and presently built another makeshift 'mill', then another – twenty in all, judiciously distributed geographically. Milling immediately became cheaper (something like 10% of its former cost one might guess). The promoter nevertheless made money out of it and became rich almost overnight: the peasants queued up at the doors of his 'mills'.[59] Had something rather like this happened in the past?

It seems the more likely when one remembers that almost from the start the mills of the eleventh, twelfth and thirteenth centuries were adapted to carry out a range of tasks: grinding grain, working tilt-hammers and pile-drivers; there were paper-mills, tanmills, fulling-mills, mills for stripping hemp. 'Following in the steps of' H. C. Darby, the eminent British historical geographer, Robert Philippe thinks it safe to say that in France too, 'the twelfth century was the nineteenth century of its time'.[60] *Mutatis mutandis*, Wilhelm Abel thinks much the same: miraculously, he claims, wages rose at the same rate as prices![61] Pierre Chaunu borrows W. W. Rostow's notion of a take-off,[62] and it is true that under the influence of a whole range of 'multipliers', western Christendom did indeed take off, France along with the rest. Even the water of the tide had been harnessed to turn mills in Normandy by the end of the eleventh century.[63]

It is not clear whether the mills were the cause or the consequence (probably both at once) of the transformation of this early Europe. It was a transformation so thoroughgoing as to be

FIGURE 26
Ancient mills (moulins) on the Indre

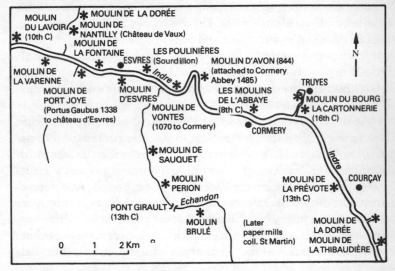

From the eighth century, the mills began to multiply. On this section of the Indre – about 15 kilometres long – together with its tributaries, there was a total of 19.

comparable with the steam revolution of the nineteenth century – with the difference that a steam engine could be installed anywhere, whereas a mill had to be fixed near running water. So whether in town or village, it was impossible to move these sources of energy, and the industries that depended on them, away from their riverside sites. This immobility, which was to last for centuries, was both a feature and a limitation of this early modern age in Europe.

Another limitation, and a more serious one, was that this revolution (setting aside a few minor developments) remained imprisoned within its own logic, repeating itself indefinitely. The later industrial revolution on the contrary, beginning in England in the eighteenth century, opened the way to a series of linked revolutions, each of them directly or indirectly giving rise to the next.

Mills unquestionably played a leading role in the creation and in the achievements of this first modern age. But if in the end its development came to a halt, one among the many reasons is that the 'revolution' of this period did not lead to any new departures, notably the invention of new solutions to the energy question.

A stroke of luck for France: the Champagne and Brie fairs

Twelfth-century Europe and the new world-economy now forming around it, became centred on the region of Troyes, Provins, Bar-sur-Aube and Lagny. This region was very soon displaying the characteristic features of all world-economies, that is, a central zone, a number of intermediate zones and a periphery. So it contained a number of different levels and inequalities, although the coherence of the whole meant that its pulse beat to the same rhythms, whether in good times or bad. There are plenty of reasons why this, the *first* world-economy to be located fully within *continental Europe*, should claim our attention.[64]

Three vital preliminary factors lay, I would argue, behind this first European economic complex: the early revival of a thriving economy in Italy, soon to have gateways on to the Mediterranean (with Amalfi, Venice, Pisa, Genoa); the emergence in the triple estuary formed by the Rhine, Meuse and Scheldt of an active economic zone, based on craft manufacture and commerce, reaching outwards and gradually extending as far as the Seine; and lastly, the establishment, on the banks of the Seine, Aube and Marne, of a point of contact for these two economic poles – the fairs held at Troyes, Provins, Bar-sur-Aube and Lagny.

According to the nineteenth-century historian, Felix Bourquelot (and Robert-Henri Bautier agrees with him),[65] the Champagne and Brie fairs embarked upon their international career during the years 1130–60 – a good deal later, we may note, than that other significant landmark, the First Crusade (1095). Did it take the repercussions from the Crusades to provide the impetus for the fairs? For whatever reason, there was a significant time lapse.

FIGURE 27
Towns in contact with the Champagne fairs of the twelfth and thirteenth centuries

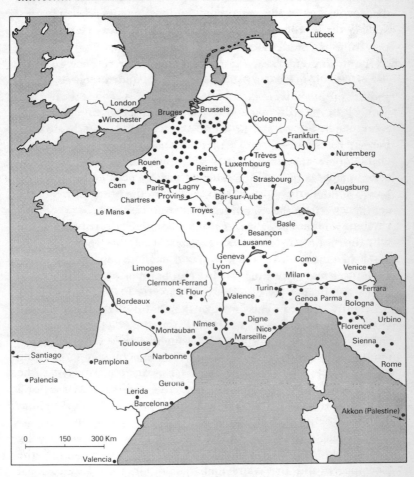

It was during the course of these years 1130–60 that the twin poles of the Low Countries and northern Italy really became connected – the current between them passing more or less along the roads of the 'French isthmus', which crossed Europe from north to south. The liberal and constructive policies of the counts of Champagne, beginning with Thibaud II in 1125, contributed to the triumph of the celebrated fairs. Products from the Levant, spices and silks, as well as credit payments from Italian merchants, were exchanged for unbleached cloth produced over a wide industrial zone from the Zuider Zee to the Seine and Marne.

One small point: how is one to explain the preference given to Troyes, Provins, Bar-sur-Aube and Lagny, and to routes which (another problem) were not old Roman roads, as against the north–south roads going by Reims, Châlons and Langres?[66] Was this 'coup' the result of the hostility of the counts of Champagne towards the episcopal cities of Reims and Châlons (which fell outside their jurisdiction)? Or was it rather because southern merchants were obliged, or tempted to be within closer reach of buyers of oriental goods – closer, that is, to the central Paris basin and the capital of the kingdom, Paris itself?

Whatever the reason, it was at the successive fairs rotating without interruption between these four towns that there became established the centre of the new world-economy embracing western Europe and governing its first corporate economic life.

The significance this choice was to have for France can never be sufficiently stressed. The fact that the centre of this new world-economy lay so little distance from Paris, that other major centre, could not fail to be important. Consequently, if Paris turned into a monster city, with at least 200,000 inhabitants by about 1300,[67] a figure unrivalled by any other town in the West; if it 'burst out of the girdle of walls – already of generous proportions – dating from Philip Augustus's reign';[68] if its university was celebrated throughout Europe; if the French monarchy flourished in Paris like the oak of justice, and allowed its central institutions to gravitate there; if Gothic architecture, born in France, spread beyond its frontiers – then the Champagne fairs, which prospered until the end of the thirteenth century, were in some sense responsible. Both in and around Paris, a series of cathedrals began to rise above the ground: Sens in 1130; Noyon in 1131; Senlis and Laon in about 1150; Notre-Dame in 1163; Chartres in 1194; Amiens in 1221; Beauvais in 1247. 'In less than a century, our ancestors planted these stone marvels. And they achieved unprecedented feats in so doing: the nave at Senlis is eighteen metres high, the nave at Beauvais forty-eight. No one would ever build higher.'[69] (The nave of Notre-Dame is only thirty-five metres high.) Since these cathedrals were a considerable time in the building, they are excellent witnesses to the whole long period. Notre-Dame was begun in 1163 but not completed until 1320.

It is hardly surprising then that Paris was already by the eleventh century 'the cultural centre of the West',[70] and that in later years, its university, in feverish pursuit of new ideas, introduced the revolutionary study of formal logic according to Aristotle – in other words what was regarded as the *science* of the day. As a result, poetry and literature, hitherto the chief subjects of study, were eclipsed by philosophy and scholasticism. In a scornful poem, the philosopher Michel de Cornubie attacked the poet Henri d'Avranches: 'I have dedicated myself to learning . . . while you prefer childish things like prose, rhythm and metre. What is the use of all that? None at all, one could say . . . You know your grammar, but you know nothing of science or logic. Why then puff yourself up, since you are ignorant?'[71]

The brilliance was not merely concentrated in the Latin Quarter, surrounding the Sorbonne, or even in and around Paris. Let me remind you once more that the Gothic architecture of France spread far and wide. From its first home, the Ile-de-France, it travelled to Germany, northern Spain, the south of England, as far afield as Crakow, and even to Milan and Siena in northern Italy, (although in general the peninsula was not very receptive to this French style). To give one small but significant example: on the great square of Siena, several *palazzi* have Gothic windows – the wealthy merchants who owned them had visited the towns of Troyes and Provins. In 1297, the municipality ruled that in order to preserve the harmony of the whole, anyone who rebuilt or repaired a house on the Campo should see that the windows on the façade conformed to this model, *a colonelli e senza alcuno ballatoio*, 'with small columns and no balcony'.[72]

FIGURE 28
Gothic architecture

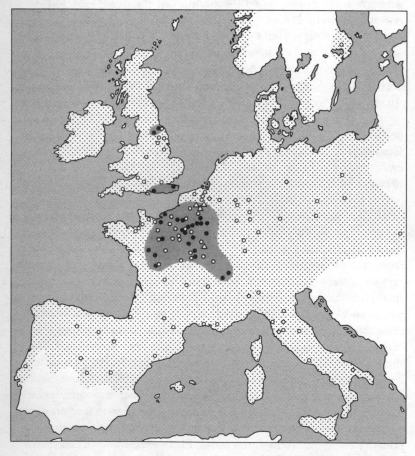

The darker shaded area shows the first wave of Gothic architecture in the twelfth century (black circles); the lighter shaded area shows the spread of Gothic architecture in the thirteenth century (white circles). Triangles indicate monuments which have been destroyed.

Geographical expansion: the Crusades

Perhaps responsibility for the rise of Europe lies with the most elementary form of growth: the expansion of the geographical area conquered by the European economy which was now being extended in every direction on the compass. English expansion was at the expense of Scotland, Ireland and Wales; in eastern Europe, Germans and Scandinavians penetrated the Slavonic and Baltic countries; the Poles and Hungarians were converted to Christianity before the year 1000; in the south, the Christian Reconquest of Spain was proceeding (with the major decisive victory of Las Navas de Tolosa); in the Mediterranean, the Balearics, Sardinia and Corsica were recaptured; the Normans settled in Sicily and southern Italy. Finally, with the Crusades, the Mediterranean and its network of trade routes was won for the West.

The Crusades were of course an immense testing ground for the destiny of Europe and in particular (*Gesta Dei per Francos*) for France. The West became very aggressive very soon (1094). It was now Europe's turn to invade, after centuries of being invaded itself; Europe's turn to act the part of barbarian towards the powers ranged against it, Islam and Byzantium; Europe's turn to conquer, to exploit and to cause suffering, in a reversal of roles. A religious passion had been kindled which would not die out for several centuries. Imperialism and colonialism were as much, or more, a matter of course as of choice. Ferdinand Lot chose to point to the shadows and dark deeds in these repeated expeditions: they were, he justifiably argued, identical to the brutal conquests of the New World, showing a similar degree of violence. The only difference – but an important one – is that European aggression in America encountered only civilizations that were either still primitive or poorly protected in a material sense. Europe was able to take root in the New World. But not in North Africa or the Muslim East, nor in the area controlled by Byzantium, which was invaded in 1204 but by no means reduced to ashes. Such reflexions, however, while relevant to the long term, take us too far from our subject – the earliest form of European expansion, a harsh but instructive gauge of the economy and civilization established in Europe, and within Europe, in France.

The downward path (1350–1450)

Is this sober title the most appropriate to describe the tumultuous hundred years which 'share with the tenth and the twentieth century', according to Robert Fossier, 'the doubtful distinction of being one of the most violent in European history' – and in French history too?[73] Would it not have been better to find a more resounding expression for these years between the misfortunes of Philip VI of Valois and the victories of Charles VII, 'the Well-Served'? 'The great depression' perhaps, or 'the satanic century'? After its extraordinary, difficult, but long-lasting upward trajectory, Europe found itself caught in a headlong plunge, massive, widespread and violent: a plunge, I would argue, that was first and foremost economic.

According to Robert Fossier, 'if the disciples of Simiand [of whom he is one whether he likes it or not, and I am an even greater devotee] sagely nod their heads and see a general economic dimension in these years, a "B" phase, as they call it,[74] a phase of recession, [that] only adds another predella to the altar-piece so to speak'.[75] For my part, I do not at all think that a Simiand-type explanation is a mere 'addition': rather it embraces all other explanations, and binds them together. It is not confined to the 'economic dimension'. For when an economy is affected at every level, and finds itself *lastingly* unable either to restore its equilibrium or to imagine adequate remedies, we may be sure that more than the economy is involved, and that many causes of disturbance are at work.

The traditional explanation used to begin with the Black Death, which struck France first in 1347, 'like a kick aimed at the human anthill', at the end of the period of demographic expansion.[76] But the chronology of the epidemic post-dates the first indications of economic depression. As early as 1315–30, a series of terrible winters had already brought famines and alarming warning signs. Further famines were to follow, in 1340 in Provence and in 1348 in the Lyonnais. The pandemic which then broke out 'prolonged and accentuated a downward [demographic] trend already well under way, hence its irreparable consequences'.[77]

It had indeed been some time since agricultural production had reached its peak, and it was no longer increasing as fast as the population. In his splendid book, André Chédeville[78] suggests that in the country round Chartres, 'stagnation had already set in between 1220 and 1230'. The reclamation of land was all but finished, and 'the last clearances of any size are recorded in about 1230. The good old days of St Louis, later to be remembered with nostalgia, were certainly not a time of serious difficulty, but [in the Chartres region at any rate] contemporaries of the pious monarch already had their best days behind them.' The country round Chartres may of course have been a victim of its location: too far north to have many vines, too far west to be drawn into the large areas of textile production, it failed, in the late twelfth century, to find that second wind that might have saved it. But elsewhere too land clearance had stopped well before the Black Death: 'by 1230 around Paris, by about 1250 in Poitou, Picardy, Normandy and Provence; by 1270 in . . . the Sologne . . .; 1290 in the Limousin, the Bordelais and the Pyrenees; 1320 in the Forez . . . and Dauphiné',[79] and between 1284 and 1350 around Bar-sur-Seine.[80]

The premature end to land clearance was itself a warning sign, as was the tailing-off of the population increase, which barely lasted into the fourteenth century. 'Between 1310 and 1320, sometimes even earlier, say 1280–90, Christian Europe seems to have reached the peak of its demographic expansion,'[81] Fossier writes. This is also the view of Robert Philippe, who suggests, using the records of the diocese of Chartres, that the crest of the great demographic wave is situated somewhere about 1280 – long before the Black Death. The fall, 'so far as we can judge . . . begins in about 1280 and is [subsequently] hastened by every adverse circumstance'.[82] Guy Bois locates 'the turning-point of the demographic curve' in Normandy, at 'about the turn of the century'.[83] I would not claim that population change, though a prime 'indicator', governed everything else, but it does provide very clear pointers to the course of a long-drawn-out process which took a dramatic turn. It is true that we only have one anywhere near reliable figure for the population of France (if it can even be called that): in 1328, the year of the accession of Philip VI of Valois, the French population apparently reached the total, fabulous in retrospect, of about 20 million inhabitants. From these heights, the descent was abrupt and swift: in 1450, a figure near 10 million has been suggested – a drop of half. It may have been even more drastic, to go by calculations relating to a small sample in Normandy: 'at the lowest point on the graph, about three people were living where once there had been ten'.[84]

But the drop was not evenly spread over the half-century of absolute decline: it took place in a series of sharp falls, interspersed with periods when the population began to increase again. Then the next fall would wipe out both the recent gains and some of the capital of the past. Thus in Haute-Normandie, after a 'first reconstructive phase' of about forty years, following the disasters that accompanied the Black Death in mid-fourteenth century, there was another sharp drop between 1415 and 1422, then a gradual recovery from 1422 to 1435, before all the gains were wiped out again between 1435 and 1450, by a terrible crisis, which Guy Bois, searching for a term appropriate to the scale of the disaster, has called 'Normandy's Hiroshima'.[85] The grim reaper pitilessly took up the scythe once more. Jakob van Klaveren has argued that left to itself, the production of human beings is the only industry that does not operate according to the law of diminishing returns. But facing the life-force and its potential, circumstances hostile or favourable may be ranged.

The Black Death and the Hundred Years' War certainly come under the heading of hostile circumstances. But there was also a remorseless law of diminishing returns at work, making it impossible to continue the previous expansion. There were still new lands to be farmed, but their soil was so poor that cultivating them would not feed anyone. There was consequently an excess of population, and when it collapsed under its own weight, other calamities were unleashed upon it: the royal tax authorities made excessive demands, imposing on the peasantry a 'surtax' which brought turmoil in 1337. Manipulation of the currency ran riot: 'between October 1358 and March 1360, silver coins changed in value no fewer than 22 times'.[86] Under these repeated blows, society itself began to fall apart: the peasantry, halted in its tracks, slumped into disaster; feudal barons saw their revenues fall and yielded to the temptations of war and brigandage. Historians have spoken of a crisis and 'the waning of feudalism', but one social order only collapses to make way for another.

The Black Death and the Hundred Years' War

In 1347, the Black Death, a calamity of double and triple proportions, took by storm a Europe which had long forgotten this scourge, since the deadly but distant epidemics of the sixth, seventh and eighth centuries. The plague was perceived as a quite unprecedented evil. Guy de Chauliac, the celebrated physician of Pope Clement VI of Avignon, wrote that no such epidemic had ever occurred before. For all previously-known plagues 'only affected a region, while this one is world-wide, the others were curable in some cases, this one in none'.[87] The only regions that escaped the Black Death of 1347–50, and then not entirely, were a few inland areas of eastern Europe, and in the West only the Béarn, Rouergue, Lombardy and the Low Countries: that is regions protected either by their isolation – having no contact with the main routes along which the epidemic travelled – or else by their exceptional prosperity, which meant a population better fed and so more resistant to disease.

The ravages of the plague were in no way comparable to those of ordinary diseases, although these had been aggravated during the preceding decades by economic hardship. In France, the first wave of bubonic plague (1348–9), sweeping through the whole country from south to north, was disastrous: depending on the region, a quarter, third, half and in some cases 80 or 90% of the population perished. France, with the rest of Europe, was completely devastated. Thereafter, plague did not disappear from the West but kept coming and going, dying out in one place only to break out some-where else, then retracing its steps. A new cycle of virulence had been opened, displaying virtually the same features as those of a thousand years previously.

To judge by the meticulous records collected by Dr Biraben, it might seem at first sight that plague was present in Europe almost uninterruptedly until 1670, the year which marked its complete disappearance (the savage outbreak in Marseille fifty years later in 1720–22 was confined to the south of France which had been reinfested, as in the past, via the sea-passages).[88] In fact, the disease struck intermittently, outbreaks occurring about every five, eight or ten years, with remissions and quiet periods in between. And it travelled around: except in 1629–36, it would never again strike the whole of France at the same time. But it circled relentlessly inside our frontiers. Its ravages became more muted over time: in the seventeenth century it caused an increase in the death rate of only 5 or 6% on average.[89] then for reasons which remain obscure, it vanished as *completely* from eighteenth-century Europe[90] as it had several hundred years earlier, after having been present for centuries on end – a surprising repetition of the same process. So one should not exaggerate the part played by strict isolation meas-ures taken against contaminated towns or regions, although they might seem eminently reasonable. The history of plague appears rather to obey some long-term biological cycle.

These remarks are intended to situate the incidence and impor-tance of the Black Death, that is the horrific opening of a morbid phase which would last three centuries. Death-dealing and persist-ent as it was however, plague conformed to the same rules as all other epidemics: great gaps indeed appeared in the population, but once the peril had passed, life reasserted itself, the wounds healed, widows and widowers remarried in haste ('the men and women who were left jostled to get married', Jean de Venette tells us)[91] and the birth rate predictably rose. At Givry in Burgundy, the nor-mal average annual number of marriages was 15; in 1349 there were 86.[92]

But the effects of the plague were compounded by the devasta-tion arising from a never-ending war. The Hundred Years' War

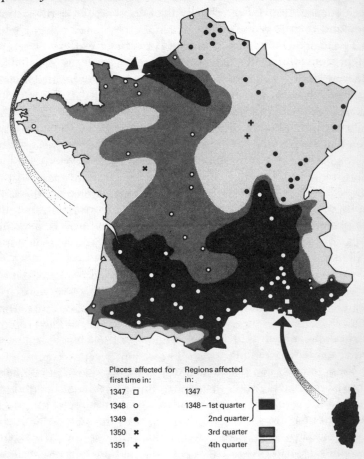

FIGURE 29
Spread of Black Death, 1347–51

Places affected for first time in:	Regions affected in:
1347 □	1347
1348 ○	1348 – 1st quarter
1349 ●	2nd quarter
1350 ✖	3rd quarter
1351 ✚	4th quarter

After Jean Favier, *La France médiévale*, 1983.

was nothing like modern conflicts of course. It would be more appropriate to call it 'a hundred years of hostilities rather than a hundred-year-war'.[93] The battles – social and anarchical as much as political – were intermittent, punctuated by truces and negotiations. On average, there was perhaps one year of actual fighting in five. But the countryside was laid waste, either by pillaging troops, who invariably lived off the land, or by scorched earth tactics, intended to deprive the enemy of supplies. Whenever they could, the peasants who had taken refuge behind city walls, returned to their land as soon as the danger had passed. Or else, as reported by Thomas Basin, Charles VII's chronicler, they contented themselves with cultivating a few patches of ground 'as if in secret', 'around or inside the towns', ready to retreat within the walls at the first alarm.[94] Many fields thus lay abandoned, and fear of war, combined with the sharp fall in the population, meant that untended land spread once more. Speaking of the previous generation, Philippe de la Boissière, prior of the commandery of the Knights Hospitallers in Breuil-du-Pas in 1441, wrote that 'this land of Saintonge, except for the towns and fortresses, was deserted and uninhabited . . . Where there had once been fine manors, domains and heritages, towering bushes grew'. In 1472, the same region still had 'deserts that were once vineyards'.[95]

One could quote a thousand similar firsthand reports from all over France. It was probably true that overall, 'there were few regions which the war marked deeply and durably', apart from those 'where the fighting was prolonged, such as the Paris region [or] those where old soldiers dug themselves in, such as Provence'.[96] On the other hand, no region escaped completely. Even the Massif Central, which was normally spared, and where Charles VII in his struggle against Burgundy found auxiliaries admirably positioned to help, was marched through by the Black Prince in 1356: the English found 'the land of Auvergne which they had never before entered . . . so prosperous and so full of all manner of goods that it was a marvel to see', writes Froissart.[97]

In Paris, Armagnacs and Burgundians vied with each other to prove how far bloodthirstiness could go: murders and massacres never ceased. When the Burgundians entered the capital in May 1418, it was littered with Armagnac corpses, 'piled up like pigs in the mud'.[98] The Parisians lived through a nightmare time of 'exhaustion and damnation', of a 'world close to its end', as the poet Eustache Deschamps[99] put it (b. 1346). Petrarch, who visited

France towards the end of the reign of John the Good in about 1360, was stupefied: 'I could scarcely recognize anything I saw. The most opulent of kingdoms is a heap of ashes; there was not a single house standing except those protected by the ramparts of towns and citadels. Where is now Paris that was once such a great city?'[100]

Paris nevertheless survived the disasters and remained, until the end of the fourteenth century and beyond, 'the centre where fashions were dreamed up, where social rituals were invented, where a way of living was defined and where the taste was formed of all those in Europe who sought to live nobly'.[101] It was a capital still, but a rotten and rotting one, up to its neck in the war and adapting to it only too well – rather like Antwerp after the arrival in 1567 of the duke of Alva, who made it the war capital of the Low Countries; or like Saigon during the Indochina war.

By the end of the agony, the French population had shrunk drastically. If in 1328, the kingdom contained 20 to 22 million inhabitants, we must accept that in 1450, it numbered perhaps 10 or 12 million at most – a figure *probably* superior to that in Charlemagne's day. But what a falling-off from its highest point!

Back to the world-economy

France was not of course the only country to be affected by the downward slide of 1350–1450 (both dates are approximate). The reader will certainly know, from the many excellent general histories available, or from the above lines, that explanations both of the expansion and of the recession relate to Europe as a whole. French history was largely *a consequence* of the surrounding environment. The Hundred Years' War, although predominantly fought on French soil, was not – how shall I put it? – a personal French tragedy. It was a sort of epidemic, sweeping the whole continent, taking root there and spreading far and wide, with much the same effects everywhere. Throughout Europe, armed bands looted shamelessly, obeying only their own captain, their *condottiere*:

The latter might put himself at the service of one prince rather than another, but it was merely a matter of pay. Sir John Chandos, Robert Knowles and Sir John Falstaff fought for the English; Du Guesclin, Gressart and Cervolle served the house of Valois; Hawkwood was working for the Pope in Rome, Colleoni for Venice; Campobasso and Villandrando for anyone who would pay them, while Francesco Sforza was out for himself.[102]

Have we French historians possibly exaggerated the events of our Hundred Years' War, as if to claim all its tragedies for ourselves? As if France alone were involved rather than France plus Europe. As if the same signs of crisis were not to be detected everywhere: a desperate currency shortage;[103] sudden and frequent variations in the gold–silver ratio; a drop in grain prices and in general of agricultural incomes, whether of landlord or peasant, as against 'industrial' wages and prices, which everywhere remained comparatively high. And everywhere there was that inequality in misfortune that gave the towns an increasing advantage: they stood up better to the storm. From Poland to the Atlantic, from the North Sea to Spain, a *single* history was being enacted.

But there could hardly be a general recession on a European scale without some disturbance, disruption and re-centring of the world-economy underlying it. Re-centring did indeed take place.

During the age of euphoria, the centre had been established for a good hundred years or so within the busy quadrilateral of the Champagne fairs. Either side of this centre, and balanced against each other, were on one hand the Low Countries, and on the other, northern Italy with its cities – the multinationals of the day – Venice, Milan, Genoa, Florence. The north stood for the cloth trade; the south for commerce and banking – tipping the scales decisively in its favour. Consequently, the decline of the Champagne fairs marked a turning-point: their prosperity, in terms of commodities, did not last beyond the end of the thirteenth century; payments from fair to fair, in other words the credit mechanism, kept going until 1320 at latest. Already by 1296, Florentine businessmen were starting to move to Lyon.[104] 'The income of the fairs [for tax purposes] fell, it is thought, from 6000 or 8000 *livres* in the thirteenth century, to 1700 *livres* in the early fourteenth, painfully climbing back up to 2630 *livres* by 1340.'[105]

Taken as a whole, this marked a decisive turning-point for Europe, and for France. In 1297, the Italians had succeeded in setting up the first direct and *regular* sea-link via Gibraltar to Southampton, London and Bruges, thanks to the great Genoese carracks, to be followed at longer or shorter intervals by other Mediterranean vessels (the Venetian galleys did not establish their first direct sailings until 1317).[106] At the same time, the busiest routes across the Alps moved further east: instead of the Mont-Cenis and the Greater Saint-Bernard passes, traffic now used the Simplon, Saint-Gotthard and Brenner. The French isthmus did not fall into disuse, but it faced competition and, essentially, failed to hold its own. Silver from the German mines was no doubt one of the forces behind these changes of route.[107]

The end result was that France, to which the Champagne fairs had brought an injection of vigour – at least in some areas such as the Rhône valley, the east, and the central Paris basin – now found itself disconnected, virtually cut off from the major routes taken by European *capitalism*. And this marginalization would be long-lasting. The countries which would benefit from the capitalism now taking shape were curiously situated on a circle surrounding France, but at a distance: a circle formed by the roads across Germany, and by the sea passages taken by Mediterranean ships, which did sometimes put in at Marseille and Aigues-Mortes, but were more likely to visit Barcelona, Valencia, Seville, Lisbon, before heading northwards straight across the Bay of Biscay, then directly to Southampton, London and Bruges. They called at no French ports unless in an emergency (with the possible exception of La Rochelle, where the Florentine merchants who protected the town were resident during the Hundred Years' War).[108] Thus France was surrounded by a circle of routes.

The new links were slow to become established, as such projects often are. But the balance now being created was tipping in favour of Italy. So during the grey and gloomy times ahead, Italy would be comparatively 'sheltered' as economists would put it.

The struggle for supremacy became all the more determined and dramatic among the great cities of the peninsula, each of which was already a major centre, linked to the international economy. Florence, which had hitherto been content to buy unbleached woollen cloth in the north and have it dyed (the function of the city's *Arte di Calimala*), now began to manufacture her own cloth as the *Arte della Lana* quickly rose to prominence.[109] The city triumphed not only in the industrial sector but also in the much riskier sector of banking and finance – one in which however it had long practice. Florence played the English card against France. Genoa, as usual the first to scent an opportunity, opened up the new, and from now on regular route northwards, via Gibraltar. Milan, at the peak of its activity, was approaching what might have been an early version of the industrial revolution.[110] Was it the recession (which did exist even in these favoured cities) that cheated the city of the triumph it never quite achieved, but which is regarded as sensational by historians of the period?

In the end, it was Venice which triumphed over her rivals, thanks to a capitalism based not on banking but on trade – a capitalism I would describe as already traditional and old-fashioned. But then, the major force behind the Venetian economy, in its international and most profitable aspects, came of course from east of Europe – from the Black Sea and the silk route, until the Mongol invasion of 1340; and after that from the Levant, particularly Egypt (depot for pepper and spices from the Indian Ocean, and gold dust from the Niger), where Venice once more had her *entrée* in about the 1340s. It was on the sea, and in the market-places of the Middle East and the Black Sea, that Genoa and Venice fought out their merciless wars. The issue remained long in doubt, for it was not until the late fourteenth century, after her victory in the dramatic Chioggia war, that Venice finally shook off her Genoese rival and could exercise her now unchallenged supremacy in peace.[111] Venetian supremacy spelled the eclipse of France, which was firmly out of the race for years to come, and would indeed remain so, even when Europe finally emerged from the tunnel.

Europe and the fate of France

Have I indicated as clearly as I would hope that the destiny both of France and of Europe was fixed irrevocably during the period between the ninth or tenth century and 1450? That these centuries hold the key to French history?

Reason No. 1: During this period, Europe was taking shape and asserting itself. Without Europe, There could be no France. Europe is our family, the condition for our existence. We live right in the middle of Europe, more firmly even than we did inside the Roman Empire. Europe came together and consolidated itself around France. We, the French are its prisoners, placed between neighbours who both watch and protect us.

Reason No. 2: Europe could only become a unit because it also represented Christendom; but Christendom, and Europe with it, could only assert its identity against some *other*. The most powerful cement binding any group of whatever kind is opposition to a third party. So, in its way, Islam played a part in the genesis of Europe – hence the importance of the Crusades.

Reason No. 3: The age of economic, political, demographic and cultural expansion gave Europe its foundations, its solid basis, its fighting strength and the sound health it would later need to face the trials ahead.

Reason No. 4: The most important of all. I have explained how Europe's early fortune was centred on France. For the latter, the Champagne fairs brought a century of comparative prosperity, but when that century came to an end, the sea passages triumphed over the land routes, and France was no longer a partner in the most advanced economic activities of Europe. It was enclosed within a circle well outside its borders running from northern Italy west, via Gibraltar, north to the Low Countries then back through Germany and across the Alps to northern Italy again. From now on, France would be an onlooker at other people's success, and on at least two occasions would be tempted by it. In September 1494, Charles VIII crossed the Alps hoping to conquer Italy: but Italy eluded him. In 1672, Louis XIV and Colbert sent the French army against

Holland, but Holland too escaped. Europe, by surrounding France, both traced and limited its destiny. It would have been better in 1494, or even earlier, to have crossed the Atlantic instead. And in 1672, France might also have been better advised to think of America. These are pipe-dreams of course – but does not imagining how history might have turned out sometimes help us to understand it better when it is irremediably written?

FIGURE 30
The European world economy in 1500

International trade travelled round the Mediterranean (with extensions into the Indian Ocean) and northwards round the Iberian peninsula to Belgium and the North Sea. Overland trade routes (dotted lines) ran through Germany, leaving France to the west.

CHAPTER FOUR

1450–1950: A Success Story

If we view as a single uninterrupted historical experience the five centuries from 1450 to 1950 (with a coda taking us up to the present day) it will at least oblige us to set aside the many dramatic episodes of France's past, while ideally it will help bring to light that deeper history which tends to be obscured by the familiar chronicle of events. A canvas ranging across several centuries affords the best perspective, the only valid one indeed for any attempt at a constructive historical balance sheet.

The demographic record will continue to occupy the foreground during this investigation. Not, I repeat, because I think it the only determining factor, but because it is in the end the most reliable of registers for measuring the forces at work in history – permanent or transitory, powerful or weak. Demography offers both synthesis and classification. Pierre Chaunu has rightly observed that 'for the historian, the demographic record provides the essential gauge, the lifeline or Plimsoll mark . . . History is about nothing if not people.'[112]

Let us then imagine the impossible: that we have at our disposal all the relevant statistics and graphs – population, production, circulation of goods, price movements – and that we can clearly distinguish all their variations. We would at least be able to draw one conclusion: in spite of all the recorded fluctuations, France *never* again experienced a catastrophic recession like that of 1350–1450. No further *mortal* blow fell, no chasm opened up to swallow a third or half of the French population. For such a disaster to happen today, one would have to envisage – as not a few people do – a nuclear catastrophe of apocalyptic dimensions.

Compared to the devastating hundred years between 1350 and 1450, such catastrophes as the Wars of Religion and all foreign wars (whether under Louis XIV, Napoleon or the Second Empire) have to be rated as of secondary significance. If I were to add to the list both the First and the Second World Wars, many historians and political writers would protest in the strongest terms; and I can well understand why. But I would stand my ground. Do not too many people assume, out of habit or laziness, that war is the driving force behind world history? All wars are wounding; they bring untold sacrifice of human life. This has always, alas, been true and the price to be paid has grown steadily, as we have approached the present day. But wounds of this kind, however grievous, are healed in time. The Hundred Years' War, when it finally ended, opened the door to the recovery of the 'long sixteenth century' (1450–1650), which would restore the population to its former size, both inside and outside France. And it should always be remembered that if the depression of 1350 to 1450 was a descent into hell, war was not the only horseman of the apocalypse. England was not the sole cause of France's troubles: war was accompanied, as I have already noted, by an underlying loss of vitality, by famine, economic collapse and recession, with plague coming as the final straw.

The Wars of Religion brought no comparable tragedy: in the first place, they lasted not a hundred years but only thirty-six (1562–98), and even these did not consist of uninterrupted fighting. Nor did the hostilities cover the whole country at any one time (see Figure 11, in Volume I). And the Spanish, although generously credited with it, did not on this occasion play the diabolical role of the English during the Hundred Years' War. Finally, the French economy remained healthy or reasonably so, as Frank Spooner,[113] Henri Lapeyre and I[114] noted long ago, though our conclusions do not seem to have influenced historiography. There are some myths that historians persist in perpetuating, come what may. However, Père Roger Mols, an expert on the history of the European population did write in his massive work of 1954: 'Demographically speaking, [the Wars of Religion] seem to have caused more alarm than real damage.'[115]

I would not, for all that, seek to minimize the impact of these fratricidal wars which I personally find horrifying. I can imagine only too well the destruction and suffering caused by the Protestant capture of Lyon in 1562; or by Coligny's heroic 'tour de France', that desperate advance during the third war, between October 1569 and summer 1570 – 'A few thousand men, spurring their battle-worn horses along the roads' and looting to 'refresh themselves'.[116] Or lastly by the two raids Alexander Farnese launched from the Netherlands, forcing Henri IV to raise the sieges of Paris (1590) and Rouen (1592). But the touchstone I always refer back to is the following: the French population *does not seem* to have declined during the thirty-odd years covered by these wars. They are therefore not comparable to the 'real' Thirty Years' War (1618–48) which would leave such bloody traces behind it in Germany.

The same considerations apply to Louis XIV's wars, fought away from French soil, or to the Revolutionary and Napoleonic Wars: once more the French population made good its losses and moved forward again. It was even true after World War I, deadly as it proved for France, with the loss of 1,500,000 to 1,800,000 French lives, all active young men; and true again after World War II, in which it is estimated that about 600,000 French people died. In 1911, France had 39.6 million inhabitants; in 1921, there were 39.2 million (but now including 1,710,000 from Alsace and Lorraine); in 1936, 41.9 million; in 1946, 40.5 million; in 1983 54.6 million.

Faced with these figures, if the reader can for a moment set aside emotional reactions, difficult though that may be, he or she will observe that independently of wars, or other accidents and tragedies of history, deep-seated forces have been at work since the fifteenth century, promoting, increasing and maintaining the population of France, as indeed of every other country, enabling it, like an ever-rolling stream, to come victoriously through its trials, misfortunes and disasters. 'The true "secret" of a population', Pierre Goubert has rightly remarked, 'may well be its capacity for survival.'[117] This is the problem I should like to tackle here.

Phases in population growth

Simplifying somewhat, we can distinguish four phases of growth. Between 1450 and 1600, the French population more or less recovered to its level of before 1350 (less rather than more perhaps); between 1600 and 1750, there may have been some minimal progress, but stagnation predominated; between 1750 and 1850, there was at first a distinct rise, which gradually ran out of steam, but never actually stopped. After 1850, the rise continued but now the problem changed its nature, as a result of developments in medical progress and public health, contraception and foreign immigration. We shall consider this final period separately, looking first at the three earlier ones.

a) *From 1450 to 1550–1600*
The first, very marked increase in the French population began before the 'Great Discoveries': Columbus's voyage of 1492, Vasco da Gama's of 1498. Similarly, in Mediterranean countries, the upturn was under way well before Christendom's belated revenge against the Turks with the decisive victory at Lepanto (1571). Nor can we identify as a possible factor promoting population growth the role played by eastern Europe, by the westbound cargoes of wheat and rye from the Baltic, since Amsterdam did not become a major centre for the redistribution of grain until the 1540s. It was *after* the steep rise in its population that the West would need food from outside.

Our conclusion then must be that France, and western Europe as a whole (which experienced the same growth) found both the reasons and the means for their regeneration within themselves: this was an *endogenous* revival.

Are we to say then that having fallen to its lowest point, the French population simply took off again of its own accord, encouraged by the return of peace? The fall had been a sharp one, and its consequences devastating. There was such a shortage of labour that trees and scrub had reinvaded large areas of once productive farmland. Greater or lesser desolation lay all about. In Normandy, a deputy to the states general of 1484 declared that 'from Dieppe to Rouen . . . there is no trace of a road; one sees no farms and no men, except for a few brigands who still infest the countryside'.[118] Between the Oise and the Marne (where the war had been particularly severe) whole villages, hamlets and farms had disappeared. Rebuilding would take money and more money, men and more men, time and more time – sometimes a hundred years. Very often, the unfarmed land would have been reclaimed by its original lord, but he might not easily find new tenants to put things to rights, restore houses and their outbuildings, and bring the fields back into cultivation. So he might be obliged to offer advantageous long-term leases to peasants or groups of peasants.

The same scenario could be seen in depopulated Languedoc: the *garrigues* had crept back over many stony hillsides. Wild beasts had multiplied:

> The brown bears of the Cévennes returned in force to the slopes of the Aigoual and the Espérou; herds of deer chased over the *garrigues* and through the woods of live oak; the Causse was full of wolves; partridges became as common as chickens; and until the beginning of the sixteenth century, the peasant was free to hunt as much as he liked, since the quantity of game seemed inexhaustible.[119]

Land was slowly reclaimed by the toil of large families, gathered under the authority of a *paterfamilias*, 'sharing a hearth and cookpot: eating and drinking the same bread and wine'.[120] And then the miracle happened: the population began to grow again, before long at a rate that impressed contemporaries. In Languedoc towards the middle of the sixteenth century it was said that 'people are multiplying like mice in a barn'.[121]

It was the same all over France. Near Bar-sur-Seine between 1477 and 1560, 'brambles, thorns and bushes retreated before the ploughshare and the pickaxe'; fields of wheat, vineyards and meadows crept over the newly claimed land.[122] Buildings as well as crops marked the return of the good times. Churches were repaired, and new ones built. At Bar-sur-Seine, the church of

Saint-Etienne, begun in 1505, was finished in 1560. The less imposing church at nearby Rumilly was built between 1527 and 1549.[123] Far away, at Saint-Antonin in the Causses, a veritable architectural renaissance took place at the end of the fifteenth century and beginning of the sixteenth.[124] Churches and new houses were appearing as fast as people. In about 1572, Brantôme gave it as his opinion that France was 'as full as an egg'.[125] A human tide was unfurling all over Europe, in England, Italy, Spain. In Germany, the Bavarian humanist Aventinus reported that people were so numerous that they were thought 'to grow on trees'.[126] Even the Turkish Empire under the Osmanlis was undergoing general demographic expansion.[127]

To return to France, the rise was most pronounced in the early years; later on it would slow down at times and even stop altogether. The 'sixteenth-century spring', to borrow Richard Gascon's expression, calmed down in about 1520. From this time on – were there already too many people? – prices began rising, and since wages did not follow suit, living standards declined. It was only an apparent paradox that during the great depression of the fourteenth and fifteenth centuries, a time of low population and low farm prices, when great expanses of land were abandoned to grazing flocks, there had been plenty of food for both peasant and town-dweller.[128] From now on, there would be less bread and wine, and in particular less meat at mealtimes; and in mid-century, between 1550 and 1560, there was a ten-year depression, broadly corresponding to the dark reign of Henri II (1547–59).

At some moment, impossible to pinpoint with accuracy, the demographic recovery was virtually complete. There were *roughly* as many people in France in about 1550–70 as there had been two centuries earlier. Pierre Chaunu has described this as compensation, recovery, the return to a former equilibrium. That is no mere figure of speech, but the beginnings of an explanation. To say this means recognizing that the return to a former balance had occurred of its own accord, that it was the result of a spontaneous and vigorous impulse, thwarted by the disorders and calamities of the preceding era.

But what kind of vigorous impulse? That is the real question. It is not so important to know whether the former population level was reached or not, and if so how exactly; or whether it was in 1550 or 1600 or later. Since we have no precise figures for the population at these dates, the debate must remain open.[129] But the moving force behind the increase does matter, since increase there definitely was. The festering wound of 1350–1450 was somehow healed; humanity rose to the challenge of history. Perhaps because the disasters (plague and famine) had abated; perhaps because of the discovery of new sources of food (inexhaustible supplies of fish from Newfoundland, cereals from the Baltic, the spread of buckwheat); perhaps because of the general good health of the economy (all wounds healed fast in the sixteenth century according to Earl J. Hamilton, and Guy Bois says the same).[130] Finally, it may have been helped by the arrival of precious metals from America, which brought new impetus to the highest levels of the economy, no doubt with repercussions everywhere else.

b) *From 1600 to 1700*

After 1600, France's population increase was limited and began to slow down. The total would remain for a century and a half at a level rising very little if at all. At the same time, economic progress slowed down as well; there were no technological breakthroughs of importance, and a series of crises occurred: five major combinations of famine and epidemic affected the entire kingdom in 1630–1; 1640–52; 1661–2; 1693–4; and 1709–10.[131] The last of these has gone down in history as particularly tragic, but for all we know the preceding crisis in 1693–4 may have been even more serious. All of them cut deeply into the population figures.

The crisis of 1640–52, which preceded the Fronde (1648–53) and continued during that violent civil war, contributed not a little to its ravages. For the French population as a whole, I believe these years to have been an even more cruel experience than the Wars of Religion, fought during an age of economic prosperity; the Fronde, by contrast, was a time of economic hardship. The towns were obliged to open their gates to peasants fleeing from looting soldiers in search of food: in Reims, the local peasants, who had 'taken refuge in the town', with their cattle, went out every night when the gates were closed, returning only at dawn 'as the gates opened', having taken advantage of the darkness to slip home to their farms for fodder for the animals.[132] The same was true of Corbie, Saint-Quentin and Péronne. The towns were burdened with unwelcome lodgers, the countryside was ravaged and neglected and the crops were lost.

Everyone suffered during these harsh times – adults, children and even unborn babies (since starvation can affect women's menstrual cycles, as has been recorded in our own century, during the siege of Leningrad for example). Emmanuel Le Roy Ladurie has spoken of a Malthusian life cycle. Infantile mortality was also rife. As Pierre Goubert put it, 'it took two children to make one adult'.[133] Death was in the midst of daily life, like the church in the centre of the village.[134] Life expectancy at birth was no more than thirty, if that.

If patterns repeated themselves, one would expect to find some kind of collapse or disaster occurring towards the middle of the seventeenth century, mirroring that of 1350: the same premisses ought to have produced the same results. But the process did not replicate itself. There was no collapse. The *overall* picture (over and above regional variations which were sometimes very marked, *vide* the contrast between Cherbourg and Alsace or Provence)[135] was one of 'extraordinary stability, with some ups and downs', sometimes quite considerable, but balancing each other out in the end.[136] The balance seems to have settled at some demographic optimum: whenever it was exceeded (for birth rates remained high) there would be a crisis and 'hundreds of thousands of poor people were carried off'. After this, a net surplus of births over deaths would be established once more. The aggregate population in the end remained comparatively stable, standing up well whether to plague, famine, civil war or later, the long War of the Spanish Succession (whose effects were not in my view catastrophic), not to mention the Protestant exodus (of some 200,000 to 300,000 people) after the disastrous Revocation of the Edict of Nantes in 1685.

Why was there such comparative stability? For a number of combined reasons, which varied from region to region, if only because of the irregular spread of new crops introduced from the New World. Maize and potatoes were not fully adopted until the eighteenth and in some places the nineteenth century. But some regions welcomed them earlier than others. The south-west took to maize from early on: by about 1640 it was being quoted on the Toulouse and Castelnaudary corn exchanges;[137] by the end of the century it had spread to the Béarn and was even 'occupying pride of place in a very intensive crop system'.[138] It was the 'cereal which ordinary people eat'. The same was true in Comminges, where maize both provided food for farmhands and brought about a revolution in the breeding of geese and pigs.

What maize was to the south-west, buckwheat – the poor man's food – was to Brittany. This was no doubt why Brittany was able to export grain throughout the seventeenth century.[139] Eastern France by contrast gave little acreage to buckwheat, but was conquered by the potato. In Dauphiné and Alsace by 1660, in Lorraine by 1680, the potato, already a familiar vegetable in kitchen gardens, began to be grown in the fields.[140] By the end of the seventeenth century, potato cultivation in Alsace was sufficiently widespread for there to be talk of including it in tithes. In the next century, after about 1740–50, and fifty years before the rest of France, this 'ready-made bread' as it was called, would be replacing cereals in the Alsatian diet, but without reducing grain production. Requiring little manure, the potato took the place of fallow land in the cycle. According to Etienne Juillard, 'this widespread adoption of the potato [soon to spread to the rest of France] marks the end of periodic food shortages'.[141]

Another reason for France's comparatively good health (and for that of Europe as a whole) was the shipment of silver from the New World. Historians used to think that this flow came to a halt, or was at any rate greatly reduced, after 1600 – such was the conclusion of Earl J. Hamilton's path-breaking study.[142] Later research, by Pierre and Huguette Chaunu, pushed the date back to 1610.[143] More recently still, Michel Morineau, using evidence from the Dutch gazettes, has decided that this crucial date may be as late as 1650.[144] There was a long age of bounty then, and a comparatively short interruption, since mining activity in the New World revived in the 1680s, so even if the shortage of silver did have an effect, it was only for about thirty years.

If we bear these dates (1650–80) in mind as a possible watershed, it is tempting to divide our period in two, either side of these thirty years: first a half-century, 1600–50, when economic life, if not exactly prosperous, at least held its own; then a less propitious hundred years, 1650–1750, outlasting the personal reign of Louis XIV (1661–1715).

The early seventeenth century may not have been that period of deep depression so often described. Otherwise, how is one to explain an enigma posed precisely by the French case: namely that following his second and definitive arrival in power in 1624, Richelieu increased taxes throughout France, doubling and even tripling them? It would only have been possible to apply the fiscal screws so vigorously if the national product (that is, the number of taxpayers and the sum of their incomes) had been rising or at least constant.

Throughout France, the horizon darkened during the Fronde (1648–53). Prices fluctuated wildly. Pierre Goubert has demonstrated the extravagant nature of the so-called 'accession crisis' between 1656–7 and 1667–8, with its abrupt variations.[145] But these irregular movements had something of the same effect as the repeated drama of bad harvests: the peasant simply withdrew into his shell like a snail (Witold Kula's favourite image)[146] then came out when things calmed down (or seemed to calm down). Prices were in fact falling overall, but is a B phase always harmful to the living standards of humble folk? If Frank Spooner's calculations are right, the gross national income held steady at about the same level, between 1,200 and 1,500 million *livres* between 1701 and 1760.[147] The population in about 1720 was approximately 20 million: above the level which Karl Julius Beloch regarded as a minimum for a great power in the past: 17 million.[148]

c) *From 1750 to 1850*
For these hundred eventful years, interrupted in the middle by the violent episodes of the Revolution and the First Empire (1792–1815) we have more precise documentation than for the preceding

ages, and the quality of the data improves the nearer we move to the present. We also have an excellent guide[149] to demographic problems and some outstanding case-studies.[150]

We need not enter into too much detail here (especially into the debates understandably provoked by the quality and interpretation of the documents). Nor need we distinguish too minutely between periods: first the very rapid population growth of 1743–70; a notable surplus of births over deaths from 1770 to 1778; a return to a climate of crisis from 1779 to 1787 (though these were mild and concealed crises compared to the seventeenth century); then eventually, after the parenthesis of the Revolution and Empire (a time of population increase, if only on a modest scale), a period of sustained growth until 1850. True, the French population rose less rapidly than that of the rest of Europe: between 1801 and 1851 there was an increase of 30% in France, as against 50% in Europe as a whole and 100% in Britain.

Once more, we find marked regional differences, but we can generally assume a healthy state of the French population as a whole: about 26.3 million in 1789;[151] 27.3 million in 1801; 29.1 in 1806; 30.5 in 1821; 31.9 in 1826; 32.6 in 1831; 32.5 in 1836; 34.2 in 1841; 35.4 in 1846 and 35.8 in 1851. This steady progression (which falters only once, between 1831 and 1836, on account of the cholera epidemic of 1834) is the major feature of the period.

But it is a surprising feature. One might well have expected an overall decrease. This period after all covers the last crisis of the *ancien régime*; the poor harvests of 1788 and 1789 which played a part in bringing that regime to an end; then the many troubles which occurred from the declaration of war in 1792 to 1815 – the emigration of perhaps 180,000 people, and losses in war (1,200,000 plus perhaps 400,000 in the terrible civil war of the Vendée). And the whole episode was accompanied by 'changes in the distribution of wealth, new prospects of social mobility, a transformation of attitudes, legal innovations – all factors which had important demographic repercussions and whose effects would be prolonged' beyond 1815.[152]

But the French population withstood all these accumulated obstacles. It would also come safely through the difficult years of the Restoration, the July Monarchy, and the short-lived Second Republic (1848–52). Here again, we may well express surprise. For historians have identified the years 1817–51 as the downward half of a Kondratieff cycle, in other words, these three regimes were accompanied by a steady and indeed accelerating deterioration in economic life, culminating in the serious crisis of 1847–8, a classic example of an 'ancien régime crisis', that is, one which, arising from an agricultural disaster, was capable of exploding to affect the entire economy.[153] This was probably the last of the old-fashioned subsistence crises, and marks a turning point. Other crises of a different kind would occur in later years, in a France by now industrialized, when the population would once more have to face the obstacles and difficulties they brought.

Traditional historians find it impossible to consider the hundred years between 1750 and 1850 as a block, both because of the political break brought about by the collapse of the ancien régime, and the economic break created by the beginnings of the industrial revolution. Historical demographers on the contrary tend to see a certain continuity in the destiny of the French population, between the reign of Louis XV and the time of the Prince-President Louis-Napoleon, later Napoleon III. If we listen to them, we may conclude that the late eighteenth century was already showing signs of a certain modernity, while the early nineteenth century still displayed traces of the ancien régime. The historian André Rémond used to say in our discussions long ago that Guizot was the last man of the eighteenth century – which is another way of saying the same thing. My own belief is that the history of the population is in some sense beyond the usual considerations and narratives of history: the events we chronicle may bite into it, but at worst they cause only temporary wounds.

Possible explanations for the demographic processes up to 1850

The history of the French population must be understood en bloc, across the entire period (1450–1950, and on to the present). It presents us with a single historical problem, since the dominant

178

trend is not in doubt: overall, this was a time of expansion. But why? What were the reasons, both general and particular?

They can essentially be summed up in two words: disease and diet. It was of significant benefit that plague vanished from France after 1720, and that the population had already become more resistant to it after 1450.

Of equal importance were the slow but steady disappearance of smallpox during the nineteenth century; the decisive transformation of medicine; from about 1850 at least, the improvement of hospital treatment; and later still, after the Second World War, the immense benefits of the welfare state – these must be regarded as milestones of outstanding significance.

But should we not be equally attentive to the changes – also of key importance – in human diet? As they say in Germany, 'Man is what he eats.' The food people ate was gradually improving. The process was slow, but real, underpinning the progress or maintenance of population levels. Advance was not rapid, to be sure, but then France like Europe was essentially agricultural; fields, crops, the surpluses that filled mouths could hardly be transformed overnight. Before 1200, the yield on one grain sowed was three grains harvested; it had risen to 4.3 between 1300 and 1500; to 6.3 between 1500 and 1820. These averages which I have taken from B. H. Slicher Van Bath's very convincing calculations may seem extremely low to us, but they did after all more than double over three hundred years.[154] They indicate an underlying trend which no doubt explains much. To this could be added the unexpected but vital contribution from the New World, already referred to, and the increase in foodstuffs from outside France: wheat from the Mediterranean, which had been coming in to Marseille for many years (in the nineteenth century Ukrainian wheat replaced shipments from North Africa and the Levant); wheat and particularly rye from the Baltic, from the latter part of the sixteenth century; the fisheries of the North Sea and in particular of Newfoundland; wheat and barrels of flour from the United States from the end of the eighteenth century. It might also be remembered that the cost of living in France during the *ancien régime* was probably lower than in her large neighbours, so there was more to go round.[155]

The result of all these improvements was a gradual rise in life expectancy, or to put it another way, an ageing of the population. Demographers have pinpointed 1750 as marking the beginning of this transformation, which has continued without interruption into our own time. Some people have expressed anxiety about this, as if triumph over death were not the major achievement and in many ways the most gratifying of modern science. We are told for instance (but is this really so?) that in the future the active population of France will not be numerous enough to finance the pensions of the oldest age groups. But tomorrow's industry will not be the same as today's. And we do not know for certain that there will be a drop in the active age groups, while the boundary between work and retirement will not necessarily remain where it is now.

I think there is a tendency to assume that Europe, which has historically exploited the poorer and less developed parts of the world, has therefore been in a privileged position; that Europe lived, moved and derived its greatness from these advantages and privileges. There is some truth in this. But the judgement should be nuanced. The European expansion which started with the Crusades and was extended with the Great Discoveries, did not lead overnight to regular and massive exploitation of the rest of the world. Migration out of Europe was always on an extremely modest scale. Moreover, if Paul Bairoch's calculations are correct, as I believe them to be, living standards in Europe as late as 1800 were hardly any higher than in other major areas of the world – China for instance.[156] It was only with the triumph of industry that Europe had an explosion of growth and made certain of a privileged future. But the industrial revolution was the product of a belated and many-sided transformation of the economy, of technology, of society and also of agriculture which had become more and more efficient and knowledgeable – that essential progress which many Third World countries have still to achieve since it depends on the accumulated effort and knowhow of generations of peasants. What I am trying to say is that Europe, and France within Europe, had to find forces within themselves for their painstaking progress. This puts a slightly better moral complexion on their history: it was a success story born partly of internal struggle.

CHAPTER FIVE

Recent Problems: the Triumphs of Medicine; Birth Control; Immigration

Do not suppose that when we come to the really contemporary period, after 1850, our problems will become clearer or easier to solve than in previous ages. We have ten or a hundred times more information. But most of the time that makes it even harder to read the true situation.

Between 1850 and the 1980s, the population, production and overall wealth of France, the possessions of the privileged and the living standards of ordinary French people all rose steadily. Each year that passed saw more vehicles, more roads, more railways, more smelters, more iron and steel, more fabrics, more cotton and silk, more students in the universities and more people living in France. There was an immense improvement in living standards. Both gross national income and per capita income grew steadily. Even in the most remote corners of France,[157] the wages of foresters, charcoal-burners and longsawyers continued to rise, in current francs. I do not say that everything was for the best in the best (or most equitable) of all possible worlds: even in Paris, the masses were often in great poverty. But setting aside the major dramas and crises (of which France has had its fair share), it was a time of visible improvement.

I do not think it necessary to provide a lengthy account of this progress, or of France's place within the ranks of a privileged section of the human race – industrialized Europe: the reader will find graphs and tables further on in the book which chart the various measurements of this unquestionable improvement. With that rather burdensome task out of the way, it will be easier for me to concentrate on three problems – to my mind essential ones – taking us right up to the present-day reality I am anxious to reach.

181

1. What exactly have been the miraculous improvements which, thanks to medical science and to the combined advance of economy and society, have in our own lifetime transformed the biological conditions affecting the French population, along with other privileged peoples of the world?

2. What role was played in our society by the now familiar spread of contraceptive practices, so often condemned in the past?

3. How are we to estimate the increasing and to some extent preoccupying role played by foreign immigration, in the present and in particular the future composition of the French population?

But before going any further, I should like to make two things clear:

1. In the following pages, I do not intend to make the still uncertain history taking place before our eyes the basis for any *solutions* to the problems that concern us. I am neither a politician, a party representative nor a moralist. If the decision were in my hands, I know that there would be an immense gap between what *ought to be done* and what circumstances would *allow me to do* (next to nothing in most cases). France will, alas, have to undergo its destiny rather than choosing it, I fear.

2. We should beware of what our conscience tells us, for it is an interested party in the debate. The present can be observed scientifically. But because we are ourselves, the *objective* present is harder to see – particularly since the social 'sciences' are still imperfect and likely long to remain so.

So how can one keep a moral perspective out of the debate? It is likely to trespass, spontaneously and logically, upon the very field of observation. In mathematics, morality does not intrude. In physics, there are only a few danger areas – though they are *very* dangerous ones. In biology, morality is always protesting and will continue to do so. In the social sciences, matters are even worse: the voice of morality is louder still, especially if one is imprudent enough to tackle the present day or the immediate future. The history of the distant past is reasonably safe. But the history of today or tomorrow is something about which everyone thinks he has something to say. So morality, and our personal moral perspectives are lying in wait for us. I shall not be able to keep them out of the debate, but will have to do my best to keep them under control.

Medicine and public health

Medical history is certainly the most fascinating of histories. But it is also the most complicated, tangled and difficult to describe. Probably because, as I have often maintained, there is no such thing as a partial or isolated history – medical or otherwise – that does not have some bearing on the broader sweep of history in general.

Many doctors today think that there is no point, no practical purpose, in studing the medicine of yesterday. It is not worth looking back any further than 1945, if that, they say. Yet the discovery of penicillin, which had been hovering within reach for decades, was made by Alexander Fleming back in 1929; heparin, a natural anticoagulant 'which made possible the development of cardiovascular exploration and treatment, was discovered in Sweden' during the last war.[158] But these developments do, it is true, belong to very recent history; and there is an ever-widening gap between today's medicine and that of yesterday.

For a course of lectures I gave at the Collège de France one year, I became very interested in the work of Ambroise Paré (c.1509–90); I had assumed there would be a certain continuity between the surgical implements of the sixteenth century and those of today. It might appear so perhaps, but there were changes even in the manner of handling apparently identical instruments, such as a simple scalpel, as has been pointed out by Jean-Charles Sournia who is both a surgeon and a knowledgeable medical historian:

> The simplest surgical gesture, for instance an incision in the skin, is not performed today as it was in the days of Hippocrates: the surgeon's scalpel does not have the same edge as it did then, nor the same point, nor the same handle.

[Today's] surgeon knows more about anatomy and controls the depth of incision, to avoid unnecessary bleeding; he watches every slip of the knife. He does not therefore hold the instrument in the same way as Abu-L-Qasim, Ambroise Paré, or even probably Farabeuf, in the last century. The wrist is differently positioned, consequently so are the forearm, the shoulder and indeed the whole body.[159]

As for the modern instruments of the most advanced surgery and micro-surgery, they are continually being improved and brought to a state of unprecedented precision and ingenuity.

It is equally clear that the history of medicine, an endless stream of ideas and actions, is an integral and informative branch of general history. How were people treated in the past? How did doctors approach knowledge of the body, of sickness and of health? How did authorities, in the towns in particular, conceive of protecting, inspecting and improving the health of the public? These are all questions of inestimable value for the study of past societies.

What is more, medicine's long past, constantly flowing into the broader course of history, can shed light on some of the features and structures even of today's medicine. Anyone who has read the books of Georges Canguilhem, the philosopher and historian of science, will know that medicine today, although it thinks of itself as a pure and experimental science, no more, no less, is still as impregnated with a priori notions as it was in the days of Marie-François Xavier Bichat (1771–1802) and his 'vitalism'. Can we call them 'myths' to quote Professor Sournia again? Such myths however, if myths they be, nowadays replace each other at breakneck speed, and the study of life mechanisms and the human cell is advancing at an accelerated and revolutionary rate.

The decisive breakthrough came in the middle of the nineteenth century. In the course of a few years, a profound revolution had taken place. It was not until then that, as Professor Jean Bernard puts it, the doctor acquired 'rational efficiency . . . with the emergence in the space of only six years (1859–65) of discoveries as fundamental as those of Darwin, Pasteur, Mendel and Claude

Bernard – laying the foundations of modern medicine and the biological revolution now taking place before our eyes'.[160] To these names, we might add at least one more, that of François Magendie (1783–1855), the teacher and precursor of Claude Bernard at the Collège de France. After the French Revolution, which had dragged down in its fall the old Faculty of Medicine, Magendie devoted himself heart and soul to the absolute pursuit of the new, and thus to an endless and merciless polemic against his contemporaries. His achievement was to relate medicine and physiology to the by then formulated sciences of physics and chemistry: a salutary step, since in so doing he was founding experimental medicine. For this, he deserves a special place in the pantheon of creative thinkers, similar to that of Evariste Galois (1811–32), his junior by some thirty years, a brilliant mathematician, who was killed in a duel at the age of twenty, but had just had time in his last paper to formulate the modern theory of algebraic functions.

Magendie, and his pupil Claude Bernard (1813–78), were uniquely aware of living at a revolutionary moment in the development of medicine. Of Magendie, Emile Littré (1810–81) wrote after his death: 'He was not interested in history, indeed he was hostile to it . . . Past systems, modes of argument, experimental methods and trends all seemed to him unworthy of the attention of a serious man. For him science had no roots in previous ages.'[161] Claude Bernard likewise unhesitatingly asserted that 'present-day science is necessarily superior to that of the past, and there is no reason whatever to go looking for any of the developments of modern science in the writings of the ancients. Their theories, inevitably mistaken because they do not include phenomena since discovered, can have no real relevance to contemporary science.'[162]

Unfair, but understandable: both Magendie and Bernard were passionately engaged in creating a medical science based exclusively on experimentation. Revolutionaries in the true sense of the term, they had to fight against a surviving *ancien régime* which surrounded them at every turn and which to an absurd degree controlled all French medical institutions of the time – hospitals, chairs of medicine, medical schools. And even after their day, the revolution they fought for still took time to become established, as all really far-reaching revolutions do, the more so since physics, chemistry and biology – the essential foundations – were themselves sciences still in their infancy, their progress still erratic and confined within certain limits. The new medicine would be conceptualized and take shape only slowly, and then thanks to hospital clinics and later to laboratory medicine. And it would only become really effective when it was taken in hand and supported by the state and the enlarged institutions of public health.

My aim here is not to analyse the slow unfolding of a revolution in itself as important as the present-day conquest of space, if not more so: there are plenty of good books which do that. I simply want to point briefly to the consequences of these miraculous achievements for the everyday lives of the French population (54 million at the last census in 1982). These consequences have already been visible for some time. In November 1949, when I took up my post at the Collège de France, I was not so young myself, but since my audience included a number of people very much older than me, I began my inaugural lecture by saying 'We can be quite sure of one thing: in the time of François I, the founder of this college, an assembly like ours, lecturer and audience included, would have been quite unthinkable. The great miracle of recent history has been the unexpected extension of life expectancy.' The fall in mortality is indeed, as Alfred Sauvy recently wrote, 'a victory won over our millennial enemy, death'.[163]

I am not suggesting that this victory was the result simply of medical advance, the impact of which was extended by many other developments: progress in communications, international emulation, the mass production of what we now call wonder drugs, vaccines, chloroform (discovered in 1831 and first applied in 1847), X-rays, lasers, the medical application of electronics, optics, deep-freezing techniques, organ transplants, open-heart surgery, the mass campaign against heart disease, the endless struggle against cancer – one could go on. Let us recognize that this many-sided war against disease – with literally millions of people saved – has made more difference to the human race than our wretched political wars, even the most horrific of them.

One result is plain to see. Life expectancy at birth in present-day France is 71 years for men, 79 for women. In 1900, it was 46 for men.[164]

This may help us to see in 'a future perspective' the situations towards which we nearly always travel with our eyes closed. But I am afraid that people tend to make prophecies based on simple linear arguments, without realizing that the future is a combination of lines and movement, some of them unpredictable. In 1942 for instance, one demographer forecast that by 1982 the French population would be 29 million: it is now 54 million. Today, another demographer tells us that, other things being equal, there will only be 17 million French people by 2100. We shall not be there to see his mistake, but a mistake it undoubtedly is. We are also told that, as things are going at present, there will not be enough young people in work to pay the contributions for their elders' pensions. But to talk like this is surely to assume unthinkingly that tomorrow will be exactly the same as yesterday and today. Does the present government (1985), still imprisoned in a former way of thinking, and faced with the problem of unemployment, realize that 'there is a contradiction between the growing proportion of elderly people [in French society] and the simple-minded notion of lowering the age of retirement?' as Alfred Sauvy put it recently.[165]

The fact is that all the dimensions of tomorrow's economy and society will have to be reformulated in terms both old and radically new. The 'young people' of tomorrow will not be the under-30s, as they are today, but the under-40s, then the under-50s. Life expectancy at birth may no longer be 71 years but 80 or even 90, who knows? And the society of the future will be one dominated to an unprecedented extent by leisure, by non-work. A special sector will have to be created to cope with the need to distract people, to help them pass the time and give them something to do. The tertiary sector – already overloaded – will be swollen even further, especially if robotics really takes off and begins performing services that create even more leisure for the so-called active population. John Naisbitt has described robots as 'the immigrant workers of tomorrow'.[166]

Birth control

Today all industrialized societies have reached a biological stale-mate. They are suffering from a deep-rooted and tenacious malady for which there is really no remedy. The voluntary restriction of births has led, or is promising to lead, to demographic collapse. When combined with the increase in life expectancy, it is resulting in an ageing society and a growing and dangerous imbalance between the active and the inactive population. Consequently all over Europe, though particularly in France, warning voices are being heard prophesying doom and bitterly criticizing contra-ceptive practices.

Let us make it clear what we are talking about. There is a whole range of practices intended one way or another to limit the number of future births. Among them are premature withdrawal (*coitus interruptus*); non-ejaculation (*implexus restrictus*), condoms, the so-called safe period (the Ogino method), spermicides and above all the contraceptive pill, available in France since the 1960s and responsible in itself for a revolution in sexual habits. Should one add chastity, celibacy, late marriage and sodomy? Unlike other commentators these days, I would not automatically include infan-ticide (as once practised in China), or abortion, which while it may be widespread is strictly speaking the prevention of birth rather than of conception.

In the past, reproduction was limited by infantile mortality. That is a scourge which has disappeared today (and France has now become a world leader in this respect)[167] but in the old days it was tragically widespread, particularly among foundlings, who were more vulnerable than other children. 'In Aix-en-Provence, between 1 January 1722 and 31 December 1767, out of 4,844 chil-dren abandoned at the Hôpital Saint-Jacques [one every three days], only 2,224 survived', that is fewer than half.[168] This is simply one example among many. Pierre Chaunu, the historian, who has regularly protested, on radio and television and in his books and articles, against the 1975 law legalizing abortion in

France (it was given permanent force in December 1979) has gone so far as to say: 'Today children are being killed before they come into the world; in the old days infantile mortality tirelessly saw to it that they died after birth'.

Contraception is certainly not a modern invention. But it is only in recent times that it has reached epidemic proportions, spreading throughout Europe, altering the old balance, and leading to a revolution in morality. It so happens that this revolution took place in France earlier than elsewhere. It was already discernible by the mid-eighteenth century. Contemporaries could not fail to notice it and imagine the consequences. In this respect, we had a good hundred years' start over our European neighbours.

This headstart turned out to be catastrophic for the development of the French population. It crept up at snail's pace, whereas our neighbours continued to expand – at even dizzier rates during the industrial revolution. France therefore lost ground, relatively speaking, within Europe. With 27 million people in 1800 (compared to 18 million in Britain and 24.8 million in Germany), France was the most populous nation in Europe, with the exception of Russia. It contained 15.7% of the European population – a percentage that had fallen to 13.3% in 1850 and a mere 9.7% by 1900. So France paid dearly for having been drawn into a vicious circle from which it has never entirely escaped, having never had the ability (or even the will) to do so with the requisite energy. It is perfectly true that the same thing eventually happened to the other European nations, once birth control had taken hold: they too would find it hard to change direction.

So did France cease to be a great power not, as is usually thought, on 15 June 1815 on the field of Waterloo, but well before that, during the reign of Louis XV when the natural birth-rate was interrupted? During the nineteenth century, as Alfred Sauvy has explained, the countries of western Europe followed patterns of development very similar to one another: everything moved more or less at the same pace – social and political change, industry, medicine and so on, with only a few years' difference. There was only one exception, concerning one country: a hundred years before the rest, 'France began to reduce its stock of young people, at the very moment when the race for world-wide expansion was beginning.' The entire course of French history since then has been influenced by something that happened in the *eighteenth* century.[169]

We ought therefore to try to analyse this precocious development, and to explore its causes. The first place to look might be the comments of contemporaries, whether economists or 'demographers' (although the word did not yet exist: *démographie*, a French coinage, appeared only in 1853).

The economist, and in my view talented writer, Ange Goudar, accused his age's taste for luxury of being a poor counsellor in this respect:

> It is the same love of ease and convenience that is filling France with bachelors . . . men who vanish from the world with all their posterity. They think it undignified to be unable to display a wife in society unless they can do so in style; and because of that they conclude that it is better not to marry at all. It is a prodigious thing how many marriages are prevented every day by a gilded coach, or a greater or lesser number of horses, servants, valets and lackeys.[170]

What was more, 'fertility is not now the consequence of conjugal union, people are afraid of it and either directly *or indirectly*, set out to hinder its progress . . . luxury makes most people regard a multitude of children as a sort of dishonour. The richer a man is, the greater his need to limit his offspring.'[171] And the worst of it was that 'the contagion [of luxury] is spreading and imperceptibly influencing the humble people on whose labour the entire edifice of civil Government is founded'.[172]

These words were written in 1756, as the Seven Years' War (1756–63) was just beginning and Louis XV still had eighteen years of his reign ahead of him, before his death in 1774.

In 1758, an abbé from the south of France, Jean Novi de Caveirac, wrote of the men who reject 'without regret the sweet name of father . . . some restrain their desires, others *cheat nature*'.[173] In 1763, Turmeau de la Morandière, an 'amateur demographer', referred to the spread of contraceptive practices:

couples want only one child, or none at all. This *profanation of the sacrament of matrimony*, this shameful meanness has spread from person to person like an epidemic', and confessors would confirm that every class in society, rich and poor alike, was affected.[174] The chevalier de Cerfvol in 1770 denounced the pernicious effect on people's health of 'this horrible behaviour' against which the Church had struggled in vain.[175] And the well-known writer Moheau was equally categorical: 'rich women . . . are not the only ones who regard the propagation of the species as an *antique absurdity*; already these *deadly secrets*, known to no animal other than man . . . have penetrated the countryside; nature is cheated even in the villages'.[176] In Normandy in 1782, if we are to believe Père Féline, a missionary of Saint-Jean-Eudes who was working in the province 'saving souls in the towns and countryside',

> the infamous crime of Onan . . . is widespread and very common among married couples . . . especially when they do not wish to have a large number of children, without wishing to deprive themselves of the pleasure they take in the married state; this unfortunate disposition is common to rich and poor alike: their motives are different but their crime is the same. Only rarely do they confess it; so it is the fatal cause of the damnation of many people.[177]

A few years later (1788), Messance condemned the 'calculation' (in other words an act implying decision and responsibility) 'which leads a man to want only one or two children; the false grandeur which leads [him] . . . to have a great number of servants, a great number of guests at table, instead of sitting down surrounded by his children; and the *greatest depravity of all*, which crowns everything, of *destroying his seed as he sows it*'.[178] The anxiety even reached government circles. In 1785, Necker expressed fears that such corruption of morals might make the number of births drop below that of deaths.

Evidence like this leaves us in no doubt that contraception was spreading, winning converts and being transmitted like a disease: the practice in question was *coitus interruptus*. But the explanations usually advanced for its diffusion are perhaps a little too simple. It

191

is generally supposed that the 'deadly secrets' were discovered and put into practice by the upper classes, passed on to the middle classes and then to the ordinary people of the towns and bourgs, before reaching the country population which 'had its eyes opened to them' only later. 'The arrival of contraception in the villages', writes one historian, 'was the culmination of a perversion invented in town.'[179] But was the countryside as 'innocent' and ignorant as we have been led to think?

A study by Guy Arbellot of five communities in Haute-Marne, not far from Joinville, has shown that in the seventeenth century children in these villages were born, depending on their parents' occupations, either after the harvest or after grape-picking.[180] The first child, whose birth is closely related to the date of marriage, can be left aside. But the others seem to have been planned. That such family planning was the result of contraceptive practice, rather than the more unlikely chastity, becomes a strong probability when one knows that at the same time in Basse-Normandie, a region where 'the fertility of married couples fell to modest levels very early',[181] contraception was regularly being condemned by confessors, including those in rural areas. In 1650 in the diocese of Coutances, a mission revealed that 'the disgraceful sin was being committed in the most monstrous fashion, and with such gross ignorance that [often the people] did not think they were committing a sin at all'.[182]

One is not surprised then to read a comment, made in 1754, (rather late in the day, but presented as a commonplace) by the so-called chevalier John Nickolls (actually a Frenchman born in Le Mans and taking this pseudonym in order to comment freely on both France and England):

> Concerning the peasants [*laboureurs*], the countryside furnishes as great examples of poverty in this class as the towns do of wealth. It is on them that the weight of state taxation falls most heavily. A peasant who has not the necessities of life dreads like the plague a large number of children. Fear of intolerable poverty prevents some from marrying; and even in this class, marriages have become less fertile.[183]

192

Similar conclusions emerge from recent research by demographers and historians, in both rural and urban milieux, using criteria and methods devised by Louis Henry, and drawing on parish records. They enable us to calculate approximately the fertility rate of married women from the regular or irregular intervals between the births of their children. A few conclusions have already emerged: contraception became part of French behaviour particularly early, compared to the chronology of the same process in the rest of Europe. And however historians choose to explain it, these practices spread like wildfire with the French Revolution, although they were evidently already in use well before 1789.

In Meulan for instance, a little town on the Seine, 47 kilometres from Paris, until about 1740 90% of couples apparently did little or nothing to limit births: the other 10% were either infertile or deliberately restricted their fertility. From 1740, the proportion of the latter increased, rising to 17% between 1740 and 1764, while a degree of birth control spread to some of the other couples; by 1765 to 1789, contraception was being practised by about 25% of the couples. But the great divide occurs in about 1790: the proportion of couples who were either childless or voluntarily restricting childbirth leaps from 24.1% to 46.5% between 1790 and 1815, and to 59.4% between 1815 and 1839.[184]

If this was true of Meulan, it was probably true elsewhere. But did it apply to the whole of France? That seems unlikely. In Rouen, J.-P. Bardet writes, 'the fall of the Bastille did not lead to any increase in contraception, which had already been well established for almost a century'.[185] He argues convincingly that

> while in 1670, there were eight children [per family], there were scarcely four by 1800. In less than 150 years the Rouen population had acquired a surprising mastery of the 'deadly secrets'. How had they managed in the space of four or five generations to reduce the number of children by half? Demographic analysis does not reveal what the contraceptive methods were, but it does enable us to trace and analyse the incidence of contraception.[186]

In three villages in the Ile-de-France by contrast – Beaumont-les-Nonains, Marcheroux and Le Mesnil-Théribus (today communes in the Beauvais district, *département* of Oise)[187] – it seems that the habit became established only in the late eighteenth century. The same is true of Châtillon-sur-Seine where, although the data covers only a short period, some limitation of family size is recorded between 1771 and 1784.[188] Whereas in Sainghin-en-Mélantois, near Lille, in a more marginal frontier area of France, the development is even later and only of modest dimensions at first, not becoming established until the mid-nineteenth century. And the Vendée, even in 1830, remained virtually untouched by the 'Malthusian revolution'.[189]

None of this need surprise us, since France showed a wide range of reactions to this growing development. The same circumstances did not necessarily lead to the same effects. Explanations which look obvious a priori can be confirmed in one place but not another. For instance, in Brittany, as in Normandy, 'egalitarian succession was the rule for commoners' and, as in Normandy, there was 'much concern for children',[190] two motives which might as a rule prompt families to restrict the number of children. But Brittany does not seem to have been as Malthusian as Normandy.

Indeed the wider the net of research is cast, the more complicated the problem becomes. Many factors have been singled out one after another: age of the parents at marriage; breastfeeding by the child's natural mother, or recourse to a wet-nurse; the family's position in the scale of occupations, its social status; the cultural milieu which, as we know, could determine the very form of the family; the laws or customs governing inheritance (which varied greatly between provinces), and lastly the efficacy of the teachings of the Church, which was deeply implicated in the debate. Any general explanation one might suggest is likely to prove inadequate for any given place or at any given period, and to have wider application only if it makes considerable allowance for discrepancies and time-lags. I accept all this, but it is still worth trying to understand how the phenomenon of contraception – destined to spread far and wide – first became established, and why it appeared so much earlier in France than anywhere else.

We should avoid the common error of attributing everything to the age of Enlightenment and the eventful and destabilizing years of the French Revolution. Contraception was not a discovery communicated in the same way as cultural values or epidemics. Nor should we conclude that contraceptive practices were invented, as some people claim, by the French aristocracy in the time of Louis XIV or Louis XV, and that a bad example was set by dukes, marquises and contemporaries of Madame de Sévigné (who was herself most anxious that her daughter should space out her pregnancies).[191]

Contraception stretches back far into the past. Some historians have claimed that voluntary birth control brought Greek civilization to an end; and fewer children than before were being born in Rome in the glorious reign of Augustus. In the Bible, Onan is the symbolic representative of *coitus interruptus*. And the penitentials of the Middle Ages, from the sixth century on, lead one to think that the 'deadly secrets' had long since penetrated the civilization of western Europe. I am inclined to believe J.-P. Bardet[192] when he says that it is hard to imagine any society that was absolutely 'non-contraceptive', for even those thought to be such included couples 'with suspicous practices'. To conclude for example, from the very low number of illegitimate births in French villages in the seventeenth century, that an extremely long period of continence was imposed on young people before they married, since contraception was unknown or even unthinkable until recent times, as Philippe Ariès argued, seems as implausible to me as it does to J.-L. Flandrin. After all, prostitutes, who have always been instructors in sexual matters, are generally agreed to have practised contraception as a matter of course. Writing of women who gave birth clandestinely, Montaigne refers to 'all the sluts [*garces*] who every day conceal their children, both in their generation and in their conception'.[193] (And the word *garce* has its present-day contemporary pejorative sense here, since it is contrasted with 'the honest wife of Sabinus'.)

Moreover if the Church fought so relentlessly, and sometimes with success, against this assault on the sacred bond and aims of Christian marriage, if confessors were worried about it and asked their bishops for guidance on how to deal with sinners, it was because there undoubtedly was a problem and a threat to the couple as construed by the Church.

The attitude of the Church

It is important to realize what the ideal representation of Christian marriage was, until fairly recent times – so far removed is it from present-day ideas. It was not a bond based on love, still less physical love. All passionate feeling, we read in sixteenth-century texts, imperils 'the honesty of the marriage bed'. The man who with his wife, 'satisfies the disordered craving of the flesh' to the point where if she were not his wife, he would 'wish to have dealings with her'; the man 'who shows himself to be rather a passionate lover than a husband toward his wife, is an adulterer'. Marriage was instituted precisely to 'preserve from sin [which consisted of seeking pleasure for its own sake] and in order to found a lineage which one may nourish in the love and fear of God'.[194] The purpose of the 'holiness of marriage' was to have 'issue among whom God is eternally blessed',[195] 'to have children that they might be brought up to the glory of God'.[196] Woe betide anyone who forgot this cardinal rule. The catechism of the diocese of Meaux, at the time when Bossuet was bishop there, taught that within marriage the greatest sin was 'to avoid having children, which is an abominable crime', unless of course the method was mutually agreed chastity. The abominable crime, relentlessly proscribed by the Church, was a mortal sin, which condemned the sinner to penitence and deprived him of the sacraments.

We should not imagine that this idea of marriage was confined to circles of bigoted piety. Montaigne wrote in terms his confessor would have approved of about 'the religious and pious bond' of marriage, and the need to remove from it all 'licence and excess'.[197] 'The shameless lasciviousness that first affections prompt in this relation', he writes, 'is not only indecent but harmful if employed towards our wives. *Let them at least learn of impudence at other hands*. They are always sufficiently aroused for our needs.'

196

The sentence in italics rings strangely in this moralizing extract. Outside marriage it seems, in adultery for instance, impudence and 'licence' are quite natural. This clearly indicates the wide gap recommended and demanded between the world of marriage, family life and dignity, and that other world of extra-marital affections, where the wild beast could be given free rein. There were thus two ways of experiencing sexual life, the shameless and the virtuous, and what was admissible in the one was not in theory proper in the other. Brantôme, who is so indulgent about the sexual indiscretions and bawdy anecdotes he recounts with amusement or tolerance, himself says that according to 'Holy Scripture . . . there is no call for husband and wife to love each other so much . . . with lewd and lascivious passion; since putting and occupying all their hearts in these sensual pleasures, and engaging in them so heartily, they neglect the love they should bear to God.'[198] He speaks elsewhere of 'sins' which 'would tarnish' marriage. But he regards the same sins (such as unorthodox positions in lovemaking) as perfectly charming when at a princely court they are cunningly presented to a group of young women in the form of drawings engraved inside the cup from which they drink. 'Several of them were corrupted into trying them, for anyone of spirit wants to try everything.'[199]

So the astonishing thing is that what was regarded as a serious offence within marriage was seen as much less serious, and indeed normal, outside marriage. More astonishing still, the Church's view and the consensus within society were at one in this. Brantôme speaks for instance quite openly of the *coitus interruptus* which certain women think it their duty to enforce in an adulterous affair, 'both to avoid their husbands thinking a child is theirs when it is not, and so as not to seem to have done them wrong or cuckolded them, so long as the seed has not entered them . . . So they are conscientious out of good intentions.'[200] It may seem an ironic conclusion, but it literally was the Church's view that avoiding the birth of a child in adultery, fornication or incest attenuated the sin. This had been the case from the penitentials of the Middle Ages – which double or triple the years of penitence imposed on the fornicator or adulterer if he was the cause of an illegitimate birth –

197

to the debates of the casuists and confessors of the seventeenth century, who concluded that in all illicit love affairs, the incomplete sexual act was a lesser evil, attenuating the sin.

Such laxity was defended by the casuists in the name of a more than specious interpretation of sin. But it was no doubt forced upon confessors, who had to grapple with everyday life, out of a straightforward desire to avoid illegitimate births. The final result could only be to encourage the contamination passing from one to the other of the two artificially separated areas of sexual life, the conjugal and the extra-conjugal. The same Père Féline who was horrified at the widespread nature of the 'abominable crime of Onan' in 1782, noted that the couples whom the Church and medical science of the day forbade to procreate during the period when a child was being breast-fed, escaped from a lengthy penitence in the same way as Brantôme's adulterous ladies, and with the same good conscience.[201]

But before long, couples would refuse to let the Church intrude upon their intimacy. This was the final stage of the long disintegration of the Christian marriage, the end of a cultural equilibrium, the breakdown of an old order, and it happened very slowly as is always the case in changes of this nature.

In theory, the Church's teaching about contraception did not change. But it was abandoned by the vast mass of Catholics themselves. This was already the case by 1842. Mgr Bouvier, bishop of Le Mans, was obliged in that year to note that:

almost all young spouses are unwilling to have numerous progeny, and yet they cannot morally abstain from the conjugal act. When asked by their confessors how they exercise their marriage rights, they are usually seriously shocked, and although warned, do not abstain from the conjugal act, nor can they be resolved upon the indefinite multiplication of the species . . . They all freely admit that infidelity to one's marriage partner and deliberate abortion are very great sins. And only a few of them can be persuaded that they are obliged, on pain of mortal sin, either to observe perfect chastity within marriage, or to run the risk of engendering a numerous progeny.[202]

The progressive lifting of the taboo reflects the rapid spread of contraception, after the later years of the eighteenth century. But it does not explain why people were unwilling to have children. In the sixteenth century, according to Montaigne, 'the commonest and most healthy part of humanity regards an abundance of children as great good fortune'.[203] Why, two centuries later, should it have become an inconvenience? And why was this unwillingness so astonishingly and visibly earlier in the particular case of France? This is the most perplexing question for the historian.

The French case

A priori, any explanation which is not differential (distinguishing between France on one hand and Europe on the other) will probably be mistaken. So we cannot say that France's prematurity in this respect results from its economic status for instance: France was economically similar to its neighbours. Nor can it be claimed that the French were the first people to discover contraception: it had long been discovered, and none of the peoples of Europe had to be instructed in it. Nor can we say too firmly that it was the growth of affection for children in the eighteenth century that led the French to have fewer children in order to bring them up in better conditions. The late eighteenth century saw a rise in the number of children callously abandoned.

I can only think of two acceptable explanations: one suggested by Alfred Sauvy,[204] which I rather hastily opposed in the past; and the other the argument I put up against him at the time. They may be compatible, but do not reinforce each other since they are different in kind: one is cultural, the other economic or, rather, demographic. And since in this area there are plenty of surprises, the surprise here is that Alfred Sauvy is not this time the demographer, but the supporter of a cultural (I almost wrote idealist) explanation.

Alfred Sauvy sees the limitation of births in France as the consequence of the liberation of Frenchmen from the teachings, the restrictions and the yoke of the Catholic Church. The Church sought to control the body, the better to control the soul. The drama played out in the eighteenth century was a sort of revenge on the part of the Reformation. Having hesitated, two centuries earlier, between Rome and Luther, or rather between Rome and Calvin, France had chosen Rome, but the choice backfired. Was that possible at two centuries' remove? Nowadays, being familiar with the perspective of the long term, I am quite prepared to say yes. I note for instance that even later, at the time of Ferdinand Buisson and others,[205] the secular primary school provides another echo of the Reformation. And there were echoes of the Reformation too in the corridors of the second Vatican Council.

But can we simply say 'Reformation'? We should not forget that non-religious education made its first appearance in France in the sixteenth century, in the new schools founded in large numbers and with much enthusiasm by that socially and culturally privileged elite whom Georges Huppert has studied with devotion. For a while, it succeeded in removing education from under the wing of the Church, until the Jesuits took things firmly in hand in the seventeenth century. Yet these men were not Protestants. They refused that particular temptation. In my view, they represent what one might describe as the hesitation, *original* to France, between Reformation and Counter-Reformation and the efforts, always discernible at least among French intellectuals,[206] humanists and 'libertines' or free-thinkers, to escape from both. This hesitation, this movement first one way then the other, this search for a separate road, was a unique feature of French culture. It was an encouragement to independence of mind, from Montaigne to Voltaire and beyond. Predictably, it would turn out to be thwarting and increasingly harmful to the Church. I think this must have played some part in French attitudes towards contraception.

I am even more prepared to believe that France, having been well-populated and developed since earliest times, may have suffered in almost chronic fashion from being an *over-populated country*. That is at any rate what Marcel Reinhard and his colleagues thought when preparing the third edition of his great history of world population (1968). It is true that over-population as a concept calls for reservations and prudence. It can only be invoked when some imbalance or threat of imbalance appears between the mass of population and the mass of available resources. In 1789, with its 26 million inhabitants and a density per kilometre rather over 50, France was certainly over-populated. Whereas England proper (rather than Great Britain), with only 8 million people and a density only slightly above the French, was not over-populated. England's gross national income was roughly the same as that of France, so its per capita income must have been much higher. The English population was up against a less rigid ceiling; it could develop within what one might call a more elastic framework. It could count, as the future would show, on a highly productive agricultural sector, expanding industry and a number of industrial towns which grew into accumulators and engines of further growth. Whereas during the French Revolution, the towns of France were, on the contrary, engines that had broken down, and would only start to work again under the Consulate and Empire. At the crucial moment in 1789–90, when the cultural elites, having already been sapped for some time, collapsed, economic life entered a crisis. Birth limitation took place against a context that encouraged its spread by aggravating the difficulties of everyday life. The Napoleonic wars may also have brought a degree of psychological disarray and anxiety about life. Edgar Quinet[207] described the worries of that generation: his own parents for instance, though highly cultivated people, had not thought it worth giving their son a proper education since he was likely to perish young on some battlefield. Such anxiety would hardly encourage large families.

Two further remarks may be added to these comments. Marcel Reinhard and his collaborators think that French over-population became established in the seventeenth century. I think it may already have been the case in the sixteenth, the time when France was 'as full as an egg', in Brantôme's phrase quoted earlier. What we may have here is longstanding over-population, causing pressure probably without parallel in Europe. Contraception would thus be a response to a pressing necessity, as had been those other choices, late marriage or celibacy – particularly in the south of France, where the authority of the patriarch could impose them.

My second and final comment is that during the first half of the nineteenth century, France saw its population grow by 30%, whereas the rest of Europe increased on average by 50% (and the English population doubled). France was poorly placed for the trial of strength of the early nineteenth century, marked in the French case by a slow, laborious and incomplete attempt to catch up industrially. Just at the moment when it would have been useful to expand the birth-rate in France, authoritative voices were raised to encourage the country in its Malthusian habits. In this respect, the prize goes to the learned Jean-Baptiste Say, that textbook writer of political economy: 'People should be encouraged to make savings not babies,' he wrote.[208]

To sum up: is the word *contraception* the most appropriate for the dramatic process that penetrated the living history of France? It is certainly the case that everyday life in France saw the deterioration of traditional Christian marriage as the Church would have wanted to maintain it – a long deterioration prepared well in advance: cultural history, despite some striking images, never really takes the form of a landslide. What happened at about the turn of the eighteenth to nineteenth century was *mutatis mutandis* the same as has happened recently, and is still happening before our own eyes, with the breakdown of matrimonial patterns that were once the social norm. What we are seeing now is the refusal even of the formal marriage in front of the mayor: it may have been a less ceremonial occasion than the church wedding, but it nevertheless represented all the constraints, demands and inconveniences called for by the law – in other words by society. So how will tomorrow's society manage to cope with and incorporate *union libre*, the couples who live together without being married? Culture can only survive over time by getting rid of certain inheritances: first Christian marriage, now civil marriage. What will it want to get rid of next?

Foreign immigration, a recent problem

I have been fortunate enough to find myself all my life on the side of tolerance. I am comfortable with it. But I cannot claim any personal credit on that account. I only really discovered the Jewish question for instance in Algeria, in 1923, when I was already over twenty years old. For the next ten years, still in Algeria, I was living in a Muslim country where I learnt to understand and respect Arabs and Berbers. Later, in 1935, living in Brazil where I taught for several years, I met black people in an atmosphere that reminded me of *Gone with the Wind*. With some exceptions, I know all the European countries and have spent long periods there with much pleasure and no difficulty.

Tolerance and yet more tolerance! That is what is needed if we are to bring a lucid eye to the large-scale proletarian immigration of which France is today the destination. And we need to understand why this time it is a problem, whereas for generations and generations past, France has received and absorbed various waves of immigrants, who have enriched the country materially and culturally.

Assimilation, if it is possible and accepted, is in my view the best recipe for immigration without tears.

This has been the way followed by all those who, individually or in small groups, have in the past *chosen* to become French: political refugees, whether Italians fleeing Fascism, Spaniards escaping the civil war, White Russians in 1917, artists, scientists and intellectuals of every nationality. These immigrants, welcomed with open arms, were quickly absorbed into the activity or the quiet corners of our civilization. Their origin no longer distinguishes them from the mass of French people. And many of those who were French by adoption have been central figures in France's greatest successes: Maria Sklodowska (1867–1934), born in Warsaw, became Marie Curie and with her husband discovered radium in 1898, winning a Nobel prize in 1911. Pablo Picasso (1881–1973) was born in Malaga; Amedeo Modigliani (1884–1920) in Livorno; Marc

Chagall in Vitebsk in 1887; Eugene Ionesco in Slatin, Romania, in 1912; Chaim Soutine (1895–1944) came from Lithuania, and is still remembered with delight in the little town of Céret: he used to wipe his brushes clean on whatever he was wearing, with unforgettable results. To list all the illustrious foreigners who have chosen to make their home in France would take too long. If they are dear to us, it is not only because they have brought us honour by their fame, but also because they were willing to join us, to become as French as the most celebrated of our compatriots, and because they added yet another rich strand to our complex culture.

But statistically more important were the massive waves of immigration: Italians in the late nineteenth century, White Russians after 1917, Poles who came to the mines and farms of northern France in about 1920, Jews who left Nasser's Egypt or Algeria after independence (Algerian Jews had had French nationality since the Crémieux decree of 1871), and the *pieds-noirs*, the European settlers who left Algeria in 1962 and entered France to no official welcome: over a million men, women and children, French in origin of course and thus returning home, but having lost everything and often left to fend for themselves like immigrants. And lastly there has been the great wave of immigrant workers of the 1960s and 1970s.

Large-scale immigration is a fairly recent phenomenon in France: in 1851, on the eve of the Second Empire, foreigners represented only 1% of the population: by 1872, at the beginning of the Third Republic, it was still only 2%. Belgians, working in the towns, mines and beet fields of the Nord, accounted for no fewer than 40% of the immigrants of those days, closely followed by the Italians. The assimilation of these foreigners, who were in fact near neighbours, was quite quickly achieved, especially once the law of 26 June 1889 made naturalization easier. By about 1914, 'the number of foreigners had stabilized at around 1,100,000 people, accounting for just under 3% of the total'.[209]

After World War I (and even before it had ended) France was short of manpower, since it was above all the active young men who were lost in the trenches. Hence a second wave of immigrants, this time from Mediterranean countries, especially North Africa, which had been incorporated (in 1830, 1881–3 and 1911) into the French colonial Empire. By 1931, there were 2,700,000 foreigners in France, 6.6% of the population.

The depression of the 1930s, followed by World War II brought this figure down: in 1946, there were only 1,700,000 foreigners, 4.4% of the population.

It was only after 1956 that the third wave of immigration rapidly took shape. By 1976, the number of immigrants was estimated at 3,700,000 or 7% of the total population. Of this total, Portuguese immigrants accounted for 22%, Algerian for 21%, Spanish for 15%, Italian for 13%, Moroccan for 8%, Tunisian for 4%, Turkish for 1.5%, and black African for 2.3% (figures from the 1975 census). Most of these immigrants were adults, men who had been selected (their mortality rate was well below the French average). The immigrant birth-rate was high: immigrants from the three North African countries had an average of 5 to 6 children per woman, Portuguese 3.3, Spanish 2.5, Italian 2. 'On average in 1975, this indicator [the fertility rate] was 3.32 for all immigrants, as against 1.84 for the French and 1.93 for the whole population resident in France.' But once the immigrants have settled in France, their fertility rate, wherever measurement is possible, tends to 'fall in parallel to the indigenous French fertility rate'.[210]

With the economic crisis of the 1970s, this third wave reached its peak. 'Will the pause, after 1974 . . . turn out to be merely a phase when some foreigners return home, or does it portend a reversal of the flow of migration? . . . Consideration of the world demographic situation inclines one to favour the hypothesis that this is only a temporary pause.'[211]

It is at any rate the first occasion, I believe that immigration has posed, at national level a sort of 'colonial' problem, located this time in France. And it has political implications which tend to conceal the complexity of the reciprocal forms of rejection, which cannot be denied, much as one may deplore them. Is it possible to look at these problems analytically?

An economic problem

The mass of immigrant workers in France represents, as it does elsewhere in Europe, 10% of the active population. Have unemployment and the current economic crisis encouraged hostility towards them on the part of French workers? In some cases no doubt. But much less than is suggested by the slogan of a certain political party: '1,500,000 unemployed = 1,500,000 immigrants too many'.

The very great majority of immigrant workers are in fact being used as cheap labour, detailed to do the most thankless tasks, or those thought to be such, which are in nine cases out of ten shunned by the 'French' workforce. If all the immigrants were to be expelled, it would quickly become clear that the unemployed, who are mostly French, would not come flocking to take up the places at the bottom of the ladder previously occupied by foreigners. It reminds me of the comment by the archbishop of Valencia when there was talk of expelling from Spain the undesirable Moriscoes in 1610: 'But who will make our shoes?' he asked.[212] If the immigrants left France, who would build our roads, do the hardest tasks in factories or the heavy labour in the building trade? These jobs would only be taken up by French nationals if some authoritarian regime were able to raise the wages for them, in an arbitrary and intelligent fashion. This was in fact tried recently for Paris dustmen: improved equipment, timetables and pay did indeed lead to the recruitment of more French workers.

Immigration, a source of workers at the lowest pay levels, is inherent in all capitalist societies. What is happening in France is happening in all the industrialized countries of Europe – even in over-populated Belgium, which sends emigrants to France but receives immigrants from Morocco; even in Italy, which has for over a hundred years been sending steady streams of emigrants to the United States and Latin America, and is still sending workers to Germany and Switzerland, but on the other hand admits Tunisians to work as fishermen in Sicily, as well as Libyans and Eritreans.

Similarly in the United States and Canada, in the industrialized areas of Latin America or Australia, unskilled labour, 'mere muscle',[213] is recruited either from outside (Toynbee's 'external proletariat', which can be exploited even from a distance)[214] or from inside the country. This is equally true of the Soviet Union, where by no means all the workers in the big industrial centres are Russian.

In fact, foreign immigration fairly closely replicates internal migration in France during the nineteenth and even early twentieth centuries. The industry of the time recruited its proletarians – who were more harshly treated than those of today – among rural immigrants. Later on, their place was gradually taken by foreigners for the most arduous industrial tasks. The incomers also filled some of the early gaps in the countryside (Polish immigrants in the Nord and Aisne *départements* in the mid-1920s). With the rapid industrial growth of the 'thirty glorious years' after the war, foreign labour had to be recruited directly from abroad.

It is a workforce often living in very poor circumstances, as can be confirmed, alas, by considering our slums, basements and *bidonvilles* (shanty-towns). These shanty-towns were still to be found in 1939 along the former boundary of the fortifications of Paris and are now in much farther-flung suburbs, as far out as Mantes-la-Jolie. In 1980, the Hauts-de-Seine *département* contained 220,000 immigrants, about 15% of its total population. An Algerian mason, Mohammed Nedjaï, aged 56 and having worked for 35 years in France, is quoted as saying: 'After building so many houses for French people, I think it would be only fair to let me have an HLM at last.'[215] But the average HLM (subsidized apartment), which costs a certain amount of money, is not big enough for families with eight or nine children. Can such families afford a 'middle-class' home? One answer might be to build houses rather than flats, but nothing like enough are built for the demand. And one remembers the expansive declarations made in the 1970s by Jacques Chaban-Delmas, the then prime minister under the presidency of Georges Pompidou: he promised to demolish the *bidonvilles* – as if in present circumstances this salutary measure was possible. No sooner is one *bidonville* destroyed than another springs up nearby. They mushroom like the *macumbos* or *favellas* in Brazil – especially since the third wave of immigrants after 1956 took France by surprise and no housing had been prepared for them. Far from satisfactory makeshift arrangements were made, and the newcomers were those who suffered.

Now that the economic tide has turned, is it right to accuse this foreign labour force of being a burden on the French economy? To criticize immigrants for receiving unemployment benefit? Or for having too many children, and contributing to the social security deficit? Such accusations are probably out of all proportion. But even if they were true, *they would be irrelevant*. Immigrants who have been in France for a long time have contributed to French economic growth, to the embourgeoisement of a section of the French working class, and to a general rise in living standards. If the nation as a whole had to pay for this today, one way or another, even at the cost of a slight fall in purchasing power, that would be no more than justice.[216]

The problem of racism

The trouble is that the economic crisis has fanned the flames of racial hatred. It becomes particularly acute in areas where two compact groups – French and North Africans for instance – find themselves face to face, often companions in misfortune and obliged to live side by side, but never really mixing, and thus in each case they are led to assert their specificity in violent fashion.

It is an old problem, and it is still with us. It is the problem of *otherness*, that is, the feeling that a foreign presence is other, a challenge to one's own self and identity, to such a degree that this real or imagined difference provokes in both parties unease, scorn, fear or hate. In order to exist, do we have to compare ourselves with the other? Nationalism has in the past brought division, madness and savagery to Europe. We French have bared our teeth at the Spanish, the English, the Germans – and they have done the same to us. In 1815, the red collars on the tunics of Prussian officers represented 'Frenchman's blood', *Franzosen Blut*, or so it was said. And perhaps the cruellist gibe devised by otherness is the scornful 'Speak white!' which the English used to address to French Canadians.

Absurd? Perhaps, but every age in history has its shameful aspects, its foolishness and prejudice, which contemporaries share without always even realizing it. Nathaniel Weyl's book describing Karl Marx as a racist[217] may entertain (though it does not necessarily convince). From his letters and writings, he argues, Marx appears to be a 'pro-slaver': 'Without slavery', Marx wrote somewhere, 'North America, that most advanced of nations, would have been transformed into a patriarchal society' (whatever he meant by that). Marx was also a colonialist, inclined to believe in the supremacy of the whites over the non-whites. In 1849, when the 'Americans' took California from the Mexicans, he wrote: 'Nothing is ever accomplished in history without violence . . . Can anyone say it was a bad thing that California was taken from the lazy Mexicans, who would not have known what to do with it?' But what does that prove? Simply that one cannot live in one's own time without being touched by it, even if one is Karl Marx. Racism did not colonize his thought, but it certainly touched it: not even Marx could live with impunity in London, the imperious and imperial centre of the world.

That said, can anyone seriously believe that racism does not inhabit our country, that it is not lying, deeply concealed perhaps, but ready to well up to the surface like bubbles from the sea bed?

The kind of evidence I prefer on this subject comes from everyday incidents – just ordinary little things but repeated many times. A friend of mine is very critical of this habit, which he says is scientifically inaccurate, but I still think I am right. The reader may be the judge: I offer here two or three anecdotes in which I was an involuntary participant, but a participant all the same. These incidents have at least the advantage over many we read about that they are not violent.

I live in a part of Paris, the thirteenth *arrondissement*, where there are many immigrants from Africa and Asia. One afternoon, my wife and I were quietly walking towards the corner where a steep street meets ours at right angles. A young black teenager, about six feet tall, and smartly dressed, came flying round the corner on roller skates, right across our path and, without stopping, swerved at top speed, missing us by inches. I exclaimed angrily – just a few words: the skater was already far away. But he immediately came back, showered me with abuse, and ended up beside himself, shouting, 'Can't you just let us be!' I thought that an extraordinary thing to say, and he repeated it. I was just an old fogey, guilty of being in his way, and my protests were nothing but racist aggression. I took comfort, not very effectively, in telling myself that a white boy on skates might have been just as rude. Ten years earlier, I might have reacted more vigorously.

The other story is that I was sitting comfortably in a taxi belonging to a company I have subscribed to for about fifteen years. I know the driver well: he is a Martiniquais, who reminds me of the black taxi-drivers in Washington. The journey was a long one, and he told me about himself, how he made some money playing in a band in the evenings, how he was married to a French woman and had three children, all very handsome he assured me. One of them is now a dentist and has a Finnish wife. 'And guess what, Monsieur,' he told me with a grin, 'I've got a blonde grand-daughter!' I liked this story of the immigrant who found happiness, and for some reason, coming back that evening, this time in a cab driven by a young woman from the same company, I decided to tell her about it. It turned out not to be a good idea. She reacted angrily, with a torrent of abuse against foreign taxi-drivers. Knowing that she and her husband, also a driver, have no children, I could not resist trying to have the last word: 'But if you had children, there would be fewer foreign taxi-drivers.'

My last anecdote may make sense only to me. I was listening to an interview on the radio with a young Algerian girl, a second-generation resident in France and now a student, describing her unhappiness, her feelings of anger and the constant problems she had to face. And she said all this in such perfect and elegant French (there must be something to be said for French schooling) that I suddenly had the cheerful and no doubt absurd feeling that, for her at least, success was just round the corner.

I will stop the personal impressions there. Each of us no doubt has a store of anecdotes of this kind, evidence of racism that invariably works two ways: rejection is reciprocal and feeds on reciprocity. And if anti-Semitism has greatly diminished in France since the days of Edouard Drumont (1844–1917), the author of the unpardonable polemic *La France juive*, it is worrying to see it being rekindled like a smouldering fire, with the racism now developing in France against other incomers, more difficult to assimilate and whose numbers are growing. Hence the daily incidents and dangers.

And yet how can anyone seriously talk of 'race' in France. The people of North Africa are of white origin, and French southerners have Saracen, Spanish and Andalusian blood. 'Look at the crowd in the [Paris] metro, or in the streets of towns like Lyon, Marseille, Lille or Grenoble,' says the sociologist Augustin Barbara:[218]

> The extreme diversity of faces and human types reveals the great richness of this population and at the same time the absurdity of those who talk of 'sending the foreigners away'. The French population is a fabric made up of various ethnic groups, of various regional populations, who have been joined, in waves of immigration going back more than a hundred years, by foreigners from Europe and further afield.[219]

So many immigrants, for so long, from prehistory down to very recent history, have succeeded in settling, without too much trouble, among the French population, that one could practically say that all French people – if we look back over the centuries and millennia preceding our own time – are the children of immigrants. France is already extremely diverse: can it not take the risk of becoming biologically even more so?

A cultural problem

There remains one last problem, the only real and worrying one: the cultural problem. What Bernard Stasi says in his excellent book applies on this point more than anywhere else: 'Serenity is the quality most lacking in the difficult debate about immigration.'[220] Here again, the words bandied about as good or bad things – integration, assimilation, insertion – serve to mask reality.

Cultural mixes are never simple, as the Jewish example demonstrates. I still remember a history professor at Strasbourg long ago. When asked to respond to something 'as a Jew', he replied, 'I am not a Jew, I am a Frenchman.' I am inclined to applaud him. But Serge Koster may have been more truthful when he replied to a recent survey by saying, 'France is my fatherland, the country of my language and affections. But I feel for [the state of] Israel, which is not my country, an undying attachment.'[221] I was once dining at the Brasserie Lipp, in 1958 I think, with Raymond Aron: he explained to me that as a Jew, he was obliged on certain occasions to act in a certain manner. I replied, 'But Raymond, you are not a Jew, you are a Lorrainer' (since his family, like that of his famous relative Marcel Mauss, came from that province). I don't remember whether he smiled at that, but I am sure he did not reply. And it is true that, when faced with various civilizations at first foreign to him, a Jew will succeed in assimilating them perfectly, becoming quite absorbed into them, while at the same time taking refuge in an inner civilization which remains dear to him, and from which he can detach himself only incompletely if at all.

And yet there are only 14 million Jews altogether, scattered all over the world (600,000 in France, the largest single group outside the United States). How is it that the striking successes with which the history of the diaspora is studded – seventeenth-century Poland, fifteenth-century Italy, sixteenth-century Spain, eighteenth-century Germany, the United States today, Brazil, France – have never led to a straightforward assimilation? Why have these Jewish communities not, like other foreign bodies, become absorbed into one or other of the many lands where they have lived so long?

Perhaps it is, as a journalist recently suggested, because 'every time . . . that the Jewish community seems to be moving towards assimilation, something happens to remind it of its origins, of a painful and persecuted past, of the ghetto'.[222] If I had met Raymond Aron before 1933, would he have spoken to me in the same terms? Probably not. After the holocaust, how can any Jew, even if he is secretly shocked by some of the manifestations of Israeli nationalism, say so in public?

The visit made by President Giscard d'Estaing to the Middle East in 1980, when he spoke in favour of the Palestinian cause, provoked in the press one of those explosions of emotion. *Tribune juive* threatened him with a 'hostile Jewish vote', a reaction which was in turn greeted by a shower of insults and accusations inspired by sheer anti-Semitism. Fortunately, there were also some appeals to lucidity from intellectuals on both sides; but the episode was a revealing one.

Compared to the virtually miraculous survival over many centuries of the tiny Jewish people, the assimilation of the first colonies of foreign immigrants to France may seem to have been extremely rapid. Yet the early years were often difficult, sometimes very painful. In 1896, there were only 291,000 Italians in France, but concentrated in the south: 10% in the Var, 12% in Bouches-du-Rhône, 20% in Alpes-Maritimes. And the 'Ritals', as they were called, were publicly accused of taking the bread out of Frenchmen's mouths, and found themselves under attack. There were violent quarrels, racist crimes and even lynchings in Alès.[223] About thirty years later, the Poles, also massively concentrated, this time in northern France, and in addition isolated by their language, living amongst themselves with their own tradesmen, were also the target of public hostility. In neither case did the Catholic religion serve as a bond – on the contrary. Neapolitan dockers who crossed themselves at work in the port of Marseille were mocked – hence their nickname of *cristos*. The forms taken by Polish Catholicism – kissing the priest's hand for instance – seemed ridiculous to the people of the Nord *département*. And the Church itself made things difficult for these newcomers who wanted to have their own compatriots as priests – otherwise, they said, how are we to go to confession?[224] All the prefects of the time declared that 'the Poles will never fit in'. But there were forces working in the other direction, above all the schools, and in some cases the action of trade unions and political parties (the Communist Party in particular for Italians). By the second or at any rate the third generation, integration was complete. Nowadays a surname or certain family traditions are all that is left of the country of origin. And one senses that for the Spanish, Portuguese and Italians of the recent wave of immigrants, apart from those who retire to their homeland with their savings, the same rapid process of assimilation is at work.

Why then, in the case of the Muslims in France, most of whom are from North Africa, does the reverse seem to be the case? It is the second-generation immigrants who are finding the greatest problem, both being rejected and themselves rejecting the assimilation that the generation of their parents and grandparents in some cases achieved. There are serious obstacles: mutual distrust, fear, racial prejudice, but there are also deep differences in beliefs and customs. What we have here is not a mingling of cultures, but a juxtaposition or confrontation – rather as in the United States where, despite the attractions of the American way of life, cultural problems remain. But in France, the situation is much more tense and unstable than in the United States, in more subtle ways: because France is an old country; because the country of origin of our guests is also an old country and a neighbour. It takes only a few hours for a North African worker to take a plane, fly to Maison-Blanche airport in Algiers and set off for Kabylia, where he is back in the world of his childhood, youth, and happiness or nostalgia. In America, the great distance from home – across the Atlantic for many – was a powerful divide. Emigrants only come home from America when they have made their fortunes and not always then. When Hernan Cortes landed on the shores of Mexico, he burnt his boats.

I have no objection to synagogues and Orthodox churches in France – neither therefore to the mosques, of which more and more are being built and attended. But Islam is more than a religion, it is a whole civilization full of vigour, an entire way of life. Cases we read about in the newspapers – the young North African girl kidnapped and confined by her brothers because she wanted to marry a French boy, the hundreds of Frenchwomen married to Algerians who, following divorce, find their children being kidnapped and sent to Algeria by fathers who consider they have sole rights over them – are more than simple news items, they are symbols of the major obstacle confronting immigrants from North Africa: a clash of civilizations. They have come into conflict with a legal system which does not recognize their own code, founded on the higher law of the Koran. Paternal authority and the status of women are no doubt the biggest problems, because they relate to the family, the very foundation of society. Every year there are about 20,000 mixed marriages on average. Two out of three end in divorce.[225] For such marriages tend to require one or other partner, or both, to break with their background. Yet without intermarriage there can be no integration.

Hence the hesitation and agonizing of the younger generation of North Africans who are having such a difficult time during the economic crisis of the West, and facing hostility in our big cities. Often having French nationality by being born in France, they may refuse citizenship out of loyalty to their people, or in a spirit of defiance, and dream of returning to North Africa – but without entirely believing or even truly desiring it.

Such internal conflicts can be mortal, and there have been deaths for which none of us can avoid feeling responsible. One young North African, after being arrested and imprisoned in Clairvaux, committed suicide, leaving this strange message: 'Every day I am dying. It hurts terribly. It is like a cancer eating me up. I leave you full of hate and love. The love I failed to find, the love I never received, the love I wanted to give.' Even if Tahar Ben Jelloun[226] who tells the story has improved on the original of this striking message, what a cry of despair it represents.

Another case described in Le Monde concerned two Vietnamese: 'Isolated in a town in the middle of France, without work, without lodging, far from home and their own country, they were unable to find the courage to live. These people died twice. We [that is, the French who ought to have welcomed them] had no right to let this happen.'[227]

Distressing as these tragic incidents may be, statistically they are overshadowed by the terrible fate of the Harkis (Algerians who served with the French forces during the Algerian war). There are about 400,000 resident in France (and the statistics do not count them as immigrants since they were granted French nationality in return for services rendered to France during the Algerian war). After the Evian peace treaty in 1962, they fled to France to escape the massacre which was the fate of thousands of them. Now they are here, some dispersed as immigrant workers, but they are kept at arm's length, especially by the other Algerian immigrants who see them as 'collaborators and traitors'. Others still live in the reception camps at Bias in Lot-et-Garonne, or Saint-Maurice-l'Ardoise in the Gard, 'to which we should add thirty-six forest villages scattered throughout the wooded regions of the Lozère, the Limousin and the Vosges'.[228] In the shacks where they live crowded together, these people subsist on the modest pensions paid by the army, having large numbers of children in order to eke the pension out with family allowances. It is impossible either for them or for their children to return to Algeria. Promises have been made, but will they be kept? We are responsible for the fate of these people, whatever the reasons for their allegiance to France in which, not always fully aware of what they were doing, they had pinned their hopes. I confess to being more moved by their fate than by any other. But sympathy is not much help in cases like this.

But is the guilt all on the French side? As always, rights and wrongs are shared. Thus North Africans who have lived rather too long in France and picked up French ways, *a fortiori* those who were born in France, may meet with a cold reception when they return, temporarily or for good to their homeland. A twenty-six-year-old Algerian student at the University of Lille writes unhappily:

> I do not know whether to return to Algeria or to stay in France. The choice may look simple, but it is like asking someone to choose between his right foot and his left. In our country of origin, we find ourselves foreigners, and are made to realize it. In the country we have come to, we are foreigners because we do not have French nationality [he had been born in Algeria] and because we have dark skins.[229]

The Beurs (the name taken by second-generation North African immigrants) do indeed feel uncomfortable, not only in France (whether or not they take up the French nationality to which they are entitled) but also in Algeria where they are regarded as part-foreigners. Why should this be? Sometimes it is explained by ostentation – the 'luxuries' they display on holiday back home, the clothes or the cars. Sometimes they themselves express scorn: 'There's nothing to eat there,' one Beur is quoted as saying on returning to France', 'it's like going back to the Middle Ages.'[230] Another said, 'It's so gloomy, there's nothing to do and the family is always watching you.'[231] But the Beurs may also shock people back home by offending, sometimes unconsciously, against local habits and manners. Hassan, who had visited Paris several times, but not settled there, said he found immigrant society 'rotten'. 'We have certain traditions which must be respected,' he explained: 'Over there, in France, you lose your personality . . . Young people born in France have completely lost all sense of tradition . . . honestly, I could not be like them. They are rude to their parents. Even if I were sixty years old, I would respect my father and mother.' In short, 'as an Algerian psychologist comments, [immigrants are suspect as] potential carriers of the danger of modernity and social evolution'.[232]

Returning immigrants retort with complaints of their own. 'Often when I am walking down the street,' a young Algerian woman reports, 'men remark out loud that I must be an immigrant, simply because I do not lower my eyes.'[233] What lengths one has to go to, to be accepted back into the community! Djamel, a young man aged twenty-two whose family are all in France, has returned home alone because, he says, he cannot live anywhere else, feeling he is a Berber 'through and through'. He is now studying medicine at Tizi Ouzou. 'The first weeks were hard: I had to fight to get the other students to accept me. I'm still treated as an émigré, but one day they will stop calling me that . . . In a few years, I'll be a doctor in some rundown clinic, at the state's expense. Things are far from perfect here . . . [But] I believe in it; I dream that things will get better, and I want to play some part in it.'[234]

But how many people can summon up such courage and determination? Amar, born in Saint-Maur, tried to go back twice. He gave up. 'It was a big mistake, that's all. I'm not going to eat my heart out over it. There's a lot of official talk about "re-insertion", but it doesn't mean a thing. They do nothing to welcome you or help you. You can't even get Arabic lessons, and all day long people call you an immigrant or a Parisian.'[235]

But the Algerian government is probably as powerless as the French when faced with these culture clashes. A young civil servant from the Algerian Ministry of Planning gave his views on the question in 1983: he had no sympathy with the 'money-grubbing immigrants' who only return to Algeria after 'making a fortune in currency deals', and who become 'a new bourgeoisie, self-satisfied and quite unbearable'. But he did not agree with 'shotgun returns', with 'forcing girls who were born in France into a surprise marriage', during a summer visit. There are some incomprehensible reactions against returning immigrants, he explained: 'in the university for instance, immigrants are isolated and boycotted. The other students tease them, and the girls are considered quite simply as prostitutes. These young second-generation immigrants don't usually last more than a few weeks. This is serious, because we need new people with different ideas. Condemning racism in France is all very well. But reproducing it here is intolerable.'[236]

Is it surprising then that recent debates have revealed two opposed schools of thought within the Muslim community in France?

The first continues actively and militantly to preach a return to source, to the Koran, 'to Islam as redeemer'. For Driss El Yazami, 'only religion can bring us together, all of us from North Africa, even the children of Harkis', it is the only thing that can preserve a North African 'identity', in the face of the French one.[237] But 'in the face of' can all too easily become 'against'. Does it encourage French people of Muslim origin to refuse to vote, seeing participation in elections as a sort of cultural betrayal, a source of conflict between religious duties in the Islamic sense and the obligations of French law, on matters such as divorce, paternal rights and so on?

Is this the right role for religion which, in a multi-cultural or multi-racial society should surely remain a private matter of faith and individual morality? During the 1980 controversy referred to above, Léo Hamon, in an attempt to reason with both parties, defined what he saw as the duties of all 'Frenchmen of the Jewish faith': they seem to me to be appropriate for any individual wishing to live in the context of a nation which, like France, has no official religion.

> The right to be different [he writes] stops at the point where the reality of a community is obscured. Every man, in modern society, has different allegiances – religious, philosophical, professional, cultural, national . . . But just as there can only be one state in a given territory, there can only be one national allegiance for the individual. The full exercise of each person's rights and the coherence of society are only to be had at this price . . . If I thought differently, if Israel was the state to which I gave my major allegiance, it would be inexcusable of me not to be living there.[238]

In short, one has to make a choice. And this is precisely the view of the other school of thought, as appears in particular from debates over the question of voting. As Belkacem, aged 26, general secretary of the Association of Algerian Workers in France, explains: 'We know that 90% of the North Africans are in France to stay. Our slogan will be: "My future is here, so I'll vote here."'[239] Slimane Tir, an economist aged 29, who has set up a North African centre for Culture, Research and Action in Roubaix, does not hesitate to say that for most immigrants, 'their real country today is France', and the idea of returning home is a 'myth', a 'flight from that reality'. They should therefore enter fully into political life, exercise their votes, gain access to 'a culture in order to achieve a new citizenship'. And in order to do that 'they must make a choice. Too many young people are stuck in a situation of non-choice.'[240]

'Choosing, taking one path rather than another, is what will decide the whole future journey,' writes Jean-Francis Held in the same number of L'Evénement du jeudi. 'The young Beurs are beginning to realize that a ballot paper carries more hope than taking refuge in the Koran or dreaming of returning to Algeria.' And he imagines a time when 'many Beurs will have worked their way up to become professors, surgeons, businessmen, MPs, mayors', and will thus be able to modify their relations 'with the majority population'.[241]

I hope he is right. When that day comes, the North Africans will have won a victory for themselves and therefore for us, and for the community as a whole. I hope so the more since the rise of fundamentalism in the world makes one uneasy about even the most sincere religious crusades. France has certainly not stopped being a Christian country, but on that score it has become a tolerant one and passions have waned. It is a long time now since Frenchmen have experienced Wars of Religion, but several centuries have not yet wiped out the memory of the cruelties of those days. Who could bear to see a new war of religion in France?

BOOK II

———◆———

PRODUCTION

A 'Peasant Economy'
until the Twentieth Century

PART III

The Rural Infrastructures

Parts Three and Four of this book offer an economic perspective on the France of the past, viewed over the long term, *la longue durée*. I shall be going only as far back as the year 1000, or better still 1450, when the evidence becomes plentiful enough for us to tackle the major questions with any hope of grasping them. But even thus reduced, the time-scale is a daunting one. What is more, my aim is to arrive at an in-depth economic history. For this and many other reasons, logic requires that priority be given to rural France, that we take it as our point of departure and evaluate the whole of French economic life in relation to the key role played by agriculture – as the title of this section suggests. But the expression 'peasant economy', which I shall be using a great deal in what follows, is not my own invention. I have borrowed it from Daniel Thorner's seminal and *emancipating* article, first published in the spring of 1964, an article in which he set out to get rid of the empty formulas that have bedevilled standard works on this subject, terms such as 'the Asiatic mode of production', fashionable at the time.[1]

By 'peasant economy', Thorner did not of course simply mean the farming sector which every economy contains and which was, in the past, massively present. His aim was to identify a type of *overall* economy in which agricultural life was dominant compared to the other activities inevitably associated with it, and which would in fact gradually expand and develop at its expense. For

223

Daniel Thorner, the ratio between rural and non-rural activities is the key feature that defines and differentiates societies. The societies of western Europe in the past (like those of many developing countries today) can be said to remain at the stage of the *peasant economy* as long as they meet the following conditions:

– if agriculture, as an integral factor of the economy, accounts for half (or more than half) of total production;

– if half (or more than half) the population is engaged in agricultural work;

– if half (or more than half) of agricultural production originates in peasant households or rather peasant families (as opposed to large estates, whether seigneurial, bourgeois or capitalist). This peasant society may be exploited in various ways, but the point is that it retains a certain independence and remains in direct contact with the market.

That having been said, the economy in question must in addition be sufficiently developed for there to be:

– some form of state actively established, accompanied by the normal state apparatus, in more or less extended form;

– regular interchange between town and countryside.

Such are the criteria of the *peasant economy* as set out by Daniel Thorner, and which I shall be adopting for my present purpose. The reader will note that, without needing to be pushed to their logical conclusions, these criteria denote a system, a *coherent whole*; finding a place for towns and the state within our *model* means that we are also allowing room for some form of regulation, for industry, various types of exchange, credit, and even the first stages of capitalism. It is also clear that the term 'peasant' draws attention, rightly, to the overwhelming importance of agriculture: the countryside is the foundation of everything else, it pervades everything else; the other activities are no more than islands in the middle of the sea – but they are islands which cannot be ignored.

Every country in Europe has passed centuries as a

peasant economy. Sooner or later, they all left this stage behind them. France took longer than some of her neighbours and this backwardness has undoubtedly deeply marked the course of French history. As late as 1947, Louis Chevalier was still writing of France that 'the peasantry in a sense [constitutes] the traditional consciousness of the country, of its possibilities and limitations. Only through the peasantry can France at any moment have a precise sense of what she might dare to do and what she must refuse.'[2] Shield and safeguard, agriculture is here seen as expressing 'a certain conception of France'. But are we to regard this deadweight, this underlying reality, this slowness to change as a *good* thing for France (I doubt it) or a bad thing, as so many historians now think?

Rather than answer this question, we shall be asking how, why, and at what cost France retained a peasant population of excessive size and diminishing usefulness. Should we blame the country's natural advantages, which were able to prolong the primacy of agriculture well beyond its reasonable span, even in hostile circumstances? Or should we rather blame a long history of conservatism, sustained by its own inertia as well as by certain undeniable successes, a history it was difficult to shake off overnight? These questions will run through the next chapter and indeed through the whole of the rest of this volume.

CHAPTER SIX

For How Many Centuries was France a 'Peasant Economy'?

The first question to be defined is that of time limits: over what length of time can one observe the peasant economy *model* actually in operation and derive from it the lessons and perspectives we are looking for? The model is obviously taking shape when one of its elements is clearly visible; it is in working order once all the elements are in position; and it may deteriorate by degrees, as its essential features fall apart one by one.

Towns and countryside – in other words order and constraint – already existed of course in Roman Gaul. Its predecessor, independent Gaul, is perhaps a more doubtful case. But even in the age of the Gallo-Roman towns, the model was not perhaps fully operational, since the villas and their slave labour in the countryside contradict one condition stipulated by Daniel Thorner, namely that at least half of farm production should come from family units with a degree of freedom of action.[3] There were certainly some independent peasants in Roman Gaul, but they probably did not represent the greater share of production. What was more, the towns were falling into decay, and before long began making way for the villa to play a leading role: this went hand in hand with a fragmentation of the territory and a reduced state presence, as a sort of prelude to the seigneurial regime which would come into being several centuries later. The fully fledged peasant economy would appear, if I am not mistaken, only after the decisive turning-point around the year 1000 and the population explosion which affected rural areas of France and Europe alike. I shall shortly attempt to show how far the French economy was by then displaying the requisite features (in more or less developed form of course). But about the first date at which it becomes visible, there can be little doubt and no great surprise.

A peasant economy lasting until our own lifetime

The surprising thing – and the surprise would have been even greater in the recent past, for Marc Bloch's generation – is that this *peasant economy* should have lasted so long in France, right down to the nineteenth century and even beyond. Peasant farmers, whether owner-occupiers, tenants or share-croppers, were working about two-thirds of the land in about 1840, according to a reliable source, the agronomist Lullin de Chateauvieux;[4] by 1881, although somewhat diminished, the income from agriculture was still almost half of gross national income; only in 1931 was the urban population finally poised to overtake the population of the countryside which had been in the majority up to then. So, burdened with its underlying realities, its constraints and demands, the 'everyday story of country folk' may well have formed the *livre de raison* of French history, to which we must refer if we are to understand anything about it. Only in very recent years have we seen the rapid, catastrophic and unexpected dislocation of that peasant France which had been handed down to us through the ages.

Maurice Parodi pronounced its laconic funeral oration in his recent book, *L'Economie et la société française depuis 1945*: 'Agriculture which was still in 1968 "the leading national industry" from the point of view of employment, occupying an active population of 3,125,000, employed no more than 2 million people in 1977.'[5] The transformation had happened in under ten years. And its consequences, which are so obvious today, will have struck us even more forcibly than the process itself, with its upheavals, the depopulation of one region after another, migration from the countryside, and the conspicuous expansion of the towns, which have all grown spectacularly. Marc Bloch could not have imagined such a cataclysm, such an upheaval, when in 1930 he published *Les Caractères originaux de l'histoire rurale française*. Neither could Daniel

Halévy, when in 1934 he visited the rural districts of central France rather as people go on pilgrimages to the Holy Land.[6]

This being so, our problem is how to link the normal and classic considerations one applies to a long-term process to the upheavals and catastrophes of the present: the latter now provide the inescapable conclusion, whether we like it or not, to a story of arrested development, for so long held back and slowed down. We have to adjust our perspective and to some extent consign the nineteenth century (previously thought of as proudly progressive, revolutionary, modernist and modernizing) to that past whose last powerful convulsions it embodies and indeed passed on down to us.

It was thus in contrast to a rural France in which little had changed that there appeared, in the comparatively recent past, the energetic modern sectors of industry, urban services, transport and the many new aspects of French life. In one corner innovation, in the other conservatism. Representatives of the modern France had long mocked and derided the old, condemning its deadweight of inertia. Already by the eighteenth century, the city-dweller of Provence was describing the peasant as 'a cunning and evil beast, a wild animal, only half civilized'.[7] One could fill an anthology with this kind of disparaging remark in the nineteenth century, when it had become a commonplace. This is surely evidence that the basic peasant economy was hanging on grimly, thwarting the desires and countering the efforts of that other France which was so anxious to enter fully into the concert of industrial nations. Jacques Laffitte (1767–1844), the banker and politician, complained that the ingenious France of the nineteenth century was trying to sell its products to consumers who were still living in the poverty-stricken fourteenth century.[8] Writing in 1824, he saw the country as clearly divided in two:

> You may find a few business centres and a few provinces that have participated in the industrial movement of our age, where capital is plentiful and can be had at very modest rates; but all the rest of the territory is given over to ignorance, routine and poverty; it is eaten up by usury and lags far behind the France one might call civilized.[9]

He was describing the survival of a France that was poor, hard-working and innocent – yet a burden on the rest – a France determined, or obliged, to live as frugally as possible, economizing on salt or on the coarse and clumsy matches acquired from smugglers; throwing ash on the fire every night so that it would still be there in the morning; baking bread only once a week, if then; being content with one set of Sunday clothes, for men or women, and that one destined to last a lifetime; producing everything at home if possible (food, clothing, house and household goods), like the peasants of the Corrèze who were still in 1806 'wearing coarse cloth woven from the wool of their own sheep, which they prepare themselves';[10] sleeping alongside the farm animals that gave warmth in winter; doing without any of the hygienic products considered necessary today and now widely available;[11] saving on candles by 'following the sun step by step', or even waking before it. 'Most of the population [rises] at first light, and everywhere the first mass of the day [is said] in winter in the thin glimmer of dawn'.[12]

Indeed, as long as there remained in place that harsh, hard-working, unchanging peasant world which people of my generation can still remember – a world we loved, with its colours, its customs, its intimate acquaintance with the land, its modest needs, its deep common sense – the history of France and the life of the French people had quite different foundations, a different resonance; a different relationship with nature.

Paul Dufournet, a man of my own generation who has an unrivalled knowledge of Savoie past and present, even thinks that 'neolithic civilization lasted almost until our own day, with the ox and the carthorse'. That is perhaps putting it rather strongly. But, as he goes on,

> on fields near my country house, where I still turn up mesolithic and neolithic arrowheads, I remember seeing a great-uncle of mine, a peasant, 'scratching'[13] the land with his hoe. I link him in my thoughts to the very first men who farmed this part of the country, perhaps five or six thousand years ago. I have spoken with the last representatives of this vanished world. In my own lifetime, I have witnessed the rapid disappearance of first-hand evidence, as we have lost

touch with oral tradition. Many ancient tracks, which go back to protohistoric times or even earlier, are disappearing under hedges, fences and crops, because they cannot be used by motor traffic. They were still usable, at least on foot, in about 1960.[14]

Tracks and paths like this, which were still visible twenty years ago but are vanishing today, are all too many. The easiest to find are the drove roads on the hills, once travelled by transhumant herds of cows or sheep. Now that thousands of sheep no longer move along them each year, shrubs and scrub have grown up and taken possession, on the slopes of the Aigoual massif and Mont Lozère for instance, where the first transhumant flocks marked out the great *drailles* perhaps four millennia ago, in about 2000 BC. The few flocks that the shepherds still take up to the high pastures have to push their way through thickets of gorse and broom – a strange spectacle![15]

When the peasant economy becomes plain to see: the eleventh century

The last traces of the peasant economy, which has been disintegrating for several decades, are now disappearing, before our eyes. But what about the other end of the story, its beginning?

It must have been at the time when the village-bourg-town network I have already described at length became clearly established.[16] Let us call it the eleventh century, or possibly the twelfth, depending on the region. I am prepared to agree with some historians that in the Middle Ages 'the village is more important than the town'[17] or to put it another way, that rural activity created the urban order and the exchanges necessary to that order.[18] But the opposite is also partly true: the growth of exchange, including long-distance trade which it would be unwise to ignore,[19] favoured the town and the town in turn fostered rural activities. Towns and villages grew in parallel, in a reciprocal relationship. The increase in land clearance was not only a response to the need for food for the ever more numerous villagers; farm *surpluses*, very largely controlled by the local seigneur, the Church, or religious communities, went to feed the towns, now gradually expanding on account of increased birth-rates, long-distance trade and the spread of craft production more sophisticated and specialized than anything in the villages.

What is certain is that the first signs of progress, pointing to the future, come with development of the *topmost* sector of ancient economic life. If we are looking for a point of *take-off* (as distinct from the very first signs) we have to consider the upper storeys of the structure then taking shape. Once they appear, the long process and reality of our so-called peasant economy can be said to be truly engaged.

Perhaps western Provence in the tenth century is too good an example to be true? The Mediterranean stimulated its early development. Cities appeared in the landscape – Avignon, Aix, Arles, Tarascon. They built suburbs, extended tentacles into the country round about, took over peasant industries if they looked promising, and increased their own craft production. The precious salt of the Mediterranean was very soon being ferried up the Rhône and Durance by boats which put in at obligatory ports of call: Saint-Gilles, Tarascon, Avignon, Pont-Saint-Esprit. Rafts of tree-trunks, 'felled in the mountains of the Gapençais and the Diois'[20] were also floated down; and grain would later be an important addition to this river traffic.

From this point on, the old markets became inadequate, and fairs began to be held in the twelfth century: one at Pont-Saint-Esprit, two at Gap (the first during the week of the Nativity of Our Lady, the other on the feast of St Arnoul), and others at Saint-Paul-des-Châteaux, Fréjus, Marseille, Avignon and Beaucaire. Caravans of donkeys carried into the dye-works of the towns loads of vermilion[21] from the villages, along with chalk for bleaching and bracken to act as mordant. Such regional exchanges were swelled by produce from far away – spices, paper and silk from the markets of the Middle East.

Thus links were forged between local trade and long-haul traffic:

When the Lombards came to the fairs of Saint-Gilles or Fréjus, it was not simply to bring spices and silk and take away furs; what they loaded into their great ships was salt which had passed through the *tonlieu* at Genoa, timber which had floated down the Rhône to Saint-Gilles, wheat . . . and bales of cloth which had passed through all the *tonlieux*.[22] In 1190, one could buy at Fréjus fair cloth from Saint-Riquier, Chartres, Etampes, Beauvais, Amiens and Arras, alongside other *panni de colore* and silk.[23]

Stimulated by the general prosperity, large-scale trading activity now began to emerge, extending its ramifications into the villages, infecting them with an insidious commercialization, which would in the long run destroy the freedom of the rural craftsmen of old.

Money played a part in this, being sent into circulation in the ninth century from the Carolingian workshops in Marseille and Arles, later from the regular minting at Pavia, and in the eleventh century from the mint at Melgueil (present-day Mauguio, near Montpellier). By the end of the century, it was starting to be used by peasants to settle their bills. It circulated even more freely in the twelfth century, as a sustained commercial boom created links between towns, countryside and large-scale trade.[24]

The precocious development of Provence was however far from being the rule. In a movement which affected all of what is now France, some regions forged ahead, but more lagged behind.

The Mâconnais for instance does not seem to have been affected very early by the increased activity that the Rhône-Saône corridor might have brought it. Was it still, at the end of the tenth century, 'a purely land-based economy'?[25] The formula is perhaps misleading. Could any *economy* be entirely confined to cultivating the land? In any case, there were plenty of thriving markets. Even before the year 1000, 'at the council of Anse of 994, the clergy thought of forbidding the faithful to buy or sell anything on Sundays "except what was to be eaten that day"; for it was normal to buy food daily', even on the Lord's day.[26] And these local transactions, as well as dues and fines, were often settled in cash. Along the Saône valley, 'intense river traffic' encouraged both long- and short-distance trade. Cluny, the new settlement which had sprung up alongside the monastery, became a centre for buying and selling, because of the crowds of pilgrims. Money was minted there, as it was at Tournus and Mâcon, very ancient towns now somewhat declined from their Roman splendour, but each with an annual fair at the end of the tenth century.[27] In 950, Létaud II, count of the Mâconnais, whose possessions were scattered over a wide area, 'derived much income . . . from exploiting the salt-mines in the Revermont' of the Jura.[28] The Mâconnais indeed imported salt, iron and even some luxury goods, such as precious silks and spices – through the good offices of its Jewish colony.[29]

It was not until the third or fourth quarter of the eleventh century however that the volume of trading activity along the Rhône-Saône corridor increased enough to make a real impression on the surrounding economy. It was now that fairs started to appear in larger numbers, at Tournus, Cluny, Mâcon. New suburbs and districts were built for a population now expanding rapidly and depending for its food supplies both on the local countryside, and on goods from farther afield. The amount of traffic on the roads increased enough to amaze contemporaries – and monasteries and noble landowners lost no time in setting up tolls.[30] The mass of money in circulation increased,[31] and alongside the artisans a new merchant class arose, living off trade and usury and no longer primarily interested in wealth from land.[32] By the very end of the twelfth century, the first merchant dynasties were appearing at Mâcon.[33]

Evidence of this is only too easy to come by: one can find it in Chartres, where money was already circulating by the Carolingian period, and flowed more briskly as time went on, thanks to the city's pilgrims and students as much as to its merchants;[34] in Paris, an extreme case, where by the reign of Philip Augustus (1180–1223) grain was arriving by river, since the usual overland supply routes could not keep pace with the capital's population;[35] in Toulouse, where in the eleventh century the weavers' guilds paraded through the town behind a giant shuttle;[36] or at the Méron tollbooth, near Montreuil-Bellay in the Saumur region, from which there survives by chance a list of goods in transit between

1080 and 1082: horses, cattle, wool, grease, feathers, wax, and 'foreign or costly merchandise [*merces peregrine vel magni precii*] carried by pedlars or on the backs of donkeys'.[37] In any of these places, one would unfailingly have found craftsmen, merchants, usable roads and stone bridges across the rivers.

So let us rather look deep inland, at the very centre of France, in the Berry, where the land had been cleared for agriculture, at least in the key region of the *Champagne berrichonne*, by pre-Roman times.[38] Guy Devailly is quite right to say that in the eleventh century 'there were several towns there . . . notably Bourges'. But, he goes on,

> they were few in number, small in size and were moreover still closely tied to rural life. The shopkeepers and artisans were [in this period] men who for the most part worked the land as well as plying their trade: they were either transforming the products of the [countryside] or manufacturing what was needed to farm it. It is still too early in the eleventh century, especially in these regions of central France, *to talk of a contrast between town and country*.[39]

I emphasize the last words, not because I disagree with the writer, far from it. The problem is not so much to bring out the contrast between town and country (which everyone is only too ready to do) as to give sufficient prominence to the forces obliging them to live in harmony. However rudimentary it may have been, the connection was certainly established in a region like the Berry, still in this period in a near-primitive situation.[40]

As for thinking that a town was not really a town if it was deeply embedded in country life, that is simply untenable. We are all well aware that until the end of the *ancien régime* and beyond, many French towns were still up to their knees in the agricultural world that surrounded them and penetrated them from all sides. In 1502, many Parisian houses sheltered 'pigeons, goslings, rabbits and pigs'.[41] In 1643, an observant visitor to Lyon noted: 'This city is very large, of considerable area, because it contains within its boundaries all its shooting ranges, graveyards, vineyards, fields, meadows and other pieces of land.'[42] At the time, this was commonplace, as dozens of examples prove.[43] To return to Paris for a moment, during the 'flour wars' a poor carter who was arrested in May 1775 turned out to be transporting manure from the Parisian stables to gardens in the city and its suburbs.[44] And as late as the end of the nineteenth century 'the perimeter of the [town] boundary [of Limoges] included meadows and market gardens, not to mention private allotments and pigstyes'.[45] But whether or not it still harboured rural activities, what really mattered was that the town should play the role of a town. That is precisely what was being created and consolidated from the eleventh and twelfth centuries onwards: the role of the town and the bourg as compared to the village.

The new system had roots reaching back into the 'dark ages' before the year 1000 of course: we can guess at some elements of continuity running through the history of both France and Europe in the years following the barbarian invasions. The problem of origins, which can never be firmly resolved, is all the more fascinating, as Anne Lombard-Jourdan's articles have brilliantly demonstrated. The centuries about which we know so little were fitfully enlivened by towns fallen from former glory, by fairs dating back to pre-Roman days and ancient Gaul. At such fairs, exotic produce was being sold: 'fine wines, spices, furs warmer than wool and consequently status symbols, and above all costly fabrics which priests bought for their altars and women for their adornment'. This 'tempting' trade was 'no longer in the hands of the Syrians who had disappeared at the end of the Merovingian period', but was being handled by the fairs, those brief but effective gatherings which revitalized the market economy and shook some life back into towns that had slumped into drowsiness.[46] The eleventh century 'Renaissance' did not spring from nowhere.

CHAPTER SEVEN

Overall Characteristics

A study of the *peasant economy* must begin with the peasantry itself – although it is no simple matter to consider and understand it properly: for as Jacques Mulliez has pointed out,[47] there is no *single* pattern of French agriculture any more than there is a single French peasantry. There are many 'peasantries', different from each other, incompatible even – as all writers on the subject have acknowledged.[48]

All the same, peasants and farming life together form a category apart, a coherent and distinct mass in the body of French history. So instead of describing the peasantry from the point of view of differences – and goodness knows there are plenty of those, as between the cereal-farmer, the vine-grower and the stock-breeder, not to mention regional ways of life! – I should like to view it first as a totality, as opposed to the rest of society: to measure the weight, the numbers, the volume of this peasant *mass* and the variable area it has occupied – to measure it in other words against what it is not. After this we shall, like all historians, be able to come back and discuss the details and differences and the explanations they call for.

The power of the natural world

The major, ever-present feature of peasant life has been its endless battle against the uncontrollable forces of nature. It is against these that peasant society has pitted its efforts, destructive or creative, down the ages. Taking this view, and following in a well-established tradition, we might easily be led to see an antithesis between history and nature:[49] with history represented by man, struggling against blind natural forces. But is this really true?

237

Man is himself in fact part of the natural world: he lives on earth, under its climate and amid its vegetation – some of it untamed, some a little more obedient, provided he is prepared to accept its demands. He lives among animals, domesticated or wild, and he depends for his life on the water of springs and streams, whether the running water that tumbles downhill to flood the plains and erode the mountains, or the water that accumulates in pools to power the village water-mill. Man is also dependent, at every moment of his life, on the sun's energy. 'In the end', as François Jacob writes, 'it is the sun that provides energy for most living things',[50] including man.

So 'man *lives* on nature, [which] means that nature is his *body*, with which he must remain in continuous intercourse if he is not to die'.[51] This striking passage by Marx opens up a historical perspective. Has not man created society as an indispensable instrument with which to dominate nature?[52]

And yet man has long nourished the illusion that he has mastered nature. Listen to François Malouet (1740–1814) whom we remember for his role in the Constituent Assembly, going into raptures over the achievements of western man: 'The works of nature, her spontaneous production and primitive creations have almost vanished under the strenuous efforts of the inhabitants of the old continent,'[53] he claims – and this was before either steam or electricity! A premature judgment to say the least. And today, in the machine age, Paul Dufournet seems to be a victim of the same illusion, that 'the natural element is disappearing and everything is becoming man-made'.[54]

It is true, particularly in a country like France, that there is today no such thing as a 'natural' agricultural landscape. The landscape before us, entirely reconstructed, is the product of an evolution stretching over many centuries: it conceals nature itself, like a garment thrown over it. But does that mean man can claim to have mastered his enemy? One has only to think of the scorching drought of 1976 in Europe; of the famines that regularly devastate the Saharan Sahel; of the unprecedented wave of cold that hit the United States at Christmas 1983, compared to which even the famous harsh winter of 1709 may have been only a minor incident.

Think of the hurricanes in the West Indies and Florida, which unleash a hundred or a thousand times more energy than the bomb that fell on Hiroshima. And these are just a few examples, chosen to make our contemporaries think again. As for society in the past, I do not think we can disagree with Jean Georgelin when he describes it as subject 'to the dictatorship of the physical environment'.[55]

This dictatorship can of course be tamed, evaded, turned to advantage. It does not govern the entire rural economy, but it does enclose it, imposing its own rhythms and timetables. And that is not counting the natural calamities, shocks and disasters it episodically deals out to humans. We should beware though of concentrating too much on the dramatic catalogue of catastrophe, engraved in folk memory, the exceptional events that figure in all the chronicles, like the cold spells that kill fruit trees and even forest oaks; the frosts that destroy wheat when it has sprouted too soon and has no protective layer of snow over it (the proverb says: 'Snow in February is as good as manure');[56] the forest fires, droughts and floods, the animal epidemics, the hailstorms that can flatten a cornfield or a vineyard in a few hours. In the Fertois region of the Vivarais, 'they used to ring the church bells to ward off storms'.[57]

Reading the documents, we are plunged into a fantastic inventory of disasters: never-ending rain; snowfalls when the wheat is in the ear;[58] cereal fields so choked by weeds that the whole crop is fit only to be cut down and fed to animals; drought lasting week after week, while the peasants try to conjure it with processions; or a grape-harvest that for the fourth year running yields scarcely enough to keep the priest in communion wine; hailstorms that break all the windows in town and slash the surrounding vineyards to shreds;[59] or floods of disastrous proportions. On 16 January 1649, 'the Seine has risen so high above its banks that we have to go along several streets by boat' (and it happened again in 1910).[60] On 21 January 1651, the Mayenne swamped Angers, 'all the lower end of town and the bridges district being flooded up to the second floor of the houses'.[61] The Loire was capable of flooding the entire valley between Roanne and Orléans, and did so at the end of June 1693, just before 'the most promising hay crop ever seen'. If the fields were mown as soon as the flood waters subsided, there might be 'some hope of regrowth by September. The trouble . . . is that almost everywhere in these provinces, once the hayfields have been cut, anyone has the right to pasture his herds on them.' No magistrate dared to rescind this privilege – so the animals would have no fodder in winter.[62] Misfortunes never came one at a time.

If we did not put these dramatic events back in proper chronological order, so as to see the years of good harvest and the comparatively uneventful times in between – which did exist – they would pile up to make a perpetual wall of lamentations. But bewailing disaster and exaggerating one's woe is after all a well-established human activity.

TABLE OF LOSSES CAUSED IN EVERY
DEPARTEMENT OF FRANCE 1807–10 AND 1814–19

Floods, hailstorms, fires and other public disasters officially recorded in order to obtain state assistance (Source: Archives Nationales F 12 560).

Year	Flood	Hail *[in francs]*	Fire	Animal epidemics and other disasters	Total
1807	869 000	2 467 664	2 533 171	450 000	6 319 835
1808	2 373 242	12 394 109	3 621 993	3 293 769	21 683 113
1809	3 807 485	12 115 710	3 073 111	17 100	19 013 406
1810	4 781 898	16 828 316	6 485 995	16 000	28 112 209
1814	796 003	3 390 109	7 097 571	4 999 845	16 283 528
1815	3 647 230	6 573 917	5 041 171	96 436	15 358 754
1816	3 868 864	9 296 203	4 133 138	51 105	17 349 310
1817	3 094 709	18 912 478	4 302 755	190 512	26 500 454
1818	109 991	4 596 305	4 315 899	360 873	9 383 028
1819	525 610	37 659 925	5 181 840	4 835 481	48 202 856
Overall total	23 874 032	124 234 736	45 786 644	14 311 121	208 206 493

The historian will be more impressed by the overall significance of these calamities, which one should try to estimate, than by anecdote. The opportunity to do so is provided by a curious statistical source from the early nineteenth century.[63] It covers the years 1807–10 and 1814–19, a total of ten years altogether, and is a record of the losses incurred throughout all the French *départements* from hail, fire, flood and other visitations, including animal disease. The total loss in round figures for these ten years is 208 million francs.

The record is interesting because it lists in descending order the incidence of these various kinds of 'disaster': well in the lead, 124 million francs, over half the total, comes hail; fires account for 46 million, floods for 23 million; and animal fevers and 'other disasters' for 14 million. This classification has almost the value of a constant. It is certainly useful to remind ourselves what outstanding devastation was wrought by hail and fire. At a time when town houses were built of wood with thatched roofs, when in Picardy, as a traveller noted in 1728, even the churches were thatched with straw,[64] it is easy to understand why fire was so destructive. In 1524 for instance, practically the whole of Troyes was destroyed by fire.[65] In the valley of the Loue in the Jura, 99 houses were burned down in the village of Mouthier in 1719; 80 went in two hours in the nearby village of Vuillafans in 1733; a hundred were destroyed at the neighbouring small town of Ornans in 1636 and the same number again in Ornans, in 1764.[66] If the two leading categories – hail and fire – soon attracted the self-interested zeal of the insurers (hail from at least 1789,[67] fire as early as 1753), it was because they both concerned a potentially large clientele – and also because both categories lent themselves to calculations of probability based on the law of averages.

But perhaps the important thing about this evidence is not so much the detail as the total of 208 million francs over ten years, that is about 20 million a year, as against a gross national income (though I shall have more to say about this figure) of the order of 8,000 million francs, of which agricultural income represented about 5,000 million.[68] As against these massive totals, losses calculated as a percentage amount to astonishingly little: between 0.25%

and 0.4%. True, this record leaves out the years 1811, 1812 and 1813, which were just as bad as 1814 and 1815. 'The vagaries of the climate no doubt played a major part in the shortages which afflicted the last years of the Empire.'[69] But then our document allows nothing at all for the 'ordinary' vagaries of the climate, the unreliability of the seasons, or cyclical shifts in the climate: the reign of Louis XIV for instance is thought to have been marked by a 'little ice age'. Poor harvests ought also to be counted, for the loss of income they represented compared to a normal year: so we should not be too ready to assume a satisfactory picture overall.

The rhythm of the seasons

The greatest natural rhythm is the succession of the seasons, coming round like clockwork as the Earth circles the Sun. Every year the pattern is apparently the same, regularly dictating the farming calendar. Depending on the combination of rain, sun, heat and cold, the year will be good, bad or indifferent for the fruits of the harvest.

In order to arrive at a better understanding of the past, we should perhaps look more closely at the way the seasons shaped the whole of life – and in particular how different things were from today in this respect. The seasons today are much the same as in the past of course, but we do not experience them the same way. We have succeeded in escaping their tyranny. In the winter of 1968, while the wind howled outside carrying showers of stinging snow, I sat in my shirt-sleeves in the university library in Chicago, like all the other readers. And if frost blights our market gardens, if rain flattens the crops, or the potatoes rot in the ground, we know that, whatever the economic consequences, we are unlikely to starve.

So let us try to imagine life as it was in the past, putting ourselves in the place of people who, even if they were town-dwellers were 'often part-time farmers'[70] themselves, and constantly pre-occupied by the temperature, the state of the vegetation, the sprouting or the ripening of the ears of corn. In 1675, a 'bourgeois of Metz' noted in his diary: 'I must not omit to mention the great rains and extraordinary cold which began just after Whitsun and lasted almost a month. This worried everyone, because the wheat would not sprout nor the vine flower.'[71] Is it so surprising that Philip II's ambassadors in their letters home, or the royal *intendants* in France in their reports unfailingly speak of rain and shine, in other words of the chances for the coming harvest?

The turning of the year did not only bring heat and cold, it also dictated the times when peasant life was busy or when on the contrary there was nothing to do.

The coming of spring, whether early or late, meant starting to labour in the fields once more: ploughing, turning the soil, sowing, digging ditches. But this was not yet the busiest time of year, so it was still possible to hire peasants for other tasks at quite low prices, as hauliers for instance, with their draught teams, or as labourers for public works.

So it is not difficult to understand the concern of the engineer Pierre de Riquet (1604–80) who was overseeing the final stages of the canal des Deux Mers (1666–81). The work was almost complete when, on 16 April 1679, he suddenly became anxious:

M. Riquet is so worried [wrote d'Aguesseau, the *intendant* of Provence] about the funds he hopes you will allow him for these works, because of the number of workmen he has on the payroll, and I have not been able to prevent him sending you an express courier to ask for instructions. The reason is that *this is the best time of year* to get this work done and unless a considerable effort is made between now and Midsummer Day, he will have difficulty getting it done at another time.[72]

The reader will also understand the anxiety of the merchant who was waiting on tenterhooks in Geneva for salt from the Peccais marshes to come up the Rhône to supply the distant canton of the Valais: 'If the weather does not relent [i.e. if there is no thaw],' he wrote on 3 January 1651, 'we shall not get all the [expected] salt sent before Easter.'[73] Human endeavours had to be adapted to nature's timetable, which could mean a long wait, often in great anxiety.

Summer and early autumn were the busiest times of year:

haymaking, harvest, grape-picking, early threshing in September – the month, an observer remarked in 1792 'when people sometimes eat the new year's grain'.[74] In Savoie there was a saying 'nine months winter, three months hell'[75] (*neuf mois d'hiver, trois mois d'enfer*). Summer did indeed set an infernal pace with the urgent tasks that had to be done as fast as possible. It is true that in a mountain region like Savoie, the frosts came early and stayed late.

All the same, the hard toil of harvest and grape-picking could also be a time of festivity: the countryside resounded with merrymaking and near-continuous feasting. And no one was out of work: townspeople abandoned their trades to help get the harvest in – a practice current throughout Europe. And this rallying round of all hands was still to be seen in France in the mid-nineteenth century.

In Maine, before the Revolution, 'in August and September every year, the clog-makers, like other workers, left off their trade to devote themselves to working in the fields, which no doubt brought them more money'.[76] In the Provençal Alps, the entire population was on the move:

> Harvest time brings practically every arm into action. Diseases contracted from cold weather or changes in the atmosphere, or from want, are thrown off when spring comes; as the summer solstice approaches, all illnesses melt away; there are no more aches and pains, inflammations, colds or fevers; chronic and debilitating maladies are replaced by rude health in bourg and village alike . . . The harvesters . . . travel to each part of the province in turn and cut the grain as it reaches ripeness . . . There are hordes of them afoot . . . The first start with the plains of Napoule then come to Fréjus, Le Puget, Saint-Maxime and Grimaud, where the harvest is always early in the fields near the sea.[77]

This ritual migration was of course a familiar story, as the *gavots*,[78] both boys and girls, flocked down from the Alps to the low-lying districts of Provence, the land of grain, vineyards and wine.

Then everything would fall quiet again. As early as 15 August,

244

according to the old saying, the peasant 'hangs his lamp on the nail'. And after grape-picking and the autumn ploughing, he would take precautions for the oncoming winter. During this dead season, as late as 1804, 'a day's labour is paid at low rates [and] farmhands work assiduously and do not talk of leaving their masters'. Where would they find work? So before that time came, those who were anxious to change masters hurried to make plans. 'As soon as work begins on the vines, with the extra labour taken on, some . . . farm workers leave their masters to go and work as day-labourers or find a better situation elsewhere'.[79]

It is hard for us to imagine the rigour of past winters, accustomed as we are to centrally heated houses, roads that are maintained and swept clear of snow, ease of transport, and rivers that are controlled and channelled, so that flooding is a rare occurrence. In winter in the old days, everything automatically got worse. Cold was a persistent visitor, dangerous and devastating. With banal regularity, the same signs recur: the ink would freeze in the inkwell as you began to write a letter[80] – indeed the wine froze at the table of Louis XIV and Madame de Maintenon; wild creatures were found frozen to death in fields or woods – and there were many other tribulations. In 1709 in Marseille, the water in the Vieux Port froze over, hard as it may be to believe[81] (and this was not the first time, since the same thing had occurred in 1506).[82] The winter of 1544 had been so severe in Maine that 'the wine had to be cut in the cask with sharp instruments'.[83] In Caen, in February 1660, 'I and others', reports Simon Le Marchand in his *Journal*, 'had to warm the bread before we could cut and eat it; and the drink froze in the casks. When we wanted to draw it, we had to light a flame under the tap to melt it.'[84]

All that is not so very long ago either. Even in the midnineteenth century, France was still suffering from the accumulated hardships of winter. In Saint-Antonin, a little country town in Tarn-et-Garonne, a document dated 11 December 1845 (a good half-century after the Revolution), tells us that 'as a result of the lack of work that winter brings, there will be very great hardship in the *commune* of Saint-Antonin' – as there would in thousands of other *communes* too.[85] From Marseille, on 18 November 1853 (the

Second Empire would be a year old on 2 December), the prefect dispatched a more reassuring report: 'In conclusion, the winter seems to be passing without too much suffering for the agricultural classes.'[86] But in the same year, 1853, and only a day later, on 19 November, the prefect of the Aube was writing:

> the general situation in the *arrondissement* of Troyes and the *département* of Aube has remained the same since my last report. But we cannot conceal apprehension about the coming winter, as a consequence of the high price of bread. However throughout the *département* and particularly in Troyes where the population is concentrated, the municipal authorities have been devising ways to remedy the situation and from Monday 7 [November] tokens for [part of the price of] bread have been distributed to the neediest families. Collections have been taken up and subscription lists launched, and if necessary emergency workshops will be opened to employ the workmen whom the manufacturers are too often obliged to dismiss when winter comes.[87]

'Emergency' workshops meant what were known under the *ancien régime* as charity workshops.

One last example, this time at Rocroi in the Ardennes, dated 27 February 1854:

> The northern *départements* are this year feeling more than any others the disastrous effects of a harsh and prolonged winter. The needy classes who live from day to day have not been able to work at their usual trades, and this has greatly aggravated their situation. However charitable measures adopted by the government have made it possible to relieve much suffering and have prompted feelings of deep gratitude to the Emperor and Empress. Public charity has not slackened for an instant; everywhere resources have been made available to the assistance bureaux, everywhere it has been possible to bring relief to the families who have not the wherewithal to live.[88]

These examples, it is true, all concern distress among the urban poor, and the problem was always unemployment and high prices, rather than famine as so often in the past. The countryside was more silent, perhaps more resigned, but it is also possible that it was not so badly affected.

I am inclined to think that the *peasant economy* remained *in situ* in France and elsewhere as long as winter continued to be a season dreaded in a way we now cannot imagine, a season when most people would have agreed with the first words of the *Soliloques du pauvre*,[89] verses in Parisian *argot* by Jehan Rictus (1897):

Merd'! V'là l'hiver et ses dur'tés
V'là l'moment de n'pus s'mettre à poils
V'là qu'ceuss'qui tienn'nt la queue d'la
* poêle*
Dans l'midi vont s'carapater . . .

[stage Cockney version:]
Gorblimey, it's brass monkey wevver
Don't go in the altogevver.
If you've got money to match your mouf,
Push off to the sunny souf . . .

Spade, hoe, pickaxe – or plough

What were man's weapons and methods in the fight against nature? In the first place, he called on the help of domestic animals, in particular the *bestiaux aratoires*,[90] beasts that pulled the plough: horses, oxen, cattle (harnessed by the horns, as was still the case in many poor regions until the twentieth century), donkeys and mules (the latter a sort of 'all-terrain vehicle' as one historian puts it).[91] *Animals* made all the difference between the Chinese mode of farming and that of western Europe, as has been remarked many times before, but it is no less important for being a truism.

In Europe, men had subjugated draught animals as a source of energy by prehistoric times: they go back a very long way. But for centuries peasants did not own enough of them to farm the great expanses of potentially cultivable land. On the eve of the Revolution, Lavoisier reckoned that there were some three million oxen (plus four million cows) and 1,780,000 horses (1,560,000 of them used for farming).[92] And yet at this period, horses, oxen and mules were still *comparatively* few in number: 'animal power' only reached its highest levels later, in the early twentieth century.

What was more, animals could not do everything: some work could still only be performed by using human energy. This gap is in its own way a revealing feature of the peasant economy, though it is not one generally recognized.

The kind of labour I am talking about is not that done by man with his bare hands (as is sometimes assumed) but by man armed with farm implements – spade, hoe, pickaxe, scythe, rake, pitchfork, pruning knife, not to mention all the particular implements with different names in every region: the tools needed to prune the vine, to dig the ground around the vine stocks, or surrounding the olive, walnut, mulberry and chestnut trees; the axes and saws of all kinds to fell timber; and at threshing time, the flail with its 'bell-like' sound, still used in the Charente among other places until the twentieth century.

'Animal power' brought men relief, liberation, new possibilities and ambitions. It would have been impossible for large-scale cereal-growing to develop as it did, had it not been for animal traction. But the assistance of animals remained only partial, among other reasons because it interfered with the balance between food and production: sometimes it was a choice between people and animals, between wheat and pasture. Often what man needed for food animals needed too – some foodstuffs were interchangeable.[93]

This may seem obvious. In sixteenth-century England, Sir Thomas More (1478–1535) noted in his *Utopia* that the 'meke and tame' domestic sheep, since pastures were being extended at the expense of wheatfields, 'eate up and swallow downe the very men them selves', depriving them of food and even work: after all, 'one Shephearde or Heardman is ynoughe to eate up that ground with cattel, to the occupiying wherof about husbandrye manye hands were requisite'.[94] In France, Cantillon (1680–1734) tackled the same question: 'The more horses a state maintains, the less subsistence there will be for the inhabitants'; 'it is either horses or men'.[95] Messance echoes these thoughts in 1788: 'The multiplication of forage crops and the great number of horses is diminishing the foods fit for men to eat.'[96] In the pays d'Auge from about 1660, and in the whole of Basse-Normandie much later, by about 1780–1820, as more fields were set to grass, the cow too became an innocent enemy of man.

So on one hand there was the labour accomplished with the aid of animals, on the other the labour that man was obliged, or chose to do himself. But what could be the extent of what used to be called *la cultivation à bras*, cultivation by hand?

In the first place, it meant gardens and hemp-patches, very similar to gardens, where sometimes flax and sometimes hemp was grown. In these confined spaces, where once dense hemp stalks might have grown six feet tall, one might just about imagine a modern rotovator being used, but in the old days a horse would hardly have had room to turn round. Here the ground had to be worked over by spade, something usually left to the women. Indispensable to peasant life and close beside the house, these patches received *extra* amounts of manure, or less frequently, human excrement. Night soil was not usually collected in the French countryside except in parts of the north[97] which tolerated the practice, or in the immediate vicinity of towns. Kitchen gardens, which formed a circle round every town, were used to receiving the tosspot or the rubbish of all sorts which servants in Laval used to pile up outside the doors of the houses on Tuesday, Thursday and Saturday evenings, so that the 'muck-farmer' could collect it.[98] The same was true of Lyons, 'where the streets are cleaned as much as possible and the night soil carried out on muleback to the farms'.[99] Around Paris, rubbish, dirt and excrement from the city was used to manure the market gardens. As late as 13 *nivôse* Year II, a certain Bridet 'had the exclusive privilege granted by the *intendant* of the *généralité* [of Paris] of reducing to powder the [faecal] matter' collected at Montfaucon and selling it.[100] But this 'vegetative powder' was not as good as the real thing, the plaintiffs argued. So they requested that the privilege be annulled. And yet for some time the cultivators of Belleville, Pré-Saint-Gervais, Pantin, Saint-Ouen and La Villette – all villages at the gates of Paris – had been forbidden to use such matter 'to manure their land until it had been left to decompose sufficiently'.[101]

More manure was certainly spread on these favoured gardens than on ordinary fields, even where wheat was to be grown. So there was often a connection between cultivation by hand and well-fertilized land. The Ile de Ré is a striking example: entirely devoted to kitchen gardens, it had no horses or mules, not even a pig! 'The hoe and the strong arms of the inhabitants are the only form of cultivation . . . One used to meet old men there who, having been bent double all their lives wielding pickaxes, were as twisted as vine-stocks, their heads down somewhere near their stomachs.'[102] According to the painter Eugène Fromentin, owners of small farms would harvest their barley 'with their bare hands', so there was 'no such thing as *buailles* [thatch]'.[103] Was it because the land was divided into tiny plots that this method of farming had developed? Or was it because it gave such high yields, thanks to the island's incomparable supply of seaweed, *start*, which was collected every night at high tide, even in stormy weather, when these strange fishermen would wade up to their waists in water. Here, the cruel sea was a blessing.

But the connection between manure and cultivation by hand does not explain why the latter should have extended to the open fields, where manure was in short supply. Only necessity can have explained it, although some agronomists dreamed of applying it systematically. In 1806, one of them, P. G. Poinsot, wrote enthusiastically on the subject:

It would be a good thing if all land could be worked with the spade. This would certainly be better than the plough, and this implement is preferred in several parts of France where the practice of using it cuts the work short, since a single man can turn over 487 metres (250 *toises*) of land to a depth of 65 decimetres [*sic*: he means centimetres of course], that is two feet, in a fortnight, and this single digging is enough, whereas the plough has to be put across the land four times before sowing is possible, if the soil is heavy; in any case, the earth is never so well turned over and shaken apart as with the spade. If people object that this would be more expensive than ploughing, I would reply that one has only to calculate the

cost of the animals and their feed, their harness and ploughing machinery, their possible sickness or death; one would
quickly discover that it is a false economy to plough when
one does not have a huge expanse to cover . . . One striking
advantage of the spade is that the soil need never be left to
rest and not the least bit of land is wasted; secondly . . . the
yields from land cultivated this way are treble those of the
rest. The spade used . . . should be at least twice as long and
strong as the ordinary garden spade; the latter could not stand
up to the efforts one is obliged to make to lift solid earth and
break it up enough. The handle should have a crossbar on
top, so that the workman can lean on it with both hands,
while putting his foot on one side of the blade to push it into
the earth. When the soil is too stony . . . a fork is used
instead, its three points easily penetrate between the stones.
It is with this that the stony regions round Lyon are cultivated. It can also be used for vines, since it does not damage
their roots.[104]

This long exposé on the virtues and methods of hand cultivation
does not mention however the indispensable contribution of
manure. The spade could indeed accomplish miracles, airing and
mixing both top and bottom soil, but if the land was not 'to be
allowed to rest' as the writer says, intensive manuring was necessary. Without fertilizer, continuous cultivation was impossible –
but it was not so easy to find it.

Manure was in extremely short supply because it was mostly of
animal origin. To get rid of draught animals, as Poinsot suggested,
would not therefore have been a good thing. 'In the Fertois, in the
seventeenth century, the land was improved by marling, which
increased yields by a third . . . In 1748, certain peasants made up a
compost from bracken and heather which they took to sell at
market in Le Mans.'[105] But I would not guarantee the value of such
compost any more than of *écobuage* (burning off the top layer)
which was almost universally practised, or the compost obtained in
the Alps from rotted down oak, ash and larch leaves, mixed with
sprigs of box, and stalks of thyme and lavender.[106] These were

palliatives at best and little used. Since human excrement was not much employed either, animals were really the main if not the only source of manure. In the Alps, peasants went to collect the dung left in the summer pastures by transhumant or local sheep – the *mison* – and this precious matter was brought down to the village on the backs of men or mules.[107] But in Châlons-sur-Marne, between the wars, 'in some of the nearby villages, one could actually rent certain roads or sections of road so as to have the right to collect horse-dung from them'.[108] Perhaps the most striking example of all comes from the Provençal Alps in the eighteenth century. Cattle had become rare there, and sheep had taken over. And yet 'nowhere are cows allowed to live to such an old age as in this region, where they are kept for their dung'.[109] Fertilizer was gold dust: the peasant would barter anything, we are told, except manure.

An unusual project

Only someone who was not a peasant could overlook the capital importance of manure – as did the author of one grand scheme which had no practical consequence but is worth pausing over since it is so extraordinary and is put forward with all the earnest conviction of one who thinks he has found the perfect solution, backed up by unanswerable arguments.

The date is January 1793, and the revolutionary times inspired many grand notions. But it was out of the blue that the proposal arrived at the Ministry of the Interior from one A. P. Julienne Belair, director-general of the works at the military camp outside Paris.[110] The said director, who introduces himself as 'a citizen . . . who is proud of his reputation', and anxious 'to make himself really useful', and 'never suggests things lightly', proposed to the government a system of cultivation which he thought beyond compare:

> Experiments carried out on a large scale and on several occasions have convinced me of the immense advantages of a system of cultivation *à bras* of my own devising, after ten years' research. In the first place, with a little advance of the crop

[this probably means starting cultivation earlier than usual] this method uses arms more than horses, spades and hoes more than ploughs, and if in [manufacturing] a machine which saves on labour is always advantageous, I am persuaded that in agriculture the labour of men cannot be replaced by harrows and ploughs (although it may be rendered easier). I carried out my main experiments on soil which normally produces on average no more than eleven quintals of wheat, cultivated, but well cultivated, by the usual methods, and in order to obtain this yield, some two quintals' seed or often more, is sown. First of all I saved 60 *livres* or three bushels Paris measure on the seedcorn, which is a definite gain; then instead of eleven quintals, I harvested 55, 56 and even 60 quintals, with straw in proportion . . . Under the old system [on the same ground] . . . they sowed two bushels to get eleven, so it took ten to get 55, whereas I sowed seven to get 280 or more. One bushel under the old system yielded 5½ [to one] perhaps six nowadays because there is less vermin around,[111] whereas a bushel under my system produces over 40 to 1. Just think what value this would add to the *biens nationaux* [redistributed land] still to be sold.

The author was proposing to farm in this intensive fashion no less than the 60 million *arpents* of arable land he thought France contained. He did recognize that it was an ambitious scheme wich would require, in order to farm the 60 million *arpents* (one *arpent* is roughly an acre), some 10 million workers 'or capitalists of labour as an economic writer has described them'. Note the proportion: one man's labour, with his tools and the strength of his arm, to every 6 *arpents*.

The project was never taken up of course. Apart from anything else, after the battle of Jemappes (6 November 1792), where would the 10 million farmhands have come from – or even the one million the author asked for to launch the scheme on an experimental basis? With the war requisitioning men and horses, French agriculture was losing much of its labour force anyway.

253

Some examples

In France cultivation by hand (or rather spade) was an ancient practice born of necessity and experience. Indeed in many cases it was the only way out of serious difficulty.

How else could farmers have cultivated steeply sloping land in mountain areas? In the Massif Central, apart from the lowlands (and sometimes even there), most farmland was dug with spades until the quite recent past. Ploughing teams were the exception. The same causes produced the same results in the Alps. Animals were out of the question there, as they were on the steep hillsides of the Oisans. In the mid-Durance valley, in Montrond for instance, 'all the work has to be done by hand, alas'.[112]

And yet, in spite of the difficulties, crops were widely grown on the mountainsides in the past, whenever the population expanded. In the Pyrenees and similar regions, new farmland was desperately sought after, as high up as 2,000 metres in Andorra, 1,600 metres in Cerdagne and Capcir. But it was something of an acrobatic feat to grow crops on the mountainside: the peasant had to leave behind his plough and team when he went up to the high ground. Climbing to the edge of the snow line, he 'would take a spade to dig over the strip of land the animals could not tackle. His wife and children would follow behind, bowed down by the weight of hods or baskets of manure. Without the latter, the work would be wasted.' And one always had to hope that this fragile strip would not be carried away one day 'by the first avalanches'.[113]

Another poor region where crops were cultivated by hand was the Maine, where ploughing teams were uncommon. Such ploughs as there were were heavy and unwieldy, rough wooden implements, 'knocked up on the farm, perhaps with a little help from the village wheelwright'.[114] Only the tips of the ploughshares were made of iron, and these penetrated the earth to the derisory depth of 10 or 12 centimetres at most, which was not even enough to cut the roots of the weeds. But because the ploughs were so heavy, each one required a team of at least six oxen or four horses and could cover only about 6 hectares a year. There were in any case very few of them. 'At Saint-Mars-sous-la-Futaie, out of 81 *closeries* [little farms] only three owned a plough.'[115] So the ordinary *closier* or *bordager* as he was called, would either get together with a wealthier farmer, or more often, 'break up the land with a hoe, pitchfork or spade [the latter made of wood covered with an iron blade]. This *émottage*, or digging by hand, was a slow and costly business. A man could dig at most two hectares a year and it was exhausting work . . . which made him old and bent before his time; and all for the sake of a paltry crop and paltry profits.'[116]

But the Maine was something of a special case: it was a region where more and more *terres vaines* were being taken over for grazing sheep and cattle. These fields were sown with cereals only every eight, ten or twelve years (notably in the Laval region in the 1770s), before reverting to grassland once more.[117] In between times, they became overgrown with gorse and 'huge thickets of broom, an impenetrable haunt for game of all kinds (hares, rabbits, partridge, snipe) which the peasants could hunt, but also for more troublesome creatures (wolves, foxes and badgers)'. Since the plough could not be taken over this kind of land, it had to be cleared by hand. The shrubs had to be hacked down with billhooks and axes, and the top burnt off before these overgrown fields could be made arable once more.

Elsewhere, the poor quality or shallow depth of the soil made ploughing impossible. An example was the *arrondissement* of Nontron in the Dordogne, about fifty kilometres north of Périgueux, a very stony little region, with a few narrow valleys. 'Since we have little growing land', explained the president of the *arrondissement*'s statistical committee in 1852,

> working it is hard and costly, and the pickaxe is more use than the plough. Harrows and rollers produce little effect; that is why we have none of these advanced implements. Scorched up by the slightest heat, our crop is under-nourished and gives little straw, what there is being short, very thin and hard to bind, so it is secured with wooden laths, which is in turn disastrous for our forest. Instead of being

converted into silage, our straw is used for fodder, and heather replaces it in the cowsheds, a very poor substitute since a cartload of straw manure is worth at least three of heather.[118]

It was by hand too that terraces in the south were cultivated (mostly for vines) and so were new crops everywhere: potatoes on their first appearance, and turnips, according to official instructions (1785).[119] The same was true of maize or 'Turkish corn' when it was first introduced. The field where it was to be sown was dug over (*pelleversé*) and this method persisted on small plots where maize was grown until 1965 – yes, 1965.[120] As a result, maize-growing was from the start practised by poor peasants.[121] The tool, the *pelleversoir* (used for other crops besides maize) was 'a fork with two prongs, very straight and strong, and a handle about a metre long. It is 'with this implement', says a manual of 1868, 'that the farm workers [of Languedoc] break up the land in winter, at an agreed price'.[122]

The increasing subdivision of peasant property in the nineteenth century prolonged the survival of cultivation by hand of course. On these tiny plots, pick and shovel were all one could use. So it is hardly surprising to find cultivation by hand practised not only in the vineyards where it was normal (the first ploughs for vineyards appeared only in the Second Empire, in the south-west[123] and Languedoc), but also increasingly in regions of intensive cereal-growing, where one would not expect to encounter it, such as Alsace or Limagne: here, an observer tells us in 1860, the population was increasing, and 'they all work the land themselves, usually with a spade'.[124]

But there is scarcely anywhere in France where one does not find traces, sometimes by chance, of the old way of farming. A historian working recently on a *commune* of the Marche (present-day *département* of the Indre)[125] came across the now obsolete term *manucottier(s)* (*manu cultores*) meaning peasants who dug over their small plots of land with spades.

This was the burdensome reality of rural France in the past: farming methods remained obstinately inadequate, since animal traction could not be used everywhere, the land could not be adequately turned over and manured, and it was hard to get rid of the weeds that grew faster than the young wheat, oats or rye. Just as not all French farmers today possess a tractor, so many, indeed the great majority, of peasants in the past did not own either a horse or a pair of oxen to pull the plough. Even in the early twentieth century, 'to have the use of two oxen was a sign [in the Charente, but elsewhere too no doubt] of a certain prosperity, that of the large farmer as opposed to the *lopiniers*, whose plough [when they had one] was pulled by a donkey or a skinny cow'.[126]

That all seems clear enough. The explanation can be turned on its head though: if cultivation by hand implies a plentiful labour supply, the very existence of that large workforce in turn implies this labour-intensive method of farming; in itself, it limits 'the use of animals for agricultural purposes'.[127] Men and beasts competed with each other for the work.

Still we do know the size of the two 'labour forces': in 1789, there were over 1,700,000 horses and 6 or 7 million oxen.[128] In 1862, there were about 3 million horses and 13 million oxen.[129] The animals had doubled in number, but the agricultural population had grown far more slowly, from 20.9 million to 26.6 million.[130] So it is not unreasonable to conclude that during this comparatively short lapse of time the peasant farmer began to be liberated from some of his toil. Despite its apparent stagnation, the farming community was in fact feeling a fairly brisk and continuous wind of change – and feeling it earlier in certain advanced regions.[131]

Which crops to grow? (1)

This question refers to the absolute necessity, in the farming world, to structure the area devoted to the various crops, to divide it into proportions which, once fixed, would thereafter vary little if at all.

There are many ways to interpret the reasons for these divisions. The first is simply that people had to eat, and could not survive by eating nothing but bread or gruel made from cereals or chestnuts.[132] They needed fats – butter, which was a luxury, lard, dripping, oil (not only olive oil: walnut oil was often used both in cooking and for lamps). And they needed protein: dairy products, eggs and meat. Pierre Deffontaines argues that the geography of the stomach mattered more than the geography of shelter,[133] which also exercised certain imperatives. All that is needed to complete the picture is the geography of clothing. In order to feed, clothe and house themselves and their families, French peasants did their best to 'live off their own fat', not only baking their own bread but producing everything from their own land. Polyculture was the inevitable consequence.

One ought probably to break with custom (and etymology) and put the word 'agriculture' into the plural, to make it cover *all* forms of husbandry: forests, orchards, olives, chestnuts and walnuts; vineyards, grazing and stock-farming; gardens and hemp- or flax-patches; the 'noble' crops on arable land, cereals above all; and the 'proletarian' crops, including newcomers, only slowly adopted – buckwheat, maize, potatoes; then there were the forage crops – known in France as artificial meadows (how were they introduced into traditional crop rotation?); and lastly a series of particular crops with 'industrial' applications: mulberry trees, tobacco, sugar beet, colza (rapeseed), sunflowers, and dye-plants like madder and woad. The point is to observe how these crops were organized over a given surface area and how they affected each other, since they were inevitably part of a balanced combination, which might shift and alter but only very slowly, even during times of so-called crisis and disruption.

It is more usual to pay attention only to two elements from the above long (but incomplete) list: cereals and livestock – the two essential kinds of farming but far from the only ones. 'In France as in Europe', noted Marc Bloch, the agricultural economy 'was based on the combination of ploughing and pasture, a feature of capital importance and one which most clearly distinguished European from Far Eastern civilization'.[134] He was far from the only person to make the point. 'Agriculture', says a document from the Ariège in 1790, 'has two parts which mutually assist one another, the farming of the land and the farming of animals.'[135] 'Mutual

FIGURE 31
The rural population and the number of farm animals (1806–1954)

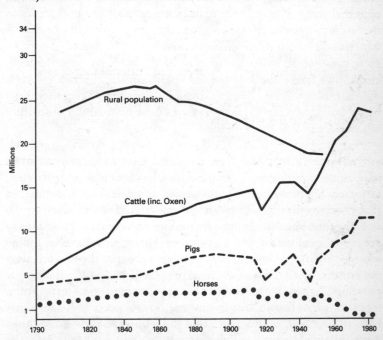

This graph shows the large increase in the number of draft animals in France between 1789 and 1860, alongside a much smaller increase in the human population of the countryside; the progressive decrease in the human population after 1860; the decrease in the number of draft animals after 1930, illustrated by the virtual disappearance of horses; and the sharp increase in cattle and pigs, corresponding to growing meat consumption.

Source: Y. Tuguault, *Fécondité et urbanisation*, 1975.

---

assistance' implied a balance with recognized benefits to both sides: this document is indeed a protest against excessive land clearance – which was taking place at the expense of grazing.

But in France, it is impossible not to give vines a special place among farming priorities. Isaac de Pinto,[136] as usual a keen observer of the realities of his time, was well aware in 1770 of the problem of equilibrium. Writing of England, he wondered whether

> there should not be a balance between these two activities [ploughing and pasture], whether it is not rather dangerous to plough up so much pasture land, and whether England may be falling into this trap by over-encouraging the export [of grain] by means of bounties.[137] In France, there are three kinds of farming to be managed: vines, pasture and arable land; the balance between these is more complicated.

To the three mentioned by Isaac de Pinto, I would add forest, which must be reckoned a major variable, if only because it draws attention to the important distinction between *bosc* and *plain*,[138] that is between trees and open country, usually farmland.

Here then are three or four variables to help us explore a long process of evolution that featured several others. We are undoubtedly simplifying, but to an acceptable degree, I hope. Readers who are familiar with old-fashioned algebra will know that the fastest growing variables eventually tend to dominate the value of a function when large numbers are concerned (as in this case: millions of hectares, millions of quintals, millions of francs, millions of animals and millions of people).

Let us try to use these notions to map out the problem. The surface area of France in about 1859, just before the annexation in 1860 of Savoy and Nice (which between them added at most about one million hectares and about 700,000 people), was of the order of 53 million hectares.[139] From this figure it is usual to deduct the 'non-taxable' areas (towns, roads, rivers etc.) leaving 50 million hectares in round figures, a convenient figure for calculations which must always be approximate on account of the unfortunately imperfect documentation at our disposal. The reasons for its inadequacy are well known: above all, the great reluctance of peasants to answer census or survey questions, since they always feared that this kind of survey concealed plans for a new tax.[140] The figures collected from mayors during the Second Empire may thus be suspect in detail; but they make it possible to establish some broad features of the overall picture.

In the first place, French territory was divided into two categories: *arable land* on one hand, land left in its natural state on the other. In the second category, we can *unhesitatingly* place all forests, natural grasslands, moors and *pâtis* – everything that I shall sometimes call 'waste' land for want of a better term. But we should on the other hand be wary of the convenient expression 'arable land': in theory it refers to land that is or can be ploughed. Would it not be better to talk about 'cultivated land', so that the term could include vines, gardens, hemp-patches and orchards? If so, the cultivated land in 1859 consisted of 25 million hectares of arable land, plus 2 million of vineyards, and 2 million of gardens and orchards, that is a total of 29 million hectares. The 'waste land' consisted of: forests, 8 million hectares; natural grassland, 5 million; heath and moorland (including land that proved resistant to agriculture and reverted to nature), 8 million – a total of 21 million hectares as opposed to 29 million. The country was not exactly divided in half: human endeavour had made its mark on the larger part, and the expansion of cultivated land at the expense of waste land, while slow, had begun early and advanced steadily. Between 1815 and 1859, about a million extra hectares were brought into cultivation, which is a not negligible figure.

How, in 1859, were the 29 million hectares of cultivated and controlled land divided up? As follows: 'gardens and orchards', 500,000 hectares; chestnut trees, 550,000; olive trees, 100,000; mulberry trees, 50,000; apple and other fruit trees, 200,000; nurseries, reed beds etc., 600,000. The 25 million hectares of arable land were divided as follows: wheat, 6,500,000 hectares; *méteil* (mixed grain) and rye, 2,500,000; barley, maize and buck-wheat, 2,500,000; oats, 3,000,000; root crops (including potatoes and beet), 1,500,000; forage crops, 2,500,000; pulses, 500,000; industrial crops (rapeseed, flax, hemp, madder, tobacco etc.) 500,000; and lastly fallow, 5,500,000.[141] As for vineyards, these occupied only 2 million hectares.

These figures are interesting for several reasons.

They indicate once more the small area occupied by vines,

which took little space (not even a tenth of the cultivated area, no more than a few tiny patches on a small-scale map).

They tell us that in the mid-nineteenth century, the 'new crops', recent or not so recent – namely root crops (including potatoes and sugar beet), maize, buckwheat, madder and forage crops – were already well established.

But even at this late date, the huge area under cereals gave the French countryside of the past the monotonous appearance remarked upon by Marc Bloch.[142] Wheat was after all 'a necessary evil',[143] an obsession. It was grown in places where it would have been wiser to grow grass, vines or fruit trees. Near Prades in the Roussillon, in order to protect the wheat against drought brought by the *tramontane* wind, the fields were even irrigated.[144] At Pontarlier in the Jura, at 837 metres altitude, Léonce de Lavergne was surprised in 1860 'to see fields of wheat above the tree line; it is harvested in September as in northern Europe, a little before the first snowfalls'.[145]

Which crops to grow? (2)

By taking the date 1859, almost halfway through the Second Empire (1852–70), have I gone beyond the chronological limit of the peasant economy? Could it still be so-called?

My answer would be that the *model* one can construct from the figures given above could easily be applied to periods much further back in the past.

Arthur Young's estimates for the end of the *ancien régime*, slightly modified by Léonce de Lavergne,[146] are quite close to our figures: cultivated land (25 + 1.5 + 1.5) comes to 28 million hectares; uncultivated (9 + 3 + 10) to 22 million. Even then, more land was cultivated than not: forests and other natural expanses amounted to less than half the total, although covering a million more hectares than in 1860.

It is tempting to carry the calculation even further back, although the risk of error increases. But we are looking for orders of magnitude at best.

In 1700, on the eve of the War of the Spanish Succession, during the latter years of Louis XIV (d. 1715), of Vauban (d. 1707) and Boisguillebert (who published *Le Détail de la France* in 1697 and *Le Factum de la France* in 1707), the national territory consisted of about 50 million hectares overall. France did not yet possess Lorraine, acquired in 1766; Corsica, bought in 1768; the Comtat Venaissin, annexed in 1790; or Savoy and the county of Nice, acquired in 1860. After taking away the 3 million non-taxable hectares, we are left with 47 million. Crops occupied 23 million hectares of arable, plus vineyards, gardens and orchards – perhaps about 26 million as opposed to 21. As the eighteenth century opened then, the division between *ager* and *saltus*, cultivated and natural, was more evenly balanced than it would be in 1789. The difference is small, but significant, pointing to the future. So Boisguillebert is exaggerating when he claims that 'more than half of France is waste or poorly cultivated'. But one would like to be able to check his estimate that even if the peasant were to clear the available land, the combination of taxes and expenses (plus, I would add, low yields) would mean that in the end 'the harvest would not belong to him'.[147]

It would certainly be fascinating to be able to go back even further. The vicomte d'Avenel tried to do so in 1894,[148] when the historical study of prices, statistics and demography had barely begun, and was certainly not easy, and when no one yet thought in terms of macro-economics and gross national income. D'Avenel was subjected to pitiless and ironic criticism by the academic historians of the past, but he has been rehabilitated now that our own price curves, worked out with every precaution from long homogeneous series, have been found more or less to coincide with those which he had to deduce from *scattered* sources. No one moreover can deny that he was prodigiously knowledgeable. His speculative, adventurous but intelligent calculations took him back to the France of Henri IV and Sully, the France of 1600 or so. This means a jump backwards of a hundred years.

In 1600, France measured no more than 44 million hectares (less the non-taxable lands – 42 million shall we say?). D'Avenel suggested that arable land represented about 32% of the whole;

uncultivated land 27%; forests 33%; meadows and vineyards 7%. If we split the last figure in half, 3.5% meadows, 3.5% vineyards – the total cultivated land would be 35.5% as against 63.5% 'waste' (or 15 million hectares for the former and 27 million for the latter).[149] Thus at a time when the 'modern' period had unquestionably begun, nature may still have laid claim to a greater area of France than man could.

I am not entirely confident in d'Avenel's figures. Was he sure of them himself? But he had an ingenious method of reconstructing orders of magnitude, when the figures were insufficient. He compared the revenue per hectare as between centuries (based on reliable samples from various French provinces); then calculated the total agricultural revenue. He concluded that between 1600 and 1890 there was threefold progress: the first was the extension of French territory from 44 to 53 million hectares; the second, which is of more interest to us, was the extension of cultivated land from 35.5% of the total in 1600 to 60% by 1890; and the third was that product per hectare, in constant francs, rose from 19 francs in 1600 to 26 francs in 1789 and a little under 50 francs in 1890. All three combined to explain the rise in gross agricultural income: 500 million in 1600, 1,000 million in 1789 (rather low, to my mind) and 2,400 million in 1890. These are the figures as calculated by d'Avenel.[150] Any historian is free to question them or better still improve on them, but the direction and significance of the evolution he detected cannot, in general terms, be questioned.

These conclusions are significant.

In the first place, they reveal how much of the background to French history is taken up by a 'natural' France: although its frontiers may have been pushed back by man over the centuries, this natural France was vast enough to withstand pick and axe, horse and plough, saw and fire. It quickly reclaimed its territory the moment man's back was turned, and it was protected by all those who had something to gain from it, whether noblemen jealous of their forests and hunting rights, or peasants clinging on to their commons. Uncultivated land was as vital to town-dwellers needing timber or firewood as it was to infant industries requiring fuel, not to mention peasants and nobles who counted on forest and wasteland to graze their flocks. A balance had somehow to be found between the *natural* and the *cultivated*.

This balance was maintained by a sort of defensive frontier, the stern *law of diminishing returns*, already in some ways prefigured by Turgot. Any land clearance extended the territory of the village and by the same token the time taken for the farm worker to travel between house and fields. And time was money. Moreover, outlying land, far away from fields that had been farmed for centuries, was notoriously infertile. Harvests from it turned out to be so meagre that they no longer fed the farmer. If some religious orders abandoned land in Champagne in about 1520,[151] it was because such land lay beyond the dangerous boundary of diminishing returns and was 'no longer worth farming'.

One is easily persuaded to see the agricultural history of France as a duel between man and nature, whether nature took the form of trees, animals or water. A sure sign of the power of this alternative natural world was the abundance of wild beasts, wolves in particular, to be found in France until the mid-nineteenth century. An informant reports that in the Franche-Comté, 'from 1775 until last March [1784], that is in nine years, there have been killed in this province 641 dog wolves, 627 she-wolves and 1,385 cubs, a total of 2,653'.[152] And this was certainly not a record. Leaving France and travelling eastwards, the presence of wolves became nightmarish: 'In the two years from 1822 to 1824, wolves have torn to pieces 25,000 domestic animals in Livonia.'[153] And going back through time, one finds wolves looming larger and larger. 'In the countryside round Troyes, in the summer of 1341, 571 wolves were captured alive and 18 killed.'[154] Not until 1850 or so did wolves die out and even then there were exceptions, the Berry for instance, where Léonce de Lavergne in 1870 says 'wolves in particular are unwelcome visitors'.[155] But sometimes devotees of wolf-hunting kept them artificially in existence for a few years, as boars are maintained here and there today.

The wild boar might have been a better example, but it does not give our chroniclers the same *frisson*, so we hear about its exploits only incidentally. The *Courrier du département du Bas-Rhin*, the official local paper, carried this unexpected information on 22 June

1817: 'There have been many complaints in the *département* of Meuse of the damage done by wild boars, which gather in herds, and devastate the potato fields.'[156] The boar, being herbivorous, escaped men's attentions more successfully than the wolf, a carnivore that was perhaps feared more than it need have been. As for ordinary game, there was plenty of that, since noble hunting preserves were numerous but not regularly exploited. With the Revolution came a spectacular expansion of hunting and a steep rise in poaching by peasants: bad news for the 'wild beasts black and tawny'.[157] At the same time alas, there were inevitably more encroachments on the forests.

A further conclusion is that although cultivated land may have advanced or receded depending on time and place (drained marshes reverting to their former state, cleared land falling once more into abandon, ransacked forests growing back across the ditches surrounding them)[158] the long-term trend was towards continuous conquest by the farmer. Cultivated, domesticated land was gradually winning the day. As generation succeeded generation, there was a *steady accumulation*: this is the phenomenon which theory should be addressing, if it is to shed more light on the slow but *not* altogether motionless history of the French countryside and indeed of France as a whole.

New crops for old (1)

Within farmland, crops vied for space. Or rather the farmer favoured some over others, with the possibility of a change of heart. Stability seems generally to have prevailed: one year's division would be much the same as the last, give or take a few changes. But the few changes could add up until a different pattern emerged.

In Normandy for instance, grassland had always occupied more space than it did elsewhere. But the real transformation, which would enshrine grass in the fields rather than cereals, was late in coming. In the pays d'Auge, *enherbage* (giving fields over to grass) became obvious on a large scale only after 1680. Basse-Normandie had to wait till about 1820. We are told that cattle took the food from men's mouths, but they certainly took their time to do so. This was a shift that took place over several centuries: despite its convenience, monocultural grassland did not triumph overnight.

I mention this major example as a useful warning. If new crops took so long to become established it was not simply because they were unknown, requiring years of observation and experiment, preferably in pilot gardens, a few steps from the house. All the new crops did, it is true, go through this trial period: buckwheat, maize, tobacco, potatoes, beans, tomatoes, rapeseed, sunflowers, sugar beet. When the chevalier de Vivens, returning from America, introduced tobacco to Clairac in 1637, the *curé* Laplaigne says, 'the seeds were sown in the gardens first'.[159] Only after the experiment seemed successful were the plants given the freedom of the fields.

But then they immediately found themselves in competition with other plants: the old crop had to be driven out, or some compromise reached. There was not always an easy answer to the dilemma: change took time.

Rapeseed or colza was grown from very early on in what would one day be the Nord *département*, but it did not reach Dieppe and Eu until about 1788, and only became really widely adopted in the 1850s.[160] Sugar beet (its industrial possibilities to be developed after 1799,[161] following the experiments of the Prussian chemist Achard in Berlin) was no exception. Napoleon as First Consul introduced it to France in 1801, and the continental blockade furthered its rise. Nevertheless, beet sugar as a rival to cane sugar took a century to become widely accepted in France.

Whenever room could be found for the newcomer alongside the old crops, the problem was easier to resolve. A field of maize could be planted in such a way that peas could be sown between the cornstalks. J.-J. Menuret (1791), a careful observer of crops on the banks of the Isère,[162] noted that the cornstalks, 'planted out at regular wide intervals, make it possible to grow peas and beans etc., in between'. This was quite usual in vineyards too, in the Loue valley of the Jura[163] in the eighteenth century for instance, or outside one village on the Langres plateau in 1900. Here, 'the vineyards', Joseph Cressot writes, 'produced garlic and shallots, haricots, beets',[164] and broad beans. A last resort was to mix up the grain for sowing: *méteil*, a mixture of wheat and rye, usually in equal parts, was found all over France (it was known in Languedoc as *conseigle* or *blé consegal*). Still in Languedoc, *basjalade* was a mixture of oats and vetch;[165] in Maine, *bréchet* was a combination of wheat and *jarosse*, a pulse, while *mélarde* combined barley and oats. Another possibility was to wait for one crop to be up before sowing in between the furrows. This was the advice given in official instructions on growing turnips, which were imported from England and assimilated to other root crops. They were sown in early June on land already planted with broad and haricot beans, which would be harvested first.[166]

These were compromise solutions of course, with newcomers prepared to take their place meekly alongside the old. Some crops were more demanding.

One such was buckwheat which, despite its name, is a member not of the *graminaceae* but of the *polygonaceae* family.[167] It arrived in Brittany at the end of the fifteenth century and its rate of growth made it very successful, particularly since it could be sown after the harvest, on soil which had formerly borne wheat, rye or oats. J.-J. Menuret tells us that buckwheat

> can be sown on stubble, after cutting the corn [and without any further ploughing, in July or August]; by the end of October it has yielded a crop not without value to the farmer; the flour made from this grain makes a heavy and nourishing bread; it can [also] be used for soups; but its chief and most valuable use is, either as grain or flour, for fattening poultry, turkeys and pigs. The straw can be usefully added to dunghills. If the plant is ploughed under at the time of flowering, it makes the field able to carry a good cereal crop at once; in regions where the harvest is later and the sowing earlier, one cannot take advantage of this interval which is too short to get buckwheat up, and it has to be sown in the spring.[168]

The text seems clear on the first two uses – either the grain or the flowering plant can be used as manure. The third is left rather to our imagination. I do not think buckwheat could be a spring cereal unless it replaced other cereals (wheat, oats or rye) in a rotating system. But what is certain is that it played an important and from now on critical role in the diet of Bretons and other peasants, in the south and the Massif Central. By the seventeenth century, it had reached the highlands of the Ariège.[169]

Maize, which arrived very early in the Basque country,[170] became effectively established only in the last quarter of the seventeenth century in Aquitaine, in particular around Toulouse. But then it took over in a big way, becoming quite indispensable. Maize literally saved the south-west from the famines and food shortages of the baroque age, in spite of complaints, in the Saintonge area for instance, 'from winegrowers who saw cheap labour flocking' towards it.[171] J.-J. Menuret is found singing its praises at the end of the eighteenth century (1791):

> Maize or Indian corn [*blé de Turquie*], a fleshy plant, bulky in stems, leaves and grain, also prefers good soil; but it derives most of its subsistence from the atmosphere; it yields a hundred to one, the stalks after harvest rot down to good silage, the extra leaves and stems are good fodder for cattle . . . The grain from it can be used in a variety of economical ways by men, poultry, pigs and even larger livestock . . . Maize grown as a forage crop on stubble would give several cuts or good grazing in spring and summer.[172]

Maize is still put to the latter use today. But it is valued above all for its grain. In the south of France, where biennial rotation was the rule, maize became a spring cereal, which had been lacking hitherto, as well as a supplement to diet, valued for animals and acceptable to humans. The peasant was prepared to eat it whenever he needed more money, saving his wheat crop for market. It was thanks to maize that Toulouse became a very large town specializing in the grain trade, notably wheat. Maize long remained a southern plant in France (see Figure 5 in Volume I) and has spread north only recently thanks to hybrid strains that can stand the cold.

The same difficulties faced the potato, another import from America, but they were gradually resolved. A new and more far-reaching revolution followed, for the potato was destined to play a major part in the French diet. The increase in the population of Europe during the nineteenth century is attributed by some historians to the spread (however slow) of vaccination against smallpox, but others, including the German economist W. Roscher, put it down to the spread of the potato.[173] Two reasons are no doubt better than one.

The European career of the potato began in the sixteenth century, when a few tubers were given to two botanists, the Englishman John Gerard in 1568 and the Frenchman Charles de l'Escluse (who was however living in Frankfurt-am-Main) in 1588. As it happened, they obtained different varieties, from which all future potato crops for a century and a half would be descended: the German variety was pink, the English yellow.

But it was not until the seventeenth century that the potato began to move out of the kitchen garden and into the fields, first in German and Austria; then in Italy, Switzerland, the Dauphiné, Franche-Comté, Alsace, the Vosges and Flanders.[174] At this period, it was thought fit only for animals, or for the poor and desperate. It was when Antoine Parmentier was a prisoner in Prussia during the Seven Years' War (1756–63), he tells us, that he discovered the joys of the potato, the only food available at the time (which he washed down with gin). Much later, during the rapid campaign that took the French armies from the Rhine to the Danube, taking Ulm (20 October 1805) and Austerlitz (2 December the same year), French soldiers ate the local potatoes. Germany was certainly a pioneer in this respect. But even in 1781, in the regions on the Elbe, no self-respecting servant would accept *Kartoffeln* to eat – he would sooner change masters.[175] England remained resistant to the potato even longer, viewing it as a botanical curiosity, whereas poverty-stricken Ireland had converted to the new food by the latter half of the seventeenth century. It was the Irish in the end who introduced the potato to English and later American farms.

In France, despite its early success, it was not until the mid-eighteenth century that the potato was regarded as truly 'worthy' to be eaten, with partisans prepared to defend it on both dietary and culinary grounds. This long reluctance may have had something to do with the questionable quality of the first varieties to become acclimatized: in 1752 there were still only two varieties in Europe; by 1757 there were 7; and by 1770, still only 9; but the number leapt to 40 in 1772, and in 1846 Vilmorin's first catalogue would be offering 177. Today there are several thousands, corresponding to differences in climate, to requirements of growers and to the methods of cooking for which they are suitable. When we learn that early consumers often tried to make bread from potatoes, we can easily picture their disappointment.

The development of the potato after the mid-eighteenth century is unquestionably explained by the rise in the population. A few clear-sighted contemporaries quickly understood the importance of the new crop. In the *généralité* of Limoges, potatoes were originally banned because they were thought to cause leprosy. When Turgot became the *intendant* there in 1761, he succeeded in dispelling this myth, with the aid of the local Agricultural Society and the parish priests, by practising what he preached and eating the dreaded tubers in public. The bishop of Castres did the same, lecturing his priests the while, with the result that the *patate* was being grown widely in the Pyrenees by about 1770.[176]

But the corner was not really turned until the severe famine of 1769–70. The following year, the Academy of Besançon set an essay competition on the subject: 'Suggest food plants which might be used in times of famine to supplement those usually eaten.' All the essays mentioned the potato – notably the winning entry, which came from Parmentier. He then embarked upon a massive propaganda campaign, deploring 'the mocking humour of our scornful citizens'. He published widely, gave advice on the growing and storing of the potato, organized gourmet dinners in his own home at which nothing but dishes made from potatoes were served (Arthur Young was one of his guests), brought to Paris all the varieties then cultivated in France and had even more shipped from America to give a better selection.[177] He finally obtained from Louis XVI, in 1786, permission to set up an experimental plantation on about 20 hectares just outside Paris in Neuilly, on the untended and infertile soil of the plain of Sablons. It was a

FIGURE 32
The arrival of the potato in Europe

Note that this map, taken from the study by György Mandy and Zoltan Csak, shows the first appearance of the potato in Europe, not its adoption as a food either for animals or humans, something which varied according to country and might be much later (over a century later in England for instance).

complete success. In his efforts to attract consumers, Parmentier concluded that the best method would be to entice people to steal his potatoes. So he ostentatiously had his plantation guarded by the *maréchaussée*, the local police – but only by day. Similarly, he advised landowners not to force potatoes on their peasants, but to plant one fine field full themselves and 'expressly forbid anyone to enter'[178] – a more subtle approach than that of Frederick II of

Prussia who sent in the troops to make the peasants plant potatoes!

That Parmentier's efforts, which are sometimes dismissed as an amiable obsession, were more than necessary (and indeed inadequate), can be seen from an official letter from the *département* of Mayenne on 29 *vendémiaire*, Year IV: 'Potato-growing is still almost in its infancy [here] since they have only been a success in gardens and on the best soil, or on land manured at great expense.'[179]

And the newcomer took longer still to penetrate central and western France. It did not appear at Huillé in Anjou until between 1790 and 1795, but made strides every year after that. It was after all useful 'to fatten the pigs', and 'to feed men in times of shortage'. By 1834, Huillé was putting 105 hectares under potatoes, almost 25% of the acreage under cereals.[180]

So J.-J. Menuret was ahead of his time when he praised the potato in 1791, but then he lived in the Isère, on the eastern side of France, where it was more quickly accepted, and in any case he grew his own:

The potato, that admirable food plant which contains a sweet and moist flesh, can be served either with the most exotic sauces or in the most simple way, being fit to be transformed into rich and delicate dishes for the tables of the wealthy [who actually avoided it for years, claiming it swelled the stomach] and providing simple and easily prepared food for every condition of Citizen . . . And [he went on] this crop, extended, encouraged and promoted on my land has brought me many advantages: potatoes have been put to economic use whether at the table of the masters, the stewards or the farmhands, or to feed the poultry, turkeys and pigs. There have been enough to give to the poor, to sell and so on. What abundant manna, and what pleasure it has brought![181]

Since potatoes had from the start been used to feed pigs, taking herds of swine out to find acorns became a thing of the past. In Saintonge whenever there was no wheat or maize left, the peasants had to fall back on eating potatoes; pig-rearing would immediately decline. The same was true in the Nivernais in the nineteenth century.[182]

Both producer and consumer had to learn how to manage the new plant. To discover what was learned, let us visit eastern France where a certain Monsieur Collot is our guide. Do not try to find on the map the town from which he writes: Libreville in the Ardennes. It was the name ('Freedom City') which Charleville took, or was given, in the early days of the Revolution. And I do not know exactly who Collot was. But he wrote a letter on 30 *frimaire*, Year III, well after the fall of Robespierre. The Convention finished sitting on 26 October 1795. But this letter makes no reference to the political situation; it is all about potatoes. How to grow them in the first place. 'This is what I shall do,' Collot writes: first of all turn the soil deeply before or during the winter, 'either with the plough or the spade'; after the frosts are over, plough the ground again, then dig holes with a spade in a straight line, four or five feet apart; one person drops in the potato which is carried by another person. Put some manure in every hole. Then fill it in. When the plants are 'a foot or fifteen inches high, I pinch the tops once, hard enough to make them put out more shoots [*margoter*]'.[183] When summer comes, weed the bed lightly. Next, and this is more important, Collot tackles the question of varieties. 'The ones I grow are of two kinds, red and yellow. The red ones are the colour of a beetroot on the outside, they are smooth, plump, and oblong rather than round – the biggest ones look like a woman's roughly-hewn clog. The second variety is yellow on the outside, the best are bigger than a fist, they are smooth like the others and roughly square. Both of these varieties are white on the inside and taste very good, so one is anxious to eat them.'[184]

The spread of the potato in the nineteenth and twentieth centuries is shown in Figure 32. Even the arrival of blight, the equivalent of mildew on the vine, which cruelly wiped out the Irish potato harvest in 1846 and the French crop the following year, did not halt its progress.

What has been said of the potato could, *mutatis mutandis*, also be said of sugar beet, of madder in the Rhône valley or in northern Alsace, where it used to be known as 'Haguenau red', or of that much earlier arrival, the mulberry tree, which would eventually lead to the marvels of the silk industry.

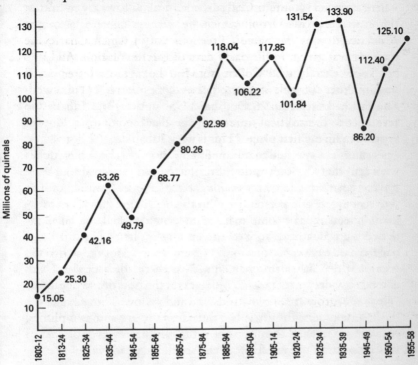

FIGURE 33
Potato production in France, 1800–1950

From J.-C. Toutain, 'Le produit de l'agriculture française de 1700 à 1958', II, *Cahiers de l'ISEA*, no. 115, July 1961.

Using fallow land

All these new crops had one great advantage: they were happy to grow on fields left fallow in rotation, without disturbing the traditional crop.

In a biennial system, land was divided into two *soles*: the fields under cultivation and those that were resting. The land *theoretically* left untended one year in two was only apparently unproductive: grass grew on it, flocks grazed there; and it would be ploughed over more than once to prepare for next year's sowing, probably of wheat.

In a triennial system, a third of the land lay fallow, the two other thirds being taken up by wheat (or rye) and spring cereals, known as *marsage* or *mars* because they were sown in March. The crops rotated in turn. Fallow land, given different names all over France,[185] also changed in character with the region: in one place it was absolute, complete or 'dead', elsewhere relative or cultivated. The fallow described as the 'shame' of agricultural life in the seventeenth century was of course the dead, completely unproductive fallow which simply lay waiting its turn.

Farmers always tried to do something about this land. The flocks were sent there as soon as the grass started growing in spring. And sowing what were known as *cultures dérobées* – 'in-between crops', such as peas, beans and lentils – was also a long-established practice. Indeed, buckwheat, maize and potatoes had all been in-between crops, at least at first – and even the plants they drove out had been in-between crops in their time. In the Morvan, when the potato, which had already been grown there for a century, was extended widely after the 1812–13 cereal crisis, it drove out buckwheat at a stroke.[186]

In the end then, the arrival of these new crops was accomplished without too much difficulty. The same cannot however be said of that innovation par excellence, the artificial meadow.

New crops for old (2): the 'artificial meadow' or forage crop

Artificial meadows are different from natural meadows, where grass grows spontaneously alongside rivers and streams. The latter have always been thought desirable: in the tenth century in the Mâconnais, a meadow was said to be 'worth twice its size in arable land'.[187] And in the Beauvaisis in 1680, an *arpent* of arable was worth 60 to 100 *livres*, wheras an *arpent* of meadow was worth 200 to 800 *livres* – an even wider gap.[188]

Artificial meadows are man-made: a field is ploughed or dug

over, manured, and sown with lucerne, clover, sainfoin or vetch. Sometimes these plants used to be sown all together, which was less convenient, since they grew at different rates and did not flower at the same time. 'This method cannot be right', said an observer in 1786, 'for the clover does not grow as high as the lucerne, so it becomes choked by the latter; and sainfoin flowers long before the others and ought to be cut earlier, so it always suffers from the delay caused by clover and lucerne. Lucerne and sainfoin should therefore be sown separately.'[189]

All the same, artificial meadows yielded two or three times more than natural ones of the same size. They provided an important addition to fodder for the animals, making it possible to keep more stock, and thus increasing the amount of manure. True, they took up space that might have been given over to the still-sacrosanct wheat, but they increased the productivity of the wheatfield by providing more fertilizer and, what was more, by fixing the nitrogen in the soil. There was less acreage under wheat, but the total harvest was greater. This may seem obvious, but according to Chaptal,[190] First Consul Bonaparte, for all his intelligence, found it hard to grasp.

In short, the artificial meadow was the motor of a powerful and necessary agricultural revolution, but one that was slow to develop in France. As late as 1823, the same Chaptal was still saying: 'Today . . . the creation of artificial meadows and sensible rotation ought to be the basis for our agriculture.'[191] But even at this date, his advice does not seem to have been universally heeded.

And yet the plants used in artificial meadows had been well known in France from at least the sixteenth century. Two hundred years later, they were being grown, but only in small patches, in Charente, Dauphiné, near Paris, in Roussillon and in Flanders.[192] And French farmers might have been aware of successful experiments with them in England by the 1730s.[193] Nor was there any shortage of encouragement for the new farming – sometimes in the form of exasperated outbursts. Here is Martin de Chassiron scolding the peasants of the La Rochelle region in 1795: 'You are rotting away in poverty and dirt because you do not organize your work properly: too many cereal fields and not enough meadows.'[194]

Equally categorical if less irascible advice had appeared in a memoir written in Metz some twenty years earlier in 1777:[195] stop trying to produce one harvest after another from 'land which is exhausted by always bearing the same grain', its author advised. What was more, the existing pattern had brought a shortage of large livestock in Lorraine and the Three Bishoprics: oxen had to be imported from Switzerland for ploughing and butchering, while horses were brought from Germany, the Ardennes and Denmark, 'for military purposes and ploughing'.

Why were people so reluctant? Why, in the late eighteenth century, when physiocrats, agricultural societies and owners of large estates (some of them eager to experiment to improve yields) were all putting 'the modern solutions of artificial meadows and root crops' at the top of their list, was this intellectual movement not translated into action? Why did 'old-fashioned rotation seem to survive on a massive scale, surrounding the few scattered reformers'?[196]

Basically because while the herbaceous plants of the artificial meadow had many advantages, they could not be 'slipped in' between crops on fallow land. Clover or vetch might, at a pinch, provide an artificial meadow once a year: if sown on fallow, they grew quickly, could be cut for fodder and then make way for wheat, leaving the soil enriched. Rotation could proceed normally.

But a lucerne field, by today's norms, can last nine years, and a meadow sown with sainfoin or clover six years. There were benefits from letting the meadow last, as was soon recognized. A long memoir on the Paris region just before the Revolution[197] tells us that 'it is when it is three, four, five or six years old that a sainfoin, clover or lucerne meadow is at its peak. After that, the plants begin to deteriorate imperceptibly, and the meadow has to be restocked.' If this practice was followed, the traditional rotation would of course be upset, so the artificial meadow if left *in situ* brought *dessolement* as it was called ('de-rotation').

There were two objections to *dessolement*.

The first was legal: tenancy or share-cropping contracts usually specified that the land had to be 'well-manured and cultivated, without interrupting rotation or disrupting [*déroyer*][198] the land, under pain of law'. Complaints from landowners came up before the *parlements*. And while in some regions landlords failed to get satisfaction,[199] *parlements* usually intervened to maintain the traditional rotation of the fields which was, they believed, necessary to keep cereal yields up.

The second obstacle concerned traditional grazing rights and the fact that rotation was not only thought of as a rational way of farming but also as a corollary of the right to graze flocks, *vaine pâture* as it was called in regions of customary law, or *compascuité* as it was called in the written code of the south.

Every village community, relying largely on its own resources, was constantly confronted with the constraints of cereal-growing and livestock-farming. No one could do without bread and no one could do without farm animals. The ancient and inveterate practices of grazing, *vaine pâture*, and transit, *parcours*, were essential to the keeping of livestock.

Free grazing, *vaine pâture*, meant that any available pasture was open to all the flocks in the village. Grazing was permitted on grassy lanes, the salvation of the poor man's cow. It was allowed on common land, the cleared space which the village owned communally, and from which rich and poor benefited alike. And as we have seen, it was authorized on fallow land, as soon as the first grass appeared in spring. It was also permitted in stubble fields after the harvest, and finally on meadows either immediately after haymaking (though this was rare) or when the grass had grown again, which was more normal. The regrowth of the grass was sometimes known as the *surpoil*. 'Since the creation of the world', says a grievance register in Lorraine in 1789, 'the second *surpoil* [that is the growth after the first regrowth] has belonged to the community.'[200]

Parcours meant the extension of the right of *vaine pâture* which a *commune* might obtain from neighbouring villages, or concede to them in turn. Village boundaries were indistinct and ran into one another. The *parcours* meant they could be disregarded. It was an advantage when flocks were being moved about and was convenient all round, since it helped livestock owners while not encroaching on cultivated fields.

FIGURE 34
The dwindling of fallow land, 1852–82

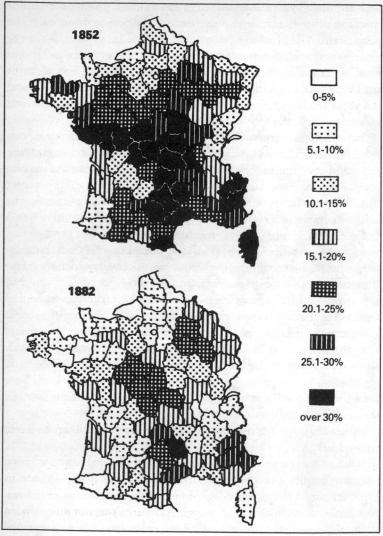

0-5%

5.1-10%

10.1-15%

15.1-20%

20.1-25%

25.1-30%

over 30%

From F. Braudel and E. Labrousse eds., *Histoire économique et sociale de la France*, III, p. 672.

But for it to work properly rotation had to be predictable so that the grazing land was open at the right time. But artificial meadows had, for their own protection, to be kept closed to the omnivorous nibbling of the herds, precisely because they were supposed to be permanent. They had to be surrounded by hedges, walls, fences or ditches, and effectively policed. The result was conflict and litigation, as rival farmers claimed rights and freedoms. Two ideas of freedom were in conflict here, the right to communal custom and the right to private property.[201] In a rich region where grassland was spreading, as in Normandy, enclosures may have been easier to enforce than elsewhere. The same was true of the Midi, where fallow land, *garrigues* and uncultivated lands were often very extensive and (provided the natural conditions were not too unfavourable) lent themselves better, with some exceptions, to artificial meadows and innovations than the open fields of the cereal-growing northeast, where the constraints of triennial rotation were more rigid and common grazing not so widespread.

The state would soon be taking the side of the rich and innovating landlords, encouraging the visible increase in production. After 1764, a series of regional edicts banned *vaine pâture* and *parcours*. The texts are clear and unequivocal. But resistance was universal and determined. Peasants fought grimly to hold on to their modest advantages. Nobles refused to give up their rights to *vaine pâture*. The *parlements* as we have seen, backed them up, and the Church also took their side, having unsuccessfully tried to extend the tithe to artificial meadows as it had to *novales*, newly cleared land. So a combination of watchful interested parties was in league against the artificial meadows.

Meanwhile the Assembly for the administration of agriculture, created in 1787, naturally came out against *parcours*, and just as firmly against the bans on *dessolement*[202] – but without any very concrete result. The provincial assembly of the Ile-de-France in 1787 granted any landlord wishing to create artificial meadows permission to enclose a field, provided its area was not more than a tenth of the property he owned.[203] This may have been an attempt at compromise, but it remained largely a dead letter. And with the Revolution, the Rural Code of 1791 would return to the communities the ancient rights they had never really forfeited.

Years passed, regimes came and went, but nothing was resolved. In 1836, the *Conseil d'agriculture* had to admit failure. The farmers of the Aisne, having been consulted, had all declared themselves in favour of keeping *vaine pâture*. It would be better, the Council's experts said, to feed the stock under cover, but in the present state of agriculture that did not seem practicable.[204]

They were not mistaken, to judge from the mini-revolution which shook the little village of Futeau (canton of Clermont-en-Argonne, *département* of Meuse) on 14 July 1861. Trouble broke out there on the afternoon of the national holiday. The mayor, who stayed at home, 'did not attempt to calm the effervescence' and 'one Dupont, François, chief of the fire brigade of the said *commune*, drummed up his men without receiving orders'. It was all in protest at the suppression of *vaine pâture*. It is true that there was a drought and the lack of grassland was becoming very serious. In the night of the 14th to 15th, 'the fences of the meadows were torn up', no doubt on the initiative of the same fire chief.[205]

What does one learn from this visit to Clochemerle? That it was not in the end King Corn, the primacy of cereals, that had been blocking the logical development of artificial meadows for over a hundred years.

By about 1861, lucerne, sainfoin and clover did nevertheless account for 2,500,000 hectares, or half the area of natural grassland in France. The revolution had taken place, but piecemeal and irregularly. By 1877, common land had almost vanished from the north-west, and with it 'the uncultivated land which in 1789 still occupied one eighth of the region'.[206] But *vaine pâture* was not suppressed by law until 21 November 1889, whereupon over 8,000 *communes* raised an outcry against a decision they considered catastrophic.[207] I remember seeing with my own eyes, in 1914 and even later, in our village of eastern France, the animals belonging to all the farmers setting off for the meadows in a single herd, as soon as the second haycrop had been cut: I can see them now, ambling along the grassy trail through the woods, by the side of the stream.

Always one step behind

If you look at all these new developments in farming in turn – buckwheat, maize, potatoes, colza, madder, sugar beet, artificial meadows – they have one thing in common. They all arrived from outside France – sometimes from far across the sea. But the decisive last step was always taken from somewhere in Europe, which surrounded France on all sides, linking us to the rest of the world but also separating us from it: buckwheat came via Holland, maize via Spain, potatoes via England, mulberries via Italy, artificial meadows via both England and the Netherlands.

Is that so surprising? Every economy, every society and culture, every political organism is constantly receiving items from the stream of cultural imports that circles the world. France was particularly well placed to receive them, being at the crossroads of so many routes: the sea-passages from the Baltic, the North Sea and English Channel; the overland routes from central and eastern Europe and Asia (along which, alas, animal epidemics could also travel); the busy Mediterranean traffic and finally the royal road of the Atlantic. Here lay the natural opening to the west, of which France did not take advantage in time, although it might have been possible to do so by employing the sailors of Dieppe, Rouen and Honfleur in Normandy or the thousands of Breton ships which were the workhorses of the European seas in the sixteenth century.

Countless cultural goods reached us along these routes: clinker-built ships for instance, and stern-mounted rudders – two revolutionary developments that came from the Baltic in the fourteenth and fifteenth centuries; or the stirrup and horse collar, which were to transform men's use of the horse between the eighth and tenth centuries, and which came from eastern Europe. Along the Mediterranean routes and up through southern France in the seventeenth and eighteenth centuries came new varieties of seed corn, plant cuttings, vegetables, fruit trees and flowers, which penetrated even our northern provinces. But all these gifts usually

283

came via intermediaries, and with some delay compared to other European countries.

Was France then in some respects a victim of its geographical position? Were the margins and extremities of the rest of Europe more sensitive than France to the teeming life of the wide world and the new things it had to offer? It was after all the 'extremities of Europe' which made the great breakthroughs: Russia in the sixteenth century annexed Siberia with its Cossack horsemen; the Iberian peninsula – with its easy access to the trade winds which like an untiring bellows blew any sailing ship westwards from the Canaries – discovered the New World. England, Holland and France came on the scene later: neither early America nor the furs and sleds of Siberia belonged to them.

But was it perhaps France's internal geography rather than its location in Europe that was to blame? Does France's great size and mass, inevitably condemning it to a fragmented life for many centuries, perhaps explain the time it took for any foreign innovation to penetrate our country, open though it stood to every wind? Is this the reason too why cultural imports made their way through France only slowly, although they all penetrated it in the end, meeting each other on their travels? This was as true of ideas and the arts as of material goods. Maize was to be found in Bayonne in 1570, but did not reach Castelnaudary until 1637 or Béziers until 1678.[208] The red and white Ugna grape, originally from Italy, had reached the Comtat Venaissin in the seventeenth century; it was not in Languedoc until the eighteenth, and only by the nineteenth had it travelled into the Saint-Emilion region of the Bordelais, and up to the Charentes, where it would eventually form the basis of cognac production.[209] The potato which Olivier de Serres was growing in the Vivarais in the sixteenth century was still unknown in many French provinces two hundred years later.

Immense and diverse, France was a constellation of different provinces: communicating only with difficulty, they were obliged, the *intendants* report, to live their own lives.[210] Some were condemned to mediocrity, remaining more attached to their old ways and customs; others, having both the desire and the means to innovate, had outstanding potential, but were to some extent exceptional and isolated by their very success. When Arthur Young left Bouchain[211] and crossed into Flanders, he went into raptures over its agricultural riches.[212] The contrast between this island of modernity and the average French province was still just as great, even in the nineteenth century.[213] In Flanders, the land yielded about 450 francs to the cultivated hectare, about three times the national average; there were 213 inhabitants to the square kilometre, one head of cattle per hectare; the manure from animals was complemented by compost from the towns, oilcake, bonemeal, sea sand and human excrement. That was what enabled the inhabitants of Flanders to 'extend their demanding crops without harming the fertility of the soil, and to show themselves to be superior even to the English as producers'.[214] And there was no fallow land here, for so-called alternative rotation had replaced it; nor were there any commons. But this region remained apart, more open to Belgian Flanders or Holland than to the rest of France. Other isolated regions, rich in themselves, were Artois, Pas-de-Calais, Normandy, Beauce and the Ile-de-France.

With their differences and lack of homogeneity, the French provinces were by no means perfectly communicating vessels. Distance and time of travel took their toll. As early as 1450, Gilles Le Bouvier defined France as 'twenty-two days long and sixteen days wide'.[215]

CHAPTER EIGHT

Animals, Vines, Cereals and Forests

Now that the main outline has been sketched in, we are faced with a mass of detail. Let us select and simplify, concentrating only on essentials (of which there are, alas, more than enough). Four main headings suggest themselves: animals, vines, cereals and forests. Rural France was governed, divided, torn apart indeed by these sectors: depending on whether priority went to livestock and grazing, vineyards and wine, cereal-growing and bread, or forestry and trees, four different Frances can be imagined, their boundaries far from clear.

Compared with the large areas devoted to cereals and livestock, or to the mass of woodland, France's vineyards might seem at first sight to take up very little space. But the wine 'industry' became a magnet, attracting population, since many hands were needed to toil in the vineyards. At times, wine-growing expanded uncontrollably: in the eighteenth century, the authorities tried in vain to restrict it, by forbidding the planting of new vines.[216] And growers took advantage of the relaxed vigilance of the Revolution to appropriate large tracts of arable land. The trend continued until about 1850 and even later. Wine-growing thus acquired at least 500,000 new hectares, a not inconsiderable area. The vine was even able in the nineteenth century to conquer the entire Mediterranean part of the Languedoc (originally the home of industry and cereals) unleashing a veritable fever of viticulture there, with consequences that are only too familiar. The fever spread to the whole of the south, once the railways were able to ferry southern wines quickly to northern markets.

In short, wine-growing, although occupying a much smaller area, was just as significant as the other three sectors, pulling its full weight in the economy. And it had some claim to be considered a more 'noble' activity. Writing of his homeland, the *Armagnac noir*,

Joseph de Pesquidoux noted in about 1920 how 'the careless shepherd or improvident ploughman of our region is galvanized into action once he sets his hand to the vine'.[217]

But in practice, none of our four sectors could do without the other three. Quite simply, they needed each other. There is an old proverb 'Qui a du foin, a du pain' ('He who has hay, has bread'), and it was quite true. In Normandy today, they still say 'If you want corn, don't plough up the meadow.'[218] One could equally well say that he who had grain had meat, or that he who had wine had bread. In Burgundy, grain was sometimes transported in casks, like wine. And anyone who owned woodland could make a living from it.

The overall picture

Where different zones abutted on each other, short- and medium-term exchanges made for good neighbours. Relations were established for instance between the horse-breeders of the *Marais poitevin* and the nearby cereal-growing plain of Fontenay-le-Comte; between the *Champagne berrichonne* and the well-watered grasslands of the Boischot and Brenne to the west; between Basse-Normandie, increasingly specializing in livestock, and the cereal fields of Argentan, Sées and Caen; between the Nivernais and the good wheat lands bordering the Loire, Allier and the Val d'Yonne;[219] between coastal Flanders and inland Flanders; between the choice vineyards on the heights of the Ile-de-France, the fields of wheat and rye to the east, and the flocks of sheep grazing on the chalk downs of the *Champagne pouilleuse*; between the vineyards of Bordeaux and the wheatfields of the Garonne valley. As for trees, they were the perpetual complement of every kind of husbandry.

Although their day-to-day activities kept arable farmers, livestock breeders and winegrowers apart, and even obliged them to be rivals, they were all imprisoned within the same force-fields, within what Paul Adam[220] has called the 'economic fields'. And these different kinds of French farming could act either as repulsive or as attractive poles within the same economic context. So to consider cereals, animals, vines and forests in one and the same breath is both a logical and necessary undertaking, ambitious and difficult though it may be.

Statistics from 1817

To give us a base-line from which to start, we need some reliable statistics. A push in the right direction comes from a useful document, which will not however take us all the way.

The document in question is a precise record dating from the end of 1817 and based on the *cadastre* (land register).[221] It provides, for each of the 86 *départements* France then contained, the income per hectare for the various sectors of production (arable land, vineyards, grassland and woodland). A fifth figure gives the income in francs of the average hectare in the *département*. In order to carry out these calculations, the areas devoted to the different kinds of production were measured.

If we look at the poorest *département*, bottom of the list – the Basses-Alpes – the five figures are as follows (arable, vines, grassland, woodland); 13, 30, 57, 2; average income per hectare was 6 francs 38 centimes. The wealthiest *département* (the Seine of course, despite being the smallest: only 10,000 hectares) was rated at 100 francs per hectare for arable (thanks to the market gardeners); 112 for vines, which were by now established around the capital; 84 for grazing land; and 108 for woodland which was becoming increasingly rare in what was left of the *département*. But the Seine *département* and especially Paris were exceptions on a truly monstrous scale.

If this massive anomaly is left aside, I wonder if you can guess which *département* was the richest agriculturally, according to average income per hectare, as calculated by this source? The answer, which may come as a surprise, is Calvados – where there were no vines, but where arable land brought in an income of 59 francs per hectare, grazing 83, and woodland 36. The average income per hectare was 78 francs 25 centimes, as opposed to over 100 for the Seine (the only *département* where the overall average was not calculated). There then comes a sizeable gap before the next names on the list: Manche 62.44 francs; Seine-et-Oise, 58.63; Nord, 58.17; Eure, 47.3; Jura, 46.4; Oise, 45.75; Seine-et-Marne, 43.35.

But our main concern at present is not this ranking order, (although it does indicate that the measurement of wealth as between *départements* was not governed by one or two simple geographical dividing lines, as people sometimes try to argue). What interests us for the moment is the competition for land as between cereal-farming, animals, vineyards and forests – to the extent that this can be deduced from the distribution of income.

It was tempting therefore to calculate for our 86 *départements*, that is for the whole of France in 1817, the *average* income per hectare of cereal land (26.8 francs); vines (47); grassland (60.9) and forest (16.4). The last figure is by far the lowest, and yet the forests were still in 1817 providing fabulous quantities of the necessary fuel both for dwellings and for the 'wood-burning industries'.[222]

Our 1817 record provides us with a matrix of 430 boxes (86 *départements* and 5 figures for each). So one could spend a long time on these calculations (see the maps and captions in Figure 35 which summarize these statistics). But alas we cannot assume the results to be either reliable or immediately comprehensible. Every *département* had all too many particular problems. Income per hectare from the different kinds of farming depended, among other factors, on the presence or absence of a local clientele to eat the cereals, drink the wine, burn or use the wood and buy the animals or their products. 'It is difficult to realize . . . what the slightest branch of the rural economy may become, once it has sufficient outlets,' remarks Lavergne, apropos the wealth that 'being near the capital' brought Normandy.[223] Income also depended on living standards and thus on wages, which certainly varied from one *département* to another. If one takes the annual wage of farmworkers for instance, this could be double in the north-west what it was in the centre or south-east.[224]

The comparative scarcity of a product and the size of the

demand for it also played a part in shaping prices and incomes. This explains why exceptionally successful vineyards might only bring in 58 francs income in the Gironde; 49 in the Marne; 46 in the Aube; 42.36 in the Côte-d'Or; but 83 in the Haute-Saône; 81 in Moselle (for the poor wine from the hillsides round Metz!); 79 in the Doubs; 75 in the Rhône; 74.64 in the Jura; 73 in the Haute-Loire, with the indisputable record being held by the Paris region – 112. A hectare of vines near the capital brought in 33% more than the best arable land in Flanders! Thus stands revealed an unusual and unexpected – but accurate – geography of vineyards and wine. For it was in regions where there were hardly any vineyards, and where their produce was of low quality, that the wine-grower made the best living – a paradox, explained by the impossibility, before the railway age, of efficient transport between an area of plenty and an area of scarcity.

Scarcity also explains the record income to be derived, unexpectedly, from grassland in the Bouches-du-Rhône. This is the highest single figure in the document: 282 francs. No other hectare in France brought in as much, even from vines. The discrepancy is explained by the scarcity of grassland between the stones of the Crau and the marshes of the Camargue, and indeed anywhere else in the *département*, and the large numbers of sheep coming down annually from the mountain pastures at the end of the summer. In the Camargue alone, 40,000 lambs were born every year, and the flocks grazed freely night and day: in about 1780, it contained '3,000 horses and the same number of oxen; the former are all white, whereas the local oxen are recognizable by their dark coats'.[225] Grazing land was at a premium for quite different reasons in Seine-et-Oise, Eure and Seine-Inférieure where it had the advantage of being close to the capital, thanks to the Dieppe–Paris highway. This was a good road, used daily by the fishmongers who brought fish to Paris as fast as they could. Dairy products took the same route, so Gournay, in the Bray, became the centre of a flourishing butter industry.

As for forests, which relied heavily on water transport, it is hardly surprising that these brought in an income of only 2 francs per hectare in the Basses-Alpes and 108 round Paris.

FIGURE 35
Average income per hectare in 1818

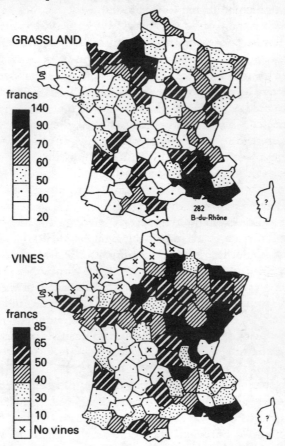

GRASSLAND

francs
- 140
- 90
- 70
- 60
- 50
- 40
- 20

282
B-du-Rhône

VINES

francs
- 85
- 65
- 50
- 40
- 30
- 10
- × No vines

Income from grassland, the highest of all, hit record levels in the Marseille area, where there was not enough of it, and in part of Normandy, which provided Paris's meat supply.

Income from vines tended to be higher than that from ploughland, and was highest of all not in areas with famous vintages, but around all the big cities, which explains why vines were grown whenever the climate did not make it quite impossible.

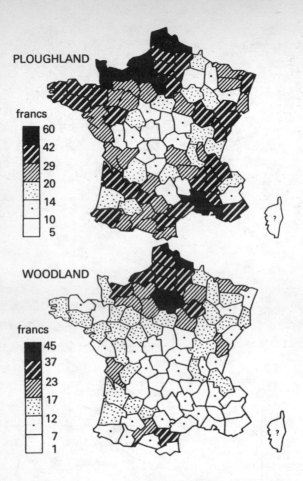

PLOUGHLAND

francs
60
42
29
20
14
10
5

WOODLAND

francs
45
37
23
17
12
7
1

High-income ploughland strikingly illustrates the poverty of central France and the superiority of capitalist agriculture in the north.

Forests brought in good incomes when they were near navigable waterways or could cater for the huge demands of big cities or fuel-burning industry.

The map showing average income per hectare once more reproduces the gap between northern and southern France.

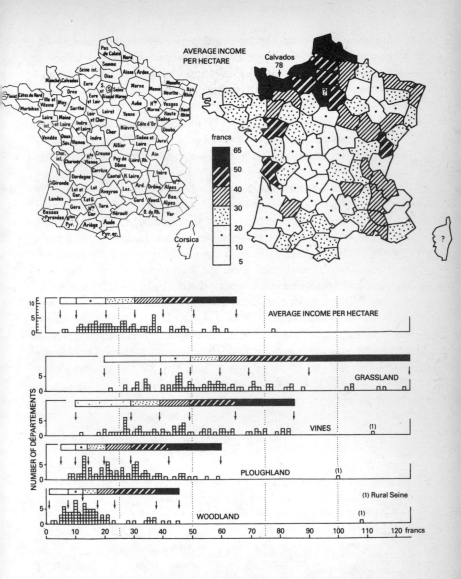

Diagrams showing distribution of départements *according to average income per hectare. (See key above).*

Such revelations may whet our appetite, but of course calculations confined to a single year will not do: we need long series of statistics both forward and backward from 1817. They are untraceable, or at any rate I have been unable to find any I regard as sufficiently reliable.

So for want of anything better, let us consider another set of figures, less satisfactory, let me say at once, and more rough and ready than the 1817 statistics. I have taken them from a rather little-known work.[226]

This suggests that in under a century – between 1785 and 1875 – French agricultural production of all sorts rose in value, in volume and in land surface area. Arable land, in round figures, rose from 24 to 27 million hectares; vines from 1.86 million hectares to 2.5; only grassland and orchards fell, and then only from 5.2 million to 5 million. The value (in this case the capital or resale value, not income) per hectare of arable land tripled, rising from 900 francs in 1785 to 2,700 in 1875; similarly, a hectare of fruit trees or grassland increased in value from 1,500 to 4,500 francs, while vineyards quadrupled, rising from 2,500 to 10,000 – a record increase. The spread of vineyards would undoubtedly enrich the French landscape, but without greatly disrupting it. Spectacular upheavals lay ahead, but vines were not responsible for them.

Old-style animal farming.
Rule no 1: the stock takes care of itself

Raising livestock in the past was not, need I say, the same as today. But the differences need explaining.

The first rule, observable almost everywhere, was that people lived at much closer quarters with farm animals than they do today, but they took far less care of them. Is this a paradox?

Nowadays, the breeder of livestock has to pay constant attention. 100 dairy cows in the shed, 1,000 pigs under cover, 10,000 battery hens – the scale of the operation means perpetual vigilance. Every farmer has to keep an eye on the fences enclosing the animals' summer pastures. Whether in the modern cowshed, scientifically organized, with a feeding-line, or in the model sheepfold or pigsty – often a building far from the farmhouse – the owner's responsibility cannot be relaxed for a moment: he has to observe a strict timetable, worry about medication and vaccination, and provide suitable feed by mechanical means. Maximum productivity, in quantity if not always in quality, can only be achieved by uninterrupted labour.

In the old days, on the contrary, most of the larger animals (cattle and horses) lived much of their lives 'abandoned to the hazards of the outside world',[227] unsupervised and often in a near-wild state.

In the first place, this was because, for most farmers, animals were a secondary resource, coming well behind wheat, barley, oats and rye. Cereals were king, and it was really because of them that livestock was kept on every farm, both for the sake of the manure and as draught animals: oxen, cows, horses, mules and donkeys were all used to pull carts and ploughs.

What was more, the peasant farmer has little time to spare, so his animals had to be raised as cheaply and with as little trouble as possible.

Leaving them to themselves had the advantage that it did not encroach on either the time or the land of the owner, since he could turn them loose to graze on heaths and moors, on waste spaces where gorse and broom flourished, on marshland, forest and hillsides. Wherever crops could not easily be grown, cattle and horses were sent, either at the beginning or the end of their lives, or indeed at any time it was convenient or necessary.

We know very little, it must be said, about this 'wild' animal-raising; historians are partly to blame for having concentrated on wheat to the neglect of livestock, with the exception of the very recent book by Jacques Mulliez.[228] One sometimes comes across a mention of it by chance – as a hunter is sometimes surprised by game.

So for instance we find an agricultural memorandum being presented to the estates of Brittany on 10 January 1731, condemning the practice of fattening an ox by turning it loose in an area of five or six *arpents* (of Breton moorland of course). Here it was left to fend for itself, except that its owner took the precaution of bringing it about five *milliers*[229] of hay of which the creature 'eats less than half, leaving the rest'.[230] It was rather an odd way to fatten cattle. But at least this stock was under some kind of supervision, since it was getting extra feed and was only temporarily abandoned. Such oxen had probably been used as draught animals before being prepared for slaughter. As Savary's *Dictionary* of 1772 tells us, an ox is 'fit to pull vehicles' at the age of three, and when it is ten years old 'it should be unharnessed from cart or plough and sent for fattening'.[231]

We find even more vivid images in the journal of the lord of Gouberville. This takes us back in time as far as the sixteenth century, but we move only a little distance from Brittany: to the tip of the Cotentin peninsula in western Normandy, where Gouberville's manor, Le Mesnil, was one day's walk from Cherbourg, in what was still very wooded *bocage* country. It was a fine estate, which Gouberville himself managed personally and with efficiency. Livestock occupied a considerable place in it, with separate buildings housing stallions, mares, cattle, sheep, pigs and goats. But most of the larger stock consisted, as Gouberville himself tells us, of *bestes saulvages*, 'wild beasts [which] graze in the forest', sometimes mingling with animals belonging to neighbouring estates, and reproducing freely. The problem was to catch them when they were needed on the farm or to sell at market. Something like a posse had to be sent out on these occasions, consisting of twenty or thirty men. And they often came back empty-handed, having failed to find the right animals, or having lost them again, perhaps after a struggle, as when a mare pushed over one of the farmhands and 'almost trampled his belly'.[232]

The entries in Gouberville's journal are quite extraordinary. On 24 June 1562, 'almost all' the cattle were rounded up: the youngest, the *veaulx saulvages*, 'wild calves', were probably branded that day, as was Gouberville's habit, and some were kept back for castrating. Another day, a hunting party was organized to go out and 'kill a wild bull' at the request of a buyer. Every so often, Gouberville would take a band of men out to *prendre du haras*, to round up his horses,[233] with varying degrees of success: he usually intended to catch young colts and fillies which would be hobbled and brought home for breaking in, or perhaps released again in the woods after branding.[234]

This sounds more like the Wild West than the French country-side, and takes us into territory even more neglected by historians than cultivation by hand, which is saying something. One is accordingly tempted to pursue the chase further, interpreting documents that are sometimes far from clear, in order to decipher a rather different landscape from the one history usually shows us.

In the eighteenth century for example, the 'calf-fatteners' of the Périgord were in the habit of buying young calves of twelve to eighteen months in the Haut-Limousin; they sent them to graze on 'poor quality grassland' until they were four or five years old, then 'after having tamed and mated them', kept a few for farm work, selling the rest.[235] It seems to me that these cattle, since they had to be *tamed*, must have been running pretty wild until then, like Gouberville's horses and bulls.

But the example of Basse-Alsace, about which we know rather more, is even more significant. The climate and vegetation allowed livestock to live out of doors for nine or ten months of the year. It was a peculiar kind of freedom, but they found plenty to eat in the forests, scrub and marshes which were more or less abandoned to them. Such grazing land, open to all, was often common land (*Allmend*), and had been so for centuries. In 1805, the mayor of Sélestat complained about the damage done by horses and cattle to the forests along the Ill, the river running through Alsace parallel to the Rhine: 'They destroy everything', he wrote, 'either by hoof or by tooth, and it is well known that a horse can do more harm to a clearing in a day than fifteen woodcutters.'[236]

But in fact grazing in Alsace had already been much modified by this date. The formerly extensive pastures had become inadequate as early as the twelfth and thirteenth centuries, as a result of land clearance and also no doubt because of the increased number of animals. In Alsace, as throughout north-eastern France,[237] regulations and enclosures appeared, fixed itineraries for moving live-stock were laid down by the authorities and eventually communal cowherds emerged.[238] Order was thereby established. Was this a pattern observable elsewhere? Would we, that is, find wild or only partly controlled grazing everywhere, if we could go back far enough? In the Bourbonnais for instance, during the Hundred Years' War, when the herds belonging to the peasants devastated the great forests, despite energetic protests from landowners?[239]

As far as horses were concerned, the old order sometimes survived as late as the nineteenth century, as Jacques Mulliez's fine book has established. Should this be attributed to the good sense of the horses – or to the laziness of their owners?

In Brittany, even in the eighteenth century, horses ran wild all year round on the partly-wooded moors and marshes. They had to survive ice and snow as best they could, digging up grass with their hooves in order to eat. If wolves attacked, they defended themselves: mares and foals would gather every night behind a protective row of stallions. Reproduction was uncontrolled. At some stage, usually rather late in the day, defective colts were castrated to prevent passing the disabilities on.

The same sight could be seen in the Béarn or in the central foothills of the Pyrenees. The so-called *navarrin* horse bred here, without any owner to take heed. Mares and stallions lived in the wild state, learning to fend for themselves from birth, to withstand the storms and early snowfalls, and to make their way surefootedly over the steepest slopes. When winter drove them down to the plains, they sometimes travelled as far as the *landes* round Bordeaux in search of grass. Small, sturdy beasts, fast and nimble once they had been broken in, they were used for hunting or light cavalry – so much so that the ending of Louis XIV's wars dealt a serious blow to the breed, from which (other factors also contributing) it never recovered. But it would take more than that to wipe it out. In August 1843, Victor Hugo, travelling in the Cauterets, discovered these horses and used one as a mount, finding it curious and original. 'These mountain horses', he wrote, 'are admirably patient, gentle and obedient. They will go up stairs and down ladders. They can venture on to grass, granite and ice. They will walk along the edge of sheer precipices. They tread delicately and with intelligence, just like cats.'[240]

An odd kind of horse-breeding also went on in the *Marais poitevin* – a region consisting largely of alluvial deposits from sea or rivers, and only partly drained by canals. The unstable soil was covered with trees and grass. An *intendant* reported that 'horses [breed] here almost without any cost or trouble . . . They are simply let loose in the pastures, where they graze summer and winter . . . Specialized breeding has led the peasants to keep only the mares, most of which are wild and never stabled, and do not know the touch of a human hand.'[241]

It was not a method that produced thoroughbred beasts of course. And we may wonder why, on the eve of the French Revolution, horses were still being raised the same way as during the Hundred Years' War. Was it because wild horses were difficult to break in? Or because horse-breeding (contrary to what one might think a priori) was less profitable than raising cattle or mules? Because it was more convenient to feed cattle in the cowshed, if only because of the milking and the benefits to be made from dairy products? There are probably other explanations too.

Rule no. 2: seasonal stabling and open air

Stabling (*la stabulation*) originally meant keeping cows in a cowshed (*l'étable*), but was extended to mean all enclosure of farm animals, whether in cowshed, stable, sheepfold or pigsty. Nowadays, animals may be kept in either permanently or seasonally. The first animal to be kept in all year round was the pig, once it began to be fattened at home, mostly on potatoes. Before that, herds of swine were taken into the woods to feed on acorns and beechmast, a practice that has still survived in some parts of Corsica. Gouberville used regularly to send his many 'hogs to look for acorns', *à la peusson* as he sometimes called it, in his oak-woods, with the loss of a few who went astray or were eaten by wolves. He also sold the right of *peusson* to other pig-keepers. But to meet the needs of his household (which consumed on average about fifteen pigs a year), he brought his beasts under cover for fattening in early autumn. No doubt this was a common practice, since acorns were regularly bought and sold. Gouberville laid in great stocks of them, sending his farmhands out 'to gather acorns', and even on occasion sold them or had them gathered by outsiders, going halves on the haul.[242]

Other farm animals were kept in only during the winter, since grazing was inadequate before the spread of artificial meadows and forage crops (that is, in most places until the nineteenth century). Keeping them in meant feeding them, not much, it is true, but at 10 pounds of hay a day for a dairy cow, one needed a well-stocked barn. They were turned out into the fields again as soon as possible, not always under supervision.

When the cold kept the animals indoors, the farmer's family lived alongside them and benefited from the warmth. Such close proximity was not without inconvenience and danger. In Brittany[243] and elsewhere, it was held responsible for poor health among the peasants. In mountain areas, men and beasts lived at close quarters for longer than elsewhere because of the intense cold of the winter. What a curious life these mountain farmers must have led, 'sleeping in winter in stables whose every crack was carefully sealed, where the moist air for want of renewal lost its oxygen, and where the stifling heat affected the natural functions' of the human inhabitants. There was a particular risk that on going out from this over-heated atmosphere, one might be exposed 'unsuspectingly to the chill outdoor air'.[244]

The animals suffered just as much, being fed, not always adequately, on hay or even straw. A Savoyard proverb had it that if the stocks of hay were only half used up by 23 February, all would be well. But it was not unusual, in Burgundy as well as Savoie, to call on emergency supplies at the end of winter: straw from mattresses and thatch from roofs might end up in the manger. The animals emerged so weak and emaciated from the experience that the cows sometimes had to be helped to their feet to get them out of the shed in spring. In Auvergne, where winters are hard, it is still traditional, even today, only to let the cows into the fields on 25 May, on the feast of St Urban, 'when neither bread nor wine will freeze . . . They must have an internal calendar, because as this date approaches they become restless. If we let them, they would walk out on their own.'[245]

Depending on the region, the release of the cattle took various forms. In many villages, they had not far to go. Out I used to go as a cowherd, in the morning or early afternoon, taking my dog and a few cows: we soon reached the narrow pasture where the herd would stop. My duties were very simple: the dog would be there to round up any stragglers tempted on to a neighbour's field (panic!). I usually had time to light a fire, and cook a few potatoes under the hot ashes. The delights of a country childhood! For it was usually children who were entrusted with this seasonal task. Joan of Arc as a child looked after her sheep in the Bois Chenu near Domrémy. In 1778, Nicolas Durival described the horses of Lorraine as 'small, degenerate . . . [but] willing and stronger than their size suggests; they are docile and nimble, obeying their master's voice; they are not prone to disease and are easy to shoe; many of them work all day and graze all night, watched by children or by dogs who are not strong enough to scare away wolves'.[246]

But most of the work, in our villages in eastern France, was done by professional herdsmen: the cowherd, the shepherd and the swineherd. They signalled their departure in the morning by blowing a horn, and the same again for their return at nightfall.

These were only small-scale migrations. In mountain regions, much larger movements took place. The animals had to go up in summer to the high pasture (*alpages*). But despite what one imagines, the usual practice whether in the Massif Central, the Vosges or the Alps was neither nomadism, nor transhumance, but migration 'within a small radius'.[247] Sheep and cattle did not go further than the pastures one could see from the bottom of the valley. If you arrived in one of the valleys before the herds were released, 'the sound of lowing would be coming from the great cowsheds, overshadowed [in the Alps and elsewhere] by spacious barns for storing hay. From the half-doors of the sheepfold, barred by hurdles, strong smells wafted out and one could guess at the sheep packed tightly inside, illuminated only by narrow cracks through which a few rays of light could penetrate the gloom.'[248] In the Vosges, a traveller tells us in 1696, the cows were capable of going up on their own to their summer pastures in spring and back down in autumn, but in the *chaumes*, the high pastures, they were watched by shepherds known as *macaires*, usually from the Swiss cantons.

They went up before the flocks and would live for months on end in wooden chalets, 'isolated from the rest of humanity and living on practically nothing but milk and cheese. Instead of bread, which they could only obtain when the price was low, they have a coarse and tasteless cheese to eat.'[249]

In the Alps, when April came, farmers had to 'make a path through to the fields, and to help the snow to melt more quickly they shovel earth on to it'.[250] Local conditions prompted different solutions. Often, where the mountain tops could not be reached at once, 'they go up by stages': there were two or three different levels of pasture. 'They stop first for a while in the "low pasture", *la montagne basse*, between 1500 and 1700 metres . . . And the same again on the way down.' Sometimes the flocks were entrusted to shepherds, hired for the most part at the crowded fair of Barcelonette. Elsewhere, as in the Tarentaise or Haut-Faucigny, the family would migrate to the summer pasture along with the flock. 'On the family farm, it is the women, taking their children with them, who go up to the mountains, watching the flocks and handling all the work, including making cheese, while the men stay down below to thresh and work the fields.'[251] According to region, the summer migrants to the high pastures lodged in individual chalets or in hamlets made up of houses clustering together like little villages.

On the return to the valley, the owner would separate his animals from others taken up to the mountains with them. He might distribute some to third parties for the winter, in return for milk or for an unborn calf. But in September most of the animals would be taken to sell at the livestock fairs.

Rule no. 3: the division of labour meant exchange, sale and resale

In the past as in the present, livestock-farming meant a distribution of tasks dictated by the division of labour, the latter more pronounced than it is today. Regions often specialized in certain livestock: the Poitou raised mules; the Perche and Boulonnais powerful horses; the Crau and Camargue, sheep; the Périgord, pigs, a production firmly controlled by the merchants of Bordeaux. In the case of cattle in particular, some regions were calf-producers, specializing in young beasts to be sold quickly; others concentrated on fattening up beef cattle; others again bought up calves and heifers and put them to work as soon as possible, handing them over to graziers when their ploughing days were done; some regions collected near-wild horses, broke them in, then took them to the fairs.

In short, the rule was that one bought to sell and sold to buy. This meant a brisk traffic between provinces, sometimes over long distances. Alpine peasants, hoping to improve their local breeds of cattle, went to buy stock in the Auvergne, the Ardèche or even the Haute-Loire. Limousins bought up beef cattle (which they would then fatten for the luxury butchers) from the farmers of the Saintonge, who had themselves bought the beasts as calves from breeders.[252] The farmers of Berry bought colts in Poitou, trained them to pull carts and ploughs and used them for comparatively light work, given the local conditions, before selling them to buyers in Normandy or Paris, where any horse in whatever condition was fit to pull a cab.[253]

In the Marche in 1768, 'peasants raised sheep of "a small breed" until the age of two or three, when they were sold in May or June at 8 or 9 francs a pair, to the Berry or the Bourbonnais'. Berry and Poitou were also in the market for young pigs, 'in August–September at 10 or 12 *livres* each, to be sold in winter for 15 or 18 *livres*, providing . . . the oak trees had produced enough acorns'.[254] The Alpine regions of Diois, Dévoluy, Champsaur and Vercors were supplied with lambs by the sheepbreeders of the Camargue, so that

> when several harsh winters, such as those preceding the Year XIII [1805] killed off the lambs of the Camargue, the prosperity of sheepfarmers in the Alps was threatened. It is easy to appreciate why when one discovers that [farmers in] the Dévoluy, which accommodated 7,000 sheep in winter, had bought 3,000 of them – almost half – in the spring.

The mountain farmers of the Isère went in search of sheep in Languedoc, those of the Beaumont travelled to the Vaucluse. I need not list further examples: the whole of France was thoroughly involved in this kind of activity.[255]

Specialization like this corresponded to various possibilities. There was grazing and grazing; not all pastureland would do for fattening. Habits and market pressures played their part too: France, like the rest of Europe, was full of fatstock fairs, which increased in number until the mid-nineteenth century. If the great international fairs like Lyon, Guibray and Beaucaire or even Bordeaux, were gradually dwindling in importance, regional fairs were still dictating the exchange and sale of both foodstuffs and livestock. For a peasant, animals were still the best exchange currency. In order to buy the things he needed, or to pay taxes and dues in cash, he would sell (often very young) his foals, calves or baby mules, which usually fetched good prices. After all, it was not unusual to sell a cereal crop while it was still in the ear. In fact the farmer only bought livestock in order to sell it again sooner or later, and those to whom he sold it, whether peasants or merchants, would hasten to sell it yet again. The result was inflation both for buyer and seller.

Animal products meanwhile – dairy goods, leather, wool – were continually despatched, if not to fairs then to markets in the towns.

The Auvergne exported its huge cheeses in every direction. They were to be found at Marseille by at least 1543,[256] and probably sooner. Cheeses from the Alps, weighing between 35 and 60 pounds,[257] were transported, sometimes in barrels, to Lombardy, Piedmont, Geneva, the Rhône valley and Provence. 'From the Tarentaise alone [which specialized] in this traffic, there annually travelled to Piedmont [in the eighteenth century] 6,000 formes of cheese, carried on the backs of mules.' [258] And as early as the Middle Ages, 'mares belonging to the Priory of Chamonix would come down to Savoy, carrying *séracs*, [259] quality cheeses and even butter'. [260] Anxious to export its goods, the Queyras had always vigilantly maintained the roads necessary for transporting its dairy products: 'the butter [of the Queyras] . . . was reputed the best in the Alps of Dauphiné or Provence; so it was sold not only at the markets of Gap and Embrun, but also on a large scale in Provence'.[261] All these exchanges were long-established. The Romans apparently knew and appreciated Roquefort, a cheese made from the sheep's milk of Larzac.[262]

But the best product was the animal itself – merchandise which had the great advantage of providing its own transport to markets and fairs and was not held up by untoward obstacles: there was no need to provide paved and well-marked roads for livestock on the hoof.

The peasants were unable to resist the regular call of the fairs, whether drawn there by necessity, ease of access, or by the promise of pleasure. They came to the fair to drink a jar of wine, to meet friends, and to hear the latest news. What self-respecting peasant could fail to drink, to dance to the sound of the pipes, or to enjoy a scrap with the mounted officers of the *maréchaussée*, if the latter were naive enough to turn up to restore order, or to try to arrest someone and haul him off on horseback? (Such was the occasion of one recorded brawl.)[263]

The most surprising thing is that after all these complicated transactions, and all the pains taken over them, profits were unfailingly low, especially if viewed by today's standards. The peasant of the past did not include in his calculations the trouble he took – on the contrary he was prodigal with it. It never figures in his accounts and this too was a rule and a more important one than it might seem.

Transhumance: the exception rather than the rule

Among all the rules we have been finding, transhumance[264] is an exception, something that was present for a long time and in many areas but an exception all the same. This was an ancient practice, as old as the world. A particular form of erosion down the ages, transhumance carved out roads, imposed its patterns of exchanges and established long–distance links between the winter pastures, in the warm plains of the Mediterranean and Aquitaine, and the summer pastures or *alpages* of the Massif Central, the Pyrenees and the Alps. In this process, the flocks rarely stayed anywhere long. It meant an orderly and well-planned movement over long distances, about 20 to 25 kilometres a day, supervised by specialized shepherds.

It does not matter very much whether the transhumance was the so-called direct or normal kind, or the inverse kind. In the first case, the owners of the flocks lived in the plain, in the second, they lived in the mountains. But in either case, this exodus of flocks and shepherds ended up, at each extremity of the journey, by being an intrusion from outside, with all the consequences and conflicts that implies.

The transhumance routes or drove roads – *camis ramaders* as they were known in the eastern Pyrenees, *drayes* or *drailles* in Languedoc, *carraires* in Provence – running as they did across regions that were both inhabited and farmed, containing villages and even towns, were always difficult to manage.[265]

Sometimes there was a coincidence of interests, when for instance a sedentary farmer hired out his fields to transhumant sheep and as a result had his land manured. Manure was always appreciated and still is today: as Rabelais put it of the sheep of Dindenault, 'in every field where they have pissed, the grain grows as if God himself had pissed on it; they need no other marl or manure'.[266]

But as a rule the sedentary farmer was the enemy. Some conflicts went on for ever. In the eighteenth century, the *intendants* of Languedoc often had to investigate the complaints of *troupeliers*, shepherds, who after being forced to give up transhumance for a few years – after an outbreak of disease for instance – had on their return found the drove roads so reduced on account of encroachment by neighbouring farmers that the flocks could not get by safely and 'the shepherds [are] ill-treated and forced back'.[267] The directory of local by-laws in the Herault *département* for 1936 tells us that most of the *drailles*, which ought to be preserved by the *communes*, had by then disappeared, 'some transformed into *chemins vicinaux* or *départementaux*, the others, although supposed to be rights of way, having been taken over by neighbouring farmers'.[268]

These flock movements, once so massive and still picturesque even today, are tending to die out. The total on the move today is about 700,000 sheep, nothing at all compared to the past. And nowadays the use of the railway or of three-tier transporter lorries, each containing up to 500 sheep, conceals from our view a sight which was traditionally to be seen in broad daylight throughout Mediterranean Europe. Photographers, scrambling to catch the last images of the old way of life, are only too aware of this.

Before they have completely disappeared, let us enjoy one of the surviving spectacles from the past, 'as in the days of the Bible and Virgil', as one commentator put it, 'an image from the depths of time'. But the year is 1980, and we are in the Pyrenean valley of the Soule, in May, when the

> great *artzain* [shepherds] [take] their flocks up to the high
> pastures which cover the ridge, the frontier between the Pic
> d'Anie and the mountain of Orry. They walk in front . . .
> surrounded by a cloud of dust, in a clamour of jingling and
> clanging bells – the *tzintzarrada*. Along the road, the flock
> moves to the respectable tinkle of small bells, but as they
> approach a village, they unload from the donkey's back . . .
> the biggest sheep-bells and attach them to the largest animals,
> so the flock sweeps through the streets like a brass band on
> the march, drawing the villagers to their doorsteps.[269]

The shepherds, 'known as the *aulhès* in the Béarnais, the *mountagnol* in the Commingeois, know how to talk to animals, to dogs and sheep, [they] can foretell the weather by the sky and heal by means of plants'.[270] Alone in their huts, with only dogs and flock for company, they spend months in the mountains. If they are at once feared, envied and scorned by the lowlanders, that is only one more example of a rule with practically no exceptions. The shepherd has always been a man apart, throughout Europe. He often had the reputation of being an *armier*, as they said in the south of France, a 'messenger of souls', an intermediary between the dead and the living, capable of communicating with the beyond, perhaps gifted with second sight. This was not exactly a question of witchcraft or black magic – although shepherds were sometimes accused of 'trafficking with the devil'[271] – but supernatural powers, a power that was both mysterious and disturbing. It was only one step away from being damned.

We might follow other guides in our search for transhumance: we might find it in the Provençal Alps with Thérèse Sclafert;[272] or we might accompany Marie Mauron who has lived alongside shepherds and described their life with infectious poetry,[273] or Anne-Marie Brisebarre who in 1978 travelled along the slopes of the Aigoual in the Massif Central, following the great *draille* of the Margeride.[274]

The difficult birth of scientific breeding

From about 1750, traditional stockbreeding was being severely criticized by French agronomists. They tried to impose upon French farmers, whom they considered ignorant and blinkered, the English model of selective breeding, by introducing foreign strains. Such attempts occasionally succeeded. In Maine for instance, in the nineteenth century, there was a clear improvement in the stock.[275]

But peasant resistance was stubborn. Too often, by the second or third generation of animals, the product had degenerated and breeders reverted to the local stock. In Normandy in about 1860, farmers were still wondering whether it was better to stick to the local breed of cattle – the Cotentin – with cows that gave 100 kilos of butter per head – or to improve it by crossing it with the English Durham; or indeed to replace it entirely by the latter.[276] The same questions were asked about the Morbihan cattle, 'of brindled black and white coat',[277] and more particularly about the Charolais, which after a series of improvements would produce the present excellent Charolais breed, known world-wide.

The royal government made determined efforts, from the seventeenth century, to promote progressive livestock-breeding in every form. Colbert set up the royal stud farms in 1665. Progress was often interrupted subsequently, but did it really cease altogether at the time of the Revolution? So thought at any rate the

Royal Academic Society of Loire-Inférieure in February 1833,[278] when it announced that the organization of the state stud farms was 'flawed' and deplored the disappearance of the old stud farms to be found in Poitou before 1789. The Vendée uprising, it further complained, had brought about the disappearance of 'stallions from England, Andalusia, Barbary, Limousin, Normandy or Holstein'.[279] Even if this was true, was it generally applicable? The pronouncements of a provincial academy are not necessarily holy writ.

It is however true that, by the end of the eighteenth century, long-standing and deserving efforts had resulted in the creation of the Percheron horse, which was bought up enthusiastically by the stage-coach service, as well as of that other successful breed, the Boulonnais. Similarly, in order to introduce the Merino sheep from Spain to Burgundy and elsewhere, an experimental sheep-farm had been created at Rambouillet in 1786. By some miracle, this farm survived the troubled years of the Revolution and Empire virtually unscathed, and after 1815, in the first years of the Restoration, it began to achieve spectacular results. This success too had taken many years, not counting the time it would later require to overcome the reluctance and ingrained habits of the French peasant.

But was the latter always wrong in preferring the breeds he knew best and which had long since adapted to their environment? According to Jacques Mulliez,[280] traditional stockbreeding conformed to 'popular common sense', as is borne out by the fact that despite all the earlier-mentioned comings and goings between breeders, fatteners and so on, clearly differentiated breeds did survive, adapting to local conditions and needs. The Montagne Noire was the home of cattle that were very small, yet capable of pulling ploughs or carts, and producing butter, cheese and milk. What would the farmers of the region be doing with the huge cattle from Poitou or the Pyrenean foothills, which provided strong teams for the ploughlands of Languedoc? It is no accident that the Tarentais or Tarin breed of cattle, described today as 'sturdily resistant to abrupt changes in temperature, as well as to hunger and fatigue' is a 'typically Alpine breed'.[281] Breeding regions were in fact *catering for the demands* of potential buyers. They maintained a homogenous herd of reproducing females, of a breed corresponding to the locality and requirements of the region they supplied, and used bulls of various origins without necessarily keeping to the same strain. So every breeder ended up producing a particular kind of cattle for a given region, whose farmers could confidently apply to him.

What was now being suggested was on the contrary that new strains be introduced to modify the breeds in such a way as to improve them. This meant the disruption of the usual markets. The new aim was to obtain 'thoroughbreds' with pedigrees to establish their purity. And the long-term intention was to select and ensure the transmission of *high-yield*, that is quantitative, capacities and thus of certain breeds, destined to supplant others on account of their superior milk, butter or wool production or, in the case of pigs for instance, for having a high ratio of meat to fat.

The breeding of pedigree herds did not really become widespread in France until the twentieth century, with the coming in the late 1950s of artificial insemination. Recently however genetics experts have become aware of the danger of a drastic reduction of the gene pool, the result of having opted for 'the extension of certain breeds, profitable under present economic conditions, and the extinction of hundreds of others'. To diminish 'intra- and inter-racial variability' in this fashion would, in the long run, threaten the *qualitative* features of the domestic breeds at present being farmed, and efforts are now being made to turn back the clock and protect endangered species.[282]

Traditional stockbreeding can perhaps only be understood properly in the limited context of available and readily accessible natural resources of the past. The only kind of stockfarming about which care was taken was the very specialized sort created by the demands of urban markets in general, and the Paris market in particular, for high-quality fatstock. This encouraged the cattle-fattening industry of the Limousin and other regions, above all Normandy, which catered for the luxury market. The Limousin method in the eighteenth century was complex and sophisticated. The animals were selected younger than usual, at about six years old. 'Since there is no shortage of young bullocks who benefit by working, the older ones are sold off when money is needed.'[283] In the *canton* of Chabanois, the beast to be fattened was turned out into a meadow, but slept under cover. When there was no grass, it fed on hay and also on a beverage prepared from walnutmeal (the residue left in the press, after the oil had been extracted) which had been soaked in warm water. These privileged creatures went outside only in fine weather. In their sheds, they drank water thickened with rye or barley flour. Their litter was dry and plentiful. Fatstock benefited from the same care and precautions, I almost wrote the same luxury, in the nearby *canton* of Pompadour where equally magnificent bullocks were reared: they grazed outdoors until the beginning of November, then came under cover to be fed on hay and cattlecake made of chestnutmeal and other cereals.

As a rule, these choice beasts were sold for high prices at the end of Lent, to celebrate the break of fasting. And yet whatever the fattening diet adopted (which varied from *canton* to *canton* within the Limousin) the whole operation brought the breeder only a modest profit. A long document of 1791 which describes this kind of farming reports that profits hardly covered the extra feed. 'Bought thin for 200 *livres*, the beast is sold fat at 300 [but] the profit [when set against expenses] is only 60 to 70 *livres*.'[284]

Stockbreeding being what it was, it gave rise to various amusing complaints, which also illustrate once more the gulf between northern and southern France. If every region produced certain kinds of stock, it was by the same token short of certain others. Poor Arthur Young complained that between Toulon and Cannes he could not find a cup of milk. And we may also smile at the discomfiture of a less well-known traveller, Pigault-Lebrun, who arrived at Orange in 1872:

There is as much chance of finding an olive tree in Siberia as a cow in the slaughterhouse at Orange. The only available animals are small sheep, very tasty actually, which are served in every imaginable manner. You sit down to soup, as you might anywhere in France; but here this first course is made with mutton. A clove of garlic masks the taste of meat. You drink sheep's milk; and you eat butter and cheese made from sheep's milk. It was certainly not for the benefit of the Provençals that Noah took a cow and bull into the ark.[285]

Can the curious history of the horse in France be explained?

When describing the cattle being fattened in the Limousin, I praised demand as if it automatically produced supply. Why then, did this pressing demand for quality horseflesh have to look abroad for satisfaction? I am willing to accept as an initial explanation – necessary but not sufficient – the argument advanced by Jacques Mulliez. He wonders whether there was not, in far-off feudal times or even earlier, an age when France *did* produce good-quality horses at home, and whether this was not gradually destroyed by Crown policy. The aim would have been to attack the nobility as a political force; to tame it and bring it to heel. It was a policy long and patiently pursued. 'When Richelieu ordered the destruction of fortified castles, he simultaneously wiped out the noble stud farms. In its desire to break the feudal system, the Crown was also destroying what had been the instrument of its supremacy: horse-breeding.'[286]

We have also to consider a longer-term explanation, it seems to me. The best horses, those whose blood was necessary to the stud farms after the seventeenth century, came from North Africa and the Middle East. These were the breeds used to launch the great stud farms of medieval Andalusia and the Italian Mezzogiorno, Naples in particular, regions which took advantage of being close to the source. The French were trying hard to acquire these magnificent horses in the sixteenth century, and no doubt earlier than that. They attempted to contact the countries of origin by direct purchase or reconnaissance trips, and even thought of setting up a permanent trading-post in Tripoli. All in vain. In the eighteenth century, 'the obstacles were almost insurmountable' for any Frenchman who wished to buy direct from source. He usually had to go through the consuls of the Barbary coast, who were not the most efficient intermediaries. When good Barbary horses were needed for 'the king's stables and stud farms',[287] a special emissary was dispatched with near-plenipotentiary powers! Did the French simply arrive on the scene too late? Was the market already closed to them? Geographical location will not do as an explanation, since England, though less well-placed, was turning out thoroughbreds before France. The only other possibility, but it is hard to prove, is that our eastern frontier, the most threatened and the greatest drain on the military budget, found it advantageous to buy cavalry mounts near at hand, in Germany or the Swiss Cantons.

Stockfarming: a one-time marginal activity

Nowadays grazing and stockfarming have taken their revenge all over France. This is the direction in which farming has moved: 55% of France's agricultural income now comes from this source. In the past, flourish though it might, livestock-farming did not find the same favour nor enjoy the same superiority. It was in a sense secondary and somewhat marginal. Indeed in most cases, it was merely the accompaniment to or consequence of farming the land.

Robert Chapuis, the attentive historian of the Loue valley – that wide cleft running east–west across the thick limestone plateau of the Jura – notes that in the eighteenth century the villages along the banks of the fast-running river kept 'only a few animals, to pull the plough, manure the field or vineyard, and provide the milk the family needed for making gruel, as well as enabling it to eat a few joints of meat when the beast was slaughtered'.[288] None of the products from this livestock ever reached the market. And contrary to what one might think, the Loue valley was not some quiet little backwater, cut off from the rest of the country. It was in fact favoured by the communications it made possible between the foothills of the Jura and the high plateaux to the east. It had its own cereal fields, gardens, and a string of reputed vineyards, as well as a series of mills and prosperous industries sited along the swiftly-flowing river. In the circumstances, it could afford the luxury of animals catering entirely to its own needs.

The Loue valley was a special case, true. But it can be the point of departure for a more general reflection. The various kinds of livestock-breeding that did well all over France had more than one feature in common. The most important was that they were *not* destined for the peasant's personal consumption. Only pigs were incorporated into the producer's own diet: he did not eat his own lambs or sheep, nor even in many cases his poultry, cattle, or the calves which Parisian butchers bought in Normandy: 'milch-calves' if under ten weeks old, 'grazing calves' once they had tasted grass.[289] In the Alps, flocks were bigger than elsewhere and provided cheese and milk, 'the [providential] solid basis of the Alpine diet'.[290] But there was little meat available for the peasants themselves to eat: every year the Faucigny sold a third of its animals on the hoof, mostly destined for Geneva.[291] This was an appreciable source of cash, a way into the market. Add to this the benefits of haulage in the winter season – a trade possible for anyone who owned a draught team.[292] It is certainly true that animals were an important supplement to the farmer's livelihood, but usually that is all they were.

Wherever livestock dominated or monopolized rural activity, it deformed and disfigured it in the eyes of the peasants, who remained attached to their polyculture. At any rate the peasant, who was until the twentieth century a figure of fun for certain sections of French society, consoled himself by venting all his scorn and ill-will on the shepherd or cowman, whose whole life was devoted to his animals. For once convinced of his superiority, the peasant found that he could poke fun mercilessly at someone else for a change. It is a strange phenomenon, and a curious kind of revenge: one finds it in Normandy for instance. The *pays* of Bray is a geographical 'buttonhole': an opening in the chalk of Picardy, uncovering the layers of clay – a land of running water, lush meadows, hard to cross on foot, planted with fruit trees. This region used to send to market in Gournay an endless supply of huge mounds of butter, for the never-satisfied Paris customers. In the Bray, the grass just grows and the animals feed themselves. The

Brayons, the local breeders, needed do nothing but leave the stock to its own devices. The cereal-growers in the neighbouring Beauvaisis had great scorn for them, and were always ready with insults for the 'lazy guzzlers' of Bray,[293] as if it were a crime to like feasting and large meals, as if it were a sin to be one of those Normans who 'made money out of their meadows . . . without lifting a finger', and who were allergic to 'spending money or making an effort'![294]

Improbable though it seems, the arable farmer's scorn for the shepherd and livestock farmer has carried on down the ages into the present day. In 1920, Daniel Halévy met in the Périgord a peasant who had migrated there from his native Corrèze and had devoted titanic efforts to working his fields and vineyard. But now old age was creeping up on him. Would he have to be content simply to keep sheep? Would he

> just sit and watch the grass grow and the sheep eat it . . .
> *Berger!* [Shepherd!] He curled his lip as he spoke this word
> . . . What he valued most was hard and unremitting labour,
> growing wheat, or flax, or vines – expert husbandry. Sheep-
> farming, according to him, was below a man's dignity. Shep-
> herd indeed! . . . When he repeated the word, it was with all
> the scorn of the sedentary farmer for the nomad, the civilized
> man for the primitive.[295]

It has often occurred to me that if Europe had not given itself over to its age-old persecution of the Jews, it might well have tormented shepherds, those men apart since the beginning of time.

The riches of the vine

The northern limit of the French vine as a *commercial* plant runs from the mouth of the Loire to about Metz or Trèves/Trier. When I say *commercial*, I mean that although the vine can be grown further north – and was in the past – it is not commercially viable to do so today.

Even south of this line, the vine's presence is often discreet. It will be found nestling in the thousands of bends in valleys and hills',[296] exposed to the first warmth of the rising sun. As one travels through France, it will appear round one corner, to vanish at the next. It is only found in large expanses in the true Midi, in Provence, Languedoc and Roussillon, but even here does not completely submerge the landscape.

The most famous vineyards are strikingly small in area. This is true of the celebrated Côte d'Or, in Burgundy: 'from the valley of the Ouche to the valley of the Rheune, [the Côte] unrolls its narrow ribbon of vineyards, bearing some of the greatest names in the world' – Nuits, Chambertin, La Romanée, Clos Vougeot.[297] And the same is true of champagne, which was in 1860 being grown 'on a sort of strip of land between Brie and Champagne', measuring some 60,000 hectares.[298] Of the 50 million hectares of French soil, wine has only occupied, at different periods, between 1.5 million and 2.5 million: between one thirty-third and one-twentieth.

But this was ultra-valuable soil, much more profitable in income per square foot than the cereal fields alongside. Hence the extreme subdivision of vineyard properties, sometimes prompted by historical circumstances. In 1898, to take one example, in the Ribeauvillé vineyards of Alsace, 'there were 894 hectares of private property . . . divided into 8,967 plots'.[299] The same would be true of the Côte d'Or, or the vineyards of the Touraine and elsewhere. Etienne Chevalier, a winegrower at Argenteuil near Paris, explained in 1790 'the *surprising difference* that he had observed in the Ile-de-France, between the population in localities dependent on the plough and that of places where thanks to the vine, *it took only an arpent* to provide for a *marriage*'.[300]

Thus it was that the vine alone, from very early times, made it possible for the independent peasant to acquire small plots of land, with all the consequences that implied. It has often been stated that France, unlike England or Germany, was essentially a country of small landowners. It should be added that it was chiefly through the spread of the vine that it acquired this character,[301] and that it was the result of a long evolution. Did the vine also encourage a more scattered habitat, as the revolutionary Raymond Lebon claimed, rather hastily perhaps in 1792, whereas cereal-growing regions were notable for large villages, separated by wide tracts of land?[302]

The history of the vine – a complicated success story full of fascinating incident – in fact raises problems at every stage of historical inquiry. Talk about vines and you are talking about society, political power, an exceptional labour process, in fact an entire civilization.

If bread stands for the body of Christ, wine is the symbol of His blood. If wheat is the prose of our long history, wine is its more recently born poetry, illuminating and ennobling the landscape. Wine, Georges Durand explains in a book dedicated to its celebration, 'does not spring from the soil, but from the pleasure of the mouth and the joy of the heart . . . Consumption of wine . . . goes beyond the mere satisfaction of a biological need, it is attached by a thousand ties to a whole art of living.'[303] In other words to a civilization. The vine has set its mark on all the countries that have adopted it, growing everywhere with astonishing vigour. And it thrives in any kind of soil.

Even in places from which the vineyards disappeared, after the major crisis for winegrowers brought about by the spread of the railways, they have left behind indelible traces. It is still possible to recognize a winegrower's house: it will be tall, and its cellar will have an immense porch big enough for the tuns in which the wine used to be kept, since the wine stores would have taken over the entire ground floor, while a staircase, often outside the building and of more than modest proportions, would have led up to the living quarters.[304] Even the landscape where vines have once grown shows telltale signs of the past: in the countryside round Laon, or Besançon or Bar-le-Duc, one can tell where the vineyards were, by the bushes and shrubs that have invaded the now untended land, and by the zigzag paths used long ago by grape-pickers at wine harvest, as they climbed up and down with baskets full of grapes. And I am not alone in thinking of the formerly viticultural valley of the Ornain (the river that runs through Ligny-en-Barrois and Bar-le-Duc) that it is the long-vanished vine that explains the unusual neatness and elegance of the old winegrowing villages – as well as the cheerful wit of their inhabitants. These are no slow-witted yokels or *houle-mottes* (turn-sods) as they used to call the villagers who worked the fields.

The spread of the vine

The vine was brought to Gaul by the Greek settlers in Marseilles in 600 BC – so it arrived well before the Romans. An early vineyard was planted near the city and the Greeks sold wine to the Gauls.

Roman viticulture came later but made more impact. It began with the occupation in 122 BC of the Narbonensis, or Provincia, broadly speaking present-day Provence and Languedoc. Vineyards were planted near Narbonne and quickly spread throughout the Provincia. In 111 BC, during the Teutonic invasion, which was finally halted by Marius at Aix-en-Provence, the barbarians went into battle intoxicated with strong drink. Plutarch tells us that 'their bodies were heavy with excessive feasting, but the wine they had drunk, by raising their spirits, had made them all the bolder'.[305]

The early success of winegrowing led to a brisk trade in wine to northern Gaul:

> The natural cupidity of many Italian merchants [Diodorus Siculus *dixit*] exploits the Gauls' passion for wine. The merchants transport their wine by boat up the navigable rivers, or by waggon across the plains, and they make unbelievable profits from it, to the point where an amphora can be traded for a slave: so that the purchaser sells his servant to pay for his drink.[306]

(This is not unlike the present-day drug trade, from which so many people make fortunes: the dealers, middlemen, smugglers and the opium-poppy growers in the countries of origin in the Far East.)

It looked as if the vine was poised for rapid extension. But at this point, for some reason, history stood still. The vine took a long time to move beyond the Mediterranean south. In northern and western France, it was faced with harmfully low temperatures,

FIGURE 36
Viticulture and the wine trade in Roman and Frankish Gaul

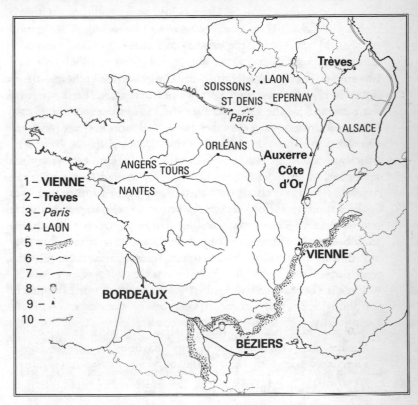

Places known to have been producing or exporting wine:

1. In the first century AD
2. In the third century
3. In the fourth and fifth centuries
4. From the sixth to the ninth century
5. Limit of the Provincia Narbonensis during the early Roman Empire

6 and 7. Main river and overland routes used to transport wine in Roman times
8. Significant remains of amphorae
9. Inscriptions or figurative monuments from Roman times concerning the commercial transport of wine by water or overland
10. Chief export routes for wine in Frankish times

Wine was already being exported to northern customers from Roman and Frankish Gaul.

Source: R. Dion, *Histoire de la vigne et du vin en France.*

which the olive tree, another Mediterranean native, would never be able to withstand. The vine, being more adaptable, did eventually overcome this obstacle, after the discovery and introduction of new vinestocks – one the ancestor of the *pinot* of Burgundy, another the ancestor of the *cabernet* of Bordeaux. Thus there came into being (possibly from the wild vine, *lambrusca*, which only vanished from French forests during the phylloxera epidemic of the last century) a type of grape capable of ripening by the first frost of the autumn. In the first century AD, the all-conquering crop spread up the Rhône, beyond Vienne, and around the edge of the Cévennes until, north of the Naurouze Gap, it reached the Tarn valley at Gaillac – a crucial link leading to the Garonne valley and Bordeaux.

Once it had travelled this far, the conquest of the rest of Gaul could not fail to follow, more rapidly in some places than others, one imagines. Vines were not established on the hillsides of Burgundy until AD 311.[307] It is claimed they were in the Rhineland by the sixth century, after the arrival of the barbarians,[308] which does not entirely convince me.[309] Both Bordeaux and Moselle wines were becoming famous by the end of the Roman Empire.[310] But the vine was encouraged in Gaul by the early increase in consumption by ordinary people. Production levels were so high in the reign of Domitian (87–96) that wine began to travel the other way, from Gaul to Italy. Was it to protect Italian vineyards and to maintain wheat production in Gaul that Domitian ordered a halt to the spread of vines in Gaul? There was even talk of pulling half of them up – not, one imagines, that it ever came to anything.[311] Two hundred years later, during the reign of Probus (276–82), the whole of Gaul was granted permission (was this still necessary?) to plant as many vines as it wanted.[312] So that by the time Roman rule came to an end, vines were to be found almost all over Gaul.

They were everywhere – even in cold regions where one would hardly expect them. The reason was the slow pace of transport, despite any images we may have of boats or waggons laden with casks of wine. The customer, the consumer, who was the motive force behind production, if not himself a producer, preferred to have wine within easy reach. So whenever it was possible (or to be more accurate wherever it was not impossible) towns had their own vineyards within sight of the houses. If the emperor Julian (331–63) recalled with pleasure the time he spent in Lutetia (now Paris) it was because the town was surrounded by gardens and vineyards, offering him a familiar sight to look out on.[313]

When Roman Gaul began to collapse, even before the great invasions of the fifth century, vines, winegrowers and wine were not swept away in the *débâcle*. Barbarian Gaul had plenty of wine close at hand, without going abroad for it. Vines were cultivated around the towns and close to the abbeys.

All the same, winegrowing did decline. It was linked to the market of wine consumers and there were fewer of them in the now dreadfully impoverished towns. The only ones to survive in any shape were the episcopal seats; consequently the bishop became the protector, inspiration and saviour of viticulture. Rich monastic orders also planted vines round their abbeys: the Church always needed communion wine in order to celebrate mass. And wine continued to be a symbol of wealth and hospitality, the obligatory offering of courtesy and friendship among the high and mighty. Princes, like monks, were protectors of viticulture. But what had almost completely disappeared was the long-distance wine trade, particularly in the Atlantic: in Roman times, there had been brisk trade with the British Isles and northern countries.

Winegrowing would flourish once more as soon as trade picked up, with the economic revival of Europe, from the eleventh and twelfth centuries. There were more rich customers in the towns and more wine-drinkers in the newly prosperous northern regions, where vines would not grow well if at all. The deprived northerners were the thirstiest drinkers of all: it was the English, in their island where the vine was only an occasional curiosity, the people of Flanders, the Low Countries and northern Germany who would rekindle the export trade that brought northern *esterlins* flooding into France. Wine is gold dust, as they said in the thirteenth century.[314]

But transport was costly, so costly that only wine of high quality, jealously preserved, could afford to travel; hence the concentration which prized some vineyards higher than others and quickly

FIGURE 37

*Towns and bourgs in Aquitaine recorded as exporting wine to
England in the thirteenth century*

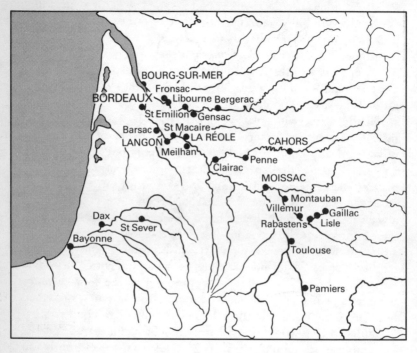

By the thirteenth century, exports to England had already led to the
development of the vineyards of Aquitaine in all the localities where
they would be found in the eighteenth century (cf. Figure 38), apart
from areas where the distillation of spirits was introduced in the
seventeenth century.

Source: R. Dion, *Histoire de la vigne et du vin en France.*

pushed them into a modernization process that can already be
described as capitalist. Such was the case of the Burgundy vineyards, which did not pass with impunity into the hands of the rich
members of the Dijon *parlement*; and of the Bordeaux vineyards,

FIGURE 38
Disposition of crops in south-west France in the eighteenth century

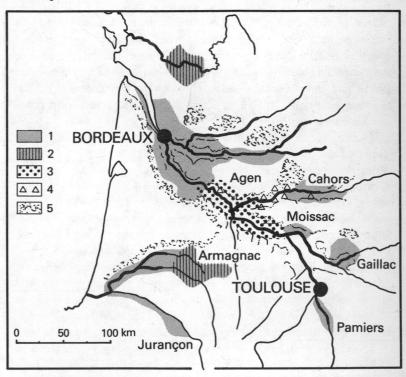

All agriculture directed towards external markets (French or foreign), was closely connected to navigable waterways; this applied to wine above all (1); to brandy and spirits (2); but also to preserved prunes from Agen (3); tobacco (4); and even the export of oak wood for making casks.

Source: P. Claval, *Eléments de géographie humaine.*

particularly prosperous ones, which fell into the hands of the aristocracy of the Bordeaux *parlement.*[315]

Export followed the easiest and cheapest routes, using waterways and sea-passages whenever possible. This explains the transport along the Loire of the wines from its own banks, including those of the Forez. The Saône and the Rhône were pressed into service too, as was the Yonne, which carried not only the logs floated down from the Morvan but also casks of Chablis. The Marne ferried the wines of Champagne, which would see their stock rise in the eighteenth century when the champagne process was successfully developed. Even the Meuse was called upon to transport the sharp wine of the Barrois towards Liège; while the Rhine had contributed from early days to the creation of the glorious vineyards of Alsace. Strasbourg was the collection point for wine in transit to the North Sea.[316]

Two early successes were encouraged by the Atlantic route. Those of the Saintonge and Aunis wines, exported via Saint-Jean d'Angély, the first window on the outside world, and La Rochelle, a thriving export centre. Then came the fortune of Bordeaux wines, later but more brilliant. Bordeaux owed its success to the fillip provided by the privileges it received from the king of England. By great good fortune, La Rochelle fell into the hands of the king of France and could no longer cater to English demand. It was this English thirst for claret that promoted the rise of Bordeaux, encouraging the cultivation of the *graves*,[317] the marshes and woodlands near the city; it also encouraged the refinement of the vintages and made the fortune of the inland vines, at least along the banks of the Garonne. Export was the spur.

So make no mistake, when the *intendant* Basville declared in 1734 apropos the wine of Alès that 'it did not travel', he was pronouncing its death warrant,[318] or at any rate condemning it to be no more than a little local wine. The same *intendant* tells us, this time of Gaillac[319] in the 'diocese' of Albi, that it

> produces the only wines that can be transported. This means there is a brisk trade in them down the river Tarn, which becomes navigable about here. They are carried to Bordeaux, where the English buy them and they have the advantage of adapting to sea-travel and improving considerably in transit.

It was a quality also possessed by the Languedoc wines which the English shipped from Sète: 'These met with great success in

London. It had been feared they would not survive the sea passage, but this turned out to be wrong, and the Navy has never had better.'[320]

Wine was sometimes accompanied on its travels by distilled spirits, from the sixteenth century and as a result of encouragement by Dutch buyers.[321] In smaller quantities for the same price, spirits were easier to ship. The length of the voyage held no terrors for them. They could be shipped from Sète (encouraging production in Languedoc) as well as from Bayonne, Bordeaux and La Rochelle, (thus promoting the brilliant success of cognac and armagnac brandies). Even in inland provinces like Burgundy, Champagne and Lorraine, grape musts were distilled. In Champagne, where (if you can believe it) beer was making progress as much as anywhere, and where wood was scarce, brandy was nevertheless being distilled.

It was during these centuries that the really *great* vineyards took on their individual character. By Colbert's time, they probably corresponded more or less to the area they occupy today. But other things have not remained equal since then, far from it. For vintage wines were not the only ones.

Popular viticulture

Vineyards, which originally belonged to the rich and powerful, were for long centuries worked by peasants as sharecroppers or wage-labourers. Their lot was probably rather better than an ordinary farmworker. But the many tasks meant continuous toil: digging, hoeing the soil between the vines, uprooting and replacing old stocks (although a vine can last a hundred years), carrying on their backs the earth that rain had washed downhill, pruning the shoots every year, whether long or short.

About pruning there were many opinions. In Bar-sur-Seine, there was a saying 'Prune early, prune late, prune in March for the best estate.'[322] In Champagne in the nineteenth century on the other hand, farmers claimed that it was 'a widespread mistake to prune the vine, and plant cuttings out, in early spring. It seems that if this work is done in early autumn, the vine will not waste its sap in useless buds and flowers.'[323] In Languedoc, in the 'diocese' of Lodève in the eighteenth century, the growers pruned their vines in winter. In spring the roots were exposed; the vineyards were ploughed 'twice a year, first in February or March, then in April, May or June; if the second ploughing was impossible because of drought, it was postponed until November'. The ploughing was done with a 'light plough known as a *fourcat*, with a metal share'. Where the vineyard sloped steeply, the peasant had to resign himself to digging with a spade, *fossoyer* as it was called. 'Many vineyards sited on terraces have to be repaired continuously.'[324]

All this careful tending was swamped at grape-harvest by the hordes of casual labourers taken on as 'pickers, carriers and tramplers, under the orders of the master of harvest. [In the Beauvaisis] the harvesters were fed copiously on solid soups and veal tripe, and received several sous a day.'[325] These were mere unskilled labourers.

The winegrower on the contrary was a craftsman. 'The winegrower is more important than the vine.'[326] For the vine, which will grow vigorously anywhere (try it yourself and see), is constantly being remodelled by the grower. He can turn it into a climbing plant with long tendrils twining round a support, or into a stocky shrub, with a gnarled trunk, requiring no stake to hold it. He can change the taste of the grape, the alcohol content of the wine, the abundance of the harvest or a particular quality, by experimenting either with grafts or with the soil of the vineyard, which he may vary to suit him – by strewing it with stones, as is the practice in some places, or on the contrary by manuring it heavily, so as to 'enrich the wine and make it less subtle and delicate'.[327] In short, the winegrower has to master many sophisticated skills.

From as early as the fourteenth century, when the vine had revived everywhere, conflict began to appear between the owners of the vineyards and the winegrowers, conflict that would only increase with time.[328] It surfaced earliest near the cities, Paris, Lyon, Orleans, Tours, Sens, Auxerre, Blois, Metz. The urban population was emerging from a time of rapid growth and the bourgeoisie was competing with the nobles and the Church.

FIGURE 39
Supplies of cheap wine to Paris in the seventeenth and eighteenth centuries

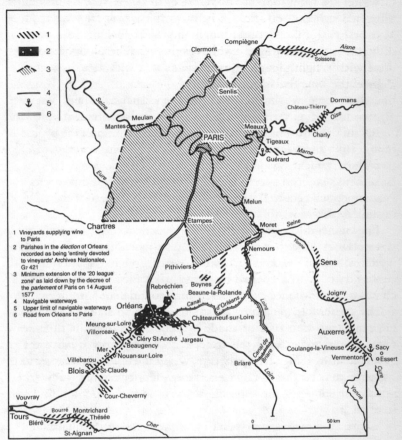

Legend:
1 Vineyards supplying wine to Paris
2 Parishes in the *élection* of Orleans recorded as being 'entirely devoted to vineyards' Archives Nationales, G7 421
3 Minimum extension of the '20 league zone' as laid down by the decree of the *parlement* of Paris on 14 August 1577
4 Navigable waterways
5 Upper limit of navigable waterways
6 Road from Orleans to Paris

In an effort to protect the quality of Parisian wines, a decree of 1577 established a zone around the capital, about 80 kilometres in radius, in which wine-shop owners from Paris were forbidden to buy wine. In practice, it became the favoured site for the production of large quantities of very poor wines which were sold in the *guinguettes* outside the city boundary. Paris also received cheap wines transported along all the waterways leading to the capital, as well as along the good road from Orleans.

Everyone wanted to possess vines and made it a point of honour to drink wine from one's own vineyard. In great demand near the towns, the vineyards shot up in price, and were split up into plots, over which quarrels broke out. But when a property was reduced to less than two hectares, it was impossible for it to support the household of the winegrower or *closier*. As a result, day-labourers, of a skilled kind of course, were called in to cultivate these numerous little bourgeois properties.

But these workmen, who were indispensable and knew it, presently developed the ambition of owning their own vines and selling their own wine. Finding a plot of land was not the problem: any land, unfit for cereals, could be turned into a vineyard. The real investment was one's labour.

Thus was born a long-lasting conflict between landowners and workers who contrived to rob their masters of part of their working day. In theory they were bound to work from sunrise to sunset. But vineyard labourers fell into the habit, in order to 'work their own vines', of either arriving late in the morning, or leaving off in the middle of the day when nones rang (three in the afternoon). If they dared so to defy their employers, it was because their struggle was a *collective* one. If we are to believe Etienne Pasquier (1529–1615), the word *tintamarre* (meaning a din) is derived from the noise the winegrowers of Blois made by knocking a stone on their *marre* (the winegrower's shovel) to let each other know it was time to leave off working all together.[329] When the town authorities, after complaints by the landowners, succeeded in making the workers stay at their posts, the same signal was used to down tools, for a sort of sit-in.

The landowners were reacting in the name of the quality of the wine, about which they were passionately concerned, both for their own glory and that of their town; whereas the workers, on their tiny plots of land, planted not noble stocks selected by tradition, but coarse grapes (*gamay* in Burgundy, *gouais* in the Ile-de-France), which were easy to grow and very productive, but of far inferior wine. If they finally triumphed over the landowners, it was because their strategy catered for a heavy demand for ordinary cheap wine, as popular wine-consumption increased. Such demand was not rural: in the countryside, wine remained a luxury for high days and holidays, and even in the eighteenth century the winegrowers themselves were content with what they called *boisson*, obtained by adding water to the grape residue left in the bottom of the press (also known as *piquette*, *buvande*, etc. depending on locality). In the towns, on the contrary, it was traditional, when the master of the house was drinking wine, to allow his servants to drink wine too, though of different quality. So domestic servants in towns were accustomed to wine, as were artisans. And as the urban population increased, so too in considerable measure did the consumption of wine, especially after the reign of Henri IV.

So there grew up a popular viticulture which 'helped the vineyard labourer to shake off the bourgeois yoke, while at the same time diminishing the quality of the vineyards by stocking them with gross vines'. Thus fine wines died out altogether from the country round Laon, Orléans, Auxerre and Paris:

> The high price of labour and its lack of goodwill, combined with the inclemency of the climate, made profits melt away. The bourgeois landowners were obliged either to sell up, or to pull up their vines. The winegrowers bought the land and hastened to plant it with high-yielding rather than fine vines.[330]

A similar process, but for quite different reasons, could be seen in the Atlantic west, favoured by trade with Holland. Whereas in Bordeaux the English clientele had developed vintages of high quality, Dutch demand in the seventeenth century had the opposite effect. The Dutch wanted spirits, either for fortifying wine or as pure alcohol. But brandy could be distilled from quite ordinary wines. As it spread quickly along the Atlantic seaboard and into the hinterland served by the Adour, Garonne, Charente and Loire rivers, it would lead to the widespread development of high-yielding but mediocre vines. The slide was rapid. As a memorandum on the Angoumois remarked in 1725, 'in the past, only the bourgeois and rich people owned vineyards. Now almost all the peasants . . . have planted their own', and there was no labour to till the property of the bourgeoisie. So it was tending to disappear.[331]

This development explains why the winegrower enjoyed a higher standard of living than other farmers. Although a mere labourer, he was able to defend himself and it was comparatively easy for him to acquire land. In Burgundy, on the eve of the Revolution, 'the winegrower eats better than the farmer on the flat land . . . He quite often eats white bread.'[332] Arthur Young remarked at about the same time upon the privileged position of the winegrower compared to the rest of the French peasantry.

Wine as an industry

Like grain, which had to go through the grindstone at the mill and the oven at the baker's before it became bread, the fruit of the vine also had to be transformed into wine, though in this case the process remained in the hands of the producer. Does it therefore count as part of farming life – or was it in fact an industry?

Industry or not, it was a highly diversified activity, as one can ascertain by turning to Savary des Bruslons's *Dictionary* of 1772.[333] He teaches us to distinguish between the *mère-goutte*, 'the wine which runs spontaneously into the channel leading from the vat, before the harvester has started to crush the grapes'; the *surmoust* or *moust*, 'the wine from the vat after the grapes have been crushed'; the *vin de pressurage*, which comes from the press containing the half-crushed grapes, with stems attached (*rafles*) from which wine has already been pressed'; the residue left after this process, the *marc*, 'which is made into *boisson*' (by pressing it again with added water); the *vin doux* 'which has not yet been boiled'; the *vin bourru* which has been prevented from boiling; the *vin cuit*, 'which has been heated before boiling, and therefore always retains a sweet taste; and the *vins de liqueur* 'including the muscats of Saint Laurent and la Cioutat in Provence; those of Frontignan and Barbantane in Languedoc; those of Condrieux in the Lyonnais; those of Arbois and Mâcon in Burgundy; those of Pouilly in the Nivernais'. If one brought his list up to date to cover present production, it would go on much longer.

If moreover one were to try to list all French wines, according to their renown, price per cask or bottle, and their customers, a whole book would not suffice. And then there were the coopers, the carriers and the whole business of storing and preserving wine, the huge cellars in Champagne round which, during the Second Empire and earlier too no doubt, 'a coach and four could quite easily have been driven'.[334] One would have to think too about the various kinds of winepress, often feudally owned, so that winegrowers were obliged to mix their grapes, a practice against which they never ceased to protest. It was not so much a single industry as a collection of industries, or of groups of industries.

Did the winemaking industry prejudice the prosperity of other industries in the area? Colbert certainly thought so. Anxious to develop textiles and in particular to increase the number of handloom weavers in both town and country, he wondered whether this would be feasible in Burgundy: 'In establishing this kind of trade', he explained, 'it should be noted that between two towns equally suitable for the purpose, one of which is in a winegrowing district and the other not, one should always choose the one without vines, for wine is a great hindrance to industry'.[335] And it was probably true that, as Roger Dion writes,

> It was non-winegrowing France, from Laval to Rouen, Cambrai and Fourmies that proved to be the habitat par excellence of the domestic looms [of rural industry]. South of the northern limit of commercial viticulture, by contrast, it rarely seems to have occurred to the rural population that a cottage industry of spinning and weaving could have been an effective remedy to their problems.[336]

Viticulture and industry it seems, did not go together. But is this perhaps a simplification?

In the eighteenth century, Languedoc was a poor and densely populated region, continually invaded by immigrants from the even poorer neighbouring areas of the Massif Central. It desperately needed something else besides cereal-growing, which was entirely in the hands of bourgeois or ecclesiastical landowners. The vine found its way on to the most unpromising land, and was moreover out of favour with the rich, so that in the countryside round Lodève for instance, as around Montpellier and other towns and villages, it was the poor people, some of them day-labourers (*brassiers*)[337] or urban artisans, who were determined to own a small vineyard and make their own wine. But this micro-winegrowing was not simply devoted to local and essentially popular consumption. It produced substantial surpluses, which were exported to Italy – notably such sought-after products as *muscat*, a fortified wine grown on the slopes of Frontignan and other villages.

Yet at the same time, Languedoc was the home of a flourishing textile industry: cloth for the army was manufactured at Lodève, and fabric for Middle Eastern markets was made at Clermont and Carcassonne. This industry underwent a series of concentrations, which made the life of the poverty-stricken weavers precarious, but their labour contributed to the rise and economic equilibrium of the province.

What is one to conclude, except that the problem in the end concerns the balance not simply between industry and wine, but between industry and living standards. Winegrowers were as a rule quite comfortably off. Why should they emigrate to the towns if they were managing perfectly well where they were? And why should they accept work under the putting-out system for rural industry, which was less well paid than the same work in the towns, if they did not need the extra income? Similar reluctance was to be found in the rich cereal-growing plain around Caen. When the town's merchants tried to recruit spinsters in the local villages, they found the peasant women unwilling to cooperate: they were prepared to take the work only if it was well paid. In this rich grain-exporting region, the peasants were by no means starving.

When in 1750, an ingenious Englishman set out to establish in France a weaving industry on the English model, capable of supplementing French production, which region did he choose? The Gévaudan: not because its vineyards were mediocre, but because the people were very poor.[338]

The three French winegrowing zones

The history of the vine can be summed up by drawing two lines across France: one to the south, marking the northernmost limit of the olive tree and embracing the whole Mediterranean region – the earliest and if you like the 'natural' vinegrowing region of France. Further north, another line marks the northerly limit of the vine as a *commercial* crop – and again I would stress the word 'commercial'. This line runs eastwards from the mouth of the Loire across the whole of Europe to southern Russia, the Crimea and Persia, where in winter the vines are earthed over against the frost.[339] This was Europe's good luck line – the luck lying to the south of it of course, hence the dominant pattern of the wine trade: after every grape-harvest, wine travelled north. Venice bought wine with high alcohol content from the Marches and Naples, but in turn allowed fleets of German waggons known as *carretoni* to carry away across the Alps the unassuming white wines of Friuli and the Veneto.[340]

Our two lines divide France into three winegrowing areas.

The most remarkable of the three is the central belt, containing the vineyards of Bordeaux, the Loire, Burgundy, Champagne and Alsace – though I would leave out Lorraine, where there are still some strips of vineyard in the region around Toul and Metz.

I hope it does not sound like boasting to say that this zone of France can claim to contain the finest vineyards in the world. (Others have thought so besides the French.) Yet in this belt, subject to winter cold, the vine had to be redeveloped, stocks had to be selected that would adapt to the climate, bearing grapes that could be harvested long after reaching ripeness, thus allowing *botrytis cinerea*, 'noble rot', to work on them, increasing their sugar and alcohol content. Sauternes grapes are even harvested with scissors, snipping the grapes off here and there, in several gatherings, taking only the fruit that has rotted.[341] This practice, which makes Sauternes 'the most elaborate wine in the world', dates back only to 1845.

The central belt of France certainly does not seem to have been predestined by nature for this exceptional role. But is that as true as it might seem at first sight? For there are vines and vines. The kind that were planted by the Romans in Gallia Narbonensis well before Christ, were not the same variety that spread up the Rhône, into the territory of the Allobroges in the first century AD. Pliny the Elder mentions this new variety as one adapted to *cold* climates, ripening with the first frosts (still the case today in Burgundy but inconceivable in the plains of Languedoc for instance).[342] And in fact the two 'noble' varieties of grape, the *cabernet* and the *pinot*, both of which can stand damp and cold, seem to be descended not from Mediterranean stocks but from local wild vines in the case of *pinot* and possibly from a Cantabrian variety in the case of the Bordeaux *cabernet*.

What was more, the central belt vineyards were favoured by their geographical location. The thirstiest consumers of wine lived, as we have already noted, in the north; so France's greatest vineyards were well placed to supply their customers. The advantages of an export trade also meant that the quality of these wines had to be maintained and protected, requiring vigilance, extreme care and investment. That is still the rule today.

The second winegrowing zone, north of the Loire, is apparently very easy to describe. Its history is simply that vineyards were planted round almost every town for local consumption, and they survived there as long as carriage remained difficult. Once transport improved, these northern vines went into decline. They had always been strangers in an unwelcoming climate, a prey to irregular harvests, for the crop could be wiped out by frost or rain. Their decline began with the rise of the great maritime routes in the twelfth and thirteenth centuries, which shipped to northern Europe the wines of the central belt; and the final blow was dealt by the railways, which carried north the abundant wines of the south. The grape thus retreated to a more 'normal' climatic zone.

But this explanation is a little too cut and dried, since northern France did, here and there, maintain wines of good quality (or could have done so). In our own day, we have seen the rebirth of *fine* wines in the Paris suburb of Suresnes.[343] So climate cannot explain everything. Roger Dion has pointed out that just at the time when southern wines first reached northern tables, farmers were experiencing a new burst of enthusiasm for the cereal-growing economy in its perfected form, whereby sugar beet or forage crops were replacing the former fallow land. Bankers, businessmen and agronomists all concurred that 'grain and live-stock are the only things worth farming'; that the industrial pro-duction of sugar beet was a hundred times better than winegrowing. In short, the retreat of the vine was not so much a consequence of the climate as of the 'frontier separating types of arable land of unequal quality'. It disappeared from all rich ploughlands; surviving by contrast (on the banks of the Loire for instance) wherever 'the soil was not so capable of bearing . . . rival crops as it was north of Paris'. As Mathieu de Dombasle said in 1829, 'We find rich farming almost exclusively confined to the northern *départements*, where the vine is not cultivated; and the prosperity of agriculture decreases the further south one goes, in virtually the same proportion as the spread of the vine.'[344]

As for the third France, the southern region, the most naturally suited to the vine, and the first in France to cultivate it, it was for many years at a disadvantage compared to the central belt, which barred its route to the good northern markets, including those of the capital.

The change seems to have begun in the eighteenth century. The terrible winter of 1709 meant that northern markets really opened up to wines from the south: the vines of the Midi had in part escaped the devastating frosts which ruined northern vineyards that year. The sudden rise in the price of wine brought casks flood-ing north from the Midi to Paris.

But the real breakthrough came with the railways. The geography of wine was turned topsy-turvy. Beaujolais now really hit the Parisian market. Further south, the Languedoc, which had hitherto divided its production between wines, manufacture and cereals, threw itself frenziedly into wine growing. The establish-ment of what was soon an overwhelming monoculture revolution-ized its economy. The phylloxera crisis (1865 to 1890) – 'the most important event of the Third Republic' as Gaston Roupnel used to

FIGURE 40
The spread of phylloxera in France

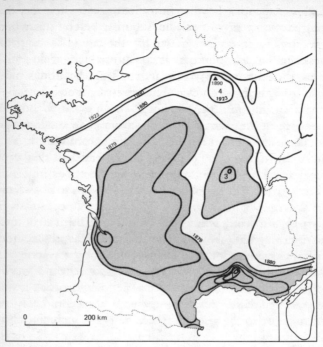

1. Pujaut (Gard); 2. Floirac (Gironde); 3. Beaujolais; 4. Champagne.
The shaded area shows the extent of infestation by 1879.

Source: P. Claval, *Eléments de géographie humaine.*

say[345] – obliged winegrowers to embark on the painful reconstitution of the French vineyards from American phylloxera-resistant vines, but at the same time the vine took over the plains of Languedoc, reaching almost as far as the coast. It was at this point that wine prices collapsed dramatically, as a result of overproduction. Small proprietors and vineyard-workers rioted, and troops had to be called out in 1907 to quell protesters distressed to find that with 'good wine' they could not even buy bread.

Should one stop here? Is it enough simply to look at the history of vineyards and wine? Or should we perhaps, if only for a moment, spare a thought for the average drinker? For the Parisian workman of the nineteenth century let us say, who every Sunday patronized the *guingettes* of the suburbs, where the wine was cheaper because it did not have to pay the city toll (*octroi*)? Or for the traveller in any century, as he unwittingly makes his way towards a local wine? Arriving in a village, he drinks his wine straight from the cask, and since he is getting it at source, he pays less for it. In 1703 (but he does not tell us in which month) Henry de Rouvière,[346] the king's pharmacist, who was travelling south, noted that it was at Montmirel, 12 leagues from Meaux, 'that we began to drink some excellent champagne, just as good as Vieux Maison' [three leagues nearer Meaux]. Stopping to drink could be worth it. Arthur Young treated himself to a bottle of Sancerre (white presumably) outside the little town of Vatan, and as a bonus it only cost him 10 *sols*, whereas it would have been 20 in town.[347]

But then who has not had the unexpected pleasure, on a journey undertaken with no thought of drink, of tasting a wine one remembers all one's life? In about 1920, some friends and I were on a cycling trip devoted to tracing the frontier between the Barrois and the *pays* of Joinville, when we came to the deep valley of the Marne, where the new season's white wine was waiting for us. Was it as delicious as my very inexperienced palate of those days told me?

Last but not least: grain or rather grains

I decided to break with convention by not beginning this chapter with a discussion of grain. I was afraid that grain, because it is so important, would simply dwarf the rest of the landscape from the beginning. And since it has reigned over a whole agricultural complex, determining and influencing it, I thought it might be preferable to look at the rest of the complex first before coming to this, the essential element.

Was it really so essential? Well, what could be more basic than eating to keep alive? But more than this, does grain not represent, as Pierre Gourou has pointed out, a *choice of civilization*, a choice made long, long before what we call history, just as the choice of rice or maize for many centuries determined the destinies of the peasantry in the Far East or in pre-Columbian America? Once such choices had been made, it would be very hard for men to extricate themselves from them.

Before going any further, let us make it clear that we should not talk about grain in the singular but about *grains* in the plural. Our ancestors may have used a single word (*blé* in France, 'corn' in England and so on) to mean any cereal you could turn into bread – wheat of course but also barley, oats, spelt, rye (still the most cultivated cereal in France in the eighteenth century),[348] *méteil* (a mixture of about equal quantities of wheat and rye), buckwheat; not to mention *petits blés*, 'small grain',[349] which referred not only to grain sown in March, such as barley and oats, but also to peas, vetch, beans, lentils and so on. As Olivier de Serres said, 'the word *bled* [*blé*] is generally taken to mean all grains, including those pulses that are edible'.[350] As late as 1898, a sociological investigator claimed that the chestnut, a vital foodstuff in the Massif Central, 'plays the role [there] of a cereal; it replaces bread. And this is a bread obtained without farming; it needs no ploughing, sowing, harvesting or threshing', in short, the writer concluded, 'it encourages the peasant in laziness and lack of initiative'.[351]

Blé then, meant anything that ended up as bread, but wheat was 'the heaviest and best of all grains . . . the one that contains the whitest flour, of the best quality and in the highest quantity'.[352] But in terms of volume harvested, rye led the field until the nineteenth century. This explains the survival of *pain bis*, or 'wholemeal' bread, which was often made from a blend of lesser cereals rather than from wholegrain wheat flour as the term means today. Desired by everyone, white bread, that is bread made from wheat, did not become widespread in France until much later than historians usually reckon, well after the revolutionary and Napoleonic wars at any rate. Raymond Lebon in 1792 stated that 'the man who constantly feeds on wheaten bread is more alert, more robust, more fit, and less subject to disease'.[353] The average Frenchman would have to wait some time to reach this happy state.

Grain and its constraints

Grain was the constant concern of the authorities, an obsession, holding them in its thrall. How was the new season's harvest looking? It was under continual observation, every change in the situation being noted. Everyone knew that only the harvest would determine whether people could breathe easily or on the contrary prepare for hardship and shortage. Although none of the so-called histories of France gives it its rightful place, grain has always been the chief character in the history of our country, at least until the nineteenth century. 'King Corn' reigned through the services it rendered, the benefits it granted and finally the constraints it imposed.

In the first place, it 'rotated', that is it was not as a rule grown two years running on the same land. It therefore made crop rotation a continuous practice. All the agronomists have their way of explaining it:

> The non-permanence of grain on a given field [says the comte de Gasparin in 1831] results from the insufficiency of manure, the impossibility of combatting the weeds which grow faster than the grain, and the difficulty of [first] clearing the ground on to which the seed is sown.[354]

Another expert in 1843[355] talks of the laws of vegetation, namely that plants are nourished by certain elements in the growing earth and eliminate their waste products into it, thus poisoning the soil if the same crop is planted twice in a row. 'We see in a natural meadow that whereas a single species of plant may have been abundant in one place, it disappears at the end of its natural span, to be replaced by others, so that the hay one gathers is never identical two years running.'

But there are other plausible explanations for the near-universal rotation of grain crops.

The growing cycle in fact took more than a calendar year, about 14 to 16 months, since the process did not begin with the usual sowing in September or October. The soil had first to be prepared, whether for winter wheat or rye, by a number of ploughings. If the furrow was deep enough (as dug by a heavy northern plough) three or four would be enough; but where the swing-plough was used, as in the south of France, more would be necessary: before the Revolution, the fields of Poitou used to be ploughed no fewer than nine times.[356] The inadequate swing-plough did no more than scratch the surface of the soil. It attacked

> the layer of earth which it turns up by undercutting it then turning it over on to its side, so that it is actually placing the ploughed layer on top of a lower layer, which it never touches; and since the first layer is no more than about four inches deep, far from burying the weeds, the *araire* simply gives them a helpful turning over . . . Soon after every ploughing, one sees them spring up again everywhere, which makes it necessary to . . . repeat ploughing frequently, so as to make the weeds disappear by dint of tormenting them.[357]

So ploughing had to be done over and over again, until teams and men were worn out. The aim, never achieved to perfection, was to expel all the plants that might threaten the crop – corncockle, vetch, cornflower, wild oats[358] – otherwise whatever one did, the weeds would overtake the growing corn, since they flowered earlier. And then one would be faced with the sad sight which met Pouget the chronicler in 1527, in the countryside near Cahors: fields 'laid waste with weeds', where there are more 'wild oats than wheat'.[359] 'Clearing the soil, and destroying the plants that grow spontaneously', writes Mathieu de Dombasle, 'is as important as fertility for the abundance of the crop one may obtain'.[360]

The area ploughed with such persistence and precaution was the fallow land, left to rest for a year precisely in order to let the plough have a chance to clear it. The final hoeing (where it was practised) was thereby rendered much easier. In Lorraine, before 1914, the farmers used to hoe the wheat to get rid of the many thistles.

This preliminary ploughing took a great deal of time and energy. And the land had also to be manured in time for the autumn sowing. This was heavy work. Even on a small farm, it took 150 cartloads of manure between the penultimate and the final ploughing – the latter to bury the sown seed. Then the harrow, with a heavy weight on top, would be hauled over the field to level the furrows, or 'plough [them] flat' as it was sometimes described.[361] The opposite practice was to plough in *billons*, with steep mounds between deep furrows, to enable surplus water to run off.[362]

But to return to the subject of crop rotation: everywhere, the fallow land would be given a first ploughing in April. By now the grain sown on other fields in September or October the year before would already be up and either sprouting or about to sprout. So the two crops coexisted, one still only a promise, and in need of further ploughing, the other ready to yield a harvest in July or August. When one thinks about it, the corn that the harvesters reaped, that the women gathered into sheaves and then piled into small ricks in the fields would have taken between 14 and 16 months to complete its cycle, if one allows for the preliminary ploughing. Whether it was 14 or 16 depended on whether ploughing began early, and whether the harvest came sooner or later. So the cycle was longer than a calendar year. Duhamel du Monceau realized that this was why crops rotated, but he pointed it out in such a terse and elliptical sentence that his meaning is not easily taken at first reading: The peasant 'cannot sow wheat every year on the same land', he writes, 'because there is not enough time between harvest and sowing to fit in the required ploughing'.[363] The agronomist and historian François Sigaut,[364] took up Duhamel du Monceau's explanation, and one of the arguments he makes is clearer than a long treatise. It refers to a significant example in Lombardy, where

the summers are very hot (it is claimed that Milan has the summers of Naples and the winters of Amsterdam) and the wheat is ripe by mid-June. This early harvest leaves a space of over four months until the next sowing in November. [The

341

farmer] takes advantage of the breathing-space to have the land lie fallow and be ploughed four times, with enriching [literally 'green'] crops[365]

– such as clover – then the wheat is sown and covered by the harrow. In this exceptional example, the wheat year fitted into a calendar year, so wheat was (or could be) sown two years running on the same soil. The necessary conditions were fulfilled: enough ploughing plus the vital enrichment of the soil, provided in this case by *cultures dérobées*, forage crops.

But important as it was, the calendar did not explain everything. It was clear that cereals, with their short roots, exhausted the top-soil. So it was important to have them alternate with root crops, such as beet, turnips or potatoes, which sent roots deep into the earth in search of nutrients, and above all fixed the nitrogen from the air. Their left-over tops, ploughed under after harvest, acted as a fertiliser.

Crop rotation (the field system)

The Milanese case – an exception – proves the rule that cereals are subject to regular rotation, a topic that has fascinated historians, so much so as to distract them from anything else.

The geography of crop rotation is extremely well known (see Figure 43). North of a line from Saint-Malo to Geneva, the dominant pattern is triennial. The arable land is divided into three *soles*: wheat, *marsage* (that is, cereals sown in March such as barley or oats) and fallow. The latter in theory means a complete rest for the land – *la jachère morte*. So if the territory is represented by a circle with three more or less *equal* sectors, the circle turns every year – wheat replaces fallow, *marsage* replaces wheat, fallow replaces *marsage* and so on indefinitely.

South of the Saint-Malo–Geneva line, biennial rotation is the rule, with half the land under wheat, the other half fallow, changing over every year.

So we have a division, a pattern typical of France, but what is the reason for it? Why were these procedures so obstinately entrenched either side of the line? The more closely one looks at an apparently simple problem, the more complicated it becomes, and easy answers recede or become ambiguous.

In the first place, the two parts of France we have identified each contain variants, not numerous perhaps, but puzzling.

There are some exceptions to the triennial rule. In the late eighteenth century, Basse-Alsace, formerly faithful to triennial rotation, suddenly switched over to biennial.[366] Much earlier, at the end of the Middle Ages, the Thiérache region had gone over to biennial rotation and allowed itself to be invaded by enclosures and hedgerows typical of the *bocage* country.[367] The *pays de Caux* has always been, as far as the records go back, a partly *bocage* region, with biennial crop rotation. But at the end of the *ancien régime*, enclosures made rapid progress there.[368] And I have already mentioned the curious case of the *Gâtine poitevine*, which shifted from *campagne* to *bocage* in the sixteenth century, as noble landowners altered the shape of the fields they possessed.[369] And that is not the end of the list: the Révermont in the Jura 'went over to *bocage*' after about 1770;[370] while the valley bottoms of the Boulonnais at about the same time were 'in the process of being enclosed'.[371]

We should also mention the perfect exception formed by farming Flanders: faithful to the 'alternating regime', it closely followed the revolutionary agricultural practice of the nearby Netherlands: the soil never rested and fallow was unknown. Beyond Bouchain, travelling north, 'you are among gardens' where the usual resting of the soil was unheard of.[372] Was it because one was leaving the land of idleness for the land of hard work and intelligence?

Another unusual case was the Ardennes. Was the fallow system (more than probably Mediterranean in origin) unable to penetrate this poor and distant region, isolated in its forest fastnesses? So François Sigaut suggests.[373] It was at any rate the practice here to cultivate only a small amount of land and to collect for its benefit all the fertilizer that could be derived from the surrounding countryside: in this special region, one crop succeeded another on the same soil.

In the much larger biennial zone, there were also exceptions, and naturally, in this larger expanse, there were more of them. Lands with three *saisons* were to be found in certain confined areas, and there were other anomalies too. South of Bordeaux, in the Landes, cereals were grown in the nineteenth century rather as in the Ardennes, concentrating Chinese-style on a small area, giving it maximum manuring, and having crops rotate without interval. Near Nîmes, according to Léonce de Lavergne (1877),

> a special kind of rotation is practised. It begins with lucerne, well manured; after four years, the lucerne is ploughed under and wheat is grown there without manure, for four years running, followed by two years of sainfoin, then another two of wheat: the whole cycle takes twelve years, six of wheat, with only one manuring.

– and it gave excellent yields.[374] This must have been a late introduction, since it depended on forage crops. But if we were to go further back into the Middle Ages, we should find triennial rotation in Brittany, and on certain land in the Toulouse area.[375] Still in the Middle Ages, in the Grasse region, a notarial lease makes it clear that everything must be done by the rule of three, *dicendo per ters*.[376]

Despite all these exceptions, biennial and triennial rotation dominated their respective areas. So the important thing is to see how these zones abutted on each other, in other words how their frontiers were defined, since borders can be instructive.

Unfortunately what we know about this huge subject amounts to very little. It seems likely on the whole that the triennial system expanded into the southern zone. Thus it may gradually, but in the end definitively, have taken over in Touraine,[377] and later, just before the Revolution, reached Poitou, between Châtellerault and Poitiers.[378] These are probably not isolated instances, but studies in this area are rare, since most historians and geographers have regarded the triennial system as unfailingly superior to the biennial. The problem would be resolved for good if the triennial really *did* always replace the biennial. This was indeed what Marc Bloch believed, as did Albert Demangeon, and so too, more recently, did as great an authority on the history of technology as

Lynn White.[379] The triennial, being a more recent invention, is assumed regularly to have driven out the older system. But were things really as simple as that?

To shed some light on the question, let us call on the defenders of the biennial system. According to Roger Dion, it was not because of its so-called inadequate structures that this system did not include a secondary spring-sown cereal, oats or barley, say, but because these plants would not have been able to withstand the dryness of the French climate south of the *Seuil du Poitou.*[380] Jacques Mulliez[381] has argued that the biennial system had the advantage of greater flexibility, thus lending itself to nineteenth-century innovations more readily than the triennial, which was often imprisoned within its rigid constraints. Lastly, François Sigaut claims that the inferiority of the biennial system has not been demonstrated and he has made some calculations which seem convincing enough at first sight, if theoretical calculation can be accepted as a valid response to the problem.[382]

His reasoning runs as follows: over a period of three years, the biennial system would provide three harvests, each obtained from one-half of the arable land. If 100 represents the annual harvest theoretically derived from the whole of the arable land, the total harvested in practice would be 150. In a triennial system, if spring cereals are reckoned, as was usual, as half the equivalent of winter-sown wheat, the latter would annually yield one-third of 100, that is 100 over three years, while the spring corn would give half that amount over the same period, namely 50, and total production would be 150 – exactly equal to the biennial.

Let us accept, other things being equal, that the two systems might end up giving much the same result. This was probably the case. But equality is not a conclusive argument. How is one to take into account the real conditions of the crops: climate, hydrography, type of seed corn, size of holding, yield of the soil, investment and equipment? On the last point, we must contrast yet again the heavy plough of the north and the light plough of the south and west, and the difference between teams of horses and teams of oxen. The light swing-plough was best for sloping, shallow and stony soil, and indeed handling the *araire* was an art, a more

FIGURE 41
Distribution of animals used for ploughing in the eighteenth century

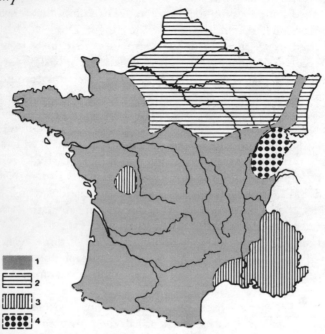

1. Oxen. 2. Horses. 3. Oxen and horses. 4. Mules.

complicated manoeuvre than driving a deep furrow with the heavy wheeled forecarriage of the northern plough. As for the comparative advantages of horses and oxen, the debate has gone on for centuries and we are unlikely to take it much further. Oxen are slower, but eat less, and are not 'machines for eating oats' like horses.[383] In short, we are dealing not with whims and exceptions, but with a series of visible adaptations to constraining circumstances.

As great an expert on the agricultural past as René Musset,[384] whose judgement was based on observation of the *cantons* of Haute-Normandie, has unhesitatingly pronounced the triennial

FIGURE 42
Swing ploughs (araires) *and heavy ploughs* (charrues)

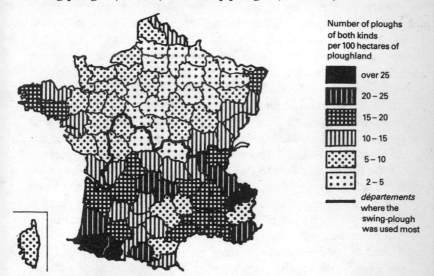

Number of ploughs
of both kinds
per 100 hectares of
ploughland

■ over 25

▮▮▮ 20 – 25

▦ 15 – 20

▥ 10 – 15

⦂⦂⦂ 5 – 10

: : : 2 – 5

— *départements*
where the
swing-plough
was used most

Source: F. Braudel and E. Labrousse, *Histoire économique et sociale de la France*.

system superior. But how can one be sure, on the evidence of particular examples (such as he has used), that they can confidently be generalized? How, alternatively, is one to appreciate the safety-net provided by spring corn in the triennial zone? If the farmer realized, during the first fine days of spring, that the main crop of wheat and rye had failed, some kind of rescue operation might be tried by spring sowing. In 1651, near Reims, the winter had been hard with much frost and flooding but no snow, and everyone knew what that meant. But 'we hope', writes a bourgeois of the town, 'to be able to sow some barley, if the soldiers do not stop us'[385] (the soldiers of the Fronde in this case, alas). Even so, once the failure of the winter wheat was certain, one had to be prepared to take the risk and substitute 'spring corn'. It was thought too great in 1740 at Gonesse – the famous bakers' village outside Paris

– where 'the farmers have not dared to plough over and bury their failed wheat crop'.[386]

Such examples are puzzling. There is no evidence that either system was superior to the other, or to explain why in certain places one system should be abandoned for the other. Perhaps the switch can be better explained within some broader transformation of which it was only one element. The progress of the triennial system south of Châtellerault, mentioned earlier, was accompanied by another factor, the arrival of the horse. For local landowners and peasants of the time, the most important and most controversial innovation was indeed the change to horses. An anonymous writer in 1784 protests indignantly that the farmers in his district have 'dropped the ancient practice of ploughing their fields with oxen and now use horses'. Preposterous! And one landowner, whose conservatism was within his rights if against his interests, stipulated in the lease he presented to his sharecroppers that 'the taker will only be allowed to use oxen'.[387]

And did not yet another factor accompany this change? 'Farm buildings in the Châtelleraudais started to be built round a closed courtyard, with a monumental entrance, as in Picardy or the Beauce, instead of the open courtyard of the *bocage*.'[388] This indication, which itself calls for further research, reminds us that the rotation of the *soles* was only one element, not the only one, going to make up an economy and indeed an entire rural civilization. 'Nature',[389] says Maurice Le Lannou, 'counts for little [well, I do not entirely agree with him about that]; the essential factor . . . is the history of a human community.' On the last point I will go along with him: we are talking about a whole civilization, the sum of many different elements and factors.

France was divided into at least three parts

Let us not therefore run away with the idea of two quite separate zones of rural France, each reducible to its method of growing crops. Geographers have in any case taught us to add to the problem of rotation that other variable, the agrarian regime, or the agrarian landscape as they sometimes call it. The agronomists are right to lump all these together and simply call them agrarian structures, that is entire agricultural complexes, all of them destined to last a long time.

Once one admits these other elements, one has to see rural France as being divided into at least three rather than two sectors.

The first is the France of the north-west and north-east, with its wide expanses, the 'openfields' as British historians, geographers and agronomists call them: a large clustered village occupies the centre of a 'clearing',[390] where there are no trees, no hedges and probably even no fences. The *saisons* or *soles* form sectors of a circle of which the village is the centre – the place everything leaves from and returns to – and they can be identified with the naked eye by their different colours. The fields are long strips, rather like the blocks in a parquet floor. This is certainly the landscape I know best, and it is no doubt the most easily recognized and understood. I well remember, returning by aeroplane from Germany in July 1945, after passing over the strange marshes of Bourtange, suddenly finding myself above the patchwork fields of Picardy, multi-coloured at that time of year, every strip neatly arranged as if drawn with a ruler, each one regularly planted, orderly and tidy, with the church steeples marking the population centres. I knew then that I had come home.

It is obvious that the spread of the disciplined and communally organized openfield, and that of triennial rotation must have gone hand in hand. Who would hazard a guess as to which came first?

The second France is that of the west and centre, the France of the *bocage*. Do not assume too quickly that it is exactly the same everywhere: there is *bocage* and *bocage*[391] and the necessary distinctions are many.

In Mayenne and Maine-et-Loire, to take only these cases (but the same applies elsewhere),

> the fields are lined with tall hedges, full of all kinds of trees [planted on a raised ridge or *talus*]; the space enclosed within them is usually planted out with apples and pear trees for

cider and perry, which gives the whole the appearance of a huge forest. The farms are of 30 or 40 hectares on average; some are much smaller, 10 to 12 hectares only and known as *closeries* because they consist of a single enclosed field.

This brief description, dating from the middle of the nineteenth century, is taken from the still useful book by Léonce de Lavergne.[392] One should add to the picture the deep lanes, the marshy moors covered with gorse and broom, and above all one should note that the appearance of continuous woodland was deceptive: trees were only a complement to the natural landscape, a means of dividing it up. 'Seen from a hill top' (there were no aeroplanes in 1870 to get a real bird's eye view), Léon, a typical region of Brittany looked like 'a chequerboard, divided into countless compartments', according again to Léonce de Lavergne.[393]

The hardest of all to define is that third France in the south-east, either side of the Saône-Rhône valley, that great trench running from the Mediterranean to the Vosges, between the Savoy, Provençal and Dauphiné Alps, the Massif Central and the Pyrenees. It contains some very different regions: the vegetation, crops, flora, trees and way of life can all alter within a short distance.

According to Marc Bloch's explanatory analysis[394] (and I shall be no more successful than he), this is the part of France whose specific features are hardest to grasp. The reader can be the judge: the essential feature here is not the biennial cereal rotation, practised everywhere and apparently dominant; neither is it the division of land into large rectangular fields, reminiscent of the Roman *centuriations* which often survive; no, it is rather the great mass of deserted and unused land, the *(h)erms*, or *gastes*,[395] abandoned after precarious attempts at cultivation, if indeed any were made. The northerner is bemused and disconcerted by the sight of this landscape stretching into the distance, with nothing but bare rocks, the stunted shrubs and bushes of the *garrigues*, the sound of cicadas and wild game, and the scent of thyme and other aromatic herbs.

As for the crops, they are as varied as the soil and the landscape.

Fruit trees are as at home here as wheat and occupy the land at the slightest opportunity. At higher altitudes grow chestnuts and walnut trees, a little lower down comes the providential olive tree, and the equally treasured mulberry, fig, apple, hazel and cherry trees. Then there are the almond trees, whose 'imprudence is proverbial, since they blossom before the end of winter', though the risk of frost is slight near the Mediterranean.[396] Round Hyères, Cannes and Toulon, orange trees and palm-trees grow out of doors, 'as in Sorrento in Italy'.[397] But every now and then a sudden cold snap brings damaging frost, capable of splitting even the gnarled trunks of olive trees and oaks.

Among the crops the climate allows, we should remember the rich plantations that once grew on the terraced hillsides, and above all the lushness of the broad valleys, the lower reaches of the Isère for instance, the valleys of the eastern Pyrenees, or the Argens valley in Provence behind the Maures and Esterel massifs. Lavergne was amazed that 'on a plot of a few square metres, one [should find] growing side by side fruit trees, olives, mulberries, wheat, vegetables, vines and flowers'.[398] Between the rows of vines were vegetables, peach trees and even olive trees, which do not fit in very conveniently with vinegrowing.[399] Along the banks of the Isère in the Grésivaudan valley, 'eternal springtime' confronted the 'eternal winter' of the mountain tops. Fields planted with mulberry or cherry trees and vines ran up to the tree line. In their shade grew wheat, barley, maize, potatoes, hemp, colza, clover, lucerne and buckwheat.[400] This scene dates from the Second Empire.

A final feature of this part of France is that everywhere there were towns, bourgs and large villages. And we should acknowledge that wealth and prosperity have not always been the rule in these sunny regions, where the summer often brought drought, where there were few herds of animals and where manure was therefore in short supply. The wealthy districts were often narrow strips, down in the plains, surrounded and towered over by a mountainous hinterland, one that was exploited and colonized by the wealthy wine- and cereal-growers of the Languedoc and Provençal lowlands.

In short, if we have to sum up the differences in a few lines, we might say that the zone of triennial rotation represented a maximum effort to cultivate the maximum area of land – expanding the *ager*, destroying the *saltus*. This conquest of arable land was the result of collective endeavour and the triumph of order, but it was a triumph bringing unavoidable consequences as we shall see. In the biennial zone by contrast, the *saltus* maintained its presence: trees grew everywhere, whether in the *bocage* or the Midi, in an apparently unending stretch of woodland. And the trees were an asset, one moreover which needed hardly any attention. The brief duration of the cold season also meant that an abundant variety of vegetables could be grown, promoting a degree of self-sufficiency in food. So outside the triennial zone, there was a greater possibility of choice; individualism could run riot there. Landscape and mentalities corresponded to each other, were responsible for each other. Cause and consequence could be reversed, depending on the reciprocity of perspectives.

Looking back in time

The previous paragraphs prove that if you start talking about grain, you always end up talking about something else. Perhaps that is inevitable. But what I have not so far said (and yet it is something that we all know from our own experience) is that the present age – by which I mean the last thirty or forty years – has in one colossal revolution completely overthrown what Daniel Faucher and others used to call 'the equilibrium of the fields', that is that legacy of habits and peasant wisdom handed down from generation to generation. After all, F. H. Gilbert, writing in 1787,[401] claimed

---

Within the two major zones – biennial and triennial, or what would in England be called a two-field or three-field system – François Sigault has identified a whole series of different 'techniques for preparing the land': this 'extremely simplified map' shows only a few of them.

FIGURE 43
Crop rotation in France in the early nineteenth century

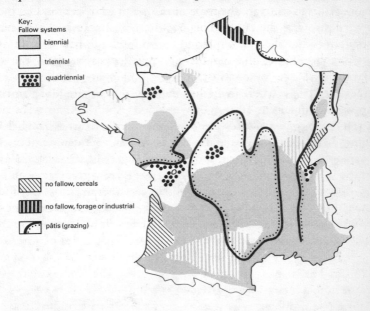

Key:
Fallow systems

- biennial
- triennial
- quadriennial

- no fallow, cereals
- no fallow, forage or industrial
- pâtis (grazing)

– Quadriennial: one year fallow then three successive cereal harvests. This was practised only in a few places, no more than 1% of French farmland, in Poitou, Berry, Savoie and lower Normandy.

– Rotation without fallow: the ideal-type example is the Landes. Two cereal crops a year (rye and millet) in uninterrupted succession. The land was heavily manured by sending flocks of sheep on to it.

– Rotation with industrial or forage crops: the ideal-type here was in Flanders, where fallow was replaced by forage crops, oil-seed plants, textile plants, etc.

– Rough grazing (*pâtis*): this is the term François Sigault uses for the practice, especially in the biennial zone, but not only there, whereby a sequence of normal rotations would be followed by a period of rest which might last several years. Typical examples in the biennial zone are the south-east of the Armorican massif, Lower Poitou and Anjou; in the triennial zone, Brittany, where two or three triennial rotations might be followed by 6 to 9 years of *pâtis*.

Source: François Sigault, in *Annales E.S.C.*, 1976.

that French agriculture had made no progress since Roman times. A slight exaggeration perhaps, but it carries some weight coming from such an excellent observer of the realities of his day.

So the great change has come recently, and over a comparatively short space of time, completely transforming what was there before. The present day cannot therefore be seen as the natural end-result of a development which it might consequently help to interpret. There was a break, and this is the phenomenon with which we must come to terms.

The only way to resolve our problem consists of working backwards rather than forwards in time. Marc Bloch[402] suggested, as a starting-point for this retrospective journey, taking the situation as it had become established in the nineteenth century, rather than the present day. From here we should work backwards, looking for clues. This makes particularly good sense since the nineteenth century is extremely well documented, and the slow changes which took place during it did not greatly distort the general picture.

François Sigaut has proposed a general outline of the situation in 1800, and his map is reproduced in Figure 43. The reader can refer to the commentary there provided.[403]

The real problems start if one goes back earlier than this: it is a task that would require years of collective work. And how far should one go? As far as Colbert? Certainly. As far as Sully? That would be more risky. And in any case would the extra years really add much? Delving down to the roots of 'the order of the fields' would require a much longer time-scale.

In the meantime, we can try drawing on *comparative history*. But what should we be comparing with what? Maurice Le Lannou[404] could tell us about Sardinia, taking us to the eastern part of the island, to the curious plain of Campidano, where triennial rotation was the rule; Xavier de Planhol[405] could take us further afield, to southern Anatolia; Jean-Robert Pitte knows about Mauritania. Well, I propose to take a trip to Russia. This may seem rather quixotic. I know that Russia imitated the experience of the rest of Europe – but in what a different context! All the same, Russia does have one advantage. It went through this experience later than the West, therefore during a period that is more visible to historians.

And since the experiment began in the central belt, where agriculture had long been established, two or three centuries before it reached the peripheral and still primitive zones, such as the Ukraine, it is possible to see several systems coexisting and evolving in the eighteenth century. The map in Figure 44, taken from Michel Confino's study,[406] makes long explanations unnecessary. It shows that the first crops to be grown on Russian soil were sown on burnt clearings and in an itinerant manner. As the population grew and tended to settle down, a biennial rotation system became established, which itself gradually gave way to a triennial pattern.

If we now imagine this process as having taken place in the West, we come face to face once more with the old explanations, the received wisdom telling us that triennial rotation succeeded the biennial model. But we still do not know why. The pre-existence of a nomadic culture, to be sure, we are prepared to accept almost without question. Prehistorians think they have detected traces of it around neolithic settlements. And perhaps some version of it continued to survive in France in what were known as *cultures non réglées*, irregular crops, the stretches of *saltus* that were episodically cleared and ploughed on the Mediterranean coast, in Brittany, the Thiérache and elsewhere, before reverting once more to heath, gorse or forest.

The Russian comparison affords us no more than a glimpse of what happened in other countries, but it nudges us towards some salutary reflexions. France should really be compared with the rest of Europe. At the Budapest conference of French and Hungarian historians in 1982, Laszlo Makkai argued that triennial rotation appeared in Hungary only in about the sixteenth century, and that it represented a restoration of order by the landowners, with harsh consequences for the peasants.[407] In sixteenth-century Brandenburg, the three *soles* of the triennial system and the introduction of sheep-farming went hand in hand with a seigneurial reaction. Triennial rotation is also found, but much earlier, in the Thames Valley, the Paris basin and the Lombardy plain, all three being regions kept under firm control.

But let us push the explanation further, even if we have to jettison it later. Hypotheses can always serve a useful purpose: it is the

FIGURE 44
Crop systems in European Russia in the eighteenth century

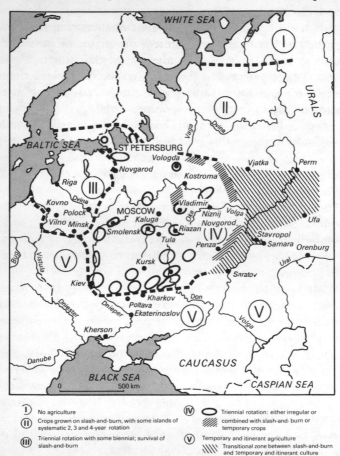

If we translate these coexisting zones into evolutionary terms, zone V represents the primitive phase of growing crops in an itinerant manner on burnt tracts; zone II shows the appearance of islands of systematic rotation, III and IV the still incomplete victory of triennial over biennial rotation and burnt tracts.

Source: Michel Confino, *Systèmes agraires et progrès agricoles. L'assolement triennial en Russie aux XVIIIe–XXe siècles*, 1969.

business of historians to make them obsolete tomorrow, if they can come up with better ones.

So let us say that southern France, with its biennial rotation and its massive fields, possibly on the sites of Roman *centuriations*, as suggested earlier, seems to represent the legacy of the Mediterranean of antiquity. Abundant mention of the two-stage system (fallow then cereals) can be found in Columella's *De re rustica* or in Xenophon's *Economics*. According to the famous agronomist the comte de Gasparin in 1831, Xenophon wrote 'as if he had before his eyes the normal practice of French sharecroppers.[408] Nothing need be added to or subtracted from these images. Nature has not changed and in a given set of circumstances, there is a system of crops adapted to it which will provide the greatest net yield.' It is a perfectly plausible hypothesis.

Much less plausible, though attractive, is the suggestion that it was the Celts, the Gauls, who invented the *bocage* system, which is admittedly to be found in Wales and Ireland as well as in Brittany. But is the *bocage* perhaps of less ancient origin than has sometimes been assumed?[409]

There remains the France of the openfields and the triennial system. We can be certain of its existence only from the twelfth or thirteenth century, when the documents mention the growing of oats (implying the existence of a second *sole*), a development which, it is thought, accompanied the introduction of horse-breeding. But the heavy Frankish cavalry which faced the Arab invasions was already established by the eighth century. Should we therefore jump several centuries and assume that the triennial system only appeared under the influence of these Germanic invaders, who favoured animal-farming and new forms of settlement? We are well into unknown territory here.

Roger Dion and Maurice Le Lannou encourage us however to take this leap into the past. They argue that the system appeared during the chaos following the collapse of the Roman Empire, particularly on its outskirts, where regrouping into tightly-knit villages and communities was primarily dictated by a concern for defence. But not all large villages necessarily adopted triennial rotation. Similarly, explanations involving the horse, as already noted, prompt some doubts: spring corn, including oats, seems to have been used to feed humans as much as animals, if not more so.[410] The only thing of which we can be certain is that the triennial system replaced a previous system of dispersed habitat and irregular field use, as archaeological digs have shown in England and indeed in France.

If we were to accept Xavier de Planhol's thesis, we would put everything down to cattle- and sheep-farming: in about the thirteenth century the flocks were brought together under the care of a single shepherd, hired by the village; the old hedges, it seems, disappeared at about the same time.[411] This is to my mind the most coherent explanation so far. The expansion of animal husbandry at the same time as the spread of arable land would have placed the peasants in an impossible situation. To resolve it, the private flock in its own field had to be abandoned and the animals brought together under a communal shepherd: they would survive by grazing on fallow land and *vaine pâture*.

Personally, I feel that Robert Specklin's[412] original and adventurous thesis, mingling geography and history, encourages us to look beyond the thirteenth century. As he sees it, the Frankish conquest (late fifth and early sixth century) brought into being south of the Loire a new *limes* or frontier with fortified points along it: to the north was a Germanicized Gaul; to the south and virtually cut off from the former lay a Romanized Gaul; in the west was Armorica, a Celtic province (possibly re-Celticized in the seventh century). The sketch-map reproduced in Volume I (Figure 8) indicates the major features of this interpretation. Can we fit into it the hypothesis about concentrated villages and self-defence? If so, one question remains: do these *limes* or marcher zones, facing the two greatest ancient massifs in France, the Armorican Massif and the Massif Central, perhaps represent some older *cultural* frontiers separating populations which had for millennia clung to the soil, adapting to agriculture and invasion and simply overlaid by the Celtic and Frankish occupations? This has been put forward as rather a wild surmise,[413] but wild surmises are not always wrong.

Present prehistorical research, seeking to discover dispersed or village-centred cultures and habitats, and going beyond the traditional study of the technical advances of the Bronze or Iron Ages brought by invaders, may perhaps prove one day that 'the bend in the Loire between the Massif Central and Brittany' is, as Lucien Gachon long ago claimed, 'more than a decorative feature on the map of France'[414] – in other words that it marks a frontier, a major articulation of French history; and an explanation.

From grain to bread

To talk of grain is to talk of bread and that takes us outside the agricultural world we have been discussing, just as wine takes us out of the vineyard.

Before it could become the loaf of bread on the table of rich or poor, grain had to undergo many processes. It had to be threshed with a flail or trodden by hoofed animals, then stored before being carried to market in bourg or town, there to be delivered to the mills and ground into flour. Flour had to be used quickly, since it did not keep well. The baker took charge of it, except when bread was to be kneaded and baked at home or in the *four banal*, the bake-oven owned by the local seigneur or perhaps by the village itself.

Each operation had its own peculiarities. The grain was not threshed until the ears were properly dry. In Poland and the north of Europe, it was still so damp after threshing that it had to be dried out in ovens. In northern regions of France, grain was left to dry in sheaves in the fields, or inside huge barns, big enough to hold haystacks as well as stooks of corn. The threshing would be carried out gradually over the winter. If the grain had been cut with a scythe, it would have been harvested before it was fully ripe, to avoid the ripe grain falling from the ear (of which there was less risk when sickles were used). It therefore required a longer drying-out period and threshing would be later still.[415] In southern regions, where it was normal to use animals to tread the grain, the process could be begun earlier.

Storing grain was not a simple matter either.

The use of silos for instance – pits or hollows lined with straw to keep the grain dry, then covered with earth – which was normal practice in Sicily, North Africa, Spain and even Hungary, was rarely found in France, apart from the Quercy, the Vivarais, Roussillon or the Gers.[416] In barns, where weevils, rodents and damp had to be kept at bay, the farmer had to be prepared to turn and air the grain every fortnight for at least six months, then to riddle it every month, if he wanted it to keep well. This was impossible in the case of large grain stores, such as rations for a town or fortress. Savary nevertheless claims that it was possible to preserve grain for tens of years. His recipe was to cover the pile with a 'layer of powdered quicklime, three inches deep', then to water it. The topmost grains, mixed in with the quicklime, would send up shoots that would dry in winter to form a protective crust, thick and very tough, insulating the mass of grain rather like a silo.[417]

In spite of all the problems, it was normal to keep grain for two, three or four years. 'The old royal ordinance of 21 November 1577, forbidding people to keep grain longer than two years, was no longer applied [in the eighteenth century] and perhaps it never had been.'[418] The wealthy, the bourgeois and religious communities were accustomed to keep their barns full all the time. Poor people, who had no emergency stocks, and peasants who were obliged to sell their harvest, always suspected grain merchants or rich landowners of hoarding grain until the price went up – and they were often right. Practically everyone speculated in grain. When an offender was caught red-handed, he might turn out to be from any class, not necessarily the richest. But hoarding was also a necessary act of prudence. Old grain added to new might help to soften the blow of a bad harvest. The sudden grain shortage which surprised France in 1816 resulted from 'a hard winter with hardly any snow', followed by sudden frosts 'during the sprouting season'[419] – but it was also partly explained by a lack of reserve stocks, the consequence of foreign invasion and the billeting of the allied occupation army on French soil.

Grain made its way to the consumer under supervision. The authorities – central government, the *intendants*, the municipal authorities, often uncooperative and quick to panic – were in charge of this. Its movement from granary to market, from market to mill, from mill to bake-oven, came under the *police des grains*, the grain police, which is well documented because of the controversies it stirred up. Would the population's sustenance not be better assured by the free circulation of grain? The authorities had certainly devised rules and regulations to the point of absurdity, and in times of serious difficulty they were applied even more stringently and consistently (if not more appropriately) than usual. And such difficulty frequently arose. In Chartres for instance, in the heart of the great cereal-growing area of the Beauce, there were, between 1699 and 1763, 25 years of abundant harvest (which led to disastrous slumps in grain prices), 17 years of high prices, representing poor harvests; and 22 years when the *setier* of grain varied between 10 and 15 *livres* – the producer only breaking even at about 12 *livres*.

In theory, grain was only sold in the public market place. If the peasants brought it in, as they were supposed to do, all would be well. And indeed this was what happened most of the time. Sales by sample took a long time to become established. So the Chartres cornmarket for example, inaugurated in 1683,[420] three times a week offered a spectacle 'still to be seen in the nineteenth century, before sale by sample became established; sacks would be heaped up all over the market place in tidy piles reaching higher than the first storey of the surrounding buildings'.[421]

Transactions on the market place were handled through official intermediaries: middlemen – or rather middlewomen, since this job was done by women known as *factrices* or *leveuses de culs de sacs*; quality checkers, valuers and finally porters. Every transaction had to pass through these hands. The porters barely earned enough to live except in winter and then not well; in order to survive, and contrary to all the guild rules, they worked simultaneously as carpenters, roofers or masons.[422] In every market place, the first hour of trading was reserved for local residents, then bakers, and afterwards outsiders and travelling grain-dealers (*blattiers*).[423]

There was grain and grain of course – just as, once the flour reached the bakers, there was bread and bread. At Chartres, the most sought-after was the top-grade wheat; then came commercial grade wheat; then *blé champart*, which in the early eighteenth century contained two parts wheat to one part rye; then '*méteil moyen*, made up of equal parts of wheat and rye; then *méteil* in which there was more rye than wheat; and finally barley and oats'.[424] In the mills, the grain was processed into flour and naturally there were as many different kinds of flour as there were types of cereal; further variations resulted from the degree of bolting (sifting).

But all flour had the same defect: it spoiled in transit even more quickly than grain. So towns needed to have mills nearby to provide a source of freshly milled flour. Paris was surrounded by windmills, on the heights of Belleville, Saint-Gervais, etc. Since large rivers tended to freeze in winter, only windmills could continue to turn, apart from a few watermills using streams close to their source. This was one of the advantages of Etampes, a great milling centre. Milling might also stop when rivers ran dry in summer. That was why in July–August 1789, when many mills came to a halt, Louis XVI cancelled the fountain display planned at Versailles for his name-day.

Flour did sometimes travel long distances. It was transported to the French and other European settlers in the West Indies where imported grain would have been no use, for want of mills. It was also shipped to the Far East, to the small colonies of bread-eaters who were unwilling to do without it. Flour from Aquitaine had proved to keep better than most: it was transported in barrels, tightly packed and well sealed, which the ships from the islands, or the vessels of the Indies Company brought back empty, to be used for the next consignment.

The baker was only the last link in this chain. But in everyday life he was the most visible, so he was regularly blamed for any change in the price of bread. It was an obsession that might turn to fury and rage. In spring 1775, during the so-called flour wars, the result of Turgot's decrees on the free circulation of grain, many Parisian bakeries were ransacked:

Yesterday [3 May 1775, declared] Catherine Le Roux, widow of Jean Chocarne, and mistress-baker in Paris, where she lives in the street and parish of Saint-Jacques de la Boucherie, during the public tumult, at about eleven o'clock in the morning, several individuals entered her premises and took the bread which was on the shelves in her shop . . . one of them who appeared to be twelve years of age opened the drawer in the counter and took nearly 80 *livres* which were there in silver and small change . . . She was robbed of three forks and one spoon from her kitchen and her shop, as well as three silver serving-dishes.[425]

Should we assume, since she owned some silver, that the plaintiff was fairly rich? Bakers under the *ancien régime* were reputed to be better off than millers.

Offences committed during the flour war (a war I am inclined to regard as of minor importance, at least in Paris) led to many arrests. Some of them seem at first sight completely arbitrary, others perhaps justified by the standards of the time. Jean L'Equillier, journeyman gauze-maker (*gazier*) aged 16,[426] was accused of taking part in the looting of the bakery belonging to master-baker Jean-Baptiste Barre, in the rue Mouffetard. At his home were found flour and bread, which he claimed to have received as charity. Unluckily for him, the bread was white, 'which is not usually given as charity'. A real-life Jean Valjean perhaps?

Since things quickly turned ugly where bread was concerned, the *intendants* kept a close watch on urban markets, intervening, threatening, providing extra supplies to bring down the price, and using armed force to keep people in order. In times of trouble, the towns were in fact better protected than the countryside. Everyone tried to protect his own interests and broke the rules in efforts to make profits. Official and unofficial grain merchants would go direct to the peasants, pay over the odds for the grain, and bring it to the warehouses they owned in town or country. 'It has been said, with some exaggeration no doubt, that grain was simply a form of contraband during the *ancien régime*.'[427] Smuggling certainly existed, but we should not blame it for everything in a system which was, as I shall try to show, the victim of irremediable weaknesses: low cereal yields (about 4.5 or 5 to 1, according to Vauban); and inefficient means of transport until the spread of the railways during the Second Empire.

The French as eaters of bread

Whether from taste or necessity or both, the French have long been great eaters of bread. They may not have been the only ones, but the caricatures depicting them as unrivalled in this respect were not far off the mark:

The inhabitant of France [wrote a citizen of Geneva in 1843] consumes proportionately more grain and less vegetables, meat and dairy produce than any other country [in Europe], so he is prepared to cultivate the production of this plant which corresponds to his most pressing needs, particularly since the best bread in the world is eaten in Paris.[428]

If we are to believe Paris-Duvernay (1750),[429] a Frenchman consumed two 200-pound sacks of grain a year, roughly the equivalent of 200 present-day kilos. In 1782, Le Grand d'Aussy more generously fixed the ration as two or three pounds of bread a day.[430] Another less well-known informant, Raymond Lebon, estimated it in 1792 as 3 *setiers* a year (a *setier* was the equivalent of 156 litres; by way of comparison, a quintal of grain is approximately 120 litres). So the annual ration would be just under 4 quintals (3.8 to be precise).[431] Now it so happens that this is exactly the average consumption calculated by historians of the Middle Ages: 10,000 quintals for a town of 3,000 inhabitants.[432] Broadly speaking then, the average consumption of bread would have remained the same from the Middle Ages to the eighteenth century – or even 1850? Average consumption implies exceptions and variations. Pottier de la Hestroye remarked in 1716 that

persons who feed on flesh and other nourishment do not eat a pound of bread a day. Domestic servants in Paris are usually given no more than 9 pounds of bread a week, which is less than a pound and a half a day, but still more than they can eat, and it is well known that they sell the extra.[433]

Domestic servants were privileged people where diet was concerned. It is only since 1950, a whole century later, that bread consumption has fallen dramatically, although it still retains its appeal for us. Bakers who have revived old recipes for yeast bread, wholemeal bread, rye bread or even (since people are more concerned about diet today) bran loaves, are making fortunes now. In present-day France, with its 54 million inhabitants, grain production is 17 million tonnes, which works out at *roughly* the average consumption per head of the past (about 3 quintals). But of this sum, 2 million tonnes are consumed on the spot; 8 million go on to flour mills and bakeries; and 7 million are sold, with some difficulty, on the international market. Our consumption has in fact fallen by half, compared with what it was at the end of the *ancien régime*.

White bread

Consumption had not yet fallen when another revolution took place, though this was later than historians usually claim: the arrival of white bread, made from wheat flour.[434] It had long been the exception, the bread eaten by the rich. All the official documents, from at least the time of Jean Le Bon, who wrote in the 1350s and 1360s, distinguish between different grades of bread.

The names given to the various qualities of bread differ widely according to time and place. In Poitiers in 1362, four kinds of bread were on sale: *choyne* bread without salt, *choyne* bread with salt, *safleur* bread (made from unsieved flour), and *riboulet*, with 90% bolted flour, containing the lightest bran, which is still known as *reboulet* in Poitevin patois today. In Paris in 1372, there were three kinds of bread, *Chailli* bread, *coquillé* or *bourgeois* bread, and *pain brode* – that is *pain bis* or 'brown' bread. In Brittany on the eve of the Revolution, besides the various kinds of bread for rich people – *pain de fine fleur, pain moussant, pain jaheur* – there was the everyday bread known as *mesléard* or *mesliand*, a mixture of wheat, rye and *paumelle* (a kind of barley).[435]

Did all rich people eat white bread? One cannot be too sure of this. As late as the beginning of the nineteenth century in

Limoges[436] 'the most stringent economy reigned in housekeeping. Most people ate rye bread, known as *pain d'hôtel*; wheaten bread was kept for visitors or occasionally for the masters of the house'. It is true that the Limousin was one of the poorest provinces in France.

Throughout the Second Empire at any rate, and probably in every *département* of France, three qualities of bread, in decreasing order of price, figure in the bakeries and the official price indexes. If the revolutionary and Napoleonic armies did much to propagate white bread in France and the rest of Europe, it only became widespread gradually, and not until the end of the nineteenth century. Until then, it was a luxury which the poor in the towns regarded with envy, while villagers rarely saw it at all. The young Valentin Jameret Duval, who was born in Arthonnay (now in the *département* of the Yonne) in 1696, when Louis XIV was still on the throne, discovered its existence one day when he was amazed to find the parish priest eating it in front of him: 'it was a different colour from what I had always known'.[437] But then one of my own friends, from a peasant family in the eastern Pyrenees, with whom I was eating lunch recently, when I passed him a basket of brown bread, said to me with a smile, 'I ate so much of this in my childhood that I only like white bread these days!' He was born in 1899.

Grain and national income

Before leaving the subject of grain, I would like to refer to a document not, to my knowledge, used by historians: the two reports by the Assembly for the administration of agriculture,[438] set up by the government of Louis XVI in 1785, following the exceptional drought which had affected all of France that year. Despite its pompous title, this committee, of which Lavoisier was a member, had a very modest role to play. It brought together some intelligent people, but being kept short of funds by the government, it had little influence. Nevertheless, its enquiries are a valuable source of information.

In the old days [one of these reports tells us],[439] one reckoned 3 *setiers* of grain were needed to feed one individual; with economic milling, 2¼ *setiers* would be enough. But this type of milling is not generally known or practised, so it would be misleading to say that on average less than 2½ *setiers* per head are consumed at present within the Kingdom . . . So consumption must be 50 million *setiers*, of which two-fifths are wheat and three-fifths rye. Included in this total are the wheat and rye that are eaten separately, and *méteil*, which is a mixture of the two grains in about equal proportions. The value of 20 million *setiers* of wheat, at 20 *livres* each on average, is 400 million [*livres*]. The value of 30 million *setiers* of rye at fifteen francs on average is 450 million [a total of 850 million].

From this text, one can draw firstly the conclusion that, given the enormous percentage of rye in total grain production, *pain bis* was not going to disappear overnight.

Secondly, this calculation assumes a population of 20 million people, not 23 or 24 million, the more usual figure for this period. The investigators had estimated that young children, who ate little bread, should be left out of the total. But if we take the figure of 29 million (resulting from the most recent research by historians) one would still have to reckon with some 25 or 26 million consumers, even if young children are again left out. Taking 26 million as our basic figure, the amount of wheat consumed would be 26 million *setiers*, and the amount of rye 39 million *setiers*, with a total value of 520 and 585 million *livres* respectively. So the total price would be 1,105 million *livres*.

Our report adds to human consumption the 'extra half', corresponding to spring-sown cereals, used for animal fodder. This adds another 425 million *livres* to the calculation, taking the total to 1,275 million *livres* if not more, an enormous share of the gross national income.

And yet grain only represented about half of 'agricultural income', which included other headings – livestock, vines, market gardens, dairy produce, woodland products (timber for carpentry, firewood, acorns, resins, pitch); hemp, flax and silk, salt mines and quarries: total 2,500 million *livres*. And when it reviewed its calculations, the committee decided that this total was still too low. For, it argued,

> this production entirely feeds and clothes for the most part, at least *24 million* (possibly *28 million*) inhabitants. Such *expense* [my italics] cannot be sustained unless three thousand million *livres*' worth of produce of every kind is harvested every year. This product must be reproduced constantly, since it is consumed annually.

In conclusion then, we have two figures: 2,500 million at least, 3,000 million at most.[440] If agricultural production was equivalent to three-quarters or half of national product, the latter must have been somewhere between 3,000 amd 6,000 million.[441] Per capita income was about 200 *livres* if that. Still it works out at rather more than the 40 *écus*, that is 120 *livres*,[442] which Voltaire thought to be the average income per head in the France of his time.

CHAPTER NINE

Is Any Kind of Summing-up Possible?

No, of course not, especially since so far we have been looking only at the lower layers, at what was literally peasant life. We shall not be able to draw up a final balance sheet until we have considered and evaluated the entire 'peasant economy' – infrastructure, superstructure and all – as I shall try to do in the next section.

For the present, let us confine discussion to the following question: could it be said of France before the railway revolution that it was autarkic, self-sufficient? In the book in which he convincingly reconstitutes the missing statistics from the eighteenth century to the present day, Jean-Claude Toutain declares that it is not his aim to find out 'whether and to what extent the supply of food provided by French agriculture was [or was not] inadequate to meet demand'.[443] But this is precisely the difficult question that I would like to tackle: demand versus supply.

For many French people, the question simply did not arise, or else they thought it settled in advance: yes of course France was amply self-sufficient. Sully displayed quite unshakeable optimism in his *Mémoires* (1603):

France [he wrote] has the good fortune to be so plentifully blessed in the distribution [of bounty] that, with the possible exception of Egypt, she is the country most abundantly provided for in every kind of good, whether necessary or merely convenient, that one could find anywhere on earth. Her cereals, grains and vegetables, her wines, ciders, flax, hemp, salt, wool, oil, woad, the countless quantity of livestock, large and small, that go to make up man's habitual diet, place France in a position where not only has she nothing to envy her neighbours as regards supplies of these goods, but she can even vie with those countries that trade solely in any one of them, such as Italy, Spain or Sicily.[444]

Optimism, pride and presumption were ever poor counsellors.

But if overweening pride was a sin, Sully was not the only offender. Antoine Montchrestien, the inventor of an expression destined for a long career, *political economy*,[445] stated in 1615 that

> France is alone in being able to do without what she receives from neighbouring countries, while her neighbours cannot do without her. She has infinite riches, both known and yet to be discovered. To anyone who reflects carefully [France] is the most complete fulfilment [literally *corps* = body] of a kingdom that the Sun could shine upon, from its rising till its setting.

Vauban had a high opinion of France too. He expressed himself with a little more caution it is true, and in the conditional tense: 'It *would* be possible for France to do without' the foreigners to whom she turns only to satisfy a craving for luxury.[446]

One could no doubt unearth hundreds and hundreds of similar pronouncements. If not, would Paris Duverney, a financier thoroughly familiar with the grain trade and the practices of suppliers, have taken the trouble in 1750 to refute the rumour current in his day that a normal grain harvest could feed the whole of France for three years? If one looked at the years 1740, 1741, 1747 and 1748, he pointed out, this was completely untrue.[447] He was right of course. But evidently, he was out of step with public opinion. In his day, it is unlikely that anybody would have contradicted the conclusions of a report from the late seventeenth century, on the economy of the Dauphiné: the author, a certain Guichard,[448] considered that if his recommendations were followed and people devoted themselves 'in every province of the Kingdom, to cultivating what nature had bestowed, France would be able to do without foreign goods, except for spices and drugs'. As we shall shortly see, this was not an altogether sustainable point of view.

France's capacity for self-sufficiency must in fact be examined from at least four perspectives:

1. Was there enough to go round, with or without calling on outside help? I have called this section 'Was France self-sufficient?' The problem concerns France's relations with other countries, as well as internal communications.

2. Shortages, hunger and famine provide a series of litmus tests: domestic supply found it hard to meet demand.

3. Peasant revolts and grain riots are a regular feature of French history from the late sixteenth to the mid-nineteenth centuries. Such disorders certainly do not show the peasant economy in the most favourable light, if its chief aim was to feed the country.

4. If substantial progress was made all the same, what form did it take?

Was France self-sufficient?

Could rural France manage to support itself on the goods it produced? And could it provide the necessities of life to non-rural France?

Broadly speaking, the answer must be yes, since the French population as a whole maintained its numbers and even increased, through all the crises and food shortages. And this success of a kind must be explained by the food and other goods derived from the soil.

All the same, shortages were frequent. The food supply often ran out or was interrupted, making it necessary to apply for help to foreign countries, something comparatively easy to arrange by the eighteenth century and even more so in the nineteenth; but rescue operations did not always restore the situation perfectly or in time.

A memorandum published in 1836 at Troyes by the Society of Agriculture, Science, Arts and Belles-lettres of the Aube does not overstate the case: an increase in the livestock of France is in its view,

> a prime necessity, since even today, France does not produce enough beasts to provide every inhabitant with three ounces of meat a day [about 90 grammes]; since no more than 12 ounces of wool [370 grammes] per head of population is

371

FIGURE 45
Cheese imports at the end of the seventeenth century

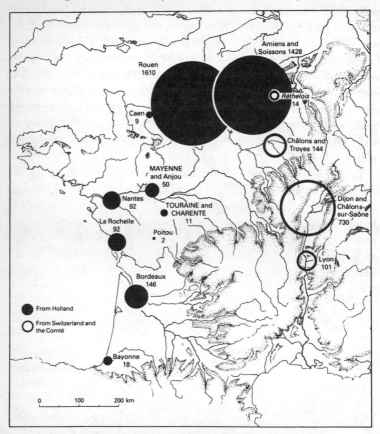

Map by F. Vergneault. Source: A.N., G⁷, 1685.

gathered, and since not enough leather is turned out to give every inhabitant of France a pair of shoes a year.[449]

It should be added that France did not produce enough butter or cheese either. The latter was by the eighteenth century being imported from Holland in 'prodigious quantities'.[450] In Louis

XIV's time, fitting out the fleet often meant making massive purchases of barrels of beef, pork or salt butter from Ireland. Cattle were bought in Germany or Switzerland. And domestic production of horses – roughly the equivalent of the motor industry today – was inadequate both in quantity and quality. The peasant of Lorraine ruined himself to buy great German horses 'of a breed which can only be maintained by a huge supply of oats'.[451] And every town needed horses to pull carts and carriages, not to mention the thousands of cabs in Paris. So even before the eighteenth century, there were long strings of horses, good and bad, making their way towards Paris, each attached to the tail of the one in front.

To supply horses for its cavalry regiments, the French army was obliged to buy thousands from Germany and the Swiss Cantons, which acted as intermediaries for places further east. This dependence lasted until the nineteenth century. During the second quarter of 1859 for instance, the Chalon-sur-Saône horse fair saw trading come to a standstill on account of 'prohibitions by the German states'. Normally, 'it is here that dealers from the north bring German, Danish or Holstein horses to sell to southerners. This year, there were only local horses for sale, from the Charolais and Morvan, and they were expensive. A cavalry detachment did however acquire some of them for the army.'[452]

Several French regions bred horses, it is true, but despite the creation of the royal stud farms in 1665, France was still not producing many really good beasts. So they were purchased abroad, leading to an annual deficit of several million *livres*.[453] In January 1792, even before the declaration of war on 20 April, the provision of mounts for the cavalry 'is costing us at the moment more than 12 [million *livres*] and all paid into foreign coffers'.[454] A telling detail of the Peninsular War is the admiration French officers expressed for the splendid horses of their English opponents: whenever one was captured, it was highly prized.

There are many signs that livestock had to be imported. Whenever, by accident or design, state vigilance along the frontier was relaxed, or whenever customs duties fell, imports of livestock on the hoof increased forthwith. But the French government itself appealed to foreign suppliers, by the decrees of 14 September and 16 October 1714, pleading the need to make good the national livestock pool, depleted by the War of the Spanish Succession, as well as to bring down the price of meat. French livestock breeders immediately raised their voices in protest.[455] A century later, in 1818, 1819 and 1820, '16,000 oxen, 20,000 cows and 150,000 sheep were brought into France'. In 1821, 27,000 oxen were imported, along with 23,000 cows and 265,000 sheep, and they travelled inland as far as the market-places of Sceaux and Poissy. A tariff introduced in 1822 'reduced the flow and cut imports to 9,000 oxen, 13,000 cows and 115,000 sheep by 1823. It went up again in 1824 and was maintained until 1830.'[456] A comparison of the value of imports and exports of cattle, sheep and pigs over six years (1831 to 1836 inclusive) reveals that 42 million francs' worth were imported, as against 16.7 million francs' worth exported, which works out at an annual deficit of about 4.2 million francs.[457]

But there was a more serious imbalance than this: France suffered from a virtually permanent *cereal* deficit – something which might seem unthinkable *a priori*. But the deficit was still there as late as the beginning of this century. Alfred Sauvy notes that in 1913, 'imports of foodstuffs to France amounted to 1,818 million [francs] and exports to only 839 million: the deficit on foodstuffs can be broadly estimated at about 12%. For wheat alone, which was an important element, the balance worked out at net imports of 15 million quintals, or one seventh of consumption.' And this was not because of an abnormally low harvest that year (87 million quintals, compared to an average of 89.6 million over the previous ten years).[458]

This was moreover nothing new. 'The myth of France cosily ensconced inside her six frontiers has always been false,' one historian writes.[459] In fact at every period in modern history, France has had to appeal for foreign cereals. That is not to deny that every year, French cereals flowed out to other countries. Certain regions were regular grain exporters – Brittany, the Aunis and Languedoc in the sixteenth century for example. Grain was exported from Languedoc to Italy every year, unless there was a really poor harvest. Small sailing ships used to carry grain from

FIGURE 46
The production, foreign trade and average price of grain in France from 1810 to 1911

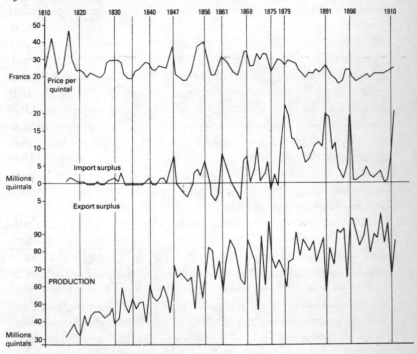

Source: *Annuaire statistique rétrospectif de l'INSEE*, 1966.

Brittany and the Aunis to Spain and Portugal: it was paid for in Seville with silver coin, in Lisbon with gold. In 1667–8, during the war with Spain, France was secretly supplying her enemy with cereals, 'because this is the trade that brings [us] Spanish gold and silver'.[460] In 1684, France was once more at war with Spain, and this time it was English and Dutch ships that loaded cargoes of grain for the peninsula at Bordeaux.[461]

Taken all round, imports against exports, the balance was not usually in France's favour (cf. Figure 46). Whenever there was a gap between two harvests, whenever there was an unexpected

FIGURE 47
Grain landed at Marseille on 8 November 1845

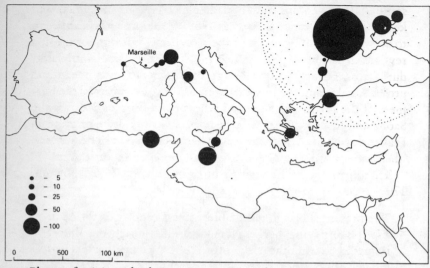

Marseille

- – 5
- – 10
- – 25
- – 50
- – 100

0   500   100 km

Places of origin and relative quantity. Dotted zone indicates area imported grain from which was quarantined (Archives nationales).

shortage, whenever the Paris food supply suddenly reached crisis point, appeals were regularly made to the Baltic (the Amsterdam grain market having replaced Antwerp in 1544),[462] or to Marseille, which was regularly supplied by the countries of the Levant and the Barbary Coast. Marseille and Genoa were communicating vessels: whenever the price of grain went up at Marseille, the Genoese dipped into their reserves and sent grain to the French port and vice versa. Paris was on several occasions supplied with Mediterranean grain, either shipped from Genoa or sent via Marseille: it often arrived in poor condition, sometimes crawling with weevils.

Another source of supply was England, which exported grain partly because of a system of bounties introduced in 1660. According to Ange Goudar, up to the year 1755, England exported to France 21 million *setiers* of wheat, 'which cost the French Crown about 200 million *livres tournois*'.[463] (21 million *setiers* is the equivalent of 27 million quintals, a spectacular amount.)

Towards the end of the eighteenth century, two new and powerful grain exporters came upon the scene, the United States and southern Russia. Ships from Philadelphia were carrying wheat and kegs of flour to France as early as 1739.[464] Ukrainian wheat began to arrive in Marseille at about the same time, but did not mean a revolution in supply for France or western Europe until later, during the Europe-wide shortage of 1817. This was cheap and providential grain, but it was dangerous. In 1819, it ruined the business of the boats which carried wheat from Burgundy down the Saône and Rhône. 'Crimean wheat' brought the price of grain in France down to less than 20 francs a hectolitre, a level below which 'the farmer is making a loss', as a contemporary report tells us.[465]

There is no lack of examples of difficult years: 1662, 1693–4, 1709–10, 1740, 1788–9:

The present shortage [a reliable witness reports on 24 April 1789] is terrifying, because it made itself felt early on, almost immediately after the harvest [of 1788] since that harvest was indeed a poor one . . . because grain hoarders are profiting shamelessly from the unfortunate circumstances to increase public misery; and finally, because the poorer part of the nation has now, in almost every province of the Kingdom, reached the depths of despair. I live near a town [Alençon] where last week there was a bloody spectacle, poor people were killed by the troops who were sent out against them. Ah Monseigneur, how terrible it is to massacre those who are crying out with hunger! And the coming harvest will certainly be even worse than the last one.[466]

The bread shortage certainly cast its shadow over the early events of the Revolution. Raymond Lebon tells us in 1792 that

over 75 million [*livres*] were spent [in 1789 and 1790] on buying grain and flour abroad to come to the aid of several regions of France, in particular Paris, [to the point that the French exchange rate with London was affected] which proves that this commodity is not in regularly plentiful supply in France, as some have claimed.[467]

This being so, it is surprising that people could always be found (Boisguillebert and Quesnay among them) in favour of exporting cereals from France, on the pretext that there was a surplus. Quite clearly, this was not the case. France as a whole (although this is merely a notional unit: there would be no 'national market' worthy of the name before the spread of the railways) had, in order simply to feed her inhabitants, to make good a frequent, almost regular deficit in cereal production. It could only be done – since everything had to be paid for in the end – thanks to the export of surplus wines and industrial products, not counting income from shipping and trade – in short by using those sectors of the trade balance that were in surplus.

We should not however exaggerate a deficit which, although visible, was not huge if set in the proper context, that is the mass of consumption.

In the first place, the importing of grain was confined primarily to Paris and coastal regions: the nodal points of the incoming grain trade were Dunkerque, Rouen, Nantes and Marseille, but also in practice any port able to handle if necessary shipments of 'sea-borne grain', at local request, even the smallest harbours. In April 1683 for instance, a letter informs us that 'there arrived a great quantity of rye from Danzig at Sables [d'Olonne] and Nantes, from where it was distributed throughout Poitou'.[468] In January 1701, a small English ship and three Dutch, laden with wheat, rye and oats, arrived at Saint-Martin-de-Ré, 'and they gave us to hope that several others were on the way'.[469] Foreign grain arriving by sea travelled up the great waterways: up the Seine to Paris, up the Loire to Orléans; up the Rhône to Lyon.

Turgot estimated that in his day the *entire* sea-borne traffic in grain in Europe came to 5 million quintals. France only received some of this (perhaps 2.5 million, or half the putative figure) in other words 5% of annual French consumption, which amounted to some 50 million quintals.[470] The 12% figure for 1913 noted by Alfred Sauvy suggests a higher percentage. If the figures can be trusted, the problem had become worse. Over this long time-scale, we should not pass too harsh a retrospective judgement on the monarchy of the *ancien régime*. It often did its best, and should not be condemned on account of the persistent myth of the Famine Pact. Should one even blame it for having too energetically forbidden grain exports and left the door open to foreign corn? Did the Restoration and the July Monarchy do much better with the 1819 law on the sliding scale and the 1832 law on customs tariffs? Did these not contribute to keeping the cost of living high, and indeed too high, as a series of grain riots and disturbances seem to suggest?[471]

What is more, we should not forget that foreign goods all too easily found their way across frontiers which were far from closely guarded in the late eighteenth century, either in France or the rest of Europe. There was continual coming and going. Would it have been possible in any case to police the grain trade, which was dispersed over thousands of minor transactions, so that small-scale dealers would often have been the only identifiable traders? 'The [French] grain trade is worth more than Peru,' Mably wrote.[472] But it was a trade fragmented to excess. Boisguillebert, who wanted freedom to export grain, a cause supported by the large landowners, claimed that imbalances of supply were easy to remedy. (In 1679, he wrote, it took only 25 to 30,000 *muids* of foreign grain to settle a harvest crisis as bad as that of 1693–4.)[473] Was he right? Yes and no. One should not over-dramatize the grain deficit – but neither should it be underestimated.

Because of problems of communication, the imbalances and disturbances *within* France combined with the export problem to create contradictions, shortages and nagging worries. A province might escape the general tribulations one year – as Brittany did in 1709–10 – only to succumb the next. So it is hard to take seriously the retrospective judgement of M. de Lamare in his *Traité de la police* (1710) that for eight years running, between 1684 and 1692, the *whole* of France had enjoyed good harvests.[474] What we do know is that when, by the decrees of 1763 and 1764, the royal government allowed cereals to be exported, provided that the price of the quintal was no more than 12 *livres*, the result was unexpected havoc, with contradictory speculation and a general price rise. The *intendants* were searchingly questioned in an effort to find out what had gone wrong. All their replies tend in the same direction: as they saw it, the grain problem was above all a domestic problem, because of the sometimes absurd disparities between prices in different provinces, even neighbouring ones. Distance divided and fragmented France, making life difficult.

How could it have been otherwise? In the early days of the Revolution, it was considered that of the 32 provinces (or rather *généralités*), 12 were regularly in deficit, 10 were in balance, and 10 had surpluses. But these inequalities did not balance each other out, since transport was slow, costly and inefficient.

War added to the normal difficulties. Hostilities on the frontier or beyond meant sending supplies long distances, sometimes to an absurd degree. The requisitions and exactions of the army's suppliers, who were granted or assumed the right to do as they pleased, threw the usual channels of supply into disarray. Consequently *intendants* frequently objected to the orders they received. When in August 1709 the government demanded from the *généralité* of Soissons a 'levy of ten thousand sacks of *méteil* or barley flour', the *intendant* Le Févre d'Ormesson replied on the 26th that this would be difficult, since 'the barley harvest is only just beginning and will not be completed until the end of September',[475] so the sacks would not be ready before the end of October. In any case the figure of ten thousand sacks might not be reached: 'this region produces next to no barley as a rule; few farmers have sown it and then only in the valleys, since this kind of grain is not grown on the best land . . . what is more, the cultivation of land in my area has been almost continuously interrupted by the constant convoys to which it has been subjected these last four months'. He meant that government requisitions of the peasants as hauliers had prevented them from working on the land. That said, d'Ormesson proposed instead to send 'unmilled oats, or oatmeal, or other lesser grains which can be used for bread' – a proposal that was apparently accepted, since in the margin of his letter another hand has written *bon* (the eighteenth-century equivalent of 'OK'). If the government yielded to the *intendant*'s arguments, it was because there was really very little choice. The supplies were intended for troops at the front: all this took place just two weeks before the battle of Malplaquet (11 September 1709), a terrible massacre, which ought to be reckoned a defeat, but which nevertheless blocked the invader's path on the northern frontier fortified by Vauban.

War also meant many troop movements back and forth. Two days after the letter quoted above, 'the remnants of the troops coming out of Tournai' descended on the district round Laon and looted 'vegetables and gardens, because they had not been paid. The townspeople had agreed to let them have bread, but the soldiers and grooms were not content with that.'[476]

Even far away from the theatre of operations (where almost anything went), and even when the fighting was over, troops were a constant nuisance and torment to town and countryside alike, since they moved round the country and at the end of every year took up winter quarters. Whether sedentary or on the move, the soldier was billeted on civilians who were obliged to feed him – a system known as *étape* and *ustensile*.[477] Reimbursement followed, but only after some delay, and through middlemen who took a percentage for themselves. In 1682, so many troops had passed through their towns that the residents of Bourg-en-Bresse, Coligny and Villars 'decided to abandon their houses since they could no longer bear the burden of billeting'.[478] Worse was to come in 1694: the harvest having been disastrous that year, the Bresse and Bugey were reduced to famine by 'the passage of over 27,000 soldiers who spent [a mere] five nights in the region of Bugey'. This was happening well before Louis XIV's wars: in August 1625 in the Saintonge, 'there are two or three regiments in the king's service who have done more damage than lightning, plague and famine put together'.[479]

War also meant increased taxation, reduced state assistance and enforced enrolment in the army. According to Pottier de la Hestroye in 1716, if the harvest was 'less abundant than in the past' during the War of the Spanish Succession, 1701 to 1713–14, the war itself must be blamed, 'since it has drained the countryside of men, not leaving enough behind to till the land'.[480]

All these hardships combined to aggravate the fragility of an economy based on agriculture. It is this fragility that Friedrich Lütge condemns, when he states that in general any region dependent principally on agricultural and artisanal production would be unable to feed its own people properly, once a certain population threshold was exceeded. Is this the explanation we have been looking for? Was France over-populated? If so, Arthur Young was right when he said of the French population on the eve of the Revolution that it contained 'six million inhabitants too many!'[481] Jean Fourastié has always pointed out in this connection, with some reason, that productivity per head of the rural workforce was low. In 1700, the labour of ten active peasants supported only 17 people, including themselves.[482]

This all helps to explain that even when France could feed its own population, it could not feed it very well. In 1700 (in constant francs of 1949) the total consumption by one individual was worth 50,000 francs; in 1972, it was worth 476,00. And to make the difference clearer, Jean Fourastié adds: 'the lowest paid worker in 1700 ate eight times as much bread as his equivalent in 1976; this was because any other food was beyond his pocket'.[483]

Penury, shortage, famine, grain riots and revolts

For centuries on end, the great majority of French people suffered from these dramatic shortages, dwelt in constant anxiety, and from time to time rebelled. Five expressions recur in the documents: penury, severe shortage (*disette*), famine, grain riots, and revolts. The word penury, the least serious, appears the least often; *disette* and *famine* on the contrary crop up frequently; indeed it was but a step from one to the other: documents refer to great shortage ('*une grande disette*'), or a 'shortage likely to produce famine'. There was however a hierarchy of hardship, as there was also a difference between the grain riot – a short-lived affair lasting perhaps a day or a few hours, on a highway, a riverbank, or a marketplace – and the popular peasant rising or revolt which might last weeks and months over a wide radius.

But penury, shortage, famine, riot and revolt were in fact closely associated. Disturbances were simply the expression of deep-seated anxiety, evidence that life in France was constantly

agitated by the tragic inadequacy of agricultural production. I say
tragic because the evidence is often distressing: in the terrible years
1661–2, 1692–3, and 1709 for instance. On 26 January 1739, the
marquis d'Argenson wrote baldly in his *Mémoires* that 'in the provinces, men are dying or eating grass'.[484] In 1652, eye-witnesses
describe the 'people of Lorraine and surrounding areas eating grass
in the fields like cattle'. In Burgundy in 1662, 'a third of the inhabitants, even of good towns', were driven to do the same and
'several ate human flesh'. In 1694, near Meulan, people were
'living on grass like animals'.[485] Since the towns were comparatively protected and given assistance, peasants who had been eaten
out of their homes by the townsfolk pressed into the cities only to
collapse and die in the streets. (The same was true all over Europe:
in Venice, peasants from the terra firma came to die on the bridges
and canal sides.) On 2 May 1694, the *intendant* of Lyon reported
that 'the shortage is becoming so pressing that the city of Lyon is
inundated with peasants, who despite all precautions have made off
with all the bread; to do so, they throw it at night over the city
walls, and we have confiscated some that was being carried off in
barrels as if it were wine'.[486]

Desmarets de Vaubourg, the *intendant* of Auvergne, had just
returned from the *élections* of Mauriac and Aurillac on 20 June
1691: 'the latter has been suffering greatly for the last two to
six months [the gap between one harvest and another] since the
peasants have entirely consumed the grain and other foodstuffs
they had stored from last year'. Bread was distributed

> once a week to all the poor who present themselves in four
> different towns in this *élection*. And there were so many at the
> distribution at Aurillac on the 8th of this month that eleven
> persons were crushed to death in the crowd, however hard
> we tried to maintain order. There are normally more than
> 6,000 people there on distribution days, and a proportionate
> number in the other towns. The distributions are made on the
> same day in all four towns so that the same poor cannot col-
> lect it from two places.[487]

The *intendant* gave 'two reasons for the distressing condition of this *élection*': the poor harvests of the previous two years and 'the increase in the *ustensile* last year, to a level of 666,000 *livres* for the Auvergne as a whole, which is a little too much for this province'.[488]

What other voices should we listen to? The parish priest of Tulle perhaps, on 11 December 1692? This little town was one of the permanent pockets of poverty in the *généralité* of Limoges. 'There are not six families within a radius of ten leagues', writes Father Melon, 'who have bread to eat, and they have used up all their beets and have no other food, the frost having wiped everything out. If the province is not succoured promptly, two-thirds of the people will perish' – an obvious exaggeration, but it was his task to soften hearts in high places.[489]

Historians tell us that France witnessed 13 *nationwide* famines in the sixteenth century; 11 in the seventeenth and 16 in the eighteenth.[490] Even supposing this list to be complete and accurate (which I doubt) it leaves out *local* famines, yet these were very frequent, occurring almost every year somewhere or other. And it cannot be said that even in the nineteenth century dearth and famine were things of the past. In 1812, France was split in two by 'terrible food shortage';[491] in 1816–17, it was ravaged by a famine which quickly spread throughout the country; in 1819, the sliding scale to regulate imports was introduced; there were a series of bad harvests between 1820 and 1830, in 1837 and again in 1846–8. The last one triggered a typical *ancien régime* crisis, that is one rural in origin, which contributed to the fall of the July Monarchy. The authorities had to resign themselves to reducing the tariffs on Russian wheat entering France, 'imported through Marseille and Toulon and carried up the Rhône by about fifty steamships'.[492] But after the extremely poor wheat and potato harvest of 1853, this source of supply could not be appealed to, because of the Crimean War, which halted all shipments from Odessa between 1854 and 1856. For three years the state was obliged to intervene energetically and in Paris Baron Haussmann had to organize a 'bakery fund' to avoid another subsistence crisis.[493]

Peasant revolts and grain riots

The peasant world was perpetually convulsed by the fluctuations of the grain harvest. Trouble would break out suddenly and as suddenly die down again. This had been the case even in the distant past: the *jacquerie* of 1356 began on 28 May of that year and ended on 10 June, following the pitiless repression dealt out by Charles the Bad.[494] Tens of thousands of peasants were massacred. The same short duration and collapse in the face of repression was typical of major uprisings in other countries too: the English Peasants' Revolt of 1381, and the Peasant War in Germany in 1525. Every peasant revolt disturbed the established order, taking advantage of some emergency or lapse of attention by the authorities to occupy the terrain, but usually proved unable thereafter to control or hold on to it. Repression had the implacable technical superiority of armed force on its side.

So popular uprisings followed a familiar, repetitive pattern. They did however change in character in France, broadly speaking after the 1680s, in the latter part of Louis XIV's reign. Before this decade, the troubles were a combination of every element: spontaneous outburst, political action, protest against the social order, tax revolt, anger born of want. They expressed themselves in large-scale riots, which spread like wildfire and were above all directed against taxation. When the Vivarais region rose up in 1670, it took over an old song from the days of the Fronde:

> *Paysan prends tes armes*
> *Sus aux vautours, aux gabelous*
> *Il faut hurler avec les loups*
> *Ton hoyau, ton pic et ta bêche*
> *A leur tour percevront l'impôt*

(Peasants, to arms!
Down with all vultures and taxmen!
You must howl with the wolves

385

Your hoe, pick and spade
Will collect the tax this time)[495]

After 1680, uprisings were more often straightforward bread riots, in town or country, breaking out sporadically and lasting a very short time – one or two days, a week at the outside. Repression quickly put them down, the not very strong *maréchaussée* being sufficient to the task. The army merely made a token appearance and doubled the number of patrols. This latter-day kind of riot was prompted by the high price or scarcity of bread. I do not entirely accept Louise Tilly's argument (1972) that bread riots after the seventeenth century represented a series of political attacks on the government:

> The simplistic economic formula shortage = hunger = riot cannot explain food riots in France after the seventeenth century [she writes]. The explanation should rather be sought *in a political context* – the development of government policy – and in the long-term transformation of the grain market.[496]

It is certainly the case that all riots were directed against the prevailing order, and in France the monarchical order had taken over from the local authorities which had previously handled questions of subsistence. So the government was automatically involved during the slightest disturbance. But poverty, shortage and fear of famine, rather than political intent, seem to me to have been the most important motives.

What does seem new to me is the increased frequency of comparatively minor troubles and their simultaneous appearance in both town and countryside. Hitherto, the town had been something of a world apart, spontaneously hostile to the peasants. In 1630, to take but one example, Dijon was briefly threatened by the neighbouring winegrowers, who had risen in protest. 'Most of the best families have transported to the countryside their most precious furniture, papers and money, out of panic lest these satyrs [*chèvrepieds*] in their bacchic fury unleash a second alarm more bloody than the first.'[497] The city gates were closed and all the companies were called to arms (between two and three thousand men) in order to capture in the end some ten or twelve offenders. For fear that other winegrowers should try to rescue them, the guard was doubled at night and all clerics, whether in communities or secular, were put on alert.

Revolts before 1680

For the period before 1680, I shall go back only as far as the last years of the sixteenth century, when popular uprisings were widespread in response to the excesses of the tax-collectors, the pillage of the Wars of Religion, and the savagery and torture committed by both troops and nobles, who literally rampaged through the countryside, whether royalists or members of the Ligue. When the situation was reversed, their violence was matched by brutal violence from the peasants. Peasant self-defence leagues appeared: between 1589 (the year of the battle of Arques) and 1593 (the year Henri IV entered Paris), there were formed the *Francs Museaux*, the *Château-verts* and the *Lipans*; later came the *Tard-venus*, the *Tard-avisés*, and the *Croquants*. This last name caught on and spread throughout the entire rebel zone which included in the end virtually the whole of western France, from the Perche and Marche to the Limousin – the centre of the revolt – and the Périgord. It was a region where few royal troops would be found, engaged as most of them were in the north and east of the kingdom.

Peasant violence went beyond anything ever known.[498] But in the end the mass of rebels (about 50,000 men in the field), although armed with muskets, were no match for the cavalry and the discipline of the small detachments of troops sent to repress them. The 1594 revolt, which began in February, ended in June that year, as soon as repressive action, organized from a distance, had had time to get going. Later on, other spectacular revolts broke out only to collapse: in the Quercy in 1624; in Poitou, Aquitaine and Vivarais in 1632; in Languedoc and Aquitaine in 1635; in the large zone stretching from the Allier valley to the Atlantic in 1636; throughout western France in 1643; throughout the Midi, south of a line from Bordeaux to Grenoble in 1645; in the Vivarais in 1670; in Basse-Bretagne in 1675. The revolt on each occasion swept over a large area, but never lasted long.[499]

The Vivarais uprising lasted from May to July 1670. The rising of the *Bonnets rouges* (Redcaps) in Brittany, which began in May 1675, ended in August. As usual, the repression was horrifying: the troops behaved worse than on enemy soil. 'Our poor *bas-bretons*', wrote Madame de Sévigné, who happened to be on the spot, 'as soon as they see soldiers, fling themselves to the ground and say *mea culpa*, the only words of "French" they know . . . There is no end to the hangings.'[500]

In between these open insurrections, one should bear in mind the many stifled revolts, outbreaks of flame that did not spread, or were quickly dowsed, perhaps to flare up once more: they add up to a substantial total. Yves-Marie Bercé has counted between 450 and 500 'sparks of revolt' in Aquitaine alone, between 1590 and 1715.[501]

Since the appearance of the French edition of Boris Porchnev's pioneering book in 1963,[502] there has been much debate among historians as to the causes and characters of these revolts. Class struggle, political revolt, anti-tax movement – all the explanations contain some truth. In a recent article,[503] Hugues Neveux concentrates on the revolts themselves and tries to reconstitute their ideology. He stresses the precarious situation of the peasant: a new tax, a further turn of the fiscal screw, an increase in social exploitation, a downturn in the economy, a fall in the price of grain – and he would be flung into poverty or even beggary. This was too much to bear. The revolts were inspired by misery and despair.

Perhaps too they can tell us something else, from their geographical distribution. If one transfers on to a map of France the regions mentioned by Porchnev as involved in successive revolts between 1623 and 1648 (cf. Figure 48), one finds that most of them took place in certain areas of the west and south. We are taken back by another route to those two congenital divisions of the country, one running north–south from the outskirts of the Armorican Massif, the other running west–east along the Loire. It is surprising, incidentally, that this geography of revolt has not, so far as I know, been the subject of more attention, except in passing, from Pierre Goubert.[504]

Such geographical concentration requires an explanation: but are we in a position to provide one? A differential history of France seems always to be slipping through our fingers at all the great turning-points of the past. Is it possible to shed any light on the problem by pointing out: 1) that the north had a better balanced economy of day-to-day subsistence; 2) that it was kept under firmer control by the royal authorities for strategic reasons, since it was nearer Paris; 3) that in the north where transport was easier, repression could quickly be mobilized; and 4) that grain riots affected all regions, but with varying intensity.

After 1680

This unbridled violence unquestionably subsided after the 1680s, if one sets aside the exasperated revolts of the Camisards in the Cévennes (1702–5), in which religion was virtually the sole cause of unrest. Why then should violence have died down after these watershed years? This is not an easy question to answer.

What happened in effect was that the country submitted to a social and political order, authoritarian in character, yet accepted and acceptable. Can it be explained by the move from direct to indirect taxation (the latter less resented by taxpayers than the former), a move begun in Colbert's time? Or can it perhaps be explained by the advance of state centralization which reinforced the power of the monarchy and taught it how to make itself better obeyed? Was it perhaps because the Church, after what we historians consider as the catastrophic Revocation of the Edict of Nantes (1685), finally came round to the monarchy, following a long period of hesitation? Frequently hostile to the government at the time of the Fronde, the clergy now changed sides.

A final possible explanation is the improvement in the living standards of ordinary people, both in town and countryside. This is hard to establish, yet it was after all in the last quarter of the seventeenth century that maize became a regular crop in the Aquitaine

FIGURE 48
Popular uprisings in seventeenth-century France

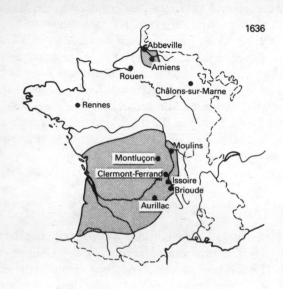

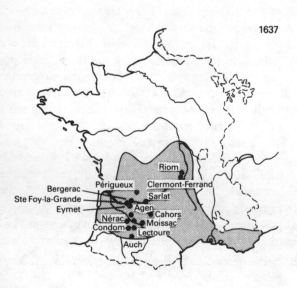

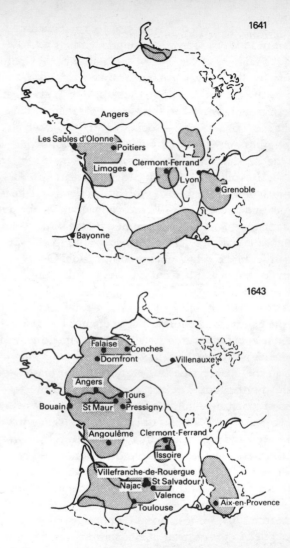

1641

1643

From the 24 maps in Boris Porchenev's study of the years 1626–1648, I have chosen four indicating the largest area and the regions most often affected.

Source: B. Porchnev, *Les Soulèvements populaires en France 1626–1648*, 1963.

basin, spreading out from the Toulouse area and eventually reaching the entire south of France, putting an end, as we have already noted, to the famines of the 'age of the baroque'.[505] Could this be one reason for the arrival of comparative calm after 1680? This would last at least until the 'flour wars' of May 1775 – that serious outbreak of trouble which, in the eyes of some historians, already carried the seeds of a potential social revolt,[506] and which affected Paris, Versailles and the nearby countryside, following Turgot's edict on the freedom of the grain trade (1774).

With the Revolution, riots and disturbances spread, without however matching the degree of violence of the past. The unrest of the summer and autumn of 1789 took advantage of the deterioration of the state and the fantasies fanned by the Great Fear. But by the autumn, the national guard formed in the towns was already restoring order in the neighbouring countryside. Oddly enough, in some regions, the peasants went on paying tithes until December 1790.[507]

One is struck by the limited nature of food riots and disturbances in the eighteenth century. The sequence of events is always the same, the apparent causes are always the same, the response of the authorities is always the same. Scarcity of grain, sharp rises in its price, in the countryside but particularly in market-places in towns, are the triggers. The reaction of the people was usually some kind of blockade – holding up grain in transit, whether it was travelling by cart, pack animals or boat, through a town, village or the open countryside; or else there might be riots by townspeople. When the protesters were successful, the grain would be appropriated, perhaps sold at prices below the current rate, or sometimes simply looted – that is if the *maréchaussée* or troops had not arrived in time.

On 2 March 1709, for instance, grain purchased in Lorraine had been stockpiled in the château of Bourbonne – at the time a 'little bourg' in what is now the *département* of the Vosges. Some of this grain was 'laden on the backs of sixty-eight mules, each carrying a sack weighing 200 pounds'. They set off for the river-port of Gray on the Saône, 67 kilometres away, where the sacks were to be embarked:

> The populace, assembled in the bourg of Bourbonne sounded the alarm bells, several men and women, armed with knives, billhooks and iron bars gave the signal, and despite the remonstrances of the provost who came running, burst open all the sacks and spilled the grain in the streets. Without further inquiry, one woman . . . and a man named Albin, a shoemaker, who had appeared to be the most furious and who had played the most part in this riot

were taken to prison in Langres.[508]

This account differs little from the report by the *intendant* Vaubourg on a popular uprising at Bar-le-Duc on 19 October 1697:

> The cornchandlers of Vitry having sent through twelve waggon loads of grain purchased in Lorraine and Barrois, three or four hundred women, claiming that these purchases sent up the price of grain, which is true, assembled and carried off several sacks, and pierced others with knives. The police force had some trouble restoring order. A few days earlier there had been similar trouble in Nancy, which the officers and garrison had promptly subdued.[509]

One might dimiss these as trifling incidents, were it not that events like this, minor in themselves perhaps, occurred so repeatedly. In 1709, a particularly bad year, disturbances broke out virtually all over France: in Châlons-sur-Marne (possibly a misreading for Châlon-sur-Saône) on 15 March;[510] at Les-Ponts-de-Cé on the Loire, on 16 March, where the crowd held up six large barges of grain about to sail, and forced the terrified merchants to sell the grain on the spot; at Angers on 18 March when the populace looted the grain-stores belonging to cornchandlers and bakers[511] (there were several deaths); in Orléans on 4, 16[512] and 27 April.[513] On the latter date, grain destined for the troops in far-off Dauphiné was being embarked to travel up the Loire. The wind was favourable, and a crowd gathered to prevent the boats from leaving, 'but the fear of the two regiments stationed here held back the populace which however wept bitter tears to see the grain leaving the town'. Similar events occurred at Coulommiers on 1 May 1709.[514] And on 16 July in Montjean on the Loire, 'all the people, both men and women, . . . with arms, sticks and stones', gathered outside the château to prevent the departure of grain which had been stored by the tenant of the maréchal de Villeroy. Only the intervention of the *intendant* and the promise to keep half the grain on the spot restored some calm. Reprisals were confined to six months in prison for a few ring-leaders so as 'not to irritate further a populace . . . already sorely tried by insistent hunger'.[515]

But such leniency was not customary: yesterday (15 June 1709), wrote the *intendant* of the Bourbonnais, Mansart de Sagone,

> I had to pass judgement on three ring-leaders of these grain looters and robbers, who had assembled in armed gatherings. They were sentenced to be hanged. Two of them were executed here [in Moulins] and I had the third sent to the scene of the crime to intimidate his fellows. I think this will have a salutary effect in the districts and that this example will stop this outbreak of robbery and brigandage. There are still some in the cells in the keep and in other places, whom I shall try when their cases are ready to be heard.[516]

The justice of the *ancien régime* was not the same as ours. It sought to make examples of offenders in order to show its strength and determination, so as not to have to react more vigorously. But its patience was quickly exhausted. Earlier the same year, in March 1709, at Pithiviers, a cavalry detachment had been sent in to quell a disturbance: the worst was avoided but twelve rioters were thrown into prison. 'I think it is necessary to make a few examples,' wrote the *intendant* of Orléans.[517]

But the troubles died out one day only to break out again the next. As one town or country district calmed down, disturbances appeared somewhere else. Every bad harvest triggered revolt. In August and September 1771, loads of grain were being stopped on all the roads. Grain was so scarce and the price so high at Cholet that nine tenths of the 3,000 inhabitants were without bread and rose up in protest: 'They said aloud that they would rather be hanged than die of hunger.' Incidents were taking place daily and would not stop, the man on the spot wrote to the *intendant*, 'unless some grain finally gets here'.[518]

In order to reconstruct the complete record of these events, one should add to these visible acts less visible thefts and the ubiquitous presence of the salt-smugglers (who did not disappear until the salt-tax, the *gabelle*, was finally abolished by the Constituent Assembly in 1790), as well as rural brigandage, and strikes by the growing numbers of artisans of the late eighteenth century. Above all, one should find a place in the picture for the streams or rather oceans of beggars. We shall have to return presently to consider this immense social drama which the *ancien régime* would bequeath to nineteenth-century France.

All the disturbances became more marked during the Revolution, calmed down to some extent under the Empire, but flared up again with the serious subsistence crisis of 1812. What matters is to recognize the continuity under the Restoration, the July Monarchy and even the Second Empire, of these riots which could occur with the same sudden and devastating violence as hailstorms. Louise Tilly's article is a salutary demonstration that grain riots went on as if nothing had changed, throughout the first part of the nineteenth century.

Precise documentary evidence makes it possible to study in detail the widespread agitation sweeping through France from autumn 1816 until the summer and grain harvest of 1817.[519] The 1816 harvest had been 50% down on the normal figure. Exhausted by devastation and the burden of feeding the foreign occupying armies of 1814 and 1815, France had no grain reserves left. Appeals had to be made for grain from the Baltic and the Black Sea, and for flour from Baltimore. But help could not reach France overnight and impatience mounted in Rouen and Marseille.

It would be an exaggeration to say that the shortages of this time were 'more artificial than real', but it is true that anxiety, rumour, and the gloomy predictions of hostile public opinion played a part in the panic which swept the kingdom. As a contemporary put it, 'the shortages that exist in people's minds are perhaps the most dangerous'.[520]

At any rate, the price of wheat shot up, markets ran out of stocks, and poor people everywhere protested and rioted. The use of force, threats, appeals to common sense and substantial shipments of grain were required before order could be restored. Every detail of these riots, alarming as they were to the authorities, is preserved in the reports in the *Archives Nationales*: here are the angry crowds, the repeated incidents in market-places, the troop movements, the calling out of the national guard, the decisions of the authorities. The impression one has is of being transported back fifty or a hundred years into the *ancien régime*. We find all the same scenarios; the same actions by rioters, the same precautions taken by the authorities (forbidding trouble-makers access to bell-towers for instance, lest they sound the alarm); the same delays, zeal and indeed the same powerlessness of the local authorities, in this small-scale war where every day brought a fresh outbreak of trouble.

For every one incident in the 1816 crisis that is recorded, hundreds more can be imagined. Here we are in Toulouse on 12 November 1816: there is much unrest, but the cornmarket is under heavy guard and the forces of order are patrolling the streets. The prefect takes up the story:

all at once, a large crowd, forcing its way up the approach roads, reached the gates of the market and renewed most vociferously and tumultuously the demand that the price of wheat should be fixed at 24 francs. I arrived at this very moment . . . My first concern was to dispose the troops in such a way as to hold back the populace which was pressing towards the *carreau*, the market square,[521] now no longer with the aim of buying grain at 24 francs but of looting it. The layout of the terrain made it very difficult for the troops to manoeuvre, since the covered market with its rows of columns is surrounded by very narrow streets, and could only be defended by hand to hand fighting. Moreover, we wished to exhaust every means of persuasion before having the troops fire on the crowd. So we braved the greatest dangers to try to make the multitude listen to the language of reason and of its own interests, without however appearing to yield to its seditious clamour. Five times, the detachment guarding the main entrance to the square seemed to sway under the assaults of the populace; five times it stood solid with our support; finally, after three hours of resistance, we tried, successfully, the bold manoeuvre of having a column of dragoons advance and they managed to clear the market and all its entrances.[522]

So in the end, the situation stopped short of tragedy: there were no shots and no arrests. Mounted cavalrymen put the crowd to flight, and the people went home. Reading this and various other accounts, one is inclined to feel some relief. There was indeed no shortage of expressions of sympathy in the official files. The sub-prefect of Verdun wrote to the minister of the interior on 15 September 1817: 'Almost always, Monseigneur, there is some justice and common sense behind the judgements of the people.'[523]

We might begin to believe that brutal repression had vanished with the *ancien régime* if it were not for certain other reports, notably the socio-drama which occurred at Montargis. It seems probable that the belated riot of 8 July 1817 threw the little town into panic. In the surrounding villages, alarm bells were sounded and crowds of peasants began converging on the town, armed with sticks and carrying empty sacks over their shoulders – fully intend-ing to loot the grain stores, as they had already looted two laden barges on the Orléans canal. But the authorities were waiting for them, some peasants were arrested and imprisoned. The crowd tried in vain to release them, the cavalry arrived and dispersed the crowd with their sabres. But nothing too dramatic occurred at this point.[524] To the sound of cries and women's screams, the demon-strators dispersed. Order eventually triumphed and the night was calm: it poured with rain. One more riot to put down to poverty, famine and failure?

How can you expect the crowd not to go to such lengths [writes one sympathetic witness] when people have no work, no bread, no money, and all their resources are exhausted? Hunger brings despair, and despair excuses everything . . . A multitude driven by hunger would be deaf to the voice of God the Father, if He tried to reason with it.

The drama took an unexpected turn the next day. The *Cour prévôtale* had travelled from Orléans to Montargis to judge 25 of the detainees. And official justice turned out to be implacable: there were five death sentences, including one passed on a woman who, being pregnant, or claiming to be so, was reprieved. The four condemned men were executed in the market-place. 'I do not know how to describe my feelings,' says our anonymous and humanitarian witness. 'I have continuous palpitations of the heart.'

Such cruel repression did not prevent further problems occurring until mid-century. As late as 1852, sacks of grain were looted at Saint Yrieix.[525]

Was the state in any condition to remedy the situation? Its only weapons were the laws which imposed or removed tariffs on imports of foreign grain. These laws were not well regarded. One of them passed in 1832 and fixing the price of imported grain at the frontier, was held responsible for the high price of bread during years of shortage, including the disturbances of 1847 for instance, which were quite serious in several regions. The riots at Buzançais (Indre) even resulted in three death sentences.[526]

Not until the railways were built would rural France finally overcome the obstacles that prevented it from providing the daily bread for its inhabitants, and wipe out at last the spectre of dearth in a country apparently rich, or at any rate better placed than many others, if not completely free from want. If one had to choose a date marking this immense change in our country's history, it would not be unreasonable to point to the abolition of the sliding scale in 1861.[527]

I continue to believe that the economic explanation is the most convincing and find near-confirmation in the sequence of events in Languedoc and Provence. Crises and bread riots were not unknown there between 1595 and 1715. But René Pillorget is categorical: 'there was no peasant war in Provence, no insurrection mobilizing the entire population, not even a district or group of communities. At no time would one find here the equivalents of the *Croquants*, the *Va-nu-pieds* of Normandy or the *Sabotiers* of Sologne.'[528] One reason, perhaps the major reason for this comparative calm was that grain continued to be imported via Marseille: it was sold at high prices, but it prevented scarcity, shortage and famine – and the panic which always accompanied them.

CHAPTER TEN

Progress all the Same

Riots, disturbances, crises, shortages and irregularities continually disrupted French life without ever, it is true, penetrating the entire country. Such unrest was nevertheless a constant indictment of the French economy from early modern times until at least 1850. But while rural France suffered, it was at the same time making progress, although domestic advances were never sufficient to deliver it from its ills. Liberation – and with it irreversible change and deterioration – would be the result primarily of outside forces.

Can we date the changes?

The old way of life lasted, I have suggested, as long as winter went on being a time of hardship, every year bringing round the same misfortunes as in the past. In this respect, it is hard to date the coming of the new age, since the winters of old meant so many things: cold weather, impassable roads, villages cut off by snow or mud, the difficulty of making ends meet between harvests, as food ran short for both men and beasts.

The old life went on, I would also say, as long as bread remained the staple food and consequently the driving force behind price movements: this remained the case until at least 1856, the year when, by pure coincidence, military fanfares marked the return of the troops from the distant but glorious Crimean war (1854–6).

Other changes one might mention include the very slow decline of craftworking, especially in the country; or the gradual triumph of coal over charcoal from about 1840.[529]

But could it not also be said that the old ways persisted, and that self-sufficiency never really died out so long as the horse remained, in town and country alike, both the means and the symbol of activities and communications which would seem desperately slow to us today? In northern and eastern France, ploughing, threshing, reaping and binding all required animal traction. The waggons of the first 'railways' were pulled by horses. In Paris, horse-drawn cabs were still in use in 1914: the new taxis, famed for their role in the battle of the Marne, were only just appearing. And in the countryside, particularly in my native north-east, the horse, which had once been the sign of an advanced economy, remained ubiquitous. Even in 1939, the French army was still hampered by its horse-drawn transport: batteries of 75 mm guns were moved about by horses, with troopers riding alongside and gunners perched on the caissons.

Such survivals from the past mark the course of history. Attending only to these, we might easily imagine that the peasant economy lasted an astonishingly long time in France. The decline of this ancient economy, with its traditional way of life, might be regarded as becoming a serious problem only in very recent French history.

On these questions of recent development, there are two schools of thought. Some historians look at the past through the eyes of the present, working backwards through the course of history and tending to pick out those signs of progress which point forward to the transformations now taking place before our own eyes. And then there are others, like myself (I began as a sixteenth-century specialist) who look at it from the point of view of the previous centuries: they tend to notice the signs of survival and the similarities between past and present, and nothing can shake them from this obstinately held view.

The only solution is to accept both perspectives and to think of the past as being extended into the present, while remaining alert to pointers to the future. France in the nineteenth and early twentieth centuries is in this respect a particularly complex field of study. I shall make no attempt to identify some irrevocable turning-point.

General progress, particular setbacks

Statistics firmly tell us that economic progress in France has been constant and widespread from the beginning of the nineteenth century to the present. The so-called peasant economy, which at some time must have stopped being whole-heartedly such, was affected in its entirety by a movement that gathered pace rapidly in the thirty or forty years following the last war, referred to by French economists as the *Trente* (or *Quarante*) *Glorieuses*. During these years, any setbacks, catastrophes, difficulties or deficits were regularly remedied or overcome. Léonce de Lavergne was already saying as much in 1870:

> Public prosperity has increased since 1815, if not continuously at any rate without major interruption, and has sometimes gone forward in leaps and bounds. Foreign trade has quintupled, industry has quadrupled its products and agriculture, which is less adaptable in the mass, has almost doubled its productivity.[530]

Constant accumulation was at work, propelling the whole economy forward. The average wealth of French people, calculated from inheritances, may have multiplied by as much as 4.5 between 1825 and 1914.[531] In the city of Paris alone, as distinct from the whole of France, fortunes increased 9.5 times.[532]

The immense gap between the capital city and the rest of the country reminds us that economic progress was uneven within society. Certain social classes saw their incomes soar to unimaginable levels in the nineteenth century. One such group were the families connected to the most advanced forms of industry: the profits of the Kuhlmann chemicals firm multiplied by 57 in the course of 45 years (1827–72), while those of the mining company Noeux multiplied by 23 in 20 years.[533] Imagine the wealth of Eugène Schneider (known as Eugène I), the founder of the ironmasters' dynasty that was to preside over Le Creusot: a regent of the Banque de France and a political figure as well, from 1837 until his death in 1875 he saw his fortune increase by 11% a year on average (that is doubling about every six years)![534] French per capita income, by contrast, barely doubled during the first three-quarters of the nineteenth century. Income from real estate doubled or tripled, but at the expense of small farmers or tenants, who suffered from falling agricultural prices until about 1840. After this, there was a reversal of the trend, with a fall in income from land, and a sharp rise in farm profits. The rise did not amount to more than a doubling over thirty years however, culminating in a crisis, and affecting in the end only a minority of farmers, above all those who produced for the market. The others only shared in the movement at some remove.[535]

In fact, in a period of rising prosperity, the less well-off suffered more than one might suppose. Were there simply too many of them, especially in the countryside? I see them as victims of persistent social inequality, of *comparative pauperization*.

France has always had its destitute, that mass of vagrants, beggars and people without work, existing on the fringes of urban and peasant society. Already a visible category in the Middle Ages, they had no doubt always existed, but their numbers were certainly on the increase in the sixteenth and seventeenth centuries. In the age of Louis XIV, *pace* Félix Gaiffe's famous book, it was not so much the unscrupulous and dishonest financiers who represented the 'underside of the *grand siècle*',[536] as these masses of beggars, who in winter besieged the towns and in summer scattered throughout the countryside, often spreading terror. In the eighteenth century, matters became even worse. One has only to think of the devastation wrought by brigands and by the sinister *chauffeurs* as they were called ('foot-burners') who were finally subdued, not without difficulty in about 1803, by mobile troops sent out after them and by military tribunals who sentenced them without mercy.[537]

Vagrants, brigands and beggars continued to haunt France in the nineteenth century. Every prefect was at odds with this endemic beggary: he would manage to rid his *département* of it for a while, and pride himself complacently on his achievement; but the poor had simply moved to the neighbouring *départements* only to return one day. They could turn up almost anywhere from time to time. During the troubles caused by the severe shortages of 1816–17, the authorities were worried by the behaviour of beggars who went round in gangs looting. Official instructions were that vagrancy was to be stamped out.[538] The Minister of the Interior declared that 'gangs of beggars are what most concerns us: the measures agreed between the Ministry of War and National Police and myself lead us to hope that such gatherings will be promptly dispersed'.[539]

This asocial category was a clear sign of the poor health of a society always on the edge of want and poverty, one that found it hard to achieve economic take-off before the end of the nineteenth century in many cases, or even later for certain poor and under-developed regions.

It was, in the end, the call of the towns that gradually rid the countryside of its itinerant population. As late as 1907, the council of the Nièvre *département* was still complaining about 'the endless exodus along public highways' of vagrants 'who live by theft, terrorizing the rural population and often being the cause of uproar in the towns', spreading, what was more, the germs of infectious diseases.[540] Similarly, in a region as poor as the Gévaudan, law reports provide many details of the thefts and violence committed by vagrants, 'until the day they finally left the *département* [of Lozère] for the towns in about 1910'.[541] Some elements of the old France survived almost until our own times.

There was admittedly in the nineteenth century some awareness of the social gravity of the problem – and this was something new. Guy Thuillier cites for example a significant case from the Nivernais region in about 1850: the debate between, on the one hand the authorities, who were seriously investigating working conditions, occupational diseases, the physical poverty of the peasants in the fever-ridden lowlands, malnutrition, the inade-quacies of medicine and hospitals, the scourge of beggary – and who proposed various administrative solutions – and on the other hand the pamphleteers who spoke out against a society which was casting aside 'those who have not been able to find a place at the great industrial banquet', and in which 'twenty-three million people . . . are a standing indictment of the inhumanity of French legislation and *mores*'.[542] One enterprising prefect in 1855 decided to organize a 'joint charity fund', asking local notabilities to channel their private good works into the voluntary subscription of money and goods in kind, entered upon for five years, to be handled thereafter by the administration and managed as a tax. The subscriptions flooded in at first but eventually slowed down and the charity disappeared, as it gradually became clear how helpless it was and how derisory its results, faced with the huge dimensions of the problem of beggary.[543]

Technical advance

In the realm of agriculture proper however, some progress was gradually taking place: not always spectacular and revolutionary, not always effective at first, but innovative in the long run.

Above all, advances were made in equipment. An important date in the history of the plough was 1824, when Matthieu de Dombasle set up his factory making ploughs in Roville (Meurthe).[544] The McCormick reaper-binder (from America) was first seen in France at the 1855 exhibition; it would spread slowly but steadily among French farmers. The steam-thresher had made its appearance slightly earlier in 1851: this thumping and noisy monster was quickly adopted, though it did not drive out horse-powered threshing-machines which remained in use until at least 1914.

Such machines did not take over from one day to the next. They were expensive. The swing-plough was still widely used in central and south-western France and even in the Vaucluse as late as 1852. At the same date, 'in the *arrondissement* of Avignon, the area most suited to ploughing, there are 3,972 ploughs without wheels [i.e. swing-ploughs] for only 737 with either wheel or shoe, and 385 with regular fore-carriage'. In the hilliest areas of the *département*, 'there are only swing-ploughs'.[545] But as late as 1921 in the Armagnac Noir, 'the grain was cut sometimes with a sickle, sometimes by scythe, or mechanical reaper'.[546] The reaper, when used for wheat, left behind it swathes of cornstalks which had to be bound into sheaves by hand.

Gradually though, machines gained the upper hand. In eastern France, the reaper-binder was in use by 1914. As harvest time approached, it was no small business checking the machinery to get it in working order. The local blacksmith was not necessarily the best of repairmen: he welded things together roughly, and insisted on patching up broken parts. Luckily, the machinery was quite sturdy. For this monster (as we thought of it) had no engine: it was set in motion by a team of three or four horses. In areas of triennial rotation, where fields lay side by side without hedges, it was important to mark off the field one was harvesting from the field alongside: a swathe was cut round the edge to provide room for the machine to manoeuvre. In the Meuse, we used to call this *décoter*. It was done with a sickle in a strip as wide as the harvesting machine, so there was a short time at the beginning of harvest that recalled the old days: behind the reaper, men and women would pick up the cut corn and bind it in sheaves to be put on one side for the moment. Later, when the field had been mown, the sheaves were piled up in *meulons* (little ricks), a practice going back only to the early nineteenth century in those parts.[547]

The new machines were spectacular indeed, but did contemporaries perhaps exaggerate their importance? Such at any rate was the view in 1913 of Daniel Zola, a professor at the École de Grignon, and someone who knew a great deal about the realities of French agriculture:

> The use of machines . . . is a very useful corrective to the rise of rural wages in every region. That is indisputable. But one should not, even in this context, exaggerate the importance of the role mechanical instruments are called on to play in farming. In many cases, human effort is indispensable. If one seeks to reduce the cost of labour, changing the crop [in other words eliminating 'incorrect' rotation], afforestation of poor soil, or the conversion of arable land to [forage crops] are much more efficient than the use of the most sophisticated implements.[548]

The real mechanical revolution in France would come much later with the petrol engine.

Perhaps one should also have mixed feelings about the advantages and consequences of the use of fertilizers. I think what really made a difference, apart from a greater use of animal manure, was increasing reliance on marl and lime. In the nineteenth century, lime-kilns sprang up everywhere, in the Maine for example. As for marl, all one needed was enough labour to dig it out, carry it to the fields and spread it like manure. It was a wearisome task, but the countryside was over-populated and there was no shortage of workers. In 1857, on a large farm in Rouvray (Seine-et-Marne), measuring 250 hectares, the owner 'marled half the land, using 50 cubic metres per hectare'.[549] In the Montmorillonnais in about 1830, at least half the acreage consisted of heathland: this dwindled over the next twenty-five years, thanks to the use of lime and marl[550] – a particularly telling example, since this was obviously an extremely poor and backward district.

Other sources of fertilizer were Chilean guano, introduced in about 1850, superphosphates (1867), sodium nitrate and suint (1882), and sulphate of ammonia (1900).[551] While these innovations were important, they were late arrivals, and agricultural progress in the early nineteenth century pre-dated the introduction of such fertilizers, which spread only slowly. In short, progress between 1785 and 1850 or even 1870 was often accomplished by using old-fashioned methods and resources. Forage crops which continued to spread, were no doubt more effective than new fertilizers. Commenting on the progress of agricultural production between 1789 and 1859, Lavergne noted that uncultivated land had diminished by only 4%, 'which is very little for such a long period', but that the farming of cultivated land had changed out of all recognition. In particular, this was because root crops (beet and potatoes) now occupied 1,500,000 hectares instead of 100,000 as previously; because wheat had spread at the expense of rye; and above all because fallow land had diminished by some 50% – 5.5 million hectares instead of 10 million, whereas forage crops now occupied 2.5 million hectares instead of 1 million.[552] Fallow land would disappear even more rapidly between 1860 and 1880.[553]

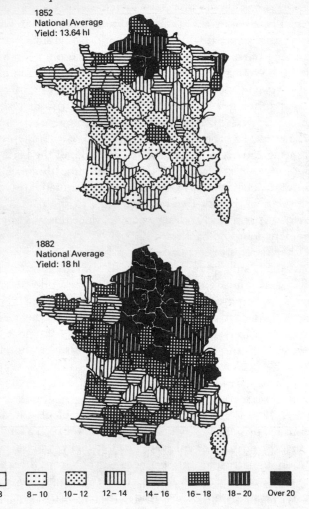

FIGURE 49
Increased wheat yields

1852
National Average
Yield: 13.64 hl

1882
National Average
Yield: 18 hl

| <8 | 8–10 | 10–12 | 12–14 | 14–16 | 16–18 | 18–20 | Over 20 |

Between 1850 and 1880, wheat yields increased generally, but that did not iron out longstanding disparities between *départements*.

Source: F. Braudel and E. Labrousse, eds, *Histoire économique et sociale de la France.*

FIGURE 50
The selective impact of new food crops

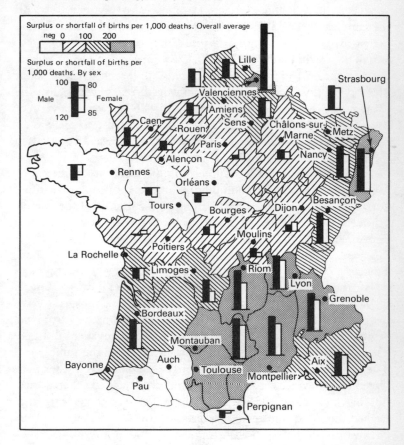

This map showing births and deaths in France in about 1787 suggests a curious difference between regions of demographic decline (such as the *généralités* of Rennes, Tours, Orleans, La Rochelle and Perpignan) and other regions which score well above the modest average rate and have a clear surplus of births over deaths: these are precisely the regions which saw the early introduction of the new food crops – maize and potatoes.

Source: F. Braudel, *Civilization and Capitalism*, vol. III.

In the end, it can be said that French agriculture witnessed progress alongside backwardness, advances alongside setbacks. Yields were very uneven and, compared to those of today, very low. All the same, between 1815 and 1880, they rose slowly but steadily and across the board, although differences between regions persisted, as will be seen in Figures 49 and 50. On a ten-yearly average, wheat yields went up from 10.5 hectolitres to 15, that is a rise of about 40%.[554] But this figure remained and would remain well below the average of other European countries: in 1886–9, despite a yield of 20 quintals in the Nord *département*, 'the national average was no more than 11.8 quintals to the hectare, whereas it was 15 quintals in Germany, 18 in Belgium and 25 in Denmark'.[555]

It was such backwardness, such low productivity, which prolonged the old peasant economy in France until our own time. André Gauron rightly remarks that 'until the middle of the twentieth century, French society remained profoundly rural and peasant-based'.[556] It was to take the upheavals of the *Trente Glorieuses* (1945–75) to shake the foundations of that peasant France.

For the backwardness of rural France has several causes. One is its heterogeneity no doubt: history, change and progress have never taken the same course nor occurred simultaneously from one region to another, one *pays* to another. When advances did take place, all the contestants did not move ahead at the same pace. There were always a few front-runners – and I have rather neglected these favoured few – but behind them lagged the majority, holding back rural society as a whole. All the same, can rural France be held entirely responsible for its destiny and its backwardness? The 'peasant economy' included not only agricultural France but also industrial France and commercial France, and it is the sum of all these that accounts for general economic progress. That is the subject of the next part of this book.

PART IV

Superstructures

> Commerce, manufacture, circulation and
> public credit are all necessary [to the prosper-
> ity of the State] . . . But each element has
> limits and there are relative proportions
> between them. So long as these proportions
> are maintained, they are of mutual benefit;
> otherwise they become mutually destructive.
>
> *Isaac de Pinto*[1]

Superstructures and infrastructures: what goes on at the
top of a given society and what goes on at the bottom.[2]
The distinction is a convenient one, provided it is not
regarded as perfect or immutable; provided that when we
consider the higher regions of the so-called peasant
economy, we do not lose sight of the basic reality – that
vast domain which accounted for the majority of people's
lives and adapted as best it could to the constraints of
successive ages, often with little success on account of its
great inertia and obstinacy in forever remaining the same.
The higher economic activities were, by contrast, more
prone to change, on account of their much smaller volume
during most of the past. They were sometimes altered by
the circumstances of the moment. As Pierre Chaunu puts
it: 'The summit shifts, but the base remains firm. Social
plasticity, relative at the best of times, is confined to the
summit.'[3]

Is the changeable nature of the superstructures one of

their revealing features? We shall try to answer this in relation to France by looking first at the towns; then at the circulation of goods, in all its forms; next at the variable and differing role of craft and industrial production; and finally at what is meant by commerce, by the various forms of credit and by capitalism itself down the centuries. And since the so-called peasant economy consists of the entire, often contradictory complex made up of infrastructures and superstructures, of permanence and change, I shall attempt as I go along to show how contrasts, convergences and imbalances have gone hand in hand with one another, in continuous coexistence, until such time as the whole complex underwent a profound upheaval, the backwardness of the infrastructure notwithstanding. At this point a different economy, a different France was born out of the rapid change and violent upheavals of the contemporary world: we have seen this happen with our own eyes.

Chronologically, the study of the superstructures will mean generally, if not always, adopting stricter time-limits than in the previous chapters. If we wish to use evidence with some statistical foundation – which seems advisable – the latter part of the eighteenth century will frequently be our starting-point. For the years before 1700 or even 1750, one is reliant on description and hypothesis. I shall of course draw on these whenever a journey further into the past seems desirable.

As for our finishing point, somewhere not too far from the present day, I have already pointed out, apropos of rural life, how difficult it is to select a date that marks a complete break. For the towns, the turning-point may have come some time after 1945; for industry there are various landmarks: 1840, 1860, 1896, 1930, 1940, 1945. And more or less the same dates punctuate the history of commerce, banking, credit and currency. Consequently, depending on the requirements of exposition, I shall stop at various points short of the present day, without in theory including our own times in the analysis. Practice may be a different matter: is it ever possible, after all, to omit from long-term analysis all reference to the present, to the time we know and have lived through? It comes unbidden to the mind of reader and writer alike, if only by implication. This is one advantage of taking a long time-scale: the movements it reveals relate automatically to the troubling questions posed by our own times.

CHAPTER ELEVEN

The Towns

There is no escaping the role of the towns in France's changing history, which they have sometimes enlivened and sometimes blocked. We are obliged for several reasons to come back to them and to begin this section by looking at them. In the first place, evidence from the towns goes back a long way and has been brought to light by the labours of many historians. So we know a great deal nowadays about their long early period which would otherwise be lost in obscurity: the trail that has been blazed ahead of us will guide our steps. Secondly, the towns provide us with an exemplary case-study: there can be no doubt that they are in themselves superstructures (more so indeed than is usually allowed).

For between towns and villages there lies an ineradicable frontier, one that has always existed, a line as clear as the Pyrenees, of which it used to be said that what was true on one side was false on the other. The superiority of the urban world could only be established in relation to the rural world alongside it, a world of completely different nature and essence, the more so for having been first dominated and then enslaved. The urban superstructure was a system perched on top of, and explained by, the underlying peasant society which was doomed to carry it on its shoulders.

10% urbanization: an ancient but provisional rule of thumb

An apparent paradox is that the balance between the urban and rural population seems to tilt the wrong way. In France, as in Europe, there were for a very long time indeed far fewer people living in the towns than in the countryside. In France this was true until 1931[4] – a date to be borne in mind, particularly if you find it surprising. It is a useful corrective.

Containing a minority of the population, the town nevertheless had certain obvious advantages: its associates (the villages) were scattered and far apart from one another. From the start, the town was aware of a difference which shaped its identity, of a ceaseless struggle inseparable from its existence and its everyday life. Concentrated in one locality, the town's enforced internal solidarity protected it from shocks, and it would quite soon be acquiring the power, culture, in a word wealth, which it would thereafter have to defend, preserve and put to constructive use. These very long-term realities were perceptible from the start.

Between about 1450 and 1500 – for want of a better starting point – the peasant population represented at least nine-tenths, that is the overwhelming majority, of the population of France. This is a percentage I am obliged to *invent*: but it is the percentage actually calculated by Heinrich Bechtel in his study of the population of Germany in the fifteenth century.[5] This figure – 10% of the population in the towns, 90% in the countryside – is an approximation of course, only *probable* at best. But even if one added or subtracted a few points, it would still be a valid indicator: nine out of ten people were living in villages.

The reader should not imagine however that this proportion represented some minimum level enabling the so-called peasant economy to become established, that is that at least a tenth of the population needed to live in towns for this to happen. In fact the ratio of 1:9, which we can detect in about 1450–1500, already represents an advanced stage: appearing just after the Hundred Years' War, this tension seems to me evidence rather of a certain maturity, the fruit of an already lengthy evolution process.

What is more, we have examples from far later periods than this of urban/rural ratios only slightly over or under the 1:9 figure. In 1812, the year of Napoleon's Russian campaign, Livonia and Estonia contained 811,000 inhabitants between them: the towns (which included the already sizeable Riga and Reval) contained only 66,000 residents; that is, approximately 8.1% of the people lived in the towns and 91.9% in the countryside.[6] About twenty years earlier, in 1796, the great but backward Russian economy was operating, after a fashion, but with only about 6 or 8% of the

FIGURE 51
Rural and urban populations, 1806–1954

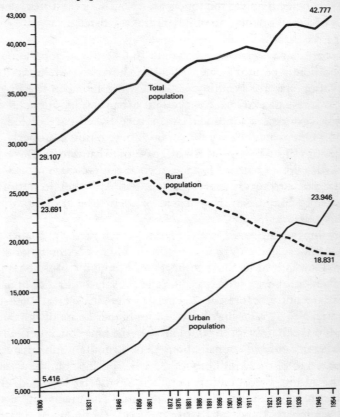

The urban population reached the same level as the rural population in 1931. Figures in thousands.

Source: Y. Tuguault, *Fécondité et urbanisation*, 1975.

population living in towns.[7] And the reader will see from the map in Figure 52 that in the early years of Napoleon I's Empire in France, certain *départements* still had extremely low rates of urbanization: Côtes-du-Nord, 3.1%; Creuse, 4.4%; Dordogne, 4.6%; Vendée, 5.7%; Corrèze, 5.9%. By way of comparison, in England at the time of the Domesday Book (1083–86), of a total of 1.5 million inhabitants (with a density of 11.4 to the square kilometre) the percentage living in the towns was 7%. Three centuries later in 1377, of a total population of 2.6 million, with a density of 20, the figure was 10%.[8]

As for China, as late as 1949, only 10.64% of the population of 542 million lived in the towns. By 1982 however, when the total population was 1,000 million, 20.83% were living in the towns. This is a case of extraordinarily rapid urbanization, but achieved only in very recent times and at the accelerated pace of today's world.[9] One would ideally like to be able to observe properly the beginnings (if such there were) of a case of urbanization. But even under-developed parts of France, such as the Gévaudan (present-day Lozère) or the Vivarais[10] (present-day Ardèche) do not offer the desired conditions. The origins of their urbanization are not readily observable.

All things considered, the 10% rate which seems probable for France under Charles VII or Louis XI should not be thought negligible. I am indeed inclined to imagine – though I could be quite mistaken – that even the expanding and prosperous France of Saint Louis, a century before the disasters of the Black Death and the Hundred Years' War, may have had no higher a rate of urbanization. It was certainly more populous than the kingdom inherited by Louis XI in 1461, which had about 12 or 13 million inhabitants as compared to 21 or 22 million in the earlier period. But the France which had lost almost half its population between 1350 and 1450 had lost more rural than urban inhabitants. The towns, protected by the ramparts they had hastily built or rebuilt, withstood the troubles of the Hundred Years' War better than the surrounding countryside. Joan of Arc had, as a child, we may remember, taken refuge inside the walls of Neufchâteau. Admittedly, the plague probably carried off more victims in urban areas than in the country, but the attraction of the towns remained such that their population returned to former levels, whereas that of the countryside waned.[11]

The growing role of towns

Medieval cities were nevertheless, with some exceptions, very modest towns. They were only just emerging from the surrounding countryside, and did not yet really dominate it. It would take time for the 'urban market to coordinate the economic life of the entire [surrounding] region and come to overshadow . . . the agricultural aspects of the town'.[12] And it would take even longer for relations between towns to shift the whole urban network on to a higher level. The process was a slow one. And if such a thing as urban capitalism existed at all at this time, it was in its early infancy. In short, one should not think of dazzling cities as having sprung up very soon.

French towns had no doubt made some progress, even before the fourteenth century, acquiring liberties and franchises (as *communes* and *villes franches*) and creating new institutions. But for one thing, their move towards autonomy came up against the two 'most solidly structured powers, the Church and the Crown'[13] – the latter in particular – so that they were willy-nilly 'drawn into a territorial policy whose dimensions went far beyond their own horizons or their immediate interests'.[14] This led to internal problems. Secondly, their autonomy itself drove them to incur debts out of all proportion to their income.[15] Finally, although they may have been strongholds and islands of resistance during the troubled age of the Hundred Years' War, they nevertheless suffered the ill-effects of this age when all growth was stifled. All the same, one element of progress, perhaps the most important, was that during the Hundred Years' War the towns gradually freed themselves from their seigneurs and the seigneurial regime,[16] a significant liberation despite the many burdensome and long-lasting remnants of feudalism which would persist until the very end of the *ancien régime*.

But after 1450, and the return of peace, the great healer, the towns came back to life with renewed vivacity. Everything was in their favour: not only the leap in the birth-rate, the rapid rise in productivity in the countryside and the revival of agricultural production, but also the flowering of urban activities, a new dynamism in craft production and the commercial economy.[17] From the mid-fourteenth century, 'industrial' prices, that is the prices of town-produced commodities, began to rise, while farm prices slumped.[18] The price 'scissors' effect operated in favour of the towns. With the lively growth and recovery of the sixteenth century, accompanied by the inflationary price revolution which boosted everything,[19] urban activity in particular, the towns expanded, became more populous, started to develop suburbs, and would soon be able to do as they pleased with the surrounding countryside, now virtually defenceless against them.

In Werner Sombart's view,[20] it was the activity of the towns, as much as (if not more than) the flow of precious metals from America, which accounted for the sixteenth-century price revolution. The towns accumulated this mobile and increasing monetary wealth, thus creating inflation, which they helped to maintain. There is some truth in this. What is certain is that the traditional history of prices, as explained by historians, primarily concerns a process centred on the towns, a superstructural process let us call it, often taking place far above the heads of the peasants.

But we should not imagine these busy towns as being anything like modern ones. For a long while to come, they would have to be self-sufficient merely to survive, drawing on resources from their own territory and earning their bread by the sweat of their own brows. Of necessity,

> they retained links with agriculture. They were embedded in a pastoral economy, and through their thoroughfares wandered cattle, sheep, poultry and pigs, the latter performing the very useful function of cleaning the streets. These stood in great need of cleaning, given the cramped conditions of urban life, the embryonic character of municipal authority and the absence of paving stones. Within their walls, and [close] outside them, the towns were responsible for vineyards, kitchen gardens and even fields. A few pleasure gardens were also planted around aristocratic or ecclesiastical dwellings. Finally, the outskirts of town were notable for

their concentration of polluting trades, such as leather- or wool-processing.[21]

This description of French towns in the twelfth century could be applied unchanged to their sixteenth-century equivalents: in his latest book, Bernard Chevalier revives their old title of *les bonnes villes*,[22] and attempts to estimate their true importance before the disruption brought by the Wars of Religion.

Statistics would of course be more satisfying than evocative descriptions. It so happens that some have survived for the town of Arles in the year 1437–8. Two-thirds of the inhabitants at that time were labourers, farmworkers, owners of flocks, shepherds, fishermen, hunters and *boscadiers* (woodmen): all these people lived off the land, that is off Arles's extensive hinterland. 'Of the other third, almost all owned or at least worked a patch of vines. Arles was a farming town . . . an agro-ville', Louis Stouff concludes.[23]

But all French towns would, for centuries after this, be in much the same position. At grape-harvest time, the winegrowers of Paris were sufficiently numerous to create disturbances and festivities throughout the city. This encroachment of the countryside upon the town is evidence of the latter's imperfect specialization, of the inadequacy of the division of labour until at least the end of the *ancien régime* and even beyond. Over the long, indeed the very long, term, it was to become a serious handicap.

Town and Crown

The towns had another handicap, this one also destined to last. While their political, economic and social importance continued to grow, the towns freed themselves from one subservience only to fall into another – sometimes willingly, sometimes less so. For once the Hundred Years' War was over, the monarchy vigorously reasserted its power, during the harsh reigns of Charles VII (1422–61) and Louis XI (1461–83), by force, legal measures or guile.

The hand of the monarchy was heaviest under Louis XI. Any town that did not submit was harshly dealt with, and brought to heel by armed force. Such was the fate of Angers, Besançon, Dole,

Arras, Cambrai, Valenciennes, Douai, Saint-Omer, Perpignan. An example was made of Arras: occupied in 1477, the town saw the mass expulsion of its inhabitants in 1479. Even its name was changed and new residents were advertised for as settlers! It has been claimed that such treatment was justified by fears for the security of the realm, though if so it was unsuccessful in the end. Nevertheless Arras had been brought to heel by force.[24]

But the required obedience was not necessarily obtained by violent means alone. Louis XI also sought to win over local leaders by setting them against the ordinary people, at the same time working to reduce local authorities to small groups of a few individuals who could be more easily persuaded than larger administrations. Inside the towns, there thus grew up a political elite, a bourgeoisie or rather an aristocracy, whose self-perpetuating dynasties appropriated local government for themselves.

Between such aristocracies and the monarchy there was thus frequently connivance and complicity. The towns placed themselves under royal protection, the better to defend themselves against the common townspeople and the peasants from the nearby countryside no doubt, but also to avoid in part paying the royal taxes re-imposed under Charles VII. As far as Crown policy was concerned, the towns were increasingly becoming the essential agents of public opinion,[25] by now a force to be reckoned with. No state in the process of modernizing could exert power without some form of social complicity. So the monarchy sought the support of the towns or at any rate of the local power elite, hoping that it would choose to collaborate. Thus were laid the foundations of France's future social and political development. Its origins were often rooted in the submission, abdication, not to say treachery, of the urban authorities.

French towns, even in the north which was less accommodating in this respect than the south, did not therefore develop into the urban republics to be found in Italy, Germany and the Netherlands. Was this a good or bad thing? Machiavelli for one thought it excellent, admiring as he did the rise in France of a central political power and of a monarchy determined to impose territorial unity. But it is clear that as a result the rise of the towns did not act as an active ferment on the history of the nation. Instead there were curbs and hindrances, and too great a thirst for power on the part of the state.

As time went by of course, and as latent antagonisms surfaced, the towns tried to shake off the yoke. Whenever the monarchical state encountered serious problems – during the Ligue at the end of the Wars of Religion for instance (particularly in Marseilles),[26] or during the troubles of the Fronde (particularly in Bordeaux)[27] – the towns tried to win back their freedom, or at least to flex their muscles a bit. But it was wasted effort, since they never had time to succeed. The course taken by France did not allow them enough strength to emancipate themselves, and in the end, to be fair, I see them as victims as much as villains. Forced to grow in hostile soil and surroundings, the plant was stunted.

Lacking the ambitions, emulation and occasionally bitter rivalries of the cities which elsewhere had grown into aggressive and expansionist states, French towns retreated into their peaceful backwaters. As a rule, the catastrophes of history hit the peasants, not the towns which complacently despised the former. In Louis XI's time and later, the towns thought themselves to be worlds apart: 'Who will ever be able to say exactly what secret tranquillity was procured for [urban] consciences by that assurance born of stout walls, high towers and firmly barred gates?' asks Bernard Chevalier. If necessary, the town could even survive on its own stocks of food, from within its own bounds. 'When domestic demand [dwindled or] collapsed, and when distant markets closed, there still remained in the hands of tax-collectors, notaries, men of law or magistrates, sufficient resources to keep traders in business and artisans in work'[28] – in other words to carry on living in peace, with modest ambitions.

The stability of the urban network

After 1450, the network of French towns remained the same as the original pattern created many centuries earlier. And it would carry on, bearing the weight of this legacy, virtually unchanged, for many centuries to come. As Jean-Baptiste Say reminded his readers in 1828, 'most of the streets [in Paris were] built before the reign of François I'.[29]

Few new towns were created between 1500 and 1789: Le Havre, dating from 1517, was founded simply as a port and took some time to become a town. Vitry-le-François was built to shelter the population of the nearby small town of Vitry-en-Perthois, which had been burnt down by the emperor Charles V in 1544. The founding of Henrichemont by Sully in 1608, and of Charleville by Charles Gonzaga, duke of Nevers and later of Mantua (on the former site of Arches) were gestures of magnificence possible only for immensely rich men. Of these, Charleville was the only one to become a real town (though it had no more than 300 inhabitants in the early seventeenth century).[30] Cardinal Richelieu in turn followed this ostentatious tradition when he founded his own town of Richelieu in 1637.[31] Sully had disguised his creation at Henrichemont by naming it after the king himself, but Richelieu did not bother to take even this precaution. His town never developed though, and today it is a rather strange museum, a fossilized seventeenth-century new town, 60 kilometres from Tours.

The same magnificent ambitions – but on the unparalleled scale of the Sun King – inspired the building in 1661–82 of the palace of Versailles, 'the stage . . . and altar of the kingdom'.[32] Around the âteau, a town grew up. Paris thereby lost some of the advantages brought by the Court, but the capital's fortunes were not seriously affected.

Finally, one should note the construction of Rochefort, which Vauban began fortifying from 1666, on an inland site but looking seawards; of Lorient, on the former site of Port-Louis, which was ceded to the French Indies Company; of Sète, which would eventually be France's second-largest port on the Mediterranean. And it is worth mentioning, just for the record, Colbert's modifications to Brest, Marseille and Toulon, while among the three hundred towns which Vauban fortified or on which he laid his mark, a few were created *ex nihilo*: Huningue, Sarrelouis and Longwy in 1679; Mont-Louis in 1681; Fort-Louis in 1687; Mont-Royal and Mont-Dauphin in 1692; Neuf-Brisach, on the left bank of the Rhine in

1698. These were small towns, in which 'the military tolerated the residents, but not overmuch'.[33] In later years, they stagnated.

All in all, the new foundations listed here can be described as exceptions proving the rule: they amount to no more than a score among a thousand towns.

Choice of site

Most French towns remained on the sites originally chosen, whether in Gallo-Roman times (the largest towns as a rule) or during the renewal of the urban fabric in the eleventh and twelfth centuries: the latter were generally intermediate towns, filling in gaps, and represented revivals in most cases rather than foundations.

There is nothing surprising about stability of location: a town's site was its point of anchorage, from which it was impossible to escape. As soon as its inhabitants numbered a thousand, or even less, a town was obliged to open up to the outside world, and this in turn meant having within reach an area equipped with water, food, wood, building materials and lastly people – since no town, until the nineteenth century, could keep up its population figures without immigrants from outside, in the first instance those from the nearby countryside. But the latter were rarely sufficient in themselves.

Paris had the good fortune to be situated in a most favoured region, one 'provided with everything'. It was thanks to these resources that the city survived the often terrible times of the Hundred Years' War.

Water was plentiful, unlike in the Beauce; the rivers contained plenty of fish; the forests were said to be well-stocked with game; the fields around Gonesse were reputed for their rich cereals; the slopes of Issy and Suresnes provided drinkable wine; the flood plains and low-lying areas were good grazing land, and a humble village like Vanves produced butter 'so excellent that the butter of Flanders and Brittany does not come near it'; there was no shortage of

425

wood; and although mineral resources were modest and the range small, as at Ferrières-en-Brie, there were useful stone quarries at the very gates of the city, starting with the suburb of Notre-Dame-des-Champs.[34]

Paris was surrounded by fields and crops, and some land had even fallen into disuse: in September 1465 (when war was raging between Louis XI and Charles the Bold), Commynes describes the mistake made by some riders who arriving in Paris in poor light, saw 'a great quantity of lances standing upright . . . Approaching . . . they found that these were large thistles',[35] covering the fields right up to the city gates.

But the immediate image a town evoked in bygone days was of a fortress. And if we are to credit Furetière's dictionary, walls were what gave it the dignity of a town.[36] This was a definition of great antiquity, according to the eminent medievalist Roberto Lopez, who reminded an interviewer on one occasion that 'the hieroglyph for a town in ancient Egypt consisted of a cross inside a circle, that is a crossroads inside a walled space'.[37] This walled space was punctuated by gates, the obligatory passages to the outside world, but also the weak links in the town's defence. Openings to the outside world were therefore kept to a minimum. Dunkerque in 1708, still as Vauban had left it, 'had only two gates on the landward side, the Porte Royale and the Porte de Nieuport'.[38] Even so, the second was opened only on market days: defence was a serious matter. By contrast, the walls built around Paris between 1785 and 1787 by the *fermiers-généraux* (tax-farmers), extended for 23 kilometres and had 17 major toll-gates and 30 smaller ones, all with their tollbooths. It may seem obvious but it is necessary to recall that despite being barricaded inside their fortifications, towns were above all points at which roads met: they were destinations or points of departure and routes ran through them from one gate to another.

The site of a town could of course be more or less convenient. In the very early days of town settlement, navigable waterways seem to have played an all-important role.[39] But there were some sites which guaranteed future prosperity: for instance a location at the point where a river became navigable; or where there was a transfer from overland routes to waterways; or at a ford or bridge

FIGURE 52
Urbanization rates by département, *1806*

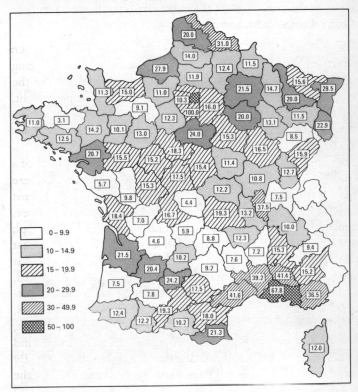

Source: Y. Tuguault, *Fécondité et urbanisation*, 1975.

enabling a river to be crossed easily. Strasbourg for example owes
its site to its strategic bridge across the Rhine, allowing the passage
of both goods and troops. Angers lies where the valley narrows to
make crossing easier. Nantes is the site of the first bridge upstream
on the Loire. Then there is Avignon with its famous bridge, built in
the twelfth century: although the Rhône is very wide at this point,
it is divided into two arms which reduces the force of the current
and originally gave the bridge a firm foundation in mid-span for a
third of its length.[40] Between Tarascon and Beaucaire, there was

once a pontoon bridge (for want of anything better) across the fearsome Rhône. Rouen also had a pontoon bridge across the Seine in the seventeenth century: inaugurated in 1630, it replaced a colossal stone-built hump-backed bridge, the Grand Pont, with thirteen arches – built on shifting foundations, this one had partly collapsed. The pontoon lasted until the nineteenth century, being ingeniously devised so as to rise with the tide, and opening to allow ships through. 'Louis XVI himself came to admire it.'[41]

But a river alone was not sufficient reason for a town: Orléans, on the Loire, had the chance to become the focus of French history, but was poorly placed to take it, lying as it did between two waste expanses – to the north the forest of Orléans, much bigger than it is today, and to the south the woods and stagnant marches of the Sologne. There could be no more dramatic instance of a failed urban history.

Towns near the sea were certainly in privileged positions, not so much at the mouths of estuaries but at the point where the water became calm enough for ships to land cargo: hence the fortunes of Rouen or Bordeaux. Such towns were indeed attracted to the outside world, made their fortunes from it, and all too often turned their backs on inland France.

Equally well placed were towns lying on the border between two different regions: inevitably they were exchange points, if only between the hills and the valleys. A string of towns grew up for this reason around the Alps.

Nevertheless, apart from Paris and Toulouse, 'most of the really big [French] towns, the ones that grew fastest, were "scattered around the edges": Nantes, Bordeaux, Marseille, Toulon, Grenoble, Lyon, Strasbourg, Lille'.[42] The interior of the kingdom, as the marquis d'Argenson keeps saying in his *Mémoires*, was virtually empty: it 'rang hollow'.

Provided its obstacles could be overcome and its possibilities exploited, location could be made to participate in a town's fortunes. Success depended on its capacity to take advantage of what was within reach. Bar-le-Duc for instance was well-placed in 1717 for smuggling, particularly for bringing into France banned fabrics from the Indies (Lorraine not being part of France at the time). It

FIGURE 53
Index of attraction between towns and rivers

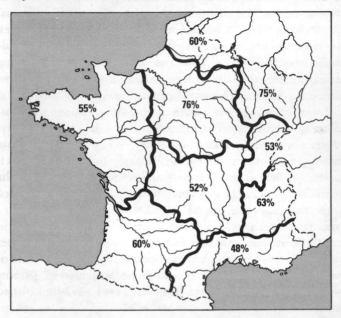

The Nord region, although well-provided with navigable rivers, scores less highly than one might expect, either because of the industrial conurbations of recent date, which were independent of rivers but figure on the map, or because some of the navigable rivers were not allowed by the scale of the original map by Vidal de la Blache (the Deule at Lille for instance).

In the Mediterranean south on the other hand, quite small rivers figure to advantage and the Rhône, flowing through independently, attracted towns which send up the regional index: even so, this is the lowest score.

Map and commentary by Jules Blache: *Revue de géographie de Lyon*, 1959, p. 19.

---

was an opportunity the town did not let escape.[43] Granville possessed for many years around 1812, 25 or 30 large 'gabares' of between three and eighteen tons, which engaged in fishing for oysters, lobster and shrimps; a few boats were sent to the cod-fishing grounds and others carried on a continuous coasting trade from Nantes to Brest and as far east as Dieppe.[44] There was sometimes danger that a town might be so preoccupied with immediate profit as to be blinded to anything else. Nantes grew rich on the Indies trade and, sad to say, the slave trade, and by the late eighteenth century had become completely cut off from its hinterland. It was so unconcerned about it that the bourgeoisie even sold off their country estates. Arthur Young was amazed: 'By what miracle has all this splendour and wealth [of Nantes] no connection with the land round about?'[45]

Overcoming obstacles, stimulating exchange and increasing trade was the business of the many fairs and markets, as they became established. In Poitou, in the reign of Louis XIV, there were in the *élection* of Luçon alone 87 annual fairs, plus 18 weekly markets (that is an annual total of 936).[46] And this was by no means an unusually busy region.

In fact the striking numbers of fairs are often a sign of the effort made by small towns and bourgs, in some relatively underprivileged regions, to stimulate trade. In the Vaucluse in 1815, the poorer the region the more fairs there were (11 a year at Bollène, 9 at Valréas, 8 in Malaucène, 5 in Apt), whereas in the more prosperous plains in the west of the *département* they were dwindling in number and importance.[47] Ornans, the site of the grain market at the mouth of the valley of the Loue, was still holding 24 annual fairs in the nineteenth century, 'on the first and third Tuesday of the month'.[48] In the northern Alps, especially Haute-Savoie, the fairs held high up in the mountains – selling cattle, sheep and mules – had for a long time been more important than the fairs held in the valleys and lowlands.

Within the many-stranded networks that bound town to bourg, town to village and town to town, ceaselessly combining to weave the basic fabric of material life in France, it was in the end the town which provided the driving force: it was in town that the moneylenders were to be found, the link with large-scale trade and capitalism; in town lay the institutions of Church and state and there too lay the seat of justice, and the machinery of administration. The town was the centre of 'written civilization'.[49] In 1851, the

FIGURE 54
France in 1841: still covered with fairs

Source: *Dictionnaire du commerce et des marchandises*, 1841. I, pp. 960 ff.

economist Adolphe Blanqui could write: 'Two different peoples [urban and rural] live on the same territory lives so distinct that they seem completely foreign to one another, although linked by the ties of the most imperious [political] centralization ever devised'.[50] These two peoples were condemned to live together and therefore formed a whole. One, the people of the towns, gave orders to the other, lived off it and exploited it, but at the same time enabled it to rise higher in the world. Urban life was the necessary condition of growth, though it was not always sufficient.[51]

People: the essential ingredient

The key problem in the towns' fortunes was in the past, as it still is today, their supply of inhabitants. Nowadays the problem is that of monstrous urban growth. Like the ogre in the fairy tale, the city swallows people up. In the past, the problem was permanent population shortage. If they were to cope with their surplus mortality and to develop even at snail's pace, the towns had continually to be replenishing their bourgeois and commercial elites, and even more urgently their workforce, whether skilled artisans or the labouring proletariat.

But French towns of the past all resolved this basic problem without inordinate trouble. They recruited a never-ending flow of people from the regions round about, sometimes from very far away (see the maps in Figure 55 and Figures 17–20 in Volume I). In response to the call, immigrants flocked towards them. Our sources rarely allow us to reckon the precise percentage of incomers in the urban population, but the geographical origins of townsfolk emerge clearly from records of marriages, or of deaths in the hospices. Whether from nearby or far afield, the immigrant took up residence either in a district near the gate by which he entered the town, or close to other immigrants from the same part of the world, often working at the same trade, who tended to cluster together in certain streets. The *quartiers* of Paris were in fact a series of mini-provinces, corresponding not only to the division of labour but also to a rigid social classification. But they also reflected the spontaneous creation of 'reception committees' for newcomers.

What is striking about these population shifts towards the towns to meet the constant demand for labour is that a problem nowadays considered troublesome resolved itself easily, almost automatically. It is true that the pool of country-dwellers was enormous by comparison with the townspeople. But the mobility of the French population, as indeed of Europeans generally, is rather surprising. It responded to all the demands or promises of the economy. Take Arles for instance: fallen from its ancient splendour and rivalled by Marseille, Aix and even Aigues-Mortes, Arles revived towards the end of the fifteenth century. And that revival was sufficient to attract immigrants, of whom quite a number came from northern France. Anything, it seems, was possible.[52] Similarly Nantes, in the sixteenth century, maintained its demographic growth thanks above all to the nearby countryside and to Brittany, but thanks also to Poitou, Normandy and the Loire valley as far as Orléans. There were even some Marseillais to be found there, rubbing shoulders with Portuguese and Italian immigrants and a sizeable Spanish colony.[53]

When, at the end of the fifteenth century, Lyon needed workers, emigrants from Savoy (which already had a diaspora covering southern Germany, southern Italy, Spain and much of France) were well placed to respond to the appeal. Contemporaries even claimed that 'two-thirds of the people in Lyon are descended from Savoyards', and that 'almost all the labourers, that is about a third of the city, come from Savoy'.[54] They were undoubtedly exaggerating: precise statistical research indicates that in 1597, Savoyards reprsented only 21.2% of the Lyon population – but that is not a negligible figure. And these migrants were a perennial source of textile-workers, outnumbering immigrants from closer at hand, from the Forez, Lyonnais and Beaujolais for instance, who represented only 18.3% combined, or the Dauphiné with 7.2%.[55] Whatever its origins, sometimes very distant (cf. Figure 20 in Volume I), this supply of labour to the great conurbation of Lyon, providing almost half the residents, was a question of life or death for the city. Its activity required newcomers, 'which it swallowed up endlessly'.[56]

Perhaps we had better not even mention Paris, an ogre with an even bigger appetite! In Sébastien Mercier's descriptions on the eve of the Revolution, we have an unforgettable portrait of its colourful population of *gens de peine*, labourers, almost all provincials: they came from Savoy and the Auvergne, from the

FIGURE 55
Immigration to five towns in south-west France

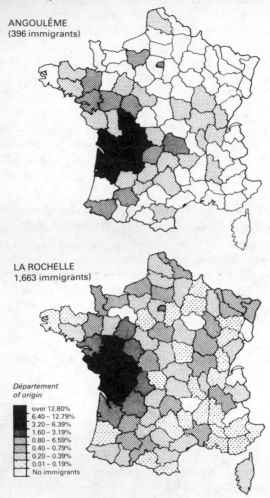

ANGOULÊME
(396 immigrants)

LA ROCHELLE
1,663 immigrants)

Département of origin

- over 12.80%
- 6.40 – 12.79%
- 3.20 – 6.39%
- 1.60 – 3.19%
- 0.80 – 6.59%
- 0.40 – 0.79%
- 0.20 – 0.39%
- 0.01 – 0.19%
- No immigrants

Each town had its own zone of recruitment and retained it, although the powerful attraction of Bordeaux was felt throughout the south-west.

Source: J.-P. Poussou, *Bordeaux et le Sud-Ouest au XVIIIe siècle*, 1983.

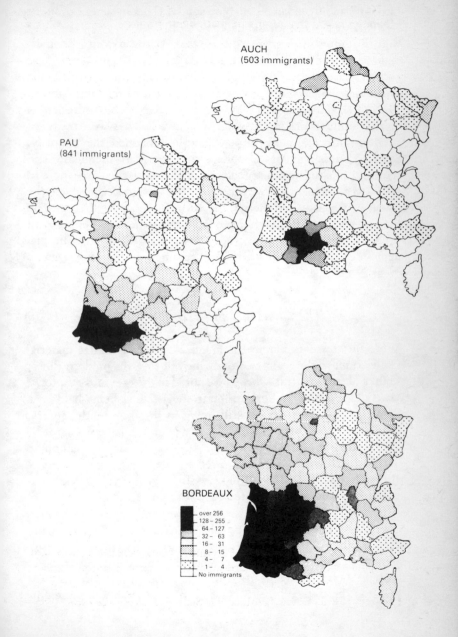

AUCH
(503 immigrants)

PAU
(841 immigrants)

BORDEAUX

over 256
128 – 255
64 – 127
32 – 63
16 – 31
8 – 15
4 – 7
1 – 4
No immigrants

Limousin and Lyonnais, from Normandy, Gascony and Lorraine.[57] But Paris really is a special case.

It is more surprising to find that Bordeaux, in the mid-eighteenth century, when it was developing its maritime and commercial activity with a vigour unrivalled by other towns in the south-west, managed with ease to attract a stream of immigrants. They flocked in as always from the nearby Gironde, but from now on they came from a much wider area as well. They were not all of rural origin, although country people remained the majority. Strong contingents of labourers, and even of merchants and traders, came to Bordeaux from other towns, particularly those of south-west France. However, and this is significant, even the towns which answered the call succeeded in retaining their grip on their own immediate neighbourhood, from which few people went to Bordeaux. It was as if every town had its own traditional demographic pool, over which it retained fishing rights so to speak.[58]

The towns and the French economy

Were the towns to blame for France's rather lacklustre material civilization, as the country slowly moved towards modern times? Unlike Jacques Laffitte who, as we noted in the previous chapter,[59] saw France's industrial expansion in the 1820s as being held back by a rural society that was still living in the fourteenth century, should one regard the towns as partly responsible too? Can it be argued that the urban power-house was not doing enough to propel rural France forward, even in the eighteenth century – although the period 1750–1800 saw such expansion that the accusation is no sooner formulated than it seems misplaced?

It was certainly true that the towns were all expanding, though not necessarily very fast, between 1500 and 1789. They all benefited from the general demographic growth which was itself enough to increase their size, prompt the building of suburbs and push up their rate of consumption. Their expansion, already clear to see in the sixteenth century, is even more visible in the eighteenth. A wind of change swept through them as they began erecting magnificent new buildings, bursting out of their medieval straitjackets, knocking down their old walls[60] (not always without qualms), laying out straight avenues and opening up cramped districts.

Already in the sixteenth century, new notions of town planning had begun to inspire a 'voluntarist' policy of which the royal government was often the agent. Italian Renaissance architecture may not have swept all before it, but it left a mark on several regions of France. The map reproduced here (Figure 56) from Jean-Robert Pitte's book is significant. It shows the energetic leading role played by the Loire valley which, as the seat of the king and Court, was for many years, until about 1525, the centre of the realm and indeed of French civilization. Paris only took the lead in the second quarter of the century, on account of the preference given it by François I (1516–47), whose Court however continued to be itinerant. In the end, the capital did not escape the influence of the new style: at the very heart of the city, on the Place de la Grève, the old *maison communale* gave way to the elegant Hôtel de Ville, the first Parisian building to be designed in the new style (1532–49).[61]

Renaissance architecture did not in fact make a very great impression on sixteenth-century French towns, but symmetry, perspectives, airiness and the opening up of long avenues from now on became part of French city architecture, and the Italian legacy would develop, from the reign of Louis XIV on, into the classical style.[62]

In the age of the Enlightenment, a renewed demand for town planning sought expression almost everywhere:

> The redesigning of the townscape reached grandiose proportions [in France, writes Jean Meyer]. If one were to blot out for a moment from the mind's eye all the buildings dating from 1650–1790, what would be left of the centres not only of our great cities but also of so many very small towns? And what was accomplished in this period was more than mere redesign, it amounted to total reconstruction. Bordeaux, the

FIGURE 56
Renaissance buildings in France, up to and including the reign of François I

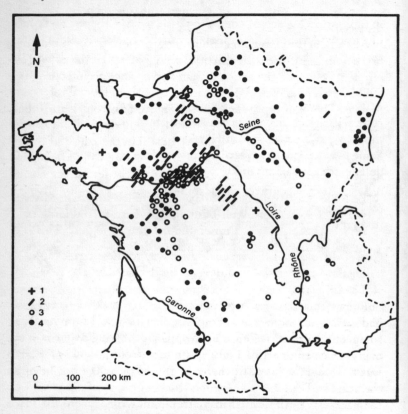

New buildings in the Renaissance style which are comparatively rare in France appeared for the most part in the footsteps of the monarchy, in other words in the Loire valley and the Paris region.

The map shows the sites of one or more buildings in Renaissance style (original or adapted) dating from the reigns of Charles VIII (key reference 1); Louis XII (2); François I before 1525 (3); and François I after 1525, the year he moved to Paris (4). List from L. Hautecoeur, *Histoire de l'architecture classique*, 1963.

Source: Jean Robert Pitte, *Histoire du paysage français*, II, 1984.

great trading city with its well-ordered buildings is, like Nancy as designed by Stanislas Leczinski, the very image of successful town planning

in this period.[63] Paris of course took the palm – 'there's no fashion like Paris fashion'. The capital was scattered with building sites, recognizable from the great pulleys used to haul materials into the air, and from the white footsteps left in the streets by plasterers coming home from work.[64]

The construction work went on into the nineteenth century, culminating in the monstrous reorganization of Paris's main thoroughfares under Baron Haussmann, appointed prefect of the Seine in 1863. But provincial towns were not far behind. As Léonce de Lavergne noted in 1860,

Le Mans, Laval and Angers have all doubled in size in thirty years; new quarters, well-built and airy, are surrounding or replacing the dirty and miserable hovels of the past. This is healthy luxury, with nothing artificial or exaggerated about it.[65]

The odd thing is that neither the state, despite its massive revenue from taxation, nor the cities, where rich men were not rare, had sufficient resources to complete all these renovation projects: some, too ambitious, had to be dropped. A constant refrain in the many histories of individual French towns is 'lack of funds'.[66] It was the same story everywhere: in Bordeaux at the height of its fortunes; in Toulouse, where the absence of the *intendant* held up the necessary permissions; in Marseille, in Lyon, where the Place Bellecour was being built; in Rouen, which had to be content to put up new buildings on the outskirts of town; or in Caen, where the financial contribution of the city to its own urban renewal was no more than 10% in the eighteenth century.

The problem became particularly acute in Rennes, following the damage caused by a disastrous fire which broke out on the night of 23 December 1720 and was only extinguished, thanks to a providential rainstorm, six days later. 945 buildings in the upper town were destroyed, including the historic heart of the city. Only 1,367 houses were left standing, most of them in the insalubrious and poor lower town.[67] But Rennes did not have enough revenue of its own to repair the damage.

So it turned for help to the state, which was not disposed to unlimited generosity, although it insisted, through a series of decrees from the king's Council, that the rebuilding should be according to its own plans, drawn up by its own architects and engineers: the state was 'tight-fisted with money, prodigal with regulations'.[68] The city tried everything: appealing to the Estates of Brittany, themselves dependent on the royal say-so; borrowing money; obtaining requisitions from the *intendant*; underpaying the peasants employed as hauliers, and the masons, some of whom had been recruited against their will, by ordinance; and haggling with the engineers in charge of the works, with the suppliers, and with the owners of the land.

Consequently the whole business dragged on a long time. The townspeople, rehoused in buildings left intact, or in the suburbs, had to remain in these cramped quarters for some considerable while to come; temporary wooden shacks, put up everywhere with official permission just after the disaster, were still standing, despite orders to pull them down, as late as 1728. It took about fifteen years for the dwelling-houses to be rebuilt, and thirty for the public buildings to be completed. This was because the over-ambitious planning schemes envisaged by the architects and the municipal authorities (themselves delayed by much dissension and argument) blocked any initiative from the owners of the land for several years, and finally came up against the impossibility of raising the necessary funds. The town itself undertook and completed part of the scheme, enough to ruin its finances, not enough to transform the townscape in a radical manner. Among various projects which had to be abandoned were plans for fountains, water conduits, and the re-routing of the river-bed to improve conditions in the lower town which was subject to regular flooding.

In the end, it was to the original site-owners that it fell to handle the rebuilding of the dwelling-houses. This was carried out quickly, for the bourgeoisie of Rennes was not short of money. Around the Place Neuve and the *parlement* building, both of which were designed by the town, there now sprang up elegant new districts, with broad airy streets laid out on a grid plan. The wealthiest residents built themselves fine *hôtels particuliers* (town houses) as well as tenements for letting out. Meanwhile the lower end of town, as well as the districts to the east and west of the upper town, remained unchanged with their filthy, twisting streets.[69]

Note the last feature: private investment in real estate. Everywhere in France, apart from the invariably partial remodelling of town centres with public money, new building was essentially carried out by rich individuals, who put up magnificent town houses (whether in Nancy, Besançon or Lille) as well as tenement houses intended for well-off tenants. They were sure to make a profit: in almost every town in France, demographic pressure resulted in a housing crisis. In Caen where, as in Rennes, 'the incompetence of the state as entrepreneur' had ended by giving way to private speculation, private building took off in about 1770, at the same time as urban rents.[70]

The urban renewal was magnificent, granted, but it was incomplete. Not all towns knocked down the walls which surrounded and in many cases stifled them. The town walls of Rennes for instance did not disappear until the end of the century, in 1774–82. And when walls came down, barriers went up – in order to collect toll and to create the still-vivid illusion of an enclosed town! Above all, no town really eliminated its medieval legacy of tortuous and evil-smelling streets. Even towns which treated themselves to grand public buildings such as a house of *parlement*, an *intendant*'s lodgings, law courts or a town hall, did not succeed in shaking off their proverbial squalor, despite efforts to improve the water supply or street-cleaning. In Lyon, rubbish was collected in sacks carried on the backs of donkeys, while in Lille, which was perpetually awash, 'the cleaning of the streets and the disposal of waste water was accomplished with carts and barrels not always as watertight as they might be'.[71] All towns, even the largest and most subject to radical planning, such as Rouen, Nantes, Bordeaux, Lyon, Marseille, Toulouse and Lille – found it difficult to escape the straitjacket of the past. Pierre Patte, in a book published in 1772, was still bemoaning the fact that in these great metropolises, filth from all directions 'is washed openly through the gutters before it reaches the sewers . . . then you have the blood from slaughterhouses streaming through the streets . . . And when it rains, you will see passers-by being drenched in dirty water running off the roofs, which by their disposition multiply by a hundred the volume of the rainwater.'[72]

Which was the least salubrious of French towns? Narbonne, in 1656, according to two would-be wits from the north (naturally) who described it in verse as an 'ancient city, deep in mire/ Of drains and sewers a shambles dire'. *Latrina mundi, cloaca Galliae*, was the verdict of some other travellers.[73] We need not take their word for it. Narbonne's problem, a serious one it is true, was to be built on very low-lying ground, all too often flooded by the river Aude. But one might equally well have put Rouen at the top of this not very honourable list. Eugène Noël tells us that the Rouen of his childhood was 'a revolting town', its streets and alleyways littered with filth, even in 'the respectable districts', while there were squalid slums in 'the frightful haunt of vice known as the Clos Saint-Marc . . . a dark and foetid labyrinth, . . . where the police feared to venture . . . A terrible stench arose from this sewer and spread over the whole city . . . You could smell Rouen from half a league away.'[74] The outbreak of cholera in 1832 prompted better cleaning of the streets, but Flaubert was still complaining in his letters to Bouilhet of the malodorous alleys, which would not disappear until the road-building programme of the Second Empire.[75]

But to return to more important things: we have seen that an essential role was played by private investment in real estate during the urban renewal of the eighteenth century (and indeed earlier: private finance – to its immense credit! – was responsible for the building, during the reign of Henri IV, of the magnificent Place des Vosges in Paris). Was this actually a sign of economic vitality? Should we agree with the habitual chorus that when the building trade is in good heart, so is everything else?

On this point, many historians are doubtful. Roberto Lopez[76] for instance has sought to show that

1) in the late Middle Ages, northern Europe, which possessed less

wealth than the great Mediterranean cities, was busy building huge churches, whereas the south built far fewer, as if it had better things to do with its money.

2) Florence under Lorenzo the Magnificent, at the time of its greatest architectural and intellectual splendour, was in fact witnessing an economic recession. Jean Georgelin has suggested the same thing of eighteenth-century Venice,[77] as has Andrzej Wyrobisz of fifteenth-century Cracow. And Witold Kula adds all the weight of his authority in support of this view: 'It seems perfectly plausible to me', he writes, 'that the building of luxurious bourgeois town houses should have coincided with periods of recession in the business cycle.'[78]

Such arguments suggest that spending money on buildings was a way to dispose of accumulated wealth for which no further useful purpose could be found. Was this true of France? One historian has pointed out that 'the consuls of Lyon, previously rather careful with the town's money, became very open-handed during the reign of Louis XIV', a time when there were a series of economic problems.[79] The apparent explanation is that all towns, whether large or small, found it easy to borrow money; they all went into debt.[80] But what about private investment? In the long run, argues Pierre Chaunu, it is clear that any demographic expansion with its inevitable corollary, a rise in urban rents, stimulates building. We can see this in Cambrai in the fifteenth century, or in Lille, which had a surplus of immigrants in the seventeenth century,[81] or in Caen, of which the *intendant* said in 1759, 'the town is so full of people, that it is impossible to find lodgings'.[82] A stagnating population on the other hand meant that building came to a stop, as was the case in Rouen between 1680 and 1720.[83]

But there is building and building. In the eighteenth century, what were being constructed in France were 'noble' dwellings, architect-designed houses made of fine stone. This 'solution, the expensive house, may have corresponded to the difficulty of capitalizing on the surplus from production. It was a better investment than gold for preserving one's [accumulated] capital.'[84] Evidence *a contrario* perhaps is that the early nineteenth century, which witnessed the first industrial expansion in France, was a time of far less building activity. The population of Paris increased by 25% between 1817 and 1827, but the number of houses by only 10%.[85] Here as elsewhere, in Lille for instance, the working class continued to be crammed into basements and attics,[86] as long as disposable capital was being absorbed by economic growth. So perhaps we find ourselves agreeing with the arguments of Roberto Lopez and Witold Kula.

The rate of urbanization

Such questions raise once more the problem of urbanization in general. It is more probable that, from the point of view of the future modernization of the French economy, urban development, even in the eighteenth century, was inadequate. French towns did expand, but not as fast as they ought to have, compared to the avant-garde economies of the time: the United Provinces and England.

What is more, if one keeps to the convention whereby a *town* is defined as any settlement of over 2,000 inhabitants, the 1,000 or so places in France answering the description accounted for only 16.5% of the French population in 1789, and 18.8% in 1809,[87] as opposed to 10% in about 1500. The urbanization index had gone up by some 6 to 9 points, but only over a period of almost three centuries. This was barely perceptible over time. And even these figures may not be accurate.

The usual cut-off point of 2,000 cannot be valid for all periods, as I have already suggested, and this question must be faced once more.[88] Marcel Reinhard was confronted with the problem apropos of France during the Revolution and Empire.[89] He came down very firmly against this criterion, arguing that no town was worthy of the name unless it could boast at least 10,000 inhabitants. By this reckoning, instead of a thousand or so towns, France had no more than 76. And all 76 combined, including Paris, contained no more than 2,564,000 inhabitants, that is barely 9% of the total population. One can of course argue whether 10,000 is the best figure, and reach different conclusions. But it is certainly true that the 2,000 limit no longer makes sense in the eighteenth century, if we are discussing a population and an economy in the throes of expansion and requiring more powerful urban motors if they were to meet the challenge of the new age.

The change in scale moreover gives fresh prominence to Paris, which would now account not for one-sixth of France's urban population (if, 2,000 is used as a base), but for a quarter if not more (if 10,000 is used as a base). The responsibility of the capital city is thus rendered greater: Paris, lacking a direct outlet to the sea, unlike London for instance, was not dynamic enough to animate the French economy. In France, the role of economic stimulus was divided among several towns, whereas in England there was little challenge to London, and in the Low Countries little challenge to Amsterdam. The French urban network thus lacked cohesion and unity, being moreover widely dispersed over the comparatively greater surface area of France.

One is in the end obliged therefore to compare the rates of urbanization as between France and its neighbours. The graph in Figure 57 tells us the answer. It takes the figures calculated by Paul Bairoch,[90] figures somewhat different from those normally cited, since in the interests of comparability he has tried to apply the same principles of reckoning to all the countries concerned. The result of these calculations is that in about 1800, France, with 12%, was behind not only England (23%), but also Italy (17%), the Netherlands (37%, the record) and even Portugal (16%) and Spain (13%) – the latter in the throes of a crisis of de-urbanization. France was however ahead of Germany (9%) as I would have expected, and just succeeds in reaching the European average (12%). So in practice, France was lagging behind. It had not achieved the rate of urbanization required for economic take-off. Even in 1850, the French figure was the comparatively low one of 19%.

Towns and the French economy
(continued)

France's towns, locked into this inadequate urbanization process, bear more or less visible witness to the backwardness of the country as a whole. But were they actually responsible for that backwardness? I am not so sure.

I do not deny that they often suffered from inertia: in many of them, life went on at a snail's pace – but what choice did they have? In the first volume of this book, I spent some time considering the case of Besançon, and also mentioned Caen, a town 'in hibernation' as its recent historian Jean-Claude Perrot has called it. One could quote dozens and dozens of other examples. For me, a sleepy town means one content to live chiefly off the immediate countryside. An office-holding class and a small stratum of property-owners, generally bourgeois, could live there quite comfortably, but the mass of townspeople led a precarious existence, comfortless at the best of times. Such was Rennes, both before and after the fire. So too were many inland provincial towns, differing in this from towns on the frontiers, which benefited from structural advantages.

One such French town, sleepy to the point of caricature, despite being quite large, was Angers, 'the black town with a thousand slate roofs'. In 1650, according to one of its recent historians, 'it had scarcely changed in a hundred years, and would hardly change over the next hundred and fifty'.[91] In 1770, for all its 25,044 inhabitants (16,879 of them *intra muros*), it was still not particularly lively. And yet it was the centre of a prosperous agricultural region, which moreover produced plenty of flax and hemp. With access to both the Maine and Loire, it was excellently placed for transport. But it showed little industrial initiative, even in the eighteenth century. Such industries as were created – woollen cloth, sailcloth, printed fabrics, or sugar refineries – did not as a rule last long. Even the slate quarries just outside the town were poorly managed. It was not that there was a shortage of

FIGURE 57
*Urbanization rates in France and neighbouring European
countries, 1800–1980*

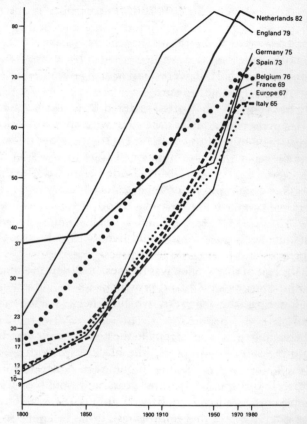

Source: Paul Bairoch, *Villes et économies dans l'histoire*, 1985, p. 288.

money, 'but its timid owners preferred the modest but reliable
income from their real estate to the risks and perils of industrial
enterprise'.[92]

The result was a 'comfortable but modest life for the high or
middling bourgeoisie which, like the nobility, kept only one foot
in the town. Almost all the bourgeoisie of Angers owned property

in the countryside, spent part of the year there, and derived a greater or lesser proportion of their income from it in cash or kind.'[93] For artisans by contrast, apart from butchers, bakers, innkeepers and tanners, life was hard, in particular if one was a weaver, spinner or spinster. Significantly, one-tenth of the population was made up of domestic servants.

As far as its upper strata were concerned at least, Angers was 'a town largely composed of lawyers, teachers, clerics and rentiers'.[94] Even in 1783, according to the tax-collector of the *généralité* of Tours, its inhabitants 'prefer the indolence in which they have been raised to the trouble and hard work that would be required by major enterprise or bold speculation. Lacking energy, the present generation is vegetating, just as the one before it vegetated, and as the one after it will vegetate.'[95] The same could well be said of many another quiet, provincial French town.

Towns containing industries give a completely different impression. They stood up for themselves, took action and made the best use of circumstances. But since they varied so much in structure, it is hard to characterize them.

In most cases, their industrial activity spilled over into the surrounding bourgs and villages. In the eighteenth and nineteenth centuries, until at least the 1850s, rural or 'proto'-industry tended to spread outwards from the towns. This was actually a revolutionary process. But it is such a familiar phenomenon, whether in France or the rest of Europe, that one has to make an effort to grasp its significance properly. In almost every case, the industrial impetus, having originated in the town, remained more or less under its control, not to say at its mercy. Rural workshops, owned and controlled by urban merchants, sprang up around Laval, Le Mans, Saint-Etienne, Voiron, Grenoble, Troyes or Lodève. The same was true in the eighteenth century around Carcassonne, one of the most active textile towns in France at the time, and comparable for woollen production to Rouen, Elbeuf, Louviers, Reims, Amiens or Sedan. In 1731, a *subdélégué* reported that

Carcassonne is one great cloth manufactory, full of carders, weavers, spinsters and cloth-shearers: the whole countryside is teeming with manufacturers and workers, indeed to excess, so that agriculture has suffered. In years when there is plenty of work available in the woollen trade, it is difficult and costly to find workers to trim the vines, or women to hoe the fields.

Similar remarks were made in 1733.[96]

Rouen is even more typical. When, in the early eighteenth century, the new cotton industry was set up there, bringing complete upheaval to the labour market and to the practices of textile production, the manufacture of *rouennerie* (a mixed linen and cotton fabric) did not remain confined to the town. It spread out towards 'the plateau of Boos, the Roumois, Cailly and above all the pays de Caux, to the point that in 1707, the syndics of the chamber of commerce of Normandy reported that 30,000 rural families were earning their living by cotton-spinning'. Many merchants immediately began sending bales of raw cotton, imported through Rouen, out into the villages, 'to Routot, Bourg-Achard and even modest parishes like Hauville, Illeville-sur-Montfort and so on'.[97] But we can tell that the city remained central to this activity, which extended all over Normandy, by the vast and rapid increase in the number of lengths of fabric (cotton, linen or a mixture of the two) which went through the excise office at Rouen: 60,000 lengths in 1717; 166,000 in 1732; 435,000 in 1743; 543,000 in 1781.[98]

It is true that the cotton industry competed with and finally killed off the ancient woollen trade of Rouen. But then Rouen was an energetic city, always prepared to move with the times. It defended its sea-going trade tooth and nail against adverse circumstances, and threw itself into every kind of enterprise, large and small. Printed fabrics, haberdashery, woollen hats, tapestries, hosiery, porcelain, paper, sugar-refining, glass, soap and starch, tanning, mechanized cotton-spinning using machines smuggled in from England, bleaching of canvas with chlorine according to the new process invented by Berthollet, lead and copper beating, the manufacture of sulphur and sulphuric acid – it was all grist to the Rouen mills, in particular to those firms which took some notice of the technical innovations of the English industrial revolution.[99]

The example of Lyon

Even more significant is the case of Lyon, perhaps the most complex, thriving and important industrial city in France in the eighteenth or indeed the nineteenth century. The way it established itself as the silk capital of Europe in the age of Enlightenment is very impressive. The silk-masters excelled themselves in ingenious devices to maintain the exports on which their fortunes traditionally rested. When Italian competitors began systematically and skilfully to imitate their silk designs, using the sample-books sent out to retailers, they found an effective means of reply. Their designers, known as 'illustrators of silk', were hired on condition they completely changed the patterns every year. By the time the copies reached the market, they were already out of date in the eyes of the snobbish and demanding clientèle for these luxury fabrics.[100]

But during the Revolution and Empire, Lyon was to suffer terribly: as a result of the uprising in the city, the siege (8 August–9 October 1793) and the brutal repression that followed, the city lost almost a third of its 150,000 inhabitants, there was much material damage, a number of industrial firms closed down and many entrepreneurs left.[101] Then came years of foreign war and with it problems for the export trade, while conscription emptied the city of yet more workers. In 1806, the population had fallen to 88,000 inhabitants. Nevertheless, Lyon managed to reconstruct the trade and, faced with a catastrophic shortage of labour, invested boldly in machines. The development of the Jacquard loom effectively brought about 'the revival of [fine] silks both in terms of tradition and of maximum profit'.[102] And the revival was maintained, since, despite the crippling crisis which once more hit the city during the last years of the Empire, business revived again almost immediately after the return of peace in 1815.

It is at this point that the example of Lyon becomes significant, since it was at this *late* stage that the silk industry suddenly began to spread out of the town and into the countryside, extending well

FIGURE 58
The spread of the silk industry into the countryside round Lyon after 1820

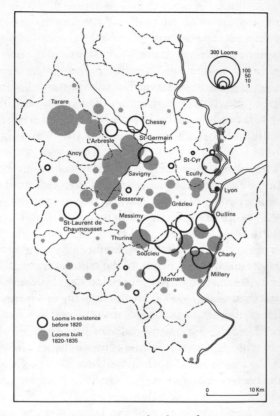

Source: Pierre Cayez, *Métiers jacquard et hauts fourneaux aux origines de l'industrie lyonnaise*, 1978.

beyond the immediate neighbourhood of the city, as is shown in Figure 58, a map taken from Pierre Cayez's excellent book. Once more, Lyon was asserting itself as a true economic capital. With all the workers employed full time, the dispersal of looms throughout the countryside represented a careful calculation: the highly-skilled weavers and the Jacquard looms remained in town, but plain silks were woven in rural areas by lower-paid labour, a strategy designed to beat strong foreign competition from Prussia and Switzerland.[103]

At the same time, Lyon began to take part in the industrial revolution, and would until about 1860 lead the way in several sectors. It dominated a vast region controlled and stimulated by the city's entrepreneurs and capital. Lyon in short was the opposite of a sleepy provincial town; it was a centre of growth which eventually came up against the expansion and hostility of the industrial power concentrated in Paris. Centralization – which was perhaps inevitable – brought no benefit to Lyon as a city. It suffered on this account in the nineteenth century and is still suffering from it today.

But it sometimes happened that a town refused to be a centre of growth for the entire region. To compare Lyon with Bordeaux is to take the full measure of what Edward Fox has called 'the other France', the France of the great sea-ports, in so many ways foreign to French life as orchestrated from Paris.[104] Describing the lively expansion of Bordeaux in the eighteenth century, the 'wealth and magnificence' of which so struck Arthur Young, and the attraction that the city was then exerting over the entire south-west on account of its growing need for labour, Jean-Pierre Poussou expresses surprise at 'how small in the end its influence was on the economic, demographic and social development' of the same south-west. Torn between two preoccupations, its vineyards and the 'powerful winds blowing from the Atlantic', Bordeaux quite forgot to become a regional capital.[105]

The example of Lille

Elsewhere, other specific situations and circumstances complicated matters. A town and its industrial environment might not necessarily form a harmonious whole. Tensions could arise. They were particularly strong in Lille.

Alongside the many textile industries which dominated the

city – wool, linen, silk, cotton, mixed weave, tapestries, printed fabrics, thread, hosiery, lace, dyeworks, bleaching and finishing – Lille was host to a whole range of other industries, from ceramics to glass, rape-seed oil-refining, sugar- and salt-refining, and brickworks. And it was subject to a series of divisions of labour which respected neither the city limits nor the boundaries of the *châtellenie*. Factors which complicated Lille's relations with the surrounding region, especially in the textile trades, were the rules governing its craft guilds, which hindered production, and also the constant political crises which were always unsettling markets. These included the occupation of part of Flanders by France in 1667, which cut the city off from the Netherlands (and notably from a nearby source of supply of Spanish wool); the constant war along the frontiers; the capture of the city in 1708 by Prince Eugene, and its occupation by the Dutch, a disaster for its industries which had to face competition from a flood of English and Dutch goods. Following Lille's liberation, it would take several years to get rid of the stocks left on its hands. Another problem was that it lay for customs purposes in what was known as a *pays étranger*, an advantage in dealing with the outside world but a hindrance in relations with the domestic French market, which had to be won over.[106]

But the basic difficulty for Lille was that its industrial countryside, the legacy of a long past, far from being under the thumb of the city's entrepreneurs, was organized more or less independently, around a number of manufacturing bourgs. Protected by ancient privilege, the bourgs remained very active, to the point of specializing in certain textiles over which they had de facto monopolies: *molletons* (combed flannel) in Tourcoing, *calemandes* in Roubaix and Halluin, *pannes* and *tripes de velours* (plush and velvet) in Lannoy.

The Lillois, meanwhile, taking advantage of their own privileges, sought to keep for themselves the manufacture of high-quality textiles and certain profitable end-processes such as dyeing and dressing. So the two groups were not complementary, rather they were rivals and competitors – and had been since the days of the emperor Charles V.[107]

453

The rural manufacturers moreover had a number of advantages: untrammelled by the guild rules, they had more freedom to manoeuvre according to circumstances. And their workers could be lodged and fed more cheaply, particularly since they could combine 'their cottage industry with a plot of land or work in the fields'.[108]

In the seventeenth and eighteenth centuries, rural industry in the area thus tended to thrive, something the city fought determinedly, using any means to hand. In order to thwart its rivals, it refused in 1670 for instance to allow entry to unbleached fabrics, which normally came into town for dyeing and finishing. Upon which the Roubaix manufacturers sent their textiles to Ghent instead and complained in high places – with some success, since it was well-known that when rural industry ran into trouble, the workers readily went across the frontier to the workshops of Bruges and Ghent. On their side, the magistrates of Lille tried to pull strings to get the state to confirm their monopoly. The complicity of certain *intendants* sometimes helped them get their way – in 1704 for instance. But any crisis – such as the Dutch occupation – could be used by the rural manufacturers to regain some of their lost ground and to obtain in turn decrees in their favour.[109]

This small-scale war was prolonged until the late years of the *ancien régime*. In the end, the government, on the advice of Vincent de Gournay and Trudaine, and tired of 'holding the balance' between town and region, finally came down in favour of the latter. The decree of 1762 very firmly ordered the city to 'cease creating obstacles which might damage the progress of industry and of that of the inhabitants of the countryside in particular'. There was such unrest following this in the working-class districts of Lille that the *intendant* intervened to suspend the measure in 1765. For the balance to come down even more decisively in favour of the region, the economic liberalism inspired by Turgot had to gain the upper hand: letters patent of 1777 (the year after his ministry actually fell) ordered the decree of 1762 to be enforced. 'The days of Lille's monopoly were over.'[110] Tourcoing celebrated with 'bonfires and firecrackers'.[111]

This brief summary cannot do justice to the bitter and eventful disputes within the region. Further research is needed to find out what really happened.

But it is clear enough for my present purpose that Lille did not play the role of a regional development centre, indeed far from it. Were the city's true interests served by its stance? Some Lillois did not think so. Taking their logic to extremes, the city authorities went so far as to forbid Lille's own manufacturers from setting up looms in the countryside, for certain fabrics at any rate. One of the mill-owners wrote a memorandum pointing out that 'labour is free everywhere in the countryside . . . surrounding Carcassonne, Rouen, Loundon, Leyden and Vervins in the Liège district'; and that 'the towns that lie in the middle of these manufacturers are all flourishing'. He claimed that to set up workshops outside town, at lower cost, would increase both Lille's production and profits from the sale of woollens, as well as from dyeing, finishing and retailing, and he called for 'this freedom', for 'the good of the region and of my fatherland'.[112] Perhaps he was right?

In this case, the problem lay inside the town, and it should warn us against generalizing too much. The lack of industrial success of the French towns under the *ancien régime* could signify different things, as we have seen in the cases of Lyons and Lille. We should not be too eager, although the parallels are tempting, to compare this with the massive shift of industrial production in our own time to Third World countries like South Korea, Hong Kong and Singapore.

To sum up then: before the revolution, the French economy was progressing on a number of fronts and the towns were deeply concerned. But they followed and accompanied this movement rather than led it. In fact they were not the only forces responsible either for the progress nor, above all, for France's comparative slowness when compared with the more advanced countries in Europe.

Apportioning responsibility

The towns should not take all the blame. True, French urban markets remained insufficiently developed, from the eighteenth century almost to the present day.[113] But such insufficiency when it existed was as much consequence as cause of a wider situation. To examine the question properly, we should ask serious questions about

1) the French state
2) the role of rural areas
3) the international economy

The state was asserting itself over the towns from early days, closely supervising their finances, tolls, debts, permission to borrow and modes of repayment. It took a close interest in their material existence and supply; it transformed mayors, aldermen and consuls into *office-holders*,[114] making venality of office widespread, thus enabling power to be bought by 'trade', in other words the bourgeoisie. It took a large share of the towns' income; and finally, it borrowed money from them.

Thus capital from the towns was mobilized and diverted by the state in a thousand ways – not always very efficiently, for as we shall later see, the *ancien régime* monarchy was poorly served by its fiscal system. Many sources of revenue were lost to it. But of the money sucked up by the state, in direct or indirect taxation, or loans, practically none found its way back into the active sectors of the economy, or into the local economy. It was all channelled 'along a straight line with no remission'[115] towards the Court, towards prestige spending, the repayment of government debts, and the needs of the army and navy. Even major public works in the eighteenth century, for example the modernization of the road network on the initiative and under the supervision of the Crown, were financed largely from regional resources. Herbert Lüthy has described the state as having 'purely parasitic activities'.[116] Perhaps this is a slight exaggeration, for the state also handled many indispensable tasks before 1789. But did its interventions always lead in the same direction as the necessities and requirements of future economic development?

As for the rural areas, we should not entirely exonerate them as being virtually autarkic and therefore innocent. They were necessarily open to the outside world, to the bourgs and towns, and at the end of the day to major trade routes. And they were developing in the eighteenth century. But demographic progress was actually a brake on their activity. Above all, there was no *agricultural revolution* in France, as Michel Morineau has shown. Yet without such a revolution to precede or accompany it (that is without the increased *productivity* that would have enriched landowners while freeing labour for other tasks), the industrial revolution is virtually unthinkable.

Take for example the case of Toulouse, an important town in its day, which despite the wealth in the local countryside did not take the path of industrialization. True, Toulouse was one of the rather sleepier French towns: here, the seventeenth and eighteenth centuries were 'two hundred years of stagnation'.[117] Yet its wealthy bourgeoisie, the families engaged in wholesale trade in particular, had accumulated capital by seizing the opportunities presented by the Revolution (the sale of the *biens nationaux*) to buy up much real estate. Thus it had greatly increased its wealth in land and by the same token neutralized its capital and potential investment, driving itself into 'a blind alley which would prevent it from having an industrial revolution and bringing rural Languedoc out of its backwardness'.[118] But at the same time, it was also helping delay an *agricultural* revolution, since the wealthy bourgeois landowners, who did not of course farm their own land, rented it out under traditional sharecropping arrangements which did not lend themselves at all to capitalist-type farming. The countryside thus trapped capital, immobilizing it and preventing it being used to the full.

Finally, we should incriminate *the world order itself*. By the eighteenth century, the primacy of Amsterdam and Holland was in decline: this was the swansong of the city-states that had once dominated the world (first Venice, then Antwerp, Genoa, Amsterdam). The resources of a city would from now on be too small to fuel mastery of world trade. World primacy was there for

FIGURE 59
Industrial and agricultural production between 1781 and 1938

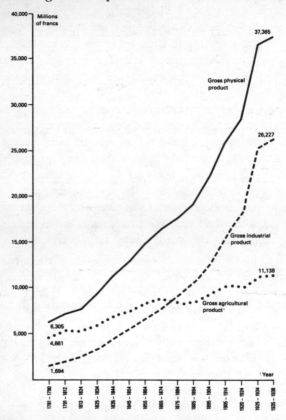

The industrial product did not overtake the agricultural product until about 1875.

Source: Jean Marczewski, *Introduction à l'histoire quantitative*, 1965.

the taking, and both France and Britain fought to gain it. I have often thought that among its other advantages over us, Britain was favoured by its comparatively small physical size: big enough to be a nation, small enough to have a unified economy. Was France, as I have come to think, doomed by its sheer size, so big that a single city, even Paris, would never have the strength to orchestrate the national economy? Was France also disadvantaged by a certain social attitude to which I shall return, an attitude not so much to money itself but to the ways deemed respectable or non-respectable of earning and using it. *Vivre noblement*, 'living nobly', whether for true or false nobles, meant keeping one's hands clean of commerce or industry. Here again, things were ordered differently in England.

By the time of the Revolution at any rate, France had already lost this decisive battle to London. By the treaty of Versailles (1783), 'England lost the war but won the peace,' as Robert Besnier once excellently remarked.[119] At the same time, England had succeeded in capturing the trade of the future United States from under the noses of the Dutch and the French. The die was cast long before Waterloo. Economic (and urban) progress would accrue to the power which had won the prize, namely the leading place in world trade. But, the reader may be wondering, since it has become

fashionable to ask this question, what if the French had won at Waterloo? Answer: it is quite possible that the same would have happened as in 1783; England would have lost the war but won the peace.

It is here that I part company with certain French historians, who see the Revolution and its consequences as a series of economic abdications, delays and disasters. They are no doubt right in part. But surely the real game had been played and lost, or at any rate seriously compromised, before 1789.

CHAPTER TWELVE

Circulation and Structures

I hesitated before choosing the word *circulation*, which was frequently heard in the eighteenth century, and was still in use in the early twentieth century, before gradually being dropped as a term of scientific explanation. To start using it again is almost like launching a new word, and a complicated one, on account of its history and the debates, reasonable and unreasonable, which it has aroused. In the early days of the *Annales* school (1929), Marxist-inclined historians criticized us for putting too much emphasis on *circulation* instead of giving proper pride of place to *production*. This was, I must say, a pointless quarrel. In the first place, we never sought to found any economic theory on circulation. Secondly, circulation has the advantage of being an easily detected and measurable process: economic history, it could be argued, had a perfect right, perhaps even a duty, to begin by tackling the easier tasks.

In any case, circulation is not to my knowledge a myth, and since the economy forms a coherent whole, approaching it by an easy way in takes one inside just the same. Is there any form of production that does not logically lead to circulation, distribution and consumption? The latter closes the circuit, and demand from consumers is what 'turns on the ignition', starting the engine again and thus stimulating production. There is no particular reason why production (still less the means of production) should have any greater claim than circulation to represent the economy as a whole. Furthermore, is it not now generally admitted that 'production is only embarked upon in response to a pre-existent market',[120] that is to an already established system of circulation?

Let us however dwell no longer on an unproductive debate. This chapter will be concerned simply to discover the elements of circulation and the means it employed: the routes, the methods of transport, the goods being carried, the warehouses, markets, fairs, exchanges, currency, credit and all the different stages of commerce. We shall also of course be looking at the people concerned, their actions and their movements. In short, what I mean by circulation is the entire range of economic movements engendered by the operation of any society, those it assumes naturally, as well as those it seeks to promote, even if its efforts are only partly successful. Every society is governed by these movements and adapts to them, and it is in this spirit that one should understand Thomas Regazzola and Jacques Lefebvre's very original book.[121]

High and low circulation

Our first task is to distinguish between the various kinds of circulation: the high road and the low road so to speak, or to use another image, the arteries and veins (high) and the capillaries and tiny blood-vessels (low).

This imagery may be misleading: contrary to what one might expect, 'low' or capillary circulation is by far the stabler of the two and the greater in volume. 'High' circulation, despite, or perhaps because of its successes, has always accounted for less traffic, being sensitive to changes in circumstances which may accelerate or slow down its flow or change its priorities. A graduate seminar at the École Pratique des Hautes Études in about 1950, studying rail traffic in what was then still French North Africa, discovered that while the main-line routes responded to changes in the overall economic situation, branch lines on the contrary had their own rhythms of activity, sometimes much harder to detect.[122] 'Low' circulation may correspond to regular everyday needs, meeting them whatever the difficulties.

Take for example the *département* Mont Blanc in about 1796: documents tell us that 'carriage [*le roulage*] is established through almost all the *département*, and it would be easy to extend it everywhere by the transverse routes [*routes de traverse*]'. *Roulage* meant wheeled vehicles travelling on main roads; *routes de traverse* were the narrow tracks used almost exclusively by laden mules, or packmen. 'The greatest good one could do this *département*', the same informant goes on, 'would be to reduce the amount of traffic carried by mules and to build carriageable roads.'[123] All very well, but for several months of the year these roads would have been closed to wheeled traffic by snow. I wonder if the reader has any idea what a snow-plough looked like, even in 1934, in the Contamines valley (Haute-Savoie)? It was 'a fantastic business. Eight horses and mules, wearing their ceremonial collars, and hung all over with bells, were harnessed two by two to an enormous wooden triangle', made heavier still by being filled with sandbags.

> Each man walked alongside his own horse or mule, cracking his whip above its head. [The beasts'] sweating hindquarters and flanks, glistening with effort, gave off a cloud of vapour which enveloped the team and moved along with it through the frosty air, to the sound of this pastoral music, accompanied by the rhythmic clatter of hooves . . .The huge drag crushed the snow, dividing it and pushing it to either side of the road which now became smooth and shining . . .

A second team of eight men, holding more horses by their bridles, followed the first, and every two or three kilometres the 'leading horses, trembling and sweating' were unharnessed and sent to the rear to have warm blankets thrown over their backs. The work lasted all day. Along the road, children came to watch, and women met the men with food and hot drinks. And that was on the 'main roads'. On the paths leading to hamlets, people had to make do with one horse pulling two wooden *billons* to clear 'a smooth track' through the snow, sufficient for sledges or the great pack-sleds used for supplies.[124] Progress, which arrived in 1934, consisted of replacing the horses with a lorry on the main roads. The traditional method, using the villagers' horses, was now transferred to the smaller roads, which were more effectively cleared as a consequence. This went on at least until horses disappeared from the farms in the valley, that is until about 1957.[125] Mechanical snow-shovels were not introduced until about the 1960s.

Here too then, there was high and low circulation – a distinction we find nine times out of ten. Even today, the closure

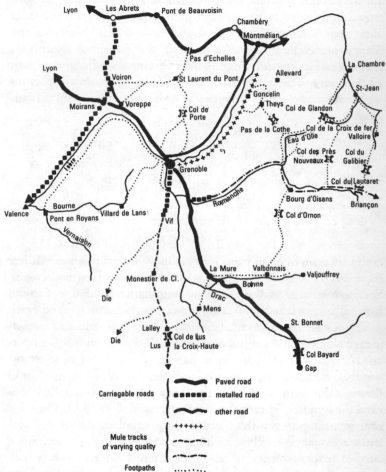

FIGURE 60
*Carriageable roads and larger tracks in the Isère Valley in the
Dauphiné*

The main roads, towards Lyon and Valence, followed the valleys
wherever possible. All the transversal routes are more or less
rudimentary tracks.

Source: Gilbert Armand, *Villes, centres et organisation urbaine des Alpes du
Nord*, 1974.

since 1940 of many branch railway lines (leaving the stations and crossing-keepers' houses deserted and falling into ruin, like so many abandoned village schools) has not destroyed these secondary 'routes' which are now used by buses, vans and private cars. The baker, grocer, butcher and postman still make their rounds from village to village – proof that these elementary communications cannot entirely die out. But speed is a privilege reserved for 'high' forms of circulation. Anyone who is in a hurry will catch a fast train from the main town in the *département*, or a plane from the nearest airport. The old dualism remains.

Statistics from the early nineteenth century make a distinction between major and minor road haulage – the former accounting for less volume than the latter. Dutens, in 1828, referring to the reports of the Committee on haulage of which he was a member, estimated goods travelling on major or 'royal' roads at 10.4 million tons, as against 30.9 million travelling on minor roads.[126] Indeed the network of capillary roads was far more developed than the main arterial highways. In 1836, the royal highways (excluding unfinished sections and those in need of repair) represented just over 34,500 kilometres: these were the very same roads (maintained, rebuilt or in need of rebuilding) which had been opened a good fifty years earlier, during the reigns of Louis XV and Louis XVI – a magnificent network, admittedly, much admired by foreign travellers, and still incomplete in 1789.[127] And it was underused, on certain stretches at any rate, if we are to believe that observant though not always complimentary witness, Arthur Young.[128] The network of second-class roads (that is those maintained by the *départements*) represented about 36,500 kilometres. But according to the same set of figures, published in 1837, the *chemins vicinaux*, that is the smallest or third-class roads, accounted for 771,000 kilometres, or ten times as much as all the other roads put together.[129] And the laws enacted in 1824 and 1836, along with injunctions addressed to villages, resulted in the repair of these elementary roads, which were essential supply-routes for the villages, as well as carrying harvest-waggons, haywains, fertilizer, timber, stone, lime and sand.[130]

Pierre Goubert is right to point to the extremely variable quality of these narrow roads: they might be footpaths leading to vineyards; or 'green lanes', bounded by protective hedges to prevent the cattle straying on their way to the pasture; drove roads for transhumant flocks; bridle-paths taken by salt-merchants (and smugglers); or foresters' tracks through the woods.[131] It was thanks to all these that the rural community was able to exist, to breathe the outside air, and learn to draw on resources other than its own. According to Léonce de Lavergne, the maintenance or revival of this basic kind of circulation, thanks to 'the 1836 law on *Chemins vicinaux*, has transformed France: agriculture is indebted to this law for most of the progress made over the last twenty-five years'.[132] Circulation, I cannot forbear from pointing out, *does* relate to production!

That said, one should not paint too rosy a picture. In France as a whole, there were at best perhaps 100,000 kilometres of these country roads actually in service, that is to say *regularly* carrying traffic. They were probably much like those in southern Germany where, in 1788, a Savoyard pedlar from Magland, Jean-Marie Perollaz, found the roads to the fairs passable enough but had difficulty 'going villaging', that is taking his wares from village to village.[133] Although still *in situ* today, our *chemins vicinaux* are under constant threat of vanishing or being widened to take motorcycles, cars, all-purpose vehicles or tractors. With their uneven cobbled surfaces and the hawthorn trees lining the way, how lovely they can be in springtime! Some of them are so straight that they have been attributed to the Romans; Gaston Roupnel believed, probably wrongly, that they went back as far as neolithic times.[134] Certainly their origins are very ancient. Here and there, they run alongside the ditches, also very ancient, still marking the boundaries of the old seigneurial forests.

Gradually, however, departmental roads began to reach most villages. Regularly re-surfaced, banked and rolled, their level has risen over time, so that a house I know in my native *département*, which was reached by a staircase in 1806, is now only a few steps above the road. Of these highways, built by the state, the village had little need, living as it did largely on its own resources. Indeed villagers avoided them, being concerned only with access to the local fairs and markets and often taking short cuts along the old footpaths. 'Thirty years before the Revolution', the villagers of the Rouergue were still 'not seeking very energetically to have roads built; some people even . . . tried to have them diverted as though they were dangerous torrents'[135] – just as today, small villages dread finding themselves on a trunk road that may bring lorries hurtling through. Apart from the noise and the many accidents, the village's own traffic might be disrupted by the intrusion.

The same distinction between high and low circulation, main roads and local roads, can be found inside ancient cities, even in Paris, where until quite recent times the many narrow, split-level or dead-end streets were an obstacle to the free movement of traffic. In the old days, the main thoroughfares like the rue Saint-Jacques or the rue Saint-Martin took a steady stream of traffic, while the back-streets gave access only sparingly to local districts. A *quartier* could be a self-sufficient island, a village in the city. Even with the coming of horse-drawn cabs, it still took a long time to travel from one part of Paris to another during the Third Republic. The massive destruction (which I still regret – perhaps unreasonably) carried out by Baron Haussmann, created long straight boulevards only in a few of the *beaux quartiers*. 'Paris is still a collection of villages as different from each other as La Muette and La Goutte d'Or' (two social extremes from the West and East Ends of town), as a journalist wrote in 1984.[136]

The major highways

France acquired, in the years after 1750, a *network* of major highways which would be complete in its first incarnation by about 1820. Many of these were of exceptionally high standard for the time. Yet they did not by any means radically affect the French economy. In any case, the network was still far from covering the country. Its star-shaped pattern took all roads to Paris, but this centralization was far from perfect in the early nineteenth century. Above all, these major routes did not adequately connect together the regional networks, designed for local purposes and largely self-contained. So before the coming of the railways, France was not really a *national market*.

The map in Figure 61, taken from a recent book by Bernard Lepetit, shows how uneven road provision was within France in about the 1820s. Once more, one can distinguish a Saint-Malo to Geneva line, dividing northern France, where there was 'maximum road capillarity' and plentiful if not perfect highway penetration, from southern and western France, where paved or stone-surfaced roads were the exception, and dirt roads were numerous. 'Southern France is characterized by a linear network, rendered more fragile by the lack of alternative routes, and without enough lateral branches to rescue from isolation the regions it goes through.'[137]

But one should not forget that at this time even major roads were fragile affairs, mere strips of presumed solid carriageway, between unsafe verges in which vehicles often became embedded. They often needed repairs. To take one example among many, in 1794, the road from Paris to Brest, an important trunk road through the *département* of Ille-et-Vilaine, is described as being 'generally . . . viable and there is no record of it having been impassable in recent years, but it is very hard going for wheeled traffic as one approaches Rennes in wet weather'.[138] Between Gravelle and Vitré, 'the ground is solid, but the surface rough, imperfect and damaged. Only a third of the funds necessary for repairs are present'; from Vitré to Châteaubourg, 'the base is solid, but the road surface is imperfect and much damaged. No funds for repairs'. Between Châteaubourg and Rennes, 'the foundations are of very poor quality, the paving uneven and very far from perfect. There is a short stretch which is very bad across the Clusaury heath. Repairs are being carried out.' Over the 25,169 *toises* (about 50 kilometres) of these three sectors, only 5,032 (a fifth) were surfaced.

This example illustrates a general reality which Bernard Lepetit's detailed research has brought to light. The official map of royal highways – the major carriageable roads – indicates on paper a good coverage of the country in 1820. But in reality, not all these

FIGURE 61
Road density by département *(gaps excluded), 1820*

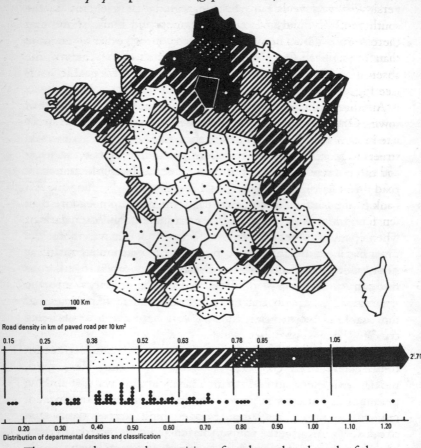

The contrast between the provision of roads north and south of the Loire is very marked.

Source: Bernard Lepetit, *Chemins de terre et voies d'eau*, 1984.

roads had even been finished: they were interrupted by gaps, by dirt roads, more or less passable according to the season, or by sections needing repair or rebuilding. Taking these imperfections into account, Bernard Lepetit has drawn up a revised map of the royal

468

roads – the good ones indicated by a thick line, the unfinished ones by a thin line – which is certainly less optimistic than the official version.[139] It reveals considerable regional deficiencies, in the south generally, and in mountain regions; and it also shows that there were 'regional networks connected to each other by no more than a single [uninterrupted] route'. In short, it betrays 'the absence of a true national network' of normal carriageable roads (see Figure 66).[140]

Another problem was that roads had to go through the middle of towns. One might think *a priori* that it was easier for traffic to circulate in town than in the suburbs or the country, if only because the streets were at least paved. But these streets were narrow, winding and often steeply-sloping, as in Vienne in the Dauphiné: the main road from Lyon to Provence ran through the town, along the left bank of the Rhône. Vienne's streets, some of them not more than ten feet wide, were steep and prone to flooding. After dark or when it snowed, vehicles courted disaster. What was more, the town had been much developed, but mainly within its fortifications, which meant the houses were closely cramped together; as the population increased, markets began to spill out into the streets, which were now 'so crammed with vehicles and horses that the residents were held up every few feet for fear of being crushed'.[141]

Yet the road-building achievements of the late eighteenth century had been considerable. New techniques were used, including deeper foundations for roads and new ways of sinking the piles of bridges into river-beds; bends were redesigned, gradients reduced and iron bridges built across rivers and streams.[142] All these transformations were noted by the observant eye of Stendhal.[143] And engineers were soon scornfully writing of the roads built in the earlier part of the eighteenth century that they were merely 'natural tracks, a little enlarged'![144] On the new highways, one travelled better, more comfortably (since carriages improved as well) – and above all faster. I shall not dwell here on the increased speeds made possible in the eighteenth century, starting with the so-called *turgotines*, or on the larger numbers of post-houses and the organization of communications, since I have reproduced in Figure 62 Guy Arbellot's maps showing these spectacular changes.[145] Even faster speeds were achieved in the nineteenth century, since the average speed of the *messageries* tripled between the late eighteenth century and 1850.[146]

Indeed for some time, carriages travelling by road continued to compete with the railways, which soon became unbeatable, but which did not reach everywhere at first. Nor were they always very fast. 'In about 1910', Jean-Claude Georges's grandmother told him, 'when I was a little girl, we would take the train to go to Benoîte-Vaux or Fontaine Saint-Avit [villages in the Meuse]. I remember that when the little train came to a hill, we had time to get out and walk through the meadows beside the embankment. We could pick a bunch of flowers and catch the train up at the top of the hill.'[147] Nowadays, I need hardly say, there is no railway line to these villages at all.

Transport of a third kind: waterways

If the trunk road was the leading transport route, and the modest local road (carrying however a greater volume of traffic) the second, the waterway, important both before and after the coming of the railways, was certainly the third. Here too, it is worth distinguishing between high and low circulation.

Alain Croix has for instance described the Loire and the Vilaine as the 'motorways' of Brittany. (The latter was the 'first river in France to be channelled by means of locks, between 1539 and 1585').[148] But small rivers, with estuaries up which boats could travel with the tide – such as the Oust, Blavet, Aulne, Trieux, Rance or Couesnon – were all 'massively used' to take goods inland, despite frequent accidents.

Being more or less equally provided with waterways, all French provinces tried to make the most of them. The great rivers were indeed like motorways, each with its own type of shipping and traditions. Travelling south (in the discomfort of a stagecoach) in 1834, Victor Hugo described seeing on the Loire convoys of five or six boats going up or down stream . . . Each boat has only one mast and one square sail. The one with the largest sail goes in front of the rest and draws them along. The convoy is arranged so that the sails decrease in size from the first to the last, in a sort of symmetrical descent, with no deviation or exception . . . I have only seen this on the Loire, and I must confess that I prefer watching the sloops and cutters of Normandy, of all shapes and sizes, as they flit to and fro [across the lower reaches of the Seine] like birds of prey, mingling their red and yellow sails under squalls, rain and sunshine, between Quilleboeuf and Tancarville.[149]

What an adventure it would be today to sail along all the water-ways in France, which not long ago were still so thronged with traffic. Pierre Goubert shares my view.[150] If historians tend to 'revive the memory of rivers that were busy thoroughfares in the distant past, fell into disuse in the recent past and are coming back to life though in a rather less picturesque way today', it is because reviving them means rediscovering the way of life of the past – one that has many charms for us, though it meant immense toil for the river boatmen.

I tried in a previous chapter to retrace the glorious shipping history of the Rhône and the Loire. Choosing two examples meant sacrificing all the others. Shall I confess that, having often had occasion to cross or to drive alongside the Canal des Deux Mers, recognizable from far away with its lines of tall poplars, I have more than once been tempted to take a boat right along its narrow length until it meets the Garonne. The Garonne is one of the two rivers – the other being the Dordogne – which Monluc in 1562 described as 'the two breasts that nourish Bordeaux'.[151]

The Dordogne, a broad river which it took over an hour to cross by boat just north of Bordeaux, 'where this river is at least as wide as the Garonne',[152] is described at length in a book brimming with images of the colourful life along its banks in the eighteenth century.[153] Towns, villages, hamlets and private houses all had a front on the river, if only by way of the *peyrats*, crude extensions of the banks,

*France's large surface area: the difficulties of establishing a
national market*

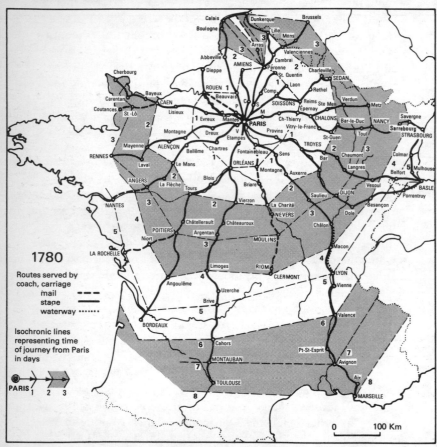

These two maps from G. Arbellot's article in *Annales E.S.C.*, 1973, at
p. 790, show 'the great highway revolution': thanks to the new roads
suited to 'coaches travelling at a gallop', and the widespread use of the
stage-coaches known as *turgotines*, as well as the increased numbers of
posting-stations, travelling times were much reduced throughout
France between 1765 and 1780, some of them even being halved. In
1765, it took at least three weeks to travel from Lille to the Pyrenees
or from Strasbourg to Brittany. Even in 1780, France was a huge
landmass which took a long time to cross.

FIGURE 62b

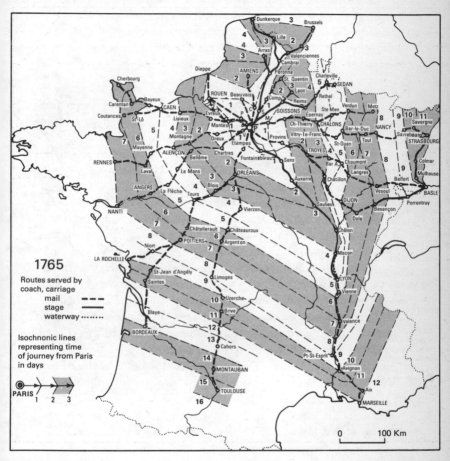

1765

Routes served by
coach, carriage
mail
stage
waterway

Isochnonic lines
representing time
of journey from Paris
in days

PARIS 1 2 3

0 100 Km

But progress in road transport affected the whole country. On the
1765 map, one can identify certain privileged itineraries: Paris–Rouen
or Paris–Péronne (just one day, the same as Paris–Melun); Paris–Lyon
(5 days, the same as from Paris to Charleville, Caen or Vitry-le-
François). On the 1780 map, the distance travelled and the time taken
roughly match, hence the almost concentric circles round Paris instead
of the skewed pattern on the first map. The length of journey
remained much the same on the formerly privileged routes from Paris
to Lyon or Rouen. The breakthrough here was the creation by Turgot
of the *Régie* (department) of Mail-coaches and Stage-coaches, in 1775.

built out into the water and strengthened with ballast, stone, faggots, *aubarèdes* [plantations of withies] and sand. Attached to the bank, the *peyrats* sloped gently down to the water to make it easy for flat-bottomed boats to moor here and take on cargoes, but they were vulnerable to the high waters of winter and spring, which undermined them, altered their shape, or washed them away down river.[154]

The boats were of all kinds, from the *filadières*, used only for fishing, to the great barges known as *couraux*, or the *gabarres* and *gabarrots* encountered on the lower Garonne, as well as *barques*, which were in theory confined to the coastal trade.[155] To go upstream, these boats of quite small tonnage traditionally depended on human haulage, until about 1740, when oxen began to compete with the hauliers, occasioning vehement disputes.[156] The upper reaches of the Dordogne were narrow and fast-flowing, and could be used for little except *la flotte* – floating loose logs, tree trunks or wooden beams down with the current. The system was less simple than it looked; the floating logs had to be watched and guided as far as 'Spontour, Argentat, or even Arroumet, the timber depot for Souillac'.[157] Timber-transporting boats took over here, for no great rafts of logs were sent floating down the Dordogne as they were down the Garonne towards Bordeaux. Firewood, planks, charcoal, were all laden on to these flimsy and short-lived boats known as *argentats* from the little town which was their obligatory port of call; like the *sapinières* on the Loire or the Allier, they made only one trip downstream before being broken up on arrival for their timbers or for firewood.[158]

Although the types of boat, their names, and the modes and problems of navigation differed from one waterway to the next, all types of river transport inevitably had much in common. On the Seine and its tributaries, one meets all the usual obstacles and quarrels. The obstacles generally arose with 'my lords the toll-owners', who were a perpetual nuisance; the quarrels were with the state, which insisted on ever more rules and formalities. Documents not always easy to interpret at first reading tell us that every ship had to have its *lettre de voiture*, (bill of lading) which amounted to a contract with the shipper of the goods;[159] the goods themselves were obliged to go through the hands of the *brouettiers*, who took them to be weighed and then on to the boat in their handcarts (*brouettes*). There was always chaos around the public weighbridge, and at the point of embarkation, and the same again for disembarkation. The whole thing seems to have been carried on in the most disorganized and haphazard manner.

But the system worked. In an article which caused a sensation in its time, many years ago, Léon Cahen remarked with surprise on the modest traffic on the waterways leading to Paris.[160] I am not sure now that he is right. In 1710, it took eight days (10 to 18 June) to ship grain from Rouen to Paris, but the cargo consisted of 4,533 sacks.[161] One isolated document tells us that at the port of Soissons on the Oise, just after the river had unfrozen, between 6 March and 13 April 1709, 805 *muids* of wheat (i.e. about 15,000 hectolitres, the Parisian *muid* being about 18) were taken on board 'to ship to Paris'.[162] On account of the prodigious development of the capital, traffic along the Seine and its tributaries, calculated in 1857 at 5,376,000 tons, outstripped that on the Rhône (3,608,000 tons) or the Loire (2,111,000).[163]

Furthermore, waterways transported not only goods but passengers and their luggage, providing a sort of luxury coach service. To travel from Agen to Bordeaux in the seventeenth or eighteenth century for instance, one took a 'water-coach' which left twice a week and took two days to reach Bordeaux. For the return journey, one could take advantage of the 'many boats which sailed up on the tide as far as Cadillac', and from there on travel by horseback, changing mounts six times before reaching Agen.[164] In Paris, timetables were printed giving passengers itineraries served by water-coaches from the capital, and informing them of the day, time and place of embarkation, plus some necessary instructions. Travellers were requested to arrive at exactly the time shown on the clock of St Paul's church. But the boat might be leaving either from St Paul's quay or the Tournelle quay, and the timetables varied in summer and winter. No voyager could be refused passage for himself and his luggage, and he would not be cheated over the price of the ticket, since the tariffs of the water-coaches, following a decision taken by the provosts, merchants and sheriffs of Paris on 29 April 1738, were 'pinned to the masts' of the said boats and 'inscribed on a tin panel'.[165]

At about the same period, travellers and businessmen, French and foreign, were flocking to take the water-coaches on the Loire at a fare of three *sols* per person per league. Passengers spent the nights at the many inns along the river. A century later, the first steamships made their appearance, but several spectacular accidents (in which the boiler blew up) kept passengers away. Hence the name given to a new type of ship in 1838, the *Inexplosibles* (Unexplodables)! By 1843, these were all the rage on the Loire and even on the Allier (70,000 passengers on the lower Loire, 37,000 on the upper Loire and the Allier). Their speed, comfort and even the excellent fare on board were much vaunted. Less was heard about the fact that, like traditional vessels, they tended to run aground – and that it took six pairs of oxen to haul them free! Despite their success, within ten years the famous *Inexplosibles* had been ousted by the railways.[166]

Rivers and canals were always being improved of course: redesigned, built or rebuilt according to necessity. From the energy with which waterways were tackled wherever possible, one can tell how important they were. There were countless proposals for improving the navigability of hitherto unused rivers. One such was unsuccessfully put forward in the Cher in 1679,[167] only to surface once more, again to no avail, in 1788.[168] In 1696, a plan was proposed for making the Charente navigable between Angoulême and Ventreuil, in order to supply timber to the naval port of Rochefort. In 1763,[169] the *intendant* of the *généralités* of Pau and Auch had works hastily carried out on the *gave* of Oléron, a tributary of the Adour, for the conveyance of ships' masts to Bayonne. In 1795, the winegrowers on the banks of the Sioule requested the improvement of the 6.5 kilometre stretch separating them from the point where it joined the Allier. The answer was no: the project would be expensive and unreasonable, since to render this very short stretch navigable would mean destroying three mills.[170]

Another project, a very ambitious one, was proposed by the chamber of commerce of Picardy on 15 June 1781: improvements to render the Somme more suitable for shipping between Amiens and the sea. This would require exceptional works, since the estimated expenditure was 900,000 *livres*.[171] The mouth of the Somme was gradually being silted up by the masses of sand brought in by both the sea and the river: traffic through Saint-Valéry had been affected by this for years. Various plans had been put forward without success in 1764, 1770 and 1779.[172] The 1781 version was on a grand scale, proposing that 'the Somme should be dammed shortly above its mouth', and that 'its waters [be] diverted via a canal leading directly to the harbour of Saint-Valéry. . . A lock would be built for the purpose of removing sand; furthermore, haulage by horses [should] replace towing by men, from the works at the Saint-Valéry end as far as Amiens.' This plan, which was no doubt originally responsible for the canalization of the river between Abbeville and Saint-Valéry, may seem obscure to us. But anyone who is familiar with the vast Somme estuary – still blocked by sand to this day – will see why there were dreams of changing the landscape.

Which was better, land or water?

Waterways were not confined to rivers of course. We must add to them the 'artificial waterways' provided by canals (1,000 kilometres in 1800, as opposed to 7,000 kilometres of navigable rivers; by 1830 there were 2,000 and by 1843, 4,000 – before the coming of the railways slowed canal-building).[173] And one should also bear in mind coastal shipping, as well as several routes using the high seas. All in all, was water a serious competitor, compared with the colossal services rendered by overland transport?

Werner Sombart's answer to this question, many years ago, was a resounding no, backed up with his usual energetically polemic demonstration. His thesis applied to Germany but could unquestionably be transferred to France. And Jean Meyer is also right to stress how even on a river regarded as *regular*, such as the Seine, periods of flooding or drought could add up to render it unusable for two-thirds of the year.[174] Further supporting evidence is that an overland route could be regarded as preferable to the waterway running alongside it. In the sixteenth century for instance, most of the convoys driven by carters from Arras, Valenciennes or Champagne, instead of transferring their loads to boats when they reached the Saône, 'went on to Lyon. Arriving at the start of the fair, they would return laden with goods bought at the fair and destined for the Netherlands.'[175] We will also bear in mind the comparative regularity of overland routes (comparative since seasonal farming activities took peasant hauliers off the job in summer), its rapidity, also comparative, as against the slow speed of river traffic, and the risks water transport posed for certain fragile goods, such as textiles. Lastly, what seems the clinching argument, the figures registered in 1828 record 4.8 million tons of goods being transported by water, as opposed to 41.3 million by land.[176] But is this really the end of the question?

I do not say that Werner Sombart and Jean Meyer are mistaken. But are they asking the right question? Should we perhaps recall the opinion of Vauban, himself no mean observer. 'A boat of reasonable size', he says, 'on a good stretch of water, can convey on its own, using six men and 4 [towing] horses . . . a cargo that 200 men and 400 horses would have difficulty conveying on normal roads.'[177] And it cannot be denied that, whenever possible, heavy or bulky goods such as charcoal or straw went by water almost as a matter of course.[178] So too did stone, iron, cast-iron, grain, wine, wood, and coal. In 1796 for instance, coal was discovered near Annecy.

But the problems of transporting this coal [an observant witness remarks] from the Annecy basin, which is surrounded on all sides by very steep slopes, will always cancel out the great profit it might bring, because of the great cost of haulage, which can be done only by waggons and carts; so it is doubtful whether one could convey the coal from this quarry from Annecy to Chambéry, nine or ten post-leagues away, as cheaply as the coal that comes via the Rhône and the Lac du Bourget from the quarries of Rive-de-Giers, although that is some thirty or forty leagues distant. This proves . . . that places where there are navigation canals will always make more progress than those which can only communicate by road, however fine and carriageable those roads may be.[179]

In June 1757, the *intendant* of finance at Courteille calculated that to transport grain in small barges of 30 to 50 tons from Caen to Paris would work out at a quarter of the cost of haulage.[180]

Waterways were thus cheaper and better at transporting heavy goods. These advantages continued to have force until the coming of the railways and even later. In July 1817 for instance, a convoy of a dozen boats loaded grain at Rouen and landed it at Poissy for Paris; each boat carried about 200 tons,[181] the equivalent of about 800 cartloads since in the late eighteenth century, despite spectacular progress in haulage which had increased the volume of goods carried by about 60%, a carter with four horses could still only carry 2.5 tons of goods.[182] And in 1827, without going into detailed calculations here, waterways were still two and a half times cheaper than the roads.[183]

Whatever the accuracy of these observations, they do not fundamentally alter the debate about the respective use of land and water. But two further remarks may be of some guidance:

1) In the figures relating to weight and volume, timber floated down rivers has not, as far as I can see, been included in the total for waterways.[184] This is probably a monumental omission. For heating alone, Paris and its suburbs were in 1786 consuming some 700 to 800,000 *voies* of timber, or about a million and a half *stères*.[185] Practically all rivers had log-rafts on them, whether the Isère, the *gave* of Pau, the Allier or the Ornain, which ferried down great *brelles*, rafts of pine-logs from the Vosges, as far as Bar-le-Duc,: they were then sent on down the Marne to Paris and Rouen.

2) Waterways were used for medium- and particularly for long-distance traffic, sometimes along the entire course of a river. A boat leaving Roanne to travel down the Loire would go at least as far as Orléans, and sometimes as far as Nantes. On the Saône, a boat would sail past Gray and usually take the obvious course and carry on to Lyon. Fruit, wine, stone, or coal, taken on board on the Allier, travelled directly to Nantes, Paris or Orléans. The canals

linking rivers were increasingly making it possible to carry on without trans-shipping. So waterways were part of the 'higher' circulation, the upper level of transport.

This is the crucial point to remember. Waterways should be compared to the main highways, still in 1827 known as the 'royal' roads. The 4.8 million tons carried by water should be compared not with the 41.3 million tons which is the total for all overland routes, but with the 10.4 million carried on the royal roads. This makes the proportion more like 1 to 2, which is the figure deduced by J.C. Toutain for the 1840s (49% on roads, 23% on navigable waterways).[186] But if one then adds on the goods carried by coasting vessels, another 25% would have to be added to the 23% for the rivers. That would make the water-borne total almost equal to the overland total. And what if we added on the enormous quantities of timber which, as I have said, are left out of the estimates?

Lastly, we might remember that the authors of improvement projects dreamed of extending even further the network of canals (already quadrupled in size between 1800 and 1843) in order to reduce the large sums that road transport was costing the French economy. It was not a new idea: Vauban had earlier proposed the improvement of 190 waterways to make them navigable, in order to unblock traffic bottlenecks.[187] Waterways could and should have been expanded. In fact, after 1830, they demonstrated their superiority over the roads in that, unlike road haulage, they kept pace with the railways in handling an increased volume of traffic, until the latter eventually won the price war.[188] So French waterways found their development blocked at a level below what it might have been. And blocked it still remains today.

Circulation as a whole: the role of the state

The French state could only become consolidated, or established, by 'domesticating' the traffic and exchange taking place within French territory. This certainly did not happen overnight. The state gained control in the first instance of the nodal points of circulation: markets and fairs, which could only be created with state permission and which remained under state protection. It was also able to control that travelling commodity par excellence, money, as it left the mints. It created and granted privileges to the postal service. And finally, it concerned itself more and more with the roads, chiefly the trunk roads and the network they formed (or should have formed) and the towns lying at important crossroads.

This task, a colossal one since it was attempted on a nationwide scale, inevitably went far beyond the much-vaunted works of Sully, which were actually of limited, not to say episodic character, in the years following the major destruction caused by the Wars of Religion. The post of Grand Voyer de France, in charge of all the roads, a post created for Sully in 1599, was abolished in 1626.[189] And indeed Sully himself in his time had made it clear that he considered 'bridges and highways not to be the concern of the King's service', but to be the responsibility of the local authorities and financing bodies.[190] During Colbert's time in office (1661–83), the monarchy did begin to engage in these grandiose road-building programmes. But once more, when Colbert had left the scene, the state's interest lapsed.

It was not until the eighteenth century, after about 1735 or rather the 1760s, that the state deliberately embarked on a task which would always exceed its means if not its intentions. In the event, it was above all the requirements of an expanding economy which inspired the building, repair and maintenance of roads, and since the technology of civil engineering had greatly improved, the costs rose steadily. As a result, the state found itself committed to a task beyond its purse; the very efforts it had to make revealed the obstacles imposed by its own structure.

For there was no such thing as the *single* French economy, rather France contained a series of provincial economies, motivated by regional considerations and therefore interested above all in medium-distance communications. These provincial economies defended their privileges, their interests and their everyday existence. And to the extent that the state long allowed them to plan their own lives, including virtually all road-building and maintenance, the roads they built tended to serve local trade circuits.

FIGURE 63
Mail routes in 1632

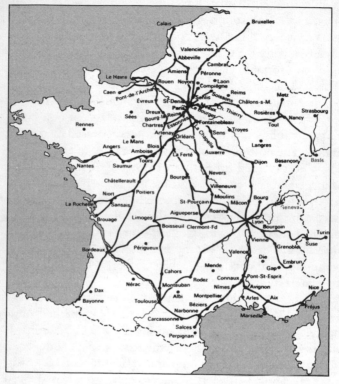

Note that they did not yet cover the whole of France, as they would in the eighteenth century: there were gaps in the east and west in particular.

Source: Alfred Fierro-Domenech, *Le Pré carré, géographie historique de la France*, 1986.

Even large-scale plans, sometimes attempted by the *intendants*, rarely went beyond the limits of regional activities and needs.

The state meanwhile was left to take charge of the essential communications, that is the national network. It gradually realized the need to bring the highway out of its local context, to 'de-

FIGURE 64
Mail routes in 1797

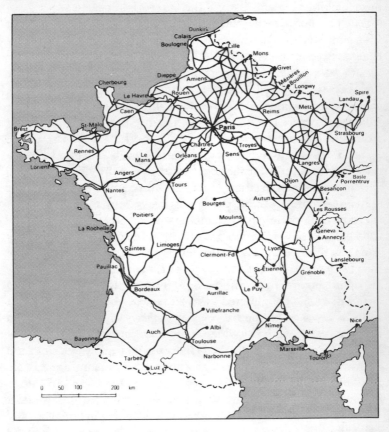

Source: after Vidal de la Blache, *Tableau de la géographie de la France* and
A. Fierro-Domenech, *Le Pré carré*, 1986.

territorialize it', to bring together 'the regional chequer-boards
created by the *intendants* within their *généralités*', in order to create
one great network, shaped like a spider's web, with all roads leading to and from Paris,[191] and thus to establish, as far as possible,
what today's economists would call a *national market*. The task

could only be accomplished slowly, since it sometimes came up against local resistance.[192] And the longer it was in the making, the more ambitious – and costly – the enterprise became.

The problem was that the monarchy of the *ancien régime* had not fully exploited the tax resources of the kingdom. Would the reader have guessed as much? It could draw only on part of its subjects' wealth. As a result, it was short of money. And the building of the highways would only be possible by requisitioning peasant labour, by the system known as the *corvée royale*. This was already established well before it was formally recognized in 1738 by a circular from the controller-general Orry: Colbert had already talked about it, and from his time on, the *intendants* had begun to introduce it, whether or not the idea was theirs in the first place.

This annual mobilization of labour – for about 12 to 30 or even 40 days – represented an extremely heavy levy in days worked. Moreover, it was desperately unfair, varying greatly, and theoretically exacted only from villagers living three or four leagues away from road-projects. As a result there were complaints and general ill-will from the *corvoyeurs de bras* or *de harnais* (that is those providing their labour with or without draught animals). It also provoked criticism from 'enlightened' writers, from Mirabeau, author of *L'Ami des hommes*, to the *Encyclopédie méthodique*. It must be agreed that the *corvée*, without which Trudaine, *intendant* in charge of Ponts et Chaussées (Bridges and Highways) from 1743 to 1769, and Perronet (1708–94) the engineer who in 1747 organized the Ecole des Ponts et Chaussées for trainees, would never have been able to build their admirable roads, was sometimes a pure waste of effort and even money. Village labour was often lacking in both skill and enthusiasm and the results sometimes left much to be desired. In 1701, the *intendant* of Montauban, following torrential rain which had swept away bridges and destroyed roads, was bewailing the loss of 200,000 man-days' labour, wiped out by the rain, on 'new roads, [where] no carriage could have passed 40 years ago'.[193]

This was why, even before Turgot's edict abolishing *corvée* (February 1776), and again after the edict restoring it (11 August the same year), several *intendants* had begun replacing the *corvée* in kind by a tax in money which enabled a specialized workforce to be hired. Approving this decision in the Berry in 1780, the provincial assembly noted that in order to build three leagues of roadway (about 12 kilometres), the days lost in men's and beasts' work amounted to 624,000 *livres*' worth of tax levied in kind, whereas 240,000 *livres* of taxes in money from various sources enabled double the distance to be built.[194] A memorandum proposing the abolition of the *corvée* in Burgundy in 1775 advanced much the same arguments. The quality of the roads and the development of new technology would be infinitely better, it explained. True, it would cost about 800,000 *livres* a year, 'a very terrible fact', but then the 98,283 requisitioned men and 69,918 horses employed for 12 days a year on this work represented 1,933,000 *livres*' worth of labour, even on a very low estimate of its cost. In other words, the latter would cost twice as much. It is a matter of urgency, the writer concluded, to introduce 'remunerated road-building'.[195]

The new tax proved difficult to levy however. Getting rid of the *corvée* in 1789 did not resolve the problem. In Year X (1802), the *conseil général* of Saône-et-Loire was actually publicly deploring its abolition. 'Only the *corvée*', it declared, 'can give the Republic back its magnificent roads, so necessary to its commerce and which were once the admiration of foreigners.'[196]

Despite such difficulties and delays, the road network did expand. There were 302 'post-houses' altogether in 1584; 623 in 1632, 798 in 1791, 1,426 (almost twice as many) in 1789, and 2,057 in 1850.[197] Admittedly, no more than a tenth of all goods, at most, was travelling on the main roads, even in 1827. But the still imperfect network all the same handled an essential part of the country's needs and ensured regular links. A hundred years earlier after all, in February 1707, the maréchal de Tessé, arriving at Grenoble after the disaster of Turin to take command of the army in the southeast,[198] had realized with horror how difficult it was to communicate with the Court. Between Paris and Lyon, messages travelled fairly quickly by the normal mail coach. But between Grenoble and Lyon, mail was carried in an ox-cart![199] Compare this with 1814, when in even more dramatic circumstances, as Napoleon was defending the approach-roads to Paris against foreign troops, the mail-coaches continued to operate as best they could, despite the invasion of France from the east and north. The mails from Strasbourg, Lille and Lyon sometimes arrived 'very late, on account of the detours they were obliged to make',[200] but they did arrive (no doubt because a country as big as France could not be completely controlled by the enemy), regularly bringing news which was more or less accurate, but always alarming. On 30 March, capitulation saved Paris 'not from occupation, but [perhaps] from fire and pillage'. When the Allies entered the capital on 1 April, 'the public was informed that mail services would leave that day as usual, and by 7 April, it was hoped that the service would be completely back to normal by the end of the week'.

The strangest aspects of this imperfect system were the record speeds reported – some of them are so extraordinary that one wonders if they are true. I am prepared to believe for instance that news of the disaster of Pavia (24 February 1525) arrived in Paris on 7 March, and that by 20 March the troops fleeing after the battle, who had only their own legs to carry them, were already on the outskirts of the capital and looting the villages.[201] On the other hand, I find it hard to credit that news of the St. Bartholomew's Massacre (24 August 1572) reached Madrid a mere three or four days later – it seems quite impossible. However the news of the fall of the Bastille (14 July 1789) certainly spread throughout France in a few days.

And here is one absolutely attested fact, which may interest the reader. At a time when the fastest stage-coaches from Paris (cf. Figure 62) took days and days to travel across France, some news sped as if on wings, even before the telegraph invented by Chappe was in position (1793). The sensational news of the arrest of the royal family at Varennes (22 June 1791) was learnt in Quimper, on the other side of France, within two days. The members of the *département* of Morbihan wrote to the Assemblée Nationale to say 'we heard of the capture of the king and his family on Friday 24 of this month at 7 in the morning'.[202]

FIGURE 65
GDP and production for the market 1785–1938

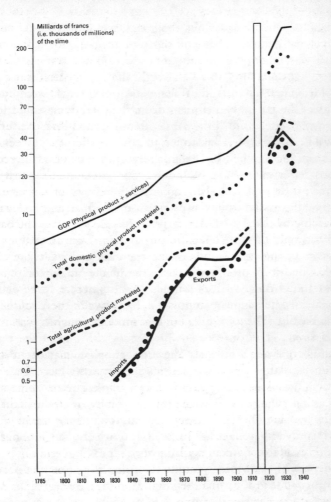

Graph based on largely decennial averages provided by Jean-Claude Toutain. The gap over about 10 years after 1920 is because we cannot compare the francs in circulation before 1914, which were attached to a metal standard, to post-World War I francs, which had undergone severe inflation.

The overall volume of traffic

To conclude anything serious about this, we must resort to retrospective calculations, above all those by Jean-Claude Toutain.[203] He has worked out the amount of production which found its way into exchange circuits, in other words, the volume that was available for commerce instead of being consumed on the spot by the producer. To do so, he deducted from the total domestic product what was needed to feed the peasant himself and his farm animals, as well as the 'industrial' products (textiles, buildings, equipment) manufactured for the use of the family. And it could no doubt be argued that of industrial production proper, notably in the towns, a certain proportion was also consumed by the producer without reaching the market. But this proportion was small and in any case impossible to calculate. So we may set it aside without it affecting the total greatly. Figure 65, based on Toutain's figures, enables one to see at a glance the results of the exercise, and clearly demonstrates the overall progress made in the nineteenth century.

But the striking feature of this development is the relation (which does not appear on the graph) between total *agricultural* production and the percentage of that production which was commercialized. This confronts us of course with one of the major questions of French history. The proportion of agricultural production available for sale represents the surplus which supported everyone who was not a peasant, that is, the entire urban population, all the ruling and privileged classes – in short all the luxury in French history. This figure, even on the roughest of calculations, which is all we have, must be a key figure for the 'sincere' history of France, as for any country subject to a peasant economy.

This key figure varied greatly according to region and period. For Languedoc in 1737, the memoranda of the *intendant* de Basville helped me to calculate the amount of production that was not consumed on the spot, which I have worked out as about 14%. And since this includes all industrial production, only a very small proportion of agricultural production can have been available for the market.[204]

The latter part of the eighteenth century witnessed extraordinary progress: the first figure advanced by J.C. Toutain for surplus *food* production between 1781 and 1790 is 30%; this had risen to 50% by 1874–5; the average for 1935–8 was 75%; and in 1980 it was 95% and could hardly be bettered.[205]

With this, we are witnessing the disappearance for good of the small local circuits. Autarky, for so long a living reality though never *total*, has been literally wiped out, so that today, even if you are in the remotest village or country cottage, you are unlikely to be eating local produce, apart from a few eggs, milk and fruit bought from the neighbours: the bread, meat, butter and wine you consume will not normally be of local origin at all. Milk and grapes are nowadays increasingly collected by farming cooperatives; the product can go anywhere in the country. Between 1903 and 1914 by contrast, 39% of all produce remained on the spot. We are a long way from that now.

So the old circuits have broken down. The regional circuit is all but vanishing and the national circuit is wide open to the produce of the whole world. If our frontiers continue to open, we shall be eating more and more Argentinian beef, New Zealand lamb, fruit from Africa, America and Australia, while industrial products will be reaching our house from all over the world. A silent revolution has transformed French circulation as it has that of all the other national economies of the globe.

Before and after the railways

So the move towards a more uniform France took place in the end, without French people having sought it or even in some cases noticing what was happening. An ancient economy, still in the fragile form of the national market so painfully achieved, has melted, like sugar in water, for the benefit of an international market under which we are gradually being submerged.

We are a long way now from the *ancien régime* which, a mere two hundred years or so ago, just before it disappeared, was still wondering how to abolish all the internal barriers, customs tariffs,

FIGURE 66
The network of royal highways, 1820

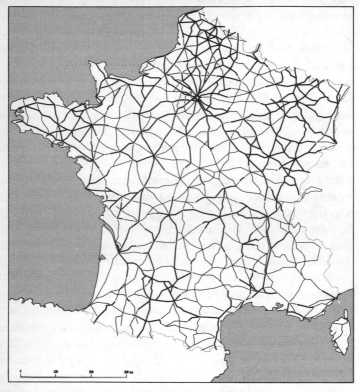

Bold lines represent roads which were actually built and carriageable;
faint lines those which had gaps.

Source: Bernard Lepetit, *Chemins de terre et voies d'eau. Réseaux de
transports, organisation de l'espace*, 1984.

tolls and duties to be found on the frontiers between provinces,
along roads and rivers, or at the entry to towns, irremediably frag-
menting the circulation of goods *within* the kingdom! As the state
had grown, it had acquired provinces, towns, *pays* and *seigneuries*,
but by the same token it had inherited customs institutions, public
and private privileges which had been clung to tooth and nail,

resisting all attempts to bring them under control, notably by Colbert.

By the eighteenth century however, especially after 1750, all the economists were calling for major reform. People may not believe it, wrote Forbonnais, but it is the literal truth that 'in order to double the mass of money in circulation within six or seven years, and thereby to increase public revenue proportionately', all that is required is to 'abolish the customs post at Valence, the two per cent levied at Arles, the baron's farthing, the *traite foraine* [foreign duty] of Languedoc on its frontier with Provence . . . to cut the duty on silk and raw materials by half . . . to abolish the tariffs levied in Lyon on all goods leaving France via Provence . . . and in general on all goods travelling between provinces'.[206] The customs post at Valence alone, 'the most destructive tax on commerce' in France, 'exhausts five or six provinces whose trade it wipes out'.[207] In addition to the customs duties, there were tolls and *octrois*, which did more damage by the constant interruptions to traffic that they occasioned than by the actual sums they cost. To give one tiny example: in 1788, a load of timber sent from Lorraine to Sète had to pay 34 different duties in 21 different places![208]

In view of this, it is easier to appreciate the remark by Catherine the Great's ambassador to Paris that there was no overall guidebook on the French mail service, only a 'haphazard collection' in three volumes about the *messageries* (mail-coaches), stage-coaches and haulage, which in fact listed an unbelievable number of rules, regulations and prohibitions each more footling than the last.[209] But then the *Encyclopédie méthodique*, published just before the Revolution, was equally scathing, describing as a 'veritable mishmash' the guidelines for the tariffs of the *Traite de Charente*, which varied according to the commodity and the place it came from.[210]

In 1786, the government seemed determined to clear away tariff barriers inside the kingdom, where theoretically the state could do as it pleased. Dupont de Nemours proposed to replace all internal customs barriers by a single systematic regime, with six classes of entry tariff and four classes of exit tariff.[211] On 20 November 1786, the Russian ambassador Simolin reported to his government on this plan to 'translate to the frontiers' all the domestic French tariffs. 'The administration is in favour of this and thinks it useful', he explained, 'but according to calculations, this measure will bring about a drop of eight to ten million a year in the King's revenues, a loss which would be difficult to sustain in the present state of the finances.'[212]

The Revolution brought about the administrative unification of the country. But that did not solve the problems of transport. What no political regime ever accomplished – not the *ancien régime*, 1789, the Empire, the Restoration or the July Monarchy – despite the expansion of the national economy and the belated but real spread of the industrial revolution, would be accomplished effortlessly by the railways after 1840. This time, technology solved a problem which had become extremely intractable.

What was the position in 1830? A considerable increase in traffic had made the road-building exploits of the previous half-century seem insignificant. The economist Dunoyer described with a critical eye the roads of France: hard, bumpy, full of potholes, where 'two carriages sometimes find it hard to pass at the same time' without being pushed on to the verge.[213] What was more, they cost too much. Both a technical and a financial ceiling seemed to have been reached. 'Far from improving continuously, the system is becoming worse and worse suited to the new needs.'[214]

At this point the railways appeared. But do not imagine them as having been built gradually, like modern motorways, according to a plan for the national network. The railways were born of local industrial initiatives, for transporting the heavy materials extracted from mines. The Coalmining Company of the Loire was the first to obtain permission from the administration of Ponts et Chaussées. On the English model, the company put down railway lines for waggons pulled by horses, carrying to Lyon coal mined at Saint-Étienne (almost 300,000 tons were extracted in 1812, but the figure had risen to 600,000 in 1825). This purely coal-carrying line was opened in 1823 between Andrézieux and Saint-Étienne (22 kilometres) and extended first from Saint-Étienne to Lyon in 1826, then from Andrézieux to Roanne in 1828. Before long, this line linking the Rhône and the Loire was carrying goods and passen-

FIGURE 67
The coming of the railways

The very first lines were purely local, and essentially linked to the transport of coals (from 1823); 25 years later, the railways had developed into the star-shaped pattern radiating out from Paris, planned by the government.

Source: T. Regazzola and J. Lefebvre, *La Domestication du mouvement. Poussées mobilisatrices et surrection d l'Etat*, 1981.

gers. Steam engines were introduced for the first time in 1831, and in 1836 the railway carried 170,000 passengers. In 1840 however, for the whole of France, there existed only the few short sections shown on the map in Figure 67.[215]

But the idea of a national network, of a railway that would be 'not only an industrial but a political revolution', one that would 'singularly [expand] relations between people and cities', was vigorously defended by the Saint-Simonians.[216] It rapidly gained converts in banking and government circles, and in 1833 the state withdrew the railway concessions from the Highways department (Ponts et Chaussées). It was however no more eager than the French monarchy in the days of *intendants* and royal highways to shoulder the financial burden: it merely reserved the right to 'guide the steps of the private companies'[217] by designing the network – one which would of course be centred on Paris: the shape of the old road network influenced the railways from the start.

The railways did not have anything like the density of the road network however. To get on to the main railway line became the subject of fierce jockeying among French towns, with politicians, capitalists and engineers acting as their mouthpieces. These were ruthlessly fought battles, not always clean fights, and on the whole a black page in French history. From them emerged a new deal on which the future would depend: thus Brive-la-Gaillarde on the direct line from Paris to Toulouse would eclipse Tulle; Grenoble would grow at the expense of Chambéry; Annecy was rescued from isolation, but Besançon fell by the wayside, and so on. A differential history would now take shape, based on the railway network and the industrialization of which it was an essential element though not, admittedly, the only one.

One should not however imagine that the railways revolutionized French life overnight. They were greeted with as much scepticism as enthusiasm at first. Adolphe Thiers described the pioneering line between Paris and Saint-Germain in 1836 as a 'big dipper', a toy to amuse the public. In the same year, Adolphe Blanqui, brother of the revolutionary and a learned professor at the Conservatoire des Arts et Métiers, stated that 'the railways will always be too expensive to attract goods traffic'.[218]

Although it took so long to become a part of French life, if only because of the high fares,[219] the railway as a graft on to the old system of circulation was not 'rejected' as we would say today. The old system collaborated with the new. At the comparatively late date of 1869, Georges Duchêne noted that 'in the transport industry, there is still competition between the *coucous, pataches* . . . carts and waggons which extend the railway journey by road'.[220] The railway left entire regions untouched; horse-drawn vehicles and pack animals carried on here as before. It was even the case that the need to link villages to the nearest railway contributed to the brisk development and maintenance of the *chemins vicinaux*, the minor roads. Trunk roads however, since they were duplicated by the railway, fell progressively into disuse and were in a thoroughly bad way by 1900.[221]

It is true that the stage-coach could not compete with the railway. In October 1856, on the opening of a new railway line, a writer in the *Journal des Débats* pointed out that

It is when one gets away from the big cities and becomes a prisoner once more of the stage-coaches, with long waits for fresh horses, sleepy postillions, broken shafts that have to be tied up with string, drags to be attached in order to go down hill, and the cramp that assails the poor passengers in these travelling prison-cells, that one realizes how much we have been spoilt by the railways.[222]

After 1860, local demands for railway lines were so numerous that in the end, in about 1880, the state had to resign itself to underwriting the costs of branch lines: 19,000 kilometres of local lines, presumably run at a loss, which private industry refused to contemplate. It was a forerunner of the nationalization to come.

The roads took their revenge when the train in turn found itself competing with the motor car. But the latter took a long time to eliminate branch lines. During World War I, men and matériel were transported by road, in lorries and trucks, leaving clouds of dust behind them. During the terrible battle of Verdun, they travelled in an unending stream along the Voie Sacrée from Bar-le-Duc to Verdun. But at the same time the narrow-gauge railway – the Varinot – with its tiny locomotive and carriages, continued without interruption to ply between Bar-le-Duc and Verdun.

As everyone knows, the march of progress continued. Soon

would come asphalt roads, electricity, the telegraph and telephone, the motorways and finally the internal airline, Air-Inter, for the delight of privileged travellers of whom I am one. I need not dwell on all this.

But for the generations who lived through these transformations, how splendid and miraculous they seemed! The telegraph, invented by Claude Chappe, was for many years exclusively reserved for government business. In the late 1830s, experiments were made with it using wires and electricity. And thirty years later, the prefect of the Loiret wrote from Orléans on 5 February 1866,

> The speech delivered by His Majesty the Emperor on the opening of the parliamentary session was the political event of January. Printed as soon as it had been received by telegraph, this important document was posted up a few hours later in the streets of Orléans, and the same night I dispatched copies to the sub-prefects and mayors so that it should be placarded in the *communes*.[223]

Fast work, Monsieur le Préfet.

Twenty years later, on 1 February 1887, Edmond Got, the celebrated Comédie-Française actor, was writing, 'The telephone operates between Brussels and Paris. Science will never stop showering us with marvels.'[224] But it is not so very long ago that I was myself marvelling to find that São Paulo in Brazil was linked to Paris by direct dialling: I hastened to call up an old friend whom I had first met in 1936, when Brazil was still over two weeks from Europe *by boat*!

In search of lost time

But the past was not a block, propelled at the same uniform speed into modern times. In pre-1850 or even pre-1914 France, local economies survived quite undisturbed in areas outside the main traffic routes.

One could quote hundreds of examples. In 1830 for instance,

the peasants of Thurins, a large village west of Lyon, carried their calves to the nearby fair at Brignais slung across the backs of mules, their hooves tied together on either side. In the 1850s, the mountain villages of the Ventoux were linked to the *chef-lieu* only by footpaths. One *commune* in the Ventoux, Brantes, sent its grain to Buis-les-Barronies, 'along 20 kilometres of bad roads, on mule-back'.[225] 'Until about 1850, the peasant of Malrace or La Figère [in Languedoc] carried his chestnuts to the market at Vans on his back: four or five hours toiling along poor footpaths.'[226] To be convinced that the progress of the highways and later the railways left large tracts of rural France virtually untouched, one has only to read Eugen Weber's magnificent book, *Peasants into Frenchmen*.[227]

Even more telling than these images of a France still lingering in the past is a fascinating little book narrating the ups and downs between 1850 and 1940 of Saint-Antonin,[228] a small town which is now a *chef-lieu de canton* in the *département* of Tarn-et-Garonne. Lying on the chalk slopes of the Causses, where they are deeply channelled by the gorges of the Aveyron and its tributary the Bonnette, Saint-Antonin has a long, prosperous past behind it (a Romanesque town hall, several Gothic houses). Once a Protestant bastion, this little town in the Rouergue was dealt a body blow in 1685 by the Revocation of the Edict of Nantes, a wound that has still not healed three centuries later. It had the reputation, according to the mayor in 1820, who regretted it, of being 'the most troublesome town in the *département*'.[229]

In 1859, Saint-Antonin (5,000 inhabitants) and the villages nearby were virtually self-sufficient: only 800 people went to buy bread from the seven modest bakers of the town, who used local flour ground in the mills on the banks of the Aveyron. The other inhabitants, who remained true country people, either had their own bread-ovens or went to bake their bread in the communal ovens, *chez les fourniers*.[230] Although stockfarming had spread with the increased use of forage crops in the region, meat was little eaten: its price seemed too high. In the mid-nineteenth century, the town was still making do with a small money supply. The local farm labourers, *brassiers* or *gagistes*, cultivated tiny plots of land, but in order to live had to work for others, usually for payment in kind . . . they hoed the maize-patches 'at 7/1' [that is, for a seventh of the crop], helped out at harvest time in return for a bushel of wheat, or picked grapes in exchange for *marc* to make *piquette*. [In short], all produce was exchanged on the spot for other produce or for labour. The miller took a percentage of the grain brought by his customers; the weaver kept part of the hemp, the blacksmith made an axe in exchange for a day's labour in his vineyard.[231]

Wine, poultry, vegetables and fruit were produced and consumed on the spot, particularly walnuts, from which essential cooking-oil was extracted.

Barter was the natural everyday form of exchange, as a matter of course. Cash was rarely seen and was used mostly for savings, 'to conserve value'. Contrary to what seems to have been the norm elsewhere, it was brought out only during crises, as a last resort, for example when a family who the year before had baked their own bread found that, following a poor harvest, they had to buy it from the baker. The little town was a perfect example of sleepy, necessary and unconscious autarky.

There were a few inroads by commerce and small industry. The calves reared at Saint-Antonin or nearby were prized at its fairs (13 a year in 1860);[232] people came from miles around to buy them, even from Rodez or Montauban. Hides were also exported, raw or tanned. Some paper was milled, on archaic equipment, since local firms did not have modern Dutch cylinders; and there were a few spinning and weaving mills. But all these activities, still of an artisanal nature, were in decline, the dilapidated legacy of a more glorious past, when the town had been a centre of the cloth trade, dyeing and tanning. Saint-Antonin figures on the registers of towns linked in the thirteenth century to the Champagne fairs.

Around the town, scattered through the country districts where roads were few and far between and so confusing to the traveller that for centuries 'the monasteries would ring their bells every day [as they did in the Massif Central], to guide lost wayfarers',[233] there were 'thousands of houses, and many hamlets, villages and towns which . . . even in 1820 were still inaccessible to wheeled

FIGURE 68
The transport revolution and social change

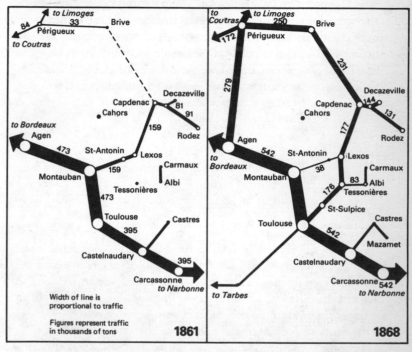

In 1861, the town of St Antonin was on the railway line which would within a year be linking Toulouse to Paris, via Brive-la-Gaillarde. In 1868, the new route for the track left St Antonin high and dry.

Source: C. Harmelle and G. Helias, *Les Piqués de l'aigle. Saint-Antonin et sa région (1850–1940). Révolution des transports et changement social*, 1982.

traffic. A secret landscape, inward-looking, lay here, dozens of kilometres away' from the Saint-Antonin road, itself but imperfectly linked to main road traffic.[234] Far from becoming modernized, this countryside in the mid-nineteenth century seemed to be plunging even deeper into a self-sufficient polyculture, for the industrial decline of the town had killed off the production of hemp and dye-plants, including woad and the plants used in leather-working.[235]

The Harmelle/Helias book traces step by step the consequences of the arrival of the railway in this environment, at the rather early date of 1858. By and large, it remained a 'foreign body'. If the Montauban–Capdenac line was the first to be built in the region, it was in order to serve the steel and coal towns of Aubin and Décazeville. When, in 1862, the line was extended from Capdenac to Brive, thus creating a direct line between Paris and Toulouse (which had previously been linked to the capital only by a connection at Bordeaux), it was a stroke of good luck – but an ephemeral one – for Saint-Antonin. In 1868, the new Toulouse line was altered, and the Montauban–Lexos line became a tiny branch line (see Figure 68). Saint-Antonin lost three-quarters of its transit tonnage. 'The breath of an industrial revolution' which had hovered over the little town, especially when steam was introduced in 1860 to the paper and textile mills, rapidly evaporated. Only the tannery and the trades directly serving farmers – wheelwrights, smiths and saddlers – were left.[236] The near-autarkic economy would carry on declining until the outbreak of war in 1914. 'The impact of the railway', Claude Harmelle concludes, 'turned out to be almost the reverse of the expectations it had aroused.'[237]

One cannot even say that it opened up the rest of France for the townspeople, or tempted them to venture beyond its narrow confines. On the eve of World War I, the price of a ticket, 'even third-class over a short distance, was still . . . an exorbitant luxury for most people'. Indeed in 1876, a 'service of horse-drawn vehicles . . . successfully competed with the train to Montauban'. But 'the usual means of transport was Shanks's pony', even for journeys 30 or 40 kilometres away![238]

Immobility, stability and autarky remained the lot of French people, at least in the greater part of the country. Nationwide circulation would be long delayed. Almost until our own day, the old peasant society has persisted in living by its own lights, through thick and thin. For this we may blame imperfect circulation and all the reasons behind that imperfection.

CHAPTER THIRTEEN

Industry and Industrialization

Industry and industrialization certainly confront us with quite new problems. Yet they are curiously reminiscent of those encountered apropos of circulation.

Just as we identified two kinds of circulation, so there seem to have been at least two kinds of industry: large-scale industry, primarily associated with adaptability, success, economic miracles, development, advance planning and mass production – in short the industrial superstructure; and small-scale industry, which long represented the bulk of production in France – scattered throughout the country, it was so to speak endemic, a widely-diffused infrastructure, to which should be added the mass of lilliputian enterprises, consisting of independent artisans in town and country.

The twofold nature of French industry was striking. 'Until at least the end of the Second Empire', writes Pierre Cayez, 'industrial production (in France and elsewhere) was propped up on two different legs.'[239] And François Caron has also singled out the expression 'twofold growth': this twofold growth, or development in tandem, lasted until about 1880 or 1900, presenting the historian with an awkward problem.

The eminent economist and 1972 Nobel prizewinner, J. R. Hicks, argued that the word 'industry' should be reserved for large-scale industry – and he was perfectly entitled to do so. Indeed I shall from time to time try to follow his advice. But the student of France can never entirely set aside that dualism which has taken so long to resolve, if indeed it is resolvable. (I am inclined to doubt it in view of what is happening today before our very eyes.) Are 'division', 'opposition', 'coexistence', and 'complementarity' perhaps inevitable, indeed necessary terms to use of France?

The word 'industry'

Industria (from the Latin *indo*, within, and *struere*, to build), long retained its original meaning of 'skill at doing things, inventiveness, savoir-faire' and by extension 'trade' in the sense of 'skilled trade'. The word only took on its modern sense in the eighteenth century, perhaps in the time of John Law.[240] But before it became established, the word 'industry' (*industrie* in French) had to displace the old terms *arts et métiers*, or *arts et manufactures*, which put up sturdy resistance, and of which the English term 'arts and crafts' is a misleading translation. They still survive today in the names of certain institutions: the *Conservatoire des Arts et Métiers*, founded in 1799, and the *Ecole Centrale des Arts et Manufactures*, founded in 1829. In the nineteenth century, every *département* would have had its own *Chambre consultative des Arts et Manufactures*.

To complicate matters further, the word 'industry' tended in the nineteenth century to mean all production, whatever its form, volume or specific character. Mathieu de Dombasle in 1835 refers for instance to 'the agricultural industry', the 'winegrowing industry', 'commercial industry', 'domestic industry' and to the relations between these various industries.[241] Georges Duchêne, Proudhon's friend, regarded 'all industries as touching, penetrating and intertwining with each other in an intimate solidarity'.[242] In official correspondence of 1853, one reads: 'Absorbed by the seedtime and harvest of agriculture, the residents [of Loudéac] pay only minor attention to anything which does not concern this branch of industry.' Three years earlier, the officers of the chamber of commerce of Morlaix (Finistère) were saying:

> While our commercial and industrial situation leaves much to be desired, we should nevertheless recognize that there has been improvement, and that that improvement would be more visible if the principal among our industries, namely agriculture, could make available more easily and at less disastrous prices, certain of its products, notably cereals.[243]

In 1857, further official correspondence concerned encouraging 'the prosperity of the agricultural industry as well as that of manufacturing industry' in the *département* of the Hérault.[244]

So if Jean-Baptiste Say is also to be found referring to 'commercial industry', 'manufacturing industry' and 'agricultural industry', he is simply using the language employed by everyone else.[245] It is hardly surprising then that even Jules Méline, the minister of agriculture in 1883–85, who was moreover a textile manufacturer from the Vosges should still be referring to agriculture as 'our leading industry'.[246]

And after all, what is so shocking about describing agriculture, transport or commerce as industries or 'trades'? The artisan's workshop is an industrial site, as too is the peasant's cottage, since it contributes to the functions of production, providing accommodation not only for the harvest, but also for the farm implements, the cowshed, the stables and the sheepfold, as well as lodging the family: a plough is after all a machine, and its team of horses or oxen an engine. Spades and pickaxes have as much right to be considered tools as those of the craftsman. Massimo Augello stresses that, in about 1830, industry was explicitly presented in France as 'the sum of all activities directed towards the production of wealth and services'. It was the view of Jean-Baptiste Say, for example, that

> All our physical possessions are created by industry, and thus they encourage us to consider industry in the broadest sense of the term, that is to say, human activity considered in all its useful applications, as the fundamental object of society.[247]

The ambiguity and wider application of the word 'industry' are not peculiar to France, since David Ricardo (1772-1822) noted in his *Principles* that Adam Smith and all British writers after him used the words *labour* and *industry* interchangeably.[248] Jean-Baptiste Say protested against this usage, himself reserving the word 'industry' for 'productive labour', that which called for the intervention of human intelligence.[249]

So we may sympathize with the perplexity of a conscientious statistician grappling in 1849 with the figures for the *département* of Saône-et-Loire.[250] The questionnaire distributed by the administration required him to classify according to pre-ordained categories the number of workers in the *département*, but without making it clear 'what was meant by industry, industrial speciality, the cultivation industry and the industry of agricultural labour'.

We can also see why historians speak quite unselfconsciously of the 'industrial' revolution in the eleventh, twelfth and thirteenth centuries, or even of neolithic or paleolithic 'industry'. To do so acknowledges that mankind and industry emerged at practically the same time, as soon as the first tools were made with human hands: split flints were early tools and so, *a fortiori*, were digging sticks, hammers, knives, scissors, spades, pickaxes, hoes and saws. So too were the first 'human-powered engines': the lever, the handle, the pedal-wheel, the pulley; not to mention animal-powered engines.

In the end, the word 'industry' did not disentangle itself from this profusion of meanings and usages – and then not entirely – until after what we now call the industrial revolution, the one that began in England in the eighteenth century and has been affecting all of our lives ever since. The industrial revolution of the water-mills between the eleventh and thirteenth centuries was merely an earlier version, one that lasted a long time admittedly, but without changing or developing in any way. The nineteenth-century industrial revolution is distinguished simply by having led to others, which have prolonged and revitalized one another. In an article written in 1978, Maria Rafaella Caroselli argued that there was a 'second' industrial revolution in the 1880s.[251] But was this not strictly speaking the third, rather than the second? And the age of atomic energy since 1945 could be described as the fourth, while the explosive mixture of computer technology and robotics which began in the 1970s would be the fifth. Or perhaps we should simply say that the industrial revolution is going on around us all the time, that it has never stopped, as I sometimes think with awe, though not always with pleasure.

It was under the impact of all this, at any rate, that the word 'industry' was transposed an octave higher, shedding its various traditional meanings and acquiring a single dominant meaning.

When we say 'industry' today, we are invariably referring to *large-scale* industry.

I need hardly add that the word 'industrialist' (*industriel* in French) which probably first appeared in 1770· from the pen of Abbé Galiani, did not take on its meaning of 'the head of a firm' until later, perhaps not until 1823, when Saint-Simon wrote about industrialization and of industrialism as a complete economic system.[252] To clarify our vocabulary thoroughly would really require us to explain certain other key words: factory, manufacturer, workers, wages, proletariat. We should find similar shifts of meaning there too. Words do not in themselves create history. But they show the direction in which it is moving.

A plea for a scientific vocabulary

Instead of these living, organic words, which are so hard to pin down, it would no doubt be preferable to construct a vocabulary of unambiguous terms: to call this a scientific language would be a bold but not unjustified claim. This inestimable service was rendered in its time by a little book now completely forgotten, Hubert Bourgin's *L'Industrie et le marché*.[253] In this essay, Bourgin argues that in every observable industrial landscape, one can distinguish, today as in the past, three types of enterprise, identifiable by their size and location:

1) *The family workshop (l'atelier familial)*, where an artisan works alone or with one or two journeymen, and usually with his own family as well; in almost all cases, this tiny group can only survive by daily mobilizing the sum of its resources. The word *atelier* itself, derived from the Old French *astelle*, a chip of wood, originally meant the carpenter's shop. It came to mean any workshop, being applied without distinction to the blacksmith's forge, to the weaver working at his loom in a basement, to the shoemaker's shop, and so on, in every case to a primary unit of production which could not be broken down further by the division of labour. And while in a town these workshops might be interconnected by guilds or trade

associations, or grouped together in certain streets, they nevertheless maintained separate premises and their own autonomy.

2) *Dispersed manufacture* (*fabriques disséminées*), consisting of a series of primary units, scattered workshops whose labour and production were controlled by a 'merchant-manufacturer'. The latter was the link between them, providing raw materials, paying part of the remuneration in advance, and collecting the finished, or part-finished products (in the latter instance finishing them himself). In particular, he controlled sales and distribution. There are countless examples of this arrangement. The classic case is the Florentine woollen industry in the twelfth century: washing, carding, spinning and weaving were dispersed all over the city and throughout the Tuscan countryside, over a zone of about 60 kilometres' radius around Florence. All these activities were controlled by the merchants of the *Arte della Lana*.[254] The dispersal of the linen industry around Laval, referred to in Volume I, is another example.[255] There, as in Florence, capitalist enterprise cast its net over the workshops of town and country alike.

It was indeed the immense expansion of rural industry that prompted the rapid and widespread rise of dispersed manufacture throughout eighteenth-century Europe. Thwarted in the cities, where labour could defend itself and take advantage both of the comparatively high wages and the solidarity of the craft guilds, merchant capitalism found compensation in the labours of the countryside. The rural artisan for his part was more free, that is less supervised in the country than in town, and the cost of living was lower.

German historians were the first to recognize and put a name to this system: they called it the *Verlagssystem*, the merchant who controlled the process being the *Verleger*. The German expression, hard to translate into French, Italian or Spanish, has become part of the international vocabulary of history. The English term for the same thing is the *putting-out system*, sometimes described as *cottage industry*, a term which rightly underlines the domestic nature of the activity. For the artisan stayed at home, literally in his cottage.

What was more, in the countryside (and even in town) 'he could be both artisan and peasant, taking part in harvest or grape-picking, and often owning a field, a garden or a vineyard of his own'. In the sixteenth century, the Florentine wool-weaver left his loom at the time of the wine-harvest, and the miner of Liège left the pit in August to gather in the grain. 'In the nineteenth century, the cottage weavers of Picardy and Cambrésis picked beets from May to September, while those of Maine regularly worked as harvesters until about 1860.'[256] But even thirty years ago, it was common in the Vosges, 'to work at Boussac [textile firm] during the day, and be a dairy farmer first thing in the morning and last thing at night'.[257]

The same system would have been found all over Europe, in Bohemia and Silesia, in Segovia in Castille, and in the whole of France. If one wanted to illustrate it with a single example, none is more telling than that of lace-making in the seventeenth century, in that region rather confusingly known as the 'pays de France', running from Paris north to Senlis or Chantilly, and from the forest of Ermenonville in the east to those of Isle-Adam and Montmorency in the west. The most specialized lace-making villages were Villiers-le-Bel, Sarcelles, Ecouen, Mesnil-Aubry, Fontenay-en-France. The lace-makers, both men and women, were peasants and worked the thread at home. Travelling merchants on horseback, countrymen themselves, distributed the raw material, the threads of gold and silver, linen and silk, and later collected the finished product. Still on horseback, they would ride into Paris to hand it over to the commissioning merchants in the rue Saint-Denis. The latter had often originally provided the thread and they handled sales of lace to the Netherlands, Germany (Hamburg especially), Spain and 'the Indies'.[258] So there was commercial and financial *centralization*, but no *concentration* of labour. At the end of the century, when the central grip of Paris became stronger, the Compagnie des Points de France (Lacemaking Company), which had obtained a state privilege, had 20,000 women lace-makers working for it, but scattered in 52 different places.[259]

3) The last observable category is *compact-site manufacture*

(*l'entreprise compacte*), bringing everything together under a single roof, whether a *manufacture* or a factory (*usine*).

In this last category, the new feature was precisely this *concentration* of labour;[260] but it would take a long time to become the norm, with all the upheavals and constraints it brought in its train. The end result would be the concentration on one site of workshops for all the different work-processes and trades: in other words this was a change in size and scale. The Gueugnon metal-works, of which the early site-plan survives in the Archives Nationales, is a good example: these brought together blast furnaces, forges and steam-hammers (before the days of the tilt-hammer), refineries, smelters, wireworks, sheet-metal works and so on.[261] These workshops, built adjacent to one another, would later expand, sometimes being brought together under one roof, sometimes divided up – as in Le Creusot,[262] Gueugnon, Hayange[263] or Niederbronn[264] – but they were always interconnected and built close together.

A few words of warning

1) It is important not to assume that one stage *inevitably* followed on from the other, namely that there was a sort of rational progression from the individual workshop to dispersed manufacture to the compact site. Industry is not a self-contained world with its own logic, merely one activity within the surrounding economic context. For industry to change speed or alter its form, there has first to be progress in the overall economy, then fresh demand has to create a regular market, or a new technology has to be perfected. Thus the *manufactures* set up first by Henri IV and later by Colbert never really thrived – with a few exceptions to prove the rule[265] – because in those days the market had not developed the capacity without which industrial progress is impossible.

2) In the absence of regular progress from one stage to another, *coexistence* was the rule. Large-, medium- and small-scale industry had to rub shoulders. And although they may sometimes have conflicted – as when the coke-burning furnaces everywhere drove out those furnaces that were still using charcoal – it was also possible

for large and small industries to give each other a helping hand. In the past, this was plain to see. And even today it is equally obvious, since in the shadow of big or even multinational firms, there gravitate smaller sub-contractors dependent upon large firms for orders. There may be many reasons for this: the weight of hierarchy, the advantages to be derived from differences in retail prices, wages or productivity.

3) Finally, if one takes the historical perspective, Hubert Bourgin's first category was not chronologically the very first stage of industry. The individual artisan was not originally a sedentary worker, installed in his workshop-cum-dwelling, but an intinerant, travelling from place to place, always ready, or obliged, to move on. In twentieth-century China and India, there are still itinerant craftsmen travelling from village to village, town to town.[266] So one is not too surprised to find a chronicler of the time of François I describing metalworking in the Gier valley, a region 'much frequented by certain breeds of poor foreign blacksmiths, who do not remain in one place, but come and go like birds of passage'.[267] (The image of the bird of passage is charming but inaccurate: migrating birds always return along the same itineraries, whereas these blacksmiths wandered about at random.)

And this nomadic tendency persisted. In the eighteenth century, despite the general expansion of manufacturing, all observers agree about the instability of the world of artisans and workers: 'An itinerant and precarious group', which does not stay in one place, says one commentator;[268] 'undoubtedly migratory' says another.[269] It is impossible to 'depend on the constancy of our artisans . . . as we can on the immobility of our fields', says a third.[270] 'If anyone anywhere offends an artisan, his baggage is quickly packed; taking his trade with him, he moves on' – the last quotation is from Jean-Jacques Rousseau.[271]

In the quite recent past after all, French villages would receive visits not only from travelling salesmen but also from itinerant artisans on the Chinese model, who would hire out their skills to anyone prepared to pay for them. It might be the tinker, the knife-grinder, the chimney-sweep, or the workers hired to do some particular job and given board and lodging by the householder as long as the work lasted: carpenters, coopers, masons, stone-cutters, ditch-diggers, tailors, chair-caners – and I will spare you the rest, for I am quoting from an endless list referring to the *département* of the Nièvre.[272]

In the *département* of the Meuse, since the villages were over-populated in the nineteenth century, migrant workers used to travel for eight to ten months of the year 'following the same unvarying itineraries'. Statistics dating from 1851 mention knife-grinders taking to the road with their grindstones from Rupt-aux-Nonains (where there were 40 of them), Condé-en-Barrois (78), Brabant-le-Roi, and Rupt-devant-Saint-Mihiel. They also mention tinplaters, of whom many came from Beaulieu-en-Argonne, Rarécourt and Souhesmes; cobblers who left their villages of Levoncourt and Brandeville to ply their trade in the Franche-Comté, Paris or even Belgium; and wicker-workers who travelled from farm to farm offering to repair winnowing fans.[273] In the Middle Ages, bell-founders used to travel from Lorraine to Spain as well as all over France. 'Some of them were in Rouen when Joan of Arc was put to death, and they testified at their compatriot's rehabilitation hearings.'[274]

André Chamson has described how, elsewhere, versatile workers used to travel within a smaller radius, between the hills and valleys of the Gard, in about 1900, 'labourers . . . hired perhaps for a day or even a few hours', but never short of work. 'They were jacks of all trades inside a week, by turns masons, woodcutters or well-diggers.'[275]

These migrants, hiring themselves out episodically here and there, for want of what would today be called full-time employment, hint at the very distant origins of the 'pre-industrial past'. Settled craftworking, wherever one finds it, indicates that a certain stage of development has been reached. Regions tucked away from the major roads – such as the northern Alps, and certainly the high Alps under the *ancien régime*, condemned to laborious if not total self-sufficiency, had to be content with the elementary craft skills of the villages.[276] But even this arrangement, modest though it seems, was already an achievement, a sign of organization, whether in this or any other backward region. We should perhaps regard the beginnings of craftworking in certain towns in the eleventh and twelfth centuries as a decisive element in the birth of Europe, the first step on the road to modern times.

Dispersed manufacture

Despite its name, dispersed manufacture was actually a primitive form of concentration and regrouping – an early reflection of the demands of industrial capitalism, while at the same time putting to use the considerable 'voltage difference' between town and countryside, of which it was tempting to take advantage.

This yoking together of town and country, which had begun at least as early as the fifteenth century, became more widespread in the sixteenth, seventeenth and particularly eighteenth centuries. In the countryside round eighteenth-century Laval, over 5,000 people were engaged in linen manufacture. The pattern was similar in Cholet, which in 1790 was sharing its textile industry with 77 dependent parishes. The Saint-Quentin region provided employment for 150,000 people, 'from the bleacheries of Senlis to the Netherlands frontier'.[277] Voiron in the Dauphiné was a hyper-industrious little town: in the surrounding area there were, in 1730, '4,915 [hemp]-weavers, and peasants or artisans who spin and weave for the manufacturers of Voiron' – the Denantes dynasty for instance, who would soon be joined by the leading merchants of Grenoble, such as the Périer family.[278] Woollen manufacture throughout France, the silk industry of Lyon, and lace-making in the Ile-de-France – all were essentially organized on the same lines.

A good example of the system is the glove-making industry of Grenoble: long-established in the town, it began to spread into the countryside in the late eighteenth century. By 1787, it consisted of no fewer than 64 master-glovers, 300 cutters, 80 master-dressers, 30 master-finishers and 10 master-dyers, assisted by 220 workmen, 5,560 seamstresses or embroiderers – a total of 6,264 people. The basic working unit, the *atelier*, often consisted of no more than 'a fairly large room in which [alongside the master] there were a number of permanent workers, as many as 10 or 20 in larger firms, but more often 4 or 5'. All the others worked at home for the master-glovers. Merchant firms provided all the leather for the workshops, while commission agents on behalf of the merchants bought the finished product and handled sales.[279] Once again, money – capital – was the key. Since capital had the power of determining prices, it penetrated and distorted the old guild system: the master-glover became a mere employee: the only difference was that he in turn employed a number of workers, earning wages like himself.

Ribbon manufacture in Saint-Etienne operated along similar lines. The master-ribbonmakers fell into two categories: the least adventurous preferred simply to 'carry out the work and run less risk'; the others went in for the commercial side of the business, abandoning the weaving trade themselves. The basic unit was still the *atelier*, in this case well-lit 'by large windows, which were [however kept] hermetically sealed as far as possible, to avoid dust from outdoors spoiling the silk'. It was an uncomfortable and difficult trade, and in the confined atmosphere problems were magnified. Ribbon-making extended well beyond the outskirts of Saint-Etienne (which was still a small town in those days), into the Jary, the Forez and the Velay, employing in 1786 a total of 26,500 people, dispersed among a huge number of *ateliers*.[280] At Sedan, the cloth-weavers were divided between town and country: 25 wholesalers employed 10,000 people over a radius of 25 kilometres round the town.[281] Cassini's map of Mazamet and district shows how, by 1789, industry had spread outwards from this little town which had been expanding since the late seventeenth century.

In metal-working, the system took several forms. The iron-masters, scattered throughout France according to the location of mineral deposits, hydraulic power and forests, worked largely to order for various clients, such as the businessman of the Nivernais who took large deliveries from Rochefort in 1689, or the contractor for the foundries of the French navy, who in 1720 placed orders in the Berry, the Nivernais, the Franche-Comté and Burgundy.[282] Regular orders were meanwhile received from manufacturers, whose capital thus controlled the entire operation,

FIGURE 69
Textile manufacturers in the inspection zone of Troyes in 1746

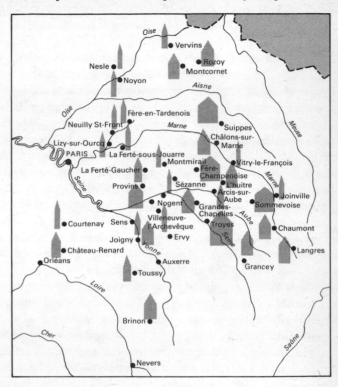

In all there were 1,138 'fabricants', each owning between 1 and 4 looms. For two of the towns, the exact number of manufacturers is not given in the document used, but has been estimated from the number of looms instead, which happens to be given (not always the case).

Source: Archives Nationales, F^{12} 748.

from the iron-making process itself to the manufacture of machinery. In Lower Normandy, to take one example among many, the manufacturing merchants would contract with the ironmasters of Maine at the cattle fairs of Domfront, of which there were about ten a year. The iron they were ordering was destined for 'a multitude of workers' employed in their own homes, 'as half-time peasants, half-time workers; [most of them] making nails' (Chanu was the nail-making capital of Normandy), but also turning out locks or ironmongery.[283]

All over France then, one would have found countless tiny industrial units. And their numbers would swell with time. So one is not particularly surprised by the figures the *bureau de commerce* of Valenciennes produced for 'the people's representative' Paires, during his mission to the north in 1795. In the five provinces of Hainault, Flanders, Artois, Cambrésis and Picardy, linen manufacture provided the means of subsistence for a million and a half people, 'growers of flax, spinners, weavers, merchants, bleachers and finishers'[284] – with an active population, that is, of some 400,000, about the same number as were employed in woollen manufacture in the Languedoc.

Not all these workers were necessarily operating within the putting-out system. But it did concern the majority of them and because of its extension, and the balance between town and country on which it depended, it would take a long time to disappear. Even the famous *manufacture* of printed fabrics founded in 1760 by Oberkampf, who was still investing heavily in it in the early nineteenth century, was largely run according to this ancient system.[285] And much later still, well into the nineteenth century, one comes across records of exchange contracts signed between a master, who provided the materials and collected the finished products, and a team of workers led by a quasi-foreman. It is not so different from the famous sweating-system in the London garment trade, based literally on the sweat of exploited workers in attics. In France, it was long the custom, even in the early twentieth century, for shops in Paris to have garments, buttons, haberdashery and so on made by peasants, both men and women, in the provinces.[286] The advantages for the entrepreneur were obvious: he had a cheap labourforce, but avoided direct contact with it or any risk of its making demands on him. The moment he no longer needed it, he could stop employing it.

But something very similar is surely happening before our own eyes: European entrepreneurs now get espadrilles, cheap clothing and radios made in South Korea, or alarm clocks in Hong Kong; a French textile magnate sends patterns to India to be woven, and receives the finished product which he then sells or even exports. The exploited proletariat may be far away, but the system is surely identical: the labourforce can be hired and fired without any trade-union interference, and the pay is low. The whole operation is a godsend to the entrepreneur and thoroughly attractive to today's industrial capitalism which is thus, without realizing it, reproducing a very old pattern.

Early forms of concentration: the manufactures

Despite the long survival of traditional versions of the putting-out system, the industrial revolution which began early in England, in the eighteenth century, would eventually spread to France and gradually disturb its ancient patterns, as industrial firms developed and became more concentrated.

As already indicated, *concentration* is here taken to mean the bringing together on the same site of the means of production, both workers and equipment, while *centralization* will be used to mean the bringing together at a higher level of the entrepreneur's capital and commercial organization. Centralization at the top took place sooner and more easily than concentration at the bottom, but the former sometimes encouraged the latter, even before the spectacular successes of the nineteenth century. So I agree with Paul Bairoch when he stresses the importance of the eighteenth century, and gives it credit for much progress and expansion which the nineteenth century in many cases simply continued.[287]

All this early activity took shape, or rather became visible, with the establishment in the reigns of Louis XV and Louis XVI of the *manufactures* (sometimes translated as manufactories, but the French term will be used throughout this chapter). The word itself does not mean very much: during the *ancien régime*, it could mean anything and everything. It was historians who decided to give it a precise meaning for explanatory purposes. I shall use it to refer to the first forms of industrial concentration to bring together the means of production on a large scale. In textiles for instance, this would mean not only looms for weaving, but warehouses for storing raw materials and finished products, vats for dyeing, baths for washing wool, hydraulic wheels for fulling, and drying-rooms with their long wooden hangers. (The 1712 building in the Van Robais *manufacture* in Abbeville was christened *la Maison des Rames*, the House of Hangers.)[288] Apart from the water-wheel and possibly some horse-power, machines were few or non-existent. What *manufactures* brought together above all were workers, a skilled labourforce, using equipment which remained traditional. There were of course advantages in bringing together the equipment and the labourforce – the latter supervised and if necessary trained by foremen (who had not yet acquired the name). So artisans found themselves transplanted from their homes, separated from their own private means of production. This represented an important break, one that would became widespread, indeed commonplace, in later years.

The government often led the way in this respect. It granted to several firms the honorific title of *manufacture royale*, which was distributed somewhat generously until 1787 and symbolized by the livery of the doorkeeper, in the king's colours of red, white and blue. More important than the honour however were the substantial privileges that accompanied it: monopolies, protective tariffs, donations, advances and loans with or without interest, exemption (critically important) from the rules and regulations imposed by the craft guilds: the *inspecteur des manufactures* alone was authorized to inspect production. And the workers were exempted from the ballot for militia service.[289]

The government's aims in applying this determined policy were not new. (Colbert had similarly attempted to bring some order to the incoherent and inadequate industrialization of his own day.) It wanted to provide more continuous work for a labourforce all too often unemployed. And above all, since France's gold and silver reserves were negligible, it aimed at developing export industries so that money and precious metals would be drawn back to the kingdom. In about 1750, for instance, the French government tried to establish silk production in the Dauphiné.[290] So this was to some extent a forward-looking policy, although it never consciously sought, and rarely achieved, the gradual concentration which would come about more or less spontaneously from the middle of the century. Only then did the *manufacture* begin to be really successful.

The scale of its success has been disputed by German historians. Examining a case very similar to that of France (since the *manufacture* phase occurred throughout Europe, as far afield as Poland and Russia),[291] they have noted that, at most, *manufactures* represented only about one-hundredth of industrial activity. Werner Sombart sharply criticizes Marx for making the mistake of assuming that the *manufacture*, which was essentially a concentration of labour, engendered the factory (*fabrique* or *usine*), the latter being the result rather of bringing in machines.[292] It is true that this sequence did not as a rule operate: the *manufacture* was not normally the precursor of a factory, although some individual *manufactures* did turn into factories.[293] But this dispute may be missing the essential point, namely that the *manufacture* is proof that, well before the industrial revolution, the process of concentration which pro-duced it and which had a long future ahead of it, was already in existence, having become essential.

The eighteenth-century *manufactures* did not, it is true, achieve the degree of concentration later to become normal. Any number of examples, when considered closely, make this plain, whether the magnificent Gobelins *manufacture* on the banks of the Bièvre, south of Paris;[294] the Saint-Gobain mirror-works;[295] the *manufacture* owned by the brothers Vialate d'Aignan in Montauban;[296] the *manufacture* of heavy cloth known as the Gros Chiens works, founded in 1660, before Colbert took office, and the Dijonval works founded in 1644, both at Sedan;[297] or, an example of a firm with a long history, the much-cited Van Robais *manufacture* at Abbeville. Receiving its royal licence in 1784, this firm had been founded in 1665 by Colbert and Jesse Van Robais, who brought about fifty workers with him from Holland. It subsequently reached such a stage of perfection that 'it equals the best examples of fine cloth produced in England', as d'Aguesseau wrote from Paris on 31 May 1708.[298] At this time, it employed over 3,000 workers, but that figure includes both the labour employed at the great *Maison des Rames* and the dispersed spinners and spinsters working at home.

It was quite normal in fact for a *manufacture* in France or elsewhere to be accompanied by a putting-out system, with its string of little *ateliers*. In textiles for instance, keeping one weaver's loom in action required the labour of at least half a dozen spinners or spinsters. Instead of housing all these workers under one roof, it was simpler and less costly to resort to the putting-out system for spinning, with its known advantages of a docile workforce, largely rural and comparatively underpaid.

We do not know exactly what proportion of the workforce was housed in the main building of the *manufacture*. There is usually little precise information about its dimensions and capacity. Even when former workers' lodgings exist (as at Villeneuvette, or on the banks of the Lergue which runs through Lodève) it is hard to tell how these buildings, which have since been altered, were originally used.[299] There are few clear answers, still less valid averages, merely a few scattered though significant figures.

Thus in the late eighteenth century, Van Robais was employing 1,800 workers on a single site in Abbeville and another 10,000 working at home.[300] The Charvet woollen firm only employed a third of its workforce in the *manufacture* at Vienne.[301] In 1789, in Orléans, one firm making hose knitted on a loom (as distinct from hand-knitted) had 800 people working on the spot and more than twice that outside.[302] In 1810, a manufacturer of *cordelats* in Mazamet was employing 'a hundred workers inside the buildings', probably dressing, dyeing and finishing the wool, and 'a thousand outside', as spinners and weavers.[303] The pattern seems hardly any different from that of a hundred years earlier in Châteauroux in 1697, where, we are told, there was 'one of the most considerable cloth *manufactures* of the kingdom. It employed 10,000 persons of all ages and both sexes, in the town and the surrounding district.'[304] But clearly the ambiguous word *manufacture* did not necessarily refer to a central building housing production, but rather to the whole of textile activity inside and outside the town which might be divided among an indefinite number of units.

Generally it seems likely that there was a 'slow move towards concentration': the number of workers per *atelier* increased visibly, especially when mechanization began. The cotton industry, which by 1765 had introduced mechanical spinning (in general use by 1800), was organized on a fairly large scale from the start. The same pattern was followed by silk-spinning and later silk-weaving (the first mechanical loom appeared in Lyon in 1747).[305] But the textile industry nevertheless remained obstinately attached to tradition. In fact, both in wool and in cotton, a curious reversal took place. Spinning, having made the transition to machines, moved in from the country to an industrial building (located near a river as energy source). And whereas in the past the spinning-wheels could scarcely keep up with the weaver, now it was the turn of the weaving trade, which had remained essentially manual, to call in reinforcements. These largely consisted of out-workers, numerous, low-paid and mostly living in the country.[306] Handloom weaving at home persisted in France as late as the 1870s, despite the introduction of steam-powered looms after about 1860.[307]

All the examples so far mentioned concern textiles. They tend to dominate the scene and rightly so, given their leading role in the former economy, even in the early nineteenth century. But there are other examples of concentration one might mention: coal-mining for instance or metal-working, paper, glass and ship-building. Some of these concentrations had taken place earlier than in textiles, having been encouraged by technical revolutions. Technology and machines were playing an increasing role in these sectors and, merely by their presence, imposed a modern form of concentration, spelling the end of rural industry. This would give a new twist to Marx's equation: *manufacture* plus machines equals factory.

This expansion in all directions is significant. It was a river which would swell to a flood once the *ancien régime* was over, increasingly moving towards modern industrialization and the factory system.

Large-scale industry and the new energy sources

Large-scale industry was the result above all of technical innovation, of newly available energy sources, and of consumer demand, which was both cause and consequence of industry's expansion.

The space-rockets we send up today are powered by several stages of engines which fire one after another. Their sequence determines the spaceship's trajectory. The same was true of industrialization. It required a series of explosions, activated one after another but at very long intervals of course. Even today, industrialization does not happen with a wave of the magic wand.

Every 'engine' in fact wears itself out, sooner or later reaching the end of its useful life. The water-power that drove mill-wheels, or the wind that powered windmills had already been exploited to their limit by the fourteenth century. Wood, as a prime source of energy, was used for so many purposes that by Sully's time supplies were running short, and the price of timber was reaching apparently prohibitive levels.[308] Animal traction could not easily be further developed, since it required fodder: as Cantillon put it, it was a choice between horses and men.[309] As for manpower, while the individual might be weak, collectively human labour could increase the energy available to industry. But the worker's wages necessarily corresponded to the vital minimum that ensured survival. Whenever the population increased, so in quick succession did the price of food and the rate of wages: high prices threatened the existing balance and slowed down industrial growth, which could not be reconciled with an increase in labour costs.

The great advantage of machines was that they did not need to eat, so they did not increase labour costs. But when the source of energy they used reached the limits of its capacity, only some technical breakthrough, followed by the application of the new energy, could carry expansion forward. This process always took time. Discovering technology is one thing, its application another. Even today it takes on average four or five years before technical innovation is introduced into the production process. The two new energy sources of the nineteenth century – coal and steam – were no exceptions. Their progress was slow.

None of this is hard to understand. Various constraints – financial, technical or psychological – prevented one system from adapting to another. There was often recourse to old-fashioned methods, *faute de mieux*. The cotton-spinning industry which developed in Paris in the early 1800s used teams of horses, just as the first English machines had done years earlier.[310] Similarly, metalworking in France was, until 1750 or later, using both charcoal and coke simultaneously in the smelting process. And hydraulic energy long remained in competition with steam. The latter developed earliest in northern France as well as along the Loire and in Alsace, whereas Brittany and the south of France remained faithful to wind- and watermills for much longer.[311] But whatever the region, steam engines spread only gradually. In Normandy, as late as 1847, 'water provided 58% of the motive power needed by the factories', and ten years on, of the 734 cotton mills in France, only 256, barely a third, on steam-power.[312]

Thanks to a study by Adrien Printz, we can follow closely the conflict between tradition and modernity as it occurred in Lorraine, at the Wendel works at Hayange, in the ancient mining valley of the Fensch.[313] Between 1825 and 1870, as production rose from 3,000 to 134,000 tonnes, everything was steadily being transformed. Coal was replacing charcoal. But it did not mean the immediate introduction of the steam engine. If the many new buildings were still, like the old ones, built along the banks of the Fensch, it was not for lack of space elsewhere but in order to use the water contained behind a series of dams. Hydraulic energy was still in use here. Admittedly an old paddle-wheel had been abandoned since it took up too much room and turned too slowly and irregularly. But even in 1860, hydraulic energy represented 500 horse-power as against 1,024 horse-power of steam energy. In 1880, the old laminating wheel was still turning. Sometimes it ground to a halt and on such occasions the workers had time to go to the café for a quick game of cards or to eat potatoes which the concièrge's wife used to cook in the hot ashes from the sheet-metal furnace. When the wheel began turning again, the workers returned to their posts. And this was in Wendel's, one of the leading French firms of the day (11.2% of overall production).

The arrival of mined coal (*charbon de terre* also known as *charbon de pierre* or *charbon fossile*) in French industry resulted from the crisis in timber supplies, which struck early and got steadily worse. France's forests, abundant though they were, could not stand up to accelerated exploitation. Wood was used for heating and cooking; as charcoal it was used in smelters for iron and steel, and it remained the indispensable raw material for traditional crafts like clog-making or cooperage, or for the construction of ploughs, carts, houses, boats and ships. The iron foundries and smelters were not the only industries dependent on fire-power; glassworks, breweries and lime-kilns were all in the same position.

France, having the advantage of many forests, withstood this potential crisis better than Britain. If Britain began using coal much earlier, to heat London's houses for instance, and if Britain pioneered the use of coke for smelting, it was partly because the British had no choice, their woodland resources being exhausted. France was better provided for, but that did not prevent a frenzy of determined and methodical prospecting for coal deposits. 'Coal fever' swept through French business circles in the eighteenth century, as can be seen from the countless requests for prospecting and mining licences sent in to the old *Conseil du Commerce*.[314]

Another advantage of coal and one that would become ever greater, was its increasing cheapness, compared to wood, for the same amount of energy. Consequently a shift to coal became irresistible. A ton of coal produces the same number of calories as 2.5 tons of wood: weight for weight, and prices being equal, coal was cheaper than its rival from the start. By the July Monarchy, it cost only a third the price of wood for the same energy, and by the Second Empire, one-sixth. This fall in the price of the new fuel was one of the causes of the industrial revolution that gathered speed in France between 1830 and 1870.[315]

In 1815, French coal consumption was a million tons; by 1827, it was 2 million; by 1847 it was 7.6 million; by 1860, 15 million; and by 1900, 40 million, a third of it imported. Of the 40 million tons, 6 went to metalworking; 4.5 to the railways; 2.5 to the mines, including coalmines;[316] and some 5 or 6 million must be reckoned to have fuelled the

77,000 machines or boilers powered by steam which, combined, represent some 1,200,000 h.p. . . . from the simplest agricultural machines, used only a few months of the year, to the factory generators, huge steam-kettles under pressure day and night.

The terms may be picturesque but they express the vicomte d'Avenel's admiration for the industrial performance of his time.[317] And in fact his figures do rather less than justice to reality, since he takes no account of the engines and horse-power of the railways. Yves Guyot therefore reckoned that in 1894 there were in France some 85,400 steam engines and a total of 6,121,000 h.p. (more than two-thirds of it on the railways).[318] As a result, coal became all-important. The 'hydraulic factories' represented less than a million horse-power. The powerful Anzin Mining Company, constituted on 19 November 1757, was already employing 4,000 workers in 1791.[319]

The problem, not to say tragedy, was that there were not enough French coalmines, and those there were proved difficult and costly to operate. The mining areas were far away from the consumers, and since transport was expensive, by the time it reached Paris, coal from Anzin cost 33 francs a ton – a very high price. Productivity was moreover low: in 1900, the French miner was extracting 200 tons of coal on average, while his counterpart in Silesia was extracting 330.[320] So coalmining was often a poor investment in France: of the 297 concessions on French soil in 1900, 123 were operating at a loss.[321] France found itself paying in the nineteenth and early twentieth centuries a high coal bill not unlike the high oil bill the country has been paying since 1945 and still is today. And as in the present, French industry was at some disadvantage as a result. As a textile manufacturer from Reims explained in 1834:

> We use coal from Liège, Mons and Anzin. Our factory uses 120,000 hectolitres at 5F 20. This price is excessive . . . It is the result of transport costs (4F per hectolitre) whereas our rivals in Leeds pay the equivalent of 0F 55 a hectolitre – ten times less.

As a result, iron cost 30 francs a quintal in Paris, but only half that in the Welsh port of Cardiff.[322] This was a serious handicap, at a time when textiles were beginning to lose their earlier predominance as coal and steel took over.

Whatever it cost, France had to procure the coal required both for industry and for heating houses, where it had replaced wood. By about 1890, Paris was buying 90 million francs' worth of coal a year, of all kinds: raw coal, briquettes, *tête de moineau*, anthracite, nutty slack, Newcastle. Parisians old enough to remember the days before central heating will have memories of the *bougnat*, invariably from the Auvergne, who sold coal and firewood: with one sack protecting his head and shoulders, and a laden sack on his back, the *bougnat*, his face black with coal dust, would deliver coal to the topmost floors of apartment blocks just as water-carriers used to deliver water drawn from fountains or the Seine. Are there any *bougnats* left at all now, I wonder?

Inventions

In the grand march towards industrialization, the procession of inventions which have all contributed to the ever-more complicated progress of industry down to the present day, France lagged behind. In 1819, Chaptal could write:

> In the old days, the inventions of scientists lay dormant among their papers, or in the memoirs of learned Academies, without the manufacturer being aware that they might be usefully applied to his business . . . Today, the closest bonds unite them: the manufacturer consults the scientist and leaning upon each other, they are moving forward to the perfection of industry.[323]

A lucid vision of the future, possibly a little optimistic as far as the France of his day was concerned. But in England, the gulf between science and technology had already been bridged.

Inventions and their applications are cultural goods and, like all cultural goods, they tend to circulate unbidden. It is a waste of time to try and keep them secret, as Britain sought to do during the first industrial revolution. The machines and processes developed in Britain were soon finding their way across the Channel. By the latter part of the eighteenth century, many English and Scottish entrepreneurs had set up business in France, including John Wilkinson who, with Ignace de Wendel, founded the Le Creusot works. They built English-type machines on the spot. British workers and foremen followed or even preceded them to Normandy, Lyon, or the Forez. Meanwhile French travellers, whether entrepreneurs or engineers, paid many visits to Britain, practising what would today be called industrial espionage.[324] After 1815, this interchange, interrupted by the Revolution, took off once more with renewed vigour in both directions. Everything worthwhile had already become available in France by the time Britain finally (in 1842) granted official permission for machines to be exported.[325] So the early engineers who built the first French railways had all learnt their skills from the British, even if they had never set foot in Britain.

Inventions have in fact always travelled beyond their place of origin, since the beginnings of human ingenuity: think of the bronze- and ironworking of prehistory; or of silk, which arrived in Byzantium in the time of Justinian; or of gunpowder, which travelled far beyond China; or nearer to our own time, the techniques of mining and printing carried by German craftsmen throughout Europe and beyond, from the fifteenth century. The British also practised industrial espionage in the early eighteenth century, when they imitated the mechanized silk mills, invented in Bologna and kept secret there for over a century.[326]

Of more recent origin on the other hand is the partnership between science and technical invention – or as I would prefer to call it technology, by which I mean a second-level science, modified by experience, whose modest practitioners often share, unconsciously, the attitude of mind that denotes a true savant. Science and technology are two storeys of the same house, and in practice their relation is a dialectical one. But while they have established a permanent dialogue today, it was not always so. In the sixteenth century, the famous mathematician Tartaglia was approached by the artisans and master craftsmen of the Venice Arsenal, at the time the most advanced technological centre in Europe. They asked him at what angle a bombard should be fired in order to reach its maximum range. The mathematician established that the optimum angle was 45 degrees.[327] But the historian would be hard put to it to find many examples of this kind before the eighteenth century. They become legion however, as soon as large-scale industrialization begins.

An extremely obvious example is the steam engine, the symbol par excellence of nineteenth-century progress. This was after all the fruit of a long partnership between technology (which led the way) and theoretical science. And once it had been constructed in its earliest form, the steam engine itself inspired, provoked and made inevitable a whole string of inventions, on account of the uses to which it was put and the suggestions for its further application. As H. J. Henderson once famously and ironically wrote, 'science owes more to the steam engine than the steam engine owes to science'.[328] That is abundantly clear. The first locomotive worthy of the name was George Stephenson's *Rocket* (1829). Stephenson (1781–1848) was an English workman who turned engineer after taking up study as an adult.[329] All credit to technology, then. But the original feature of the *Rocket* was that it used a tubular boiler devised by a French engineer Marc Seguin (1786–1875), nephew of Joseph Montgolfier.[330] So theory deserves credit too. And scientific theory in turn drew profit from the experiments initiated by the use of the steam engine: the 1860s saw the birth of thermodynamics, a new and fruitful branch of physics.[331] The very imperfections of steam became the source of inquiry and indeed obsession. Inside the compression cylinder of the locomotive for instance, steam developed the annoying habit of disobeying Mariotte's (or Boyle's) law and suddenly losing between 15 and 50% of its power – until the day in 1870 when the Alsatian industrialist, Gustave Adolphe Hirn (1815–90, a devotee of metaphysics incidentally), solved the problem: the answer was to prevent water forming and condensing inside the cylinder.[332]

And this interlocking history was of course destined to continue, with improvements to locomotives and rolling stock, to rails and sleepers, to couplings, wheels and carriages, making it possible for trains to take curves more smoothly. The interchange between science and technology, technology and science, that inexhaustible subject, is particularly illustrated by the many changes in metallurgy, both in France and elsewhere. 'The nineteenth century was remarkable for the increased use of iron and steel, whether in completely new applications, such as railways, or as a substitute for wood as in the case of girders, bridges and scaffolding.'[333] Here it was the customer who called the tune, imposing specifications, stimulating production and inspiring new inventions. The replacement of charcoal by coke led to the cheap production of high-grade steel. The names of Bessemer, whose invention dates from 1856–9, of Martin (1864), of Thomas and Gilchrist (1878), mark the stages of a 'metallurgical revolution' and the coming of a 'scientific steel industry', the result primarily of the need to build railway lines that could withstand wear and tear. Quality products were particularly sought after – the secret of the Wendel firm's fortunes under the Second Empire.[334] And research into new alloys gradually developed, resulting in more laboratories and a network of scientific information. Thus there grew up an extremely diversified scientifically-based metallurgy.

The same dialogue between science and technology occurred in electricity. But here the process worked the other way round. As François Caron says, 'electricity was a science before becoming an industry'.[335] The theoretical advances on which all else depended were made by Ampère (1775–1836), Arago (1786–1853), Faraday (1791–1867) and Clerk-Maxwell (1831–79). It was later that practice and experience came on the scene, thanks to Louis-François Bréguet (1804–83), watchmaker and physicist, Werner von Siemens (1816–92), artillery officer, engineer and entrepreneur, and perhaps the most striking of all, Zénobe Gramme (1826–1901). This extraordinary inventor was born near Liège into a large and far from well-off family. Always 'at war with spelling', he was a poor scholar, became a joiner and made only a meagre living despite being prodigiously skilled. 1855 found him in Paris, still a joiner and still poor. In 1860, he took a job as a cabinet-maker with the Société L'Alliance, a firm specializing in electrical appliances. These literally fascinated him, and when he took another job, at the Christophle goldsmithing factory, where galvanizing technology was practised, he began to imagine a new type of machine. Needless to say, nobody took the slightest interest in his ideas and it was with the aid of his wife that in 1869 he 'set up the elements of his machine on the kitchen table'.[336] The Franco-Prussian war intervened, and it was only afterwards that he was able to display to the Académie des Sciences his electric dynamo, the Gramme machine, worked by turning a handle, which was still to be seen in the physics labs in schools a few decades ago. Instead of being powered by an electric current, it could be worked the other way round, using a steam engine to generate electricity. The inventor had of course reproduced ideas from an earlier age without realizing it. And scientists now tend to pooh-pooh historians who praise the inventive joiner. But the historians are, I think, right. In the great chain of inventions and industrial progress, Gramme is an essential link.

Things certainly moved quickly after him. Until about 1870, 'the production of electricity . . . was chiefly used to meet the very modest needs of telegraphy',[337] that 'first sign', as Maurice Daumas puts it, 'of modern industry', which had appeared during the 1830s. But electricity only entered everyday life much later. It was in 1879 that Siemens built the first electric train; in 1883, that Deprez created an electrically powered line between Vizille and Grenoble (14 kilometres); and in 1888 that an electric tramway was inaugurated in Paris.[338] By 1906, the capital had 671 kilometres of electrical cables for lighting as against 250,000 kilometres of pipes for gaslamps.[339] In the meantime, electro-chemistry had completely revolutionized the heavy chemicals industry. And a new source of energy appeared with hydro-electricity (known in France as white coal, *houille blanche*), which was by the 1890s competing with both coal and steam to generate electricity.

But anyone living today will be well aware how industry has completely transformed technology and ways of life. I well remember, in the village in the Meuse to which I used to return every year until 1924, the light from our big oil-lamp, hanging over the dining table in a white porcelain bowl, with a shade of the same translucent material. And I can also remember the gas-lamp with a fragile Auer mantle, by which I used to study as a schoolboy in Paris until 1920.

More memories come to mind as I write: my extreme puzzlement in about 1910, as my mother tried unsuccessfully to explain to me what the cinema was; or the first time I saw an aeroplane fly over Paris in 1913, in the company of my marvellous Latin master at the Lycée Voltaire, Alexandre Merlot. At about the same time, I very gingerly approached my first telephone. And in September 1913, I recall my parents, in Tréveray (Meuse), describing to me, one after the other, their night ride in the motor car belonging to one of our neighbours who ran the draper's shop in the village.

After the how, the why

Hubert Bourgin's schema, which I have been using here, even when modified and fleshed out with examples, simply helps us to classify and describe. Is it possible to find out the reasons for the stages of industry listed there, to get some sense of evolution and of the behaviour that accompanied it? Looking back over the uninterrupted history of French industry, the difficult question is whether there are any discernible rules, repeated on different occasions and likely to produce similar consequences in the right circumstances: Georges Gurvitch would call these 'tendencies' rather than 'laws', believing (rightly) that the latter term is not really appropriate for the human 'sciences'.

Arguably the first rule (or tendency) is what used to be known as the 'second providence' explanation. This unusual formula is to be found in a rather late writer, Antoine Caillot: industry, he wrote, 'forever active, [is] like a second providence' – for the poor, he meant.[340] The *idea* was not new, since it was already to be found in Savary des Bruslons' *Dictionnaire de commerce* of 1760, where we read that 'the prodigies of industry have always arisen from the bosom of necessity'.[341] Basville, the *intendant* of Languedoc in 1730, hailed human ingenuity rather than Providence, 'as if nature were compensating for the losses suffered by people whose land is sterile and barren by [providing them with] industry and . . . the talents appropriate to commerce'.[342]

A well-known example of this kind was the Gévaudan, a poor

and hilly region, where the bitterly cold winters obliged the peasants to take refuge indoors. It did not even require the stimulus of a *Verleger* for them to devote themselves to spinning and weaving coarse but marketable cloth from the wool of their sheep. 'There are about 5,000 handloom weavers in the Gévaudan,' a memorandum of 1740 tells us.[343] But about half the weavers forsook their looms during the fine season, 'which is suitable for tilling the land'. Peasants in summer, they returned to the loom once they 'were driven back into their cottages by the ice and snow which for six months of the year grip the land and the hamlets'. Selling their cloth in the lowland fairs helped these mountain-dwellers to eke out a precarious living.

The same could be said of the nearby Cévennes, or the Ariège, in particular the diocese of Mirepoix, a particularly poor *pays*: the only well-off residents were to be found in the workshops. Around Mazamet, the land being for the most part 'completely barren', the inhabitants were obliged to take up textile working.[344] A memorandum of 1733, about the Languedoc in general, suggests that the owners of fertile land, 'occupied with farming in which they place all their hope', had difficulty making ends meet, whereas the peasants living on poor land, and dissatisfied 'with the gifts of nature . . . apply themselves to industry', which provides the 'poorest with the means of subsistence and of paying their dues'.[345] This may well have been true. But the advantage of rural industry was that it could be added on to the produce of the soil, however meagre that might be: it was a 'second providence'. It never ruled out tilling a patch of land, or a garden at the very least, or keeping a few animals.

In the towns, the rules were different. Here there had always been craftworking, arising spontaneously from the needs of any urban settlement and the surrounding region. But was it always a second providence, a safeguard against poverty? One would have to define what one means by poverty, its characteristics and its causes. But the towns were certainly not immune.

In Lille for instance, over-population hastened industrial growth and diversification. Whereas average density in France was 51 inhabitants to the square kilometre, the Nord *département* had a density well over 100, while the figure for Lille was 255! Under this demographic pressure, all industries prospered, striving to overcome the obstacles of the French domestic market and to meet the demands of foreign trade. Almost throughout the town's existence, there had been overcrowding, with the proletariat crammed into attics and cellars. Lille was an extreme case, a town ahead of its time. The city hummed with looms, indeed all its strength was absorbed into their activity which extended into the countryside, the *plat pays*, as well.[346] These considerations are still relevant since the same causes may produce the same effects: in today's world, Singapore, Hong Kong and South Korea have witnessed spectacular commercial and industrial growth, but it is based on an economy of low wages, and excessive working hours. And all to meet the powerful call of foreign markets, since in this case the process, not to say the problem, operates on a world scale. But is it right to talk of a second providence in this case?

Let us rather say that industry provided an ever-present way out of difficulty. It was always possible to take this road if the need arose. It was the solution invariably adopted in the end, though not necessarily with lightness of heart; so despite periodic collapses and intervals, it always recovered and always advanced. Industry was like a river, sweeping away obstacles, its flow forever swelling as if by some natural process. Even the Hundred Years' War and subsequent crises did not interrupt this movement. Industry might collapse in one town or region, only to revive in another, as if some kind of law of compensation was at work. The long War of the Spanish Succession (1701–13/4) has often been mentioned in these pages. Would it lead, in its final years, to the disasters and depressions so regularly predicted? A government inspector, in Reims on 6 April 1708, wrote to the Controller-General: 'I can presently assure you, Monseigneur, that by extraordinarily good fortune, the trade of this town has suffered little if at all from the present war and there is not a single worker unemployed.'[347] I would not wish to generalize from this example – the words 'extraordinarily good fortune' rule that out. And I would not deny that French artisans were to suffer, especially in the following year, with extra hardship caused by the cruel winter of 1709. But the river kept flowing just the same, and that was the main thing. Things would of course have been better if France had not been at war, and things did indeed improve with the coming of peace in 1713–14.

But France during the Revolution and Empire is an even better example. Some historians persist in calling these years catastrophic; they are no doubt sincere, but are they right? It is true that there was a dramatic fall in foreign trade (imports and exports totalled 1,000 million *livres* in 1789; 550 in 1795; and 622 in 1815). But foreign trade was only part of French trade as a whole, and in this period it did not have 'the importance for the whole of [French] industrial production that it was to have during the Second Empire after 1852'. More strikingly, the index of industrial production 'of the Napoleonic period [was] higher than it had been at the end of the *ancien régime*'.[348] So I am inclined to agree with Serge Chassagne that there was continuity and stability, both in the structures and in the volume of industrial production between the *ancien régime* and post-Thermidorian France, and even later, despite the great losses of the Napoleonic wars.[349] What France lacked was an industrial revolution. But that is not quite the same problem. The industrial revolution was the culmination of the long-term growth which only Britain had achieved in the seventeenth and eighteenth centuries. As far as France is concerned, the die was cast before 1789.[350]

But is the argument I have been outlining valid for the nineteenth and twentieth centuries, in the face sometimes of terrible odds? Were these ever really overcome? The Franco-Prussian War of 1870, painful though it was for French national pride, did not ruin the French economy. That much is clear. But can the same be said of the colossal disasters of the First and Second World Wars? Jean Bouvier relieves me of answering that question:

> The two world wars of the twentieth century proved to be disruptive only in the short term to [France's] industrial growth. They did not destroy it. And on both occasions, they led to periods of rapid recovery and growth, culminating, in the third quarter of the century, in unprecedented volumes of production (and consumption): between 1944 and 1977

(including recovery) industrial production multiplied 12.8 times.[351]

So here too there was continuity, survival and recovery. The same thing was true of economic crises, despite their impact: industrially speaking, France successfully negotiated the dangerous moment of the 1929 crash, less easily, it is true, than it had the 1857 crisis or that of 1810, which according to some historians was more disastrous to the Empire than the Peninsular War. But come through them France did, and we are gradually coming through the crisis that began in the 1970s and has wrapped us in its toils ever since.

This onward march, this silent progress, persevering in the face of all obstacles, whether the absurd policies of governments or international recession, is in the end the dominant feature of the history of industry, which is too often narrated in short sections and episodes, without any sense that these sections and episodes form a series, marked by continuity, progress and expansion. It is time we reconsidered the usual explanations, since these processes and their articulations have repeated themselves over time, influencing and controlling one another, and existing side by side. For one thing, industry cannot emerge until there is surplus agricultural production; secondly, since industry needs manpower, the surplus rural population must be prepared to engage in it; thirdly, industry has to be able to sell its products – Lodève, which made cloth for soldiers' uniforms, made a fortune during the revolutionary and Napoleonic wars;[352] Mazamet sold its *cordelats* to Canada; Laval its ginghams to Latin America, and so on. Trade was therefore the key. And trade, like industry, depended on credit, on banking, in other words on capitalism: would it not be said over and over again that if French industry did not expand faster, it was because bankers did not come promptly enough to its aid? And the French state always had something to say, sometimes productively sometimes obstructively, but never failing to intervene. The tide carrying industry forward was like a river propelling and carrying a boat: it was a general impulse, a compulsion, a vital necessity.

Repeated fluctuations

But to argue that economic life propels and calls forth by its very movement continuous industrial activity, and that this continuity is an essential feature, is surely to contradict what we perceive to be the rhythm of industry itself. How many triumphant launches are matched by collapse, recession or stagnation! Considered individually, industrial enterprises seem to obey some kind of law of discontinuity, their lives being so often cut short. We have all heard of deserted villages. We might do well to remember the deserted factories!

Maurice Daumas in his study of 'industrial archaeology' has compiled a catalogue of all the defunct factories and buildings abandoned to ruins or reconverted to other uses throughout France. He compares the 'permanence' of the buildings to the 'transitoriness' of the enterprises they once housed.[353] Tracing his steps, we can visit the great *manufactures* on their original sites.

At Lodève in the Languedoc, some huge buildings in a semi-circle still loom above the banks of the Lergue, a little river running through the town.[354] Not far away is the curious *manufacture* of Villeneuvette, built, like so many others, among the foothills of the Montagne Noire, from which flow the swiftly running streams once essential for the washing of wool, the fulling of cloth and the turning of millwheels. This old textile mill has beaten all records of longevity. Founded in 1677, it did not completely close down until 1954, after a long period of decline. Its survival means that the visitor can today walk in and find 'almost intact, a replica'[355] of industrial organization as it was in the eighteenth century: from the master's house one can walk into the great vaulted halls of the warehouses, the machine-houses and the workers' dwellings, laid out in several streets, which served both as lodgings and as weaving workshops; finally there are the great hydraulic works for the water supply. A dozen villages scattered round this capitalist fortress worked closely with it.[356] In Abbeville, Sedan, Louviers, massive buildings like castles, now in decay, bear witness to the fragility of great textile mills: they are born, flourish and die. In his search for old furnaces, steel mills, refineries and other elements of the archaeology of metallurgy, Maurice Daumas takes us all over France, from the Périgord to the Haute-Marne, the Châtillonais, the Côte d'Or or the Franche-Comté, from the Landes to Brittany, noting with surprise on the way that the only blast furnace classified as an ancient monument is that of Cons-la-Granville on the Chiers in Meurthe-et-Moselle, built rather late, in 1865, and abandoned fifteen years later.[357]

But rather than dwell on this fascinating mine of documentation, unknown though it is, my purpose is simply to point out how fragile and short-lived was the activity, not to mention the prosperity, of most industrial concerns. In so doing, I am echoing Walter Hoffmann's theory, formulated with reference to Britain after the industrial revolution,[358] but which could safely be applied to France in the eighteenth and nineteenth centuries. Formulated as a general proposition, it can easily be extended beyond its already generous chronological limits.

Rather than a theory, it is a rule, indeed for once I will hazard to say a law. For Walter Hoffmann, *any* industry, whatever its location and purpose (and I would add whatever its period) follows a parabolic curve from its inception, with a comparatively rapid rise, a ceiling reached over time, and a downward phase that may be vertical. We need not dwell on the examples he cites, which prove the point. In another book, I tried out 'Hoffmann's law' on a few quantifiable examples, alas only too rare, from the sixteenth century.[359] But one thing stands out: the days of any industry are numbered, even if its beginnings are spectacular, even if at the height of its powers it seems to be in perfect health. All industrial activity will sooner or later obey this predestined curve, whatever the ups and downs of fortune on the way.

In short, while any village community has hundreds of years stretching behind and ahead of it, an industrial establishment can never be sure – with some exceptions that merely prove the rule – that it has more than a century of prosperity ahead of it. Industry, we must conclude, is a comparatively short-term phenomenon. Since it depends essentially on a voluntarist history – that of the individual entrepreneur trying his luck – it proves in its way that human activity can control only the short term: the long and especially the very long term is beyond man's reach.

Despite the apparent contradiction, these remarks do not prevent me from returning to the original proposition to which I remain faithful, namely that industrial activity has an *overall* progressive continuity when considered within the context of a given national economy. The industrial tide as a whole does not ebb, rather its inherent tendency is to expansion. If failures and setbacks are one rule, vigorous upsurges are another. The whole scene is the sum of pluses and minuses, so to speak. I would maintain that the slightest encouragement from outside – whether a well-judged governmental measure, the opening-up of a new market, a favourable upturn in the business cycle, or the elimination of a rival – enables the whole industrial sector to move forward. This is to take an optimistic view. But I imagine that T.J. Markovitch, far and away the leading expert on the industrial history of France from the eighteenth century to the present, would support me in this. He establishes a three-fold division among French industries: the new ones which provide dynamism for the whole sector; those which have peaked but which are still holding their own; and those which are stagnating and have reached the end of their career.[360] This schema basically reflects Walter Hoffmann's analysis, and the diagram reproduced in Figure 70, from Markovitch's book, shows it clearly enough: industrial progress depends on innovation. As I come to the end of these rapid reflections, I find myself aligned with economists such as Mensch, André Piatier and no doubt many more: innovation is the spring of youth for industry, the reward of intelligently applied and necessary technology.

We still have to account for failure and exhaustion, for the recurrent need for rejuvenation. What are the reasons for the regular fluctuations which mark the history of industry? In the old days, even for a historian as scrupulous and well-informed as Henri Sée, the period under observation tended to be defined by political history: what was the French economy like under the Restoration, the July Monarchy or the Third Republic?[361] Then we began to consider the economic phases defined by François Simiand: the downward trend from 1817 to 1852, a rise from 1852 to 1876, another depression between 1876 and 1896, followed by an upward trend, encompassing the First World War, which lasted until 1929. Now

FIGURE 70
Dynamic, progressive and declining industries

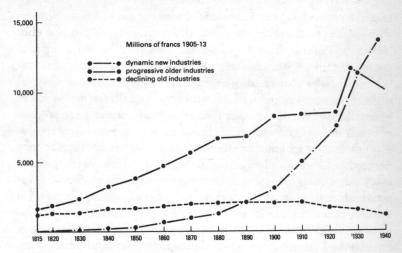

Source: T. J. Markovitch, *L'Industrie française de 1789 à 1964*, Cahiers de l'ISEA, 1966.

the awkward fact seems to be emerging that industry may sometimes develop more quickly during a B or downward phase than during an A or upward phase.[362] Should we simply give up on the problem and dismiss it as insoluble? Or can we reconsider it from the perspective of crisis? Might it not be suggested that growth, which attenuates conflicts and competition, which swells both profits and demand, may enable everyone to survive, even lame ducks? In short, growth may act as a force for conservation. Economic crisis, on the other hand, precipitates long-term collapse, reduces profits, increases national and international competition, strengthening the strong and further weakening the weak.[363] It may be that this cold wind also encourages innovation, pushing people to look for new solutions, for a new way out of the crisis. But that brings us to a different problem and one perhaps even more insoluble than the first: how to explain the crisis itself.

In conclusion: the survival of the small firm

Historians are all agreed today that, under the *ancien régime*, France, with its large area, latent wealth, and numerous population (the largest in Europe apart from Russia) was the leading industrial power in Europe. But that pre-eminence was founded on ancient methods and processes, and on small units of production. Capital was concentrated in certain large cities (Lyon, Lille) in ports such as Marseille and Bordeaux, but these financial centres preferred to put their money into something less risky than industrial enterprise – as entrepreneurs knew to their cost. The only major capital concentration likely to allow itself to be attracted by manufacturing was Paris, although it too was drawn more towards trade and commerce than to textiles or steel, more inclined to import Spanish wool or to retail cloth from Sedan or Elbeuf, than to invest in the woollen industry in which, however, merchants and clothiers in the city had shown more than theoretical interest in the seventeenth century. In short, France in 1789, whatever the health of the economy, had an industrial sector set in its old ways – with only a few exceptions, in cotton, mining, and metallurgy. The industrial revolution, which was on the whole imported from Britain, would have difficulty extracting itself from this ancient straitjacket: the two had to exist side by side.

This industrial *ancien régime* which survived throughout the nineteenth century and as late as 1914 or beyond, was characterized by what might be termed second-rank industry, or as T. J. Markovitch has called it 'craft production in the broader sense', as opposed to industry proper, that is large-scale industry with a concentration of resources and manpower. The results of the four major surveys carried out under the July Monarchy and Second Empire (1840–5, 1848, 1861–5) are summarized in the following tables (figures in millions of francs).

According to these surveys, 'in the twenty years between 1840 and 1860, the total industrial product increased by 42.36%; industry proper . . . by 111.29%, and craft-working in the broad sense by only 19.08%. So structural change was very great. The share of industry proper rose from 25.2% to 37.5%.'[364] This structural shift

	Total industrial product	Industry proper	Craft production (in the broad sense)
		(annual averages)	
1835–44	6,385	1,612 (25.2%)	4,773 (74.8%)
1855–64	9,090	3,406 (37.5%)	5,684 (62.5%)

is even clearer, if one compares the respective proportions of profits and wages in the context of industry proper: profits rose from 56 to 60.4% while wages fell from 44 to 39.6%. 'This comparative fall in the proportion of wages in expanding (or 'dynamic') industries is typical of the nineteenth-century industrial revolution.' But it was accompanied by a rise in the price of raw materials. Should we see this, as our guide does, as one reason for colonial expansion, for the imperialism of the major powers?[365]

But in any case, even if it was declining in importance, small-scale industry still represented the lion's share of French industry as a whole: 62.5% in 1860. And even this figure is an underestimate, since the very debatable criterion selected by the enquiry teams to distinguish between large- and small-scale industry was the use of machinery. So in the statistical records of 1866, a tailor or dressmaker owning a Singer sewing-machine (a relatively recent invention) and employing two assistants, would count as 'large-scale industry'! T. J. Markovitch rightly prefers to distinguish between industry and craft-working, 'depending on whether the employer manages the enterprise without actually *working* himself, or whether he is at once manager and workman'. He thus includes under the craft label small-scale workshops, the ever-present rural industries and domestic industrial production, essentially for the needs of the household. If the calculations are revised according to the new criteria, the share of 'industry proper' about 1860 is no longer 37.5% but a mere 19.8% – in other words merely a fifth of all industrial production.[366] So large-scale industry, still the exception, was surrounded on all sides by traditional production, above which it stood out like an island in the sea. Traditional production meanwhile continued to maintain itself and even increase: industrial progress was indeed twofold – spectacular in the case of large-scale industry but real enough for small firms too.

T. J. Markovitch's revised calculations in the end accord with the imperturbable statements of the historians who were my generation's mentors, and who wrote the copious but now obsolete *Histoire de la France contemporaine*, edited by Ernest Lavisse: Sébastien Charlety and Charles Seignobos. The latter, writing in the 1900s, that is well into the Third Republic, so quite a distance from the Second Empire, used the records available to him which all spoke of the immense progress made by French industry:

> The average number of workers per firm was still estimated, in 1866, even in the most concentrated industries, as only 84 in metallurgy, 21 in mines and quarries, 17.4 in chemicals. By 1906, it had risen to 711 in steel-working, 449 in mining and 96 in glassmaking . . . By 1896 only 36%, and by 1906 only 32% of the workforce was still employed in small firms with less than 10 workers.[367]

With a third of French workers in small firms, and two-thirds in large-scale industry, the hour-glass had been reversed, but the minority percentage remains quite a large one.

Should it be thought that the continued survival of small businesses hampered larger industries? Or on the contrary that the larger concerns needed the small ones, that coexistence bred links? What is certainly true is that large-scale industry did not advance as fast as it might have. Partly this was its own fault: the great innovations – cars and aeroplanes for instance – made headlines when they first appeared, but if I am not mistaken, their development was sluggish. More particularly, French banks did not contribute with the requisite generosity, hesitating to commit themselves to the long-term investment needed by industry. Like France's great sea-ports under the *ancien régime*, the banks were tempted to operate on a world scale rather than a national one. Industries consequently had to help each other out, granting mutual delays for settlement of sales and purchases. I shall have more to say about these problems which have loomed so large in recent French history. Was capitalism to blame? Since its reputation is not untarnished, it cannot escape some responsibility.

Hervé Le Bras proposes another rather attractive explanation. He points out in the first place that, significantly, the Geneva–

Saint-Malo line once more separates two halves of France, one in the north, extensively industrialized, the other in the south, which resisted industry and where the family firm remained tenaciously entrenched. 'The two halves remained in opposition, one engaging in heavy forms of production, the other in light; in one, production was concentrated, while in the other its sites were scattered; one half was covered with small landholdings, the other with large farms employing agricultural labourers.'[368] Resisting the development of modern industry in the form of the working-class conurbation, the south saw its *manufactures* and traditional workshops, left over from the eighteenth century, driven out of business by competition from the factories. So the south began to fall far behind the rich and ever-richer France north of the Loire (cf. Figure 71). Already in 1827, Baron Dupin was writing:

> Fellow-southerners, it is to you that I dedicate the description of northern France [a book entitled *Forces productives et commerciales de la France*] . . . You will be astonished when you see the differences in population, in territorial, manufacturing and commercial wealth between the two great divisions of France which our ancestors distinguished as the *langue d'oïl* and the *langue d'oc*. [And he exhorted them to] serious and fruitful studies necessary for your *départements* . . . because today you are experiencing physical and moral privations which render your individual needs more numerous and pressing.[369]

But the south was not to be drawn by this appeal to industrialize: its population, the last in France to remain on the land, would not go to swell the working-class population of the north. (This would be largely composed of immigrants.) And when, in the end, the south too saw a rural exodus, it would be to the tertiary sector, to the services, the professions, and the civil service, and hardly if at all to industry. In fact the south of France remains even today *culturally* hostile to the industrial way of life.

This being so, during the nineteenth century, northern France where industrial production was concentrated, ought to have developed it energetically. But compared to the rest of Europe, its growth was comparatively slow (at least until after the Second

FIGURE 71
'Inequalities in the economic geography of France' in 1830

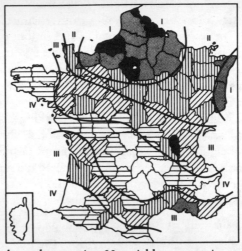

This map has been drawn using 33 variables concerning every aspect of the economy (agriculture, transport, industry, incomes, wealth etc). It shows the disparity of regional development in France in 1830: to move from the dark areas to the pale ones and from I to IV is to move from riches to poverty.

Source: B. Lepetit, forthcoming article in *Annales E.S.C.*, 1986.

World War). Hervé le Bras's explanation is a political one. In the last century, he argues, the French state was concerned with the north-south divide, to the point that 'the industrial imperative was eclipsed by the political imperative of unity'. Government investment – that is the wealth of the north – went into developing the south, thanks to a policy of nationwide education (the Jules Ferry laws), the railway system, and the administrative penetration of the territory, thanks too to an 'immense public and private building programme, often considered by economists as a diversion from productive investment'. This, in his view, is the chief explanation why France 'lagged behind in industrial growth rates between 1860 and 1914'. 'By tempering the inequalities unleashed by the first wave of industrialization, France [may have] limited its industrial growth, while succeeding in creating political unity.'[370]

CHAPTER FOURTEEN

Commerce: Always One Jump Ahead

From the number of studies devoted to it, one would think that commerce, whether in France or anywhere else, was the most important of all economic activities. The illusion does not however stand up to confrontation with the available figures. In 1837, Baron Dupin calculated what we would call the GNP of France under Louis-Philippe: agriculture accounted for 6,000 million francs; industry for 3,000 million; and commerce for a mere 1,500 million.[371] Such figures introduce a sense of proportion. All the same, during the constant economic progress of the nineteenth century, French commerce developed proportionately faster than the two other sectors. In fact it would have been the fastest-expanding sector, if banking is discounted. (But after all, banking is itself a kind of commerce, dealing in money.) I quoted earlier Léonce de Lavergne's comment in 1870 that since 1815, France's foreign trade had quintupled, industry had quadrupled and agriculture had doubled.[372] But this rhythm of development, with industry outstripping agriculture and trade outstripping industry, was not new. According to Pierre Chaunu, between the last years of the seventeenth century and 1800, the income from agriculture in Europe multiplied by 1.5, that from industry by 3, and that from trade by at least 10 and perhaps 20 – an extraordinary commercial explosion.[373]

There are no doubt many explanations. One thinks of the law formulated by William Petty (1623–87), the first of the English 'arithmeticians', that 'more money is made in industry than in agriculture, and more in commerce than in industry'.[374] Profits were clearly part of the answer. Nor was the division of labour as neutral as some have suggested. It created a hierarchy, distinguishing between levels, giving prestige to some and depreciating others.

Indeed it may itself have been the result of the different rates of development. And there may also have been a hierarchy connected to numbers: there were far more peasants than artisans, and more artisans than merchants and their employees: while the latter in turn exceeded the very small number of bankers. Economic progress may have been in inverse ratio to the numbers of people concerned.

Whatever the reason, the commercial sector expanded faster, preceding, pulling along and dominating the others. I have already discussed this at length apropos the *Verlagssystem*, and shall return to it at the end of this chapter apropos commercial, or as I prefer to call it merchant capitalism. Here I would merely note in passing that industry was primarily, if not uniquely, dominated by the impact of trade. Where progress was concerned, industry may have been the daughter of technical inventions marking a series of new departures, breaks and revolutions, but it was equally the child of innovations in marketing, as any number of examples conclusively prove.

Take the case of the fine woollens industry. It arrived in France in the seventeenth century: even earlier than this, fine wool had begun to replace silk for furnishing fabrics and particularly for luxury clothing. The market was already in existence and was being catered for by foreign cloth. It was the capture of this market, thanks to the drapers of Paris, which made possible the creation of the *manufactures* of Sedan, Elbeuf and Louviers. To take another example, the cloth made in Languedoc in the seventeenth century (and indeed until the Revolution) corresponded to the opening-up of the distant market of the Middle East, the export link with Smyrna and Constantinople being handled by Sète, a port created by Colbert in 1666, as well as by the major port of Marseille. So it is not surprising if in the documents of the *manufacture* of Villeneuvette in Languedoc, we find lists of ships from Marseille and Provence, with their litany of protective saints' names: the *Saint Joseph* and the *Crowned Dauphin*, the *Child Jesus*, the *Notre-Dame de Garons*, the *Notre-Dame de Bon Rencontre*, the *Notre-Dame de Grâce*, the *Saint Louis* and the *City of Aleppo*. And we have noted other examples too: the linens of Laval which were shipped to

Latin America in the eighteenth century, and the *cordelats* of Mazamet which sold well in Canada.

Even agriculture needed the services of the merchant. When trade boomed in eighteenth-century France, the various provinces emerged from their isolation and engaged in profitable specialization: inland Provence planted vines, other provinces shook off the straitjacket of arable farming and began to raise livestock. Under Catherine II, the Russian authorities were trying to break into western markets with exports of grain, flax and timber. In Marseille, the activities of the Russian consul Peschier (a member in fact of the colony of Swiss merchants in the city)[375] eventually inaugurated the export of Ukrainian wheat through the ports on the Black Sea (which had to be built from scratch). If he did not single-handedly introduce mass cereal-growing to Russia – itself a new departure – he certainly lent it a hand. Trade could bring things into being by waving its magic wand.

How many people were 'in trade'?

Even in a country like France, where the development of commerce never rivalled the records set up by the Italian cities or by Holland, or before long by England, one should not imagine that trading was a minor activity. Many people were involved, for there were traders and traders: the captains of commerce, sometimes described as wholesalers, for whom the term *négociants* gradually came into use (and will be used in this chapter); and all the others. Turgot rightly saw the world of commerce as extending 'from the woman who spreads out her herbs on the market stall to the shipbuilder of Nantes or Cadiz'. Or as a Rouen document puts it, 'from the humblest worker to the greatest merchant'.[376]

The commercial *sector* covered hundreds of trades and functions, accounting for an entire population of its own. In the fourteenth century, in Avignon and the Comtat Venaissin, it accounted for about 2 to 5% of an undoubtedly privileged society. In 1800, in a France of about 30 million inhabitants, perhaps one and a half million persons were engaged in trade. And by about 1825, if Dupin's calculations are correct, about 10% of the population was thus employed. However Jean-Claude Toutain reckons only about 1,900,000 people to have been employed in the various branches of trade in 1856. Admittedly, his statistics take account only of *established* commerce.[377]

At the top of the pyramid at any rate were a few very wealthy *négociants*, habitués of the Paris Bourse. Below them came the many medium-sized merchants, surrounded by their assistants and services. Then came the small traders, the 'small-timers' or as the French said, *marchands de basse étoffe*, or *marchands de moindre plumage*;[378] and lastly the countless artisan-shopkeepers, not to mention the humble market-traders.

At this lowest level, one would place the vendors of vegetables, butter and poultry who set out before daybreak from the Paris suburbs, and jogged into the city in their carts, still half-asleep. They would be found in Lyon too, where in 1643, the year of Louis XIII's death, a traveller described how

> everything that can be bought is peddled here: fritters, fruit, firewood, charcoal, grapes, celery, fish, mushy peas, oranges . . . Lettuces and greens are hawked about from a handcart, to the cries of the vendor. Apples and pears are sold ready-cooked. Cherries are sold by the pound weight.[379]

In Caen,

> the sale of everyday goods was handled by a host of small market-traders without shops of their own (apart from the pottery-sellers, one of the poorest guilds). They set up stalls here, there and everywhere in the streets. . . These vendors had no pack-animals and carried their entire stock in two or three baskets; they would come in on foot every morning from the villages round about.[380]

Is this the very lowest level of exchange? One doubts it, for several reasons. I imagine that the lowest level of all consisted of elementary barter of goods and services: milk for butter, cheese or bacon – as we saw in the case of the little town of Saint-Antonin.

Should one place slightly above this level the itinerant pedlars –

gypsies travelling in their covered waggons – or hawkers? Yes for the former, but one is less certain about the latter.

What we do know is that the trading population increased steadily – as was only to be expected with the general increase in population, in agricultural surpluses, in industrial production and in transport.

We have abundant evidence that this growth was *continuous*. As early as 1515, as the reign of Louis XII drew to a close, Claude de Seyssel, the bishop of Marseille and later archbishop of Turin, wrote:

> Everyone now dabbles in commerce, and for one merchant in the time of King Louis XI [1461–83] you would find over fifty in the present reign [Louis XII, 1498–1515] and thus there are now in the small towns more merchants than would once have been found in great leading cities.[381]

This is valuable but isolated evidence. By the seventeenth century, the picture is much clearer. An epidemic of trade was sweeping through the cities of Europe: all of them were being literally taken over by shops. Clustered together by speciality, according to ancient regulations, they were now starting to appear along both sides of the street, taking up the whole frontage. In December 1656, two Dutch visitors to Paris discovered the rue de la Ferronnerie, near the cemetery of the Innocents, 'a remarkable street, in that almost all the merchants of iron, tin, copper and pewter have their shops there'.[382]

The expansion was even greater in the eighteenth century. In 1716, Pottier de la Hestroye reported that

> the retail trade is handled not only by special merchants but by the artisans themselves, who often open a shop, run by themselves or their wives, to sell the goods they have made. These *shopkeepers* must make up one of the largest categories of the people.[383]

They were soon selling not only their own wares, but those of other people.

Further expansion followed in the nineteenth century, after the return of peace in 1815. A disgruntled observer in Limoges in 1817 commented that

> a large number of our fellow-citizens have gone in for trade, as offering much profit for little pains. Clerks, servants and labourers have all opened shops. Today in Limoges [for about 10,000 inhabitants] there are 25 drapers, 76 grocers, 97 haberdashers, 41 manufacturers, 14 goldsmiths, 18 ironmongers, 5 bureaux of hired carriages, 23 cafés and 85 wine-shops.[384]

Similar local surveys provide us with a few figures, rather doubtful ones in most cases, for example in Grenoble in 1725,[385] or Savoy in 1789.[386] For a certain number of towns in these regions, we therefore know the percentage of heads of families living off trade: 12.5% in Cluses; 8.5% in Thonon; 7% in Evian; 6.1% in Aix-les-Bains; 3.5% in Bonneville; 15% in Annecy; while Chambéry had something between the 15% in Annecy and the 12% in Grenoble. But what is one to make of this? That sedentary tradesmen were more numerous in large towns than in small ones (the latter often relying more on the trade conducted at fairs)? That is hardly news. But it is impossible to calculate an overall percentage, including towns, bourgs and villages, nor above all to estimate how fast the undeniable expansion of the commercial sector was taking place.

If I am dwelling at some length on these details, which may seem obvious, before embarking on the necessary analysis of the history of commerce in France, it is because they are easily overlooked by statisticians, who are usually dazzled by the spectacle of long-distance international trade. But this superstructure, while obviously very significant, accounted for only a *quite small* proportion of the real world of trade. Domestic trade was far larger, both in volume and value, than the long-distance trade which looked beyond the frontiers.

Maurice Block, one of the earliest statisticians in France, pointed out this disproportion at national level in the mid-nineteenth century:

Domestic trade, of which people do not generally have a very clear idea, includes in its vast embrace all the transactions of every kind taking place between the individuals in a single nation. These transactions far exceed those of external trade, and it is probably an underestimate even to say that they account for ten or twenty times as much as the latter. It is in any case quite easy to visualize the difference between the two types of trade, if one notes that external trade serves only to top up a country's supplies or to get rid of its surplus production. Think on the other hand of the enormous amount of business that is transacted every year between the 36 million inhabitants of France; consider that there is practically no commodity which has not passed through the hands of three or four intermediaries before reaching the consumer, thus giving rise to several commercial transactions; and add to these actual sales and purchases the operations carried out by banks and other credit institutions, which are the necessary accompaniments to commerce – then one will realize that it is not excessive to attribute a value of at least 35,000, or 40,000 million francs to the volume of domestic trade, that is, over a thousand francs per head of the population.[387]

There are plenty of other indices of the scale of this domestic commodity market: its role in exports, its role for the acquisition of indispensable raw materials for industry and for the nation's survival. And at the date when Maurice Block was writing, the size and profits of domestic commercial enterprises were also rising. Even in Voltaire's time, the famous Petit Dunkerque shop was not negligible. But by the mid-nineteenth century, the big department and chain stores were starting to appear: Félix Potin in 1850;[388] the Bon Marché in 1852; the Louvre in 1855; and the Samaritaine in 1869. Some of the 'sedentary' tradesmen in the big cities were making as much money as wholesale *négociants* by then.

But to return to the figure of 35,000 or 40,000 million francs for domestic trade, which is posited, as its author admits, without any possibility of verification: uncertain and arguable as it may be, it does prompt some useful reflections. Note in the first place that it includes, as Turgot also thought proper, 'transactions of every kind', from the pedlar's pack to markets, fairs and shops. Secondly, the same goods might change hands several times, thus entering the account every time they were bought, sold or resold, not to mention the credit arrangements, bills of exchange and money orders, which are all equally included in this 'volume of domestic trade'. It is hardly surprising then if one arrives at a figure greater than the total physical product of France, which was about 25,000 million francs. As for foreign trade, imports and exports combined, this was estimated in 1872 to be only 7,800 million francs (not counting re-exports, which came to just under a quarter of the total).[389]

8,000 million as against 35,000 million: this ratio echoes the findings of certain British historians[390] who have estimated British domestic trade as representing four or five times the volume of foreign trade. It was only a short step from there to considering domestic trade as the chief motive for the industrial revolution, and they took it. After all, Defoe had long before pointed out the multiplying role played in eighteenth-century England by the sharing-out of commercial transactions among many intermediaries, whose small profits in the end added up to a huge total, swelling the national market.

So domestic trade was characterized by a multitude of small gains. But what about foreign trade? Galiani was well aware of the difference between the modest everyday profits provided by the massive grain trade within France (divided among countless agents), and the profits made by the large-scale dealer who only indulged in this trade in times of shortage, by speculating on international price differences. Such profits, made perhaps on small quantities but concentrated in the hands of a single importer, could be enormous: 300% for the Ximenes firm in 1591 for instance.[391]

And this is where we should locate the comparison between internal and external trade, as is excellently demonstrated in an article by Michel Morineau.[392] It is well known that in the eighteenth century, according to the trade-balance records, 'French trade with its colonies in America was largely in deficit except occasionally in time of war.'[393] For instance in 1750, France imported 62 million francs' worth of goods and exported a mere 27 million.[394] Yet as everyone also knows, this trade, which would triple or quadruple during the eighteenth century, was the secret of the growing wealth of France's Atlantic ports. The paradox is explained by a memorandum of 1729 containing very detailed accounts of the voyage to Saint-Domingue and back by a ship from Bordeaux. The value of the cargo on the outward trip was 37,149 *livres*, on the return journey 92,895: officially then this represented a trade deficit of 55,746 *livres*. But the merchant responsible was not making a loss at all. The outward-bound cargo (wine, spirits, flour, salt meat, butter, candles and glassware) would double in price or more when sold at Léogane, bringing in 81,678 *livres*. The return cargo (composed of indigo, sugar and tanned hides), having been bought for 78,603 *livres*, would be sold at Bordeaux for 92,895 *livres*. Taking into account all the expense involved, including paying off the ship, the profit was 35.6%, a percentage which probably applied to the whole of the West Indies trade and which is substantial considering that these were *regular* voyages, in no way speculative. Vauban estimated trading profits at about 10% on average.

This brings us to the problem which really preoccupies me. I do not intend to compare internal and external trade – something beyond my resources. Nor am I concerned to accept or reject the views of the British historians, who may well be right when they ascribe a leading role in the British industrial revolution to internal trade (in which case, I might be inclined to say that the progress made by the French home market may have been the motive force behind our own industrialization). What concerns me above all is that paradoxically, in the development of *capitalism*, which inspired, shaped and controlled the progress of industrialization while growing rich on it, it was *foreign trade*, so much smaller in volume, which really made the decisive difference. This requires some explanation (or explanations) and obliges us to look more closely at the foreign traders themselves, the *négociants*.

Wholesale traders (négociants) *and long-distance trade*

Négociants can easily be distinguished from other kinds of merchants. The latter were simply shopkeepers: the customer could just walk in and ask for something. The *négociant* by contrast owned a warehouse, stacked with goods which would only emerge from it 'under canvas and rope' and in large quantities. Jean Maillefer, a merchant of Reims, writing in the time of Richelieu and Louis XIII, remembered his apprenticeship, first of all with 'a merchant who sold retail goods', then one after another, with two merchants *en magazin*, 'owning warehouses'. It was when he was with the second of these,

> who had dealings with Italy . . . that I saw the openings for very good business, and realized that the wholesale trade had connections everywhere [*des chesnes*] and something noble and attractive about it which was not to be found in the retail trade, the latter being subordinate and tying one down and obliging one indeed to exercise a deference not called for in the wholesale trade.[395]

But in order to be a *négociant*, one had not only to be rich, but to have a rich family and to be able to count on it in moments of need. What temptations, what risks and what resources it represented! Money was so quickly ventured and took so long to return! Every balance sheet contained active debts but also irrecuperable ones. In this world, any trading-house was vulnerable. So at every point in its career, the family had to be behind it as the indispensable underwriter, whether launching it, lending money, helping it out of a tight corner or avoiding the dishonour of bankruptcy. And if there were no family, this role might be played by other merchants, thanks to partnerships and later to associations between shareholders, *sociétés en commandite*.[396] No one who wanted to be rich could afford to be isolated.

Another condition was that the *négociant* was invariably engaged in long-distance trade, with dealings in distant lands far beyond the frontiers of France. Overseas trade meant shipping of course, a point which has never escaped the writers of literature: whether in *The Merchant of Venice*, *The Count of Monte Cristo* or a Balzac novel, a merchant 'is always waiting for a ship to come in. His fate is linked to the safe arrival of a cargo, harbinger of wealth.'[397] Among these rich cargoes were the pepper, spices and drugs which for centuries made the extraordinary fortune of the Levant; other goods included costly saffron, sugar and rich fabrics. 'A pound of saffron cost as much as a horse [in about 1500]. And a pound of sugar [from Cyprus] cost as much as three sucking-pigs.'[398] In the thirteenth century, '30 metres of Flanders cloth sold at Marseille [reached] two to four times the price of a Saracen woman slave'.[399] These prices may leave us 'pondering the mentality of the age, the price set on human life, the extraordinary value placed on a length of drapery from the Netherlands, and the considerable profits to be made from it by producers and *négociants*'.[400] *Mutatis mutandis*, trade with 'the islands' (the West Indies) in the eighteenth century, or exchanges with America and the Far East obeyed similar rules.

And then there were the lucky breaks, the unexpected opportunities one had to be shrewd enough to seize. The traders of Saint-Malo, in the late seventeenth and early eighteenth centuries, for a while succeeded in obtaining silver coin and ingots at source – in Chile and Peru, after a long voyage through the South Seas. Their profits reached as much as 800%.[401] Similar opportunism was shown by the merchants who in the 1780s succeeded from time to time in sending into Russian ports a large ship laden with luxury goods. It was rather like letting off a depth-charge, fetching 'millions of roubles' out of Russia in exchange. The Tsarist government, anxious to protect its recently created domestic manufacturing industry, tried hard to 'forbid entry to [such] frivolities which catered to luxury',[402] but for the shipper the risk was evidently worth running.

The slave trade was also a risky undertaking in the eighteenth century, and profits accordingly reflected the degree of risk: 300% in 1782, in exceptional circumstances, it is true, during the American War of Independence. But profits of 50, 60 or even 80% were commonplace during the century.[403] It was no doubt 'a hazardous and scabrous business', as one shipowner of Nantes, Deguer, remarked in 1763, and it could end up in a loss, if only because so many slaves died on the voyage.[404] But since it was practised alongside the trade in colonial produce, which was a safer proposition, traders regularly took a chance on it. Every port on the Atlantic, from Dunkerque to Bayonne, was deeply involved in slave-trading.[405]

German historians long ago drew attention to the importance of *Fernhandel* (long-distance trade) and the *Fernhändler* (the traders). It had never been a secret. Contemporaries well knew that profits were usually greater 'when trade and traffic is carried on in distant countries and by means of shipping'.[406] Father Mathias de Saint-Jean, the curious early precursor of the Dutch, noted in 1646 that 'trade in foreign goods is always the best and the most profitable'.[407]

In the eighteenth century, it came to be seen as having another advantage: making the merchant bourgeoisie 'independent of the King' – free men in other words.[408] Whereas domestic trade was closely supervised by the local authorities, seeking to control everything and believing that they did, foreign trade crossed frontiers. Once the ship was out of harbour, the captain (and consequently the merchant) was master on board. The king of France was left behind, as the *Conseil du commerce* was only too aware:

> The greater part of trade and that which calls for most attention [it explained] is that carried on with the outside world. Internal trade is under the government's eye and one can from day to day issue orders suitable for controlling it.

We meet once more the domestic–foreign comparison. The *Conseil du commerce* had no hesitation in stating that foreign trade was more important than domestic trade. So too thought Maurepas, Secretary of State for the Navy, when he wrote in a report for Louis XV on 3 October 1730: 'Foreign trade brings gold and silver into your kingdom and gives impetus to domestic trade, which can only go well when the former is conducted to your subjects' advantage.'[409] But keeping it under effective supervision was another story. In the document quoted above, the *Conseil du com-*

merce noted that 'we have not heard for over a year any news about dealings in the Levant ports; the same is true for the ports of Spain. We do not at present know on what footing trade is being conducted there.'[410]

Does such freedom from control explain why external trade links were sometimes easier to set up than internal ones, as the British economist Sir Kenneth Berrill has found in developing countries in the twentieth century?[411] 'International trade', he points out, 'is often much cheaper and easier than internal trade [in these countries] and specialization between countries is often much easier than specialization between regions of the same country.' One might accordingly wonder whether historically, being easier to establish, foreign trade may not have actually preceded internal trade and *at first* at least, exceeded it in volume – contrary to the schema I previously outlined. The historian Marcello Carmagnani has firmly claimed this to be true in the case of Chile, which was still in the early stages of growth between 1680 and 1820. 'The values of external trade there', he writes, 'were far higher than those of the other sectors',[412] that is of domestic trade. Was the same true of other parts of America, as they moved towards a more European pattern? And if so, might Europe itself in the early days also have obeyed the rules we have observed of *every economy once it reaches a certain maturity*?

But such speculation takes us away from the original problem, namely why and to what extent long-distance trade came to generate large profits, and above-average accumulation, leading directly towards capitalism. The question is worth raising, since for the last twenty or thirty years most historians, especially in France, have preferred to stress collective realities rather than the achievements of elites. Pepper, spices and overseas trade have been somewhat neglected.[413]

Such neglect may have misled analysts, as was suggested by the debate that took place when Vitorino Magalhães Godinho was defending his major thesis at the Sorbonne. On this occasion, Ernest Labrousse raised the question whether in Portugal, where the king was the chief trader in pepper and spices, this luxury trade outweighed, either in value or in volume, the grain trade within the country. The answer of course is no, it did not. But that proves nothing. For as we have already seen, the grain trade was, with a few exceptions,[414] dispersed among thousands of dealers. If profits were made, they were shared out in tiny portions and were quickly swallowed up in the everyday accounts. All long-distance trade in precious commodities, on the other hand, led to a division of the profits among a very small number of European merchants, whether in Venice, Genoa, Marseilles or later in Amsterdam, as Paul Adam clearly perceived:

> Confronted with a trade which was fragmented both at the supply end, that is in the east, and at the demand end, in western Europe, the Mediterranean cities [in the age of the sea's greatest prosperity] found themselves controlling a 'bottle-neck'. Trade was concentrated in the hands of a small group of merchants.[415]

They had the great *strategic advantage* of controlling the point at which all incoming trade routes converged before fanning out again. Take a typical example, the merchants handling the fine woollen *étamines* produced in Le Mans in the early eighteenth century. In those days, they had not yet established direct links with the foreign markets on which these fine woollen fabrics mostly ended up. They sold them in bulk at the great fairs of Paris, Rouen, Lyon, Bordeaux, Limoges or Tours through middlemen. The merchants did not attend the fair in person, not even the nearby Guibray fair outside Caen. They did not need to. By making sure to control the dyeing and finishing processes, they also made sure the goods were concentrated in their hands at the end of the production process, thus enabling them to control prices on the supply side and having a strong voice in fixing them on the retail side. It used to be said in those days, in about 1710, that 'freedom to put a price on one's wares was the soul of commerce'.[416] Such freedom would be even greater for the few Le Mans wholesalers who after 1720 sent permanent representatives to Italy, Spain and Portugal, where they could make contact with the colonial American markets. By about 1740, this international trade was monopolized by less than a dozen powerful merchants.[417]

Not many winners

Needless to say, our merchant did not always bring off the perfect deal. But he was privileged in belonging to a tightly-knit group. The game was not really open to all comers. Innocents who did venture into these waters – which they might when the economic climate looked set fair – could be swept away by the first squall when the going became rough. The true *négociant* was the one who could survive stormy weather.

As a rule, I must stress once more that *négociants*, that is shippers and wholesalers, whether in Venice, Lisbon, Cadiz or Amsterdam, were comparatively few in number and in any one centre would all be known to one another. In France, again in the early eighteenth century, they were indeed *abnormally* few in number. In Cadiz, the landing-point for American silver, and the most sophisticated and important trading centre in Europe, there were only 26 French merchants in 1703,[418] all of them commission agents, none operating on their own account. There was not a single *négociant*, or super-merchant, among them.

A year later, in 1704, Pottier de la Hestroye, later to be an opponent of Vauban's *Dîme royale*,[419] offered a pessimistic judgement on France as a whole: 'there are few [French] merchants', he wrote, 'trading on their own account'. Whether they were not adventurous enough, or whether they were not wealthy enough to consider it, most of them

> confine themselves to acting as commission agents for the English or Dutch, especially the latter, a situation which far from making France rich, is only making her poorer . . . [For] it is not commission agents for foreigners we need in France – attached to the cheap profit of a commission, they only think of the profit of foreigners and are little concerned with that of the state . . . we need true merchants, trading on their own account.[420]

This inferiority, which dated from before the early eighteenth century, was a heavy legacy. In the international division of labour, France was poorly placed, did not occupy a leading position, and paid the price for it. Until the age of Mazarin, Italian merchants had had everything their own way throughout the kingdom, whether in Lyon or Paris. Next it was the turn of the Dutch, who had taken control of France's most profitable frontier, the coast-line from the North Sea through the Channel to the Atlantic, from Dunkerque to Bayonne. Colbert would not be able to get rid of them. And it was after watching them at work that Jacques Savary, author of *Le Parfait Négociant* (1675), was moved to exclaim that French merchants ought to consider carefully 'how the greatness of the state and of their own fortunes, and the way to become rich, lies in trading by means of long-distance voyages'[421] (evidence that this was not yet being done on a large scale).

There would be little improvement until the age of Law's system, if we are to believe Jacques-Marie Montaran (1701–82), *maître des requêtes* and *intendant* of trade from 1744, whose functions gave him some authority to speak on this subject. In 1753, he made a rather strange statement: 'Peace has fructified these ancient seeds . . . Until 1720 or so, there were only merchants [*marchands*] in France; trade having become more active, has turned them into *négociants*.'[422] Was this thanks to foreign trading practices, revealed to the French through the capture of enemy merchantmen during the long War of the Spanish Succession? Or was it a product of the upheaval wrought by Law's system? Or of the launch of the West Indies trade, which would turn Bordeaux, hitherto rather a sleepy town, into a trading port of the first rank? Or was Montaran himself deceived, and thus unconsciously deceiving posterity?

For there certainly had been some *négociants* in France before 1720, the shipowners of Saint-Malo for instance, or wealthy businessmen like Samuel Bernard or Antoine Crozat, marquis du Châtel (of whom more later). And there were also important wholesalers to be found in Paris, as was revealed by the conflict between the *merciers* and the *drapiers* in the late seventeenth century. The mercers, who had the privilege of being able to engage in all kinds of trading, provided they did not themselves manufacture anything, may have been as many as 2,000 at this time. The most powerful of them engaged in the export trade. The drapers, being specialized dealers in cloth, numbered no more than about forty. But a small clique or elite from among the mercers decided to put some money into the new industry of fine woollen cloth, expanding rapidly just then. They took advantage both of this new situation and of their solid trading connections to dominate not only the large Paris market – the leading market in France – but also re-export abroad. The complaints lodged by the drapers were apparently successful. In 1687, a decree from the *Conseil d'Etat* confirmed their privilege: they had the exclusive right to market woollen cloth in Paris. But it was left open to the mercers, if they so desired, to 'join without charge' the worshipful company of drapers. And in October 1687, seventy mercers did indeed choose to do so, among them Jacques Cadeau, Rieulle de Lamothe, Denis Rousseau, François Celière, François Mignot and Gilbert Paignon. In the end, nothing had really changed. 'For at least fifty years, the bulk of the fine woollen industry in France was controlled by a small group of Parisian *négociants* all doing business within the small rectangle between the Halles and the Châtelet.'[423]

Not far away, around the rue Saint Denis at about the same time, one might have found another group of true *négociants*, the merchants mentioned earlier who handled the luxury lace trade in silk and gold, mostly destined for the export market, from Hamburg and Warsaw to Vienna and Nuremberg, from Copenhagen and Stockholm to Madrid and Lisbon, from Seville to Latin America.

So we should not necessarily believe Pottier de la Hestroye or Jacques-Marie Montaran: France, although less penetrated by capitalist concentration than its great neighbours, did not escape that centralization of capital without which the operations of these *négociants* would not have been possible. It is true that we still know little about their dealings in Paris, where they remain shadowy figures in a history yet to be fully explored. But it is easy enough to recognize that trade was expanding in France's active sea-ports in the eighteenth century.

Evidence from the major trade circuits

This will become clear from the examination of three case studies.

The first port of call is Marseille, which can illustrate what the classic Levant trade really meant for France; next we shall move to Saint-Malo between 1702 and 1723, to analyse its trading links with Latin America; and finally, we shall make a visit to Bordeaux, to have some idea of what the profitable West Indies trade represented: although rather more than a flash in the pan, it was all the same an episode of limited duration.

We shall thus be comparing similar processes at work in these important cycles which begin, flourish and fall away – almost persuading one that William Hoffmann's law about the industrial cycle could be applied to trade cycles as well. Were they longer or shorter-lived on the whole? The history of human volition is likely to keep us within the short term. But at this stage, that is what most concerns us: the role played by capitalists.

The Levant trade corresponded to a very ancient pattern of exchange. It had existed since time out of mind between the countries lying between Syria and the Persian Gulf, or across the narrow barrier of Mount Sinai, bringing together two sets of economies and civilizations, those of the West and the Far East. It also drew on the commodity traffic of the Black Sea (the Pontus Euxinus of antiquity), the Red Sea and the Indian Ocean. It was through the Levant trade that the Roman Empire discovered pepper, spices, silk and drugs. The early centuries of the Middle Ages were a time of undoubted decline in Mediterranean trade. This falling-off, though never complete, was accentuated by the Arab conquests: almost deserted, the sea was sailed neither by Christian nor Muslim ships.

But in the eleventh century, European trade revived. During the Crusades, the Italian cities forced open the gates of the Levant: pepper, spices, silk and drugs returned to the West, as Europe took up again where Rome had left off – to an even greater degree since medieval Europe had an inordinate taste for pepper and spices.

Marseille was very soon shipping in these precious goods, as were Montpellier and Narbonne. But pepper long remained a scarce commodity there, 'more or less like gold dust, since it was used as an exchange currency and many taxes [in the port] were paid in pepper'.[424] Marseille was in fact something of a poor relation at the Levant banquet, as the Italian cities jostled for pre-eminence there, elbowing aside lesser trading partners. They would only yield when brute force was eventually applied, as in the fifteenth century by the Catalans.

As for Marseille, which came under the French Crown only after 1482, it was boosted to the ranks of the leading sea-ports not so much by French pressure as by the activities of the Turks. The latter, newcomers to the Levant trade, had disturbed the old patterns and unwittingly introduced a new deal. The first Turkish triumph, the conquest of Constantinople in 1453, and in particular the occupation in short order of Syria in 1515 and Egypt in 1516, changed all the rules. From now on, the Ottoman Empire controlled the gates of the Levant. To have closed them would have been out of the question, cutting the Empire off from considerable sources of income. But the Turks gave short shrift to the old masters of the trade, the Italians, welcoming, rather, their rivals. In 1530 what must have been the first Marseillais trading house was founded in Istanbul. And François I even allied himself with the Sultan in 1535, to the great scandal of Christendom.

There remained one major obstacle: Venice, with its colonies of merchants in Istanbul, Aleppo and Alexandria. It was in the end the slow decline of the Queen of the Adriatic, during her conflicts with the Turks, which paved the way for Marseille's fortunes in the east. Only two years after the great victory at Lepanto, in which it had played such a leading part, Venice capitulated to the Turk by the peace of 1573. Marseille, which had already chalked up some successes during these wars (1569–73), immediately moved in. From 1573, consulates were set up, in the name of the city and of the king of France, in many of the Levant ports, and soon became established there. The first capitulations (treaties) were signed with Sultan Muhammad III in 1597; the French ambassador, the comte de Brèves, signed the second set in 1604; and the marquis de Nointel signed the third, which consolidated the position of the Marseille merchants, in 1673, during the sultanate of Muhammad IV.[425]

The Marseillais arrived at just the right moment, precisely the time when spices and pepper were starting to return to the Levant. Captured by the Portuguese voyages of discovery, notably Vasco da Gama's rounding of the Cape of Good Hope in 1498, many of the Far East's cargoes of pepper and spice had been sailing directly to the Atlantic, to the greater benefit of Lisbon and almost immediately afterwards of Antwerp. But this rich traffic had begun to return to the Levant by the 1570s, following the influx of Spanish silver, which circulated throughout the Mediterranean via Genoa.[426] Trade returned more or less to the old basis: Asia sent vegetable products – spices, pepper, dyestuffs, soda, drugs, bales of silk, cotton and wool. And the Levant also exported cotton fabrics (the exception to prove the rule). They were woven in the Aleppo region, and were not unlike those of India. In return, Europe dispatched high-quality textiles and silver coin, which eastern countries melted down to manufacture their own currencies. So this was an exchange between nature on one side and industry on the other. As Marseille's fortunes grew, so did those of the cloth manufacturers of Languedoc, at least until the eighteenth century.

It is true that this revival of the Levant trade in the Mediterranean attracted the British after 1579 and the Dutch after 1612 – bringing competitors who were active, aggressive, and ready to turn pirate if need be. But there was room in the Levant for all the merchants of the West.

Marseille attracted investment from outside the city, from Montpellier, Lyon, Genoa and even Paris. The harbour was full of ships and cargoes ready for dispatch to other Mediterranean ports, or up the Rhône valley to Lyon. It is no surprise to find that the import trade from the Levant was by 1563, and earlier too no doubt, concentrated in the hands of

a dozen wealthy merchants . . . [In 1587] the best known of these, Ascanio Roncalhe, Pierre Albertas, Martin and Jean

562

Covet, had between them a turnover of 50,000 *écus*. They had 3 galleons and two smaller boats sailing to Tripoli [in Syria]; 2 galleons and 6 smaller vessels on the route to Alexandria [in Egypt]; and for [the island of] Chios one boat, that is a total of 14 vessels.[427]

Their prosperity lasted into the seventeenth century, until about the 1650s. In 1614, out of 585 ships leaving Marseille, 67 were bound for the Levant, namely '48 merchantmen, 2 polaccas, 2 galleons and 15 barques'. 26 were bound for Alexandria, another 26 for Syria, and 15 for 'Greek' ports (Chios, Constantinople, Smyrna and Zante). In 1618, there were 23 departures for Syria, 7 for Egypt and 10 for the Greek ports.

Taking one year with another, and despite variations in the pattern, the Levant trade retained its priority. Of the hundreds of ships leaving and returning to Marseille every year, only a few dozen actually went eastwards: they often sailed empty on the outward voyage, except for a few sacks full of Spanish pieces of eight; but they returned with rich cargoes which kept the Levant at the top of the list for trade and profits. As usual, the bulk of this trade was handled by a few trading houses owned by the wealthiest merchants.[428]

About 1650, the Levant trade began to change. Neither pepper nor spices had disappeared from it – Jacques Savary mentions them still being shipped from Cairo in 1712[429] – but from now on, they made up a more modest proportion of cargoes, almost nothing by comparison with coffee, which had begun crossing the Mediterranean from Egypt, or with silk, wool, leather, and before long raw or spun cotton. Vasco da Gama's route round the Cape had been re-opened a century after his voyage by the Dutch, in 1595, and they were soon monopolizing the fine spice trade from the East Indies.

The Atlantic route was once more, and with renewed vigour, short-circuiting (or perhaps one should say long-circuiting) the Levant and the Mediterranean. What was even more significant, Europe seemed to be weaning itself (more or less rapidly, depending on the country) from the craving for strong spices – a desire that had lasted over five hundred years. Had this been, as Franco

Borlandi has suggested, because westerners, who ate a lot of meat, wanted to season it strongly so as to disguise the possible taste of decay? Whatever the reason, the reduced demand for spices marked the end, or substantial decline, of a very ancient cycle of exchange.

Another cycle was however beginning. The more the Turkish Empire opened up to trade with Christian merchants, the more it was penetrated and colonized by them. The decline of the 'sick man of Europe' was beginning, although its armies, if not its navies, were still a force to be reckoned with in battle. The fate of the Turkish Empire – to be eaten alive – was not unlike that of the Byzantine Empire which Venice had greedily devoured long before, in the days of the Crusades. A sign of the times, the spices, sugar and coffee of the East Indies were by 1750 actually coming to the Levant via the Atlantic, reversing the former flow.[430]

Marseille took its share of the spoils. Every year it shipped not only cloth but huge quantities of piastres to Turkey, thus forcing open the market. Even when Marseille had, in the eighteenth century, become a 'world-rank' port, trading with India, China, Black Africa and America, the Levant was still its most profitable route. Meanwhile, the city's merchants had increased their bases in the east, settling in Cavalla on the Thracian coast, in Salonika, an up-and-coming port in the eighteenth century, in the Greek islands, on the Albanian coast, in Cyprus, in Canea on Crete, Modon in Morea and finally in Smyrna itself, the old and thriving port to which the headquarters of the Levant trade had by then been transferred in a move northwards, possibly in order to bring it nearer the heart of the empire. Marseille had also captured what was known as the 'caravan', that is the coasting trade along the Turkish seaboard in the Mediterranean, which fell entirely into French hands when Venice had to abandon it during the series of wars with the Turks. Partly because of this coasting trade, Marseille was sending up to a hundred ships to the eastern Mediterranean, accomplishing what Dutch ships (in other circumstances of course) had succeeded in creating along the French Atlantic seaboard: a sort of maritime blockade. French merchants had even set up a communications network, by means of bills of exchange, between these ports and Constantinople: the pashas themselves made use of the network to send the surplus from their coffers to the *miri*, the Sultan's treasury. They were thus avoiding the risk involved in sending cash by land or sea, but the bill of exchange network was not of course free of charge. Imagine if you like a British company setting up telephone links in a Latin American country, but retaining operating rights.

But by this time, the merchants or rather *négociants* of Marseilles were not personally visiting the Levant ports as they had in the past. Instead, 'commission agents' represented them on the spot, earning a commission which could be as high as 60%, an exorbitant rate, 'yielding a substantial profit, and thus enabling them to make a living and even to save money which, after several years in the Levant, they return to spend in France . . . [This is] the origin of several prosperous trading-houses in Marseille'.[431]

If by the end of the eighteenth century, Marseille was not managing to sell as many bales of Languedoc cloth in the souks of the east, it was because Turkey was by now ailing and poverty-ridden – bad news for Languedoc, which was thrown into severe crisis. As for Marseille, the city survived by dispatching more silver coin, preferably Maria Theresa thalers, minted in Milan.

Saint-Malo makes a good centre for understanding French trade directly with Latin America, *à longueur de pique* as it was called, that is avoiding middlemen. Between 1698 and 1724, the ships of Saint-Malo were more or less clandestinely visiting the ports of New Spain, in particular Vera Cruz, and more especially the ports and bays of Chile and Peru on the distant Pacific coast. These dates are absolute limits for what was at most a quarter-century of high activity,[432] and was essentially a mere episode in the history of trade.

The real *fons et origo* of the adventure was the general cycle of American silver, which had begun arriving in Spain by 1503, a mere ten years after Columbus's first voyage from Seville. Imported silver was quickly seized upon by the avid European and even Asiatic economies: a substantial quantity of precious metals was regularly reaching India and China. By the end of the seventeenth century, the Pacific had in turn been crossed from east to west; silver from New Spain and Peru was being dispatched to China via the Philippines, discovered in 1543 by the Spanish, who founded Manila in 1571.

In the course of this major development, one rule was observed almost without exception. The Spanish of the past were no more able to keep American silver to themselves than the Gulf states, about whom we read every day in the newspapers, can extract their oil without selling it. Silver became a commodity, to be exchanged for other much-needed goods: grain, timber, beams, textiles (both woollen and linen), ironmongery. Cadiz, the central departure point for American trade in the seventeenth century, was flooded with a prodigious 'quantity of goods of every type of manufacture, from France, England, Flanders, Holland, Hamburg and Italy'.[433] All of Europe crowded into the port to offer its wares, since the trading balance of Europe required a continuous supply of silver, whatever the cost. In this redistribution, a significant role was played by the constraints of the trade balance, as well as by the demands of the empire Spain was still maintaining in the Netherlands. When the latter rebelled in 1567, they provoked the dispatch of the duke of Alva in August that year with a task force, and the occupying army would remain there until 1714. All in all, it would mean two centuries of costly military expenditure.

What was more, since the beginning of the *Carrera da Indias*,[434] contraband had been endemic along the endless South American coastline and especially in the Caribbean, with its many intersecting routes. It also flourished clandestinely in the port of Seville, the obligatory landfall on the return voyage from America, and to an even greater degree in Cadiz, which took over this role in the seventeenth century. At Seville, in the river port on the Guadalquivir, upstream from the Triana bridge, a degree of effective control of smuggling was possible. But in the great bay of Cadiz, it flourished unconfined.

Saint-Malo was from very early days a party to this siphoning off of American silver, naturally so since its sailors had long been familiar with the Iberian peninsula. Notorious as 'les rouliers de la mer' (sea-rovers), they were already, in the fifteenth century, trading and privateering along the entire Atlantic seaboard from north to south, as far as Madeira.[435] In the sixteenth century, Breton 'barques' were carrying wheat to Lisbon, where it was exchanged for gold, and to Seville, where it was exchanged for silver. By 1570, ships from Saint-Malo had reached the Mediterranean and were putting into Civita Vecchia to embark alum from the papal mines at Tolfa. Later, when American demand got under way, they shipped into Seville and Cadiz enormous quantities of Breton-made textiles, which were then re-exported to the New World. It was at about the same time that Saint-Malo, which had for a good half-century been working the Newfoundland fisheries, began shipping dried or salt cod to Spain, Marseille and Genoa. In return, silver coin or ingots travelled north.[436] Lastly, the gates of Spain were opened wide to French trade, and consequently to the entrepreneurs of Saint-Malo, by the treaty of the Pyrenees (1659), as Mazarin's political victory was accompanied by an economic victory.

Trading by Saint-Malo ships, based on a triangular commodity circuit of textiles, cod and silver, now reached a new intensity in the Iberian peninsula. The correspondence of the French consuls in Cadiz provides ample evidence about their comings and goings. On 1 April 1702 for instance,[437] four frigates from Saint-Malo arrived from Morlaix, having made the journey from Brest to Cadiz in eight days, 'without meeting any enemies',[438] and laden with 'sailcloth estimated at 500,000 piastres, which pleased our merchants, since they had been afraid the ships might have been waylaid'.[439] (War had broken out once more in Europe the previous year.) 500,000 piastres was the equivalent of at least 1,500,000 French *livres*. This figure gives some indication of the prosperity now reached by Saint-Malo. In the same year 1702, on 15 October, the consuls reported that 'there arrived here last night a Saint-Malo vessel en route from Chapeau Rouge [one of the great Newfoundland fishing banks] with a half-cargo of cod'.[440]

Twenty years earlier, in 1682,[441] a routine consular report gave a list of silver exports to Europe over the preceding year: to Genoa and Livorno (especially Genoa) – 4,500,000 *écus*; to Holland, 3,500,000; to Britain, 2,500,000; to Saint-Malo, Le Havre,

FIGURE 72
The short trade cycle between Saint-Malo and the South Seas

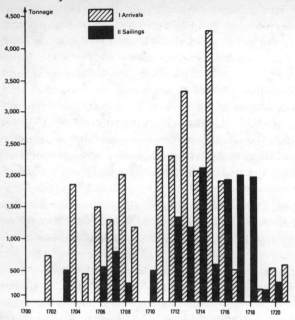

I: arrivals in Saint-Malo of ships from the South Seas
II: departures from Saint-Malo for the South Seas between 1701 and
1720
The departures are more significant than the arrivals, because while all
the ships returned to France, some of them were unloaded in other
ports. The major arrival of 1709 for instance does not figure here since
it landed its cargo at Auray.

Source: Jean Delumeau and colleagues, *Le Mouvement du port de Saint-
Malo, 1681–1720*, 1966.

Dunkerque and Marseille, 2,500,000 – of which Saint-Malo alone
probably received 2 million, thanks to twelve of its trading vessels.
One small detail: 'several of our [i.e. French] merchants have sent
good sums of money to England and Holland, claiming that money
earns slightly better interest there than in France'.

One could fill pages with evidence of this kind. Let me cite just
one final example, relating to a dramatic incident which remains

rather enigmatic and mysterious, but which allows a glimpse of the fraud involved in certain trading operations. The year was 1672. War between France and Holland had broken out in March; and the French army had invaded the United Provinces in May – but Spain had not yet intervened against France. On 16 October, a Spanish vessel, equipped with 50 cannon, and commanded by the duke of Veraguas, admiral of the fleet, came broadside on against the *Saint-Jacques*, a Saint-Malo vessel anchored in the bay of Cadiz, which was armed with 40 guns and carried a crew of 150. Veraguas ordered the French boat to stand by and be inspected by the Spanish authorities; the French refused; a second command met a second refusal; whereupon the Spanish ship fired at point-blank range. The French riposted but their powder-store caught fire and the Saint-Malo ship blew up, killing 100 men, including the captain. Did the *Saint-Jacques* have contraband goods aboard, as seems likely? Possibly, but then in Cadiz which ship did not? The *Saint-Jacques* however, according to the French consul, was 'carrying 300,000 *écus* in bars and many goods from the Indies'.[442]

The incident did not however – according to the documents I have read – have any direct consequence for French trade with Cadiz, even when Spain did enter the war. It is true that war in those days very rarely disrupted trade to any great extent. Ten years later, in 1682, a Saint-Malo ship left Cadiz, 'laden with over 200,000 *écus* in silver for French merchants', escorted by two French warships, the *Portefaix* and the *Tardif*. In 1689, French ships exported from Cadiz 1,884,000 *écus* bound for France and 205,000 bound for Genoa.[443] In short, links between Saint-Malo and Cadiz were maintained even during the fraught years of the Spanish war, and despite the blockade of the Spanish port by the Dutch and English. Such blockades could not last for ever. American silver unfailingly reached Cadiz and was re-exported all over Europe as if there was no war on at all.

It is in this international context that the extraordinary ventures of the ships of Saint-Malo in the South Seas should be placed, to be properly understood. Even so, early stages of this episode remain obscure. It seems to have begun in 1695. France and Spain were still at war (the peace of Ryswick was not signed until 1697). On

3 June 1695, a squadron of ships belonging to the king, under the command of one Monsieur de Gennes, 'who had a reputation for enterprise', sailed out of La Rochelle. Their destination was the Strait of Magellan on the way to the South Pacific. But the squadron failed to get through the Strait. Buffeted by fierce winds, it turned back into the Atlantic and moored at São Salvador in Brazil, before stopping for some time at the French island of Cayenne. It did not return to La Rochelle until 21 April 1697. It should not be concluded that the voyage was entirely fruitless; on the contrary, it seems to have been the first visible sign of a plan to reach the Pacific via the Strait route.[444]

This unsuccessful expedition had in fact been inspired by the tales of privateers returning to France, who had spent the previous ten years or so raiding with impunity the coasts and small merchant vessels of the Pacific. Piracy had therefore pointed the way. It may even be supposed that the Saint-Malo captains had obtained from the pirates information about the route to the Pacific and the secrets of successful operations there.[445] That at any rate is how I would interpret some of the details and admissions in the correspondence between the Parisian businessman Jourdan, the Saint-Malo shipowner Noël Danycan, and Pontchartrain, secretary of state for the navy, who protected these men and gave them the go-ahead. The associates wrote to Pontchartrain on 4 March 1698, just before going into action, that

> on the basis of the trade which the French, English and Dutch are carrying out illegally [*en fraude*] along the coasts of Mexico and the Coast of Cartagena, [they] have resolved to attempt something similar along the Spanish coasts of the southern sea.[446]

Along this coastline, bounded by immense deserts and where there were few European settlers, it would probably be easier to evade Spain's prohibition on foreigners trading with its colonies in America.

A few weeks later, on 20 May 1698, Jourdan and Danycan announced to Pontchartrain that they had formed a company to 'send 4 armed vessels to the South Sea, via the Strait of Magellan, in order to seize the said passage and set up establishments on the coast of Chile, even as far as California,[447] since they are occupied by no European power'.[448] This original company was very quickly transformed into a second[449] on 17 November the same year, Jourdan taking on his own account 13 of the 20 *sols* or shares[450] into which the company's capital was divided, with five other participants taking one each and the seventh, one Begon, taking two.[451] The details do not matter; more importantly, six months later, on 18 December 1698, Jourdan informed Pontchartrain that the 'starting pistol' had been fired at La Rochelle and that the four ships equipped for the South Seas would be 'setting sail at dawn' the following day.[452]

This operation, in which Saint-Malo's shipowners and captains would be the chief actors, was quite different from the 'wartime privateering' which had by the seventeenth century been to some extent codified between states, to the point of being regarded as legal *during wartime*, and in which Saint-Malo was a regular participant.[453] This new venture (since peace had been signed with Spain in 1697) was privateering pure and simple, although every attempt was made to conceal its character. This no doubt explains the creation in Saint-Malo – again in 1698 – of a *Compagnie de Chine* (China Company), whose founders declared that the two trades, China and the South Seas, were inseparable. Officially then, China was the destination of the expeditions.

But on 1 November 1700, Charles II of Spain died, and his designated heir was Louis XIV's grandson, the duc d'Anjou, who became Philip V. So until 1713, the crowns of France and Spain were united. The idea quickly dawned on the men of Saint-Malo that it might be possible to reach the Pacific with the agreement, the blessing and even the cooperation of the new king of Spain. This was indeed the gist of a proposal put forward by Jourdan on 30 July 1702, an unprecedented one, signed at Versailles, so probably devised in the corridors of power, and advanced according to Jourdan, 'both on my own behalf and that of M. Danycan of Saint-Malo, who gave me the order'. So far as I can tell, this project was never actually put into operation, but the plan is nevertheless a revealing one. Every year, it was proposed, two merchantmen and a frigate with 30 to 40 cannon – French vessels but flying the Spanish flag and under commission from the king of Spain – would sail for Peru and then on to the Philippines and China. They would be fitted out at Cadiz or La Corunna, and would return to a Spanish port, paying regular dues to the Spanish king. The avowed intention of the expedition (barely credible though it seems) was to rid the South Seas of interlopers, such as the Dutch and English, and also to interrupt the China trade with New Spain and Peru, which was costing Spain 3 million *écus* a year.[454] Should one call this naïvety or effrontery?

Probably the latter: the China Company set up at Saint-Malo was indeed intended to serve as a smokescreen for expeditions to the Pacific coast. I interpret in this sense one of Jourdan's letters to Pontchartrain: 'truly, China and the South Sea are so indivisible that it would be the ruin of either if they were to be separated'.[455] So one aim was certainly to bring together the gold of China and the silver of Potosi – in itself a most profitable enterprise[456] – having the ships call in the South Pacific both on the outward voyage to China and on the way back. Yet it was this very link between China and Peru, so injurious to Spanish interests, that the 1702 proposal was supposed to be preventing.

The Indies Company was another useful smokescreen. Being on the verge of bankruptcy, this company allowed the China Company to handle its far-off trade, the latter paying for the right to trade in Canton, which was a partial infringement of the former's monopoly. The operation did not bring immediate profits, but things improved for Saint-Malo with the sub-contracting agreements which followed between 1706 and 1714. The two last agreements, in 1712 and 1714, amounted to the virtual cession of the Indies Company monopoly. And in 1715, with the backing of Antoine Crozat, one of the great financiers of the time, a company was set up bearing the name the Saint-Malo East Indies Company. Between 1708 and 1713, Saint-Malo sent fifteen ships to the Indian Ocean – quite a feat in wartime.

What was more, after the outbreak of hostilities again in 1702, Saint-Malo had as usual immediately fitted ships to take part in 'wartime privateering'. A few years earlier, in 1696, a little fleet commanded by Duguay-Trouin, the son of a rich shipowner of Saint-Malo (who had entered the royal navy in 1693) had captured three ships of the Dutch East India Company. 'My backers', the victor declared, 'had returns of twenty to one'.[457] In October 1711, the same commander forced his way into the roads of Rio de Janeiro and held the city to ransom.

Finally, we might ask what was the result of these voyages to the Pacific – long and often uncomfortable ones: 'twenty to twenty-six months in 1701–9, at least three years after 1710'.[458] The ships had to put frequently into port for fresh water and rations, both in the Atlantic and the Pacific. At the end of the voyage, on the other hand, comfort was at hand. On the coast of Chile, at Concepciòn or Arica, small French colonies had been established, which could provide stopping-off points for food and trade. And manufactured goods, especially fabrics, could be exchanged without difficulty even in Callao, the port for Lima, where the ship put in on the pretext of embarking rations and water – all with the connivance of the local Spanish authorities. The goods were exchanged for silver, which was accepted in every form, coin or ingots. The Saint-Malo ships had a virtual monopoly here. 'Out of 133 French ships sent to the west coast of America between 1698 and 1724, for commercial purposes, 86 – that is two-thirds – were fitted either by the *négociants* of Saint-Malo or by the shipowning firms' which they managed.[459]

It is a wonder that none of the ships participating in this venture was wrecked, or rather perhaps one should pay tribute to the seamanship of the Saint-Malo sailors: the voyage was less risky, it is true, once the itineraries stopped using the dangerous Strait of Magellan in favour of sailing round Cape Horn. Were the Saint-Malo ships the first to round the Horn? Or were the Dutch first to do it as seems more likely? It does not greatly matter, for the point is that communications became so regular that very small boats of about 100 tons were making the trip, alongside merchantmen of 700 tons and frigates of between 250 and 400.

This was not only a feat for the ships and their crews, it was also a coup for the trading companies. Only the first expedition, in 1698, had made a loss. After that profits were often in the region of 200%.

And to add to the good fortune, the return voyages brought back to the French economy and the public coffers the silver which was indispensable both for trade and for heavy military expenditure. In 1709, a convoy of nine Saint-Malo ships, escorted by a royal vessel commanded by Chabert, carried to Auray in southern Brittany silver bullion officially reckoned to be worth 16 million *livres* (and probably nearer 30 million, since fraud and deception were not unknown). Did this shipment save Louis XIV's finances from disaster in that terrible year? It is not impossible.[460]

The surprising thing – but is it so surprising after all? – is that Saint-Malo's fortune, which was of very ancient origin, did not long outlast the end of the war (1713), although expeditions were still sailing to the Pacific until 1724.[461] Few details are known of these last voyages. In 1713, 'it is reported that there were still about 30 ships off the coast [of Peru], almost all of them French'.[462] But then, given the length of the voyage and the attraction of spoils, it was hardly possible to disengage from the South Sea trade overnight.

The upshot in any event was that the withdrawal sooner or later began to affect Saint-Malo. There were several reasons: the return of peace and the end of wartime privateering; the shift of prosperity towards the Atlantic and to the trio of seaports which would in the eighteenth century grow rich on the West Indies trade: Nantes, La Rochelle and Bordeaux; the revival of Spain under the Bourbons, who set about restoring order, with some success, on the coasts of Chile and Peru, if only after the voyage of Martinet's fleet in 1716. Indeed the French government provided assistance for this, at Spanish request. In fact, it was faced with the choice between illegal trafficking or official trade through Cadiz. It was essentially on the latter – always a profitable business – that the overall economic equilibrium of France depended.

Besides, the South Sea trade had required huge outlay, with expenses running at as much as a million *livres*, or even two, for every large ship. These were beyond the resources of the little port of Saint-Malo. Consequently this venture (and also the Indies trade and privateering expeditions) had begun to draw in capital from Paris, Nantes, Rouen, Marseilles and elsewhere. Even the prosperous shipowners of Saint-Malo – Magon (de la Lande and de la Chipaudière), Le Fer de Beauvais, Guillaume Eon, Naillon, Locquet de Granville, De La Haye, Gaubert, Danycan – who all seem to have been *bona fide* and very wealthy *négociants* – were not however in the same league as the great financiers and bankers of the later years of Louis XIV's reign, such as Samuel Bernard or Antoine Crozat, both of whom did have a finger in the Saint-Malo pie. So is it stretching the argument too far to wonder whether Saint-Malo had some underlying weakness, some inadequacy which was concealed during the years of prosperity, but appeared once more in leaner times? What had happened was that much of the available large-scale capital in France had been mobilized for privateering, for the South Sea trade and the voyages to China and India, guided by the hand of Pontchartrain, one of the secret masters of the country and a man who had personal contacts and sympathies with Saint-Malo. But on the death of Louis XIV, Pontchartrain was abruptly expelled from office. The Indies Company soon slipped out of Saint-Malo's hands, and after being reconstituted by John Law in 1719, it escaped the disasters of his famous System.

So after about 1713 to 1719, Saint-Malo lost the cooperation of the government and of French capital. The port returned to its former status. Its ships continued to go cod-fishing on the Newfoundland banks, and landing fish in Spain and throughout the Mediterranean; it retained its regular links with England and Holland, and still sent ships to Cadiz where they landed dried fish, Breton textiles and sometimes grain, bringing home silver in return, since they were regarded as safe transports.[463] But Saint-Malo's moment of glory was over. We know this since its most dynamic entrepreneurs went elsewhere to seek their fortunes, to other French ports like Nantes, or to Cadiz, or the Indian Ocean. Another significant point is that the town had no foreign-exchange market.[464] And despite many requests, it did not obtain the status of free port which might perhaps have saved it from its slide back to mediocrity.

But Saint-Malo's ultimate fate is not the most important problem raised by the story of these ventures in the early eighteenth century. It seems rather to me that what was happening in these action-packed years was that the port's enterprise was exerting an influence over the whole history of the kingdom. Already before the War of the Spanish Succession, France had opted for the silver of Cadiz. It would opt once more in its favour after the war, preferring safe and peaceful dealings with Cadiz to risky ventures in the South Seas. Was it a choice made unhesitatingly? At about the same time, the English, by the Methuen Treaty (1701), were opting for Lisbon and the gold of Brazil and the Braganzas. It was surely because of the Portuguese connection that England would soon, almost unintentionally, be going on to the gold standard, and that the other capitalist powers, Holland, Genoa, probably Venice, would also choose gold. France meanwhile remained faithful to silver. Napoleon in turn would allow himself to be tempted by the Spanish mirage.

Our last example is *Bordeaux in the eighteenth century*. Through the fortunes of Bordeaux, one can find out about the important West Indies trade in sugar, coffee, cotton, tobacco and indigo. This was a luxury trade, and essentially an episode, although it lasted a century, thanks to continual injections of energy.

Bordeaux, although the leading port for the import and resale of goods from the Caribbean, was not the only French port concerned. There was also Rouen, which provided an endless list of manufactured articles for export; Nantes, the capital of the slave trade; Dunkerque; and Marseille.

Nor did the West Indies represent all French interests in the New World: Canada and Louisiana were both French, though these vast expanses were slow to develop. La Rochelle was the chief port for Canada. But I have deliberately chosen to restrict the field of observation to the West Indies.

The first problem is to sort out which islands were French, which is no simple matter, since they are part of a vast complex of land and sea. The Spanish had gradually settled in the West Indies after Columbus's first landfall on 12 October 1492, on the island of Guadahani in the Bahamas, to which he gave the name San Salvador. They subsequently occupied Santo Domingo (1496), Puerto

Rico (1508), Jamaica (1509) and Cuba (1511). The last island, the largest of all, would be the base from which Cortez set sail for Mexico. Havana grew up at the meeting-point for the two fleets of the *Carrera de Indias*. The exactions of the Spanish and the diseases they brought with them decimated the indigenous population, while cattle brought from Spain reverted to the wild state and propagated themselves in the islands.

But the Spanish did not long remain unchallenged. The existence of these wild herds of cattle, which were easy prey, tempted adventurers – mostly French – to the islands. The name *boucaniers*, buccaneers, given to these marauders, comes from the *boucan*, the wooden grill on which they smoked the meat of the beasts they caught. By about 1630, the Dutch and the English were appearing in greater numbers. They destroyed the herds, forcing the buccaneers to turn pirates, joining the corsairs of Tortuga (Ile de la Tortue).[465] Were they eventually wiped out by the rival nations jostling for supremacy during the War of the Spanish Succession? Perhaps; or maybe the rewards of piracy were dwindling. At all events the pirates moved to the South Sea during the last two decades of the century. Meanwhile the English, French and Dutch had moved in to take possession of the islands, and to begin growing crops there. The English drove the Spanish from Jamaica in 1655. The Dutch seized Curação in 1634. The French took Martinique and Guadeloupe in 1635 and in 1659 occupied the western end of the Spanish island of Santo Domingo, possession of which was only recognized by the peace of Ryswick (1697). This was the largest French possession in the Caribbean (30,000 square kilometres)[466] and to the immense jealousy of the English, it was to be the scene of the greatest economic success of the region. Among other reasons this was because Saint-Domingue (the French name: it is now Haiti) had plenty of virgin soil to be exploited, which needed no fertilizer.

But until the end of the seventeenth century and even later, these overseas possessions were not really very significant. It was only with the cultivation of sugar cane and the development of the sugar industry that major change came in the eighteenth century.

Sugar cane was native to the plains of the Indus and Ganges, and spread slowly through tropical and semi-tropical regions. It reached China in the east, and its westward expansion took it through what Savary called the 'torrid zone', in other words the warmest zone of the Mediterranean, reaching Egypt in the tenth century, then the coastal plains of Cyprus: in the fifteenth century Cyprus had its 'sugar barons', the noble Venetian Cornaro dynasty, who owned vast plantations. During the enterprising fifteenth century, sugar cane was planted in Sicily, Valencia, the Sous valley in Morocco, then travelled to the Atlantic islands – Madeira, the Canaries, the Cape Verde islands. Finally, in the 1550s, the Brazilian coastline, from Santos in the south to Recife in the north, was planted with sugar cane: this was the age of the *enghenos de assucar* (sugar mills) which crushed the cane and extracted molasses, the age of the *senhores de enghenos*, seigneurs almost in the medieval sense – and it was the age of black slavery.

In the middle of the plantation stood the *case grande*, the master's house, and around it the *senzalas*, the houses of the slaves. Every sugar plantation in the eighteenth century reproduced the same pattern, the 'great house' as it was called in Jamaica, the slaves' dwellings and the industrial installations. When the Dutch captured the Brazilian Nordeste, the Recife region (the state of Pernambuco), it was the sugar plantations which they seized and exploited between 1630 and 1654. When they were expelled from their colony, there followed a wave of emigration by planters and sugar technicians, mostly 'New Christians', who went to seek their fortunes elsewhere. As Alice Piffer Canabrava long ago pointed out, the fortunes made from sugar in the West Indies were the result of this transfer of men and technology.[467] It was after this, at different dates and with varying degrees of success, that trade really took off in the Caribbean, in sugar above all, but also in *rocou* (orange dye), cotton, cocoa, ginger, tobacco and later coffee. Martinique and Guadeloupe began to prosper in about 1654, Saint-Domingue a little later, in about 1680, but it was very soon leading the way in production and trade.

The French West Indies were slightly reduced in extent in the eighteenth century. By the treaty of Paris in 1763, France had to cede the very small islands: St Kitts, Antigua, Montserrat,

Dominica, St Vincent, Barbados, Tobago, Grenada and the Grenadillos. The treaty of Versailles in 1783 brought back Tobago and St Bartholomew: but these losses and gains all concerned very small territories. The French position remained fairly stable, both in territorial possessions and in trade: the same products went on being sent back to France – more than half the total consisting of sugar. This Indies trade, originally in the hands of the Dutch, was taken over by the French in Colbert's day, with the establishment in 1664 of the French West Indies Company.[468] But it lost its privilege two years later. After that, 'all French vessels [were] equally welcome' to the islands.[469]

Exports from France to the West Indies also remained broadly the same. Food supplies had to be sent to islands now devoted to growing cash crops for export: so there were regular cargoes of flour, salt beef, pork, herring and cod, wine and oil. Then there were manufactured articles, many of them shipped via Rouen: needles, pins, shoes, beaver hats, silk and woollen hose, textiles, blankets, glassware, copper boilers and vats for the processing of sugar. Bordeaux, which had links with Aquitaine, sent casks of flour (ground by the mills along the Garonne), wine and various industrial products, since the town had good communications with almost all the provinces where they were manufactured. The islands were also provided with slaves from the Guinea coast: the slave-traders usually sailed from Nantes on a regular three-sided itinerary (Nantes, Guinea, the islands, then back to Nantes). They took special cargoes to be used for barter on the African coast – spirits, cotton cloth, guns – which were exchanged for slaves. In the Indies, the holds of the slave-ships were re-arranged in order to carry cases of sugar or sacks of coffee back to France. Meanwhile there were more and more black slaves in the islands: 500,000 on Saint-Domingue just before the Revolution. A series of disturbances, revolts, attacks and escapes culminated eventually in the uprising of 1791.

Traffic between France and the islands was considerable (for the time) as is evident from the number of French ships doing the crossing: over a thousand during the prosperous period that followed the Seven Years' War (1756–63). Up to 80 ships could be seen landing or embarking goods on the Martinique coast. In 1778, the value of this trade reached 210 million *livres*, that is a third of all France's foreign trade.[470]

The formal monopoly by France of all colonial trade continued to operate, despite some local smuggling, and the French merchants and authorities controlled all trade links, watching jealously over what they regarded as their private property, defending it against allcomers, through the ups and downs of war. Strictly speaking, from the point of view of the trade balance, this trade regularly operated at a loss, but we have already noted[471] what really lay behind the deficit: a vast network of controlled trade in which goods sent from Bordeaux regularly doubled in price on the other side of the Atlantic. The dates of voyages and the volume of cargoes were moreover calculated in such a way that European goods remained sufficiently scarce in the islands for the price to remain high, while the sugar was collected soon enough after harvest to be still good value for money.[472] On the homeward voyage, in the examples studied by Michel Morineau, the value of the return cargo also went up by about 20%. This was however the riskiest part of the operation, depending on prices of colonial produce in Europe, where there was Dutch and English competition. Bordeaux in fact re-exported most of its imports: 87% of the sugar, 95% of the coffee and 76% of the indigo, in about 1787 for instance.[473]

So the West Indies trade was part of a 'complex exchange system', in which wine and flour came from the Gironde valley, salt beef was often bought directly from Ireland, and where Bordeaux *négociants* were not above even speculating in money itself, which was treated as merchandise. In 1729, a 'register of the cargo of 123 vessels leaving Bordeaux for America' pointed out that a true record would include 'a list of the "short" piastres which *négociants* have been sending to America for the last two or three years, and which bring back a sure profit of 50%' – this trade being kept secret since it was 'expressly forbidden'.[474]

In short, the profits from the West Indies trade were substantial; and they played a vital part in the rise of Bordeaux in the eighteenth century. In 1700, the city had 45,000 inhabitants; by 1747 there were 60,000 and on the eve of the Revolution over 110,000. This was a far faster rate of increase than would have been found in Marseille, Paris or any other French city.[475] In fact, the transatlantic trade brought a belated revolution to Bordeaux. Having so long been a wine port, having grown rich on wine, and become used to seeing foreign fleets and merchants taking Bordeaux wines all over Europe, Bordeaux had never been a centre for shipbuilding, nor did it have a large population of sailors. The sharp fall of its traditional exports during the War of the Spanish Succession, and the opening up of the English market to Portuguese products, including port wines, had severely affected the French city. This crisis, followed by government measures – in particular the letters patent of 1717 which designated Bordeaux and twelve other ports as the only authorized departure points for trade with 'the French islands in America', and finally the initiatives launched by new men, all contributed after 1720 to make the city a naval and shipowning centre.[476]

These new men, some of them bourgeois of Bordeaux, others foreign merchants who had come as immigrants, grew rich very quickly. Examples are the Schylers, originally from Hamburg, or the great Jewish Gradis dynasty originally from Portugal; the Bonaffés, from the Languedoc, who made a fortune from shipfitting and commissions; the Journus, whose fortune was based on drugs and who set up a network made up of members of a particularly large family, scattered in all the strategic ports.[477] But these *négociants* remained very few in number, a small fraction of the 800 'merchants and *négociants*' who represented *the entire trade* of the city in about 1790, making up 11% of the population.[478] Similarly in Rouen, the *Almanach* of merchants for 1779, which draws a distinction between the two, lists only 61 shipowning merchants and export dealers, the 'capitalists of the period', and the most important people in the city.[479]

It is clear that French transatlantic trade in the eighteenth century was an interlocking system. The islands were under a slave-owning regime harsher even than in antiquity, but extremely productive, particularly since it contributed to a fast-expanding capitalist regime back in France. The difference in voltage was one of the secrets of success. Obviously, contained as it was within a theoretically[480] closed circuit, the system was vulnerable to risk and damage. War was a major threat, but the system survived this more or less intact. In any case, the planters in British-owned Jamaica did everything to prevent their country from annexing the French islands which were their direct competitors. Another possibility was that the supply of black slaves from Africa might have run out – but this never happened. And freight prices on the Atlantic run might have become prohibitive, but that never happened either.

In the end it was the very success of the system which brought about its downfall: too many black slaves. On 28 March 1790, the Constituent Assembly granted them their freedom and political rights. In 1791, there was an uprising in Saint-Domingue, led by Toussaint L'Ouverture. After this it became impossible to restore white domination and the colonial order in the island. Sugar was in any case being produced elsewhere (in Guadeloupe and Martinique among other places) and was not in short supply in Europe, where sugar beet would soon be appearing. Besides, the Indies trade, a luxury trade of archaic type on account of its reversion to slavery on the ancient model, conflicted with changing attitudes in Europe. And international trade was also changing: in the nineteenth century, the chief goods carried would be bulky raw materials such as coal, iron and grain.

Problems still seeking an answer

Trade in France, as elsewhere, witnessed a series of successive cycles, long-lived in the case of Marseille between 1569 and 1650; almost as long in the case of Bordeaux and the West Indies between 1720 and 1791; more short-lived in the case of the Saint-Malo venture which lasted at most from 1698 to 1724. If the history of trade ever moves beyond the descriptive stage, it may one day be able to explain the patterns and regular features of these commercial cycles. The three examples examined here suggest few explanations beyond the most obvious ones: all these trade links depended on the many networks operating in the world as a whole. Nowadays these are established or broken more quickly than in the past. Even so, successes which lasted a century or so, such as those of Marseille or Bordeaux, remained very much the exception in the past. We have somehow to explain such exceptions, if only by Europe's collective passions which sometimes reached fever pitch, such as the medieval taste for spices; the later cravings for spirits, coffee and tobacco; or in our own time the unhealthy addiction to hard and soft drugs. Success might also depend on good organization: no commerce was possible without good contacts, local representatives and established networks.

The question of the trade balance brings a different perspective to bear on what is essentially a similar problem. Any positive balance was the result of a production effort, with the mobilization of a large surplus of labour. If in the nineteenth century the balance went into deficit, it was because the export of French capital allowed such a luxury – for luxury it was. In our own time, on the other hand, the foreign-trade deficit which preoccupies governments so much must be reckoned to be a weakness, or at any rate a dangerous luxury, since it creates debts, prejudicing the future. But in normal times, exports and imports have tended to be roughly in balance; compared to national income as a whole, the trade surplus or deficit is usually only a small percentage. So it still remains a problem to discover how this phenomenon, basically of minor proportions, is still able, today as in the past, to influence the entire course of the national economy.

I do not know what the answer is. But perhaps matters would be clearer if it were possible to work from the bottom up and demonstrate something I feel in my bones to be the case, namely:

– that the lowest levels of the economy balance out spontaneously within a certain number of local trade circuits, which change comparatively little over time, and that these short-distance flows provide their own energy, which is entirely expended at this level;
– that the foreign-trade side of the economy rarely has any contact with this elementary level, that it limits the impacts which its own mechanisms create; by being thus delimited, the flow of foreign trade is in fact strengthened;

– that foreign trade in part depends on the international economy, which may limit or encourage it, but in all cases controls it.

That said, we should not imagine that the entire economy of any nation would be capable of responding at every level to the stimulus of foreign trade. Only a section of the economy is really affected – like the smock windmills one used to see with a mobile top section that swivelled according to the wind. So simplifying wildly, let us imagine a straight line passing through Paris, and being able to swivel at that point. If the line runs east-west, you have a picture of France in the fifteenth century, divided in half: the south is being stimulated by the proximity of the Mediterranean, while the north remains more backward. After the sixteenth century, the axis tends to move into a longitudinal position: the west begins to open up to the Atlantic, taking advantage of the creation of the ocean-going trade, and receives an inflow of silver. Meanwhile the eastern half, Burgundy for instance, is still using copper currency. In the seventeenth century, the axis shifts back to a more latitudinal position, with this time the north as beneficiary. There is a clear pull in the direction of Holland: it was Amsterdam, rather than the Sun King, which determined the French climate. Later still, it would be London, probably until the eve of World War II. And what about France today? The so-called 'French desert' is mostly in the west, while eastern France is under the sway of the dominant German economy.

This outline is suggested as a theoretical model, one that needs to be verified at detailed level, in the first place by establishing with precision the itineraries of the major trade circuits: there is still an entire geometry and geography of trade to be reconstituted. And one must bear in mind that mobility is always located at the higher levels of the economy, compared with the relative inertia of the base.

What we can at present glimpse of French commerce, although as yet without enough evidence, draws attention to these higher levels, which were more alert, easier for people to move and develop with the times, and located at the cutting edge of what I consider to have been the essential capitalism emerging in French history.

CHAPTER FIFTEEN

At the Pinnacle of the Hierarchy: Capitalism

To have introduced the word *capitalism* at the end of this long section does, I admit, complicate our task. But how else could this investigation be completed? The words *capital, capitalist* (and *capitalism* which broadens their scope) occupy key positions in any field of economic observation. So how can one leave them out if the picture is to be complete?

Capital, according to the most usual definition, represents accumulated previous labour, which is reintroduced into the production process. In this sense, it is present in every sector of human life, and in all eras. According to the economist Charles Gide (uncle of the novelist André Gide), 'capital . . . is as old as the first stone axe-head';[481] one might equally say as old as the first digging stick, 'the most primitive agricultural implement',[482] or *a fortiori* the pickaxe or plough.[483]

Capitalism, used of capitalists, but meaning 'nothing more than the mobilization of capital' – an obviously very minimal definition[484] – also has an extremely long pedigree. So, unlike some critics, I am not at all shocked that Marcel Laffont Montels should have called the book he wrote in 1938 *Les Etapes du capitalisme de Hamourabi à Rockefeller* (*The Stages of Capitalism from Hammurabi to Rockefeller*), nor that Theodore Mommsen, the great historian, should have spoken of capital and capitalists apropos of ancient Babylon – to Marx's great disapproval.

But neither *capitalists* nor *capitalism*, unlike *capital*, enjoy the privilege of being ubiquitous in a given economy or society. They are in practice confined to the highest and most sophisticated levels of economic life, where they are normally to be found. Capitalism does, it is true, inevitably spill over on to lower levels, but it remains above all a superstructural phenomenon, at the pinnacle of all hierarchies. To look down from this height would be to survey the whole of the economy from above, which is why I like to use the word *superlative* of capitalism.

Capital, capitalists and capitalisms

Jacques Laffitte, in 1824, suggested a distinction which may seem a little late and a little too clear-cut, but it does enable us to consider the possible diversity that has always existed between types of capital, types of capitalist and consequently between varieties of capitalism.

> Capital [he writes] does not *always* belong [my italics] to those who use it. On the contrary, those who own capital and are popularly known as 'rich men' [Turgot and his contemporaries would in fact have said *capitalists*, well before Laffitte's day] tend not to put it to use themselves, but to lend it to others who are obliged to work, on condition they receive a share of the product, thereby enabling them to live without exertion.[485]

This dividing line is a major frontier in economic life, perhaps the most important one, but it would be wrong to think of it as clear-cut. As an owner of capital, it would be quite possible for me to finance my own enterprise, while being at the same time both a *rentier* capitalist, and an employee in someone else's enterprise. But if we accept Laffitte's distinction, we should not simply assume, as his illustrious contemporary David Ricardo did, that the distinctive function of the banker begins at the point 'where he uses other people's money'. This famous formula could have been applied equally well to a merchant, a *négociant* and before long to an industrial entrepreneur, all of whom were also 'using other people's money'.

Thus, if I am not mistaken, the higher level of the economy can be divided into two parts: one in which capital accumulates, stagnates, and if hoarded may even become sterile; and another in which it is poured into the production process, as water is channelled towards the millwheel. This distinction makes it easy to understand why capital drawn into production should be considered 'true' capital, fulfilling its proper function, while the other kind, 'false' capital, is to be condemned as lying idle, having been withdrawn from production and the public weal. Joseph Chappey once spoke of 'dead money': is there such a thing as 'dead capital'?[486]

I have to say that I think this view fundamentally mistaken. I will not risk trying to justify the accumulation and hoarding of capital. But setting moral considerations aside, I am persuaded that active capitalism is only possible thanks to the capitalist pool made up of those who possess money. The latter is the condition of the former, the reservoir from which water-courses and streams are constantly released, at greater or less rates of flow. I even doubt whether there is any such thing as dead or inert capital: the volume of water (or money) creates such pressure that some must always be spilling over the top.

I am reminded of a little story, not even an event really, which occurs in the *Mémoires de Monsieur de Gourville*.[487] It dates from the beginning of Louis XIV's reign, in 1663. The memorialist had returned to Brussels, which he tells us,

> I found more agreeable than anywhere else. Monsieur le marquis de Sillery was good enough to visit me, and since he told me he would like to go to Antwerp, I accompanied him there. I took him to see, as a person out of the ordinary, Monsieur de Palavicine,[488] one of the richest men in the world, but who did not think himself so. I told [M. de Palavicine] that he ought to go to some expense on our behalf . . . offer us a few meals, and that he ought to provide at least a coach and six for us to travel about in. He took it upon himself to explain to Monsieur de Sillery that he was not as rich as people thought, and showing us a cabinet alongside his bedroom, he gave us to understand that there were a hundred thousand *écus*' worth of silver bars in there, which did not

587

fetch him in a penny . . . and that he had a hundred thousand *livres* in the Bank of Venice which did not even pay him three per cent, and that in Genoa, his native city, he had four hundred thousand *livres*, which paid him scarcely any more interest, and he always ended up saying that it did not bring him in much at all. After we had left him, Monsieur de Sillery confessed to me that he could scarcely credit . . . what he had seen, and since then, he has several times said to me that after returning to Paris he regretted not having told Molière about it, so that he could have put this scene in his comedy *L'Avare* [*The Miser*]

– which would have been theoretically possible, since *L'Avare* was only performed on stage for the first time in 1668.

I do not quote this story – which in any case takes us outside France – simply as an example of avarice. It is admittedly interesting to hear of a capitalist who took his cautious – and apparently resigned – inactivity to such extremes. And it is also interesting to find incidentally that the heir to the great Pallavicini dynasty, which had been fabulously wealthy in Genoa before the fifteenth century, was still a man of fabulous wealth. So contrary to what both Henri de Pirenne and the vicomte d'Avenel believed, not every fortune, not every form of capitalist activity lapsed *ipso facto* as if by some inexorable law, after two or three generations, to make way for the rising stars. Pallavicini at least shows us that. But above all, this example surely proves that capitalism apparently dormant and buried was often only apparently inert. Not only because the silver bars were so to speak their owner's nest-egg, something to count on, so that if the need should arise, he might sell one or more of them on the Antwerp money market, but also because his deposits in Venice and Genoa were, without his knowledge, being channelled into the world of business by these solidly established banks which enjoyed universal confidence. His capital was in fact being put to work.

So by virtue of its very mass and the need to put it somewhere, 'immobile' money was in fact circulating and 'living again'. Other outlets for it were inheritances and their surprises, or the money the prodigal threw out of the window; then there were dowries, moral obligations within the family which could not be completely ignored; there was the temptation to invest some of one's capital via the reassuring mediation of the notary, or the banker, or to advance some of it to the *partisans*, the tax-farmers who lent money to the king.

In short, there was inevitably some communication between living capital and more or less inert capital, with part of the latter always turning into the former. And this phenomenon is all the more significant, today as in the past, since (as the lists of those paying the wealth tax in France since 1981 would probably demonstrate), the richest people in the country are not necessarily the most active capitalists.

The weight of sleeping capital

This store of hoarded money constituted a mass of reserves, securities and guarantees for the whole economy. It was like a sponge saturated with water. The question is, did it release it regularly, playing its proper role in France?

It certainly did so very inadequately, but the answer must be that yes, it did, after a fashion – for credit was never really organized during the *ancien régime* or indeed until about 1850. In Paris, there were about a hundred bankers – of varying significance – but then Paris was Paris and this was in 1789. At the same time, Rouen, although a leading city and an important commercial centre, had only four bankers.[489] So to obtain 'advances' one had perforce to approach the 'gentlemen with fat purses', to go cap in hand and very often to wait a long time to get anything.

Jean-François Fréal for instance, a textile manufacturer and merchant of Laval, borrowed in 55 different operations between 1746 and 1770 a total of 282,093 *livres* at 5% (that is 13,625 francs in interest) from noblemen, clerics, bourgeois, notaries and even artisans, on the strength of mere promissory notes.[490] He cannot have done so without problems and arguments, or so I imagine from the chance survival of documents from the same period giving a day-by-day record of the incredible and indeed insoluble difficulties encountered by a leading merchant of Rouen, Robert Dugard, in his search for capital. In 1749, he had founded at Darnetal, a suburb of Rouen, a textile mill and dye-works. Now he needed more money to get the enterprise off the ground. His Paris associate, Louis Jouvet le Jeune, moved heaven and earth trying to find backers, who kept defaulting. 'Hold on,' he wrote to the impatient Dugard, 'everything takes time, especially this kind of enterprise, where one cannot be too circumspect . . . Anyone less timid or with more wit than I might have obtained money at first asking, but I am afraid to have doors closed against me, because once they are shut, there is no point in applying there again.' The venture ended in failure.[491]

I could quote similar examples from Dijon or Armagnac in the nineteenth century, but it would be much the same story. And what concerns us here is that the abnormal difficulty in obtaining credit in France, as compared with England, coexisted with considerable amounts of 'sleeping' capital. One only realizes how much there was in this, the second sector of capitalism, when these reserves of money were provoked into the open by extraordinary circumstances. If a region was hit by some natural disaster for instance, money appeared as if by magic from its secret hiding-places to meet the emergency and help its owners through hard times – to the great surprise sometimes of eye-witnesses.

In 1708 for instance, the War of the Spanish Succession had been going on for seven years; the state's coffers were empty and proving hard to fill, so a cash loan was needed. There was no shortage of money. The problem was that the treasury had been issuing paper currency since 1701, and had been doing so increasingly without saying so, as a correspondent of the controller-general of finance explained in a letter from Rennes on 6 March that year:

> One of the leading townsmen of this city . . . being, through his present commerce, of which he has long experience on both land and sea, well acquainted with the best-known *négociants* of the province . . . assured me that he knew for a fact that there were more than 30 million piastres hidden away and over 60 millions in gold and silver which would

never see the light of day until paper money[492] . . . has been thoroughly exhausted, and until cash is in moderate supply and commerce restored to better health.[493]

So poverty-stricken Brittany was concealing buried treasure. The explanation, in 1708, may be that thanks to its merchants, the provincial authorities and its own Hôtel des Monnaies (mint), Rennes had come to share in the dazzling fortunes of Saint-Malo, whose sea-captains had succeeded in obtaining bullion from the mines in Chile and Peru. Rennes was the gainer and its reserves swelled. But they would only be disbursed with the greatest caution.

Twenty years later, and still in Brittany, this time in Nantes, the date is 20 March 1726:

> We only became aware of the strength and resources of our city [a report reads] on the occasion of the project devised by our merchants either to embark on their own account in the King's commerce [i.e. the Compagnie des Indes, the French Indies Company] or to associate themselves for the same purpose with the merchants of Saint-Malo who are very powerful. The latter course has been chosen, in order not to hinder one another and the association is to be known as the Saint-Malo Company. It turns out that the subscriptions from our merchants amount to 18 million, whereas we thought they would not be able to put up more than four million altogether. Nine ships are being made ready to set sail as soon as the freedom of shipping is restored . . . We hope that the huge sums being offered at Court in order to procure the ending of the exclusive privilege of the Indies Company, which is ruining the kingdom, will encourage it to make trading free generally.[494]

We may note in passing that this time it was the merchants who were hoarding cash.

Otherwise, this quotation requires no comment. It well illustrates the point I am making, namely that France (like China or India, *mutatis mutandis*) was the graveyard of precious metals, swallowing them up and turning them all too easily into accumulated savings. This propensity, for better or for worse, would last well beyond the *ancien régime*. In the nineteenth century, the mass of money accumulated in France was comparable to that in the rest of Europe put together. During the short but sharp international crisis of 1857, beginning in the United States, where banks crashed one after another and 5,000 firms went bankrupt, first England was affected by the panic, then virtually the whole of Europe in a chain reaction – Germany, Denmark, northern Italy, Vienna, Warsaw. France escaped to some extent, because French banks, despite some expansion in the early years of the Second Empire, were simply not an exposed enough target: deposits totalled only 120 million francs, 'whereas hoarded savings were estimated at 3,000 million. The famous woollen stocking [full of coins] helped France to escape disaster. But it was a brake on the growth of French companies and remains so today.'[495]

If we jump another fifty years, we find Alfred Neymarck, the economist and statistician, going into raptures in 1906 at the proverbial latent wealth hidden under French mattresses. 'Why on earth', he wondered, 'should France be the biggest reservoir of capital in the world?.'[496] The 1929 crisis, a far more serious one than 1857, affected France only belatedly. Was it partly because people were able to live on their savings? In 1945, Léon Schick, a banker with a taste for history, set out to reassure the French by calculating the immense amount of gold they still possessed![497]

This passion, or mania, for saving, which is a constant in French history, was by no means confined to the rich or even comfortably off. There were the many small savings of the poor and the not so poor, the fruits of often desperate efforts to introduce some security to lives perpetually under threat. Pitifully little money ever fell into such people's hands, but royal taxation had forced open the village economy, obliging the peasants to engage in what Pierre Goubert calls 'the difficult quest for hard cash'.[498] The only way to provide for a rainy day was to obtain a gold or silver coin and keep it carefully hidden away. In 1786, disastrous flooding in 'a rich province', obliged the peasants to 'dip into their secret hoards, and everyone was astonished to see suddenly in circulation a remarkable quantity of gold *louis*, in mint condition, dating from the re-coining of 1726: they had come literally out of the ground'.[499] This widespread peasant hoarding increased in the nineteenth century. And paradoxically, it was the poorer regions, as an observant witness remarked in 1815 of the Morvan, which were 'richer in coin than the more prosperous farming regions, . . . for contrary to all the maxims of modern economists, it is always in places where the least money is available that more is left'.[500]

Certainly the passion for hoarding on the part of ordinary people, since there were so many of them, in itself immobilized the greater part of money in circulation. Herbert Lüthy, the historian of Protestant banking, wrote of France under Louis XIV that it was a 'land without banks and a land of frequent devaluation of the currency . . . as well as a land of hoarded treasure, where precious metals seem to have been swallowed up by the earth'.[501]

Not all French savings were reduced to the fate of dormant capital hoards, of course. But Turgot, recalling the view of his mentor Vincent de Gournay (1712–59), put his finger on the trouble, when he expressed fears that rich men would be unwilling to take the risk of investing in business, preferring the quiet life offered by investing at a guaranteed rate of interest. Thus at every turn and change of circumstances, there would be a more or less attractive interest rate, which would determine the movement of capital. This was indeed the role played by 'rent' (la rente) in France since the sixteenth century: rent was a sort of perpetual annuity, registered before the notary and transmissible to one's heirs. A similar kind of investment was the prêt à la grosse aventure (large-scale loan) which was one way for négociants, usually associated in partnership (commandite) for maritime ventures, to obtain money from outside the clan for a particular expedition.[502]

Maritime insurance was another kind of loan. And there were also simply short-term loans, made through a banker or notary, in which case the lender trusted the intermediary to choose borrowers who were a good risk. This was the option chosen in the 1820s (at a time when interest rates were low, about 4 or 5%) by a former settler on St Thomas in the Virgin Islands, who had retired to his estate in Armagnac to produce brandy.[503]

Beyond these simple and recognized forms of investment, it is not always easy to trace the streams into which dormant or so-called dormant capital might be channelled. The nobility for instance was supposed to be living off its income from the land. Active capital was in a sense ruled out for it, and ancient noble families suffered sometimes acutely from falling incomes in the sixteenth century. I shall have occasion to refer to this later, but to suggest the complexities of this issue briefly, what would you make of the two pieces of 'society' gossip which the Russian ambassador at Versailles passed on to his government in November 1785? The first was the death of the duc d'Orléans (the father of Philippe-Egalité) who left his heir an income of 4,800,000 *livres* 'and no debts';[504] the second was the marriage between Necker's daughter and Baron de Staël. Necker's personal fortune, we are told on this occasion, provided him with an annual income of 100,000 *livres*. Setting these two figures side by side gives one to reflect: ancient accumulation (of land in theory, but also of allowances and pensions from the king) amounted to far more than the income from financial capitalism – not working flat out it is true, since from the day Necker entered the government probably no more than half his wealth, if that, was invested in banking. As for the fortune of the duc d'Orléans, it was certainly not dormant or inert: it was managed by trusted men, who invested in a series of enterprises – canals, property speculation and so on.[505] There is a good thesis subject there somewhere.

Another good subject would be a general study of the *sociétés en commandite*, or limited partnerships (difficult as it would be to penetrate the maze of notarial acts). These partnerships financed most industrial investment in the eighteenth century and the principal shareholders were originally wealthy merchants, financiers and Parisian bankers – few in number but rich in resources. Then, towards the middle of the century, noblemen began investing heavily in mines (as at Anzin), in the glassworks at Saint-Gobain, the foundries of Cosne and so on.[506] The nobility had converted to active capitalism.

Credit remained hard to find however and industrial investment short of funds, in the eighteenth and even the nineteenth centuries. The great event in this context was the creation after 1850 of provincial branches of the main banks, which soon became numerous and for the first time succeeded in tapping the reserves locked up in savings. This brought about a decisive acceleration in the circulation of the money supply as important, according to one historian,[507] as the railway revolution – and who would disagree? Its large quantities of specie made France the richest country in Europe, by the criteria of Colbert and Cantillon, for whom wealth meant gold and silver. But in economic terms, as I must keep stressing, France was very far from leading the field. Indeed it was not even immune from cash shortages – 'money famine' was not uncommon throughout the country.

The volume of dormant capital must be regarded as partly responsible for this paradox. Boisguillebert, a more lucid observer than the mercantilists, said: 'the body of France suffers when money is not in perpetual motion'.[508] What was the good of a blood supply if it did not flow? But absence of movement is not entirely explained by the gap between inert, motionless money and living, circulating money. It can also be attributed to the relation between the mass of coin and that of paper money, the 'pseudo-money' which was so much easier to move about. France was in fact one of the last countries in Europe to change over from metal to paper. Before 1750, 93% of all transactions in France were made in metal and only 7% in banknotes.[509] By 1856, the proportion of banknotes had miraculously risen to 20% – but at the same date in England, paper money accounted for 67% of the total![510] So the history of capital accumulation in France is the history primarily of metal coin.

Metal coins: stocks and flow

French economists in the early nineteenth century went to enormous lengths to explain to their readers that cash in hand, metal coins, did not account for the whole of so-called capital goods. This may seem obvious, but Jean-Baptiste Say (1767–1832), the leading academic economist and the author of what was to be for years to come the economists' bible, thought it necessary in 1828 to issue a long warning: 'Despite all the various forms capital can take', he wrote, 'why is the habit so entrenched of regarding a sum of *écus* as the only kind of capital, and of measuring the capital wealth of a country by the number of *écus* to be found there?'[511] 'French capital', he goes on to say later, 'consists of many other values besides the currency.'[512] It is of course impossible to quarrel with him. But should one all the same play down the role of liquid cash? It was after all the most convenient, valid and expeditious form of capital good; protean in character, it was by far the most commonly used form of capital. What was more, it held its value. For the *négociant* or merchant, Marx's formula is quite correct: start off with money, exchange it for goods, then turn it back into money again.

But nothing so distorts analysis as the very banality of the every-day occurrence: something one sees happening all the time tends to become invisible. By the time of Jean-Baptiste Say, the monetarization of the French economy, while not complete, was an established and normal phenomenon. In earlier times, it had been natural for observers to express surprise at the role and power of money. Eon for instance, writing in 1647, sang its praises:

> Consider now, I beg you, what would become of us, if we were reduced to losing all use of money by a general collapse, and if we had to take an ox or a cow to the draper's shop in order to buy some cloth. And what a hardship it would be to have to go travelling on a long voyage of two or three hundred leagues, without a single penny in our pockets.[513]

This engaging passage reminds us that money released people from barter.

Turgot himself, a century later, in about 1770, was still not speaking the same language as Say. He did make a distinction between capital in kind (houses, property), and in value, in 'masses of money'. But he stressed that money (that is currency), 'repre-sents any accumulated value or *capital* [my italics] and that the circulation of money . . . being useful and fructifying . . . stimulates all the labours of society'.[514] Turgot will bring more comfort than Say to those historians who regard money as having been originally, as Pierre Chaunu[515] puts it, 'the accelerator par excellence of communication' – or as I would rather say 'of circulation' or better still, 'of increased economic activity'. It was also the ultimate weapon of the modern state in its struggle against other states, and indeed its 'indispensable foundation'.[516] And it was the basic guarantor and reference of value, that vague and disturbing word in all economic theory. 'All values and even certain businesses', wrote the Dutchman Van der Meulen in 1779, 'bear a direct relation to the universal measure, that is to say to money, and not to paper or credit which serves only to depreciate it.'[517]

Coin, cash in hand, which has played so conspicuous a part in French history, did not of course represent all economic life. But flowing through the economy, stimulating it and in turn being stimulated by it, money did impose certain constraints on economic life, and at the same time offered it certain possibilities of action, to which I would like to draw attention. It is the case that active capitalism has always manipulated currency, even tending to identify itself with this indispensable instrument. Consequently, it displays a certain number of typical characteristics. J. F. Soulet has even described capitalism in the age of Turgot as 'real and monetary'.[518]

We should not forget that the mass of money in question was already quite considerable by the sixteenth century.

In 1500, there were some 30 million *livres tournois* in circulation in France; by 1600, perhaps 80 million.[519] By the time of Colbert, between 1661 and 1683, the total money supply may have been as much as 200 million. A report probably dating from 1706,[520] estimates it at 250 million *livres*, 'in cash', to which should be added 50 million in paper money, 12 of which the government envisaged reimbursing, about 300 million in all. But these 300 million *livres* are probably only a fraction of the real money supply, representing what was effectively in circulation. The mass of 'dead money' was approximately equivalent to the mass in circulation, if we are to believe Jean-Baptiste Say, who thought that France divided its money supply in two: 50% in circulation, 50% hoarded away. So too thought François Mollien (1758–1850), Napoleon's treasury minister, who in 1810 estimated that at most two-thirds of the money supply was 'actively employed'. So when Pottier de la Hestroye, in his criticism of Vauban's *Dîme royale*, affirms that France had a total circulation of 460 million *livres* in 1704 (not counting 'what private individuals have kept at home without exchanging it'),[521] should one conclude that this sum, almost double the total mentioned in the report of 1706, corresponded to the real total – that is, what was in circulation plus what was hoarded?

Much later, in 1786, Necker estimated the total French money supply as 2,200 million *livres tournois*.[522] Arnould at about the same time put it at 1,900 million. Let us say roughly 2,000 million. And in 1809, since the money supply of Europe as a whole was estimated at 9,000 million,[523] the figure for France alone was probably about 4,000 to 5,000 million – about half the currency of Europe. It had certainly grown rapidly. The mercantilists of the eighteenth century would have been delighted. Goudar, one of the last of the faithful, was quite categorical in 1756: 'I maintain that . . . the more specie there is in a state, the richer and more opulent that state is.'[524]

The superabundance of specie is undeniable, but wealth was another matter. As we have seen, shortages of currency and cash-flow crises were frequent. In Orléans in February 1691, when newly-minted coin failed to arrive, and was unobtainable, there was 'a breakdown in commerce such as you would not believe'.[525] In November 1693, in Tours,

> the scarcity of money is so strongly felt in this province . . . that yesterday there was not enough money to employ the workmen, virtually no one came to change. This shortage is attributed to the conveyance to Paris which the *fermiers-généraux* and other persons, and the king's tax collectors arrange, of all the money they receive, without spending any of it here.[526]

But even in Paris, there was tension. As one anxious correspondent wrote to the Controller-General Desmarets, 'Your Eminence is informed of the disturbance caused by the lack of circulation of money, causing most businessmen to be unable to settle their debts honourably, although they have plenty of goodwill and paper currency.' Every year, depending on circumstances, cash was plentiful in some quarters, scarce elsewhere. As late as 1838, Autun, a town where there were many wealthy landed proprietors but not much commerce, was overflowing with money, while it was in short supply comparatively nearby, in Dijon.[527] Distance and freight charges played their part in these imbalances. Within France, until 1848, there was a sort of internal exchange market, with the Paris franc or *livre* having a different value from that in Lyon or other cities.[528]

Metal itself was part of the explanation. If France had more cash than any other nation in Europe, but was still capable of running short, it was not simply as Ange Goudar thought in 1756, because French coins had 'the vice' of being turned into gold and silver objects or plate. It was also, perhaps especially, because metal was heavy to move around. 200,000 *écus* weighed a ton; transport between Lyon and Paris required at least ten days.[529] Finally, large as it was, the mass of money played a limited role. The very dimensions of the kingdom, 400,000 square kilometres, inevitably had an effect on the velocity of circulation.

When all is said and done, the monetarization of the French economy remained terribly incomplete: it is scarcely exaggerating to say it irrigated only the uppermost level. At the beginning of the eighteenth century, in Picardy and Artois, which were far from poverty-stricken provinces,

> payment in cash [by the peasants] was still rare . . . specie was in short supply, coin was in limited circulation and was not indispensable, since exchange in kind was still much practised. Payment in kind was therefore imposed by circumstances . . . In 1720, the return on grain was still so unfavourable in the *généralité* of Soissons that tenancies were paid for in grain, since it would have been so hard to obtain payment in cash.[530]

In the eighteenth century of course, the situation changed, monetarization advanced, but was still very far from applying to all transactions. Well after 1789, there were still regions in France practically outside the reach of money. Corsica – an extreme case it is true – remained so until 1914.[531]

The money supply operated to the advantage of the merchants and the state. The latter had insisted that taxes be paid in cash. Since taxpayers often paid their dues in copper coin, this had to be changed into silver or gold currencies – regularly provided by the customs service out of the duties levied on foreign trade. In Colbert's time, this state levy, out of a circulation of perhaps 200 million *livres*, was of the order of 80 million – a huge sum, which the state first confiscated then by its expenditure sent back into circulation, only to levy it once more: the wheel came full circle. But it did not result in a healthy and even distribution throughout the kingdom. The king's money was spent almost entirely on the expenses of the court, on the army and foreign wars, or on servicing the royal debt. There was no outflow to the provinces, no reinvestment in local economies.

As for the poorer classes, the money supply circulated largely above their heads. Some traditional wisdom must be revised. No, the 'monetary manipulation by Philip the Fair had no appreciable influence on public wealth, nor on the price of goods . . . [among] the mass of people; the poor were not affected'.[532] And until recently historians were too inclined to be mesmerized by the rumours and spectacular dealings of the rue de Quincampoix: we now know that Law's famous System did not in fact cause chaos at every level of French life.

The history of currency then, in France as in Europe, is a hierarchical history: what was going on at upper levels was not necessarily the same as what was happening on the ground floor.

The Crown's money

The monarch had to conquer the money supply just as he had conquered the provinces that enlarged his kingdom, supervising coinage, fixing its values and controlling circulation. It was the king's money that made the king.

But money was an elusive commodity, always slipping through

one's fingers: the authorities were forever chasing after it with bans and admonitions. Between 1295 and 1328, 15 edicts were issued in France concerning gold coins, 27 concerning silver; the price of the gold mark[533] fluctuated by 75%, that of the silver mark by 100%.

Another worry was that, whatever the authorities did, French coin left the kingdom and foreign currencies slipped in, whether prohibited or not. Only certain foreign coins were welcome. In 1601, Sully[534] favoured a ban on all foreign coin, 'except [you will not be surprised to learn] Spanish money [both gold and silver] since to be suddenly deprived of these would create too great a vacuum in commerce'. But like it or not, a mixture of foreign and domestic currencies was the rule throughout Europe. In 1614, there were no fewer than 400 different currencies circulating in the Netherlands – at the time it is true, the commercial centre of the world; in France alone there were 82,[535] and possibly more, since in an edict of 1577 there is mention of 180 types of coin 'belonging to a score of sovereign currencies'.[536] By at least 1526, Spanish coins were circulating in Poitou.[537] And in 1611, it was claimed that 'the regions of Picardy, Champagne and Burgundy contained more [foreign currencies] than French ones'.[538]

Foreign powers were always anxious to attract good coins out of France and to get their own bad coins in, especially those made of copper and overlaid at most with a thin layer of silver. The metallic equivalent of the *assignat*, these 'black' coins had no intrinsic value at all, so selling them was all gain to the monarch at home, and just as good if they could be palmed off on a neighbour. Faced with such invasions, it was only prudent to put a ban on them. Venice successfully imposed bans in the sixteenth century, and so did Portugal. But these were two powers particularly sensitive to the necessities of trade, and neither had to operate over territories as vast as the kingdom of France. There was very little the latter could do. The French Crown could express irritation, against the *escalins* which invaded the northern provinces in the late seventeenth century, or the *sous* of Lorraine which could be smuggled in across the complicated frontier between the duchy and France.[539] But expressing irritation, issuing threats and at most punishing the odd offender, to make up for all the others who got away, was about the measure of it. In about 1780, according to Mollien,[540] the English were manufacturing and offloading into France 'French' copper coin at below even the face value. (If one was trying to make money, there was no point in doing things by halves.)

In short, while money in France theoretically belonged to the king, it had to compete with other currencies and was obliged to respect certain balances.

When Cardinal Richelieu controlled French currency between 1640 and 1641, he preferred to mint coins that were the same denomination and value as those that were commonest among our neighbours, than to continue the denomination and weight which had previously been in use in France. He preferred, that is to say, to disrupt the system of coinage previously practised in the Kingdom than to miss the chance of introducing here the same coins as were current among our neighbours. Instead of quarter-*écus*, he had silver *écus* made as we have them today [in 1706] of the same weight and denomination as Spanish pieces of eight.[541] The Spanish *pistole*[542] was at the time the commonest gold coin among our neighbours. Instead of gold *écus*, previously the currency of the French kingdom, he had golden *louis* minted of the same weight and denomination as the Spanish *pistole*.[543]

The English guinea, minted after 1661, was also modelled on the *pistole*.[544]

Another worry was the adjustment of the gold-silver ratio, which depended on the official or market price for gold and silver, as well as on the different denominations of coin. It had long been believed that there was a 'natural' ratio between gold and silver of 1 to 12: gold being worth 12 times an equal weight of silver. In fact the ratio varied up and down. As a result, there were periods when silver was at a premium against gold, others when it was the other way round. In the 1560s for instance, silver lost ground to gold; the Genoese, who had seen this coming as far back as 1558, speculated in gold ahead of everyone else and did very well out of it.

But governments could also play on the gold-silver ratio in

order to influence currency movements. In 1726, by stabilizing the *livre tournois*, Louis XV's government undervalued gold (1: 14.5) and as a result gold moved abroad to Holland, England and Genoa, while silver came into France where it was worth more. In 1785, Calonne readjusted the relative values of gold: this time gold was worth 15.5 times more than silver, going up a point: as a result silver, being undervalued and therefore cheap, left the kingdom, letting gold in. This was one way a country could choose a sort of standard, gold or silver, before such a thing truly existed.

Internal currency operations

French currency constituted a system similar to all those in use throughout modern Europe. It had its own rules, its own internal permutations. It was based not on bi-metallism (gold and silver) but on tri-metallism (gold, silver and copper). Copper was used as an alloy to strengthen gold and silver coins and, more importantly, it was the metal from which small change was minted. Sometimes a little silver was included in these lower denominations, but so little that the copper soon showed through, and all such coins eventually turned black: this was the 'black money' of the poor, a fiduciary currency of which the legal tender was arbitrarily fixed, bearing no relation to its metallic value.

Small denominations had to be used because of the low wages and expenditure of the poorer classes. It was the currency of the artisan, the low-paid worker, for everyday transactions. These coins in fact 'went straight from hand to mouth', since wages were barely at subsistence level. So they circulated faster than silver coin, the prime currency for commercial transactions, and *a fortiori* faster than gold, which was used for long-distance trade.

Thus described, the monetary system does not seem very hard to grasp, but there are one or two difficulties to be resolved.

1) The specificity of the *livre tournois* – a money of account, that is to say a fictional or 'imaginary' unit. It was worth 20 *sols*, and one *sol* was worth 12 *deniers*. But neither the *livre* nor its subdivisions

were real coins you could have held in your hand. They were used in accounting, so that all the various metal denominations could be reduced to a single unit of account.

The *livre tournois* had been both inherited and chosen. It was a legacy received by several countries after the break-up of Charlemagne's empire. In the days of the emperor, following his monetary reform of 781, the *livre* as a money of account corresponded exactly to one pound weight of silver, out of which 240 *denier* pieces were cut, of a convenient size to handle. It was therefore a real currency, although not in fact materialized. But under Charlemagne's successors in most of Europe, the *denier* began to vary, diminishing constantly in weight. So the *livre* ceased to be a real currency. Accounts and contracts continued to be drawn up in *livres*, but these represented a variable number of *deniers*, as the values of metal currencies fluctuated. For instance in France, the *livre* was worth 260 *deniers* in 1290, 300 in 1295, 400 in 1301. To add to the confusion, within French territory, before the Capetian accession, there were several *livres* of account, of different values – the *livres* of Roussillon, Languedoc, Provence, Dauphiné, Burgundy, Lorraine as well as the *livre parisis* (Paris) and the *livre tournois* (Tours). So 'between 1200 and 1300, Languedoc was using the *livre raimondine* (the money of the counts of Toulouse) which was worth six times less than the [*livre tournois*]; in 1207, 9 *livres raimondines* were worth only 30 *sous tournois*'.[545] In order to be chosen as the king's currency, the *livre tournois*, which was at this time worth about four-fifths of the *livre parisis*,[546] therefore had to eliminate its rivals. Logically, one might have expected the *livre parisis* to be chosen: and indeed it was not abolished until 1667. If the *livre* of Tours was preferred, it was above all because it opened up to the Capet monarchs the possessions of the Plantagenets. Having become the royal currency, it quickly took over as money of account, even 'in provinces whose overlords are very jealous of their prerogatives'.[547]

So the *livre tournois* became a sort of measurement scale, against which real currencies were quoted at such and such rates. The exchange rate varied. Devaluation in the old days was quite a simple process. All one had to do was to raise the value of the coinage, which thus devalued the *livre* by which they were measured. Another procedure was to remint coins, the new ones holding the same face value as the old, although their metal content was inferior. So in 1621, president Pasquier was able to say that he did not like the proverb applied to someone of bad reputation that 'he was cried down like old money . . . because the way things are going in France now, the old money is better than the new which has been worth less and less over the last hundred years'.[548]

If the correlation between the *livre* and some real gold or silver currency had been fixed at some point, the *livre* would have been consolidated. This was tried in 1577: the weak government of Henri III, on the advice and under the pressure of the merchants of Lyon, decided that the *écu d'or en or*, a standard coin, would from now on be worth three *livres*, or 60 *sols*. The *livre* was now a real currency attached to gold. But the operation failed almost before it had begun: the *écu d'or en or* shot up, and was soon being exchanged at 63, 64 or even 70 *sous*.[549]

2) I wrote just now that under the old system, the *livre tournois* had no material form. There are two exceptions to this, neither terribly important. If banknotes were issued, they were expressed in *livres*. This happened under Louis XIV. But the banknote was quickly devalued, so it never became consolidated. The other exception was small change, which represented a certain number of *sous* and *deniers* – that is subdivisions of the fictional *livre tournois*, not sub-divisions of actual gold or silver coins. But these were also fiduciary currencies and might just as well have been made of paper.

3) There were then three ways one could devalue the *livre tournois*:
    a) by raising the legal value of actual gold and silver coins:
    b) by reminting coin, keeping the same face value but diminishing the metallic content;
    c) by reducing the official price of subdivisions of the money of account: the three-*denier* piece was reduced to two *deniers* in 1668 for instance.

The *livre tournois* was in fact constantly being devalued, as can be seen from the graph in Figure 73, taken from a book by Frank

FIGURE 73

Value of the livre tournois *in* francs germinal *on the gold and silver standard*

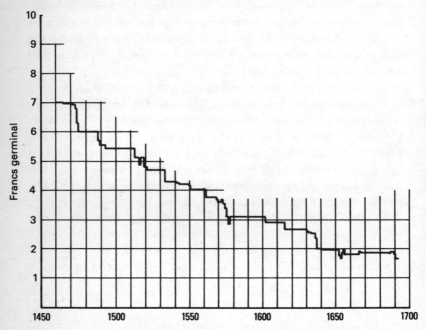

In two and a half centuries, the *livre tournois* lost three-quarters of its value, continuing its uninterrupted decline since the thirteenth century.

Source: F. C. Spooner, *L'Economie mondiale et les frappes monétaires en France, 1493–1680*, 1956.

Spooner, and registering changes only after 1450, when the process was already well under way. If the value of the *livre tournois* in 1258 is set at 100, its value was no more than 53 in 1360, 36 in 1465, and 11 in 1561! Inflation had never stopped.

The *livre* was not stabilized until 1726, and this time it was attached to silver: 54 *livres* were cut per mark of silver. Calonne consolidated the reform in 1785, by modifying the gold-silver ratio, as I have already mentioned (it went up from 14.5 to 15.5:1).[550] After the monetary chaos of the Revolution, the creation of the *franc germinal*, on 7 April 1803, prolonged the spirit of these *ancien régime* measures. The stabilization now introduced was to last over a century, until the law of 25 June 1928 creating the *franc Poincaré*, also known as the *franc de quatre sous*, since it was indeed worth only a fifth of the *franc germinal*. But this time the franc was pegged to the gold standard, no longer to silver, and gold mono-metallism thus became the norm in France.

This attempt to maintain a fixed parity for the franc in relation to the gold standard was, as we know now, the last. Before long inflation was getting under way once more and after 1945, it set off at a gallop.

But it has to be said that the inflation we have endured for half a century of French history is really nothing compared to what France suffered in the old days, for centuries on end. It is to this inflation that I would like to return.

To grasp the difference between the two, we must first return briefly to some definitions. I have been using the word 'monetarization' in the general sense of the spread of the monetary economy. I should now be more precise – the spread of money really means the spread of the services it could render to commerce:

– providing it with a reference, a scale, preferably fixed, such as the gold standard or the silver standard, or the double gold–silver standard as was the case in 1726, 1785 and 1803;

– allowing it to operate normally, in other words making possible what is known as the market economy;

– providing it with a guarantee of value;

– lastly allowing for the creation of credit mechanisms – money in a different shape.

The old monetary system provided varying degrees of satisfaction according to these four criteria.

It made credit possible, in the form of those pseudo-currencies the bill of exchange and the bank note: for a long time bills of exchange had to be paid for in gold. The *écu de marc* of the Lyon fairs was something like the US dollar of today.[551]

FIGURE 74
Monetary devaluation as a general phenomenon in Europe

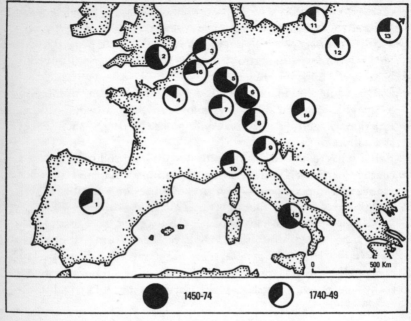

1. New Castile; 2. England; 3. Holland; 4. France;
5. Frankfurt; 6. Wurzburg; 7. Alsace; 8. Augsburg; 9. Venice; 10.
Genoa; 11. Danzig/Gdansk; 12. Poland; 13. Moscow;
14. Austria; 15. Naples; 16. Spanish Netherlands.

Source: *Cambridge Economic History of Europe*, vol. IV, 1967.

The old system also offered a means of preserving value –
savings – since in the general flow of exchange and transactions,
metal coins would constantly be passing through my hands. If I
decided to lock them up in my treasure chest, they would still have
kept their value the day I took them out again, because of their fine
metal content. Nowadays, to protect against inflation, one can
actually buy gold currencies such as gold napoleons, or ingots, but
they are commodities; there is also real estate, land, stone walls, as

people say, or paintings and works of art. All these possibilities existed before 1789, and there were also precious metals in the shape of gold or silver plate and jewellery. 'In France at present', wrote Ange Goudar in 1756, 'we have over 1,300 millions in gold and silver ornaments, jewellery and plate.'[552] I do not vouch for the figure, but such treasure certainly existed. Baron Dupin, one of the earliest statisticians, gives more precise figures: according to official records, he says, 'French families – would you believe it? – [have] increased their possessions of gold and silver plate and jewels to the tune of 20 million francs a year', between 1818 and 1825.[553] But the essential point here is that until 1914, just as much as before 1789, the monetary system was self-protecting in terms of value, its gold and silver coins being worth saving without any need for transformation. It is true that once the determined and effective policy of the Banque de France reassured the French people about the worth of the bank note, the woollen stocking under the mattress might be stuffed with notes as well as coins. But coins played a role for centuries on end. The historical society of the Périgord[554] records that

in 1420, in Limoges, coins minted in 817, that is six hundred years before, bearing the image of Louis the Pious, were still very common. At about the same time one would have found coins stamped with the names of Charlemagne, Odo or Pippin of Aquitaine – minted between 752 and 890. It is true that coins went on being stamped in the image of kings long after their death, but it is curious all the same.

Equally curious, less significant perhaps, but worthy of note are the following observations: 'In 1892, peasants in Lower Normandy, when they took their animals to the fair, expressed their prices in *pistoles* and *demi-pistoles* [last current in the time of Louis XIV]; Breton peasants often expressed prices in *réaux* [pieces of eight], the last trace of Brittany's commercial links with Spain.'[555]

All metal coins, old or new, could be used for any transactions. They were heavy to carry but they travelled all over France and Europe in every combination. Every time we have records of a detailed payment, we get a surprise. In 1670, the official at the salt-store of La Ferté-Bernard (in what is now the Sarthe), sent a sack to Laval containing the sum of 7,173 *livres*, 2 *sols*. The sum was made up of 86 gold *louis* at 12 *livres* each, 86 gold *louis* at 110 *sols* each, 12 Spanish *pistoles* at 4 *livres* 5 *sols* 10 *deniers*, 8 gold *écus* at 5 *livres*, 13 *sols* 9 *deniers*, plus silver *louis* to the value of 1,000 *livres* and *douzains* to the value of 450 *livres*.[556] So it is easy to see why having a money account was absolutely essential! But one can also understand the irritation expressed by Sébastien Mercier in 1788 at the sight of the rue Vivienne. On the 10th and 20th of the month, so many cash payments were transacted in this street that it was thronged with cashiers bowed down by the weight of their satchels. A great chance for a bank raid, a modern criminal might think. Specie was not of course easy to handle in large sums. But merchants and *négociants* avoided some of the problems by using bank notes and bills of exchange, or the magic clearing operations at fairs and deposit banks.[557]

In short, the old monetary system, consolidated or not, which in practice remained the underpinning of the French economy until 1914, lasted so long because it was viable, compatible that is with the rhythms and demands of the economy. So I do not think it should automatically be dismissed as disastrous, even before the stabilization of 1726.

But all that being granted, what about the long-term inflation which this system allowed, provoked and in part sustained? Should one consider this inflation, the constant depreciation of the *livre tournois*, as the root of all evil? Or was it more symptom than cause? From Figure 74 it will be seen that inflation was a pan-European phenomenon, the rule that exceptions could only prove: certain currencies were stable only thanks to the good health of the underlying economy – examples being Florence, Genoa, Venice, later Amsterdam and finally and spectacularly, London. In France, a stabilized currency was the result after 1726 of the greater prosperity of the eighteenth century, just as the collapse of the *franc germinal* in the 1920s reflected exhaustion and the consequences of a war and a victory for which France had paid an exorbitant price. Even the 'Thirty Glorious Years' did not enable France to return to the gold standard. But is inflation in the end not a way of encouraging growth, a more or less deliberate choice? As R. Sédillot so excellently put it: 'since Gaul became France, money has usually been used to pay for wars, but that is how a country is built'.[558]

Money also pays for many other things, and takes many things into account. Perhaps Antoine Barnave (1761–93), the famous Girondin, has been credited with too much clairvoyance. But his ideas, if literally interpreted, do indeed look far ahead. He argued that political regimes are determined principally by the uses to which the countries concerned put their wealth. This in turn is closely linked to all the consequences of their particular situation, whether as an 'inland state' or a 'maritime state'. Traian Stoianovich may be right to conclude then that French currency, at the beginning of the Revolution, was still the currency of an essentially agricultural country, it was money based on the land, with all the attendant likelihood of getting bogged down, held up by every kind of obstacle, or falling down potholes. English money on the other hand was linked to commerce and sea power, so it was agile, fast-flowing and well equipped to power and animate an economy more modern than that of France, more suited to promoting modern capitalism.[559]

The capitalism of the future was really the key issue here, and once more, alas, we find a contrast between France and Britain. Why did the latter, as early as the reign of Elizabeth I, when it was far from being the dominant power in Europe, succeed in stabilizing the pound sterling? The only explanation that seems to lead anywhere is that monetarization of the English economy was earlier and more far-reaching than in France. According to Phelps-Brown and Hopkins, the proportion of wages paid in money (rather than in kind) was already reaching about a third of the population by the first half of the sixteenth century.[560] In France, although workers in Paris were paid in copper coin,[561] as were the small woad-growers in Toulouse in the sixteenth century, I do not think the situation was anywhere near as advanced. But why was England so far ahead? After all, it had had to contend with serious drawbacks at first. Paul Adam has suggested that the later reasons lie with the struggle against France, the need for a fixed rate for the notes issued by the Bank of England in 1797, and the establishment of an industry obliged to undertake mass production: these constraints, he argues, made for precipitate industrialization. True, but Britain's smaller geographical dimensions also made it possible to set up a denser network, amounting to a national market, well before this was possible in France.

Vertical exchange

The monetary system being what it was, why should capitalism not have learnt to live with it, and incidentally to take advantage of it? Capitalism's future lay of course in the use, spread and eventual triumph of paper currency, pseudo-money. But to the extent that capitalism was a malleable, adaptable and changeable process, it could be moulded to any shape, like hot wax. And that is indeed what happened: early capitalism made use of both coin and paper.

The real buying power or commercial value of a metal coin did not necessarily coincide with its face value. One could always buy more in the market-place with a silver *écu* than with the equivalent in copper coin, which had no intrinsic value and might see its face value cried down overnight – one of the mechanisms for devaluing the *livre* as we have seen. In August 1738, the marquis d'Argenson noted that 'this morning, there was posted a devaluation of the value of the two *sols* coin, to the tune of two *liards*, a quarter of the total [25%] which is considerable'.[562] There was also perpetually established what José Gentil da Silva has elegantly if somewhat confusingly described as a 'vertical exchange rate', that is an exchange relationship between higher and lower currencies, which always worked in favour of the former.[563]

It was therefore the practice, in their own interests, for merchants and other well-off persons, or indeed the state,[564] in any payment they made, to use up first the 'black money' they happened to have received from a tenant, a farmer, the poorer taxpayers, or simply by virtue of the ancient usage which obliged creditors to accept copper coin in part payment. This obligation, which Necker abolished in 1780, was restored during the Revolution, and the reform of the *franc germinal* in 1803 had maintained it for one-fortieth of any sum due. Mollien, as treasury minister, finally abolished it altogether in 1810: as he explained, if in 'repayment of a sum of 100 francs, one received 98 francs in silver coin and two francs in coin whose real value was no more than one franc',[565] thus losing one per cent of one's money, it was easy to see why 'those in the know hold on to good coins, while the bad ones [remain] in the hands of the ordinary people'.[566] The bankers of Lyons, in the sixteenth century, had a regular policy of 'monopolizing gold crowns'. Agents collected these for them, in the city itself, sending canvassers out to the local inns.[567] And in even a small-scale transaction like that between a modest money-lender and his debtor in 1645, good coin was promised: the borrower, a share-cropper, seems to be apologizing in his letter for a slight delay – he has nothing but *deniers*, and is 'afraid to give you poor repayment', but in a few days, he promises, when he returns from the Saint-Berthommieu fair, 'I shall have some good silver and will bring it to you.'[568]

The result was that while black coins, which were always being recycled downwards to the lower layers of the economy, circulated very fast, good coins were trapped by the rich and tended to stay put, hoarded away in coffers until some appropriate use for them was found after a few weeks, months or even years.

This tendency of 'noble' currency to float to the top was a constant force in monetary history. Gentil da Silva sees it indeed as a form of expropriation, the 'starting-point' and source of modern capitalism itself, whether in France or anywhere else.[569]

Then there was the more subtle speculation in gold and silver. To the very richest merchants, who were also of course the best informed, the different currencies in circulation did not greatly matter. Indeed it hardly mattered to them whether or not the *livre* should be stabilized on such favourable terms as it was in 1726. They were personally above all such problems. But they were all the same capable of the basically simple strategy of hanging on to good, or at any rate less bad, coin. Gascon has described how the Lyon bankers collected gold crowns. Carrière, the historian of Marseille, repeatedly reminds us how the *négociants* of Marseille in the eighteenth century hoarded the silver piastres which they could put to such good use in the Levant. The Saint-Malo merchants of the early eighteenth century speculated in American silver. Between 1720 and 1750, the Magons, wealthy *négociants* of Saint-Malo, speculated in Chinese gold: to take silver to China and exchange it for gold meant huge profits, since silver was grossly over-valued there. Towards the end of the century, Jean Joseph de Laborde, a court banker who was to die on the scaffold in 1794, speculated, like many others, in silver from New Spain and gold from Portugal, that is from Brazil.

These were elementary kinds of speculation, admittedly, but one had to be well placed in the first instance to be able to practise them. José Gentil da Silva's explanation remains the essential one. But this 'vertical exchange dealing' was only one form of siphoning off savings, the surpluses hoarded from labour without which capitalism could not exist. One could argue after all that some form of vertical exchange dealing operated between French banks under the Second Empire and Third Republic, with the public sale of shares in limited companies. Public money flooded in, and the board of the company disposed of it as it thought fit. This was the system denounced in 1869 by Georges Duchêne and in 1911–12 by Lysis, the enemy of speculative raids by bankers using the money of small savers.[570] The principle remained the same.

The slow takeover by paper

Paper currency did not revolutionize things overnight, nor would it aggravate matters or precipitate sudden crisis. It had been at work for a long time, as a substitute for specie, but had only been adopted slowly, despite being so simple: a few lines of script, one or two signatures and that was that. To those who did not understand how it worked – and they were the great majority – paper was shocking, a manoeuvre of the devil. For others, it was a brilliant device, a short cut and a miracle. It undoubtedly stood for modernity moving into the subtle world of high finance. But this modernity only imperfectly filtered down to the level of ordinary life: only businessmen and careful observers were aware of it. One such was the modest editor of the *Journal de la Régence*, Jean Buvat, who had been following the extremely instructive vicissitudes of Law's famous System. As he explained to his readers in April 1720,

What is meant by credit in general is a written or unwritten promise, by one or more persons, the said [promise] being a substitute for money. . . Thus throughout the world, most commerce is carried on every day by the use of paper alone. Businessmen do not send express couriers or ships to carry coin to all the places where they have credit. Their notes [i.e. bills of exchange] suffice not only for them to be lent all the money they need, but also to load ships with all the goods in the kingdom . . . So the use of paper which it is at present proposed to introduce to France [i.e. Law's System] merely confirms by public credit what private Bankers are used to doing every day through their private credit.[571]

Not a bad summing-up.

But promissory notes (IOUs), company shares or loans launched by town authorities did not release masses of paper on to the market. The state took the whole thing much further. It had very early on issued interest-bearing bonds: the famous *rentes sur l'Hôtel de Ville*, in Paris in 1522, with payment guaranteed on what would today be called dividends. Were these bonds really the equivalent of cash, as we would unhesitatingly think today? Isaac de Pinto thought so in 1771,[572] but he is somewhat hesitant in saying so:

Although the analogy [with money] is very close in some respects, public bonds do not exactly stand for specie, but they increase the amount of money by merely being created: they become a form of property like land or a house; they bear interest without requiring repairs or labour; their greatest advantage is that they make money and its equivalents circulate more swiftly, and it is in this sense, to some extent, that one may consider them as representing cash, since they often perform the same function. On the London stock market, one can convert bonds worth a hundred thousand pounds sterling into cash within twenty-four hours.

But such a transformation was only possible through an active Stock Exchange, such as did not truly exist in Paris before the Edict of Fontainebleau (1724). Until then municipal bonds, 'far from entering into commerce', were difficult to negotiate: it took time, required witnessing by a notary, and cost money. During Louis XVI's reign however, stock-exchange practices developed in France, and speculation on rising or falling values became as lively as in Amsterdam, which is saying something, or even London. More than one observer noted this with alarm, as did the government itself. In 1789, a page every day in the *Journal de Paris* or the *Affiches* was devoted to quoting prices on the Bourse: shares in the Compagnie des Indes, royal loan bonds, the Caisse d'Escompte, and bonds on the city of Paris. In the early days of the Revolution, these various pieces of paper represented 8,000 million *livres*, no less than double the GNP, or four times as much as the cash actually in circulation.[573]

Of this total, it was the 3,000 million *livres* of the royal debt which was to destroy the *ancien régime*. Economic historians find it hard to understand how this should have come about: the rule today is that a national debt does not run any immediate danger so long as it does not exceed twice the GNP. By this reckoning, the monarchy ought to have been well within the margin of safety, with a debt of only 3,000 million. But today's rules do not necessarily apply to the past. Much obloquy has been heaped on Calonne,[574] a man of outstanding mind, and a bold modern economist (he has even been described as 'Keynesian') who nevertheless took all the wrong decisions for the French state. But at the time, was it possible to take the right ones?

To return to the history of paper money, this meant above all bank notes, *billets de banque*. The name did not emerge until later, being first applied to the notes printed by the Banque de France (founded 1800). Before this date, they were referred to simply as *billets*, and long remained marginal in everyday commerce. Paper was above all an expedient, and indeed a poor one, to which governments with empty coffers tended to resort. This was what Louis XIV's government did after 1701: its notes were devalued with amazing speed, dwindling away in the wallets of businessmen who did not know how to get rid of them, or falling into the all-too-skilled hands of all the usurers and embezzlers in the kingdom. The correspondence of the marquis d'Argenson, chief of police in Paris, mentions many tricks and frauds which prove the naivety and perplexity of ordinary holders of paper money. Anxious to change it into hard cash, at unbelievable rates, they trusted middlemen who simply forgot to pay them. It happened in Paris and it happened in Lyon. This was the first really serious attempt to introduce paper money to France and it did not work. A memorandum, probably dating from 1706, rather plaintively says: 'Paper money must be acclimatized to France, like a fragile plant.'

The next experiment in this area was the System devised by Law: at first it operated smoothly and efficiently within the context of a general reform of taxes and their collection. Then the machine began overheating, and broke down, bringing disaster. In the course of the débâcle, Louis XIV's debt was cancelled out, and one is tempted to say bravo! But the awful memory of Law's paper currency cast a deadly and inhibiting shadow over all banking institutions. It inspired some vengeful verses:

> *Un écu est un écu*
> *Un billet de banque un billet de banque*
> *Un écu est un écu*
> *Un billet de banque un torche-cu*

> A gold crown is a gold crown
> A bank note is a bank note
> A gold crown is a gold crown
> A bank note is a bum-wipe[575]

I do not think this is one of those cases where as the proverb has it in France, *tout finit par des chansons*, all ends in song, and no more is heard about it. The fact is that the 'electric shock of inflation between 1718 and 1720' played a long-lasting role in delaying the development of French banking.[576] The creation of the Caisse d'Escompte in 1776 was effected with the utmost discretion. The word 'bank' was avoided altogether and the large notes issued by the Caisse concerned only 'high' commerce and speculators, rather than the public at large. Could anyone have foreseen that during the Revolution France would see something even worse than Law's System, with the issue of *assignats* and *mandats territoriaux*? The *assignat*, established by the Constituent Assembly, in the face of stiff internal resistance in April 1790, had within a few months become a virtual note to bearer when the Assembly made it legal tender. In no time at all, it became impossible to buy grain or live-stock in fairs and markets unless one paid cash. Paper was devalued to a frightening extent. On 15 *nivôse* Year IV, in Chambéry, 43 or 44 *livres* in cash would obtain 10,000 *livres* in *assignats*. One old man in 1838 remembered the old days of 1797: 'An income of 30,000 *livres* would hardly have bought a pair of boots.'[577] Allowing for the different circumstances, this is rather reminiscent of the inflation during the Weimar Republic in Germany in 1923.

The banknote proper did not really become part of French financial life, I repeat, until the founding in 1800 of the Banque de France, which was granted the privilege for fifteen years of issuing bank notes for the Paris region only. In the provinces, local banks issued notes which only circulated in the *départements* covered by that bank. But since Parisian banknotes were accepted everywhere, while provincial notes were not accepted in Paris, exchange rates came to depend on the flow of money into and out of the capital. In fact, the Banque de France's main activity was dis-counting. This enabled it to send banknotes into circulation in the business world, notes which could always be exchanged for coin. But since the only denominations were for large sums of 500 francs or more, the Banque de France was virtually operating as a service to high-level commerce, where of course its caution paid off every time.[578]

Oddly enough, it took the 1848 Revolution (which caught everyone by surprise, governor, deputy governors and regents) for the situation to become more flexible. The regional banks were now effectively annexed by the Banque de France, which thus covered the whole of French territory. The issue of smaller notes, worth 50 francs, brought the Bank into closer touch with lower levels of commerce, if not with the general public, which remained

FIGURE 75
Percentage of paper money and metal coins in the French money supply, 1820–95

	Total money in circulation				
	Total millions of francs K	Coin (%) L	Notes (%) M	Deposits (%) N	Total (%) O
1820–1824	2.30	80.1	8.5	11.4	100.0
1825–1829	2.56	80.6	7.9	11.5	100.0
1830–1834	2.86	81.0	8.1	10.9	100.0
1835–1839	3.27	81.4	7.6	11.0	100.0
1840–1844	3.49	80.7	8.6	10.7	100.0
1845–1849	3.83	79.7	9.8	10.5	100.0
1850–1854	4.58	77.2	12.6	10.2	100.0
1855–1859	5.49	77.6	12.4	10.0	100.0
1860–1864	6.24	76.2	12.3	11.5	100.0
1865–1869	7.23	70.8	14.8	14.4	100.0
1870–1874	7.30	53.0	32.6	14.4	100.0
1875–1879	8.02	53.1	28.8	18.1	100.0
1880–1884	9.02	52.7	29.0	18.3	100.0
1885–1889	9.24	49.1	28.7	22.2	100.0
1890–1894	9.48	41.2	32.1	26.7	100.0

Source: F. Braudel and E. Labrousse, *Histoire économique et sociale de la France*, III/1, 1976.

wary of it. Fixed exchange rates, which remained operative between 1848 and 1852 and met no widespread resistance, encouraged the spread of banknotes.

But as can be seen from Figure 75, their progress was slow. Credit was still very much the province of local moneylenders and above all notaries. There would be no great developments on this front until after 1860, when the creation of provincial branches of banks succeeded in attracting a larger share of the public's savings into the banking sphere. Although coins retained an unusually prominent place in French monetary circulation until the eve of World War I,[579] the banknote, governed by the wisdom of the Banque de France, had become domesticated and was now an everyday item in credit and exchange. It was the banknote which gradually ousted the bill of exchange, about which I must now write at some length.

The role of the bill of exchange

The foregoing explanations have cleared the ground a little. By that I mean that we have already dealt with the *livre tournois* and the bank note, and can therefore turn to an even more important item, the bill of exchange, which poses a number of problems because of its very early appearance, and which sheds light on the entire history of the European economy from the twelfth to the nineteenth centuries. The problems it raises seem to multiply with the progress of historical research. Resolve one, and another immediately appears. One might have thought, after the work of André-E. Sayous, Raymond de Roover and Giulio Mandich, that everything had been said on this subject, and indeed well said. But I have now seen in manuscript a new book, by three young economists, *Monnaie privée et pouvoir des princes* (*Private Money and Princely Power*) which raises more problems and offers some brilliant solutions, leaving one with the impression that further problems will be provoked by it, since it takes the story only to the end of the sixteenth century.

The bill of exchange was a 'flying paper', about the same size as a present-day banknote. If you turn to the manuals of commerce, they will tell you how to draw one up, according to a virtually sacrosanct model, unvaried for centuries. The same precautions, the same formulas, the same invocations are religiously reproduced. To read one of them is to read thousands – for thousands of them are preserved in the archives.

A bill of exchange was theoretically the means of sending a sum of money from one financial centre or fair to another, where it would be paid in different currency: a bill sent from Lyon to

Medina del Campo would be made out in *écus de marc*, the exchange currency used in Lyon, and would be paid in *maravedis*, the money of account in Castile, at the Medina exchange rate; if it was drawn on Antwerp, it would be calculated on arrival in *livres de gros*. It is not hard to work out that four persons were concerned in the operation – four people who were given generic (though variable) names in merchants' jargon. But it was the mechanism itself and the need for four participants which caused the problems. I will try to explain this by means of an example the reader may find too simple.

In 1945, it was difficult, but not impossible, to transfer money from France to Italy. There was a quite well-known agency in Paris: you paid it a sum of money in French francs, and the agent's contact in Venice, Genoa or Rome paid the equivalent in lire to a person named by you. So there were two intermediaries, one in Paris, one in, say, Venice – and it was essential that they have absolute confidence in each other. Then there was the Frenchman who paid in the francs. He would have received a piece of paper – a receipt – in exchange, which he could then send to Venice, where his nominee would draw the equivalent in lire, less the handling costs. There are our four participants. And if in fact I was myself the traveller who drew in Venice the funds paid by myself in Paris, I was simply playing a twofold role and counted as two people. The number of agents remains four.

In fact what emerges from this demonstration is that there is a contact system – between the two agency colleagues – and, at either end, two customers who do not have their own contact system. And the receipt obtained in Paris, whether a 'flying paper' or not, probably hastily scribbled out, is the twentieth-century equivalent of the famous bill of exchange. Now let me add a few extra remarks:

1) Clearly in our example, Paris–Venice in 1945, the transfer could have worked either way, from Paris to Venice or Venice to Paris: in any given finance centre, the outgoing bill was a draft (*traite* in French); an incoming one a remittance (*remise*). As J. Trenchant put it in his *Arithmétique* (1561), to exchange money was to 'take money from one city to give out the same value in

another, or on the contrary to pay it out in one place and take back the equivalent in another.'[580]

2) As a rule, the centres or fairs operating this exchange were not in the same country or state or even in the same monetary system. But there were also bills, wrongly known as 'of exchange', in circulation within a single state: thus in the sixteenth century, bills could be exchanged between Lyon and Paris, Rouen, Tours, Nantes, Bordeaux, La Rochelle and Marseille. In both cases, the distance between the dispatch and receipt of the bill was compensated for by a difference in the sum actually paid out. So the transfer was paid for by a percentage, which we should call interest, but it could vary as between exchanges. There was therefore an element of uncertainty and 'risk' involved, which is why the Church, which forbade any loan at interest as usury, tolerated the bill of exchange and so to speak absolved it of any charge of usury. This concession opened the door to capitalism certainly, but then the Church, with revenue dispersed all over Europe, was faced with exactly the same problems as the merchants. Note however that it sanctioned the bill of exchange only if there was a *genuine* transfer of funds from one centre to another.

3) As for the four partners in the bill of exchange transaction, they would inevitably have been either banks, or *négociants*, or merchants or exchange dealers. The bill of exchange was not available to any Tom, Dick or Harry who could read and write. It was monopolized by tightly-knit groups of specialists. Condillac knew that 'in the centres of commerce, the greatest praise one can heap on a merchant is to say: "he understands exchange dealing"'.[581] The difficulty of 'understanding' related of course to the monetary speculation underlying the exchange of bills. Actually drawing up a bill was a very simple matter. It was merely a question of reproducing an invariable formula, full of precautionary clauses, and filling in the relevant details (names of people, places and the sum of money in the appropriate currency). It was understood that the bill was a *holograph*, that is penned in one's own hand and that one's correspondent, as an extra precaution, would have samples of one's writing.

4) Over time, the bill of exchange altered its nature while extending its functions. As early as the sixteenth century, merchants were trying to make it a negotiable asset, but endorsement took a long time to be accepted. On the other hand, a very early development (condemned incidentally by the religious authorities) was that a bill could be sent to another city and come back to its original signatory, after having been sent to one or more intermediary stations, all by previous agreement: this arrangement was known as the *ricorsa* pact. The practice became established in Italy in the sixteenth century, but was not unknown in Lyon, where references are found to *rechange* or *rescontre*, which is the same thing. Giulio Mandich reports finding one bill of exchange which had been on its travels for six years! And I myself have come across one bill of exchange sent by Philip II of Spain to the German firm of Fugger, issued in 1590 but apparently not settled until 1596. In both cases, this was really a loan at interest without admitting it. *Rechange* even made possible fictitious if not fraudulent transactions, known in French as *cavalerie*. But whether it was an instrument of credit or pure speculation, re-exchange called for the expertise of a specialist in *arbitrages*, that is the choice of itineraries, since one could be much more advantageous than another. Jacques Laffitte, an employee of the Perrégaux bank, who succeeded his boss when the latter died in 1808, claimed to be an expert at this kind of deal, which his old master had not understood at all.[582]

The final stage to note, by which time the bill of exchange had lost any importance compared to the bank note (and even more to the bank cheque, introduced to France from England in about 1865) was probably the law of 7 June 1884,[583] which permitted 'the creation of a bill of exchange at the place of payment, regularizing a de facto situation'. The sacrosanct requirement of transfer between two places had disappeared.

Did the bill of exchange create 'intra-European' links?

This 'internal' history of the bill of exchange has been central to research by economic historians. But once more, we are here concerned with external factors, with the role played by the bill of exchange in relation to the early development of capitalism, and the initial stages of the European economy which acquired coherence at an early stage.

The best way to move outside so to speak is probably to take an example. Leaving France for a moment, I have chosen a Castilian example with which I am completely familiar. Simon Ruiz, a merchant in Medina del Campo, whose entire correspondence has been preserved, did many things in his life, but towards the end, in the 1590s, he contented himself with speculating in handling bills of exchange from Medina del Campo to Florence (drafts) and from Florence to Medina del Campo (remittances). He enhanced his capital by playing on these transactions – so this was no longer a simple matter of transferring funds, the origin of the bill of exchange.

Let us assume that Simon Ruiz had just bought, from a wool merchant in Medina del Campo, a bill of exchange on Florence, where the merchant could by this bill mobilize for him the price of his bales of wool, which were usually shipped from Alicante to Livorno and then to Florence, and for which he was owed payment. He sold his bill of exchange to Simon Ruiz in order to obtain immediate settlement, which he would otherwise have received only much later, given the transit period and allowing the necessary three months for a bill of exchange to arrive from Florence. He was thus receiving his payment in advance – it had been discounted for him. As for Simon Ruiz, he sent off his bill to a compatriot living in Florence, Baltazar Suarez, whose credit was excellent and in whom Ruiz had complete confidence. Baltazar received the bill, collected on it and bought another in Florence, payable to Simon Ruiz in Medina del Campo. So six months after the first bill had been dispatched, the latter recovered his outlay, usually accompanied by 5% profit. Since the operation happened twice yearly, the annual profit was 10%.[584]

Where did these profits come from, since the transfer did not give rise either to commission or to interest? The answer is from several sources, which altered over time, as the bill of exchange did itself.

According to the authors of *Monnaie privée et pouvoir des princes*, until the end of the sixteenth century, the user of bills of exchange could not fail to make a minimum automatic profit. They provide convincing evidence for this proposition, explaining in particular why centres which quoted their own money of account ('certain value') in terms of foreign currency ('uncertain value') – in Lyon for instance the *écu de marc* against the Genoese crown – always offered a higher exchange rate than centres which quoted the 'uncertain' against the 'certain' (thus in Genoa, the *écu de marc* was quoted in Genoese crowns but – and this was the nub of the matter – at a different rate from Lyon). The explanation, which refers to the whole currency system within each state, to actual currency and the relation between its face value and its intrinsic value, takes up almost half the book, and the reader anxious to know more is referred to it. Even more important than this automatic profit is the fact that it was based on a hierarchy of European financial foci, centred on a key fair (at first the Lyon fair, later the Genoese 'Besançon' fair), which called all the shots. Each finance centre was allotted a role: it had either to quote the certain against the uncertain or vice versa, so profitable itineraries for bills of exchange virtually selected themselves. As a result, 'the merchant bankers [of the sixteenth century] were sure of making a minimum profit on the exchange by transferring money between two countries and back', whatever the economic circumstances of the moment. In the example quoted, of Lyon and Genoa, the certain against the uncertain, the profit was 1.8% per transaction, or 7.3% a year.[585]

This system could only function to the extent that the bill of exchange was – and had long been – a closely guarded privilege, the monopoly of a very small group, the privileged caste of Italian bankers. 'Organized in a veritable network which covered virtually all of Latinate Christendom in Europe', they operated quite independently, both of the merchants, whose needs they were turning to their own account, and of princely powers. The system collapsed quickly after the monetary reforms of 1577. But for decades it had made the bill of exchange a permanent road to riches, to be added to the vertical exchange dealing described by José Gentil da Silva.

Alongside the 'automatic' profit, there were other benefits to be derived from the bill of exchange, less certain ones, but developing steadily during the seventeenth and eighteenth centuries. Among the privileges of the trading nations, wrote Galiani in 1770, let us not forget 'the profits to be made from exchange dealing; it almost always operates to their advantage . . . Thus the trader appears to be selling without gain, whereas the exchange rate alone gives him quite a satisfactory profit.'[586] According to Savary's *Parfait Négociant*, in 1710, that profit might be 'two, three, four, or even ten to fifteen per cent, depending on the value of the currency, or on the abundance or otherwise of money, or the scarcity or otherwise of bills of exchange on the market'.[587]

Bills of exchange, in other words, merely reflected monetary movements between countries, themselves determined by the trade balance or requests for credit. So Simon Ruiz had a sudden disappointment in his dealings in bills of exchange. A surplus of specie had hit Florence, and his correspondent could only buy a bill for Medina at a high price. 'The exchange rate is such', the latter wrote, that 'anyone who has money has to give it at the price asked by the taker.' The only way of safeguarding Simon Ruiz's profit was to make the bill transit through Antwerp or Besançon.[588] On the other hand, when specie was scarce in any one centre, and if I were a merchant needing funds, I could make out a bill of exchange, sell it, and only have to repay six months or a year later. In the interval, the merchant banker in possession of the bill – for which he had paid me – would be circulating it between various places of his choice, before calling it in again, now enlarged by the profits it had made for him en route. This was the *ricorsa* process mentioned earlier. The bill of exchange therefore made it possible to advance loans to businessmen, lords and princes.

The bill of exchange was also, thanks to the exchange fairs (but also thanks to deposit banks like that in Venice) a means of compensation, known in Italy as *riscontro* and later in England as 'clearing'. The Académie Française in 1985 expressed the wish that the word 'clearing' (used increasingly by French economists) should be replaced by *compensation*, but did not suggest a return to the archaic term *rescontre*, which is now obsolete. It is not to be found in Littré, and Savary's *Dictionnaire* contains only the verb *rescontrer*.

Compensation, or clearing, was the main role of the exchange fairs. When Lyon was the central fair, until 1539 or even 1579, a mass of bills of exchange would flood in at the end of every quarter of the year. In fact these bills balanced each other out: a plus cancelled out a minus. Claude de Rubys, the Lyonnais historian (1533–1618) expressed wonder that in a morning a million francs' worth of debt could be cancelled out without a *sou* changing hands. Clearing was further simplified since any remaining debts could always be carried over until the next fair – becoming known then as 'deposits', a credit instrument which usually brought in 2.5% per fair, or 10% per annum. When, in the seventeenth century, Lyon lost its leading position, deposit went on operating there, attracting money 'lying idle'. This was one of the regular resources which Lyon money-lenders took good care to keep for themselves – it was a very safe means of income.

We may now approach the key problem referred to in the title of this section, with some hope of ascertaining its significance. It does not greatly matter, in this obscure debate, that we do not know when or how the bill of exchange first appeared in the West. Perhaps in the twelfth century; probably in Italy; possibly within the context of Genoese trade, for the transfer of money in the Mediterranean, or more likely to meet the needs of intra-European trade centred on the Champagne fairs. It may simply have been invented by the Jews, in their efforts to recover property left behind when they were forced into exile, another hypothesis which has been plausibly suggested. But in that case, was it perhaps an imitation of the bill of exchange which we know to have been circulating very early on among the merchants of Islam, from Tunisia (Ifriqya) to India? The bill of exchange may have been a cultural transfer, just like paper itself, the cotton bush, sugar cane or gunpowder. I have several times pinned my banner to this explanation, which is however unhesitatingly rejected by specialists on Islam, including Ashtor, though so far without any decisive evidence. Let us move on though, since it is the future of the bill of exchange which concerns us here.

Its existence unquestionably meant that the merchants and bankers had created a form of currency which was beyond the reach of princes, a quasi-currency that crossed all the political and monetary frontiers of Europe, constituting a unique level of exchange, over and above all the various metal currencies, where initiates could do what they pleased unhindered by the Church which, despite its long dispute with them over usury, was powerless against them. As for princes, while they might forbid the export of specie, the bill of exchange was beyond their grasp. In the end, it succeeded in creating what the authors of *Monnaie privée et pouvoir des princes* call 'inter-Europe', something which to my mind has all the characteristics of a world-economy, constituted within the continent of Europe, as long ago as the age of the Champagne fairs. I am inclined to accept this view, subject to a few clarifications and reservations.

In the first place, Christian Europe was in existence well before the twelfth century, and had of necessity established a network of relations throughout the continent. Such contacts inevitably led to transfers and movement of specie, for despite being both heavy and closely watched, coin did move about, as we know simply from the number of foreign coins in any one place referred to in documents. The bill of exchange merely duplicated the circuits of cash transfers; it did not eliminate them.

So metal coin had in any case already created a kind of 'European community', albeit an imperfect one, an achievement which both followed and accompanied the movement of goods and people.

The advantage of the bill of exchange was that it flew through the air. It operated at the top level, where some kind of centralization was necessary, because the system, depending on the quarterly fairs (rather than on the financial centres where turnover was quicker) required a central clearing house if some order was to be brought into a circulation artificially inflated by thousands of repeated transactions. 'Commerce', as François Mollien remarked in 1810, 'has every year set in motion twenty times the sum of the real wealth of gold and silver in Europe, perhaps even more, ever since it invented that miraculous universal currency known as drafts and remittances'.[589] So some kind of simplification or deflation was required, and clearing institutions emerged almost unbidden.

Was this really so extraordinary? If I were an individual businessman, I would surely find my incomings and outgoings to be roughly in balance, as a rule, and the balance would be visible, provided there was some kind of settling of accounts. This was the role played by Lyon, unquestionably the central clearing fair, during the period of the *écu de marc*, created in 1533 and only abandoned in 1575 in favour of the *écu soleil*. Lyon's decline as a commodity fair had admittedly begun as early as 1562, but exchange dealing continued to flourish there until 1575.[590] This was a significant extension, comparable to what happened to the Champagne fairs: they too ceased to be commodity centres in about 1300, but continued to provide exchange dealing until 1335.

But with Lyon in decline, another centre had to be found. From 1579, the so-called Besançon fair was held at Piacenza (about 40 kilometres from Milan). This was as strictly controlled by the Genoese as the Lyon fairs had been by the Florentines. Genoa's fortune was the natural consequence of a series of favourable circumstances, which enabled its merchant bankers to gain control of the immense mass of *political* money belonging to the king of Spain and circulating all over Europe, but which was particularly needed in the Netherlands because of the rebellion there. After 1557, the Genoese became the king of Spain's bankers, replacing the German firms of Fugger, Welser and others; they eventually took over the role formerly played by Antwerp. The war had cut communications between Spain and the North Sea in 1569: the Atlantic was out of bounds, so the Mediterranean came into its own. Spanish galleys in the king's service now carried ingots and chests of *reals* no longer to Antwerp but to Genoa, where they were sold to cities like Venice and Florence, which needed them for their trade with the Levant. Meanwhile by means of bills of exchange, the Genoese made available on the Antwerp money market the gold coin needed to pay the troops in Flanders.

Thus there came about the 'age of the Genoese', from 1558 to 1627, close on three-quarters of a century. While it lasted, all the trade of Europe centred on the Italian city and the fairs it had established at Piacenza.

Should we agree with the recent specialists on the subject, to whom I am indebted for this account, that the Genoese were actually 'perverting exchange'? Was it now no longer tied to underlying trade circuits, but dependent on transfers of *political* money from Spain? It was the artificial nature of the exercise, they argue, which explains why Piacenza, not to say Genoa itself, lost its extraordinary pre-eminence so quickly in the end.[591]

These new explanations ought to please me, but I am not convinced. Things look rather different to me. The bill of exchange, floating like a banner on top of the economy, was based both on liquid money, gold and silver, and on commodities. And while Genoa was amply provided with silver, it was not a major centre of trade in goods. Its merchant fleet was modest, despite having the cargo vessels of Ragusa at its disposal. The great *trade* route – for timber, grain, cloth and fabrics of all kinds, or ironwares – was monopolized by Dutch flyboats. Silver too eventually found its way on to the Atlantic route between Spain and the North Sea. From 1630, surprising as it may seem, English ships were carrying bullion on behalf of the king of Spain, while after 1648, even Dutch ships were joining in! Business was after all business. What was more, *marrano* bankers, converted Jews (sometimes of doubtful conversion), were also acting for Spain through the good offices of the Count Duke Olivares. Spain would gradually be drawn into their network, as France was later into that of the Protestant bankers. It was for these reasons, in my view – and not because of artificial manipulation of the bill of exchange – that the age of the Genoese came to an end. The city itself in any case remained fabulously wealthy.

From all the foregoing, conclusions emerge which require us to revise our views of the world-economy in general and of that constructed in Europe in particular, the one in which France was willy-nilly engaged. A world-economy, as already defined, is an autonomous economic zone, located in a given region of the planet. It tends to have a cardinal point, and in Europe that role was played in turn by Venice, Antwerp, Genoa, Amsterdam and

London. But if one bears in mind the key role played by the clearing fair, one has to accept that the European world-economy had two poles of attraction, a dominant city and a crucial fair. So that complicates the concept of the world-economy. In the days of the Champagne fairs, Genoa was already the dominant city from the point of view of exchange dealing. When the fairs declined, Venice moved into first place, associating itself with the fairs and the financial centre of Bruges. Antwerp came to be dominant later only through the link with Lyon, control of which it shared with Florence, the latter pulling the most important strings. Genoa, in its second period of glory, controlled a clearing fair very close to home, at Piacenza. But when the financial and commercial centre of Europe moved first to Amsterdam and later to London, the dual polarity between city and clearing fair lapsed. Amsterdam had everything, fairs and a Stock Exchange. London brought everything together, first in the Royal Exchange, founded by Gresham in 1571, then in its successor the Stock Exchange, created two hundred years later.

Have we now dealt with the bill of exchange and the strings of problems it caused? Not entirely, I dare say, as the reader can ascertain by looking at the diagrams in Figures 76 and 77. The first draws on data from the very rich archives of Francesco di Marco Datini, dating from the later fourteenth and early fifteenth centuries. The destination and departure points of the bills of exchange he sent and received – Naples, Rome, Florence, Milan, Genoa, Venice, Barcelona, Montpellier, Avignon, Bruges – give a fairly good idea of the bases of the prevailing European economy, from Italy to the North Sea: they clearly reveal the axis of the early modern phase of capitalism. The second diagram represents the network of bills of exchange and transfers of money traceable from the Piacenza fairs (known in Italy as the 'Bisenzone' i.e. Besançon fairs), controlled by the Genoese, at the turn of the sixteenth to seventeenth centuries. This network covered the whole of France and a large part of northern and eastern Europe, with the Frankfurt fair serving as a relay point for Vienna and Cracow. Two hundred years after Francesco Datini, 'inter-Europe', in other words the European world-economy, had considerably expanded.

FIGURE 76
The bill of exchange network in 1385–1410

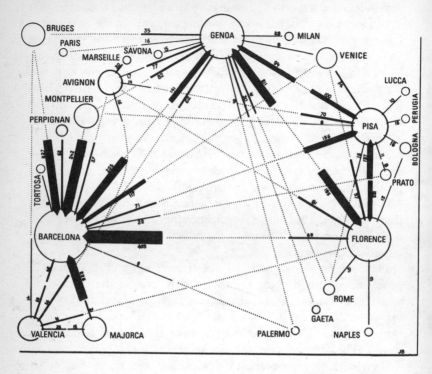

The arrows represent the movements and numbers of bills of exchange between one centre and another. When the bill made a return trip, the figure refers to the receiving centre. For example, Majorca sent 226 bills to Barcelona and 25 to Valencia; it received 31 from Barcelona and 15 from Valencia. (Map by Jacques Bertin).

This diagram is based on an exceptional source: the complete record, catalogued by Elena Cecchi, of bills of exchange circulated by Francesco di Marco Datini, merchant of Prato. Centred on the three major poles of Florence, Genoa and Barcelona (which were such important places in the fourteenth century), these bills trace for us the financial and commercial arena of international trade at the time; Italy, the French and Spanish Mediterranean coasts, with a 'branch' reaching up to Bruges and the north.

FIGURE 77
The triangle of bills of exchange and world specie movements

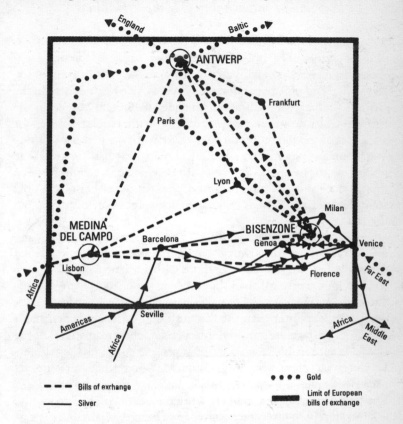

This diagram represents the situation two hundred years later than Figure 75, with the network of bills of exchange and movements of specie (silver from America or the Far East), controlled by the Genoese bankers. Centred now on the three essential poles of Piacenza (the so-called 'Bisenzone' fairs), Antwerp and Medina del Campo, the European network had expanded considerably to the east and north.

Finance and banking (1): the beginnings

If you leave the window open and the lamp on in summer, moths will be irresistibly drawn towards the light. Capitalists and moneyed men were equally drawn towards the ever-lit lamp of the state. They did not always burn their wings. In every country in the world, whether Ming China, India under the Grand Mogul, or the countries of Europe, the state was always the biggest business of all, a sort of suction pump for money. I do not say that life was one long round of paying taxes and dues, but it was hard to avoid the obligation to pay up: taxation had after all existed for centuries – in France since at least Philip Augustus, the true begetter of the Capet state. He had the French making their useful contributions from the start.

Means of escape were possible of course: fraud, evasion – and even straightforward poverty. Lucien Febvre used to say that the dirtiest villages in France were those with a seigneur, because they tried to look worse off than they were in order to deceive the seigneur about their capacity to pay. But perhaps it was harder to trick one's local exploiter than the distant king of France. 'The richest man in the village', reported the *grand bailli* (chief magistrate) of the Ile-de-France in 1709, 'would not at present dare kill a pig, unless he did it at night without people knowing [difficult surely?] because if he killed a pig in public, his taxes would be raised.'[592] The taxpayer took good care too to avoid settling his bill promptly, lest this should be interpreted as a sign of being well off and the signal for raising the rates. It was preferable to sit back and wait for the long and costly legal wrangle his delay would provoke.

The great mass of money, credit, receipts and expenses set in motion by the state was the biggest financial affair in *ancien régime* France, as well as in later times. It represented at least 5% and possibly 10% of the national product from the start, in France as in other European countries. Over time of course, the percentage increased. In present-day France, the state accounts for something like 50% of GNP, a massive proportion, which has a powerful impact on the entire economy and is pushing French society towards an order which may or may not be considered appropriate but which inevitably provokes grumbles.

Alongside the potential and overwhelming wealth of the state, the fortunes of families like the Medicis, the Fuggers, the Welsers or the Rothschilds were derisory. The wealth of the Rothschild family in France in 1840 was estimated at 123 million francs – about 2% of the money supply in France at the time.

But the state treasury was a strange one, with stocks that forever varied and fluctuated. It was a pool overflowing one minute, dry the next, only to fill up and be emptied once more. The state grabbed people's money, then gave it back or redistributed it, while sometimes holding some back: Sully had treasure piled up in the Arsenal and the Banque de France has its gold reserves in the vaults. Flowing first in one direction then in the other, called in then sent out, the state's money represented a sort of giant sweep-stake with success virtually guaranteed. What capitalist would not wish to put some money into it in order to become one of the players? In the private sector, whether one was dealing in exchange or commodities on the great trade circuits of Europe, one had to be prepared to wait, to take risks and to calculate accurately. Serving the state, while not forgetting to serve oneself, might look a more attractive option.

Certainly turning state revenues into private income is a very old game. So we may suppress a smile when a journalist writing about Morocco 'discovers' that the colonies were a way of turning public investment into private profit, or when today's economists condemn present-day collusion between capitalists and the state. Was there ever a time when this was not true? Can one imagine any state doing without the services of merchants, financiers and bankers? Are we to disapprove of Louis XIV for (in Saint-Simon's words)[593] 'prostituting himself' by receiving at Marly Samuel Bernard, the 'king of the merchants' in France and Europe; or of the Empress Eugénie for welcoming James de Rothschild to the court of Napoleon III? These were calculated and rational gestures. During the War of the Spanish Succession, revenue from indirect taxes had dwindled: the lease of the Ferme Générale had fallen by

1703 to 42 million *livres* – 20 million less than it was producing in 1683. Faced with such a decline, the tax farmers refused to renew their contracts. The tax farms were therefore operated directly by the state, as *régies*, but by 1709, they were only yielding 31 million *livres*.[594] Circumstances obliged the state and capitalism to proceed hand in hand.

Perhaps the most interesting aspect of this is that because of the state, a kind of fault line runs through French economic history: on one side, to use present-day language, is the public sector, on the other the private sector. If life were simple – unfortunately it is not – we could say that *finance* operated on the state side, being more or less confined to the public sector, whereas *banking* dealt in affairs that were no concern of governments, and of which bankers soon acquired complete control. If things were as clear-cut as this, we could distinguish once and for all between bankers and financiers as two separate breeds. This is of course impossible. In the fifteenth century, the term financier was applied without distinction both to royal office-holders who were responsible for managing public money, and to men of means with private status.[595] It was only later that the two words came to mean different things. A financier, according to the eighteenth-century *Encyclopédie*, was 'any person known to have an interest in tax-farms, *régies* or business to do with the king's revenue'.[596] In the nineteenth century, the two words tend to become confused once more, probably because the Revolution had restored to the state officials (as *régies*) the task of collecting both direct taxes (as had only partly been the case before) and indirect taxes, abolishing that abnormal excrescence the Ferme Générale. After that, in theory and legally, the state was master of its own finances.

That said, in what follows I shall assume a theoretical distinction between the private and the public sector, between banking and finance, one which was fairly clear during the centuries of the *ancien régime*.

It should nevertheless be understood

1) that this is by no means a hard and fast dividing line: it was often crossed, with bankers turning financier and financiers turning banker;

2) that the vantage point chosen for observation is not that of the 'fiscal state' as constituted since Philip Augustus, with the creation of the tax system, but the 'finance state', *l'Etat financier*, to use Pierre Chaunu's formula, that is to say the state which could not survive without the aid of its suppliers of cash, wherever they stood in regard to our demarcation line. They were the men who provided that 'money which is the blood coursing through the veins of the state', to borrow the words of an *intendant-général*.[597] How then was the state served – or not served? And how did it react?

To this last question, the answer is that it reacted by turns either too leniently – when it had little choice – or too harshly. It assumed the right, through brutal prosecutions carried out by special tribunals, to make its servants pay dearly. Jacques Coeur, Semblançay and Fouquet were all victims of state vengeance. John Law probably would have been if he had not left the country. In 1793, the Convention executed the *fermiers-généraux*, including Lavoisier. Should that particular tragedy be described as one of the continuities between the Revolution and the *ancien régime*? If we are talking about continuity, a better example perhaps is Napoleon, who unexpectedly called on the survivors of the Ferme Générale to administer indirect taxes during the Empire. At least they had plenty of experience.

Jacques Coeur (c.1395–1456), Charles VII's financier, restored currency coherence to the kingdom in 1436, and lent the king the 2 million *livres* which enabled him to reconquer Normandy. He was clearly on both sides of our dividing line, being both a financier for the king and a banker and *négociant* on his personal account, with interests in many mining enterprises and contacts in all the major European centres: Bruges, Marseille, Montpellier, Genoa and Venice. He kept a fleet of at least seven galleys at Aigues-Mortes and engaged successfully in the Levant trade. He was an extra-ordinary man, 'a brilliant emulator of the Italian businessmen of his time'[598] and a great servant to the king. But he discovered to his cost how dangerous it could be to trespass on the territory of the prince, in particular by being too rich and influential. On the absurd charge of having poisoned Agnès Sorel, Charles VII's favourite, the 'Dame de Beauté', he was thrown into prison in

1451 and a trial prepared. Fortunately for him, he escaped, dying in 1456 in Cyprus, in the service of the Pope. A romantic story and a significant example for our purposes.

A similar but more tragic lot befell Jacques de Beaune, baron de Semblançay (1445–1527), one of a family of merchant bankers from Touraine, where the frequent visits by kings of France had led to a number of local fortunes being made. He served first Charles VIII, then Louis XII, and at first had his own banking house. In 1518, he became *surintendant des finances* to François I. The king's mother, Louise of Savoy, made use of his services, then turned against him, which she was notoriously capable of doing to people who had become a nuisance. She even accused him, unjustly it seems, of having diverted to his own account the pay of the army campaigning in the Milanese. An enquiry cleared him of the charges. But he was unwise enough to refuse funds and to protest against another expedition which resulted in the reconquest of the Milanese and the bloody disaster of Pavia on 24 February 1525. François I was taken prisoner on the battlefield, and Louise of Savoy became regent in his absence. With the complicity of certain others, she lodged charges against the *surintendant*. Semblançay was condemned to death and hanged on the gibbet at Montfaucon.

History repeated itself with Nicolas Fouquet, who became sole *surintendant* in 1659, having previously shared the post with Servien. He too fell into disgrace, was arrested on 5 September 1661 and, surprisingly, condemned to life imprisonment rather than death. He died after twenty years harsh incarceration in the fortress of Pignerol in 1680. Even his death is mysterious. Did he perhaps know too much?[599] Historians today are inclined to be on his side rather than on that of his triumphant masters, the wretched Colbert and the wretched Louis XIV.

The Fouquet affair was the last of these tragic episodes. But what might have happened to John Law, after the disastrous collapse of his 'System', if the Regent had not facilitated his flight to Venice? Did he, like Fouquet, know too much? And it is possible that even Necker, after his dismissal on 11 July 1789, might have been put on trial if the attempt to reassert royal authority had not failed.

Returning to the distinction between banking and finance, we might note that Fouquet, unlike Jacques Coeur and Semblançay, was a financier, with no banking interests, reflecting perhaps the spirit of his age.

It seems to me that the reign of the financiers proper – also known as *traitants* or *partisans* – began at the great turning-point halfway through the sixteenth century. This was when the slow but eventually total elimination of foreign bankers took place. Thereafter, the French king tried to restrict his requests for money to his own subjects (*regnicoles*). But he still needed just as many loans and advances. Moreover, the French monarchy was incapable of collecting unaided the income from direct and indirect taxation. It just did not have enough staff – civil servants as we should call them today. So a particular system became established whereby the tax collector became the state's provider of funds.

Regarding indirect taxation, the French solution was the same as that adopted by the republic of Venice, where taxes were farmed out at auction to the highest bidder. These Venetian tax farmers were usually men of comparatively modest means, but behind them were patricians who underwrote the operation, that is they took part in it clandestinely, advancing funds and receiving their share of the profits. Although there was no formal imitation of the Venetian system, exactly the same applied to the king's tax farmers in France, who had such a bad reputation. It was a reputation which went beyond the bounds of malice, for these financiers were neither jumped-up nobodies nor arrant rogues. If they were able to advance huge sums to the king, it was because they had the backing, as in Venice, of a mass of investors who entrusted their capital to others in hope of returns. They were middlemen above all. The system would survive somehow until the Revolution, having reached the peak of its extension with the creation of the Ferme Générale in 1669, in Colbert's time.

As for direct taxation, the final operation was entrusted to officiers de finance, office-holders who had bought their posts: *receveurs-généraux, généraux des monnaies, sous-receveurs*. And they too unofficially became endless providers of funds.

As has often been commented, the monarchy was thereby

signing away its own powers. But what was the choice? It could have chosen differently it is true, if like Britain in 1688 (always one jump ahead of the continent), it had set up a modern inland revenue department. As we have seen, such was not the case. So France had to be content with this twofold and undoubtedly archaic system. Two recent studies by Françoise Bayard and Daniel Dessert both nevertheless concur that at the end of the day, the 'remarkable vitality', and 'extreme' or 'extraordinary suppleness' of the system did allow French state policy somehow to survive all the troubles of Louis XIV's reign, 'through all the scares and bankruptcies'.[600] The king, who was cheated, losing quite a substantial share of the tax levied on his subjects, was also, they argue, well served – essentially because the fund-providers concealed behind the financier were often richer than the latter: they belonged to the monied and socially most select classes, 'the noblesse d'épée, de robe et d'Eglise',[601] including grandees and ministers. The operation afforded substantial profits and theoretically there was no risk, since all loans were pledged against the king's tax revenues. The lenders' anonymity was respected with punctilious discretion[602] (given finance's bad reputation, no such men would wish to be publicly associated with it). So the financiers had little difficulty in meeting the state's requests. They had abundant capital at their disposal, invested by people hoping for rewards. In short, the system could be said to have the merit of bringing sleeping capital out of strong-boxes.

The king's debts however went on rising, as did the fiscal demands made on the mass of tax-paying subjects. Our two authors conclude, rightly, that the France which bore this crushing burden must have been richer than is usually thought, and that the trade balance must have been far more positive than previously assumed, since the enormous sums of money collected by the financiers were always in specie, in hard cash.

These cool-headed conclusions open the door to a rehabilitation of the royal finances of the *ancien régime*. We ought to set aside Felix Gaiffe's famous book *L'Envers du Grand Siècle*, of somewhat overblown reputation. And we should not take too literally the caricatural insinuations of the theatre of the time, which was particularly ferocious towards financiers, claiming they had come from the lowest classes of society, which is untrue; that they were wasteful and dishonest, which is possible; and that they were made fools of by the ladies of the aristocracy whom they kept in funds. Despite Lesage's bitter portrait of the financier in *Turcaret*, he was not as a rule a small-time usurer, 'selling silver at the price of gold' and hoodwinking the naive.

In any case, the system could scarcely be said to have been chosen. It was, rather, imposed by circumstances. It can really only be understood, I think, if one goes back earlier than the seventeenth century, at least as far as the reign of Henri II: a wretched time, remarkable for some wretched characters, but that did not stop the economy or war from carrying on as normal. And since war was in full swing, the government spent a great deal of money. In order to do so, it borrowed on the rich Lyon money market, and not merely as in the past from the Italian bankers and merchants who had long controlled international finance. As early as 1542–3 (when François I was still on the throne), Cardinal de Tournon (1489–1562), archbishop of Lyon, had managed to put public finance in touch with private French capital in his city. He repeated the operation, on a much larger scale, just before the last battle in the Italian wars in 1555. This loan became known as the *grand party*: the French bankers advanced the king 2,600,000 *écus* over 41 successive fairs, interest on each being 4%, plus 1% depreciation. As there were four fairs a year, annual interest was thus 20% over ten years. As well as taking money from the bankers, the *receveur* in Lyon accepted investment from any private individuals, in exchange for the waiving of obligations. So a mass of small subscribers hastened to invest: 'Everyone came running to put his money into it . . . even servants who brought their savings. Women sold their jewels, widows diverted their annuities into it'. Foreigners could also subscribe, 'not only the Swiss cantons, German princes and others, but Turkish merchants and pashas using the names of their factors'.[603]

This loan, which appealed to both bankers and the general public (the bankers as usual lending other people's money) was thus extremely 'modern', virtually similar in every point to the procedure used in the seventeenth and eighteenth centuries for Dutch loans;[604] or indeed much later, after 1840, when the Rothschilds were great organizers of French government loans. In short, the *grand party* was outside the ordinary run of financial solutions. There was no comparison between this feverish launch and the prudent issue of *rentes sur l'Hôtel de Ville*, in Fouquet's own time – although in fact the latter carried fabulously high rates of interest.

At this point, the French suffered the terrible defeat at Saint-Quentin (10 August 1557) the last straw before the peace of Cateau-Cambrésis, followed not long after by the tragic and unexpected death of Henri II (10 July 1559).

The debt left by the king was enormous. The paper bonds of the *grand party* fell progressively to 80, 70, 50 and 40 per cent of their value.[605] This brought about the collapse of French finances, and the near-rupture between the state and the financiers, or more accurately between the state and a modern version of capitalism. For many years I shared Frank Spooner's view that the centre of gravity of the French economy then moved from Lyon to Paris, a transfer which my British colleague compared to the shift from Antwerp to Amsterdam. I have now changed my mind about this and think that Paris did not in fact take first place from Lyon until the late eighteenth century. But in about 1559, some Italian firms certainly did move to Paris: the Capponis for instance, or that colourful individual Sebastian Zamet.[606] They were simply moving closer to the favours distributed by the French crown.

The 1559 scare was the more worrying since the crisis had become pan-European, affecting Antwerp and Venice, Spain, Cracow and Lyon, the 'central fair'. These shocks and disasters also coincided with the opening years of the 'age of the Genoese', which was not very good news for France and positively catastrophic for Lyon; and this betokened a new orientation in the European economy, which now looked, as in the ancient past, to the Mediterranean. Hauser, Mousnier and Hartlaub all agree with me about this. Henri Hauser has even written that 'the 1557 crisis . . . probably hindered the evolution of commercial capitalism'.[607]

Finance and banking (2): a lost opportunity

The financial system established by the latter half of the six-teenth century remained in use throughout the reign of Louis XIV. Frequent wars placed strains on it, but for want of a better solution to hand, they ended up reinforcing and maintaining it. Faced with deadlines and urgent demands for payment, the French treasury called on its office-holders, its *traitants* and *fermiers-généraux* and on the administrators of the many tax-farms. (The latter were created rather at random and often to suit the buyer, since the government lived in a hand to mouth manner, in constant panic that it would run out of money.) It is true that the *traitants* and office-holders were not in theory creating concrete debts for the government, since in both cases they were advancing loans against future public revenue, in other words the taxpayers' money.

But taxpayers' money had its limits. Taxpaying France was essentially peasant France, which still lived to a large extent on the margins of the money economy and whose prosperity or hardship depended on the harvest: if the harvest was too good, it meant that prices collapsed; on the other hand, if it was poor it brought food shortages and indeed repeated famine. The system was therefore prone to problems and breakdowns. The War of the Augsburg League (1686–97) placed considerable strain on it: by the end of the war, the *traitants* and office-holders had exhausted all their available resources. The almost immediate outbreak of further hostilities in 1701, with the death of Charles II of Spain and the War of the Spanish Succession, found them in complete disarray. They were obliged to turn to the bankers, and it was at this point that so-called Protestant banking, which had already played a walk-on part before 1697, came to occupy a leading role in the history of the French monarchy.

The story of this international banking community, an 'intra-European' one, is similar to that of the 'new Christians' of the Iberian Peninsula. Driven from their homeland, the latter had travelled the world, establishing contacts and keeping up business links. Banking is unthinkable without some kind of world-wide network. I mentioned earlier how the new Christians had managed to get hold of the king of Spain's political money, from their bases in Holland – a feat which is almost worthy of fiction. Newcomers to a foreign land, and enemies of Spain to boot, they succeeded in imposing on Spain their necessary and (almost) loyal services, while the Castilian authorities continued to make accusations against them, sometimes of the most gratuitous kind and not always religious. Protestant banking would come to play a far more important role in France than the new Christians in the reign of Philip IV. But its origins are almost exactly the same.

There had been a certain number of Protestant bankers in France before the Revocation of the Edict of Nantes in 1685: Protestants were barred from careers in state service, so they tended to go in for industry, commerce and finance. But the bankers were not irreducible pillars of their faith, far from it: with the aid of the crown authorities themselves in Paris, and under a little pressure, they converted to Catholicism, perhaps paying it no more than lip service, but without fuss. There were many Protestant bankers and merchants however who chose the path of exile and left for Geneva, Basle, Frankfurt, Amsterdam and London, thus setting up, without necessarily intending to, that international system of contacts without which banking cannot successfully operate. It is no paradox that the Revocation of the Edict of Nantes was in fact a shot in the arm for Protestant banking, if it did not actually create it from scratch, since it offered it a new role, making possible the barely clandestine return of its financiers to Lyon and Paris, without even obliging them this time to conceal their Protestantism. This should not be seen simply as a miraculous example of just deserts and moral revenge. Having travelled to America, in the late 1930s, on boats full of unhappy refugees from Nazi Germany, I have often thought since that for some at least this exile brought good fortune – in the domain of banking and business among others.

During the War of the Augsburg League, Protestant banking had already been pressed into Louis XIV's service by circumstances. With the rest of Europe up in arms against him, Geneva was the only 'corridor' through which France could negotiate with the rest of Europe and obtain credit from Amsterdam – for although Holland was at war with France, business relations between them had not been broken off. Through Geneva, France received the indispensable gold and silver bullion without which French mints could not have continued to produce coin; and without coin, how was the army to be paid? Under the breakneck pressure of these transfers, Geneva, still a small town at the time, was transformed: the industry which had hitherto been its means of support declined (silk production in particular) and the guilds protested loudly at the decision of certain wealthy families in the town to move from industry and commerce into banking.

Thus Geneva first became involved with the French Crown's finances. The involvement deepened during the long War of the Spanish Succession, the major drama of the last years of Louis XIV. This time France was fighting on the same side as Spain, of which the duc d'Anjou had become king, as Philip V. Once more, the rest of Europe was lined up against the Sun King. With Spain as an ally, France was no longer short of bullion supplies, but its financial system was in disarray, so it was to the Protestant bankers, in Geneva in the first instance, that appeals were made to rescue the Crown's finances. At the centre of these dealings was Samuel Bernard, one of the *religionnaire* bankers who had remained in France after 1685, having abjured his faith in December that year under pressure from the authorities. He had made a fortune, paradoxically, or perhaps one should say in mysterious circumstances, just after the Revocation. No doubt he had acted as banker for émigré Protestants, holding their capital for them while waiting to get it out of the country. At all events, he boasted that he had never borrowed money in France.[608] This fortune of obscure origin enabled him to aspire to, and indeed reach, a leading position. His success marks 'the *first triumph* of banking – cosmopolitan and Huguenot what is more – over the old-fashioned financiers who were now relegated to the more modest role of tax collectors'.[609]

It fell indeed to the old system – which took on this role with a bad grace – to arrange for the reimbursement of loans by means of revenues collected for the king. Bankers – or rather Samuel Bernard – advanced the money required for immediate payment, thanks to the issue of the bills of exchange, which were indispensable so long as the war was essentially being waged beyond French frontiers, in Germany, Italy and Spain. He was in a way 'discounting public and semi-public assets',[610] and this, the authors of *Monnaie privée et pouvoir des princes* would probably say, was another 'perversion' of the bill of exchange – but then was it not through successive perversions of its original function that the bill of exchange contrived to renew itself? This time, it was used first to provide funds for the royal treasury and then to transfer them. The problem was repayment of the money, and this was where the precipice yawned.

It was through a mixture of folly, inexperience, greed for profit (since discounting rates were as high as 36%), and the impression that they were on to a good thing, not to be given up at any price, that the Genevan bankers (the Hogguer brothers for instance, after Huguetan, the first victim who fell irretrievably bankrupt) got into dire straits. In the end, their families came to the rescue, not without difficulties. Samuel Bernard, being more experienced, having funds lodged with André Pels (*négociant*, shipowner and banker, one of the wealthiest businessmen in Holland),[611] and above all being in closer contact in Paris with the all powerful controllers-general of finance, survived, sailed with the tide, made advances, and more or less monopolized bills of exchange. But the moment of truth came for him too in 1708. He was supposed to settle in Lyon a mere trifle of 14 million *livres* in cash: a huge sum, which he did not possess. All he had was 18 million in banknotes issued in 1705, which had depreciated by over 80%. It is true that in 1704, Samuel Bernard had been one of those who advised having recourse to paper currency, and that he had not imagined at first that it would be so quickly devalued. But reality had caught up with him. If Bernard's credit remained good in foreign markets, notably Amsterdam, the same was not true of Lyon, a centre where he had little influence, where his position was unsure and where he was detested as much as he was feared. Lyon stood for the old system.

True the government had provided Bernard with a whole series of tax assignments and rescriptions: 'on the Ferme Générale, on the duties on Tobacco and Post, on registration tax, on the king's secretaries, on Boues et Lanternes (street-cleaning and lighting), on the Butcheries of Paris, on the Saisies nobiliaires and on the *receveurs-généraux*'[612] – in short on all manner of revenues old and new (new ones being invented, one imagines, from day to day), as well as on the treasury, which saw only a trickle of the revenue due to the king. Later, he was assigned revenue from the Caisse de l'Extraordinaire. But these were all promises. And time was money, so any delay meant disaster. Several bankers in Lyon advanced money and Samuel Bernard, with their agreement, issued bills of exchange on them, the usual 'cavalerie' device. But everyone was impatient for the 'horses' (i.e. bills) to return to the stable. Tired of waiting, and with treacherous motives too, two of his creditors, Lullin and Constant, sold off the royal treasury notes that had been given them as pledges, at 70% of their value. This was a serious blow for all paper instruments.

It would take too long to go into the details of Samuel Bernard's on-off bankruptcy. He was saved *in extremis* by a reprieve signed on 22 September 1709 by the new controller of finance, Nicolas Desmarets, a man who held his post until the death of Louis XIV in 1715, and whose personal lucidity, intelligence and energy must deserve our esteem. But Desmarets was a man of the Ferme Générale, the *ancien régime* – on principle or of necessity? At any rate, he was the man who saved Samuel Bernard in 1709, but could it not be said that the moratorium he granted Bernard was also needed by the public treasury, in order to settle its own debts? How is one to explain the actions of these two men? In the case of Bernard, we must note his boundless ambition, his desire to be the king's sole banker and to keep to himself for his personal profit the goldmine of the royal finances. Desmarets, unlike his predecessor Chamillart, was a reliable and lucid expert on financial questions, but when he took over in 1708 from the man who had so long been his boss, he found himself bound practically hand and foot. It was impossible to avoid appealing to the bankers, and notably to Samuel Bernard.

Chamillart himself had tried to do the same, in the year that he resigned. The French armies, except those in Spain, had been driven back inside the frontiers. So payments outside France, by way of Milan and Amsterdam, were no longer required. Chamillart gave orders for 'all available money to be collected directly from the provincial treasurers, that it may be carried straight to the armies without intermediaries and without recourse to drafts and payments abroad'.[613] Unfortunately, this was not a solution. The armies demanded to be paid *regularly* and transfers of cash, difficult to organize and irregular by definition, could not be spaced over time to meet the deadlines for regular troop paydays and expenses. Once more, appeals had to be made to Samuel Bernard and his rapid transfers by bill of exchange. So, whether with or without a heavy heart, Desmarets was obliged to allow Bernard's adventurous intervention to continue. His delay in granting the moratorium leaves wide open the question about the secret motives behind his conduct – if secret there was. Did he like the rather arrogant banker, or detest him?

Perhaps something of a wedge was further driven between them by a project which failed, alas: the creation of a Royal Bank. Samuel Bernard had pressed for this with all his might. It would have been a link between the monarchical state and private credit. For the bank would not have been under government control. It would have taken on the royal debt – hundreds of millions of paper notes which it would have called in, in order to issue new ones, worth more than the old. This was the policy adopted, but on a small scale and under pressure of day to day needs, by the Caisse des receveurs-généraux, known as the Caisse Legendre, set up by Desmarets.

What would have become of such a bank, which was so sorely needed both by France and the monarchy? It would almost certainly have become a deposit and issuing bank on the model, well-known to all parties, of the Bank of England created in 1688. But Samuel Bernard and the bankers would have been in control of it. It was the financiers of the Ferme Générale and the *receveurs-généraux* who rejected the project. And so too (though their reasons are harder to see) did the *négociants*. And Desmarets himself was apparently hostile to its creation. So it was back to the old system, to the France of the financiers. The Caisse Legendre was a false bank, I am almost inclined to say a counter-bank. The time had not yet come when the bankers would be deeply involved in the royal finances. As things turned out, with their bills of exchange, their deposits, their investment in major projects – such as the Louisiana scheme of Antoine Crozat, the Saint-Malo expeditions, and wartime privateering – they remained in the centre of overseas and European trade. They continued to be many-sided businessmen, like their predecessors and indeed their successors. But an opportunity had been lost.

Finance and banking (3)

So, with the consent or tolerance of Desmarets, the old system of 'publicans' was allowed to continue. It had a new lease of life, and once more, despite all its faults and drawbacks, it enabled the monarchy to exist and to survive miraculously, until the end of the War of the Spanish Succession. I will not go so far as to say that the system led logically to the *chambre de justice* of March 1716, entrusted with inquiring into 'embezzlement and abuses . . . committed to the detriment and on the occasion of the royal finances', but it was after all the monarchy's habitual reaction, as unjust and brutal as in the past. Desmarets was dismissed on the death of Louis XIV, and with his departure the Caisse Legendre collapsed for good. 8,000 financiers were investigated and 4,410 condemned to fines and repayments, some of them being sent to prison.[614]

The system was certainly not to blame for that other, more famous 'System', launched by John Law (1716–23), a sequence of extraordinary and well-publicized events which clearly indicated that it was still impossible for the French economy to accept the processes of modern capitalism. Across the Channel, the collapse of the South Sea Bubble, the equivalent of Law's venture, certainly distressed England, but the English economy absorbed the disturbance, and regained its balance – the government having supported the defaulting South Sea Company – whereas in France by

649

contrast, everything vanished without trace: the entire Law experiment left nothing behind.[615]

I am not convinced by the at best partial explanations historians have given of this affair. Thiers, for instance, claims that Law made the mistake of resorting to 'fictional capital', and the 'doubtful value' of shares, in short of meddling with metal specie, which was at the time and would long remain the foundation of economic life in France.[616] Jacob van Klaveren, the subtlest analyst, puts it all down to the failure of the Louisiana project (the Mississippi scheme), the unsuccessful South Seas venture, and also countermanoeuvres by grandees like the princes de Conti and Condé. He does not attach so much importance to the frantic speculation in the rue Quincampoix, the unofficial open-air bourse. Law himself – but how reliable a source is he? – later blamed the outbreak of plague in Marseille which paralysed a quarter of France in 1720 to 1721, and according to him, wrecked his experiment.

All the explanations have some truth in them, but they must be combined, and furthermore some underlying responsibility must be attached to the French economy as a whole, which was archaic in its practices. The graft of the new did not take. Law managed to flee the country, thanks to the Regent who, according to rumour, had received his share of the pennies from heaven. The Tuscan representative in Paris did not hesitate to write home on 30 September 1720: 'Il Reggente ne deve certo avere accumulato al meno per trecento miglioni.'[617] It seems highly likely indeed that the Regent should have both been involved and made something out of the 'system', but to what extent? (Three hundred million francs as the writer suggests?) Was it his fault if, after the dust had settled, France returned to the old ways (the *visa* being one more chamber of justice, the last one); and if, after the débâcle, he had to compensate the financiers by abandoning to them the liquidation of Law's legacy? This did indeed mean returning to the old system, so fiercely criticized in 1715, and to the dreadful Pâris brothers, but what was the choice? This was the only card left to play.

But should we, on the other hand, as too many historians tend to, exaggerate the importance of Law's System? To read some of them, one would think he had revitalized the French economy, and helped a few more gold coins find their way into the peasant's woollen stocking. The experience undoubtedly served to discredit paper currency in the minds of the French people. But was the whole thing really any more than a summer thunderstorm? Earl J. Hamilton has shown, in some very precisely argued articles, that the System did not cause either the runaway prices or the spectacular ruins that have been claimed. In Paris, prices did double for a brief moment, then rapidly fell back to their normal level. But these articles do not seem to have been read, or remembered, by many historians. In another study, this time of notarial activity in Paris and Versailles, Jean-Paul Soissons has also noted that their business seems to have been carried on very much as usual, whereas one might have expected a frantic flurry of activity.[618] Stirring events may, like summer storms, be more sound and fury than anything else.

The old system re-emerged at any rate, and the level of the king's debts returned more or less to that of 1718. Cardinal Fleury, whose period in office (1726–43) was beneficial, despite what the marquis d'Argenson says and repeats in his *Journal*, turned the clock back in 1726 and reinstated the Ferme Générale (since 1703, it had been replaced by direct commissions, *régies*).

It would serve little purpose from our point of view to retrace in detail the monotonous history of the monarchy's financial services from this point. The whole machine swung implacably into motion again, with all the old devices, the good intentions and the harsh injustices of the past. The financiers and the Crown did not quarrel until late into the century, after 1770 and the energetic reactions of the triumvirate. Louis XV no doubt restored the balance of the monarchy for a further two decades. Terray, promoted to Controller-General, brought much upheaval but little renovation.

The real change, as so often, came from outside the closed system, from the deep levels of the French economy. An amazing revival was taking place in the old kingdom, as if new sap were rising in springtime. It was this revival, as Jean Bouvier has commented, that released credit, giving it strength and vigour, and extending its volume and its impact.[619] Protestant and cosmopolitan banking had never forsaken the kingdom – indeed how could it? – but now it came back with a vengeance. The house of Thélusson (known by several names in later years, most famously as Thélusson-Necker from 1757 to 1768) had set up in Paris at the beginning of the century and by 1715, as peace returned, it had branches in Genoa, London, Amsterdam and Geneva. Vernet came to France in 1742; Perrégaux in 1781; Bidermann and Clavière in 1782; Hottinguer in 1785.

The great name of Necker towers over this period. Becoming Controller-General in all but name in 1777, Necker was forced to resign on 19 May 1781. But further deterioration in the crown's finances brought his recall in August 1788. He was dismissed once more on 11 July 1789. Two days later, Paris was up in arms. That a banker should be so popular, that bankers should in 1789 be supporting the Revolution, are questions certainly dramatic enough to warrant attention. But they are not our present concern.

From 1789 to 1848

Moving faster now, I should like to look at the whole period from 1789 to 1848, from one long and tempestuous revolution to another revolution, no less profound but which did not have time to work itself through. Contrary to custom, I am deliberately treating the French Revolution, the Empire, the Restoration and the July Monarchy as a single period, since they are in fact linked, forming a meaningful sequence for our purposes. This was the age when finance began to recede in importance, and banking, while retaining its identity, came to the fore to occupy the vacated terrain, in other words, the bankers moved closer to the state and entered its service. But banking continued to be essentially separate from the state, thus retaining its freedom of manoeuvre.

In fact the Revolution dictated the sequence of events to a greater extent than is usually allowed. In the first place, it cleared the ground. Next, it preserved and rebuilt. And lastly, it was a selective test for those banking houses which remained active or semi-active, in spite of everything.

The Revolution, for better or worse, made a clean sweep:

by abolishing indirect taxes (though they were reintroduced in practice), and by collecting direct taxes inefficiently if at all, the state authorities destroyed the fiscal machinery: consequently, they were very soon obliged to start printing paper, issuing *assignats* and *mandats territoriaux*.

The urgently needed restoration of order was the first task of the Consulate at the end of 1799. It was now that the administration was created, with at its head a Ministry of Finance (to centralize revenue) and a Ministry of the Treasury (to organize expenditure). 'France today is too big', said Bonaparte, 'for a Ministry of Finance to control everything! And I need a guarantee of good financial administration: I should not have that with a single ministry.'[620] It is of course his first sentence – France is too big – which is music to my ears. Underneath this double ministry then, there was created a great bureaucratic machine of tax-collectors, inspectors, *receveurs*, all appointed by the state, and each of whom had to pay a sizeable caution on his own account. In this reorganization however, many men and many arrangements from the *ancien régime* remained intact. The new *receveurs-généraux*, for instance, were allowed a period of grace before paying the money they had received in to the central authorities: in the meantime they had an opportunity (rather like the old *receveurs-généraux*) to invest the money they held, before handing it over. There was thus some temptation for the treasury to turn to them for advances. Nevertheless, the new machinery was quite different from the old: the reign of the publicans was over.

The new régime destroyed, but it also preserved, innovated and protected. By creating the Banque de France in 1800, the Consulate intended to protect banking and trade, which stood in great need of it. The bank was in fact set up by reorganizing the Caisse des comptes courants, created in partnership by a group of bankers, but which had had difficulty operating properly (24 *pluviôse* Year VIII to 13 February 1800). Three years later, the new bank obtained the exclusive privilege of issuing notes, in practice only of very high denominations, so that at first and for some time to come it was essentially at the service of big business rather than of the state. 'It was understood', Bertrand Gille notes, 'as a sort of cooperative mutual benefit society [for the rich]. The price of shares in it – 5,000 francs – put them out of the reach of small traders.' It belonged to the bankers who were the majority of the first generation of 'regents': Périer, Robillard, Perrégaux, Mallet, Lecoulteux, Récamier, Germain. Among them there were however some *négociants* and one notary. Was it shocking that the heirs of the Revolution should have allowed the new bank to be very largely taken over by the private sector? Since the old finance sector had been put out of action, there was in fact no other viable solution. All the same, it was a goldmine for the favoured few who were in at the beginning. On 29 February 1800, the new bank opened its counters.[621]

The intervention of the Banque de France, during the Consulate and Empire, smoothed out many of the problems encountered by commerce and banks in Paris and even in the provinces. It played a triple role: as a deposit, discount and issuing bank. It was prudent from the start, and circumspection remained its immutable rule of conduct: no discounting without at least three signatures, no discounting over more than three months. It did on some occasions help out established houses in difficulty, and also came to the rescue of the government when it was short of advances, without however letting the state get a foot in the door. It was a very aloof establishment – so aloof indeed that the crises of 1803, 1806 and 1810 did not affect it – which is more than can be said of the Paris bankers.

As I have already suggested, during a period of expansion, banking tended to advance more rapidly than commerce, which nevertheless made some progress, while industry and agriculture lagged behind at a respectful distance. But during times of recession or stagnation, agriculture, tortoise-like, kept creeping forward, and industry continued to progress, while commerce fell off rapidly, dragging credit, in other words banks, down with it. This is more or less what happened between 1789 and 1815. Nevertheless, the chief Parisian banking-houses (among them Perrégaux, the mysterious 'banker of the Committee of Public Safety') had survived the difficult revolutionary period without too much trouble.[622] During these tempestuous times, wisdom naturally counselled keeping a low profile and playing safe. 'The Mallets followed just such a policy: their capital stood at 800,000 *livres* in 1788, 525,000 in 1792, 240,000 in 1794 and zero during the heyday of the *assignat*.'[623] They had invested widely in property and land. The Périers had also bought up large estates, and shares in the Anzin coalmines. The return of strong government, with Bonaparte, brought hope and some revival to the banking sector. But the fresh outbreak of war, the crises and the bankruptcies that followed in 1803, 1806 and 1810, were all very grievous blows to Parisian banking, which would not really recover until the Restoration.[624]

So from the point of view of credit, the Consulate and Empire were lean times. It even seems that there were throwbacks to the past. Gabriel Ouvrard, the great businessman of Napoleon's time, was really an old-style merchant banker: he speculated in *biens nationaux*, in colonial produce, in supplies to the army, in massive purchases of grain in Holland and England, during the shortages of 1801; in 1804, when Spain was threatened with famine, he shipped in food supplies and had himself paid in piastres in Mexico and New Spain, getting his silver brought back to Europe in English ships. Ouvrard was a larger than life figure, but surely a man from the old days: high-living, a gambler, prevaricating if necessary and completely shameless.[625]

France in 1815 was in a sorry state. While he paints rather too black a picture, Dupin's summing up is not far from the truth: 2 million men mobilized, one million dead, 700,000 ex-soldiers looking for peace-time employment, two invasions representing 1,500 million francs' worth of destruction, plus expenses of about the same to support the foreign occupation, until the evacuation of foreign troops in 1817.[626] Life began again nevertheless, and agriculture, industry and trade recovered. As usual, peace was a great healer. Movement was in the air and certain modern sectors pointed the way towards the changes they were helping to bring about: financial operations, trading firms, the new metal and chemicals industries, the Lyonnais gaslighting companies, canals, steamboats, railways. 'Every day', noted Adolphe Blanqui the economist, 'we see the disappearance of workshops, scattered outworking and handlooms. Industry is now housed in great factories, like barracks or convents, equipped with imposing machines, worked by motors of infinite power'.[627] An exaggeration perhaps, but contemporaries surely had cause to marvel at what the age had to offer: the world was undeniably moving in a new direction. Progress was all around, symbolized in particular by the railways, which would be regulated by law in 1842.

And since these huge undertakings required money, ever more money, and credit, ever more credit, the limited company (*société anonyme*), legally devised in 1807, finally began to appear: between 1825 and 1837, 1,039 companies were still *en commandite* (accounting for 1,200 million francs capital) as against 157 limited companies (393 million francs capital). This was just the beginning – everything has to start somewhere. The limited company, in big business, would give full powers to the board of directors; small shareholders were fleeced by this handful of privileged men and, needless to say, the top level was exploiting the lower echelons, but what was new about that? The secret of the resilience of the old rules of society is that they are infinitely adaptable to new circumstances. Here again, nothing was really new in the visible changes at the top of the economy. Limited companies, the foreseeable consequence of the *Code du commerce* of 1807, existed potentially before they began to spread. The rise of the banks was another change which had been on the way for some time. After their eclipse and problems during the Revolution and Empire, the rapid revival of banking did not mean new foundations (usually ephemeral in any case) so much as the return to business of old houses, a good third of which had been active under the *ancien régime*.[628] If the 1830 Revolution and the July Monarchy included bankers like Jacques Laffitte and Casimir-Périer among its new ministers, it was because *la haute banque* (high finance) had swiftly reaffirmed its position. It would further strengthen it later, with the sudden extension of its field of operations during the Second Empire and the Third Republic.

The expression *haute banque* remained in use until 1914 and probably beyond. It referred to the great Paris banks, solidly established, active throughout France and moreover deeply engaged in international finance. The dynasties at the head of these banks, mostly long-standing foundations, weighed heavily in French economic, social and political life: Jacques Laffitte, the successor to Perrégaux, Hottinguer (from Zurich), Hentsch, Périer, Delessert, Fould, James Rothschild – a total of twenty to twenty-five houses, many of foreign origin. But there again, this was surely a very old rule, the *sine qua non* in all the cases known to us. Foreign contacts were absolutely essential in big business. In 1820, Meyer Amschel Rothschild's five sons had settled in various European cities, Amschel in their native Frankfurt, Solomon in Vienna, Nathan in London, Karl in Naples and James in Paris. From these vantage points, they could survey and do business with the whole of Europe, the scene of their spectacular rise. And according to another very old rule, they did a bit of everything: deposits, discounting, exchange, government loans and large-scale commission work, connected with trade. James, the Paris brother, 'had, to back up his vast financial concerns, docks in le Havre and ships at sea; he had gradually become the sole importer of tea to France, and was a major buyer of wool, cereals and silk'.[629] Casimir-Périer, who was briefly prime minister under Louis-Philippe, but died of cholera in 1832 on the brink of a great political career, 'had a hand in everything: shipbuilding, banking, property speculation, public and private credit, metalworks, glassworks, sugar refineries, soap factories, mills: and all on the grand scale'. In other words, these bankers still had strong connections with trade and industry.

Rothschild however, who was on excellent terms with Louis-Philippe, was more deeply involved than any other banker in state finance. He gradually acquired a near-monopoly in government loans. The operation was much the same as in the old days, on the lines introduced in Amsterdam in the eighteenth century. The banker's function was to advance to the government the total of the loan before it was launched, and to buy the attached stocks, under par of course. The bidder satisfied with the lowest rate of interest would get the contract. Once the stocks or bonds were put on sale to the public at full price, he could also benefit by pushing up their price on the Bourse, so as to sell at a profit those he had kept back for himself. Once more, these were age-old practices, which 'ensured huge gains at little expense or risk'.[630] From now on the banker was closely in touch with the state, and the words *finances* and *financier* lost their distinctive meaning.

But was the state as inert and weak as it appeared? The rules all changed at any rate, after the February Days of 1848, which took the business world by surprise. The Second Republic was an unsettled and difficult time, hostile to 'cosmopolitan finance'. The Hope bank quite simply emigrated to England. As for Rothschild, who had just, in August 1847, underwritten a large loan of 250 million francs, he found himself obliged to cease issuing bonds on it, because of the huge problems involved.[631] With the Second Empire, the business and banking world breathed again, but Rothschild, having been edged out by Fould, no longer had the same access to power as previously under Louis-Philippe. Indeed in 1854, Bineau, the Minister of Finance, looking for underwriters for the 250 million franc loan required for the Crimean War, rejected Rothschild as intermediary and allowed himself to be persuaded by two other financiers, Dassier and Mirès, to launch the loan directly, by national subscription. Success was total, the loan was covered within a few days, and 'Napoleon III welcomed with satisfaction this manifestation of "universal suffrage by capital"'. This was a heavy blow for *la haute banque*, which thus lost its virtual monopoly on government loans.[632] The state had regained control of its borrowing (as indeed had often been the case under the *ancien régime*) but that did not prevent it appealing once more to the bankers, now led by Alphonse de Rothschild, for the underwriting of the loan launched after France's defeat in the Franco-Prussian war of 1870–71, to pay the 5,000 million francs demanded by the victors.[633]

There were compensations however for the financial aristocracy. For after the pronounced economic crisis of 1846–8, France, along with the rest of Europe, entered on a period of sustained euphoria. The entire European economy was expanding. Was this because of the goldmines discovered in California and Australia in 1848 and 1851, which swamped Europe with enormous quantities of gold – 'in the space of twenty years, almost as much as had been extracted since the sixteenth century'?[634] France received in ten years 3,380 million francs worth of gold, losing on the other hand 1,100 million francs in silver, which was exported massively to the Far East to pay for French trade there. In 1861, 80 *départements* were consequently short of 5-franc coins and other small silver.[635] Goldmines and railways, it was claimed in 1865, 'are the twin secrets of the industrial and commercial prosperity of Europe'.

Railways, the object of government favours after 1842, were precisely one of the sectors in which Parisian bankers had invested. The banks took on the task of collecting the millions of francs needed to build them, in debentures guaranteed by the state. Neither they nor their competitors lost by the deal. And the massive upheaval that followed served to take the banks outside their many commercial interests, while their connection with industry, mining, metalworking and the new sector of insurance, already a close one, since 1820, was further strengthened.

The crisis of 1846–8 had however demonstrated the inadequacy of credit in France and serious imbalances. On the whole, banking and discounting activity, even in 1840, was essentially serving Paris and large-scale foreign trade. The provinces, the other commercial cities and rural market towns were by contrast poorly served.[636] Parisian notables deliberately prevented the extension into the provinces of their own credit and discount institutions, for fear of over-production, the result of which would be to 'overload markets with a glut of products and thus compete with and perhaps ruin men who have been established for forty or fifty years' (this remark dates from 1840).[637] They were even more strongly opposed – and their opposition was effective because the agreement of the Conseil d'Etat was required – to the creation of independent provincial banking circuits. During the first half of the century then, industrialization, except in sectors in which Parisian bankers were directly interested, was a hand to mouth affair, with firms and their major customers giving each other mutual aid, if only by agreeing to delayed settlement or short-term loans. In 1827 for instance, the textile industry in Alsace was being financed by the cotton importers of Le Havre and *négociants* in Paris, Lyon and Basle; in 1844, the 400 industrialists in Lyon were drawing on credit put up by 70 local silk merchants and 180 commission agents, French and foreign. But this kind of short-term credit, dependent on trade circuits, was fragile; domino-style bankruptcies were possible, and that was what happened in 1846–8.[638] The prolonged breakdown of the economy called for urgent measures.

It was in these circumstances that on 8 March 1848, a few days after taking power, the provisional government, bypassing the approval of the Conseil d'Etat, created a Comptoir National d'Escompte (Discount Bank) in Paris, with branches in all the major French cities based on the Paris model.[639] From now on, the Parisian stranglehold was broken, and during the vigorous banking and industrial expansion following Napoleon III's coup d'état (not unlike the Trente Glorieuses after 1945), there was a sort of fever of creativity, of 'competitive disorder between kinds of banks and bankers'.[640] Among the institutions founded then which have lasted until the present day are the Crédit Foncier (founded, like the Crédit Mobilier, in 1852); the Crédit Industriel et Commercial (1859); the Crédit Lyonnais (1863); the Société Générale (1864). Historians have consequently said that after 1848, or rather 1852, a new generation and a new pattern of banking sprang up, making the Rothschild formula a thing of the past. Is this entirely true?[641]

The old-fashioned *haute banque* houses, having remained, in spite of everything, individual family firms, were not of course built on the same scale as the commercial banks with branches everywhere – banks like the Crédit Lyonnais and the Société Générale which would soon be nationwide and attracting the savings of the French people. But in the first place, if one looks closely at the situation in say 1860, Maurice Lévy-Leboyer argues that the new-style credit institutions had hardly modified the methods used by the old private banks, either as concerns the granting of credit or in their financial policy.[642] The big changes lay in decentralization which was extremely beneficial, and in the general expansion of the economy. But one ought not necessarily to 'confuse the development of the economy and the action of the banks' – and first credit the latter with the expansion during the Second Empire, and thereafter blame it for the slowing in growth after 1860.[643]

Secondly, it seems to me that the commercial and deposit banks were, like the stock exchanges, the fairs of the past, and the old-fashioned market an instrument, a means to an end, whose function fluctuated with the economy. It is perhaps an error of judgement to compare these juggernauts with the great capitalists, of the kind seen in Europe and soon emerging in the United States. In other words, I am suggesting that the capitalists continued after all to be the leading actors. *La haute banque* did not in fact remain aloof from the new wave of banking: members of the old banks were to be found on the board of the Banque de France with great regularity from 1800 until 1890, just as they were to be found taking part in the founding of Second Empire institutions. They put up 20% of the capital for the Crédit Foncier, 50.5% for the Crédit Mobilier (taking 8 out of 12 seats on the board), 23% of the Société Générale, etc.[644] So if the big lending banks, in the latter part of the nineteenth century, launched into loans and business in the outside world, if the Société Générale seemed to be acting like an entrepreneurial capitalist of the old days, embarking on adventurous and far-flung dealings – in Latin America, in Bolivia and Peru, bottomless pits incidentally, in which European money was always being swallowed up – was it really on their own initiative? They were after all clearly national rather than international in inspiration. Is it not more likely that it was because *la haute banque* was at their side, egging them on through participation on their boards, gaining a position of power within them and holding on to it?

These thoughts are provoked by Jean Bouvier's brilliant article analysing both the profit rates and the policies of French banks after 1850.[645] With the exception of the Banque de France and the Crédit Foncier, they remained 'many-sided concerns for the most part', and risky ones until the First World War. The general rise in their profits (interrupted by two periods of stagnation, from 1872 to 1882, and from 1893 until 1901) was achieved by a re-orientation of policy: a substantial drop in interest rates and therefore of the productivity of capital, after 1873, was compensated for by an extension of the credit offered to the French economy, and the lower rate of profit from the domestic market was compensated for by vast and more promising operations on the *foreign market*. And the inspiration behind this policy, 'the financial groups which controlled major dealings on the Paris money market – in particular the launch of foreign loans – always consisted until 1914 of a tightly-knit group of private bankers from *la haute banque*, the deposit banks and the commercial banks'. It was perhaps only after the two world wars that *la haute banque* ceased to be the chief influence on the entire French banking scene.

I hope to return to these questions in the later sections of this book concerned with society, where they could appropriately be discussed, for this heavy superstructure has been a more decisive force in the history of France than the political crises and foreign alerts with which the historical chronicle is punctuated.

The happy few?

It is always at the topmost levels of economic life that one finds power, decision-making, effective privilege – whether this is logical or not, and whether or not we should regard it as morally defensible today. It was centralization, a blind or at most semi-conscious process, which conferred these benefits on groups which were invariably restricted in number. They might change their composition – less however than has been claimed – but the newcomers were no more numerous than the outgoers.

In Lyon, at the peak of its prosperity, in about 1550, exchange dealing and the clearing fairs were in the hands of no more than 80 families of Italian merchants. When in 1590, Piacenza became the new clearing fair, the centre of all European money transfers, everything depended on about sixty *banchieri*. Daniel Dessert has in a recent book made a study of the *traitants* and *partisans*, the financiers who helped Louis XIV by collecting taxes from his subjects, and advancing to the crown the money they would later receive back from the taxpayer. These key men were few in number: between 1668 and 1715, the total of those who signed contracts with the king was 693. If one counts only those who signed at least 6 and up to 50 or more contracts, the total is a mere 242.[646] These 'financiers' were mostly 'from the northern half of the country, north of a line between Nantes and Geneva' – yet again.[647] And all of them had settled in Paris, 'the centre of financial affairs'.[648] Soon they were building sumptuous houses for themselves around the place Vendôme. So centralization observed two rules: unity of place; restriction of personnel.

In the small world of tax farmers, the Ferme Générale was the essential bastion, representing the pinnacle of ambition. After the Falconnet contract of 1680, it was given responsibility, in return for advances, for the collection of a whole set of indirect taxes, *gabelle*, *aides*, *traites*, and entry duties. One historian who has studied it closely notes that

> regional distinctions [the Languedociens had entered it with enthusiasm in the eighteenth century] are of little significance here, on account of the intermarriage that linked tax farmers' families, to such an extent that systematic genealogical research might quite possibly find that they were linked in two or three families – or even a single family group.[649]

But this very small group of ultra-rich people, forming a kind of 'super-capitalism', had a whole army of people at its service scattered throughout the kingdom.

> The Tax Farms [wrote Goudar in 1756] have attracted out of the countryside over fifty thousand citizens, most of whom would have been agricultural workers today instead of clerks. The tax farmers only employ about twenty-five people whom they pay; but . . . the number of citizens connected with the Farms is more considerable.[650]

One has indeed to reckon with the *sous-fermiers*, to whom the Ferme sub-contracted certain taxes, standing to them in just the same relation that the Crown stood in to itself. If we are to believe their masters, these were the people most detested of all. It was certainly against *sous-traitants* and *sous-fermiers* that popular violence was most often directed.[651]

In short, the significant aspect of this case which can be studied at close quarters is the great mass of the iceberg, whereas we usually only see the tip. No powerful group was without an underlying mass of servants, dependants or slaves.

A few pages earlier, I described how something as significant as the Levant trade was concentrated in just a few hands. In eighteenth-century Marseille, a thriving port at the time with ships sailing to the Atlantic by agreement with Saint-Malo, and later to the West Indies, there were, according to Charles Carrière, no more than 80 *négociants* – again, a little privileged world. In Rouen in 1779, there were only 61.[652] *La haute banque* in Paris, during the Restoration and later, consisted of a mere 25 families.

The rule of small numbers is far more general than these few examples would indicate: it has every appearance of a law – an immoral one if you like, but is Mariotte's law immoral? Does society need a commanding élite in order to survive? At any rate, whether or not one approves of the law (and different views are possible) it seems to have applied straightforwardly nine times out of ten in other societies too – France was not the only country subject to its constraints.

The regents of Holland, who were masters of the towns and of the merchant companies, long dominated the most brilliant economy in Europe.[653] In Cadiz, the most sophisticated city in the eighteenth century, the Consulado of Seville was still all-powerful, for the ancient city had not relinquished its power. And a French merchant could write on 12 December 1702,

> The consulate [of Seville] consists of four or five private persons [Basque merchants], who manage trade to suit their own particular ends; the galleons and fleets leave harbour when these men see fit, and return when they desire it; they have their own people in the [West] Indies, who obtain all the fruits [i.e. profits]. In a word, there are but these five persons making their fortunes, and it is at the expense and to the ruin of the *négociants*.[654]

But if we are talking about *laws* – which are as rare in history as in other human sciences – they must be valid in other sectors besides those concerned with wealth. And indeed power, in all its forms, has belonged to minorities who have triumphed to the point of being able to navigate serenely and profitably above the vast ocean of the unprivileged, as we are reminded by the title of Pierre

Goubert's famous book, *Louis XIV et vingt millions de Français*. The twenty million French people, a disconnected and disunited mass, put France, that is to say their own persons, their property and their labour, at the disposal of a tiny aristocracy, which headed determinedly towards the Court. I confess that, following my early tutors,[655] I used for a long while to view the *ancien régime* as a race in two stages: the first step was to get to Court, the second to get into the government and power. When in 1614, Cardinal Richelieu became chaplain to Anne of Austria, the French queen, he had taken the first step. It was like a politician entering parliament for the first time. I must say then that I was surprised, but confirmed in my opinion, when I read from the expert pen of Claude-Frédéric Lévy, who is a marvellous connoisseur of the eighteenth century, this quite categorical statement: 'In the last years of Louis XIV's reign, effective power was exerted neither by the now-failing monarch, nor by his devout companion [Madame de Maintenon], but by two ministerial families, the Colberts and the Phélipeaux.'[656] This gives a little extra savour to the reaction of the Regency against Louis XIV and his régime, as it does too to the disgrace of the Controller-General Desmarets, who had 'saved' the monarchy from the brink of bankruptcy – and who belonged to both families.

Leaving France and turning to England during the Napoleonic wars, I confess that I was also surprised, on reading the keen observations of the *mestre de camp* Pillet, that England in the early nineteenth century was governed by ten families. And that the Duke of Wellington, though laden with honours, was no more than an upstart, a servant and a minor character by comparison to these families. Was very high society really the arbiter, discreet or otherwise, of all manifestations of power?

Even cultural history does not seem to escape the rule of small numbers. Lucien Febvre used to say that every age was governed by a dozen or so great writers and thinkers, and if one knew their works and read them well, one would be thoroughly acquainted with the ideas of their time. A quick glance over French literature brings to mind the Pléiade of the sixteenth century, or the *philosophes* of the eighteenth, Diderot at their head. In painting, one thinks immediately of the banks of the Loing, the forest of Barbizon, the Bâteau Lavoir or Montparnasse . . .And in the long history of religious passions and ousted minorities, one remembers Fénelon and his circle; while thoughts of minorities which succeeded but did not triumph reminds me how fascinated I have been reading and re-reading *Port-Royal* by Sainte-Beuve.

But I must cut short these thoughts, hoping to return to them at leisure in the next part of this book.

I have given much attention, in no spirit of accusation, to capitalism, which lodged itself at the topmost level of French life. It was a capitalism already visible in the rich profusion of the late eighteenth century. To cut a long discussion short, I think it took a long time to penetrate French society, perhaps because of its small volume, even in the time of James de Rothschild, and perhaps also because, having really hit its stride only in the second half of the nineteenth century, it was too inclined to prefer the outside world, foreign markets and the colonies, to France itself (an argument one will find in the reasonable and well-informed diatribes of Lysis). At any rate, it seems to me that France was somehow resistant to capitalism, that France was never consumed by the necessary passions for the capitalist model, by that unbridled thirst for profits without which the capitalist engine cannot get started. Is it perhaps both France's tragedy and the secret of its charm that it has never really been won over to capitalism? France's charm is that it has had a way of life different from that of many countries; but France's tragedy was that it was not aware of its riches and possibilities, that it never fully took part in the struggle between the great powers of the world.

In other words, France was not capitalist enough? It might be one answer. On the other hand, France was certainly exploited by capitalism, as could easily be demonstrated by looking at the present day. But I shall content myself with quoting Sébastien Mercier, whom history insists on regarding as a lively journalist, with a gift for the pen and an astonishing sense of reality. But this was a man who could think too. Listen to what he has to say just a few years before the Revolution. His article is entitled 'Capitalists':

The people have no more money; that is the great problem. And what little they have is taken away from them by the infernal workings of a murderous lottery and by dangerously seductive loans which are always being launched. The pockets of the capitalists and their associates conceal a sum of at least six hundred million. It is with this mass that they are eternally doing battle with the citizens of the realm. Their wallets are in league and this sum never gets back into circulation. Lying stagnant, as it were, it calls all wealth towards it, dictates everything, crushes and destroys every would-be rival, is foreign to agriculture, industry, commerce and even the arts. Devoted to speculation, it is lethal, both by the vacuum it creates and by its obscure and perpetual action in trampling the nation underfoot. Within five or six years, all the money in the country will be violently and forcefully seized by the capitalists who are in league to devour anything that is not one of them.[657]

Towards an Overall Conclusion

In 'these two volumes [the first part of the original project], I have tried to evaluate and re-evaluate some of the basic realities in the history of France: its different areas, its population, its economy.

I often told myself as I went along that at the end of the day it would be possible to fill in the gaps, and perhaps to correct the approximate nature of some of my explanations. The conclusion of a book, and that is the point I have now reached, is often offered as the moment for regrets, doubts and uncertainties. But I have realized, in the course of writing this book, that I shall not be altering very much the images suggested, or pressed upon me by observation. There will be room at most for a few finishing touches. So this will not be the kind of conclusion that throws everything into question. It will simply sum up what has been a long journey, and will at least have the virtue of brevity.

Diversity and oneness

Yes, France is certainly diverse. And that diversity is visible, lasting and *structural*. Vauban was already writing of 'the diversity of the land of which all the provinces in the kingdom are composed'.[1] Michelet and Lucien Febvre pointed it out in turn, and so have many others: it is a diversity which breaks up, divides, and sets one region against another. But what is the reason for this heterogeneity, this perpetual and obsessive variety, which Frenchmen readily assume to be a major characteristic of their country – but which they are perhaps wrong to think unequalled anywhere else in the world? In 1982, in Göttingen University, I found myself speaking unthinkingly about France's 'unparalleled' diversity, which proves that one can blithely repeat received wisdom and add one's voice to the chorus of claims probably made in all innocence by one's compatriots. In the discussion that followed, my audience pointed out forcefully and good-humouredly, that Germany too was a country of great diversity, as they were ready to prove. And I knew very well myself that Italy, Spain, Poland and Britain could all lay claim to diversity. So any explanation, if there is one, should be sought outside the frontiers of France, even if not all these diversities are quite as intense as each other in the end.

Perhaps what happened, inside and outside France, was as follows: very small human groups, tiny prehistoric communities, took up residence in given areas, preferably areas with a number of different characteristics, since diversity means more resources. Then the area in question became individualized, adapted to the number of people it held, to their means and the implements they had devised, to the potential movements of a community which had given up nomadic wandering and settled down once it began to till the soil, but in which people still had to travel from their homes to their gardens and fields and back again. This settlement and adaptation determined the conditions of the habitat for centuries to come, for the latter would never thereafter free itself from the pattern laid down in earliest times. A tree puts down roots for good.

If this apparently reasonable explanation is right, the economy was the deciding factor in the first instance, and human settlement would originally have observed the rules formulated by Von Thünen.

These original communities and their homelands were not, moreover, closed in on themselves. There have always been openings linking these small groups to the outside world. The outside world in fact holds the community in its grip, since even if its inhabitants never move far from home, they are obliged to keep communications open, if only a crack. So we can set aside explanations of diversity purely in terms of the *natural world*: this merely provides the background. The economy is thus once more an important explanatory factor: it is relevant because no group can live in isolation, because diversity appeals to diversity, as in electricity the positive attracts the negative. One can observe this process at work in what one might call laboratory conditions so to speak, wherever the circuits of exchange are incomplete, where the village-bourg-town network is not properly established: the western Bourbonnais for instance, or better still the Velay, in the nineteenth century. Gaps in the network had to be filled *faute de mieux* by fairs. Usually held on a 'non-urban' site, these fairs were the scene 'for several days on end, of tumultuous gatherings in the open air, in places without any special facilities'. They reproduced the 'very archaic pattern also to be found in isolated regions in the southern Massif Central (the Gévaudan, the Rouergue or the Haut-Vivarais) in the age of the traditional peasantry'.[2] Am I justified in seeing these examples, which could still be witnessed not so long ago, as a sort of proof of the hypothesis? Groups with imperfect communications were making up for this deficiency by a sort of compensatory *kermesse*, the fair. The economy was asserting itself.

But while the economy was undoubtedly a decisive factor, it was not the only one. The need for social intercourse, *la sociabilité*, the need to meet other people, also exerted some pressure. Going to the bourg or the town gave the peasant the chance to travel, to leave home, to escape from a life where one was all too often cut off from other people. Going to town meant going towards bustle, noise, gossip, and convivial drinking companions in the taverns. The trouble is that sociability does not leave behind as much historical evidence as economic constraints do. It is harder to detect. We find more traces of it, it seems to me, in dispersed habitats than in large villages, or at least one imagines that social interchange was more lively, more necessary between the inhabitants of hamlets or scattered houses than elsewhere. The 'oneness' of France begins with these elementary contacts, by means of which man was asserting himself as a social animal. But there was nothing of the beehive or the ant-hill about these links. They stopped short of such totalitarian patterns.

The outside world: an insistent presence

In the chapter entitled 'Was France invented by its geography?', [in Volume One, Part Three] I ended the story with the siege of Toulon in 1707. Was this some kind of milestone? Not at all. France is bounded by the sea and by continental Europe, and I wanted to emphasize these frontiers, to bring out their importance. They have been decisive in France's domestic history. But frontiers look outwards as well as inwards.

I referred rather briefly, as others have before me, to France's failure to become a *maritime power*, to achieve that control of the seas which was the key to world domination. And I mean to return to this question at length at the very end of my project. But I could and should also have referred to the heavy pressure from Europe, which has modelled and moulded our destiny as the sculptor moulds the clay with his thumb. Europe can be felt inside France, just as the larger world can be felt inside France.

From the days of Julius Caesar or earlier, until the great barbarian invasions of the fifth century, French history was part of Mediterranean history. What went on in the Mediterranean, even in places very far from French shores, had an effect on life in what is now France. But after the great invasions (and with a few exceptions such as the belated Italian wars) France has above all had to face central and eastern Europe. I confess that during my travels, which tend to create illusions, I have dreamed of a Europe starting on the banks of the Somme, the Meuse or the Rhine and stretching away to Siberia and distant Asia. Such thoughts came to mind because, from the Rhine to Poland, I kept coming across the same rural architecture as in the Lorraine countryside of my boyhood: the same clustered villages, the same open farming, the same cornfields, the same triennial rotation, the same images. Flying over Poland, one looks down on fields in long narrow strips biting cleanly into the dark patches of forest, an obsessive image that forever haunts my mind.

If we had to imagine a diagram of France within the economy of the outside world, I would represent it as a circle. In the centre I would put Paris, which is of course from a geometrical point of view well off centre: the *true* centre – Bourges – was important historically for only one brief moment, in the reign of Charles VII. Around the circumference would be the great sea-ports: Marseille, Bordeaux, La Rochelle, Nantes, Saint-Malo, Rouen, Dunkerque – and on the continental side, the landlocked frontier cities of Lille, Strasbourg and above all Lyon. All these cities were attracted to the outside world: they were only half-attentive to inland France. The contrast between interior and exterior is a classic one. Historians have long referred to inland Spain and peripheral Spain for instance. But was there also a sort of pendulum movement, with first the outside then the inside getting the upper hand? Perhaps the reason why inland France seemed so deserted to the marquis d'Argenson in the midst of what we now consider to be the great expansion of the eighteenth century, was because the French economy was being pulled too quickly towards the periphery, towards the outside world?

The pattern I have described at any rate conflicts with notions of *world-economies* in which the periphery is represented as poor, backward and exploited. It is the task of economists and historians to try to reconcile such contradictions. But surely any rational community is obliged to pay special attention to its outer limits if it is to take its place in the world order? The periphery is the place where the national meets the international.

These are problems of forbidding complexity and I hope to return to them in my final section entitled 'France outside France'. It would probably be wise of me to leave until then my proper voyage round the world, after completing my journeys to and fro through the equally forbidding mass of France's own history, that is to say history considered within the frontiers of French territory.

But I think it useful at this stage to make the point that these frontiers are not to be seen as barriers – if they had been, France would not only have exerted less influence in the world, but also undergone less suffering.

The collapse of peasant France

To my mind, the spectacle that overshadows all others, in the France of the past and even today, is the collapse of a peasant society. There have been plenty of other upheavals – in industry, urbanization, means of transport, technology and science. And we know that tomorrow's industry will not be the same as that of today: the upheaval will go on.

But if I end here, with rural France, it is because I believe (barring accidents, such as another major oil crisis) that it is likely to remain for a long time to come as it stands at present, with the equilibrium that has now been reached. And the present equilibrium calls for an explanation difficult to formulate. But if we could get it right, it would shed some partial but helpful light on the other changes that have taken place in France.

I have described at sufficient length how an ancient peasant France, a France of bourgs, villages, hamlets and scattered houses survived more or less unchanged until at least 1914 and some would say 1945. After 1945, it fell victim to the 'Thirty Glorious Years', that period of unprecedented expansion which lasted until the 1970s, and will unquestionably be even more constructive and destructive once it takes off again, than it has been so far.

That is not to say that before 1945 or even 1914, the French countryside did not witness considerable progress. There was progress in the area of farmland under cultivation, progress in productivity, progress in cultivation methods, with the use of fertilizers, the different stages of which have been described. From at least 1822, progress was made in the design of the plough, and later a series of effective machines with petrol engines were invented for threshing, reaping and binding.

More significant even than this was the way French society managed to absorb its rural poor, a wandering and sometimes dangerous population, by the early years of the twentieth century. It was the call of the towns which gradually rid the countryside of its floating population, a previously incurable affliction. The least well-off regions were liberated later than the others, naturally. In 1907,[3] the departmental council of the Nièvre was still condemning 'the incessant exodus along the public roads of "travellers", who live by looting, terrorize the country people and are often the source of disturbances in the towns', not to speak of the infectious diseases they carried. And in a region as poor as the Gévaudan, legal records detail the thefts and violent crimes comitted by vagabonds, 'until the day they finally left the *département* [of Lozère] and settled in the towns, in about 1910'.[4]

Another development that brought change was the appearance of large landed estates, some of which were already in existence before 1789, especially around Paris. They represent the arrival of active capitalism in the countryside.

All these changes gradually drove the old peasant economy into the ditch. One of the most decisive blows, I think (because it was one of the last, but for other reasons too), was the introduction of the tractor, a machine which could pull anything: the most advanced plough, the huge combine-harvester (a mobile factory), or carts piled high with bales or (these days) compressed blocks of hay and straw. If it has been possible to amalgamate properties (the process known in France as *remembrement*), and if the size of farm which a family can now handle has increased, it is very largely thanks to the tractor. How else could the huge fields we now see in so many farming areas even be ploughed? It would take a whole army of horse-drawn ploughs working together up and down, as I remember seeing on the land of the French settlers in Algeria as late as 1933. But by that time, the tractor was reaching Algeria too, and before long they could be seen operating at night with their headlamps on. Peasant France as a whole was not yet working at this kind of speed. It was really only after 1945 that things moved quickly. Animal teams, whether of horses or oxen, have almost completely disappeared since the war. The last time I visited my native village in the Meuse in 1980, there was only one horse left, and that one was out to grass, on the farm belonging to my elderly cousin. The expansion of trade has everywhere favoured regions that were already privileged and left the poorer regions to sink or swim, usually sink. In some parts of France, new deserts and wastelands have appeared, abandoned to scrub and wild boar.

I will say no more now about the effects of this great upheaval, of its headlong career since 1945. The French peasantry, being diverse itself, was affected in different ways, as is easy to see.

But it is the other side of this problem that interests me and which I find literally enthralling. Why did this upheaval happen so late? No doubt one should look to the whole economy for an answer. But is it perhaps for the simple reason that peasant life offered, to what was certainly an over-abundant population, a balanced way of life? Near Céret, where I live, the Aspre valley has now reverted to nature: today only brambles, shrubs and broom flourish on the poor and untended soil. Here, 'the equilibrium based on almost complete self-sufficiency, combined with a little trading, which had more in common with barter than with imports and exports, was lost for good in about 1950', Adrienne Cazeilles writes to me (20 January 1985). The population gave up, leaving everything just as it stood, as if evacuating an untenable position in wartime. But before that the position had been perfectly defensible. Life in the Aspre was not wretched: people were poor certainly, and it was a hard life, but that is not the same thing. As one of my friends, born in 1899 in a peasant family, used to put it humorously but accurately: 'The only thing we were short of was money.'

I think that historians may have been rather too ready to pity the lot of the peasant. They have perhaps been overcome by a conscientious and sincere exaggeration of the hardships of the past.

We have little reliable testimony about how tolerable the balance of rural life was in the past. I have gone to some lengths to question men of my own generation, whose early years at any rate were spent in a France very different from that of today. No doubt if one were to be spirited back into a French farmhouse of, say, the 1920s, one would have plenty of cause for complaint. Working the land was hard, and there was no end to it, despite a deceptive freedom. One had a choice yes, but only between equally backbreaking kinds of work. Nevertheless, people did not complain to each other, whether about the lack of running water (it had to be fetched from the well or the village pump), or about the poor light at night (no electricity), the drab clothes, only occasionally renewed, or the lack of conveniences and distractions to be found in the towns. Everyone had enough to eat, thanks to the kitchen garden, to the fields, which now included potatoes as a crop, thanks to preserved fruits and vegetables, butcher meat on Sundays and the family pig, which was usually killed and eaten at home. But can I count as a reliable source my own childhood memories? Or those of Jean Petit, about upland Burgundy before 1914? Or those of Michel Sageloli, former mayor of Céret and president of the council of Pyrénées-Orientales? Or those of a certain professor of philosophy who was also brought up in Lorraine?

We shall have to leave that question open. Until we have more evidence, I shall go on believing that the old peasant way of life survived by combining hard work, wisdom, and *comparative* comfort in a country which was after all rich in resources. Indeed, I cannot really bring myself to look back on it with regret, since retrospectively the survival of the old balance looks like an eminently reasonable solution. It is by no means clear that today's farming, which is developing in the direction of technology and social change, is necessarily and *everywhere* the best answer. Although agriculture now concerns itself only with the best land, abandoning the rest, there are still great differences of productivity. I have much enjoyed some recently published books describing country upbringings, perhaps a little romanticized and not necessarily accurate (such as Emilie Carles's *Une soupe aux herbes sauvages* about the Maurienne region in the Alps, or Claude Courchay's *Retour à Malaveil*) – indeed they are perhaps too enjoyable to be regarded as impartial evidence about peasant France today or in the past. But I admit to having been struck by some sentences which seem to be piercingly true: 'In the old days, one could survive by producing one's own food. Now there are instalments to pay every month. Once you have started, there is no end to it. By the time you've paid for the tractor, it is only good for scrap. In the end you are just working for the Crédit Agricole [the bank].' And I would add: in the old days you were working for the seigneur; in more recent times, you were working for the landowner. In the recent past and today, you will have been working for the state and the

677

banks. 'There is no problem for the banks,' Claude Courchay writes. 'They are opening branches everywhere. The more things change, the more it's the same old story. The land has never brought anything to those who work it.' In the France of today, some things have not changed.

La longue durée

I hope that the reader who has come this far will have become accustomed to the particular language of history viewed in the long term, *la longue durée*. Using this approach to reach that underlying history whose movement has drawn along and shaped all the various Frances of the past was our ambitious programme; and the next part of *The Identity of France* will continue the quest, the search for those underground rivers, this time as they relate to the state, culture, society, and to France's relations with the outside world.

When one tries to explain what is meant by *la longue durée*, many metaphors crowd to mind. Perhaps it is wisest to avoid them altogether, but they are hard to escape. And television provides us with more: pictures of the foaming and perilous rapids of Zaire, the fantastic explorations of underground caverns, or deep-sea divers prospecting on the ocean bed. But let us please not talk of the 'groundswell' of history. That is too strong a term. I prefer to think of a vast expanse of almost motionless water to which shipping takes naturally. Moving scarcely at all, at the slow speed of the secular trend, it nevertheless draws everything irresistibly along, whether our own fragile skiffs or the proud ships of the captains of history. That is why there is bound to be some continuity in history's slow progress, some monotonous repetition, some reactions which are easy to predict since they are always or almost always the same.

Of course there are breaks and discontinuities too, but never such that history as a whole is cut in two. The history of the *longue durée* is thus a sort of reference by which every national destiny is not so much judged as situated and explained. It offers us the possibility, if I am not mistaken, of distinguishing the essential from the accessory. It helps us to take the measure of France in an unusual way, to enlarge its history, to arrive at what the identity of France *might be*. In the end, this history, coming from the depths of time and stretching on into the future its gently rolling course, poses all the old problems at once. Can we say that it limits – note that I do not say eliminates – both men's freedom and their responsibility? For men do not make history, rather it is history above all that makes men and thereby absolves them from blame.

[Fernand Braudel died before he could complete the further planned volumes of *The Identity of France* referred to in this conclusion.]

Notes

The notes, particularly to the later chapters of this volume, had to be reconstructed from Fernand Braudel's papers. He worked with a card-index system based on abbreviations which only he could easily decipher. It was decoded for the French edition with the kind and painstaking assistance of Annie Duchêne, Marie-Thérèse Labignette and Josiane Ochoa, who had worked with Fernand Braudel over the years. A few incomplete references nevertheless remain.

Notes to Foreword

1. Joan ROBINSON, *Economic Heresies*, 1981, p. 141.
2. Guy BOIS, *Crise du féodalisme*, 1976, p. 16.

Notes to Part I

1. Alfred SAUVY, letter to the author, 29 February 1980.
2. Pierre CHAUNU, *La France*, 1982, p. 33.
3. Henri LERIDON and Michel Louis LEVY, 'Populations du monde: les conditions de la stabilisation' in *Population et Sociétés*, December 1980, no. 42.
4. Ange GOUDAR, *Les Intérêts de la France mal entendus*, 1756, vol. I, pp. 255 and 342.
5. Jean MARKALE, *Le Roi Arthur et la civilisation celtique*, 1976, p. 9.
6. Quoted by Gilles DELEUZE and Félix GUATTARI, *Capitalisme et Schizophrénie, l'anti-Oedipe*, 1972, p. 169.
7. Ferdinand LOT, *La Fin du monde antique et le début du Moyen Age*, 1968, pp. 11–13; 1983, pp. 28–9.
8. Colin RENFREW, *Before Civilization. The Radio-Carbon Revolution and Prehistoric Europe*, London, 1973, p. 22.
9. Isaac NEWTON, *The Chronology of Ancient Kingdoms amended*, in *Complete Works*, 1779–85, vol. V, quoted by Colin RENFREW, op. cit., p. 22.
10. Colin RENFREW, op. cit., p. 249.

11. On this radical re-thinking, see C. RENFREW, op. cit., chapters 3–5 and *passim*.

12. Gabriel CAMPS, *La Préhistoire*, 1982, pp. 125–40.

13. *Ibid.*, p. 54.

14. *Ibid.*, pp. 55 ff.

15. André LEROI-GOURHAN, quoted by G. CAMPS, *ibid.*, p. 59.

16. Jean GUILAINE, *La France d'avant la France, du Néolithique à l'Age de fer*, 1980, p. 14.

17. Henri DELPORTE, 'Les premières industries humaines en Auvergne', in Henri de LUMLEY, ed., *Préhistoire française*, I, *Les Civilisations paléolithiques et mésolithiques de la France*, 1976, p. 803.

18. H. de LUMLEY, S. GAGNIERE, L. BARRAL and R. PASCAL, 'La grotte du Vallonet Roque-brune-Cap-Martin (Alpes-Maritimes)', in *Bulletin du Musée d'Anthropologie préhistorique de Monaco*, 10, 1963, pp. 5–20.

19. Franck BOURDIER, *Préhistoire de la France*, 1967, pp. 55 ff, and *Préhistoire française*, I, op. cit., chronological table, p. 10.

20. We now know that in the far distant past, continental drift moved entire continents. India for example was originally attached to Antarctica, but eventually reached Eurasia, north of the equator, and became joined on – in a process that took 50 million years.

21. H. de LUMLEY *et al.*, art. cit. (cf. note 18).

22. E. W. PFIZENMAYER, *Les Mammouths de Sibérie. La découverte des cadavres de mammouths préhistoriques sur les bords de la Berezovka et de la Sanga-Iourakh*, 1939, *passim* and pp. 17–21.

23. H. de LUMLEY, J. RENAUL-MISKOVSKY, J. C. MISKOVSKY, J. GUILAINE, 'Le cadre chronologique et paléoclimatique du Postglaciare', in *La Préhistoire française*, II, *Les Civilisations néolithiques et protohistoriques de la France*, ed. J. GUILAINE, 1976, p. 3.

24. Marie-Antoinette de LUMLEY, 'Les Anténéanderthaliens dans le Sud', in H. de LUMLEY, ed., *La Préhistoire française*, I, op. cit., 1976, p. 547.

25. Jean ABELANET, *Le Musée de Tautavel*, 1982, pp. 32–6.

26. *Ibid.*, pp. 11 and 25.

27. G. CAMPS, *La Préhistoire*, op. cit., p. 157.

28. *Ibid.*, pp. 380–1.

29. *Ibid.*, p. 381, and F. BOURDIER, *Préhistoire de la France*, op. cit., pp. 223–4.

30. G. CAMPS, op. cit., pp. 162–76; F. BOURDIER, *Préhistoire de la France*, op. cit., p. 208.

31. Philip LIBERMAN, 'L'Evolution du langage humain', in *La Recherche*, 1975, pp. 751 ff.

32. G. CAMPS, op. cit., pp. 173–4 and 178.

33. F. BOURDIER, op. cit., p. 262.

34. André LEROI-GOURHAN, 'L'Art paléolithique en France', in *Préhistoire française*, op. cit., I, pp. 741 ff; G. CAMPS, op. cit., pp. 203–7.

35. Pierre GAXOTTE, *Histoire des Français*, 1951, I, pp. 16–17.

36. G. CAMPS, op. cit., p. 194.

37. *Ibid.*, pp. 187–90; F. BOURDIER, op. cit., pp. 240–4.

38. F. BOURDIER, op. cit., pp. 249–56.

39. G. CAMPS, op. cit., pp. 229–32.

40. Robert ARDREY, reference not found.

41. J. GUILAINE, *La France d'avant la France. Du Néolithique à l'Age de Fer.* op. cit., p. 29.

42. *Ibid.*, pp. 29–30.

43. Raymond RIQUET, 'L'anthropologie préhistorique', in *La Préhistoire française*, II, ed. J. GUILAINE, 1976, p. 151.

44. J. GUILAINE, *La France d'avant la France*, op. cit., p. 34.

45. *Ibid.*, p. 37.

46. R. RIQUET, art. cit., see note 43, p. 140.

47. J. GUILAINE, *La France d'avant la France*, op. cit., pp. 40 ff.

48. The term megalithic is applied both to constructions made from enormous blocks of stone, as in Carnac in Brittany or Stonehenge in England, and to chambered cairns such as those found on the Ile Longue in Brittany, which are built with small stones.

49. J. GUILAINE, op. cit., pp. 66–7.

50. *Ibid.*, pp. 94 ff.

51. *Ibid.*, p. 94.

52. R. RIQUET, art. cit., see note 43, p. 144.

53. J. GUILAINE, op. cit., pp. 95–6.

54. *Ibid.*, p. 103.

55. An ivory statuette found in the Grotte du Pape (the Pope's Cave) at Brassempouy (Landes).

56. J. GUILAINE, op. cit., pp. 104–5.

57. *Ibid.*, pp. 129–30.

58. *Ibid.*, p. 131.

59. *Ibid.*, p. 149.

60. In primitive societies in modern times, the blacksmith is always someone set apart, respected and usually feared as well.

61. J. GUILAINE, op. cit., pp. 160–1.

62. *Ibid.*, p. 167.

63. *Ibid.*, pp. 174 ff.

64. *Ibid.*, p. 177.

65. G. RACHET, reference not found.

66. J. GUILAINE, op. cit., p. 203.

67. *Ibid.*, p. 241.

68. *Ibid.*, pp. 241 ff.

69. *Ibid.*, pp. 242 ff.

70. *Ibid.*, pp. 248–50.

71. It has, however, recently been questioned whether the remains are those of a woman.

72. J. GUILAINE, op. cit., pp. 254–5.

73. Jacques HARMAND, *Les Celtes au second Age de fer*, 1972, pp. 16–17.

74. Venceslas KRUTA, *Les Celtes*, 1976, pp. 68–70.

75. *Ibid.*, pp. 34–5.

76. Barry CUNLIFFE, *Celtic World*, 1979, p.14.

77. On the extraordinary unified civilization of the Middle East in the second millennium BC, see W. CULICAN, *Le Levant et la mer, histoire et commerce*, 1967.

78. Jacques HARMAND, *Les Celtes*, op. cit., p. 15.

79. *Ibid.*, p. 40.

80. *Ibid.*, p. 42.

81. Jules MICHELET, *Histoire de France*, 1876 edn, I, p. 12.

82. *Ibid.*, p. 15.

83. Jan de VRIES, *La Religion des Celtes*, 1963, p. 14.

84. Henri HUBERT, *Les Celtes et l'expansion celtique jusqu'à l'époque de la Tène*, 1950; *Les Celtes depuis l'époque de la Tène et la civilisation celtique*, 1950.

85. Gustave BLOCH, 'La Gaule indépendante et la conquête romaine', in *Histoire de France*, ed. Ernest LAVISSE, II, 1911, p. 33.

86. Vital-Fleury VIMAL de SAINT-PAL, 'Le Celte, homme de cheval', in *La Cavalerie celtique*, 1952.

87. J. HARMAND, *Les Celtes*, op. cit., p. 80; B. CUNLIFFE, op. cit., p. 120.

88. Karl Ferdinand WERNER, *Les Origines*, in Jean FAVIER, ed.,

Histoire de France, 1984, I, p. 202.

89. Paul-Henri PAILLOU, *L'Anti-César*, 1965.

90. J. HARMAND, *Les Celtes*, op. cit., pp. 88–9.

91. See below, part IV.

92. *Dictionnaire archéologique des techniques*, Editions de l'Accueil, II, p. 1008, article 'Transports'.

93. Alain GUILLERM, 'L'Etat et l'espace de la guerre', typescript, 1982, I, pp. 37 ff. and 49.

94. G. BLOCH, in LAVISSE, ed., *Histoire de France*, op. cit., II. p. 43.

95. Venceslas KRUTA, *Les Celtes*, op. cit., pp. 112–15.

96. *Ibid.*, p. 105.

97. *Ibid.*, pp. 102–3, 108–10.

98. G. BLOCH, in LAVISSE, *Histoire de France*, op. cit., II, p. 42.

99. CICERO, *De provinciis consularibus*, quoted by G. BLOCH, *ibid.*, p. 37.

100. G. BLOCH, *ibid.*, p. 95.

101. Albert GRENIER, 'Aux origines de l'économie rurale: la conquête du sol français', in *Annales d'histoire économique et sociale*, 1930, pp. 32–3.

102. A. GUILLERM, 'L'Etat et l'espace', op. cit., p. 66.

103. Pierre BONNAUD, 'La ville: deux origines, deux filières', in *Géographie historique des villes d'Europe occidentale*, proceedings of the conference held in 1981 at the Sorbonne, I, *Villes et Réseaux urbains*, ed. Paul CLAVAL, 1984, p. 29.

104. Emmanuel de MARTONNE, lecture given in São Paulo, Brazil.

105. Colin RENFREW, *Before Civilization*, op. cit., pp. 143.

106. Raymond RIQUET, 'L'anthropologie préhistorique', in *La Préhistoire française*, ed. J. GUILAINE, op. cit., II, pp. 150–1.

107. Ferdinand LOT, *La France des origines à la guerre de Cent Ans*, 5th edn, 1941, p. 8.

108. Colin RENFREW, *Before Civilization*, op. cit., chapter 7.

109. K. F. WERNER, in *Histoire de France*, ed. J. FAVIER, op. cit., p. 71.

110. Louis-René NOUGIER, *Le Peuplement préhistorique*, 1950, p. 65.

111. G. CAMPS, *La Préhistoire*, op. cit., pp. 310–11.

112. R. RIQUET, in *La Préhistoire française*, op. cit., p. 146.

113. Quoted by André ARMENGAUD, Marcel REINHARD, Jacques DUPAQUIER, *Histoire générale de la population mondiale*, 1968, p. 43.

114. G. BLOCH, in LAVISSE, ed., *Histoire de France*, op. cit., p. 35.

115. Eugène CAVAIGNAC, quoted in ARMENGAUD, REINHARD and DUPAQUIER, op. cit. (see note 113), p. 43. The authors regard this figure as 'fairly firmly established'.

116. K. F. WERNER, in *Histoire de France*, ed. J. FAVIER, op. cit., p. 167.

117. Jean BERNARD and Jacques RUEFF, *Hématologie géographique*, 1966, I, quoted by M. BORDEAUX in 'Voies ouvertes à l'histoire des coutumes par l'hématologie géographique', *Annales E.S.C.*, 1969, p. 1275 and map on p. 1282 for example.

118. Robert FOSSIER, *Histoire sociale de l'Occident médiéval*, 1970, p. 22; Michel ROBLIN, *Le Terroir de l'Oise aux époques gallo-romaine et franque. Peuplement, défrichement, environenment,*

1978, p. 297.

119. G. BLOCH, in LAVISSE, ed., *Histoire de France*, op. cit., p. 101.

120. A. GUILLERM, 'L'Etat et l'espace', op. cit., p. 44.

121. J. MICHELET, *Histoire de France*, op. cit., I, p. 52.

122. Jérôme CARCOPINO, *César*, 1936, p. 707; Camille JULLIAN, *Histoire de la Gaule*, 1971 edn, II, pp. 437–47 and 449–52.

123. G. BLOCH, in LAVISSE, ed., *Histoire de France*, op. cit., I. p. 101.

124. *Ibid.*, p. 104.

125. Ferdinand LOT, *La Gaule*, 1947, p. 170.

126. C. JULLIAN, *Histoire de la Gaule*, op. cit., pp. 508–9.

127. K. F. WERNER, in *Histoire de France*, ed. J. FAVIER, op. cit., p. 137.

128. A. GUILLERM, 'L'Etat et l'espace', op. cit., p. 143.

129. Siegfried Jan de LAET, 'Romains, Celtes et Germains en Gaule septentrionale', in *Studia historica gandensia*, 1964, p. 92.

130. *Ibid.*, p. 93.

131. Marcel LE GLAY, 'Les Gallo-Romains' in *Histoire de France*, ed. Georges DUBY, 1970, I, p. 114.

132. Maurice BOUVIER-AJAM, *Dagobert*, p. 19; Pierre LANCE, *La Défaite d'Alésia. Ses causes dans la société celtique, ses conséquences dans la société française*, 1978, pp. 155 ff.

133. André PIGANIOL, *Histoire de Rome*, 1962, p. 273.

134. Jules MICHELET, quoted in François GEORGE, *Histoire personnelle de la France*, 1983, p. 91.

135. Pierre LANCE, *La Défaite d'Alésia*, op. cit., *passim*.

136. Pierre BONNAUD, *Terres et langages, Peuples et régions*, 1981, I, pp. 37–9, and 45: 'The situation of the Gauls in relation to Latin during the early Middle Ages reminds one . . . of that of the Occitanian language in relation to French since the sixteenth century.' Cf. Yves FLORENNE, 'Les peuples fidèles' in *Le Monde*, 21 July 1983.

137. J. MARKALE, *Le Roi Arthur*, op. cit., p. 24.

138. Jan de LAET, 'Romains . . .', art. cit. (cf. note 129), p. 91.

139. Reference mislaid.

140. F. LOT, *La France*, op. cit., p. 69.

141. Karl Julius BELOCH, *Die Bevölkerung der Griechisch-Romischen Welt'*, 1886, p. 507.

142. See note 115 above.

143. K. J. BELOCH, 'Die Bevölkerung im Altertum', in *Zeitschrift fur Sozial und Wissenschaft*, II, 1899, pp. 512 and 619. This article is fifteen years or so later than the one cited in note 141.

144. Robert FOSSIER, *Histoire sociale de l'Occident médiéval*, op. cit., p. 51.

145. Heinrich BECHTEL, 'Städte und Burger vom 13.–15. Jahrhundert' in *Wirtschaftsgeschichte Deutschlands*, 1951, p. 256.

146. F. BRAUDEL, *Civilization and Capitalism*, I, *The Structures of Everyday Life*, p. 268.

147. F. LOT, *Histoire de France*, op. cit., p. 397.

148. R. FOSSIER, exact reference mislaid.

149. Jean-Louis VATINEL, *Les Années terribles du IIIe siècle en Gaule*, 1978, p. 17.

150. Lucien MUSSET, 'Les Gallo-Romains', in *Histoire de France*,

ed. G. DUBY, 1970, I, p. 159.

151. André PIGANIOL, quoted by R. FOSSIER, *Le Moyen Age*, I, *Les Mondes nouveaux (350–950)*, 1982, p. 33.

152. Michel ROUCHE, 'L'éclatement des mondes anciens', in *Le Moyen Age*, op. cit., I, p. 107.

153. Pierre DOCKÈS, *La Libération médiévale*, 1979; 'Révoltes bagaudes et ensauvagement' in *Sauvages et ensauvagés; analyse épistémologique et histoire économique*, March 1980, no. 19, pp. 145 ff.

154. M. ROUCHE, op. cit. (see note 152), p. 108.

155. Roger AGACHE, 'Détection aérienne des vestiges protohistoriques, gallo-romains et médiévaux dans le bassin de la Somme', in special number of *Bulletin de la Société de Préhistoire du Nord*, no. 7, 1970, pp. 179–80.

156. Guillaume FOVET, *Gallia*, supp. 20, 1969.

157 Roger AGACHE, 'Archéologie aérienne de la Somme' in special number of the *Bulletin de la Société de Préhistoire du Nord*, no. 6, 1964, plate 32: figs 103 and 104.

158. Monique CLAVEL, *Béziers et son territoire dans l'Antiquité*, 1970, pp. 606–7.

159. Pierre DURVIN, *Essai sur l'économie gallo-romaine dans la région de Creil*, 1972, p. 46 and note 9.

160. Apollinaris SIDONIUS, *Letters* (French edn, 1970).

161. Henri DUBLED, 'Quelques observations sur le sens du mot *villa*' in *Le Moyen Age*, 1953, 1–2, pp. 1–9

162. P. DURVIN, *Essai sur l'économie gallo-romaine*, op. cit., p. 68.

163. Lucien GACHON, *La Vie rurale en France*, 1st edn, 1967, 3rd edn, 1976.

164. Michel ROUCHE, in *Le Moyen Age*, ed. R. FOSSIER, op. cit., p. 57.

165. *Ibid.*, p. 59.

166. Marie-Bernadette BRUGUIÈRE, *Littérature et droit dans la Gaule du Ve siècle*, 1974, p. 321. Lampridius, a friend of Apollinaris Sidonius, was murdered by his slaves; the same Apollinaris Sidonius reports that a woman was kidnapped and sold as a slave in the market at Clermont.

167. Régine PERNOUD, in *Histoire du peuple français*, ed. Louis-Henri PARIAS, I, *Des origines au Moyen Age*, p. 29.

168. Pierre DOCKÈS, *La libération médiévale*, op. cit., p. 118.

169. Pierre DOCKÈS, *Révoltes bagaudes*, op. cit., pp. 152–4.

170. Henri HUBERT, *Les Celtes depuis l'époque de la Tène*, op. cit., p. 184.

171. Salvian retired to the abbey of Lerins in 420, then to Marseille where he was ordained a priest in 430. This passage is taken from *De gubernatione Dei*, where he describes the barbarians, sent by God to chastise the Roman Empire, as the promoters of a regenerated society.

172. Quoted by Robert FOSSIER, *Histoire sociale de l'Occident*, op. cit., p. 45.

173. M.-B., BRUGUIÈRE, *Littérature et droit dans la Gaule*, op. cit., p. 53.

174. P. DOCKÈS, *Révoltes bagaudes*, op. cit., p. 237.

175. Jan DHONDT, *Le Haut Moyen Age (VII-XIe siècles)* (French translation), 1976, pp. 27–8.

176. Hans DELBRUCK, *Geschichte der*

Kriegskunst in Rahmen der Politischen Geschichte, I, 1900, pp. 472 ff.

177. Henri PIRENNE, lectures given in Algiers, 1931.

178. Lucien ROMIER, L'Ancienne France, des origines à la Révolution, 1948, p. 45.

179. Ferdinand LOT, 'La civilisation mérovingienne' in Gustave GLOTZ, ed., Les Destinées de l'Empire en Occident de 395 à 888, Part I, De 395 à 768, p. 383.

180. P. DOCKES, La Libération médiévale, op. cit., p. 109.

181. Reference mislaid.

182. R. FOSSIER, Histoire sociale de l'Occident médiéval, op. cit., pp. 33 ff.

183. Paul DUFOURNET, Pour une archéologie du paysage, 1978, p. 163.

184. Robert FOLZ, André GUILLOU, Lucien MUSSET, Dominique SOURDEL, De l'Antiquité au monde médiéval, 1972, pp. 94–9 and 243.

185. Robert FOSSIER, Histoire sociale de l'Occident médiéval, op. cit., p. 36.

186. Jean-Louis VATINEL, Les Années terribles du IIIe siècle en Gaule, 1969, p. 29.

187. Collection des historiens de France, quoted by Emile LEVASSEUR, La Population française, I, 1889, p. 107.

188. Paul-Albert FEVRIER, Le Développement urbain en Provence de l'époque romaine à la fin du XIVe siècle (archéologie et histoire urbaine), 1964, p. 212.

189. Henri LABROUSSE, Toulouse antique. Des origines à l'établissement des Wisigoths, 1968, p. 571.

190. Alexander RUSTOW, Ortsbestimmung der Gegenwart,

II, Weg der Freiheit, 1952, p. 243.

191. Edmond FREZOULS, 'Etudes et recherches sur les villes en Gaule' in La Gallia romana, Proceedings of conference of the Accademia Nazionale dei Lincei (held in Rome, May 1971), 1973, p. 174.

192. M.-B. BRUGUIERE, Littérature et droit dans la Gaule, op. cit., pp. 391 ff.

193. Numa Denis FUSTEL DE COULANGES, La Monarchie franque, 5th edn, 1926, p. 520.

194. Marc BLOCH, 'Le problème de l'or au Moyen Age', in Annales d'histoire économique et sociale, V, 1933, p. 18.

195. Etienne SABBE, 'L'importation des tissus orientaux en Europe occidentale au haut Moyen Age', in Revue belge de philologie et d'histoire, XIV, 1935, pp. 811 and 1261.

196. François-Louis GANSHOF, 'Notes sur les ports de Provence du VIIIe au Xe siècle', in Revue historique, 184, 1938, p. 128.

197. Elyas ASHTOR, A Social and Economic History of the Near East in the Middle Ages, 1976.

198. Pierre BONASSIE, La Catalogne du milieu du Xe à la fin du XIe siècle, 1975, I, p. 379.

199. I do not believe that the warming-up of the climate after the eighth century – another plausible recent explanation – really takes us very far on the question of causes and consequences.

200. A. ARMENGAUD, M. REINHARD and J. DUPAQUIER, Histoire générale de la population mondiale, op. cit., pp. 62 and 64. K. F. WERNER, in Histoire de France, ed. J. FAVIER, op. cit., p. 360.

201. K. F. WERNER, in *ibid.*, p. 302; Lucien MUSSET in R. FOLZ, A. GUILLOU, L. MUSSET and D. SOURDEL, *De l'Antiquité au monde médiéval*, op. cit., pp. 118–20.

202. L. MUSSET, 'Les migrations barbares', in *Histoire de France*, ed. G. DUBY, I, 1970, p. 165, and Pierre RICHE, 'Les temps mérovingiens, VIe–VIIe siècles', *ibid.*, I, p. 171.

203. Renée DOEHAERD, *Le Haut Moyen Age occidental. Economies et sociétés*, 1971, pp. 125–6 and 223–4.

204. *Ibid.*, p. 223.

205. Michel ROUCHE, 'L'éclatement des mondes anciens', in *Le Moyen Age*, ed. R. FOSSIER, op. cit., p. 97.

206. Jean-François LEMARIGNIER, *La France médiévale, institutions et société*, 1970, p. 52.

207. Pierre RICHE, in *Histoire de France*, ed. G. DUBY, op. cit., I, p. 170.

208. Léopold GENICOT, 'Aux origines de la civilisation occidentale, Nord et Sud de la Gaule', in *Miscellanea L. Van der Essen*, 1947, pp. 1 ff.

209. *Ibid.*, p. 89.

210. Renée DOEHAERD, *Le Haut Moyen Age*, op. cit., pp. 90 ff.

211. Thomas REGAZZOLA and Jacques LEFEVRE, *La Domestication du mouvement. Poussées mobilisatrices et surrection de l'Etat*, 1981, p. 20.

212. Marc BLOCH, quoted by Michel LE MENE, *L'Economie médiévale*, 1977, p. 26.

213. Henri PIRENNE, 'L'instruction des marchands au Moyen Age', in *Annales d'histoire économique et sociale*, 1929, p. 18.

214. P. RICHE, in *Histoire de France*, ed. G. DUBY, op. cit., I, p. 170.

215. *Ibid.*, pp. 180–1.

216. R. FOSSIER, *Histoire sociale de l'Occident médiéval*, op. cit., p. 52.

217. Jan DHONDT, *Le Haut Moyen Age*, op. cit., p. 73. On the treaty of Verdun, see *The Identity of France*, vol. I above, and Figure 33, p. 314.

218. J. DHONDT, *Le Haut Moyen Age*, op. cit., p. 75.

219. Jacques MADAULE, *Histoire de France*, 1943, I, p. 77.

220. That is an event with long-term repercussions which thus stretches over a period of time far beyond its own duration.

221. Ernst Robert CURTIUS, *La Littérature européenne et le Moyen Age*, 1956, p. 23.

222. Neculai IORGA, *History of the French People* (in Romanian), 1919, p. 93.

223. P. BONNASSIE, *La Catalogne*, op. cit., I, p. 131.

224. R. FOSSIER, *Le Moyen Age*, op. cit., I, *Les Mondes nouveaux 350–950*, p. 14, and II, *L'Eveil de l'Europe, 950–1250*, p. 7.

225. J. DHONDT, *Le Haut Moyen Age*, op. cit., pp. 2–3.

226. The *fisc* – the product of the various contributions levied in the provinces of the Roman Empire. The word later came to mean the personally owned domains of the sovereign or the state, and the product of the seigneurial dues which the king collected as owner or overlord of fiefs.

227. The *counts* were the governors of provinces and had administrative, judicial, financial and military authority. The *Missi Dominici* were created by Charlemagne to keep an eye on the counts.

228. The name *honor* or *honos* was given in Carolingian times to

the land, revenues or tax delegations that the king conceded as livings to his chief administrators to provide them with an income for the period that their functions lasted.

229. See *The Identity of France*, I, above, pp. 304; and J. DHONDT, *Le Haut Moyen Age*, op. cit., p. 55.

230. *Ibid.*, p. 55.

231. *Ibid.*, p. 58.

232. Lucien GACHON, *La Vie rurale en France*, 3rd edn, 1976, p. 42.

233. Paul ROLLAND, 'De l'économie antique au grand commerce médiéval. Le problème de la continuité à Tournai et dans la Gaule', in *Annales d'histoire économique et sociale*, 1935, VII, pp. 245–84.

234. Anne LOMBARD-JOURDAN, 'Du problème de la continuité: y a-t-il une protohistoire urbaine de la France?', in *Annales E.S.C.*, 1970, 4, p. 1127.

235. Jakob van KLAVEREN, 'Die Wikingerzüge in ihrer Bedeutung für de Belebung der Geldwirtschaft in frühen Mittelalter', in *Jahrbuch für Nationalökonomie und Statistik*, 1957, Bd 168, H 5/6, pp. 405ff.

236. Maurice LOMBARD, 'Mahomet et Charlemagne', in *Annales E.S.C.*, 1948, no. 2, p. 197.

237. Michel ROUCHE, 'La rénovation carolingienne', in *Le Moyen Age*, I, *Les Mondes nouveaux 350–950*, 1982, p. 371.

238. T. REGAZZOLA and L. LEFEVRE, *La Domestication du mouvement*, op. cit., p. 19.

239. *Ibid.*, p. 23.

240. See for instance the plentiful evidence collected by Renée DOEHAERD about sales made by royal cities as well as by lords, abbeys and the peasants themselves, *Le Haut Moyen Age*, op. cit., pp. 224–30.

241. The document is the *Edictum Pistense* of 864, contained in Alfred BORETIUS and Victor KRAUSE, *Capitularia regum Francorum*, II, in *Monumenta Germaniae Historica*, 1890.

242. J. DHONDT, *Le Haut Moyen Age*, op. cit., p. 194.

243. *Ibid.*, p. 36, and on long-distance trade, pp. 152 ff.

244. *Ibid.*, pp. 172–90.

245. *Ibid.*, pp. 160 ff.

246. Renée DOEHAERD, *Le Haut Moyen Age*, op. cit., pp. 103–9.

247. The Mozarabs were Christians in Spain under Muslim domination.

248. A polyptic was a register folded into several sections in which the official record of the property and dues of an abbey was set down.

249. J. C. RUSSELL, quoted by Marcel REINHARD in *Histoire générale de la population mondiale*, op. cit., p. 64.

250. Karl Julius BELOCH, 'Die Bevölkerung Europas im Mittelalter', in *Zeitschrift für Sozialwissenschaft*, 1900, p. 408.

251. M. ROUCHE, in *Le Moyen Age*, op. cit., pp. 460–1.

252. On the concept of the world-economy, see F. BRAUDEL, *Civilization and Capitalism*, III, *The Perspective of the World*, pp. 21 ff.

253. Henri PIRENNE, *Histoire économique et sociale du Moyen Age*, 1969 edn, p. 20.

254. J. DHONDT, *Le Haut Moyen Age*, op. cit., p. 183.

255. *Ibid.*, p. 189.

Notes to Part II

1. Jan DHONDT, *Le Haut Moyen Age (VIIIe–IXe siècles)*, French translation, 1976, p. 186.
2. Guy BOIS, *Crise du féodalisme*, 1976, p. 299.
3. 70% in Normandy, 64% in Haute-Provence, 70% in the Champsaur region and almost as much around Paris. Figures quoted by Guy BOIS, in *Crise du féodalisme*, op. cit., after Edouard BARATIER, *La Démographie provençale du XIIIe au XVIe siècle*, pp. 81and 59; Alfred FIERRO, 'Un cycle démographique: Dauphiné et Faucigny du XIVe au XIXe siècle', in *Annales E.S.C.*; Guy FOURQUIN, *Les Campagnes de la région parisienne à la fin du Moyen Age*, 1964, pp. 364–6.
4. Guy BOIS, *Crise du féodalisme*, op. cit., part 3, 'Les étapes de la crise'.
5. Cf. Karl Ferdinand WERNER, *Les Origines*, in *Histoire de France*, ed. J. FAVIER, I, 1984, p. 432.
6. *Ibid.*, p. 431.
7. *Ibid.*, p. 433.
8. *Ibid.*, p. 426. By the eleventh century in northern Burgundy.
9. Friesia, a country with a long maritime tradition, was integrated into Lothair's kingdom at the treaty of Verdun in 843, and exported to long distances the products of its textile industry. Jan DHONDT, *La Haut Moyen Age, VIIIe–IXe siècles*, 1976, pp. 143–4.
10. Edouard PERROY, *La Guerre de Cent Ans*, 1945, p. 41.
11. *Alleu – allodium*: freehold inheritance, as opposed to feudal fief.
12. 'What would begin to be called a "fief" by the end of the eleventh century', Jean FAVIER, *Le Temps des principautés: de l'an Mil à 1515*, *Histoire de France*, op. cit., II, 1984, p. 22.
13. Charles PFISTER, *Etudes sur le règne de Robert le Pieux (996–1031)*, 1885, pp. 167–8.
14. E. PERROY, *La Guerre de Cent Ans*, op cit., p. 18.
15. François SIGAUT, 'Moulins femmes, esclaves', in *Colloque Techniques, technologie et histoire dans l'aire méditerranéenne*, Aix-en-Provence (proceedings of the conference held at Aix-en-Provence in October 1982, forthcoming).
16. K. F. WERNER, in *Histoire de France*, ed. J. FAVIER, op. cit., p. 424; J. DHONDT, *Le Haut Moyen Age*, op. cit., p. 27.
17. J. DHONDT, *ibid.*, pp. 24–5, and Georges DUBY, *L'Economie rurale et la vie des campagnes de l'Occident médiéval*, 1962, I, pp. 100–2.
18. On the rise of these two poles of economic activity, see F. BRAUDEL, *Civilization and Capitalism*, III, *The Perspective of the World*, op. cit., pp. 89 ff.
19. *Ibid.*, p. 94 and note 17.
20. Josiah C. RUSSELL, 'Late ancient and medieval population', in *Transactions of the American Philosophical Society*, 1985, pp. 95 ff, quoted by Wilhelm ABEL, *Crises agraires en Europe (XIIIe–XXe siècle)*, 1973, pp. 35–6.
21. Georges DUBY, Robert MANTRAN, *L'Eurasie: XIe–XIIe siècles*, 1982, p. 18.
22. J. C. RUSSELL, 'Late ancient and medieval population', art. cit., p. 96.

23. W. ABEL, *Crises agraires*, op. cit., p. 37.

24. G. DUBY, R. MANTRAN, *L'Eurasie*, op. cit., pp. 18–19.

25. *Ibid.*, p. 85.

26. Amédée THALAMAS, *La Société seigneuriale française 1050–1270*, 1951, p. 46, note 18.

27. Marc BLOCH, *Les Caractères originaux de l'histoire rurale française*, I, 1976, pp. 5 and 9.

28. A. THALAMAS, *La société seigneuriale*, op. cit., p. 43.

29. M. BLOCH, *Les Caractères originaux*, op. cit., I, p. 9.

30. Louis BADRE, *Histoire de la forêt française*, 1983, p. 27.

31. E. MOREL, 'En Champagne, le bois dont on fait les villages', in *Marie-France*, October 1982.

32. On the use of wood, see F. BRAUDEL, *Civilization and capitalism*, I, *The Structures of Everyday Life*, p. 362.

33. The Multien is an ancient region of France between the Marne and the Ourcq.

34. The Orxois is a little *pays* in Brie.

35. Pierre BRUNET, *Structure agraire et économie rurale des plateaux tertiaires entre la Seine et l'Oise*, 1960, pp. 430 ff.

36. See the astonishing aerial photographs by Roger AGACHE: these reveal the sites of former Gallo-Roman villas, invisible today, and the villages built parallel to the sometimes irregular boundaries of the villas. This suggests that the villages were first settled at a time when the villas were still being farmed. R. AGACHE, 'Archéologie aérienne de la Somme, recherches nouvelles', in *Bulletin spécial de la Société de Préhistoire du Nord*, no. 6, 1964, figure 218; and 'Détection aérienne des vestiges protohistoriques gallo-romains et médiévaux dans le bassin de la Somme et ses abords', in *ibid.*, no. 7, 1970, figure 637 and figure Q, pp. 210–11.

37. Emile MIREAUX, *Une province française au temps du Grand Roi, la Brie*, 1956, pp. 70 ff.

38. P. BRUNET, *Structure agraire*, op. cit., p. 434.

39. François JULIEN-LABRUYERE, *Paysans charentais, histoire des campagnes d'Aunis, Saintonge et Bas-Angoumois*, I, 1982, p. 43.

40. Guy BOIS, 'Population, ressources et progrès techniques dans un village du Mâconnais (Xe–XVIIIe siècles)', in *Des labours de Cluny à la révolution verte*, proceedings of the *Colloque Population-Ressources*, 1985, p. 38.

41. J. DHONDT, *Le Haut Moyen Age*, op. cit., pp. 115–17 and note p. 330.

42. J. FAVIER, *Histoire de France*, op. cit., II, *Le Temps des principautés de l'An Mil à 1515*, 1984, p. 58.

43. Cf. F. BRAUDEL, *Civilization and capitalism*, III, *The Perspective of the World*, p. 96, note 19.

44. *Ibid.*, note 18.

45. J. FAVIER, *Histoire de France*, op. cit., II, p. 56.

46. Guy BOIS, *Crise du féodalisme*, op. cit., p. 264.

47. K. F. WERNER, in *Histoire de France*, ed. J. FAVIER, op. cit., I, pp. 426–8.

48. *Ibid.*, p. 58.

49. *Ibid.*, p. 60.

50. Pierre CHAUNU, *Le Temps des Réformes*, 1975, p. 77.

51. Robert PHILIPPE, *L'Energie au Moyen Age: l'exemple des pays d'entre Seine et Loire de la fin du Xe siècle à la fin du XVe siècle*, unpublished thesis, I, 1980, p. 173.

52. André CHEDEVILLE, *Chartres et ses campagnes, XIe–XIIIe siècles*, 1973, p. 196.

53. *Ibid.*, p. 194.

54. Since the average energy of a mill was 6 horsepower, the total mobilized was 120,000 hp, whereas the horse as a draught animal averaged 1/7 hp and a man 0.3 hp (but one also has to reckon with the intermittent nature of the labour provided by men or horses and the seasonal intermittence of the mills).

55. By Robert PHILIPPE in one of our discussions.

56. Robert PHILIPPE, 'Les premiers moulins à vent', in *Annales de Normandie*, no. 2, June 1982, p. 100, note: 'In 1802, there were 66,000 water-mills and 10,000 windmills; in 1896, there were 37,051 mills of all kinds and in 1921, 20,168.'

57. P. BONNAUD, *Terres et langages*, op. cit., I, p. 18.

58. Even if we do not accept Russell's very low figure, cited earlier, of 6,200,000 inhabitants, the population at the beginning of the twelfth century cannot have been more than 10 million at most, and the active population therefore about 2 million. If we accept that the 20,000 mills working at this time were the equivalent of 600,000 workers (see above and note 54), they would have increased the available workforce by a third. This is all hypothetical, of course, but it suggests an order of magnitude.

59. First-hand account by the 'mill-builder' himself, met while travelling.

60. R. PHILIPPE, *L'Energie au Moyen Age*, op. cit., I, p. 15.

61. W. ABEL, *Crises agraires*, op. cit., chapter I, esp. pp. 49–51.

62. P. CHANAU, *Le Temps des Réformes*, op. cit., p. 13.

63. Léopold DELISLE, *Etudes sur la condition de la classe agricole, et l'état de l'agriculture en Normandie au Moyen Age*, 1850, quoted by R. PHILIPPE, *L'Energie au Moyen Age*, op. cit., p. 66.

64. For further details of this, the first European world-economy, see F. BRAUDEL, *Civilization and Capitalism*, vol. III, *The Perspective of the World*, pp. 89 ff.

65. Félix BOURQUELOT, *Etudes sur les foires de Champagne*, 1865, I, pp. 72–5; Robert-Henri BAUTIER, 'Les foires de Champagne', in *Recueils de la Société Jean Bodin*, V, *La Foire*, 1953, p. 14.

66. Michel BUR, 'Remarques sur les plus anciens documents concernant les foires de Champagne', in *Colloque Les Villes, contribution à l'étude de leur développement en fonction de l'évolution économique*, Troyes, October 1970, 1972, p. 60.

67. Philippe DOLLINGER, 'Le chiffre de la population de Paris au XIVe siècle: 210,000 habitants ou 80,000 habitants?', in *Revue historique*, July–September 1956, pp. 35–44.

68. E. PERROY, *La Guerre de Cent Ans*, op. cit., p. 16. Charles V (1356–80) built the quarter of the Marais outside the walls.

69. 'Georges Suffert fait le point avec Régine Pernoud: des cathédrales à recolorier', in *Le Point*, 24–30 January 1983, pp. 112–22.

70. Ernst CURTIUS, *La Littérature européenne et le Moyen Age latin* (French translation), 1956, p. 68.

71. *Ibid.*, pp. 588–9. Michael

Blaunpayn, also known as Michael of Cornubia, a native of Cornwall, studied at Oxford and Paris.

72. Lando BORTOLOTTI, *La Città nella storia d'Italia*, 1983, p. 36.

73. Robert FOSSIER, *Le Moyen Age*, III, 1983, p. 55.

74. François SIMIAND distinguished between the A or upward phase and the B or downward phase of cyclical crises.

75. R. FOSSIER, *Le Moyen Age*, op. cit., p. 21.

76. Guy BOIS, *Crise du féodalisme*, op. cit., p. 10.

77. *Ibid.*, p. 11.

78. André CHEDEVILLE, *Chartres et ses campagnes, XIe–XIIIe siècles*, 1973, p. 528.

79. R. FOSSIER, *Le Moyen Age*, op. cit., III, p. 25.

80. Michel BELOTTE, *La Région de Bar-sur-Seine à la fin du Moyen Age*, doctoral thesis, 1973, p. 37.

81. R. FOSSIER, *Le Moyen Age*, op. cit., III, p. 44.

82. R. PHILIPPE, *L'Energie au Moyen Age*, op. cit., I, p. 265.

83. G. BOIS, *Crise du féodalisme*, op. cit., p. 52.

84. *Ibid.*, p. 62.

85. *Ibid.*, p. 299.

86. Adolphe VUITRY, *Etudes sur le régime financier de la France avant la Révolution de 1789*, 1883, II, pp. 195–9, quoted by G. BOIS, *Crise du féodalisme*, op. cit., p. 267.

87. Jean-Noël BIRABEN, *Les Hommes et la peste en France et dans les pays européens et mediterranéens*, 1975, I, p. 55.

88. From the Middle East, where plague had not disappeared as it had from Europe (cf. note 90).

89. J. N. BIRABEN, *Les Hommes et la peste*, op. cit., I, p. 309.

90. Plague continued to rage in the Ottoman Empire, making quarantine necessary in all Mediterranean ports; it eventually disappeared, as it had from Europe, but not until 1850 or so. Daniel PANZAC, *La Peste dans l'Empire ottoman 1700–1850*, doctoral thesis, Aix-en-Provence, 1982.

91. Jean de VENETTE, *Continuations de Guillaume de Nangis (1300–1368)*, II, 1844 edition, quoted by Noël COULET, 'Le malheur des temps 1348–1440' in *Histoire de la France*, ed. Georges DUBY, op. cit., p. 11.

92. J. N. BIRABEN, *Les Hommes et la peste*, op. cit., p. 159.

93. N. COULET, in *Histoire de la France*, ed. G. DUBY, op. cit., II, p. 9.

94. Thomas BASIN, *Histoire de Charles VII*, 1933 edn, pp. 88–9.

95. F. JULIEN-LABRUYERE, *Paysans charentais*, op. cit., p. 132.

96. N. COULET, in *Histoire de la France*, ed. G. DUBY, op. cit., II, p. 18.

97. Jean FROISSART, *Chroniques*, V (1356–60), quoted by N. COULET in *Histoire de la France*, ed. G. DUBY, op. cit., II, p. 14.

98. *Journal d'un bourgeois de Paris (1405–1449)*, 1881 edn, quoted by N. COULET, *ibid.*, p. 32.

99. *Ibid.*, p. 9.

100. Emile LEVASSEUR, *La Population française*, 1891, I, p. 179.

101. N. COULET, in *Histoire de la France*, ed. G. DUBY, op. cit., p. 28.

102. R. FOSSIER, *Le Moyen Age*, op. cit., III, p. 65.

103. John DAY, 'The Great Bullion Famine of the 15th Century', *Past and Present*, May 1978, pp. 3–54; and 'The Question of Monetary Contraction in late

Medieval Europe', in *Nordisk Numismatik Arsskrift*, 1981, pp. 12–29.

104. F. BOURQUELOT, *Etudes sur les foires de Champagne*, op. cit., I, p. 90.

105. André LEFEVRE, 'Les finances de la Champagne aux XIIIe et XIVe siècles', in *Bibliothèque de l'Ecole des Chartes*, 1859, p. 69, quoted by M. BELOTTE, *La Région de Bar-sur-Seine*, op. cit., p. 156.

106. Renée DOEHAERD, 'Les galères génoises dans la Manche et la mer du Nord à la fin du XIIIe et au début du XIVe siècle', in *Bulletin de l'Institut Historique Belge de Rome*, 1938, pp. 5–76.

107. F. BRAUDEL, *Civilization and Capitalism*, II, *The Perspective of the World*, p. 119.

108. Enrique OTTE, 'La Rochelle et l'Espagne. L'expédition de Diego Ingenios à l'île des Perles en 1528', in *Revue d'Histoire économique et sociale*, 1959, I, p. 44.

109. F. BRAUDEL, *The Perspective of the World*. op. cit., p. 116.

110. *Ibid.*, pp. 550 ff.

111. *Ibid.*, p. 118.

112. Pierre CHAUNU, Georges SUFFERT, *La Peste blanche*, 1976, p. 57.

113. Frank C. SPOONER, *The International Economy and Monetary Movements in France, 1493–1725*, 1972.

114. F. BRAUDEL, *The Mediterranean*, op. cit., II, p. 896.

115. Père Roger MOLS, *Introduction à la démographie historique des villes d'Europe du XIVe au XVIIIe siècle*, II, 1955, p. 516.

116. Jean H. MARIEJOL, *La Réforme et la Ligue. L'Edit de Nantes (1559–1598)*, vol. VI of *Histoire de France*, ed. LAVISSE, op. cit., p. 111 ff.

117. Pierre GOUBERT, *Beauvais et le Beauvaisis de 1600 à 1730. Contribution à l'histoire sociale de la France du XVIIe siècle*, 1960, p. 30.

118. E. LAVASSEUR, *La Population française*, op. cit., I, p. 189.

119. E. LE ROY LADURIE, *Les Paysans du Languedoc*, 1966, I, pp. 149–50.

120. *Ibid.*, p. 163.

121. *Ibid.*, p. 189.

122. M. BELOTTE, *La Région de Bar-sur-Seine*, op. cit., p. 266.

123. *Ibid.*, p. 310.

124. Claude HARMELLE, *Les Piqués de l'aigle. Saint-Antonin et sa région (1850–1940)*, 1982, p. 22.

125. Pierre de BRANTOME, *Oeuvres*, IX, 1779 edn, p. 249.

126. Quoted by Karl HELLEINER, in *The Cambridge Economic History of Europe*, ed. E. E. RICH and H. J. HABAKKUK, IV, 1967, p. 24.

127. Omer LUTFI BARKAN, quoted in F. BRAUDEL, *The Mediterranean*, op. cit., pp. 396–7.

128. F. BRAUDEL, *Civilization and Capitalism*, I, *The Structures of Everyday Life*, op. cit., pp. 187 ff.

129. It probably depends on the region. In Normandy, for instance, Guy Bois points out that the maximum reached in about 1550 is clearly about 25% lower than the maximum reached at the end of the thirteenth century; op. cit., p. 71.

130. F. BRAUDEL, *Civilization and Capitalism*, II, *The Perspective of the World*, op. cit., p. 86. Guy BOIS, *Crise du féodalisme*, op. cit., p. 10, gives a striking illustration of this: in 1473, the northern part of Normandy was devastated by the Burgundians: villages were wiped out, crops

burnt, and the damage was the same as a century earlier, but this time, because of the vigour of the economic revival, normality was restored within only a few years.

131. André ARMENGAUD, *La Famille et l'enfant en France et en Angleterre du XVIe au XVIIIe siècle*, 1975, p. 81.

132. Oudard COQUAULT, *Mémoires (1649–1668)*, 1875 edn, I, p. 34.

133. Pierre GOUBERT, 'Le régime démographique français au temps de Louis XIV', in *Histoire économique et sociale de la France*, ed. F. BRAUDEL and E. LABROUSSE, II, 1970, p. 37.

134. Jean FOURASTIE, 'De la vie traditionnelle à la vie tertiaire', in *Population*, 1959, no. 3, p. 418.

135. André ARMENGAUD, Marcel REINHARD and Jacques DUPAQUIER , *Histoire générale de la population mondiale*, 1968, pp. 175–6.

136. *Ibid.*, p. 195.

137. F. BRAUDEL, *Civilization and Capitalism*, I, *The Structures of Everyday Life*, op. cit., p. 164.

138. Charles HIGOUNET, ed., *Histoire de l'Aquitaine*, 1971, p. 303.

139. Alain CROIX, *La Bretagne aux XVIe et XVIIe siècles*, 1981, I, pp. 44–5.

140. F. BRAUDEL, *Civilization and Capitalism*, I, *The Structures of Everyday Life*, op. cit., p. 169.

141. E. JULLIARD, *La Vie rurale dans la plaine de Basse- Alsace. Essai de géographie sociale*, 1953, pp. 213–15.

142. Earl. J. HAMILTON, *American Treasure and the Price Revolution, in Spain*, 1934.

143. Huguette and Pierre CHAUNU, *Séville et l'Atlantique 1504–1650*, 1955–60.

144. Michel MORINEAU, *Incroyables gazettes et fabuleux métaux, les retours des trésors américains d'après les gazettes hollandais, XVIe–XVIIIe siècles*, 1985.

145. P. GOUBERT, *Beauvais*, op. cit., p. 382 and note 77.

146. W. KULA, *Théorie économique du système féodal*, op. cit., p. 48.

147. Frank SPOONER, *The International Economy*, op. cit., p. 306.

148. Karl Julius BELOCH, 'Die Bevölkerung Europas zur Zeit des Renaissance', in *Zeitschrift für Sozialwissenschaft*, 1900, pp. 774 and 786.

149. A. ARMENGAUD et al., *Histoire générale de la population mondiale*, op. cit., pp. 241–71, 328–39.

150. Charles-Henri POUTHAS, *La Population française pendant la première moitié du XIXe siècle*, 1956; P. GOUBERT, 'Les fondements démographiques', in *Histoire économique et sociale de la France*, ed. F. BRAUDEL and E. LABROUSSE, op. cit., II, pp. 9–84; André ARMENGAUD, 'Le role de la démographie' in *ibid.*, III, 1976, pp. 161–238.

151. A. ARMENGAUD et al., *Histoire générale de la population*, op. cit., p. 252.

152. A. ARMENGAUD in *Histoire économique et sociale de la France*, ed. F. BRAUDEL and E. LABROUSSE, III, p. 163.

153. C. E. LABROUSSE, *La Crise de l'économie française à la fin de l'Ancien régime et au début de la Révolution*, 1944.

154. B. H. SLICHER VAN BATH, *Yield Ratios 810–1820*, 1963, p. 16.

155. Richard GASCON, 'La France du mouvement: les commerces et les villes', in *Histoire*

économique et sociale de la France, ed. BRAUDEL and LABROUSSE, op. cit., I, 1977, p. 238, quoting MACHIAVELLI.

156. Paul BAIROCH, 'Les grandes tendances des disparités économiques nationales depuis la révolution industrielle', in *Regional and International Disparities in Economic Development since the Industrial Revolution*, 7th international economic history conference, 1978, pp. 43–5.

157. L. M. POUSSEREAU, 'Changements survenus depuis un siècle dans la condition des bûcherons et des ouvriers forestiers du département de la Nièvre', in *Bulletin de la Société scientifique et artistique de Clamecy*, 1927, pp. 36–54.

158. Jean-Charles SOURNIA, *Histoire et médecine*, 1982, p. 236.

159. *Ibid.*, p. 235.

160. Jean BERNARD, quoted in 'Le 28e Congrès d'histoire de la médecine, tromper la mort', in *Le Monde*, 8 September 1982.

161. Emile LITTRE, *Journal des débats*, 18 June 1856, quoted by J. C. SOURNIA, *Histoire et médecine*, op. cit., p. 237.

162. Claude BERNARD, *Introduction à l'étude de la médecine expérimentale*, quoted by J. C. SOURNIA, *ibid.*, p. 236.

163. Alfred SAUVY, Preface to *Demain le Tiers Monde: population et développement*, special number of *Revue Tiers Monde*, XXIV, no. 94, April–June 1983, p. 236.

164. Alfred SAUVY, *La Population*, 1963, p. 66.

165. A. SAUVY, 'Notes de lecture', *Le Monde*, 14 September 1982.

166. John NAISBITT, *Megatrends*, quoted by Jacques DUQUESNE, 'Special 1983–2000, l'agenda du futur', *Le Point*, 7 November 1983, p. 4.

167. Ten per thousand in 1980, eighth in the world, behind Sweden, Japan, Finland, Switzerland . . . but ahead of the United States and Germany (*Population et Sociétés*, August 1982, no. 160). By 1983 the figure had fallen to 8.3 per thousand (*ibid.*, no. 200).

168. Georges VALRAN, *Misère et charité en Provence au XVIIIe siècle*, 1899, pp. 22–3.

169. A. SAUVY, ed., *Histoire économique de la France entre les deux guerres*, II, 1974, pp. 340–1.

170. Ange GOUDAR, *Les Intérêts de la France mal entendus*, op. cit., 1756, I, pp. 271 and 275.

171. Jean AUFFRAY, *Le Luxe considéré relativement à la population et à l'économie*, 1762, pp. 29–30.

172. A. GOUDAR, *Les Intérêts*, op. cit., p. 96.

173. Jean NOVI DE CAVEIRAC, *Paradoxes intéressants sur la cause et les effets de la révocation de l'Edit de Nantes, la dépopulation et repopulation du Royaume, l'intolérance civile et rigoureuse d'un gouvernement*, 1758, p. 253.

174. Denis-Laurian TURMEAU DE LA MORANDIERE, *Appel des étrangers dans nos colonies*, 1763, p. 21.

175. Chevalier de CERFVOL, *Législation du divorce*, 1770, pp. 62–3.

176. M. MOHEAU, *Recherches et considérations sur la population de la France*, 1788, p. 27.

177. Père FELINE, *Catéchisme*, 1782, p. 11, quoted by Jean-Marie GOUESSE, 'En Basse-Normandie aux XVIIe et XVIIIe siècles: le refus de l'enfant au tribunal de la

pénitence', in *Annales de démographie historique*, 1973, pp. 255–6.

178. M. MESSANCE, *Nouvelles recherches sur la population de la France*, 1788, p. 27.

179. Jean-Pierre BARDET, *Rouen aux XVIIe et XVIIIe siècles, les mutations d'un espace social*, I, 1983, p. 263.

180. Guy ARBELLOT, *Cinq Paroisses du Vallage, XVIIe–XVIIIe siècles. Etude de démographie historique*, 1970, p. 225.

181. J. M. GOUESSE, *En Basse-Normandie*, art. cit. (see note 177), p. 231.

182. *Ibid.*, p. 251.

183. John NICKOLLS (pseudonym of PLUMARD DE DANGEUL), *Remarques sur les avantages et désavantages de la France et de la Grande-Bretagne par rapport au commerce et autres sources de la puissance des Etats*, 1754, pp. 18–19.

184. J. DUPAQUIER and M. LACHIVER, 'La contraception en France ou les deux malthusianismes', in *Annales E.S.C.*, 1969, no. 6, p. 1401.

185. J. P. BARDET, *Rouen*, op. cit., p. 265.

186. *Ibid.*, p. 272.

187. Jean GANIAGE, *Trois Villages d'Ile-de-France au XVIIIe siècle*, Cahier INED no. 40, 1963, p. 131.

188. Antoinette CHAMOUX and Cécile DAUPHIN, 'La contraception avant la Révolution française: l'exemple de Châtillon-sur-Seine', in *Annales E.S.C.*, 1969, no. 3, pp. 662–84.

189. Raymond DENIEL and Louis HENRY, 'La population d'un village du Nord de la France, Sainghin-en-Mélantois de 1665

à 1851', in *Population*, 1965, 4, pp. 563–602. On the Vendée, see J.-L. FLANDRIN, *Les Amours paysannes (XVIe-XIXe siècles)*, 1975, p. 242.

190. J.-M. GOUESSE, 'En Basse-Normandie', art. cit., p. 232 and note 6.

191. Marquise de SEVIGNE, *Lettres*, Pléiade edn, I, 1953, pp. 432, 433, 450; see also *Prévention des naissances dans la famille, ses origines dans les pays modernes*, Cahier INED no. 35, 1960, pp. 156–9.

192. J. P. BARDET, *Rouen*, op. cit., p. 264.

193. Michel de MONTAIGNE, *Essais*, Pléiade edn, I, 1962, essay XIV, p. 58.

194. Sixteenth-century texts, quoted by J.-L. FLANDRIN, *Les Amours paysannes*, op. cit., pp. 83 and 86.

195. Saint-Jean-Eudes, quoted by J.-M. GOUESSE, 'En Basse-Normandie', art. cit., p. 253.

196. Bricquebec, September 1708, quoted *ibid.*, p. 258.

197. MONTAIGNE, *Essais*, op. cit., I, essay XXX, p. 196.

198. Pierre de BRANTOME, *Les Dames galantes*, ed. Maurice RAT, 1917, quoted by J.-L. FLANDRIN, 'La vie sexuelle des gens mariés dans l'ancienne société: de la doctrine de l'Eglise à la réalité des comportements', in *Communications*, 1982, pp. 108–9.

199. P. de BRANTOME, *Les Dames galantes*, op. cit., pp. 32 and 27–8, quoted by J.-L. FLANDRIN, 'Contraception, mariage et relations amoureuses dans l'Occident chrétien', in *Annales E.S.C.*, 1969, no. 6, pp. 1383–4 and note 4.

200. P. de BRANTOME, *Les Dames*

galantes, pp. 38–9, quoted by J.-L. FLANDRIN, *ibid.*, p. 1385.

201. J.-L. FLANDRIN, 'L'attitude à l'égard du petit enfant et les conduites sexuelles dans la civilisation occidentale', in *Annales de démographie historique*, 1973, pp. 182 ff.

202. Quoted by Hélène BERGUES, *La Prévention des naissances dans la famille*, op. cit., Cahier INED no. 35, pp. 229–30.

203. MONTAIGNE, *Essais*, op. cit., I, essay XIV, p. 62.

204. A. SAUVY, 'Essai d'une vue d'ensemble', in *Prévention des naissances dans la famille*, op. cit., pp. 389–90.

205. Ferdinand BUISSON, *Souvenirs (1866–1916)*, 1916, pp. 30–2.

206. On this group and its social role in the sixteenth century, see George HUPPERT's *The Idea of Perfect History*, 1970, and *Les Bourgeois Gentilshommes*, 1977. On the founding of the new schools, see George HUPPERT, *Public Schools in Renaissance France*, 1984.

207. Edgar QUINET, *Histoire de mes idées. Autobiographie*, 1878, pp. 78–9.

208. Quoted by A. ARMENGAUD, M. REINHARD and J. DUPAQUIER, *Histoire générale de la population mondiale*, op. cit., p. 336.

209. Michel-Louis LÉVY, 'Les étrangers en France', in *Population et société*, July–August 1980, no. 137. The preceding figures come from the same article.

210. *Ibid.*

211. *Ibid.*

212. Quoted in F. BRAUDEL, *The Mediterranean*, op. cit., II, p. 795.

213. Augustin BARBARA, 'Un muscle seulement?', *Le Monde*, 25 July 1980.

214. In 1984, in the United States, certain leading industries found it more advantageous, to cut costs, to resort to off-shore manufacturing, usually in Asia, than to employ Mexican labour.

215. J. F. DUPAQUIER, 'Immigrant families do not want to play the bourgeois, but with eight or nine children, they are barred from subsidized housing', *Le Quotidien de Paris*, 27 March 1980.

216. This is what most French people think, apparently: according to a Figaro–SOFRES poll in November 1985, 90% thought it quite normal that immigrant workers who paid contributions should receive unemployment benefit and family allowances; at the same time 71% thought that illegal immigrants should be sent back home.

217. Nathaniel WEYL, *Karl Marx, racist*, 1980.

218. Article in *Le Monde*, 25 July 1980.

219. As is confirmed by a biological survey carried out by INSERM, on thousands of blood samples, both in relation to blood groups and to genetic combinations. The samples were taken from families who had lived in their region for at least three generations, and proved 'the great diversity of our ethnic origins', with sometimes surprising regional differences, revealing very ancient currents of migration. Franck NOUCH, 'Une étude biologique démontre le "métissage" du peuple français', in *Le Monde*, 25 October 1985.

220. Bernard STASI, *L'Immigration, une chance pour la France*, 1984, p. 13.

221. 'After Begin's accusations, are the French antisemitic? Yes, says Serge Koster, who thinks there can be no innocent statement about Israel', *Le Quotidien de Paris*, 12 August 1982.

222. 'Un équilibre sans cesse remis en question', in *Le Quotidien de Paris*, 2 April 1980.

223. J. F. DUPAQUIER, 'Quand les bougnoules étaient ritals', in *L'Evènement de jeudi*, 13–19 June 1985, pp. 48–9, reference to J. B. DUROSELLE and E. SERRA, *L'Emigrazione italiana in Francia prima del 1914*, Milan, 1978.

224. J. F. DUPAQUIER, 'Quand les bougnoules étaient polaks', *ibid.*, pp. 50–1.

225. Judith SAYMAL, 'Si ma soeur épouse un Français, je la tue!', in *L'Evènement du jeudi*, 13–19 June 1985, pp. 40–1.

226. Tahar BEN JELLOUN, 'Les jeunes et la mère amnésique', in *Le Monde*, 25 July 1980.

227. G. LECLERC-COUTEL, 'Ne pas mourir deux fois', *Le Monde*, 25 July 1980.

228. Jean ANGLADE, *La Vie quotidienne des immigrés en France, de 1919 à nos jours*, 1976, pp. 105 ff.

229. Debate, 'Les immigrés parmi nous', *Le Monde*, 19–20 June 1983.

230. Jean-François MONGIBEAUX, 'L'album de voyage de petits maghrébins au Maghreb', in *Le Quotidien de Paris*, September 1982.

231. Investigation carried out in Kabylie by Jacques MAIGNE, 'Le double exil des immigrés qui choisissent "le grand retour"', *Libération*, 7 November 1983.

232. Investigation in Algeria by Michel AREZKI, 'Les émigrés, ces étrangers de l'intérieur', *Libération*, 9 November 1983.

233. *Ibid.*

234. J. MAIGNE, article in *Libération* cited above (note 231).

235. *Ibid.*

236. *Ibid.*

237. J. F. DUPAQUIER, 'L'Islam ou le bulletin de vote?', in *L'Evènement du jeudi*, 13–19 June 1985, pp. 34–8.

238. Léo HAMON, 'Une seule appartenance', *Le Monde*, 23 May 1980.

239. J. F. DUPAQUIER, article in *L'Evènement du jeudi*, cited above (note 237), p. 37.

240. J. F. DUPAQUIER, 'Le pays réel c'est la France', *ibid.*, p. 41.

241. Jean-Francis HELD, 'Comment faire des Français avec du Beur?', in *L'Evènement du jeudi*, 13–19 June 1985, pp. 32–3.

Notes to Part III

1. Daniel THORNER, 'L'économie paysanne. Concept pour l'histoire économique', *Annales E.S.C.*, 3, May–June 1964, pp. 417–32.

2. Louis CHEVALIER, *Les Paysans, étude d'histoire et d'économie rurale*, 1947, pp. 223–4.

3. D. THORNER, article quoted, p. 418.

4. Frédéric LULLIN DE CHATEAUVIEUX, *Voyages agronomiques en France*, 1843, I, pp. 40 ff.

5. Maurice PARODI, *L'Economie et la société française depuis 1945*, 1981, p. 81.

6. Daniel HALÉVY, *Visites aux*

paysans du Centre (1903–1934), 1935 (now in Livre de poche, 1978).

7. G. VALRAN, *Misère et charité en Provence au XVIIIe siècle*, 1899, p. 29.

8. Jacques LAFFITTE, quoted by S. CHARLETY, *La Restauration*, in Ernest LAVISSE, ed., *Histoire de France contemporaine*, IV, 1921, p. 307.

9. Jacques LAFFITTE, *Réflexions sur la réduction de la rente et sur l'état du crédit*, 1824, p. 6.

10. Archives Nationales (A.N.), F²⁰ 130.

11. Alain CORBIN, *Archaïsme et modernité en Limousin au XIXe siècle (1845–1880)*, 1975, I, p. 58, note 31: 'since [in 1866] the country people had never seen a cesspit'.

12. Michel-Christophe KIENER, Jean-Claude PEYRONNET, *Quand Turgot régnait en Limousin: un tremplin vers le pouvoir*, 1979, p. 32.

13. *Ecrouter* – to turn only the surface of the soil.

14. Paul DUFOURNET, *Une communauté agraire sécrète et organise son territoire à Bassy (Haute-Savoie)*, 1975, p. 551.

15. Anne-Marie BRISEBARRE, *Bergers des Cévennes. Histoire et ethnographie du monde pastoral et de la transhumance en Cévennes*, 1978, p. 26.

16. Cf. Volume I, Part II.

17. Robert FOSSIER, *Le Moyen Age*, II: *L'Eveil de l'Europe*, 1982, p. 292.

18. Georges DUBY, *La Société aux XIe et XIIe siècles dans la région mâconnaise*, 1971, p. 362.

19. Jean SCHNEIDER, 'Problèmes urbains dans la France médiévale', in *Actes du 100e Congrès national des Sociétés Savantes*, 1977, p. 139.

20. Jean-Pierre POLY, *La Provence et la société féodale, 879–1166*, 1976, pp. 226–7.

21. *Vermillon* (vermillion) was the popular name for the *kermès*, a kind of cochineal beetle which lives on the evergreen oaks of the south of France.

22. J.-P. POLY, *La Provence*, op. cit., p. 231. The *tonlieu* was a tax levied on the right to display goods at fairs.

23. Hektor AMMAN, 'Deutschland und die Tuchindustrie Nordwesteuropas im Mittelalter', in *Hansische Geschichtsblätter*, 1954, p. 8.

24. J.-P. POLY, *La Provence*, op. cit., pp. 233–7 and 248–9.

25. G. DUBY, *La Société . . . dans la région mâconnaise*, op. cit., p. 53.

26. *Ibid.*, p. 50.

27. *Ibid.*, pp. 46–7.

28. *Ibid.*, p. 93.

29. *Ibid.*, p. 48.

30. *Ibid.*, pp. 264–6.

31. *Ibid.*, pp. 275 ff.

32. *Ibid.*, pp. 309–10.

33. *Ibid.*, p. 316.

34. André CHEDEVILLE, *Chartres et ses campagnes, XIe–XIIIe siècles*, 1973, p. 434.

35. Nicolas de LAMARE, *Traité de la police*, II, 1710, p. 727.

36. R. FOSSIER, *Le Moyen Age*, op. cit., II, p. 285.

37. Anne LOMBARD-JOURDAN, 'Les foires aux origines des villes', in *Francia: Forschungen zur Westeuropäischen Geschichte*, X, 1983, p. 483. List from cartulary of Saint-Aubin d'Angers.

38. François-P. GAY, *La Champagne du Berry*, 1967, p. 50.

39. Guy DEVAILLY, *La Berry du Xe au milieu du XIIIe siècle*, 1973, p. 197.

40. *Ibid.*, p. 553.
41. N. de LAMARE, *Traité de la police*, op. cit., I, p. 539. The Provost of Paris banned the keeping of pigeons, goslings, rabbits and pigs within the city, 4 April 1502.
42. Elie BRACKENHOFFER, *Voyage en France 1643–1644*, 1925 edn, p. 110.
43. Jean PITIÉ, *Exode rural et migrations intérieures en France. L'exemple de la Vienne et du Poitou-Charentes*, 1971, p. 672.
44. A.N., Y 10558 A.
45. A. CORBIN, *Archaïsme et modernité en Limousin*, op. cit., I, p. 69.
46. A. LOMBARD-JOURDAN, 'Les faires', art. cit., p. 441. The *Syri* or Levantine merchants brought precious goods from the East to the West until the end of the sixth century.
47. Jacques MULLIEZ, 'Du blé, "mal nécessaire". Réflexions sur les progrès de l'agriculture de 1750 à 1850', in *Revue d'histoire moderne et contemporaine*, XXVI. January–March 1979, p. 8.
48. In the south of France, for instance. Charles HIGOUNET, 'Sources et problématique de l'histoire des campagnes', in *Actes du 100e Congrès National des Sociétés Savantes*, 1979, pp. 181 ff.
49. Oswald SPENGLER, *L'Homme et la Technique*, French edition, 1958, p. 90.
50. François JACOB, *La Logique du vivant, Une histoire de l'hérédité*, 1970, p. 261.
51. Karl MARX, *Economic and Philosophic Manuscripts of 1844* (tr. M. Milligan, Moscow Progress Publishers edition 1959, pp. 70–1).
52. Maurice GODELIER, *L'Idéel et le matériel. Pensée, économies, sociétés*, 1984, pp. 9 ff.
53. François MALOUET, *Mémoires*, I, 1868, p. 111.
54. Paul DUFOURNET, *Pour une archéologie du paysage. Une communauté agraire sécrète et organise son territoire*, published version of his 1975 thesis, 1978, p. 9.
55. Jean GEORGELIN, *Venise au siècle des Lumières*, 1978, p. 14.
56. A.N., F^{20} 561, Dordogne.
57. André BOUTON, *Le Maine. Histoire économique et sociale, XVIIe et XVIIIe siècles. L'administration de l'Ancien Régime. Ses classes sociales, ses misérables*, 1962, p. 495. Alain MOLINIER, *Stagnations et croissance. Le Vivarais aux XVIIe et XVIIIe siècles*, 1985, p. 33.
58. A.N., F^{10} 242, Aveyron, 1796.
59. *Gazette de France*, 12 October 1772, p. 378.
60. *Ibid.*, 16 January 1649, p. 60.
61. *Ibid.*, 21 January 1651, p. 135.
62. A.N., G^7 521, Tours, 30 June 1693.
63. A.N., F^{20} 560. *Tableau des pertes causées dans chaque département par les inondations, grèles, incendies, épizooties . . . de 1807 à 1810 et 1814 à 1819.* A similar table for the years 1826–35, not entirely comparable because it includes frosts in the list, gives much higher figures (three times as high) but with the same classification; hail and fire came at the top of the list, *ibid.*
64. *Voyage d'Angleterre, d'Hollande et de Flandre fait en l'année 1728*, Victoria and Albert Museum, 86, NN2, fol. 4.
65. M. CRUBELLIER ed., *Histoire de la Champagne*, 1975, p. 204.
66. René CHAPUIS, *Une vallée*

franco-comtoise, la Haute-Loue. Etude de géographie humaine, 1958, pp. 16–17.

67. A.N., H 1517, 222–7.

68. Charles DUPIN, *Le Petit Producteur français,* III, 1827, pp. 1–2.

69. Léonce de LAVERGNE, *Économie rurale de la France depuis 1789,* 1877, p. 39.

70. J. PITIÉ, *Exode rural,* op. cit., p. 672.

71. Joseph ANCILLON, *Recueil journalier de ce qui s'est passé de plus mémorable dans la cité de Mets, pays messin et aux environs, de 1675 à 1684,* 1866, p. 13.

72. A.N., G⁷ 293, Montpellier, 16 April 1679. This was the father of d'Aguesseau the chancellor.

73. Stockalper Archiv, Brig, Sch. 31, n° 2998.

74. A.N., F¹⁰ 226, 1792.

75. Philippe ARBOS, *La Vie pastorale dans les Alpes françaises. Etude de géographie humaine,* 1923, p. 234.

76. André PIOGER, *Le Fertois aux XVIIe et XVIIIe siècles. Histoire économique et sociale,* 1973, p. 297.

77. M. DARLUC, *Histoire naturelle de la Provence,* I, 1782, pp. 129–30.

78. The name given in Provence to the inhabitants of the Gap district and to mountain dwellers from the Alps in general.

79. A.N., F¹ᶜ V (1) Hérault, meeting of the departmental council, session on agriculture, Year XII.

80. *Journal de Nicolas de Baye, greffier au Parlement de Paris, 1400–1417,* ed. A. TUETEY, 1885, I, p. 211, 17 January 1408.

81. Charles CARRIERE, *Negociants marseillais au XVIIIe siècle,* I, 1973, p. 108.

82. Edouard BARATIER ed., *Histoire de Marseille,* 1973, p. 151.

83. Robert TRIGER, *Observations agricoles et météorologiques sur les années remarquables de 1544 à 1789 dans la province du Maine . . . ,* 1881, p. 4.

84. *Journal de Simon Le Marchand, bourgeois de Caen, 1610–1693,* ed. Gabriel VANEL, 1903, p. 166.

85. Claude HARMELLE, *Les Piqués de l'aigle. Saint-Antonin et sa région (1850–1940), révolution des transports et changement social,* 1982, p. 46.

86. A.N., F¹ᶜ III, Bouches-du-Rhône 7.

87. *Ibid.,* Aube 4, 19 November 1853.

88. *Ibid.,* Ardennes 6, 27 February 1854.

89. Jehan RICTUS, *Les Soliloques du pauvre,* 1971 edn, p. 9.

90. The term used by the provincial assembly of the Ile-de-France in 1787, p. 245.

91. Pierre-André SIGALAS, *La Vie à Grasse en 1650,* 1964, p. 86.

92. Antoine Laurent de LAVOISIER, *De la richesse territoriale du royaume de France,* in Collection *des principaux économistes,* XIV, 1847, 1966 edn, p. 595.

93. A. CORBIN, *Archaïsme et modernité en Limousin,* op. cit., I, p. 67.

94. Sir Thomas MORE, *Utopia,* Everyman edition, pp. 23–4.

95. Richard de CANTILLON, *Essai sur la nature du commerce en général,* 1755, pp. 97–8.

96. MESSANCE, *Nouvelles Recherches sur la population de la France,* 1788, p. 85.

97. Léonce de LAVERGNE, *Economie rurale de la France depuis 1789,* 1860, p. 75.

98. Jules-Marie RICHARD, *La Vie privée dans une province de*

l'Ouest. Laval aux XVIIe et XVIIIe siècles, 1922, p. 5.

99. Elie BRACKENHOFFER, *Voyage en France, 1643–1644*, 1925 edn, p. 111.

100. A.N., F[10] 295, 141 and H 1517, 207–11.

101. N. de LAMARE, *Traité de la police*, op. cit., I, p. 569, 12 December 1697.

102. François JULIEN-LABRUYERE, *Paysans charentais. Histoire des campagnes d'Aunis, Saintonge et bas Angoumois*, I: *Economie rurale*, 1928, p. 218, note 1.

103. *Ibid.*, p. 269 and note 18.

104. P. G. POINSOT, *L'Ami des cultivateurs*, 1806, II, pp. 39–41.

105. A. BOUTON, *Le Maine*, op. cit., pp. 497–8.

106. P. ARBOS, *La Vie pastorale*, op. cit., p. 196.

107. *Ibid.*, p. 174.

108. André GERDEAUX, 'Evolution de l'agriculture et métamorphoses des paysages de la Champagne châlonnaise', in *Châlons, 2000 ans d'histoire, mélanges d'histoire, de géographie, d'art et de traditions*, 1980, p. 243.

109. P. ARBOS, *La Vie pastorale*, op. cit., p. 173.

110. A.N., F[10] 212 AB.

111. During the Revolution, hunting reserves were suppressed and the supply of game dropped considerably.

112. Alfred LEROUX, *Le Massif Central. HIstoire d'une région de la France*, 1898, II, p. 45. Alain MOLINIER *Stagnations et croissance*, op. cit., pp. 179–80. P. ARBOS, op. cit., pp. 172–3.

113. Jean-François SOULET, *La Vie quotidienne dans les Pyrénées sous l'Ancien Régime, du XVIe siècle au XVIIIe siècle*, 1974, pp. 84–5.

114. A. BOUTON, *Le Maine*, op. cit., p. 502.

115. *Ibid,*, p. 501.

116. *Ibid.*, p. 502.

117. F. BRAUDEL, *Civilization and Capitalism*, I, *The Structures of Everyday Life*, op. cit., p. 118.

118. A.N., F[20] 561.

119. A.N., H 1462, printed paper, 1785, p. 3.

120. Roger BRUNET, *Les Campagnes toulousaines. Etudes géographique*, 1965, p. 163.

121. Pierre DEFFONTAINES, *Les Hommes et leurs travaux dans les pays de la Moyenne-Garonne (Agenais-Bas-Quercy)*, 1932, p. 220.

122. Gustave HEUZÉ, *La France agricole, Région du Sud ou région de l'olivier*, 1868, p. 91.

123. J. PITIÉ, *Exode rural*, op. cit., p. 307.

124. L. de LAVERGNE, *Economie rurale*, op. cit., p. 387; Robert LAURENT, *Vignerons de la 'Côte d'Or' au XIXe siècle*, 1958, p. 177.

125. Michel AUBRUN, 'La terre et les hommes d'une paroisse marchoise. Essai d'histoire régressive', in *Etudes rurales*, 1983, p. 252.

126. F. JULIEN-LABRUYÈRE, *Paysans charentais*, op. cit., I, p. 224.

127. Pierre VALMARY, *Familles paysannes au XVIIIe siècle en Bas-Quercy. Etude démographique*, 1965, pp. 15–17.

128. *Réflexions d'un citoyen-propriétaire sur l'étendue de la contribution foncière et sa proportion avec le produit net territorial, converti en argent*, 1792, p. 8. A. de LAVOISIER, *De la richesse*, op. cit.

129. *Annuaire statistique de l'INSEE*, vol. 58, 1951, p. 119.

130. Jean-Claude TOUTAIN, *La Population de la France de 1700 à 1959*, in *Cahiers de l'ISEA*, 1963, pp. 54–55.

131. In the *élection* of Clermont, in Picardy, in the eighteenth century there were 1,850 *arpents* farmed by hand and 76,665 ploughed; Albéric de CALONNE, *La Vie agricole sous l'Ancien Régime en Picardie et en Artois*, 1883, p. 261.

132. Gruel was the basic element of diet in the Pyrenean region of Ariège; chestnuts in the Limousin and Gévaudan.

133. Louis-René NOUGIER, *Géographie humaine préhistorique*, preface by Pierre DEFFONTAINES, 1959, p. 8.

134. Marc BLOCH, *Les Caractères originaux de l'histoire rurale française*, I, 1952, p. 24.

135. A.N., F10 221 1.

136. Isaac de PINTO, *Traité de la circulation et du crédit*, 1771, p. 12.

137. England had begun encouraging exports in 1689 by offering bounties, cf. Peter MATHIAS, *The First Industrial Nation*, 1969, p. 71.

138. Jean CHAPELOT, Robert FOSSIER, *Le Village et la maison au Moyen Age*, 1980, p. 147.

139. Jean-Claude TOUTAIN, *Le Produit de l'agriculture française de 1700 à 1958*, I, *Estimation du produit au XIXe siècle*, in *Histoire quantitative de l'économie française*, ed. J. MARCZEWSKI, *Cahiers de l'ISEA*, series AF, no. 1, July 1961, p. 23.

140. Georges d'AVENEL, *Histoire économique de la propriété, des salaires, des denrées et de tous les prix en général depuis l'an 1200 jusqu'en l'an 1800*, I, 1894, p. 268.

141. L. de LAVERGNE, *Economie rurale*, op. cit., pp. 402–3.

142. Marc BLOCH, *Les Caractères originaux de l'histoire rurale française*, I, 1952, p. 22.

143. J. MULLIEZ, 'De blé, "mal nécessaire"', art. cit., pp. 3–47.

144. Around Prades in 1859, for instance, 'it is usual to water the wheat and rye three times, namely when it sprouts, when it is in the ear and at the beginning of June, so that the earth will retain enough moisture until the grain is quite ripe. There are some years when it has to be watered four or five times', report by the *sous-préfet* of Prades, A.N. FIC 111, Pyrénées-Orientales, in *Documents d'histoire économique 1800–1914*, Service éducatif des Archives départementales Pyrénées-Orientales, 1974, p. 10.

145. L. de LAVERGNE, *Economie rurale*, op. cit., p. 139.

146. *Ibid.*, p. 50.

147. Pierre LE PESANT DE BOISGUILLEBERT, *Le Détail de la France*, 1697, 1966 edition, pp. 253, 254.

148. G. d'AVENEL, *Histoire économique de la propriété*, op. cit., 1894–1912, 6 vols.

149. *Ibid.*, I, p. 406.

150. *Ibid.*, I, pp. 394 and 405–7.

151. *Ibid.*, I, p. 275.

152. Moscow, State Archives, 84/2.418, p. 7 v°.

153. Heinrich STRODS, *Die Einschränkung der Wolfsplage und die Viehzucht Lettlands*, 1970, pp. 126–31.

154. G. d'AVENEL, *Histoire économique*, op. cit., I, p. 273.

155. L. de LAVERGNE, *Economie rurale*, op. cit., p. 350.

156. A.N., F11 2740.

157. F. JULIEN-LABRUYÈRE, *Paysans charentais*, op. cit., I, p. 479. 'Tawny' was used by hunters to mean game of this colour, such

as hares, deer etc., as opposed to 'black' game (wolves, wild boar).

158. The boundaries of forest property were usually marked by a ditch, often still visible today.

159. André MATEU, *Un Village gascon au temps de Louis XIV, Fals-en-Bruilhois ou la chronique de l'abbé Laplaigne*, 1978, p. 10, note 16.

160. L. de LAVERGNE, *Economie rurale*, op. cit., p. 185.

161. *Ibid.*, p. 75.

162. J.-J. MENURET, *Mémoire sur la culture des jachères*, 1791, p. 28.

163. R. CHAPUIS, *Une Vallée franc-comtoise*, op. cit., p. 65.

164. Joseph CRESSOT, *Le Pain au lièvre*, 1973, p. 65.

165. Michel COINTAT, *Tresques en Languedoc, ou l'histoire vivante dans le Midi*, 1980, p. 263.

166. A.N., H 1518, on the cultivation of turnips.

167. Family of plants including annual and perennial herbs and shrubs (such as sorrel, rhubarb, persicaria, bistort or snakeweed – and buckwheat).

168. J.-J. MENURET, *Mémoire*, op. cit., pp. 18–19.

169. Michel CHEVALIER, *La Vie humaine dans les Pyrénées ariégeoises*, 1956, p. 217.

170. Emmanuel LE ROY LADURIE, *Les Paysans du Languedoc*, 1966, I, p. 71 (section not translated in English version).

171. F. JULIEN-LABRUYÈRE, *Paysans charentais*, op. cit., I, p. 302.

172. J.-J. MENURET, *Mémoire*, op. cit., pp. 28–9.

173. R. M. HARTWELL, *The Industrial Revolution and Economic Growth*, 1971, p. 127.

174. Ernest KAHANE, *Parmentier ou la dignité de la pomme de terre Essai sur la famine*, 1978, pp. 38–41.

175. F. BRAUDEL, *Civilization and Capitalism*, I, *The Structures of Everyday Life*, op. cit., p. 170.

176. E. KAHANE, *Parmentier*, op. cit., pp. 52–3.

177. *Ibid.*, pp. 67, 73–5, 84, 91.

178. *Ibid.*, p. 74.

179. A.N., F^{10} 242, 29 *vendémiaire*, Year IV.

180. Claude CHÉREAU, *Huillé, une paroisse rurale angevine de 1600 à 1836*, 1970, p. 120.

181. J. J. MENURET, *Mémoire*, op. cit., pp. 21–2.

182. Guy THUILLIER, *Aspects de l'économie nivernaise au XIXe siècle*, 1966, p. 17.

183. *Margoter* or *marcotter* is to plant out cuttings that have taken, in order to propagate a plant.

184. A.N., F^{10} 210, Libreville, 30 *frimaire*, Year III.

185. François SIGAUT, in his article 'Pour une cartographie des assolements en France au début du XIXe siècle', in *Annales E.S.C.*, 3, 1976, gives several names for the *jachère* (fallow): '*guéret*, . . . *versaine, sombre, somart, cultivage, estivade, cotive,* etc.', p. 633.

186. G. THUILLIER, *Aspects de l'économie nivernaise*, op. cit., pp. 52–3.

187. André DELEAGE, *La Vie rurale en Bourgogne jusqu'au début du XIe siècle*, 1941, I, p. 188.

188. Pierre GOUBERT, *Beauvais et le Beauvaisis de 1600 à 1730. Contribution à l'histoire sociale de la France du XVIIe siècle*, 1960, p. 169, note 81.

189. A.N., H 1514, Alfort, Maisons and Créteil, 14 June 1786.

190. Quoted by J. MULLIEZ, 'Du blé, "mal nécessaire" ', art. cit., p. 7.

191. Jean Antoine Claude CHAPTAL,

Chimie appliquée à l'agriculture, 1823, I, p. xlvi.

192. *Histoire des faits économiques jusqu'au XVIIe siècle,* ed. Robert BESNIER, no. 502, 1963–4, p. 42.

193. *Ibid.,* 1962–3, pp. 63 ff.

194. F. JULIEN-LABRUYÈRE, *Paysans charentais,* op. cit., I, p. 202.

195. A.N., H 1515, n° 60.

196. Ernest LABROUSSE, 'L'expansion agricole: la montée de la production', in F. BRAUDEL and E. LABROUSSE (eds.), *Histoire économique et sociale de la France,* II, 1970, pp. 435–6.

197. A.N., H 1514, Alfort, Maisons and Créteil.

198. The word used is *déroyer* or *desroyer,* to throw into disorder (*Dictionnaire de la langue française du XVIe siècle*).

199. E. LABROUSSE, 'L'expansion agricole . . .', art. cit., pp. 436–7.

200. M. BLOCH, *Les Caractères originaux . . . ,* op. cit., p. 215.

201. On the 'incompatibility of *vaine pâture* and forage crops', in Lower Auvergne, see Abel POITRINEAU, *La Vie rurale en Basse-Auvergne au XVIIIe siècle,* 1965, pp. 243 ff.

202. A.N., H 1514.

203. *Procès-verbal de l'Assemblée Provinciale de l'Isle-de-France,* session of 15 December 1787, p. 370.

204. A.N., F[10] 1576, 22 April 1836.

205. A.N., F[1C] III Meuse, 11, 25 July 1861.

206. L. de LAVERGNE, *Economie rurale de la France,* op. cit., pp. 10–11.

207. Pierre BARRAL, 'Le monde agricole', in F. BRAUDEL and E. LABROUSSE, (eds.), *Histoire économique et sociale de la France,* IV, 1979, pp. 359–60.

208. E. LE ROY LADURIE, *Les Paysans du Languedoc,* op. cit., I, p. 71 (section not translated in English version).

209. *Ibid.,* p. 59.

210. 'In 1700, the *intendants* were agreed that the provinces grew only enough grain for their own consumption', J.-C. TOUTAIN, *Le Produit de l'agriculture française . . . ,* op. cit., I, p. 4, note 5.

211. Chef-lieu of the canton of Nord, 19 km from Valenciennes.

212. Arthur YOUNG, *Travels during the Years 1787, 1788 and 1789 . . . [in] the Kingdom of France,* 1792, London, I, p. 309 (in *Observations*).

213. L. de LAVERGNE, *Economie rurale de la France,* op. cit., pp. 73 ff.

214. *Ibid.,* p. 75.

215. Gilles LE BOUVIER (or BERRY), *Le Livre de la description des pays . . . ,* ed. E. T. HAMY, 1908, pp. 30–1.

216. A.N., F[10] 212 A–B.

217. Joseph de PESQUIDOUX, *Chez nous. Travaux et jeux rustiques,* 6th edn, 1921, p. 106.

218. André PLAISSE, *La Baronnie du Neubourg,* 1961, p. 193.

219. J. MULLIEZ, 'Du blé, "mal nécessaire" ', art. cit., pp. 40–1.

220. Paul ADAM, *Systèmes économiques et histoire. Essais sur la violence dans les guerres et la paix,* 1980, pp. 197 ff.

221. A.N., F[20] 560.

222. Total production in 1835, 32 million *stères* of wood, *ibid.*

223. L. de LAVERGNE, *Economie rurale de la France,* op. cit., pp. 95–6.

224. *Ibid.,* p. 435.

225. M. DARLUC, *Histoire naturelle de la Provence,* op. cit., I, pp. 263–4.

226. *Statistiques de la France esquissées par Hubert, le long d'une période de 90 ans, 1785 à 1875*, 1883, pp. 20–1.

227. Pierre BONNET, *La Commercialisation de la vie française du Premier Empire à nos jours*, 1929, p. 93.

228. Jacques MULLIEZ, *Les Chevaux du royaume. Histoire de l'élevage du cheval et de la création des haras*, 1983.

229. That is, thousands of old pounds, about 450 kg.

230. A.N., H¹ 262, 10 January 1731.

231. Jacques SAVARY DES BRUSLONS, *Dictionnaire universel de commerce*, 1759 edn, I, col. 550.

232. Abbé Alexandre TOLLEMER, *Journal manuscrit du sire de Gouberville*, op. cit., pp. 381–4.

233. In its old sense, *haras* (now = stud farm) meant both the farm itself and the 'stallions and mares contained in the farm' (LITTRÉ).

234. A. TOLLEMER, *Journal . . . du sire de Gouberville*, op. cit., pp. 367–9.

235. A.N., F¹⁰ 222, memorandum on the fattening of cattle in Limousin and adjacent regions, February 1791.

236. A.N., F¹¹ 2740.

237. Xavier de PLANHOL, 'Essai sur la genèse du paysage rural de champs ouverts', in *Annales de l'Est*, proceedings of international conference at Nancy, 2–7 September 1957, pp. 418–19.

238. *Ibid.*

239. André LEGUAI, *De la Seigneurie à l'Etat. Le Bourbonnais pendant la Guerre de Cent Ans*, 1969, p. 20.

240. Victor HUGO, *Les Pyrénées*, ed. Danièle LAMARQUE, 1984, p. 170.

241. A.N., F¹⁰ 628, 1733.

242. A. TOLLEMER, *Journal . . . du sire de Gouberville*, op. cit., pp. 391–9.

243. 'The dangerous practice country people have of living side by side with their animals' is condemned as a cause of depopulation in Côtes-du-Nord (Normandy) in the Year IX. Cf. Octave FESTY, 'La situation de la population française d'après la session de l'an IX des conseils généraux de département', in *Revue d'histoire économique et sociale*, 1954, p. 288. Cf. also the report by Dr Bagot, quoted in Jean-Pierre GOUBERT, *Maladies et médecins en Bretagne*, op. cit., pp. 192–3.

244. JAQUET, *Mémoire sur la statistique de l'arrondissement de Suze . . .* , An X, p. 9. edited by Charles MAURICE in *La Vie agricole au XVIIIe siècle dans l'ancien Ecarton d'Oulx*, reprinted 1981.

245. Jean ANGLADE, *La Vie quotidienne dans le Massif Central au XIXe siècle*, 1971, p. 162.

246. Nicolas Luton DURIVAL, *Description de la Lorraine et du Barrois*, 1778, I, pp. 288–9.

247. P. ARBOS, *La Vie pastorale dans les Alpes françaises*, op. cit., pp. 12 ff.

248. *Ibid.*, p. 21.

249. Dom Thierry RUINART, *Voyage littéraire . . . en Lorraine et en Alsace*, 1862, p. 50.

250. Jean and Renée NICOLAS, *La Vie quotidienne en Savoie aux XVIIe et XVIIIe siècles*, 1979, pp. 21 ff.

251. *Ibid.*, p. 23.

252. A.N., F¹⁰ 222, memorandum on fattening cattle in Limousin and adjacent regions, February 1791.

253. J. MULLIEZ, *Les Chevaux du royaume*, op. cit., pp. 38–9.

254. Noëlle BERTRAND, *Colondannes, village creusois (1632–1802)*, 1975, p. 43.

255. P. ARBOS, *La Vie pastorale dans les Alpes françaises*, op. cit., p. 203.

256. Archives of Bouches-du-Rhône, admiralty of Marseille, B IX, 14.

257. M. JAUFFRET, *Petite Ecole des arts et métiers . . .*, I, 1816, p. 49.

258. P. ARBOS, *La Vie pastorale . . .*, op. cit., pp. 183–4.

259. Second-rate cheeses.

260. P. ARBOS, *La Vie pastorale . . .*, op. cit., pp. 167–8.

261. *Ibid.*, p. 185.

262. L. de LAVERGNE, *Economie rurale de la France*, op. cit., p. 317.

263. A.N., Z^{1C} 430–1.

264. From *trans* = across, and *humus* = earth.

265. F. BRAUDEL, *The Mediterranean*, op. cit., I, pp. 85 ff.

266. Quoted by F. JULIEN-LABRUYÈRE, *Paysans charentais*, op. cit., I, pp. 402–3.

267. *Archives départementales* of the Lozère, C 480, quoted in A.-M. BRISEBARRE, *Bergers des Cévennes*, op. cit., pp. 99–100.

268. A.-M. BRISEBARRE, *Bergers des Cévennes*, op. cit., pp. 103–4.

269. Bernard DUHOURCAU, *Guide des Pyrénées mystérieuses*, 1973, pp. 119–20.

270. René NELLI, 'Le berger dans le pays d'Aude', in *Folklore, revue d'ethnologie méridionale*, Spring 1952, pp. 3–13.

271. Jean-Pierre PINIES, *Figures de la sorcellerie languedocienne*, 1983, p. 45 (*arma* = *âme*, soul, in the archaic language of the Languedoc).

272. Thérèse SCLAFERT, *Cultures en Haute-Provence: déboisements et pâturages au Moyen Age*, 1959.

273. Marie MAURON, *La Transhumance du pays d'Arles aux grandes Alpes*, 1952.

274. A.-M. BRISEBARRE, *Burgers des Cévennes*, op. cit.

275. Jacques MULLIEZ, 'Pratiques populaires et science bourgeoise: l'élevage des gros bestiaux en France de 1750 à 1850', in *L'Elevage dans les hautes terres*, proceedings of the conference at Clermont-Ferrand, 1982, p. 299.

276. L. de LAVERGNE, *Economie rurale de la France*, op. cit., pp. 90–1.

277. *Ibid.*, p. 212. Cf. also the *Larousse agricole*, edited by Jean-Michel CLEMENT, 1981, under the entry 'Bretonne Pie Noire'.

278. A.N., F^{10} 1574.

279. *Ibid.*

280. J. MULLIEZ, 'Pratiques populaires . . .', art. cit., p. 299.

281. *Larousse agricole*, op. cit., caption of first photograph between pp. 208 and 209.

282. *Ibid.*, pp. 55–6.

283. A.N., F^{10} 222, memorandum on the fattening of cattle in Limousin and adjacent regions, February 1791.

284. *Ibid.*

285. Charles PIGAULT LEBRUN and Victor AUGIER, *Voyage dans le Midi de la France*, 1827, p. 31.

286. J. MULLIEZ, *Les Chevaux du royaume*, op. cit., p. 81.

287. J. SAVARY DES BRUSLONS, *Dictionnaire*, op. cit., article 'Cheval', I, cols. 1057 and 1060.

288. R. CHAPUIS, *Une vallée franc-comtoise*, op. cit., p. 73.

289. A.N., F^{12} 67, fol. 98–9, 4 April 1720.

290. Georges de MANTEYER, *Le Livre journal tenu par Fazy de Rame en langage embrunais (6 juin 1471–10 juillet 1507)*, II, 1932, p. 85.

291. P. ARBOS, *La Vie pastorale*, op. cit., p. 182.

292. 'A peasant who has a cart and a pair of oxen is well-off', wrote the *intendant* of Guyenne in 1713, quoted by Jean-Pierre POUSSOU in *Hommage à Philippe Wolff*, *Annales du Midi*, 1978, p. 409.

293. Antoine LOISEL, *Mémoires des pays de Beauvaisis . . .* , 1617, p. 27, quoted by P. GOUBERT, *Beauvais et le Beauvaisis*, op. cit., p. 111.

294. Gabriel DU MOULIN, 1631, quoted by René DUMONT, *Voyages en France d'un agronome*, 1951, pp. 376 and 379.

295. D. HALEVY, *Visites aux paysans du Centre*, op. cit., p. 217.

296. Edouard DEMOLINS, *Les Français d'aujourd'hui*, 1898, p. 133.

297. Robert LAURENT, *Les Vignerons de la 'Côte d'Or' du XIXe siècle*, 1958, p. 18.

298. L. de LAVERGNE, *Economie rurale de la France*, op. cit., 1870, p. 123 of the 1877 edition.

299. E. DEMOLINS, *Les Français d'aujourd'hui*, op. cit., p. 137.

300. Roger DION, *Histoire de la vigne et du vin en France des origines au XIXe siècle*, 1959, p. 650 of the 1977 edition.

301. E. DEMOLINS, *Les Français d'aujourd'hui*, op. cit., p. 133.

302. A.N., F[10] 226, p. 35.

303. Georges DURAND, *Vin, vigne et vignerons en Lyonnais et Beaujolais*, 1979, p. 11.

304. Renée CHAPUIS, *Une vallée franc-comtoise*, op. cit., p. 17.

305. Quoted by R. DION, *Histoire de la vigne*, op. cit., p. 101.

306. Diodorus of Sicily, quoted by R. DION, *ibid.*, p. 102.

307. André DELEAGE, *La Vie rurale en Bourgogne jusqu'au début du XIe siècle*, 1941, I, p. 154.

308. Charles LAMPRECHT, *Etudes sur l'état économique de la France pendant la premiere partie du Moyen Age*, 1889, p. 23.

309. Alfred LEROUX, *Le Massif Central. Histoire d'une région de la France*, 1898, II, p. 50.

310. Gustave BLOCH, *Les Origines. La Gaule indépendante et la Gaule romaine*, in E. LAVISSE, ed., *Histoire de France*, 1911, II, p. 425.

311. R. DION, *Histoire de la vigne*, op. cit., p. 129.

312. *Ibid.*, p. 148.

313. *Ibid.*, p. 165.

314. *Ibid.*, p. 202 and p. ix.

315. F. BRAUDEL, *Civilization and Capitalism*, II, *The Wheels of Commerce*, op. cit., p. 265.

316. Philippe DOLLINGER, ed., *Histoire de l'Alsace*, 1970, pp. 158 and 175. Jean-Pierre KINTZ, *La Société strasbourgeoise 1560–1650*, 1984, pp. 319 ff.

317. 'The pebbly alluvial formations known as the *graves* have certain physical qualities which make the great wines of Bordeaux', R. DION, *Histoire de la vigne*, op. cit., p. 34.

318. Nicolas de LAMOIGNON DE BASVILLE, *Mémoires pour servir à l'histoire du Languedoc*, 1734, p. 252.

319. *Ibid.*, p. 258.

320. *Ibid.*, p. 271.

321. F. BRAUDEL, *Civilization and Capitalism*, I, *The Structures of Everyday Life*, op. cit., p. 243.

322. Michel BELOTTE, *La Région de Bar-sur-Seine . . .* , op. cit., p. 45.

323. A.N., F[20] 221.

324. Emile APPOLIS, *Le Diocèse civil de Lodève*, 1951, pp. 421–2.

325. P. GOUBERT, *Beauvais et le Beauvaisis*, op. cit., p. 168.

326. Mariel JEAN-BRUNHES DELAMARRE, *Le Berger dans la France des villages*, 1970, p. 20.

327. A.N., F[20] 221, Marne.

328. R. DION, *Histoire de la vigne*, op. cit., pp. 462 ff.

329. *Ibid.*, p. 469.

330. *Ibid.*, p. 491.

331. *Ibid.*, pp. 459–60.

332. Pierre de SAINT-JACOB, *Les Paysans de la Bourgogne du Nord au dernier siècle de l'Ancien Régime*, 1960, p. 539.

333. J. SAVARY DES BRUSLONS, *Dictionnaire universel du commerce*, 1762, IV[1], article 'Vin', cols. 1213 ff.

334. L. de LAVERGNE, *Economie rurale de la France*. op. cit., p. 123.

335. P. CLEMENT, *Lettres, instructions et mémoires de Colbert*, 1861–1882, II, pp. 624–5.

336. R. DION, *Histoire de la vigne*. op. cit., p. 33.

337. *Brassier* – one who has only the strength of his arm (*bras*) with which to earn a living, synonym of labourer (*manouvrier*).

338. F. BRAUDEL, *Civilization and Capitalism*, II, *The Wheels of Commerce*, op. cit., p. 320.

339. *Voyages du chevalier Chardin en Perse et autres lieux de l'Orient*, IV, 1811, p. 107.

340. F. BRAUDEL, *Civilization and Capitalism*, I, *The Structures of Everyday Life*, op. cit., p. 234.

341. Pierre CHERRUAU, 'Sauternes fait main', in *Le Monde*, 22 September 1984.

342. R. DION, *Histoire de la vigne*, op. cit., pp. 119–20.

343. 'Le vin de Suresnes', in *Le Monde*, 22 September 1984.

344. Quoted by R. DION in *Histoire de le vigne*, op. cit., p. 25.

345. Gaston ROUPNEL, *Histoire et destin*, 1943, pp. 61–2.

346. Henry de ROUVIERE *Voyage du tour de France*, 1713, p. 56.

347. Arthur YOUNG, *Travels*, op. cit. 1892 edn., p. 20.

348. POTTIER DE LA HESTROYE, *Réflexions sur la Dîme royale*, 1716, I, p. 52.

349. J. SAVARY DES BRUSLONS, *Dictionnaire*, op. cit., I, 1759, p. 531.

350. Quoted by Jean CLAUDIAN, 'Quelques réflexions sur l'évolution du vocabulaire alimentaire', in *Cahiers de Nutrition et de Diététique*, IX, p. 163.

351. E. DEMOLINS, *Les Français d'aujourd'hui*, op. cit., p. 84.

352. J. SAVARY DES BRUSLONS, *Dictionnaire*, op. cit., II, 1766, col. 785.

353. A.N., F[10] 226.

354. Adrien de GASPARIN, *Cours d'agriculture*, 1831, 1860 edn, pp. 1–2.

355. Frédéric LULLIN DE CHATEAU-VIEUX, *Voyages agronomiques en France*, 1843, I, pp. 283 and 287.

356. A.N., H 1510 n° 16, quoted by Marc BLOCH, *Les Caractères originaux de l'histoire rurale française*, 1952, p. 54.

357. F. LULLIN DE CHATEAUX-VIEUX, *Voyages agronomiques*, op. cit., II, pp. 331–2.

358. A. de GASPARIN, *Cours d'agriculture*, op. cit., V, p. 3.

359. *Le Livre de main des Du Pouget (1522–1598)*, edited by Louis GREIL, 1897, p. 20.

360. Christophe MATHIEU DE DOMBASLE, *Traité d'agriculture*, 1862, p. 213.

361. *Procès-verbal de l'Assemblée provinciale de l'Ile-de-France*, 1787, p. 245.

362. Jean MEUVRET, *Le Problème des subsistances à l'époque de Louis XIV*, 1977, p. 111.

363. Henri-Louis DUHAMEL DU MONCEAU, *Elements d'agriculture*, 1762, bk II, ch. IV, p. 221.

364. François SIGAUT, 'Pour une cartographie des assolements en France au début du XIXe siècle', in *Annales E.S.C.*, 1976, pp. 631–43.

365. François SIGAUT, 'Quelques notions de base en matière de travail du sol dans les anciennes cultures européennes', in *Les Hommes et leurs sols: les techniques de préparation du champ dans le fonctionnement et l'histoire des systèmes de culture*, special number of the *Journal d'Agriculture et de Botanique*, 1977, p. 155.

366. Etienne JUILLARD, *Problèmes alsaciens vus par un géographe*, 1968, p. 112. [In England, this was usually known as the two-field or three-field system. The French terminology has been kept here. – Tr.]

367. Jean-Robert PITTE, *Histoire du paysage français*, 1983, II, p. 62 and note 551 on p. 150, after Gérard SIVERY, 'Les noyaux de bocage dans le nord de la Thiérache à la fin du Moyen Age', in *Les Bocages*, 1976, pp. 93–6.

368. J.-R. PITTE, *ibid.*, II, p. 63.

369. Louis MERLE, quoted by J.-R. PITTE, *ibid.*, II, p. 63 and note 555, p. 150.

370. René LEBEAU, quoted by J.-R. PITTE, *ibid.*, II, p. 63 and note 556, p. 150.

371. J.-R. PITTE, *ibid.*, II, p. 63.

372. Arthur YOUNG, *Travels during the Years 1787, 1788 and 1789*, op. cit., 1792, I, pp. 308–9.

373. François SIGAUT, 'La jachère en Ecosse au XVIIIe siècle: phase ultime de l'expansion d'une technique', in *Etude rurales*, Jan.–March 1975, p. 99.

374. L. de LAVERGNE, *Economie rurale de la France*, op. cit., p. 257.

375. Germain SICARD, 'Le métayage dans le Midi toulousain à la fin du Moyen Age', in *Mémoires de l'Académie de législation*, Toulouse, 1955, p. 36.

376. Paul Louis MALAUSSENA, *La Vie en Provence orientale aux XIVe et XVe siècles*, 1969, p. 87.

377. Roger DION, 'La part de géographie et celle de l'histoire dans l'explication de l'habitat rural du Bassin Parisien', in *Publications de la Société de Géographie de Lille*, 1946, p. 72.

378. Pierre MASSÉ, *Varennes et ses maîtres*, 1926, p. 24.

379. Lynn WHITE, *Mediaeval Technology*, 1962, p. 72, quoted by F. SIGAUT, 'Pour une cartographie . . .', art. cit., p. 635.

380. R. DION, 'La part de géographie', art. cit., p. 59.

381. J. MULLIEZ, 'Du blé, "mal nécessaire". . .', art. cit., p. 11.

382. F. SIGAUT, 'Pour une cartographie . . .', art. cit., p. 636.

383. J. MEUVRET, *Le Problème des subsistances*, op. cit., pp. 108–9.

384. René MUSSET, 'Les anciens assolements et la nourriture', in *Mélanges géographiques offerts à Ph. Arbos*, 1953, p. 176.

385. *Mémoires de Oudard Coquault bourgeois de Reims (1649–1669)*, edited by Charles LORIQUET, 1875, I, p. 183.

386. A.N., F¹¹ 222.
387. P. MASSÉ, *Varennes et ses maîtres*, op. cit., pp. 23–4.
388. *Ibid.*, p. 23.
389. Maurice LE LANNOU, 'Les sols et ses climats', in *La France et les Français*, ed. Michel FRANÇOIS, 1972, pp. 23–4.
390. Pierre de SAINT-JACOB, 'Etudes sur l'ancienne sommunauté rurale en Bourgogne', in *Annales de Bourgogne*, 15, 1943, p. 184.
391. *Les Bocages, histoire, écologie, économie*, Round Table organized by the CNRS, Rennes, 1976, I, *Géographie*. Pierre FLATRES, *Rapport de synthèse*, pp. 21–30.
392. L. de LAVERGNE, *Economie rurale de la France*, op. cit., p. 186.
393. *Ibid.*, p. 208.
394. Marc BLOCH, *Les Caractères originaux*, op. cit.
395. *Herms* or *erms*, a southern word for wastelands, cf. *terre gaste*, in George BERTRAND's chapter 'Pour une histoire écologique de la France rurale', in George DUBY, ed., *Histoire de la France rurale*, 1975, p. 4.
396. L. de LAVERGNE, *Economie de la France rurale*, op. cit., p. 264.
397. *Ibid.*, p. 269.
398. *Ibid.*, p. 270.
399. P. L. MALAUSSENA, *La Vie en Provence*, op. cit., p. 84.
400. L. de LAVERGNE, *Economie de la France rurale*, op. cit., pp. 246–7.
401. François Hilaire GILBERT, *Recherches sur les moyens d'étendre et de perfectionner la culture des prairies artificielles*, 1787, ed. Ch. DUFOUR, 1880, p. 35.
402. Marc BLOCH, *Les Caractères originaux*, op. cit., 1931, 1952 edn, pp. x and xiv.
403. François SIGAUT, 'Pour une cartographie . . .', art. cit., p. 632.
404. Maurice LE LANNOU, *Pâtres et paysans de la Sardaigne*, 1941, p. 195.
405. Xavier de PLANHOL, 'Essai sur la genèse du paysage rural de champs ouverts', in *Annales de l'Est*, 1959, p. 416.
406. Michel CONFINO, *Systèmes agraires et progrès agricoles. L'assolement triennal en Russie aux XVIIIe–XIXe siècles*, 1969, *passim* and pp. 29–46.
407. Laszlo MAKKAI, 'Grands domaines et petites exploitations, seigneur et paysan en Europe au Moyen Age et aux temps modernes', in *Eighth International Economic Congress*, Budapest, 1982, 'A' Themes, pp. 10–11.
408. Comte de GASPARIN, *Cours d'agriculture*, V, p. 6.
409. J.-R. PITTÉ, *Histoire du paysage français*, op. cit., pp. 40 and 117.
410. R. MUSSET, 'Les anciens assolements . . .', art, cit., p. 172.
411. X. de PLANHOL, 'Essai sur la genèse . . .', art. cit., p. 417.
412. Robert SPECKLIN, *La Géographie de la France dans la littérature allemande (1870–1940)*, 1979; and 'Etudes sur les origines de la France', in *Acta Geographica*, 2nd quarter, 1982.
413. Olivier LAUNAY, *La Civilisation des Celtes*, 1975, p. 170.
414. Lucien GACHON, 'Regards sur la campagne française', in *Les Nouvelles Littéraires*, 10 February 1940, p. 2.
415. François SIGAUT, *Les Réserves de Grains à long terme*, 1978, p. 32.
416. *Ibid.*, p. 21.
417. J. SAVARY DES BRUSLONS, *Dictionnaire*, op. cit., 1762, pp. 524–5, article 'Blé'.

418. Geneviève ACLOQUE, *Les Corporations et le commerce à Chartres du XIe siècle à la Révolution*, 1917, p. 212.

419. Maurice BLOCK, *Du Commerce des grains*, 1854, p. 59.

420. G. ACLOQUE, *Les Corporations*, op. cit., p. 214.

421. *Ibid.*, p. 215.

422. *Ibid.*, pp. 218–20.

423. These *blattiers* were 'small-time travelling dealers who go out into remote districts with pack-horses and mules, in search of grain, loads of which they then bring back to markets, or river-banks, where they sell it to the merchants who supply the . . . big cities', Nicolas de LAMARE, *Traité de la police*, II, 1710, p. 738.

424. G. ACLOQUE, *Les Corporations*, op. cit., p. 215.

425. A.N., Y 105 58a (4 May 1775).

426. A *gazier* was a textile worker, making gauze. (The modern meaning is a gasfitter.)

427. François SIGAUT, *Les Réserves de grains*, op. cit., p. 37.

428. F. LULLIN DE CHATEAUVIEUX, *Voyages agronomiques*, op. cit., I, p. 62.

429. A.N., F^{12} 647–8.

430. Pierre LE GRAND D'AUSSY, quoted by Jean CLAUDIAN, 'L'homme et son pain', in *Cahiers de nutrition et de diététique*, VII, 1972, p. 269, note 1.

431. A.N., F^{10} 226.

432. Georges DUBY, *L'Economie rurale et la vie des campagnes dans l'Occident médiéval*, I, 1962, pp. 223–4.

433. POTTIER DE LA HESTROYE, *Réflexions sur la Dîme royale*, op. cit., I. pp. 122–3.

434. Not necessarily what we would call white bread today: this is made from very finely sifted flour, which was only made possible by the cylindrical mill in the last years of the nineteenth century. It remained a rarity when sieving was done by hand. In the past, pure wheatflour, which was still whiter than other flour even when quite crudely sieved, was a luxury in itself; see Henry BEAUFOUR, *Le Préjugé du pain blanc*, 1931, pp. 8–9.

435. F. BRAUDEL, *Civilization and Capitalism*, I, *The Structures of Everyday Life*, op. cit., p. 136; Jean MEYER, *La Noblesse bretonne au XVIIIe siècle*, 1966, pp. 446–7.

436. Jacques-Joseph JUGE SAINT-MARTIN, *Changements survenus dans les moeurs des habitants de Limoges depuis une cinquantaine d'années*, 1817, pp. 14–15.

437. Valentin JAMERET-DUVAL, *Mémoires*, 1981, p. 112.

438. A.N., F^{10}* 1B (1786) and A.N., H 514 (1787).

439. A.N., F^{10}* 1B.

440. Jean-Claude TOUTAIN, in his retrospective statistics, calculated a figure for the years 1781–90 not far from this, between 2,420 and 2,850 million *livres*. *Le Produit de l'agriculture française de 1700 à 1958*, I, p. 215.

441. J. MARCZEWSKI, 'Y a-t-il eu un "take-off" en France?', in *Evolution des techniques et progrès de l'économie, Cahiers de l'ISEA*, March 1961 (series AD, n° 1), p. 72.

442. J. SAVARY DES BRUSLONS, *Dictionnaire*, op. cit., I, 1760, article 'Écu', col. 250.

443. J. C. TOUTAIN, *Le Produit de l'agriculture française*, op. cit., I, p. 8.

444. SULLY, *Mémoires*, op. cit., III, 1822 edn, p. 485.

445. Antoine de MONTCHRESTIEN, *Traité de l'économie politique*, Rouen, 1615, 1889 edn, pp. 23–4.

446. VAUBAN, *Projet d'une disme royale*, 1707, p. 26.

447. A.N., F^{12} 647–8.

448. A.N., F^{12} 673 (about 1696).

449. Memorandum published by the Société d'Agriculture, Sciences, Arts et Belles-Lettres de l'Aube, 1836, p. 151.

450. J. SAVARY DES BRUSLONS, *Dictionnaire*, op. cit., II, 1760, col. 781, article 'Fromage'.

451. F. LULLIN DE CHATEAUVIEUX, *Voyages agronomiques*, op. cit., I, p. 298.

452. A.N., F^{IC} III, Saône et Loire.

453. No less than 300,000 *écus* for a single purchase in Switzerland in March 1710. A.N., G^7 1511 (1711).

454. A.N., F^{10} 226 (30 January 1792).

455. A.N., F^{12} 1904.

456. A.N., F^{10} 1576 (1837).

457. Jean-Henri SCHNITZLER, *Statistique générale méthodique et complète de la France comparée aux autres grandes puissances de l'Europe*, IV, p. 40.

458. Alfred SAUVY, *Histoire économique de la France entre les deux guerres (1918–1931)*, I, 1965, pp. 239–40. For the average 1903–12, see *Annuaire retrospectif de l'INSEE*.

459. René GIRAULT, 'Place et rôle des échanges extérieurs', in F. BRAUDEL and E. LABROUSSE (eds)., *Histoire économique et sociale de la France*, IV, 1979, p. 199.

460. Arthur de BOISLISLE, *Correspondance des contrôleurs généraux des finances avec les Intendants des provinces*, I, 1874, p. 11 (M. De Ris, *intendant* at Bordeaux, to the Controller-General, 8 January 1684).

461. *Ibid.*

462. B. H. SLICHER VAN BATH, quoted by Immanuel WALLERSTEIN op. cit., p. 96.

463. Ange GOUDAR, *Les Intérêts de la France mal entendus*, 1756, I, p. 19.

464. A.N., F^{10} 226; and F. BRAUDEL, *Civilization and Capitalism*, I, *The Structures of Everyday Life*, op. cit., pp. 124 ff.

465. A.N., F^{IC} III, Côte d'Or, 7 (1819).

466. A.N., H 1517 (Dufriche de Valazé to M. de Tarlé).

467. A.N., F^{10} 226 (1792).

468. A.N., G^7 449 (Thouars, 27 April 1683).

469. Archives du Ministère de la Guerre, A 1 1524, 6 (Rochefort, 2 January 1701).

470. A. SAUVY, *Histoire économique de la France*, op. cit., I, 1965, pp. 239–40.

471. Alfred RAMBAUD, *Histoire de la civilisation contemporaine en France*, 1888, 1926 edn, p. 488.

472. Abbé de MABLY, *Le Commerce des grains*, *Oeuvres*, XIII, pp. 291–7.

473. Pierre LE PESANT DE BOISGUILLEBERT, *Le Détail de la France*, 1697, 1966 edn, I, p. 381.

474. Nicolas de LAMARE, *Traité de la police*, op. cit., II, 1710, p. 1038.

475. A.N., G^7 1651, fol. 26.

476. *Ibid.*, fol. 27.

477. *Ustensile* was the right of troops to claim bed, board and a place by the fire and candle from the local inhabitants (LITTRÉ).

478. A.N., G^7 156 (Dijon, 12 July 1682).

479. Yves-Marie BERCE, *Histoire des croquants*, 1974, p. 65.

480. POTTIER DE LA HESTROYE, *Réflexions sur la Dîme royale*, op. cit.

481. Arthur YOUNG, *Travels*, op. cit., 1792, I, p. 469: France would be 'infinitely more flourishing if she had five or six million fewer inhabitants'.

482. Jean FOURASTIÉ, *Machinisme et bien-être*, 1962; in 1899, they would have provided for 43 people (and today the figure would be 300).

483. Jean FOURASTIÉ, *Les Trente glorieuses*, 1979, p. 159.

484. Marquis d'ARGENSON, *Mémoires*, 26 January 1732, 1859 edn, ed. J. E. B. RATHERY, II, p. 72.

485. F. BRAUDEL, *Civilization and Capitalism*, I, *The Structures of Everyday Life*, op. cit., p. 78.

486. A.N., G^7 1633 (Bérulle).

487. A.N., G^7 103 (Desmarets de Vaubourg).

488. *Ibid.*

489. A.N., G^7 346.

490. F. BRAUDEL, *Civilization and Capitalism*, I, *Structures of Everyday Life*, op. cit., p. 74.

491. A.N., F^{11} 704 (30 April 1812).

492. Philippe SUSSEL, *La France de la bourgeoisie, 1815-1850*, 1970, p. 70.

493. Toschio HORII, 'La crise alimentaire de 1853 à 1856 et la caisse de la boulangerie', in *Revue historique*, Oct.–Dec. 1984, pp. 375 ff.

494. E. LAVISSE, *Histoire de France*, 1911, IV, pp. 132 ff.

495. *Ibid.*, VII, p. 349.

496. Louise A. TILLY, 'La révolte frumentaire, forme de conflit politique en France', in *Annales E.S.C.*, 1972, p. 731.

497. Arsenal, Mss 4116. *Chèvrepied* – one who has goat's feet, as of Pan, fauns, satyrs, the devil etc., and by extension men capable of aggression and violence.

498. Auguste POIRSON, *Histoire du règne de Henri IV*, 1862, I, pp. 593 ff.

499. Boris PORCHNEV, *Les Soulèvements populaires en France de 1623 à 1648*, 1963, *passim*.

500. E. LAVISSE, *Histoire de France*, op. cit., VII, 1, p. 355.

501. Y. M. BERCÉ, *Histoire des croquants*, op. cit., II, p. 681.

502. B. PORCHNEV, *Les Soulèvements*, op. cit.

503. Hugues NEVEUX, 'Die ideologische Dimension der französischen Bauernaufstände im 17. Jahrhundert', in *Historische Zeitschrift*, April 1984.

504. P. GOUBERT, *Beauvais et le Beauvaisis*, op. cit., p.l.

505. F. JULIEN-LABRUYERE, *Paysans charentais*, op. cit., I, p. 302.

506. Georges RUDÉ, 'The growth of cities and popular revolt, 1750–1850', in J. F. BOSHER, *French Government and Society 1500–1850*, 1973, p. 176; E. LABROUSSE, in F. BRAUDEL and E. LABROUSSE (eds.), *Histoire économique et sociale de la France*, II, p. 729; Jean MEYER in Jean FAVIER (ed)., *Histoire de France', III, La France moderne*, p. 448.

507. Jean NICOLAS, 'L'enjeu décimal dans l'espace rural savoyard', in *Prestations paysannes, dîmes, rentes foncières et mouvement de la production agricole à l'époque industrielle*, ed. Joseph GOY and Emmanuel LE ROY LADURIE, pp. 66, note 20; 674, note 64; and 690.

508. A.N., G^7 1642, 396.

509. A.N., G^7 415–6.

510. A.N., G^7 1642, 403.

511. François LEBRUN, *L'Histoire vue de l'Anjou*, 1963, I, pp. 169 and 170.
512. A.N., G⁷ 1646.
513. *Ibid.*
514. A.N., G⁷ 1647.
515. F. LEBRUN, *L'Histoire vue de l'Anjou*, op. cit., I, pp. 170–1.
516. A.N., G⁷ 1646, 342 (Moulins, 16 June 1709).
517. A.N., G⁷ 1646, 369 (Orléans, 20 March 1709).
518. F. LEBRUN, *L'Histoire vue de l'Anjou*, op. cit., pp. 192–4.
519. A.N., F¹¹ 2740.
520. TOULOT, *Subsistances 1816. Vues générales sur la nécessité de faire des achats de grains à l'étranger pour parer à l'insuffisance de la récolte de 1816*, 20 Janvier 1817, p. 5.
521. The *carreau* was the open space around the covered market (*les halles*).
522. A.N., F¹¹ 726.
523. A.N., H 1517.
524. A.N., F¹¹ 728.
525. *Ibid.*
526. Alfred RAMBAUD, *Histoire de la civilisation contemporaine en France*, 1888, 6th edn 1901, p. 488.
527. L. de LAVERGNE, *Economie de la France rurale*, op. cit., p. 440, note 1.
528. René PILLORGET, *Les Mouvements insurrectionnels de Provence entre 1595 et 1715*, 1975, p. 989.
529. Pierre LEON, 'L'épanouissement d'un marché national', in F. BRAUDEL and E. LABROUSSE, eds., *Histoire économique et sociale de la France*, op. cit., III/1, 1976, pp. 301–2.
530. L. de LAVERGNE, *Economie de la France rurale*, op. cit., p. 45.
531. Yves LEQUIN, *Histoire des Français*, II, *La Société*, p. 307.

532. Adeline DAUMARD, *Les Fortunes françaises du XIXe siècle*, 1973, p. 192.
533. P. LEON, in F. BRAUDEL and E. LABROUSSE, *Histoire économique et sociale de la France*, op. cit., III/2, pp. 604–6.
534. Alain PLESSIS, *Les Régents et gouverneurs de la Banque de France*, 1985, p. 204.
535. R. LAURENT, in F. BRAUDEL and E. LABROUSSE, eds., *Histoire économique et sociale de la France*, op. cit., III/2, pp. 740–4.
536. Félix GAIFFE, *L'Envers du grand siècle*, 1924, pp. 117 ff.
537. L. de LAVERGNE, *Economie de la France rurale*, op. cit., p. 38.
538. A.N., F¹¹ 2740 (Amiens, 23 and 28 April).
539. A.N., F¹¹ 2740 (Paris, 3 June 1817).
540. Guy THUILLIER, *Aspects de l'économie nivernaise au XIXe siècle*, 1966, p. 82.
541. Elisabeth CLAVERIE, Pierre LAMAISON, *L'Impossible Mariage. Violence et parenté en Gevaudan, XVIIe, XVIIIe et XIXe siècles*, 1982, p. 339.
542. G. THUILLIER, *Aspects de l'économie nivernaise*, op. cit., pp. 75–6.
543. *Ibid.*, pp. 81–2.
544. Louis LEOUZON, *Agronomes et éleveurs*, 1905, p. 232.
545. Paulette SEIGNOUR, *La Vie économique du Vaucluse de 1815 à 1848*, 1957, p. 101.
546. Joseph PESQUIDOUX, *Chez nous. Travaux et joies rustiques*, 6th edn, 1921, p. 141.
547. Personal memory.
548. Daniel ZOLA, *L'Agriculture moderne*, 1913, p. 13.
549. L. de LAVERGNE, *Economie rurale de la France*, op. cit., p. 105.
550. *Ibid.*, p. 194.

551. Aimé PERPILLOU, 'Essai d'établissement d'une carte de l'utilisation du sol et des paysages ruraux en France', in *Mélanges géographiques offerts à Philippe Arbos*, 1953, p. 197.

552. L. de LAVERGNE, *Economie rurale de la France*, op. cit., pp. 51–2 and 402–3, where the figures from p. 52 are partly corrected.

553. Robert LAURENT, 'Tradition et progrès, le secteur agricole', in F. BRAUDEL and E. LABROUSSE, *Histoire économique et sociale*, op. cit., III/2, p. 672.

554. *Ibid.*, p. 682.

555. Pierre BARRAL, 'Le monde agricole', in *ibid.*, IV/1, 1979, p. 361.

556. André GAURON, *Histoire économique et sociale de la Cinquième République*, I, *Le temps des modernistes*, 1983, p. 19.

Notes to Part IV

1. Isaac de PINTO, *Traité de la circulation et du crédit*, 1771, p. 218.

2. I am not of course using these words in the Marxist sense.

3. Pierre CHAUNU, *La Civilisation de l'Europe classique*, 1970, p. 26.

4. See Figure 51.

5. Heinrich BECHTEL, *Wirtschaftsgeschichte Deutschlands von der Vorzeit bis zum Ende des Mittelalters*, I, 1951, p. 255.

6. François-Gabriel de BRAY, *Essai critique sur l'histoire de la Livonie*, III, 1817, pp. 22–3.

7. Hugh SETON-WATSON, *The Russian Empire 1801–1917*, 1967, pp. 21 ff.

8. Julius BELOCH, 'Die Bevölkerung Europas im Mittelalter', in *Zeitschrift für Sozialwissenschaft*, 1900, p. 409.

9. Figures kindly provided by Gérard CALOT of INED, 28 May 1984.

10. Even in the late eighteenth century, there were 'only the beginnings of an urban network in the Vivarais' (Alain MOLINIER, *Stagnation et croissance. Le Vivarais aux XVIIe–XVIIIe siècles*, 1985, pp. 46–7 and 67 ff); they were no more than *bourgades*, large villages, of very ancient foundation but having stagnated for many years. cf. Pierre BOZON, *Histoire du peuple vivarois*, 1966, pp. 263 ff. The same was true of the Gévaudan.

11. Guy BOIS, *Crise du féodalisme*, 1976, pp. 61 and 66–7.

12. Yves RENOUARD, *Les Villes d'Italie de la fin du Xe siècle au début du XIVe siècle*, 1969, I, p. 15.

13. Jean SCHNEIDER, 'Problèmes d'histoire urbaine dans la France médiévale', *Actes du 100e Congrès National des Sociétés Savantes* (Paris, 1975), 1977, p. 150.

14. *Ibid.*, p. 153.

15. *Ibid.*, p. 152.

16. Well described by Bernard CHEVALIER, *Les Bonnes Villes de France du XIVe au XVIe siècle*, 1982.

17. Guy BOIS, *Crise du féodalisme*, op. cit., pp. 311–14.

18. Edouard PERROY, 'A l'origine d'une économie contractée, les crises du XIVe siècle', in *Annales E.S.C.*, 1949, pp. 167–82; Wilhelm ABEL, *Crises agraires en Europe (XIIIe–XXe siècles)*, 1973, p. 75, quoted by G. BOIS, *Crise du féodalisme*, op. cit., p. 84, note 32.

19. F. BRAUDEL, *The Mediterranean*, I, pp. 516 ff.

20. Quoted by Friedrich LUTGE, *Deutsche Sozial- und Wirtschaftsgeschichte*, 1976 edn, p. 207.

21. Jean-Robert PITTE, *Histoire du paysage français*, I, 1983, p. 149.

22. B. CHEVALIER, *Les Bonnes Villes*, op. cit.

23. Louis STOUFF, 'La population d'Arles au XVe siècle: composition socio-professionnelle, immigration, répartition topographique', in *Habiter la ville XVe–XXe siècles*, proceedings of round table organized by Maurice GARDEN and Yves LEQUIN, Lyons, 1984, p. 8.

24. Henri SEE, *Louis XI et les villes*, 1892, *passim*.

25. *Ibid.*

26. F. REYNAUD, 'Du comté au royaume (1423–1596)', in Edouard BARATIER, ed., *Histoire de Marseille*, 1973, p. 132.

27. S. A. WESTRICH, *L'Ormée de Bordeaux. Une révolution pendant la Fronde*, 1973.

28. B. CHEVALIER, *Les Bonnes Villes*, op. cit., p. 310.

29. Jean-Baptiste SAY, *Cours complet d'économie politique*, 1852, 1966 edn, III, p. 612.

30. J. R. PITTE, *Histoire du paysage*, op. cit., II, p. 25.

31. *Ibid.*, pp. 31–2.

32. Thomas REGAZZOLA, Jacques LEFEBVRE, *La Domestication du mouvement. Poussées mobilisatrices et surrection de l'Etat*, 1981, p. 123.

33. J. R. PITTE, *Histoire du paysage*, op. cit., II, p. 40.

34. Bernard QUILLIET, 'Les Corps sd'officiers de la prévôté et vicomté de Paris et de l'Ile-de-France, de la fin de la guerre de Cent Ans au début des guerres de Religion: étude sociale', doctoral thesis, University of Paris, IV, 1977, reproduced by Lille thesis service, 1982, I, p. 145.

35. Philippe de COMMYNES, *Mémoires*, ed. J. CALMETTE, 1964, I, pp. 73–4.

36. FURETIERE's *Dictionnaire*, 1690, defines a town as a 'settlement consisting of a fairly large number of people, ordinarily surrounded by walls'.

37. Roberto LOPEZ, *Intervista sulla città medievale*, 1984, p. 5.

38. A.N., G⁷ 1692–259, f° 81 ff.

39. Jules BLACHE, 'Sites urbains et rivières françaises', in *Revue de géographie de Lyon*, vol. 34, 1959, pp. 17–55.

40. Daniel AUCHER, *L'Homme et le Rhône*, 1968, p. 179.

41. Jean-Pierre BARDET, 'Un dynamisme raisonnable. Dimensions, évolutions (1640–1790)', in *Histoire de Rouen*, ed. Michel MOLLAT, 1979, p. 214.

42. Jean MEYER, *Etudes sur les villes en Europe occidentale (milieu du XVIIe siècle à la veille de la Révolution française)*, I, 1983, p. 68.

43. A.N., F¹² 673, Metz, 6 June 1717; the same happened in 1712, G⁷ 1697, 127, 7 September 1712.

44. A.N., F²⁰ 215.

45. Quoted in Paul BOIS, 'La Révolution et l'Empire', in *Histoire de Nantes*, ed. P. BOIS, 1977, p. 245.

46. Reference mislaid.

47. Paulette SEIGNOUR, *La Vie économique du Vaucluse de 1815 à 1848*, 1957, p. 77.

48. Robert CHAPUIS, *Une vallée franc-comtoise, la Haute-Loue*, 1958, p. 125.

49. J. MEYER, *Etudes sur les villes*, op. cit., I, p. 69.

50. Adolphe BLANQUI, 'Tableau des populations rurales de la France en 1850', in *Journal des économistes*, January 1851, p. 9.

51. E. A. WRIGLEY, *Towns in societies*, 1978, p. 298.

52. L. STOUFF, 'La population d'Arles', art. cit., p. 10.

53. Alain CROIX, *Nantes et le pays nantais*, 1974, pp. 163–99.

54. Roger DEVOS, 'Un siècle en mutation (1536–1684)', in *Histoire de la Savoie'*, ed. Roger DEVOS, 1973, p. 258.

55. Olivier ZELLER, 'L'implantation savoyarde à Lyon à la fin du XVIe siècle', in *Habiter la ville*, op. cit., p. 27.

56. Maurice GARDEN, 'Trois provinces, une généralité (XVIIe–XVIIIe siècles)', in André LATREILLE, ed., *Histoire de Lyon et du Lyonnais*, 1975, p. 227.

57. Louis-Sébastien MERCIER, *Tableau de Paris*, V, 1783, p. 282; VI, 1783, pp. 82–3; IX, 1788, pp. 167–8; and F. BRAUDEL, *Civilization and Capitalism*, op. cit., I, p. 490.

58. Jean-Pierre POUSSOU, *Bordeaux et le Sud-Ouest au XVIIIe siècle. Croissance économique et attraction urbaine*, *passim* and pp. 100–1 and 369 ff.

59. See above, chapter 6.

60. Jean-Claude PERROT, *Genèse d'une ville moderne: Caen au XVIIIe siècle*, 1975, I, pp. 23ff and II, chapters X and XI, discusses the attitudes and interests working for and against the new urban development; the demolition of the fortifications, which began in 1751, was not complete until 1787. Bordeaux hesitated too,

61. J. R. PITTE, *Histoire du paysage*, op. cit., II, p. 16.

62. *Ibid.*, II, chapter 1.

63. J. MEYER, *Etudes sur les villes*, op. cit., I, p. 14.

64. L.-S. MERCIER, *Tableau de Paris*.

65. Léonce de LAVERGNE, *Economie rurale de la France depuis 1789*, 1860, 1877 edn, p. 192.

66. Jean-Pierre POUSSOU, 'Une ville digne de sa fortune', in Charles HIGOUNET, ed., *Histoire de Bordeaux*, 1980, p. 238. J. GODECHOT and B. TOLLON, 'Ombres et lumières sur Toulouse (1715–1789)', in Philippe WOLFF, ed., *Histoire de Toulouse*, 1974, pp. 370–2; A. BOURDE, 'Le mentalités, la religion, les lettres et les arts de 1596 à 1789', in E. BARATIER, *Histoire de Marseille*, 1973, p. 237; Jean-Pierre BARDET, 'Un dynamisme raisonnable', art. cit.; J.-C. PERROT, *Genèse d'une ville*, op. cit., II, p. 585.

67. Clause NIERES, 'L'incendie et la reconstruction de Rennes', in J. MEYER, *Histoire de Rennes*, 1972, pp. 213 ff.

68. *Ibid.*, p. 229.

69. *Ibid.*. p. 233.

70. J. C. PERROT, *Genèse d'une ville*, op. cit., II, pp. 592 and 615–17.

71. Louis TRENARD, 'Le Paris des Pays-Bas (XVIIIe siècle)', in *Histoire d'une métropole, Lille-Roubaix-Tourcoing*, 1977, p. 278.

72. Pierre PATTE, *Mémoire sur les objets les plus importants de l'architecture*, 1772, p. 6, quoted by Claudette DEROZIER, 'Aspects de l'urbanisme à Besançon au XVIIIe siècle', in *L'Information historique*, 1984, p. 82.

cf. *Histoire de Bordeaux*, ed. C. HIGOUNET, p. 236.

73. Jean-Marie CARBASSE, 'Pesanteurs et fastes de l'Ancien Régime', in Jacques MICHAUD and André CABANIS, eds., *Histoire de Narbonne*, 1981, p. 244.

74. Eugène NOEL, *Rouen, Rouennais, rouenneries*, 1894, pp. 164–72.

75. J.-P. BARDET, 'La maison rouennaise aux XVIIe et XVIIIe siècles, économie et comportement', in J.-P. BARDET, P. CHAUNU *et al.*, eds., *Le Bâtiment. Enquête d'histoire économique XIVe–XIXe siècles*, I, *Maisons rurales et urbaines de la France traditionnelle*, 1971, pp. 319–20.

76. Roberto LOPEZ, Harry A. MISKIMIN, 'The economic depression of the Renaissance', in *Economic History Review*', XIV, 3, 1962, pp. 115–16.

77. Public defence of his thesis, 27 May 1972.

78. Witold KULA, report by A. WYROBISZ and discussion, 6th Prato conference, 1974.

79. Sébastien CHARLETY, *Histoire de Lyon*, 1903, p. 129.

80. In 1789, Lyon's debt stood at 40 million *livres*, Marseille's at almost 19 million, that of Aix-en-Provence at 1.8 million and that of Arles at 1 million.

81. Pierre CHAUNU, 'Le bâtiment dans l'économie traditionnelle', in BARDET *et al.*, *Le Bâtiment*, op. cit., pp. 19–20; Hugues NEVEUX, 'Recherches sur la construction et l'entretien des maisons à Cambrai de la fin du XIVe siècle au début du XVIIIe', *ibid.*, p. 244.

82. J.-C. PERROT, *Genèse d'une ville*, op. cit., II, p. 615.

83. P. CHAUNU, 'Le bâtiment', art. cit., p. 20.

84. *Ibid.*, p. 25.

85. Louis CHEVALIER, *Classes laborieuses, classes dangereuses*, 1958, p. 217.

86. P. CHAUNU, 'Le bâtiment', art. cit., p. 31.

87. Jacques DUPAQUIER, 'Le réseau urbain du Bassin Parisien au XVIIIe et au début du XIXe siècle. Essai de statistique', in *Actes du 100e Congrès National des Sociétés Savantes, Histoire Moderne II* (Paris, 1975), 1977, p. 125.

88. Cf. above, vol. I, p. 180.

89. Marcel REINHARD, 'La population des villes sa mesure sous la Révolution et l'Empire', in *Population*, 1954, no. 2, pp. 279–88.

90. Paul BAIROCH, *De Jéricho à Mexico. Villes et économies dans l'histoire*, 1985, p. 288.

91. François LEBRUN, 'La tutelle monarchique (1657–1787)', in F. LEBRUN, ed., *Histoire d'Angers*, 1975, p. 83.

92. *Ibid.*, p. 101.

93. *Ibid.*, p. 103.

94. *Ibid.*, p. 103.

95. *Ibid.*, p. 101.

96. Rémy CAZALS, Jean VALENTIN, *Carcassonne, ville industrielle au XVIIIe siècle*, 1984, pp. 3–4.

97. Pierre DARDEL, *Commerce, industrie et navigation à Rouen et au Havre au XVIIIe siècle*', 1966, p. 118.

98. *Ibid.*, pp. 118–19.

99. *Ibid.*, pp. 123–39.

100. F. BRAUDEL, *Civilization and Capitalism*, op. cit., I, pp. 324 ff.

101. Pierre CAYEZ, *Métiers jacquard et hauts fourneaux aux origines de l'industrie lyonnaise*, 1978, pp. 79 ff.

102. *Ibid.*, p. 107.

103. *Ibid.*, pp. 154–5.

104. Edward FOX, *History in*

geographic perspective. The Other France, 1971.

105. J.-P. POUSSOU, *Bordeaux et le Sud-Ouest*, op. cit., pp. 411–14.

106. M. BRAURE, *Lille et la Flandre wallonne au XVIIIe siècle*, 1932, II, pp. 85 ff and 369 ff.

107. *Ibid.*, II, pp. 376–7.

108. *Ibid.*, p. 376.

109. *Ibid.*, pp. 378–9.

110. *Ibid.*, pp. 378–9 and 387.

111. L. TRENARD, 'Le Paris des Pays-Bas', art. cit., p. 245.

112. Mémoire by Antoine de SURMONT, quoted by M. BRAURE, *Lille et la Flandre*, op. cit., pp. 379–90.

113. P. CAYEZ, *Métiers jacquard*, op. cit., p. 94.

114. After 1692: Maurice BORDES, *L'Administration provinciale et municipale en France au XVIIIe siècle*, 1972, p. 199.

115. T. REGAZZOLA and J. LEFEBVRE, *La Domestication du mouvement*, op. cit., p. 123.

116. Herbert LUTHY, *La Banque protestante en France, de la Révocation de l'Edit de Nantes à la Révolution*, I, 1959, p. 314.

117. Jean SENTOU, *La Fortune immobilière des Toulousains et la Révolution française*, 1970, p. 25.

118. *Ibid.*, p. 174.

119. Robert BESNIER, *Histoire des faits économiques jusqu'au XVIIIe siècle*, 1965, p. 42.

120. Arghiri EMMANUEL, *L'Echange inégal. Essai sur les antagonismes dans les rapports économiques internationaux*, 1969, p. 43.

121. *La Domestication du mouvement. Poussées mobilisatrices et surrection de l'Etat* (1981).

122. Charles MORAZE's seminar.

123. A.N., F¹⁰ 242. Reply of the *département* of Mont-Blanc to the Committee of Public Safety on questions concerning

agriculture, manufacture and commerce, Year IV. (Savoy became the *département* of Mont-Blanc on 27 November 1792.)

124. Extract from the childhood memories Saint-Gervais and the Vallée des Contamines, before the tourist invasion which my friend Roger VERLHAC had begun to write down at my request, before his premature death. In 1820, the same system would have been found in the Jura near Les Rousses; cf. Abbé M. BERTHET, 'Les Rousses', in J. BRELOT et al., *A travers les villages du Jura*, 1963, p. 285.

125. Information provided by Gilbert BLANC, forest-ranger and guide, of Saint-Gervais.

126. Joseph-Michel DUTENS, *Histoire de la navigation intérieure en France*, 1928, I, pp. ix–x, quoted by J.-C. TOUTAIN, *Les Transports en France de 1830 à 1965, Cahiers de l'ISEA*, series AF-9, Sept.–Oct. 1967, p. 38.

127. Bernard LEPETIT, *Chemins de terre et voies d'eau: réseaux de transports et organisation de l'espace en France, 1740–1840*, 1984, p. 91.

128. Arthur YOUNG, *Travels in France*, op. cit., several references.

129. *Statistique générale de la France, Territoire et population*, 1837, p. 47.

130. A.N., F¹⁰ 242, op. cit.

131. Pierre GOUBERT and Daniel ROCHE, *Les Français et l'Ancien Régime*, 1984, I, p. 55.

132. L. de LAVERGNE, *Economie rurale de la France depuis 1789*, op. cit., p. 434.

133. Dr MORAND's private papers, kindly put at my disposal.

134. P. GOUBERT and D. ROCHE,

Les Français et l'Ancien Régime, op. cit., I, p. 55.

135. Alexis MONTEIL, *Description du département de l'Aveyron*, Year X, quoted in Claude HARMELLE, *Les Piqués de l'aigle. Saint-Antonin et sa région 1850–1940. Révolution des transports et changement social*, 1982, p. 75.

136. Marc AMBROISE-RENDU, 'Géographie parisienne, les révélations du nouvel atlas démographique et social de la capitale', in *Le Monde*, 30–31 December 1984, p. 1.

137. B. LEPETIT, *Chemins de terre*, op. cit., p. 81.

138. A.N., F²⁰ 197.

139. B. LEPETIT, *Chemins de terre*, op. cit., pp. 67–71.

140. *Ibid.*

141. René FAVIER, 'Une ville face au développement de la circulation au XVIIIe siècle: Vienne en Dauphiné', in *Actes du 100e Congrès des Sociétés Savantes*, Paris, 1975, pp. 54–5.

142. Pierre FUSTIER, *La Route. Voies antiques, chemins anciens, chaussées modernes*, 1968, pp. 228–36 and 249–54. The first iron bridge was built across the Rhône in 1824 by Marc Seguin, between Tain and Tournon.

143. STENDHAL, *Mémoires d'un touriste*, 1838, 1929 edn, I, pp. 73 and 309–10.

144. T. REGAZZOLA and J. LEFEBVRE, *La Domestication du mouvement*, op. cit., p. 112.

145. Guy ARBELLOT, 'Les routes en France au XVIIIe siècle', in *Annales E.S.C.*, May–June 1973, p. 790 and figure, also quoted in F. BRAUDEL, *Civilization and Capitalism*, III, op. cit., pp. 316–7.

146. French Ministry of Public Works, statistical documents on roads and bridges, 1873, quoted by J. C. TOUTAIN, *Les Transports*, op. cit., p. 15.

147. Jean-Claude GEORGES, *De la Beholle à la Falouse*, 1985, p. 75.

148. Alain CROIX, *La Bretagne aux XVIe et XVIIe siècles*, I, 1981, p. 39 and note 95.

149. Victor HUGO, *Les Pyrénées*, 1984 edn, p. 18.

150. Pierre GOUBERT, Preface to Anne-Marie COCULA-VAILLIERES, *Un fleuve et des hommes. Les gens de la Dordogne au XVIIIe siècle*, 1981, p. 7.

151. Blaise de MONLUC, *Commentaires (1521–1576)*, Pléiade edn, 1964, V, p. 515, quoted by A.-M. COCULA-VAILLIERES, *Un fleuve*, op. cit., p. 15.

152. Antonio PONZ, *Viaje fuera de España*, 2nd edn, 1791, I, p. 56.

153. A.-M. COCULA-VAILLIERES, *Un fleuve*, op. cit.

154. *Ibid.*, p. 34.

155. *Ibid.*, pp. 79 ff.

156. *Ibid.*, pp. 110–14.

157. *Ibid.* p. 73.

158. *Ibid.* pp. 76–8.

159. These contracts included not only a list of goods carried and the cost of freight, but also a deadline for delivery (usually about three weeks). In one register belonging to a seventeenth-century merchant, they have been written in and signed by two witnesses. O. GRANAT, 'Essai sur le commerce dans un canton de l'Agenais au XVIIe siècle, d'après le "livre de comptes et de raisons de Hugues Mario, marchand", de Montaigut en Agenais, aujourd'hui Montaigut-du-Quercy (1648–1654)', in *Revue de l'Agenais*, 1901, xxviii, pp. 425–40.

160. Léon CAHEN, 'Ce qu'enseigne un péage du XVIIIe siècle: la Seine, entre Rouen et Paris, et les caractères de l'économie parisienne', in *Annales d'histoire économique et sociale*, 1931, III, pp. 487–518.

161. A.N., G[7] 1647, no. 345, 14 June 1710.

162. *Ibid.*, no. 326, 20 April 1709.

163. Maurice BLOCK, *Statistique de la France comparée avec les divers pays de l'Europe*, 1875, II, p. 250.

164. O. GRANAT, 'Essai sur le commerce', art. cit., pp. 437–8.

165. A.N., F[14] 168, printed paper.

166. Henriette DUSSOURD, *Les Hommes de la Loire*, 1985, pp. 85 ff.

167. A.N., G[7] 124.

168. A.N., H 94, dossier VI, document 74.

169. *Gazette de France*, 15 April 1763.

170. *Histoire de la navigation sur l'Allier en Bourbonnais*, ed. by Service Éducatif des Archives Départementales de l'Allier, 1983, p. 30.

171. A.N., F[12] 1512 C.

172. Adrien HUGUET, *Histoire de Saint-Valéry*, 1909, pp. 1191 ff.

173. J. C. TOUTAIN, *Les Transports*, op. cit., pp. 74–5.

174. J. MEYER, *Histoire de Rennes*, op. cit., p. 36.

175. Richard GASCON, *Grand Commerce et vie urbaine au XVIe siècle. Lyon et ses marchands*, 1971, p. 157.

176. Joseph-Michel DUTENS, *Histoire de la navigation*, op. cit., I, pp. ix–x, quoted by J. C. TOUTAIN, *Les Transports*, op. cit., p. 38.

177. VAUBAN, *Mémoire sur la navigation des rivières*, in *Mémoires des Intendants sur l'état des généralités, dressés pour l'instruction du Duc de Bourgogne*, ed. A. M. de BOISLISLE (1st edn 1761), 1881 edn, I, p. 401.

178. For instance, according to annual records of shipping on the Allier in 1837 (the only year for which detailed statistics exist), 29 boats carried to Paris 870 tons of charcoal, and 18 boats carried 360 tons of straw from Pont-du-Château to Moulins. *Histoire de la navigation sur l'Allier*, op. cit., pp. 34–5.

179. A.N., F[10] 242.

180. J. C. PERROT, *Genèse d'une ville*, op. cit., p. 211.

181. A.N., F[11] 3059.

182. J. LETACONNOUX, 'Les voies de communication en France au XVIIIe siècle', in *Vierteljahrschrift für Sozial- und Wirtschaftsgeschichte*, VII, 1909, p. 108.

183. J. C. TOUTAIN, *Les Transports*, op. cit., p. 40.

184. The statistics for shipping on the Allier, quoted above (note 178), give for the year 1837 a table of the weights and values of all goods transported (wine, coal, charcoal, timbers and planks, stone, wooden boards, straw, fruit etc.), then mention '108 log-trains' without further detail, and these are not included in the totals on the table.

185. A.N., F[12] 653, January 1786.

186. J. C. TOUTAIN, *Les Transports*, op. cit., p. 248.

187. VAUBAN, *Mémoire sur la navigation*, op. cit., p. 413.

188. T. REGAZZOLA and J. LEFEBVRE, *La Domestication du mouvement*, op. cit., p. 132; J. C. TOUTAIN, *Les Transports*, op. cit., p. 252.

189. Marcel MARION, *Dictionnaire des institutions de la France au*

XVIIe et au XVIIIe siècle, 1976 edn, p. 561.

190. T. REGAZZOLA and L. LEFEBVRE, *La Domestication du mouvement*, op. cit., p. 97.

191. *Ibid.*, p. 111.

192. Ch. DEPLAT, 'Les résistances à l'implantation de la route royale dans le ressort de l'intendance d'Auch et de Pau au XVIIIe siècle', in *Annales du Midi*, 1981.

193. T. REGAZZOLA and J. LEFEBVRE, *La Domestication du mouvement*, op. cit., p. 105.

194. M. MARION, *Dictionnaire*, op. cit., pp. 153–4; Gaston WIMBEE, *Histoire du Berry, des origines à 1790*, 1957, p. 245.

195. A.N., H 160, Mémoire by M. Antoine, *sous-ingénieur* in Burgundy, on the abolition of *corvée* in Burgundy, 1775.

196. M. MARION, *Dictionnaire*, op. cit., p. 154.

197. Guy ARBELLOT, 'Le réseau des routes de poste, objet des premières cartes thématiques de la France moderne', in *Les Transports de 1610 à nos jours. Actes du 104e Congrès des Sociétés Savantes*, Bordeaux, 1979, 1980, I, p. 107 and note 4.

198. See Vol. I of *The Identity of France*, p. 355.

199. Pierre DUBOIS, *Histoire de la campagne de 1707 dans le Sud-Est de la France*, typescript, p. 28, letter from Tessé.

200. Madeleine FOUCHE, *La Poste aux chevaux de Paris et ses maîtres de poste à travers les siècles*, 1975, pp. 84–5.

201. Pierre CHAMPION, *Paris au temps de la Renaissance. L'envers de la tapisserie, le règne de François Ier*, 1935, p. 32. Diego de Zuñiga wrote to Philip II on the very day of the St

Bartholomew Massacre (24 August 1572) to announce the news; Philip received the letter on 7 September and greeted it with joy. Philippe ERLANGER, *Le Massacre de la Saint-Barthélemy*, 1960, p. 203.

202. A.N., F[10] 221–1, Quimper, 27 June 1791.

203. Figures kindly provided by J. C. TOUTAIN, who has been collecting them for a forthcoming book.

204. According to chapter VI of the *Mémoire pour servir à l'histoire du Languedoc*, written in 1737 by the *intendant* de Basville.

205. Percentages calculated by J. C. TOUTAIN:

1781–90	30%
1803–14	32%
1825–34	37%
1845–54	45%
1875–84	52%
1895–1904	58%
1920–24	65%
1925–34	72%
1935–38	75%
1980	95%

206. Quoted by M. MARION, *Dictionnaire*, op. cit., p. 540.

207. *Ibid.*, p. 188.

208. *Ibid.*, p. 437.

209. Moscow, State Archives, 35/6, 381, f[os] 170–1.

210. Quoted by M. MARION, *Dictionnaire*, op. cit., p. 541.

211. *Ibid.* p. 540.

212. Moscow, State Archives, 13/6 439, f° 168 and v[o].

213. T. REGAZZOLA and J. LEFEBVRE, *La Domestication du mouvement*, op. cit., p. 158.

214. *Ibid.*

215. *Ibid.*, pp. 152–4.

216. Michel CHEVALIER, *Système de la Méditerranée*, 1832, quoted *ibid.*, pp. 160–1.

217. *Ibid.*. p. 165.

218. Pierre BONNET, *La Commercialisation de la vie française, du Premier Empire à nos jours*, 1929, p. 82.

219. C. HARMELLE, *Les Piqués de l'aigle*, op. cit., pp. 152 and 162.

220. Georges DUCHENE, *L'Empire industriel. Histoire critique des concessions financières et industrielles du Second Empire*, 1869, p. 297.

221. Pierre FUSTIER, *La Route*, op. cit., p. 256.

222. Jacques LOVIE, 'Chemins de Savoie: la route d'Italie à l'époque romantique (1815–1860)', in *Les Transports de 1610 à nos jours*, op. cit., p. 80.

223. A.N., F1C III Loiret, 7, no. 307.

224. Edmund GOT, *Journal 1822–1901*, II, 1910, p. 245.

225. P. SEIGNOUR, *La Vie économique du Vaucluse*, op. cit., p. 91.

226. Elie REYNIER, *Le Pays de Vivarais*, quoted in René NELLI, *Le Languedoc et le Comté de Foix, le Roussillon*, 1958, p. 51.

227. Eugen WEBER, *Peasants into Frenchmen. The Modernization of Rural France 1870–1914*, 1977.

228. C. HARMELLE, *Les Piqués de l'aigle*, op. cit.

229. *Ibid.*, p. 53.

230. *Ibid.*, p. 93.

231. *Ibid.*, pp. 92–3.

232. *Ibid.*, p. 222.

233. Alexis de MONTEIL, *Description du département de l'Aveyron*, Year X (1802), quoted in C. HARMELLE, *ibid.*, p. 75.

234. C. HARMELLE, *ibid.*, p. 77.

235. *Ibid.*, pp. 110–11.

236. *Ibid.*, p. 235.

237. *Ibid.*, p. 320.

238. *Ibid.*, pp. 152 and 162.

239. Pierre CAYEZ, exact reference mislaid.

240. Paul HARSIN, 'De quand date le mot industrie?', in *Annales d'histoire économique et sociale*, 1930, pp. 235–42.

241. C. J. A. MATHIEU de DOMBASLE, *De l'avenir industriel de la France*, 1835.

242. G. DUCHENE, *L'Empire industriel*, op. cit., p. 45.

243. Letters to the prefect of Côtes-du-Nord, Loudéac, 24 February 1853, and to the prefect of Finistère, Morlaix, 14 January 1850, A.N., F12 4476, c.

244. A.N., F1C V Hérault 3, 1837.

245. Jean-Baptiste SAY, *Cours complet d'économie politique pratique*, 1966 reprint, pp. 100–1.

246. Pierre BARRAL, 'La crise agricole', in F. BRAUDEL and E. LABROUSSE, eds., *Histoire économique et sociale de la France*, op. cit., IV, p. 371.

247. Massimo AUGELLO, 'Il battito in Francia su economia e società 1814–1850', *Rassegna economica*, 1981, pp. 21–2. The quotation, paraphrasing Say, is from Charles DUNOYER, 'Notice historique sur l'industrie', in *Revue encyclopédique*, February 1827, p. 178.

248. David RICARDO, French edition of *Principles of political economy*, 1817, pp. 3–8.

249. *Ibid.*, p. 7 note I, by Jean-Baptiste SAY to the French edition of RICARDO.

250. Eugène de BOULLAY, *Statistique agricole et industrielle du département de la Saône-et-Loire*, 1849, p. 10.

251. Maria Rafaella CAROSELLI, 'I fattori della seconda Rivoluzione industriale', in *Economia e Storia*, 1978, pp. 389–418.

252. Albert DAUZAT, Jean DUBOIS, Henri MITTERAND, *Nouveau*

Dictionnaire étymologique et historique, 1964.

253. Hubert BOURGIN, *L'Industrie et le marché. Essai sur les lois du développement industriel*, 1924.

254. F. BRAUDEL, *Civilization and Capitalism*, op. cit., II, p. 300.

255. See Vol. I of *The Identity of France*, pp. 231 ff.

256. Serge CHASSAGNE, 'Industrialisation et désindustrialisation dans les campagnes françaises: quelques réflexions à partir du textile', in *Revue du Nord*, January–March 1981, p. 43, note 26.

257. Pierre GEORGE. 'Histoire de France, le recours à la terre', *Le Monde*, 27 October 1984.

258. Béatrix de BUFFEVENT, 'Marchands ruraux de l'ancien "pays de France" au XVIIIe siècle', in *Le Developpement urbain de 1610 à nos jours. Actes du 100e Congrès National des Sociétés Savantes*, Paris 1975, 1977, pp. 171–84.

259. Pierre LEON, 'Les transformations de l'entreprise industrielle', in F. BRAUDEL and E. LABROUSSE, *Histoire économique et sociale de la France*, op. cit., II, 1970, p. 262.

260. The word can have various meanings even in industry today, as pointed out by Yves MORVAN, *La Concentration de l'industrie en France*, 1972, pp. 15 ff. It may refer simply to the size of the unit of production (as in the example of the *manufactures*) or the bringing together of different trades for producing a single commodity (like the Gueugnon).

261. A.N., F^{14} 4481, documents 1 and 7.

262. Christian DEVILIERS, Bernard

HUET, *Le Creusot. Naissance et développement d'une ville industrielle 1782–1914*, 1918, pp. 36–49.

263. Adrien PRINTZ, *La Vallée usinière, histoire d'un ruisseau, la Fensch*, 1966, pp. 57–67.

264. *Société lorraine des anciens établissements de Dietrich et Cie de Lunéville 1880–1950*, 1951, p. 9.

265. Alexandre MOREAU de JONNES, *Etat économique et social de la France depuis Henri IV jusqu'à Louis XIV*, 1867, pp. 59–60.

266. F. BRAUDEL, *Civilization and Capitalism*, op. cit., p. 117.

267. *Le Monde des affaires en France de 1830 à nos jours*, 1952, p. 83.

268. Isaac de PINTO, *Lettre sur la jalousie du commerce*, in *Traité de la circulation et du crédit*, 1771, p. 287.

269. François VERON de FORBONNAIS, *Principes et observations économiques*, 1767, I, p. 205.

270. Pierre Samuel DUPONT de NEMOURS, *De l'exportation et de l'importation des grains*, 1764, pp. 90–1, quoted by Pierre DOCKES, *L'Espace dans la pensée économique du XVIe au XVIIe siècle*, 1969, p. 288.

271. Jean-Jacques ROUSSEAU, *Emile ou de l'Education*, 1961 edn, p. 226.

272. Louis GUENEAU, *Les conditions de la vie à Nevers (denrées, logements, salaires) à la fin de l'Ancien Régime*, 1919, pp. 99 ff.

273. *Bulletin de l'Association Meusienne*, April 1984.

274. Paul VIDAL de LA BLACHE, *La France de l'Est, Lorraine, Alsace*, 1917, p. 38.

275. André CHAMSON, *Les Hommes de la route*, 1927, p. 76.

276. Gilbert ARMAND, *Villes, centres*

et organisation urbaine des Alpes du Nord. Le passé et le présent, 1974, pp. 85–6.

277. On Laval, Cholet, Saint-Quentin, see Serge CHASSAGNE, 'Industrialisation et désindustrialisation', art. cit., pp. 37–40.

278. G. ARMAND, *Villes, centres et organisation urbaine*, op. cit., p. 92.

279. *Ibid.*, pp. 88–9.

280. Jacques SCHNETZLER, *Les Industries et les hommes dans la région de Saint-Etienne*, 1976, pp. 50–1.

281. Pierre LEON, 'La réponse de l'industrie', in F. BRAUDEL and E. LABROUSSE, eds., *Histoire économique et sociale de la France*, op. cit., II, 1970, p. 252.

282. *Ibid.*, pp. 252–3.

283. François DORNIC, *Le Fer contre la forêt*, 1984, p. 40.

284. Eugenii K. TARLE, *L'Industrie dans les campagnes en France, à la fin de l'Ancien Régime*, 1910, p. 48.

285. S. CHASSAGNE, 'Industrialisation et désindustrialisation', art. cit., pp. 49–50.

286. Georges DESBONS, *Capitalisme et agriculture*, 1912, p. 19; and Charles SEIGNOBOS, 'L'évolution de la IIIe République', in Ernest LAVISSE, ed., *Histoire de la France contemporaine*, VIII, 1921, p. 460.

287. Paul BAIROCH, *Révolution industrielle et sous-développement*, 1974, p. 276.

288. Maurice DAUMAS, *L'Archéologie industrielle en France*, 1980, p. 106.

289. Louis-Marie LOMULLER, *Histoire économique et industrielle de la France de la fin du XVIIe siècle au début du XIXe siècle. Guillaume Ternaux, 1763–1833, créateur de la première integration industrielle française*, 1978, p. 56, note 9.

290. M. DAUMAS, *L'Archéologie industrielle*, op. cit., p. 98.

291. Jacob van KLAVEREN, 'Die Manufakturen des "Ancien Régime"', in *Vierteljahrschrift für Sozial- und Wirtschaftsgeschichte*, 1964, pp. 145 ff.

292. Werner SOMBART, *Der Modern Kapitalismus*, 15th edn, 1928, II, p. 731. Cf. also F. BRAUDEL, *Civilization and Capitalism*, op. cit., II, pp. 302 ff.

293. Pierre LEON, 'La réponse de l'industrie', in F. BRAUDEL and E. LABROUSSE, *Histoire économique et sociale de la France*, op. cit., II, 1970, pp. 257 ff.

294. M. DAUMAS, *Archéologie industrielle*, op. cit., pp. 134–5; A.N., O^2 871–906.

295. Claude PRIS, *La Manufacture royale des glaces de Saint-Gobain 1665–1830*, 1973.

296. M. DAUMAS, *L'Archéologie industrielle*, op. cit., p. 106.

297. *Ibid.*, pp. 111–14.

298. A.N., G^7 259 f° 9.

299. M. DAUMAS, *L'Archéologie industrielle*, op. cit., pp. 98–106.

300. P. LÉON, 'La réponse industrielle', art. cit., p. 260.

301. *Ibid.*

302. Frederick Louis NUSSBAUM, *A History of the Economic Institutions of Modern Europe*, 1933, pp. 212–13.

303. Rémy CAZALS, *Les Révolutions industrielles à Mazamet 1750–1900*, 1983, p. 79.

304. Louis François DEY de SERAUCOURT, *Mémoire sur la généralité de Bourges, dressé par ordre du duc de Bourgogne en 1697*, 1844.

305. P. LÉON, 'La réponse industrielle', art. cit., pp. 259 and 243.

306. F. BRAUDEL, *Civilization and Capitalism*, op. cit., III, p. 593.

307. Albert SOBOUL, 'La reprise économique et la stabilisation sociale 1797–1815', in F. BRAUDEL and E. LABROUSSE, eds., *Histoire économique et sociale de la France*, op. cit., III, *L'Avènement de l'ère industrielle (1789-années 1980)*, 1976, p. 107; P. LEON, 'L'impulsion technique', in *ibid.*, III/2, 1976, p. 485; R. CAZALS, *Les Révolutions*, op. cit., pp. 114–15.

308. Cf. L. S. MERCIER, *Tableau de Paris*, op. cit., VII, p. 147.

309. Richard CANTILLON, *Essai sur la nature du commerce en général*, 1755, 1952 edn, p. 36.

310. Pierre BONNET, *La Commercialisation de la vie française du Premier Empire à nos jours*, 1929, p. 12. Walter ENDREI, *L'Evolution des techniques de filage et de tissage du Moyen Age à la Révolution industrielle*, 1968, p. 145.

311. Hervé LE BRAS, *Les trois Frances*, 1986, p. 237. (Seen by F.B. in manuscript.)

312. P. LEON, 'L'impulsion technique', art. cit., p. 498.

313. A. PRINTZ, *La Vallée usinière*, op. cit., pp. 57–67.

314. F. BRAUDEL, *Civilization and Capitalism*, II, p. 328. A.N., F^{12} 682 (9 January 1727).

315. Tihomir J. MARKOVITCH, 'L'Industrie française de 1789 à 1964, Conclusions générales', in *Cahiers de l'ISEA*, IV, 1966, p. 59.

316. *Ibid.*, but exact reference incomplete.

317. Georges d'AVENEL, *Le Mécanisme de la vie moderne*, 3rd series, 1900, pp. 215–16.

318. Yves GUYOT, 'Notes sur l'industrie et le commerce de la France', in *Journal de la Société de Statistique de Paris*, 1897, p. 287.

319. Marcel GILLET, *Les Charbonnages du Nord de la France au XIXe siècle*, 1973, p. 28.

320. G. d'AVENEL, *Le Mécanisme*, op. cit., p. 214.

321. *Ibid.*

322. Sébastien CHARLETY, reference incomplete.

323. Jean-Antoine CHAPTAL, *De l'industrie française*, II, 1819, quoted by P. LEON, 'L'impulsion technique', art. cit., pp. 482–3.

324. P. LEON, 'La réponse industrielle', art. cit., pp. 239–43.

325. P. LEON, 'L'impulsion technique', art. cit., p. 481.

326. Carlo PONI, 'Archéologie de la fabrique: la diffusion des moulins à soie *alla bolognese* dans les Etats vénitiens des XVIe et XVIIe siècles', quoted in F. BRAUDEL, *Civilization and Capitalism*, op. cit., III, p. 551.

327. Charles SINGER, Eric J. HOLMYARD *et al.*, eds., *A History of Technology*, 7 vols., 1954–78, Vol. III.

328. Quoted by François CARON, *Le Résistible Déclin des sociétés industrielles*, 1985, p. 66.

329. Jacques PAYEN, 'Machines et turbines à vapeur', in *Histoire générale des techniques*, ed. M. DAUMAS, IV, 1978, p. 18.

330. *Ibid.*, p. 118.

331. Jules GUERON, 'L'énergie nucléaire', in *Histoire générale des techniques*, op. cit., IV, 1978, p. 42.

332. Jacques PAYEN, 'Machines et

turbines à vapeur', art. cit., pp. 46–51, and François CARON, *Le Résistible Déclin*, op. cit., p. 67. N.B. Mariotte's Law is also known as Boyle's Law.

333. F. CARON, *Le Résistible Déclin*, op. cit., p. 57.

334. F. CARON, 'La croissance économique', in Pierre LEON, ed., *Histoire économique et sociale du monde*, IV, 1978, pp. 91–2.

335. F. CARON, *Le Résistible déclin*, op. cit., p. 87.

336. Louis LEPRINCE RINGUET, *L'Aventure de l'électricité*, 1983, pp. 46–52.

337. F. CARON, 'La croissance économique', art. cit., p. 93.

338. Robert MOISE and Maurice DAUMAS, 'L'électricité industrielle', in *Histoire générale des techniques*, op. cit., IV, pp. 418, 364 and 423.

339. Reference mislaid.

340. Antoine CAILLOT, *Mémoires pour servir à l'histoire des moeurs et usages des Français*, 1827, I, p. 134.

341. SAVARY des BRUSLONS, *Dictionnaire de commerce*, article 'Commerce', II, p. 113.

342. Nicolas LAMOIGNON de BASVILLE, *Mémoires pour servir à l'histoire du Languedoc*, 1734, p. 39.

343. Moscow, Lenin Library, FR 374 f° 159.

344. R. CAZALS, *Les Révolutions industrielles à Mazamet*, op. cit., p. 14.

345. *Ibid.*

346. Louis TRENARD, *Histoire d'une métropole: Lille-Roubaix-Tourcoing*, 1977, pp. 248–9 and 318–9.

347. A.N., G⁷ 1691, 63.

348. T. J. MARKOVITCH, 'L'industrie française', art. cit., p. 142.

349. Serge CHASSAGNE, 'L'industrie lainière en France à l'époque révolutionnaire et impériale 1790–1810', in *Voies nouvelles pour l'histoire de la Révolution française* (Mathiez-Lefebvre conference, 1978).

350. F. BRAUDEL, *Civilization and Capitalism*, op. cit., III, pp. 556 ff Pierre BONNET, *La Commercialisation*, op. cit., pp. 17–53, in his discussion of French backwardness compared to England, considers the Revolution and the Napoleonic wars among the 'apparent causes', whereas the real causes were technological, social, legislative and above all to do with the 'hegemony of land' – in other words, they were structural.

351. Jean BOUVIER, 'Industrie et société', in F. BRAUDEL and E. LABROUSSE, eds., *Histoire économique et sociale de la France*, op. cit., IV, 1982, pp. 1724–5.

352. Emile APPOLIS, *Un pays languedocien au milieu du XVIIIe siècle, le diocèse civil de Lodève*, 1951, p. vi.

353. M. DAUMAS, *L'Archéologie industrielle*, op. cit., p. 30.

354. *Ibid.*, p. 99.

355. *Ibid.*, p. 106.

356. *Ibid.*, pp. 98–106 and Claude ALBERGE, J. P. LAURENT, J. SAGNES, *Villeneuvette, une manufacture du Languedoc*, in *Etudes sur l'Hérault*, 1984, no. 12.

357. M. DAUMAS, *L'Archéologie industrielle*, op. cit., pp. 185–6.

358. Walter G. HOFFMANN, *British Industry 1700–1950*, 1955, quoted in F. BRAUDEL, *Civilization and Capitalism*, op. cit., II, pp. 346 ff.

359. F. BRAUDEL and F. SPOONER,

'Prices in Europe from 1450 to 1750', in *Cambridge Economic History of Europe*, IV, pp. 454 and 484.

360. T. J. MARKOVITCH, 'L'industrie française', art. cit., p. 196.

361. Henri SEE, 'Esquisse de l'évolution industrielle de la France de 1815 à 1848, les progrès du machinisme et de la concentration', in *Revue de l'histoire économique et sociale*, 1923, no. 4, pp. 473–97.

362. P. LEON, 'L'impulsion technique', art. cit., p. 479.

363. F. BRAUDEL, *Civilization and Capitalism*, op. cit., III, pp. 85 ff and 267 ff.

364. T. J. MARKOVITCH, 'Salaires et profits industriels en France (sous la Monarchie de juillet et le Second Empire)', in *Economies et Sociétés, Cahiers de l'ISEA*, April 1967, p. 79.

365. T. J. MARKOVITCH, 'L'industrie française', art. cit., p. 86.

366. Conclusions taken from a summary and report written specially for Fernand Braudel by T. J. Markovitch in 1984, incorporating the essential findings T. J. Markovitch had drawn from the seven volumes so far published on *Histoire des industries françaises*.

367. Charles SEIGNOBOS, *L'Evolution de la IIIe République*, in E. LAVISSE, ed., *Histoire de la France contemporaine*, 1921, p. 460.

368. H. LE BRAS, *Les Trois France*, op. cit., p. 223.

369. *Ibid.*, p. 236.

370. *Ibid.*, pp. 228–9.

371. Reference mislaid.

372. Léonce de LAVERGNE, *Economie rurale de la France depuis 1789*, 1877, p. 45.

373. Pierre CHAUNU, *La Civilisation de l'Europe classique*, 1966, pp. 328–9 and 342.

374. 1905 French edition of William PETTY's economic writings, quoted by Pierre DOCKES, *L'Espace dans la pensée économique du XVIe au XVIIIe siècle*, 1969, p. 152.

375. Cf. his correspondence in the Moscow archives. The Swiss *négociants* in Marseille often handled foreign consulates, notably for Denmark, Austria and England: Gaston RAMBERT, ed., *Histoire du commerce de Marseille*, IV, 1954, pp. 529–30.

376. Anne-Robert-Jacques TURGOT, *Réflexions sur la formation et la distribution des richesses*, 1766, in E. DIARE, ed., *Oeuvres de Turgot*, 1844, reprinted 1966, I, p. 43; A.N., G^7 1697, 165, 23 December 1712.

377. J. C. TOUTAIN, *La Population de la France, de 1700 à 1959*, in *Cahiers de l'ISEA*, AF 3, 1963, tables, pp. 136–7.

378. A.N., K 1351, 'Le compagnon ordinaire des marchands', 1700.

379. Elie BRACKENHOFFER, *Voyage en France 1643–1644*, tr. Henry LEHR, 1925, pp. 115–16.

380. J. C. PERROT, *Genèse d'une ville moderne, Caen*, op. cit., I, p. 182.

381. Claude SEYSSEL, *Histoire singulière du roy Louys XII*, 1558, p. 113.

382. *Journal de voyage de deux jeunes Hollandais (MM de Viliers) à Paris en 1656–1658*, ed. A. P. FAUGERE, 1899, p. 30.

383. POTTIER DE LA HESTROYE, *Réflexions sur la dîme royale*, 1716, pp. 104–5.

384. Jacques Joseph JUGE SAINT-MARTIN, *Changements survenus*

*dans les moeurs des habitants de
Limoges*, p. 90.

385. Edmond ESMONIN, 'Un
recensement de la population
de Grenoble en 1725', in
Cahiers de l'histoire, 1957, also
published in *Etudes sur la France
des XVIIe et XVIIIe siècles*, 1964,
pp. 429–61.

386. Gilbert ARMAND, *Villes, centres
et organisation urbaine dans les
Alpes du Sud*, op. cit., p. 83.

387. Maurice BLOCK, *Statistique de la
France comparée avec les autres
Etats de l'Europe*, II, 1860,
p. 225.

388. Pierre BONNET, *La
Commercialisation*, op. cit.,
pp. 170–1 and 173.

389. M. BLOCK, *Statistique de la
France*, op. cit., II, p. 286.

390. Peter MATHIAS, *The First
Industrial Nation, an economic
history of Britain 1700–1914*,
1969, p. 18; R. M. HARTWELL,
*The Industrial Revolution and
Economic Growth*, 1971,
pp. 180 ff.

391. F. BRAUDEL, *Civilization and
Capitalism*, op. cit., II, p. 405.

392. Michel MORINEAU, 'Quelques
recherches relatives à la balance
du commerce extérieur français
au XVIIIe siècle: ou cette fois
un égale deux', in *Aires et
structures du commerce français au
XVIIIe siècle*, Paris conference,
1973, pp. 1–45.

393. Ruggiero ROMANO,
'Documenti e prime
considerazioni intorno alla
"balance de commerce" della
Francia dal 1719 a 1780', in
Studi in onore di Armando Sapori,
p. 1291.

394. M. MORINEAU, 'Quelques
recherches', art. cit., p. 3.

395. *Mémoires de Jean Maillefer,
marchand bourgeois de Reims
(1611–1684), continués par son
fils jusqu'en 1716*, ed. Henri
JADART, 1890, pp. 10–12.

396. F. BRAUDEL, *Civilization and
Capitalism*, op. cit., II, pp. 438–9.

397. Robert BIGO, *Les Banques
françaises au cours du XIXe siècle*,
1947, p. 272.

398. Friedrich LUTGE, *Deutsche
Sozial- und Wirtschaftsgeschichte*,
1966, p. 235.

399. L. BLANCARD, *Documents inédits
sur le commerce de Marseille au
Moyen Age*, 1884 (21 March
1248), quoted by Gérard
SIVERY, 'Les orientations
actuelles de l'histoire
économique du Moyen Age
dans l'Europe du Nord-Ouest,
in *Revue du Nord*, 1973, p. 213.

400. *Ibid.*

401. Jacques ACCARIAS DE
SERIONNE, *Les Intérêts des
nations de l'Europe developpés
relativement au commerce*, 1766, I,
p. 93.

402. Moscow State Archives, 50/6,
522–105 Amsterdam,
20 September and 1 October
1784.

403. Dieudonné RINCHON, *Les
Armements négriers au XVIIIe
siècle, d'après la correspondance et
la comptabilité des armateurs et
capitaines nantais*, 1955, *passim*
and pp. 83, 73 and 75.

404. This happened on 11 voyages
financed by the Chaurand
brothers between 1783 and
1792, *ibid.*, pp. 128–9.

405. *Ibid.*, p. 12.

406. Louis TURQUET DE MAYERNE,
*La Monarchie aristodémocratique
ou le gouvernement composé et
meslé des trois formes de légitimes
Républiques*, 1611, p. 122,
quoted by Roland MOUSNIER,
'L'opposition politique
bourgeoise à la fin du XVIe

407. Jean EON (Father Mathias de Saint Jean), *Le Commerce honorable ou considérations politiques . . . composé par un habitant de la ville de Nantes*, 1646, pp. 21–2.

408. Jean-Baptiste PERIER, *La prospérité rochelaise au XVIIIe siècle et la bourgeoisie protestante*, 1899, II, p. 5.

409. B.N., Fonds Français (French collection).

410. A.N., F¹² 116, 99 ff.

411. Immanuel WALLERSTEIN, *The Modern World System. Capitalist Agriculture and the Origins of the European World Economy*, 1974, p. 127.

412. Marcello CARMAGNANI, *Les Mécanismes de la vie économique dans une société coloniale: le Chili (1680–1830)*, 1973, p. 14.

413. F. BRAUDEL, *Civilization and Capitalism*, II, pp. 403 ff.

414. Vitorino MAGALHAES GODINHO, *L'Economie de l'Empire portugais aux XVe et XVIe siècles*, 1969; F. BRAUDEL, *Civilization and Capitalism*, op. cit., II, p. 403.

415. Paul ADAM, 'Les inventions nautiques, médiévales et l'emergence du développement économique moderne', in *Systèmes économiques et histoire*, typescript, 1980, p. 58.

416. François DORNIC, *L'Industrie textile dans le Maine (1650–1815)*, 1955, p. 43; Nicolas de LAMARE, *Traité de la police . . .* , II, p. 725.

417. François DORNIC, *Histoire du Mans et du pays manceau*, 1975, pp. 146–51.

418. A.N., A.E., B1 280 (29 March 1703).

419. POTTIER DE LA HESTROYE, *Réflexions sur la dîme royale*, op. cit., was published in 1716.

420. A.N., G⁷ 1687, 33.

421. Jacques SAVARY, *Le Parfait Négociant ou Instruction générale pour ce qui regarde le commerce de toute sorte de marchandise tant de France que des pays étrangers*, 1675, II, p. 156; see also J. EON, *Le Commerce honorable*, op. cit., p. 167.

422. Jacques-Marie MONTARAN, quoted in Charles CARRIERE, *Négociants marsellais au XVIIe siècle*, I, 1973, p. 245.

423. Jean-François BELHOSTE, 'Naissance de l'industrie du drap fin en France', in *La Manufacture du Dijonval et la draperie sedanaise 1650–1850*, *Cahiers de l'Inventaire*, no. 2, 1984, p. 14.

424. Régine PERNOUD, *Le Moyen Age jusqu'en 1291*, in *Histoire du commerce du Marseille*, ed. G. RAMBERT, I, 1949, p. 56.

425. Affaires Etrangères, Mémoires et Documents, Turquie, 11. *Capitulations* was the usual word for treaties with the Turks.

426. F. BRAUDEL, *The Mediterranean*, op. cit., I, pp. 493 ff and 545 ff.

427. According to the enquiry of 3 February 1563, and Joseph BILLIOUD, 'Le commerce de Marseille de 1515 à 1599', in *Histoire du commerce de Marseille*, op. cit., III, 1951, p. 445.

428. Louis BERGASSE, 'Le commerce de Marseille de 1599 à 1660', in *Histoire du commerce de Marseille*, op. cit., IV, 1954, pp. 95, 91 and 94.

429. *Le Parfait Négociant*. op. cit., 1712, part II, pp. 385–7.

430. Robert PARIS, 'De 1660 à 1789. Le Levant', in *Histoire du*

commerce de Marseille, V, 1957, pp. 557–64.

431. A.N., Affaires Etrangères, Mémoires et Documents, Turquie, 11.

432. André LESPAGNOL, 'Saint-Malo, port mondial du XVIe au XVIIIe siècle', in *Histoire de Saint-Malo et du pays malouin*, 1984, p. 113.

433. A.N., Affaires Etrangères, B1 211 (9 May 1669).

434. *Carrera de Indias*: the name of the fleet serving Spanish America. Its trade was the monopoly of the king of Spain and it was organized, protected and controlled by the military.

435. A. L'ESPAGNOL, *Histoire de Saint-Malo*, op. cit., p. 79.

436. *Ibid.*, pp. 102 ff.

437. A.N., Affaires Etrangères, B1 214, f° 282.

438. *Ibid.*

439. *Ibid.*

440. *Ibid.* (Cadiz, 15 October 1702).

441. A.N., Aff. Etr., B1 212 (19 October 1682).

442. *Ibid.*, 211 (16 October 1672).

443. *Correspondance des contrôleurs généraux*, ed. A. M. de BOISLISLE, I, 1874, p. 173, 18 February 1689.

444. Reference missing, probably as note 445.

445. Abbé PREVOST, *Histoire générale des voyages*, 1753, XI, pp. 47–63, Relation du voyage de M. de Gennes.

446. A.N., Colonies, F² to 15 (4 March 1698).

447. Baja California, occupied by the Spanish in 1602, and part of present-day Mexico.

448. A.N., Colonies F² to 15 (20 May 1698).

449. *Ibid.*, reference incomplete.

450. *Sol*: it was normal to divide the capital of a firm into 20 parts or *sols*, on the analogy with the 20 *sols* or *sous* in a *livre*.

451. A.N., Colonies, F² to 15 (17 November 1698).

452. *Ibid.*, 19 December 1698.

453. Both Saint-Malo and Dunkerque were very active in wartime privateering, A. LESPAGNOL, *Histoire de Saint-Malo*, op. cit., pp. 114–20. (The Saint-Malo captains occupied what are known in English as the Falkland Islands, but in French as *les Iles Malouines* and in Spanish as *Las Malvinas*.)

454. A.N., Colonies, F² to 21, 30 July 1702. On the problems caused for the Spanish by trade between the Philippines and Peru, see F. BRAUDEL, *Civilization and Capitalism*, op. cit., III, pp. 417 ff.

455. A.N., Colonies, F² A21, Paris, 12 June 1700.

456. F. BRAUDEL, *Civilization and Capitalism*, op. cit., III, pp. 413 ff.

457. A. LESPAGNOL, *Histoire de Saint-Malo*, op. cit., p. 121.

458. *Ibid.*. p. 124.

459. *Ibid.*, p. 123.

460. *Ibid.*, pp. 126–7; Pierre GOUBERT, 'Le tragique XVIIIe siècle', in F. BRAUDEL and E. LABROUSSE, eds., *Histoire économique et sociale de la France*, II, p. 364.

461. A.N., F¹² 681 106.

462. A.N., G⁷ 1701 137 f° 57; Anne MOREL, 'Les armateurs malouins et le commerce interlope', in M. MOLLAT, ed., *Les Sources de l'histoire maritime en Europe, du Moyen Age au XVIIIe siècle*, 1962, p. 313.

463. A. LESPAGNOL, *Histoire de Saint-Malo*, op. cit., pp. 129 ff.

464. Jean MEYER, 'Le commerce nantais du XVIe au XVIIIe siècle', in Paul BOIS, ed.,

Histoire de Nantes, 1977, pp. 135–6.

465. Off present-day Haiti.

466. The Spanish half of the island was 48,000 km² in area, while the area of Cuba is 114,000 km².

467. Alice PIFFER CANABRAVA, *A industria de açucar nas ilhas inglesas e francesas do mar das Antilhas (1697–1755)*, 1946, typescript.

468. Jacques SAVARY des BRUSLONS, *Dictionnaire*, op. cit., V, col. 1462.

469. *Ibid.*, V, col. 1466.

470. Ruggiero ROMANO, 'Documenti e prime considerazioni intorno alla "Balance du commerce" della Francia dal 1716 al 1780', in *Studi in onore di Armando Sapori*, 1957, pp. 1274, 1275, 1291.

471. Cf. above, chapter 14.

472. F. BRAUDEL, *Civilization and Capitalism*, op. cit., II, pp. 417–18.

473. François CROUZET, 'Le commerce de Bordeaux', in F. G. PARISET, ed., *Bordeaux au XVIIIe siècle*, vol. V of C. HIGOUNET, ed., *Histoire de Bordeaux*, 1968, p. 233.

474. M. MORINEAU, 'Quelques recherches', art. cit., pp. 32–3; Jean CAVIGNAC, *Jean Pellet, commerçant de gros 1694–1772. Contribution à l'étude du négoce bordelais du XVIIIe siècle*, 1967, p. 103.

475. J. P. POUSSOU, *Bordeaux et le Sud-Ouest au XVIIIe siècle*, op. cit., p. 20.

476. J. CAVIGNAC, *Jean Pellet*, op. cit., pp. 31–2.

477. J. P. POUSSOU, 'Les structures démographiques et sociales', in *Bordeaux au XVIIIe siècle*, op. cit., pp. 344 ff.

478. J. P. POUSSOU, *Bordeaux et le Sud-Ouest*, op. cit., pp. 27 and 31.

479. Pierre DARDEL, *Commerce, industrie et navigation à Rouen et au Havre au XVIIIe siècle*, 1966, p. 141.

480. In practice, English contraband was never interrupted: the local inhabitants, whom it provided with flour, salt beef, horses and mules, were in league with the smugglers, and the king's officials usually closed their eyes to it. J. CAVIGNAC, *Jean Pellet*, op. cit., pp. 172–3.

481. Charles GIDE, *Cours d'économie politique*, 5th edn, 1919, I, p. 198.

482. Maxime RODINSON, *Islam et capitalisme*, 1966, p. 27.

483. Emile SAVOY, *L'Agriculture à travers les âges*, I, 1935, p. 119.

484. René SEDILLOT, *Histoire des marchands et des marchés*, 1964, p. 188.

485. Jacques LAFFITTE, *Réflexions sur la réduction de la rente et sur l'état du crédit*, 1824, p. 14.

486. Joseph CHAPPEY, *La Crise du capital*, I: *La Formation du système monétaire moderne*, 1937, p. 189.

487. Jean HERAULT, Sieur de GOURVILLE, *Mémoires de Monsieur de Gourville*, 1665, 1724 edn, II, p. 2.

488. The name was originally Pallavicino.

489. P. DARDEL, *Commerce, industrie*, op. cit., p. 159.

490. François DORNIC, *L'Industrie textile dans le Maine et ses débouchés internationaux (1650–1815)*, 1955, pp. 182–3.

491. F. BRAUDEL, *Civilization and Capitalism*, op. cit., II, pp. 389–90.

492. Notes issued under Louis XIV and rapidly devalued, see below.

493. A.N., G⁷ 1691, 35, 6 March 1708.

494. Copy of a letter sent to the Radziwills in Poland; Warsaw, Archives, AD Radziwill.

495. Jean DUCHE, *Le Bouclier d'Athéna. L'Occident, son histoire et son destin*, 1983, p. 487.

496. Alfred NEYMARCK, 'Le développement annuel de l'épargne française', in *Revue internationale du commerce, de l'industrie et de la banque*, 1906, p. 7.

497. Léon SCHICK, *Suggestions pour une reconstruction française*, 1945, pp. 38 ff.

498. Pierre GOUBERT, 'Le tragique XVIIIe siècle', art. cit.

499. Emile VINCENS, *Des Sociétés par actions. Des banques en France*, 1837, pp. 117–18.

500. G. THUILLIER, reference incomplete.

501. H. LUTHY, *La Banque protestante*, op. cit., I, p. 95.

502. J. MEYER, *L'Armement nantais dans la deuxième moitié du XVIIe siècle*, 1969, passim.

503. Fernand LAURENT, *En Armagnac il y a cent ans. La vie d'un aïeul (1761–1849)*, 1928, ch. X, pp. 198 ff.

504. Moscow State Archives, 93/6–428–174: the figure seems enormous. But Guy CHAUSSINAND-NOGARET, *La Noblesse au XVIIIe siècle*, 1976, p. 78, confirms, with figures to prove it, that the high nobility possessed immense fortunes: 'The incomes of princes could be reckoned in millions,' he says.

505. Beatrice F. HYSLOP, *L'Apanage de Philippe Egalité duc d'Orléans (1785–1791)*, 1965, chs. 1 and 2.

506. P. LEON, 'La reponse de l'industrie', art. cit., pp. 255–6; G. CHAUSSINAND-NOGARET, *La Noblesse*, op. cit., pp. 119, 161 and 44.

507. Jean LABASSE, *Les Capitaux et la région. Etude géographique. Essai sur le commerce et la circulation des capitaux dans la région lyonnaise*, 1955, pp. 9 ff.

508. Quoted by R. BIGO, *Les Banques françaises*, op. cit., pp. 41–2.

509. E. VINCENS, *Des Sociétés par actions*, op. cit., passim and pp. 114 ff.

510. R. BIGO, *Les Banques françaises*, op. cit., p. 41.

511. Jean-Baptiste SAY, 'De la production des richesses', in *Cours complet d'économie politique pratique*, 1966 reprint, I, p. 131.

512. *Ibid.*, I, p. 132.

513. J. EON, *Le Commerce honorable*, op. cit.

514. Jean-François FAURE-SOULET, *Economie politique et progrès au siècle des Lumières (1750–1789)*, doctoral thesis, 1964, pp. 94–5.

515. P. CHAUNU, reference incomplete.

516. Fritz WAGNER, *Europa im Zeitalter des Absolutismus und der Aufklärung*, vol. 4 of Theodore SCHEIDER, ed., *Handbuch der europäische Geschichte*, 1968, p. 104.

517. VAN DER MEULEN, *Recherches sur le commerce*, II, 1779, p. 75.

518. J. F. FAURE-SOULET, *Economie politique*, op. cit., p. 101.

519. Cf. F. BRAUDEL, *Civilization and Capitalism*, op. cit., III, pp. 312–14.

520. A.N., G⁷ 1622.

521. POTTIER DE LA HESTROYE, *Réflexions sur la dîme royale*, op. cit., passim.

522. Louis DERMIGNY, *La Chine et l'Occident. Le commerce à Canton*

au XVIIIe siècle, 1719–1833, 1964, p. 740 and note 3.

523. Michèle de SAINT-MARC, *Histoire monétaire de la France, 1800–1980*, 1983, p. 36.

524. Ange GOUDAR, *Les Intérêts de la France mal entendus*, 1756, II, p. 20.

525. A.N., G⁷ 418.

526. A.N., G⁷ 521, 19 November 1693.

527. R. BIGO, *Les Banques françaises*, op. cit., p. 42.

528. *Ibid.*, p. 114.

529. F. BAYARD, *Finances et financiers*, op. cit., p. 107; R. GASCON, *Grand commerce*, op. cit., I, p. 188.

530. Albéric de CALONNE, *La Vie agricole sous l'Ancien Régime en Picardie et en Artois*, 1883, p. 70, quoting departmental archives of the Aisne, c 765.

531. F. BRAUDEL, *Civilization and Capitalism*, op. cit., I, p. 445.

532. G. d'AVENEL, *Histoire économique*, op. cit., I, pp. 21–2.

533. M. T. BOYER et al., *Monnaie privée et pouvoir des princes*, op. cit., typescript, p. 128.

534. Maximilien de BETHUNE, duc de SULLY, *Mémoires*, 1788 edn, III, p. 6.

535. Barry E. SUPPLE, 'Currency and commerce in the early seventeenth century', in *Economic History Review*, December 1957, p. 240, note 1.

536. M. T. BOYER et al., *Monnaie privée*, op. cit., p. 55.

537. Paul RAVEAU, *Essai sur la situation économique et l'état social en Poitou au XVIe siècle*, 1931, p. 92.

538. Germain MARTIN, 'La monnaie et le crédit privé en France aux XVIe et XVIIe siècles: les faits et les théories (1550–1664)', in *Revue d'histoire des doctrines économiques et sociales*, 1909, p. 28.

539. Reference mislaid.

540. François-Nicolas MOLLIEN, *Mémoires d'un ministre du Trésor public 1780–1814*, II, 1845 edn, p. 469.

541. A piece of eight or piastre, was a coin worth 8 reals, the first silver coin minted by the Spanish in America in 1535.

542. The pistole was first minted in 1537 with gold from the New World.

543. A.N., G⁷ 1622, about 1706.

544. Jean RIVOIRE, *Histoire de la monnaie*, 1985, p. 33.

545. G. d'AVENEL, *Histoire économique*, op. cit., I, pp. 39–40.

546. J. RIVOIRE, *Histoire de la monnaie*, op. cit., p. 21.

547. G. d'AVENEL, *Histoire économique*, op. cit., I, p. 37.

548. F. BRAUDEL, *Civilization and Capitalism*, op. cit, I p. 466.

549. Richard GASCON, *Grand commerce et vie urbaine au XVIe siècle, Lyon et ses marchands*, 1971, II, p. 760.

550. M. MARION, *Dictionnaire des institutions*, op. cit., p. 384.

551. José GENTIL DA SILVA, *Banque et crédit en Italie*, 1969, I, p. 284.

552. A. GOUDAR, *Les Intérêts*, op. cit., II, p. 120.

553. Charles DUPIN, *Le Petit Producteur français*, I, 1827, p. 24.

554. *Société historique et archéologique du Périgord*, 1875, p. 50, and 1880, p. 397, quoted by G. d'AVENEL, *Histoire économique*, op. cit., I, p. 37.

555. G. d'AVENEL, *Histoire économique*, op. cit., I, p. 35.

556. André PIOGER, *La Fertois aux XVIIe et XVIIIe siècles. Histoire économique et sociale*, 1973, p. 196.

557. F. BRAUDEL, *Civilization and Capitalism*, II, pp. 90–1.

558. R. SEDILLOT, quoted by M. SAINT-MARC, *Histoire monétaire*, op. cit., p. 208.

559. Traian STOIANOVITCH, *The Commercial Revolution*, typescript, pp. 68–9.

560. E. H. PHELPS-BROWN and S. V. HOPKINS, 'Wage rates and prices: evidence for population pressure in the 16th century', in *Economica*, XXIV, 1957, p. 293, quoted by I. WALLERSTEIN, *The Modern World System*, op. cit., p. 79.

561. Jean MEUVRET, 'Circulation monétaire et utilisation économique de la monnaie dans la France du XVIe et XVIIe siècle', in *Etudes d'histoire économique, recueil d'articles*, 1971, p. 132 and note 8.

562. Marquis d'ARGENSON, *Journal*, op. cit., p. 52; cf. F. BRAUDEL, *Civilization and Capitalism*, op. cit., II, p. 426 and note 157.

563. J. GENTIL DA SILVA, *Banque et crédit*, op. cit.

564. J. MEUVRET, 'La France au temps de Louis XIV: des temps difficiles', in *Etudes d'histoire économique*, 1971, p. 27.

565. F. MOLLIEN, *Mémoires*, op. cit., III, pp. 471–2.

566. *Ibid.*, p. 478.

567. R. GASCON, *Grand commerce*, op. cit., II, pp. 569–70.

568. Yves-Marie BERCE, *Histoire des croquants*, 1974, I, p. 42, note 105.

569. J. GENTIL DA SILVA, *Banque et crédit*, op. cit., p. 404; cf. F. BRAUDEL, *Civilization and Capitalism*, op. cit., II, pp. 423–8.

570. Georges DUCHENE, *L'Empire industriel*, op. cit., *passim*; LYSIS (pseudonym of Eugène LETAILLEUR), *Les Capitalistes français contre la France*, 1916.

571. Jean BUVAT, *Journal de la Régence*, B.N., Ms Fr. 10283 III, pp. 1352–1409. Quotation from the unpublished section of the *Journal*, entitled Idées générales du nouveau système des finances.

572. Isaac de PINTO, *Traité de la circulation et du crédit*, 1771, p. 148.

573. A.N., G^7 1622, about 1706.

574. Guy THUILLIER, 'La réforme monétaire de 1785', in *Annales E.S.C.*, 1971, p. 1031, note 3; H. LUTHY, *La Banque protestante*, op. cit., II, pp. 687–8 and 706.

575. *Journaux inédits de Jean Desnoyers et d'Isaac Girard*, ed. Pierre DUFAY, 1912, p. 90, note 2.

576. Jean BOUVIER, 'Vers le capitalisme bancaire: l'expansion du crédit après Law', in F. BRAUDEL and E. LABROUSSE, eds., *Histoire économique et sociale de la France*, op. cit., II, 1970, p. 302.

577. A.N., F^{10} 242; article in the *Moniteur* of 30 September 1838.

578. J. RIVOIRE, *Histoire de la banque*, op. cit., p. 50.

579. Jean BOUVIER, 'Rapports entre systèmes bancaires et entreprises industrielles dans la croissance européenne du XIXe siècle', in *L'Industrialisation en Europe au XIXe siècle* (CNRS conference, Lyon, 1972), 1972, p. 117.

580. Jean TRENCHANT, *L'Arithmétique*, 1561, p. 342, quoted in M. T. BOYER *et al.*, *Monnaire privée et pouvoir des princes*, op. cit., p. 20.

581. Etienne BONNOT de CONDILLAC, *Le Commerce et le gouvernement*, in *Collection des*

principaux économistes, XIV, 1847, p. 306.

582. Jean BOUCHARY, *Le Marché des changes à Paris au XVIIIe siècle*, 1937, p. 37.

583. R. BIGO, *Les Banques*, op. cit., p. 69.

584. Felipe RUIZ MARTIN, *Lettres marchandes échangées entre Florence et Medina del Campo*, 1965.

585. M. T. BOYER et al., *Monnaie privée*, op. cit., p. 235.

586. Ferdinand GALIANI, *Dialogues sur le commerce des grains*, in *Collection des principaux économistes, XV: Mélanges d'économie politique*, II, 1966 reprint of 1848 edn, p. 51.

587. J. SAVARY, *Dictionnaire*, op. cit., I, p. 187.

588. F. RUIZ MARTIN, *Lettres marchandes*, op. cit.: these were the letters exchanged between Simon Ruiz and Baltasar Suarez; see letter of 30 March 1590.

589. F. MOLLIEN, *Mémoires*, op. cit., III, p. 471.

590. M. T. BOYER et al., *Monnaie privée*, op. cit., pp. 115–16.

591. *Ibid.*, pp. 302–3.

592. Reference mislaid.

593. Louis de ROUVROY, duc de SAINT-SIMON, *Mémoires*, II, Pléiade edn, 1969, p. 1029.

594. Adolphe VUITRY, *Le Désordre des finances et les excès de spéculation à la fin du règne de Louis XIV et au commencement du règne de Louis XV*, 1885, pp. 27–8.

595. Jean BOUVIER and Henry GERMAIN-MARTIN, *Finances et financiers de l'Ancien Régime*, 1969, p. 6.

596. *Ibid.*, p. 5.

597. *Mercure de France*, XI, p. 557.

598. J. BOUVIER, H. GERMAIN-MARTIN, *Finances et financiers*, op. cit., p. 40.

599. Georges MONGREDIEN, *L'Affaire Fouquet*, 1956, pp. 240 ff. Daniel DESSERT, *Argent, pouvoir et société au Grand Siècle*, 1984, says of the trial that many questions were left unasked in order not to compromise important people, including Mazarin and Colbert himself, pp. 279–310.

600. Françoise BAYARD, *Finances et financiers en France dans la première moitié du XVIIe siècle (1598–1653)*, typescript, 1984, p. 1851; D. DESSERT, *Argent, pouvoir et société*, op. cit., p. 365.

601. D. DESSERT, *Argent, pouvoir et société*, op. cit., p. 209.

602. *Ibid.*, p. 207.

603. Jean BODIN and Claude de RUBYS, quoted in H. HAUSER and A. RENAUDET, *Les Débuts de l'âge moderne*, 1938, pp. 572–3.

604. Cf. F. BRAUDEL, *Civilization and Capitalism*, op. cit., II, pp. 386 ff.

605. Full reference mislaid. See H. HAUSER and A. RENAUDET, *Les Débuts*, op. cit., p. 573.

606. On Zamet, his extraordinary career and his close acquaintance with Henri IV, see F. BAYARD, *Finances et financiers*, op. cit., IV, pp. 1141–6.

607. Henri HAUSER, 'The European Financial Crisis of 1559', in *Journal of European Business History*, 1930, pp. 241 ff., quoted by I. WALLERSTEIN, *The Modern World-System*, op. cit., p. 185.

608. Letter from Bernard to Chamillart, 12 October 1707, quoted by H. LUTHY, *La Banque protestante*, op. cit., I, p. 121.

609. *Ibid.*, I, p. 122.

610. *Ibid.*, I, p. 111.

611. *Ibid.*, I, p. 121.

612. Jacques de SAINT-GERMAIN, *Samuel Bernard, le banquier des rois*, 1960, p. 193.

613. H. LUTHY, *La Banque protestante*, op. cit., I, p. 195.

614. *Ibid.*, I, pp. 283–5.

615. *Ibid.*, I, pp. 414–15.

616. Adolphe THIERS, *Histoire de Law*, 1858, pp. 175 and 178.

617. Florence, State Archives, Francia f° 105 v°.

618. Jean-Paul SOISSONS, *Notaires et sociétés*, 1985, pp. 309 ff. Earl J. HAMILTON, 'Prices and wages at Paris under John Law's System', *Quarterly Journal of Economics*, vol. 51, 1936–7, pp. 30–69, and 'Prices and wages in Southern France under John Law's System', *Economic History Supplement* to the *Economic Journal*, vol. IV, 1934–7, pp. 442–61.

619. J. BOUVIER, 'Vers le capitalisme bancaire', art. cit., p. 321.

620. Georges PARISET, *Le Consulat et l'Empire*, in E. LAVISSE, ed., *Histoire de la France contemporaine*, II, p. 40.

621. Bertrand GILLE, *La Banque et le crédit en France de 1815 à 1848*, 1959, p. 41.

622. *Ibid.*, p. 39.

623. *Ibid.*, p. 40.

624. *Ibid.*, pp. 46–7.

625. Jean SAVANT, *Tel fut Ouvrard, le financier providentiel de Napoléon*, 1954.

626. Charles DUPIN, *Le Petit Producteur français*, I, 1827, pp. 5 ff.

627. Quoted by J. BOUVIER, 'Les premiers pas du grand capitalisme français. Le système de crédit et l'évolution des affaires de 1815 à 1848', in *La Pensée*, no. 72, March–April 1957, II, p. 67.

628. B. GILLE, *La Banque et le crédit*, op. cit., pp. 52–4.

629. F. DUCUING, *De l'organisation du crédit en France*, 1864, quoted by R. BIGO, *Les Banques françaises*, op. cit., p. 124.

630. R. BIGO, *Les Banques françaises*, op. cit., p. 125, note 1.

631. Guy PALMADE, *Capitalisme et capitalistes français au XIXe siècle*, 1961, p. 122.

632. R. BIGO, *Les Banques françaises*, op. cit., pp. 125–6.

633. G. PALMADE, *Capitalisme et capitalistes*, op. cit., pp. 133–4.

634. *Ibid.*, p. 128.

635. R. BIGO, *Les Banques françaises*, op. cit., pp. 133–4.

636. Maurice LEVY-LEBOYER, 'Le crédit et la monnaie: l'évolution institutionnelle', in F. BRAUDEL and E. LABROUSSE, eds., *Histoire économique et sociale de la France*, III/1, pp. 354–5.

637. *Ibid.*, pp. 363–4.

638. *Ibid.*, pp. 372–3.

639. Rondo CAMERON, *La France et le développement économique du l'Europe, 1800–1914*, 1971, pp. 128–30.

640. Jean BOUVIER, *Les Rothschilds*, 1967, pp. 199 ff.

641. M. LEVY-LEBOYER, 'Le crédit et la monnaie', art. cit. pp. 393–400.

642. M. LEVY-LEBOYER, 'La spécialisation des établissements bancaires', in F. BRAUDEL and E. LABROUSSE, *Histoire économique et sociale de la France*, III/1, pp. 470–1.

643. M. LEVY-LEBOYER, 'Le crédit et la monnaie', art. cit., p. 353.

644. *Ibid.*, p. 395.

645. Jean BOUVIER, 'Les profits des grandes banques françaises des

années 1850 jusqu'à la première guerre mondiale', in *Studi Storici*, April–June 1963, pp. 223–9.

646. D. DESSERT, *Argent, pouvoir et société*, op. cit., p. 80.

647. *Ibid.*, p. 88.

648. *Ibid.*, p. 71.

649. Guy CHAUSSINAND-NOGARET, *Les Financiers du Languedoc au XVIIIe siècle*, 1970, p. 236.

650. Ange GOUDAR, *Les Intérêts*, op. cit., I, pp. 70–1 and note.

651. F. BAYARD, *Finances et financiers*, op. cit., p. 918.

652. M. LEVY-LEBOYER, 'Le crédit et la monnaie', art. cit., p. 350.

653. F. BRAUDEL, *Civilization and Capitalism*, op. cit., III, p. 196.

654. Seville Archives, Marine B7 226, quoted by E. W. DAHLGREN, *Les Relations commerciales et maritimes entre la France et les côtes de l'océan Pacifique (commencement du XVIIIe siècle). I, Le Commerce de la Mer du Sud jusqu'à la paix d'Utrecht*, 1909, p. 36 and note 1.

655. Emile Bourgeois in particular.

656. Claude-Frédéric LEVY, *Capitalistes et pouvoir au siècle des Lumières*, II, *La Révolution libérale 1715–1717*, 1979, p. 10.

657. Louis Sébastien MERCIER, *Tableau de Paris*, III, 1782, pp. 198–9.

Notes to Conclusion

1. VAUBAN, *Mémoire sur la navigation*, in *Mémoires des intendants*, op. cit., p. 164.

2. P. BONNAUD, *Terres et langages*, op. cit., II, p. 23.

3. G. THUILLIER, reference incomplete.

4. Elisabeth CLAVERIE and Pierre LAMAISON, *L'Impossible Mariage, Violence et parenté en Gévaudan*, p. 339. *Les Financiers de Languedoc au XVIIe siècle*, 1970.

Glossary

aides: a form of excise duty on certain goods, especially drink; the principal indirect tax in *ancien régime* France

alpages: summer pastures in the Alps and, by extension, elsewhere

ancien régime: used of the historical period and system of government in France before 1789

araire: light swing-plough, or ard as opposed to heavy wheeled plough (*charrue*)

arbitrages: speculative buying and selling on eighteenth-century money markets

arpent: a land measure, slightly larger than an acre

arrondissement: territorial division within a *département*; in Paris, refers to the twenty postal districts

arts et metiers/arts et manufactures: industrial arts and crafts, trade skills

assignat: paper money issued during the French Revolution, non-convertible to cash but capable of being 'assigned' against sale of Church lands; in practice the *assignats* depreciated very fast

atelier: workshop, often of single artisan; used here to denote the smallest unit of production in Bourgin's classification

barque: usually an open boat

Beur: a second-generation immigrant from North Africa

bidonville: shanty-town, especially of poor housing in which immigrants lived in France in the inter- and post-war years

biens nationaux: all land nationalized during the French Revolution, whether belonging to private individuals or the Church

bocage: the landscape typically found in north-west France, where fields are divided by many hedges and woods

bordager: peasant smallholder, see *closier*

boucanier: 'buccaneer', adventurer in French West Indies, who survived by barbecuing meat of wild cattle, *boucan*

bourg: settlement, something between a large village and a small town, always the site of a market

Bourse: the Paris Stock Exchange

brassier: day labourer

cabernet: type of grape, cultivated early in south-west France

cadastre: register, originally for tax purposes, of land division and ownership *canton*: administrative division within an *arrondissement*

carreau: tiled area under covered market

cavalerie: financial term referring to multiple operations regarding bills of exchange, verging on fraud

centuriation: rectangular division into lots of Roman colonies, still visible on the ground in some parts of Provence

chambre de justice: extraordinary tribunal, especially investigating financiers in the seventeenth and early eighteenth centuries

Champagne pouilleuse: the dry part of Champagne (literally 'flea-bitten') north of Troyes, as distinct from 'la Champagne humide', 'wet Champagne', south of Troyes, or 'la Champagne berrichonne', round Bourges

charbon de bois/terre: charcoal and mined coal

châtellenie: judicial division lower than a *prévôté*

chauffeurs: name given to peasant rebels in some areas in the early nineteenth century, who burnt the feet of victims to make them talk

chaumes: the high mountain pastures in the Vosges

chef-lieu: the administrative centre of a given area: the *chef-lieu* of the *département* is the *préfecture*

chemin vicinal: road joining two villages; upkeep is the responsibility of the *commune*, as distinct from the *chemins* or *routes départementaux/ales*, for which the *département* is responsible

closier: peasant with a smallholding (*closerie*)

commandite: see *société en commandite*

commune: municipality; the smallest administrative unit in modern France. A *commune* can be a city or a village, but it is always headed by a mayor. The 'communal movement' of the Middle Ages refers to the towns' acquisition of autonomy from feudal overlords.

Conseil d'Etat: a legal body, consulted by the government on administrative affairs and legislative texts

Conseil du Commerce: advisory council in the eighteenth century, with representatives from the main commercial cities of France

conseil général: the elected council administering the *département*

contrôleur-général: sometimes translated in the text as controller-general; minister of finance under the *ancien régime*

cordelat: a type of woollen fabric made in the Mazamet area of south-west France

corvée: compulsory labour owed to a feudal lord

côte: a hillside; the Côte d'Or is the long range of low hills south of Dijon where many famous vineyards are located

coucou: a kind of post-chaise, nineteenth century

cour prévôtale: the lowest court of justice, something like a magistrate's court

croquants: generic name applied to various peasant rebels under the reigns of Henri IV and Louis XIII

cultures dérobées: 'in-between crops', such as peas, sown between harvests

curé: parish priest

denier: the twelfth part of a *sou*

département: administrative division of France introduced in 1790 and (until very recent changes in local government) administered by the prefect. Its subdivisions are the *arrondissement* and the *canton*.

dessolement: interruption of regular crop rotation by planting, say, a field of clover with a life of several years

dîme (royale): the word *dîme* is used of tithes (=one-tenth). In 1699, Vauban proposed a general direct tax, payable in proportion to income, to be known as the *Dîme royale*, but his suggestion met fierce opposition and was never tried.

disette: severe food shortage, verging on famine

douzain: coin worth *douze deniers*, or one *sou*

draille: old drove road used by transhumant sheep

écu: unit of currency, of variable value, but worth several *livres* or francs; 'crown'

écu de marc: exchange currency used at Lyon fairs

écu d'or en or: gold crown (currency)

élection: under the *ancien régime*, the *généralité* (q.v.) was subdivided into *élections*, originally coinciding with dioceses, which were basic units for tax purposes. They were administered by an *élu* (later a *subdélégue*). This arrangement was confined to provinces without provincial estates (*états*); so there were *pays d'élections* and *pays d'états*.

émottage: digging a field by hand and spade

escalin: French form of *schelling*, currency in the Netherlands

essarter: clearing woodland or scrub to create arable land

esterlin: French form of sterling, medieval currency of northern Europe

étape (avec ustensile): the system whereby troops were billeted on civilians, who had to provide bed, board 'and a place by the fire'

fabrique: works, mill, early version of factory, not necessarily mechanized

Ferme Générale: syndicate of the forty leading tax-farmers, created in the late seventeenth century to reduce numbers

fermiers-généraux: members of the *Ferme générale*: tax-farmers, who advanced money to the French Crown and reimbursed themselves by collecting royal taxes *flûte*: can mean either a warship or a heavy transport ship

four banal: bake-oven in a *seigneurie* to which tenants were supposed to bring bread for baking, paying a fee to the *seigneur*

frimaire: third month in the republican calendar: 21–2 November to 21–2 December

gabarre or *gabare*: flat-bottomed boat or barge on the Loire

gabelle: tax on salt, which was a state monopoly under the *ancien régime*

gamay: type of grape grown in south-east France

garrigue: typical landscape in the Mediterranean area: arid limestone covered with scrub

gastes: wasteland

gave: name for stream or river in the Pyrenees

généralité: the 32 areas into which France was divided under the *ancien régime*, roughly equivalent to a province and administered by an *intendant*

généraux des monnaies: direct tax-collectors, holding state office which they had bought during the *ancien régime*

grand party: state loan launched in 1555

grand siècle: the term used of the age of Louis XIV, latter seventeenth century

graves: wine from the Gironde, named from the gravelly soil in which it is grown

guingette: popular tavern, usually with a garden for open-air drinking and dancing

HLM (habituation à loyer modéré): 'low-rent housing', i.e. subsidized housing in twentieth-century French towns

haras: stud farm

haute banque: high finance, leading Paris banking families

hectare: land measure: 10,000 sq. m or 2.47 acres

(h)erm: local name for an uncultivated grass steppe in the south of France

houille blanche: literally 'white coal', used of hydraulic energy in the Alps

inspecteur des manufactures: inspectors who saw that government regulations were respected in the *manufactures*, under the *ancien régime*

intendant: overseer of a *généralité* or province, representing the Crown, acting as the eyes and ears of the central power and having certain powers of decision

jachère: fallow land

jacquerie: peasant revolt

laboureur: well-off peasant farmer

landes: heathland, especially in south-west France

langue de'oc, oïl: see *oc, oïl*

liard: a coin worth three *deniers*, or a quarter-*sou*

livre (tournois):   unit of account in *ancient régime* France, originally minted in Tours and worth a pound of silver (later devalued) worth 20 *sous*, independent of silver equivalent; also means a pound in weight

longue durée, la: literally 'the long term', an expression drawing attention to long-term structures and realities in history as distinct from medium-term factors and trends (*la conjoncture*) or short-term events (*l'évènement*)

lopinier: a peasant who farmed a tiny plot of land (*lopin*)

louis: a gold 20-franc piece

macaire: cowherd in the Vosges, usually of Swiss origin

maître des requêtes: judicial official sent on special missions under *ancien régime* (today, counsel in *Conseil d'Etat*)

mandats territoriaux: paper money issued during the French Revolution, similar to the *assignat* (q.v.)

manufacture: forerunner of the factory; building in which manufacture was concentrated, usually manual, later with some mechanization. The word *usine* was applied to the factory in the modern sense, housing machines, when it appeared.

maréchaussée: rural police force, commanded by the *prévôt-maréchal*

mars, marsage: cereals sown in March

messageries: originally royal service for carrying documents and money, later general mail service

méteil: mixture of rye and wheat, sown and harvested together

molletons: wool or cotton textile, combed on one or both sides, like flannel

muid: measure of capacity, roughly 268 litres liquid or 1,872 litres dry goods; 'hogshead'

muscat: fortified wine, a speciality of certain southern vineyards, e.g. Frontignan

négociant: wholesaler, import-export merchant

noblesse d'épée, noblesse de robe: nobles who had acquired their nobility either by feats of arms (*épée*) or by holding Crown office (*robe*)

oc, oïl: literally the forms of *oui* = 'yes' in the dialects of southern and northern France respectively. Hence the *langue d'oc* and *langue d'oïl* to denote both language and area

octroi: toll on goods entering towns

pain bis: brown or rye bread

parcours: the right to graze flocks in transit on the land of a neighbouring village

parlement: not a parliament in the modern sense, but a judicial body under the *ancien régime*, one of the 'sovereign courts'; there was a Paris *parlement* and a number of provincial *parlements* which sat in cities like Grenoble, Bordeaux etc.

partisans: another word for tax-farmers, those who signed a contract known as a *parti*

patache: a cheap and uncomfortable stage-coach; 'rattletrap'

patate: popular word for potato (*pomme de terre*)

pâtis: poor land, often left for grazing animals; 'rough pasture'

pays: within France used of districts or regions with their own identity

peusson: ancient right to graze pigs in oakwoods

pied noir: European settler in French Algeria

pinot: type of grape early cultivated in Burgundy

piquette: drink obtained by adding water to grape residue (*marc*) after pressing

Ponts et Chaussées: literally Bridges and Highways: the highways department, corps of civil engineers

quartier: district of town, esp. Paris: the *Quartier Latin*, the Latin quarter; *les beaux quartiers*, the wealthy districts, 'West End'

réal: silver Spanish coin; piece of eight

receveurs-généraux: collectors of direct taxes who bought their offices and were direct agents of the state (unlike tax-farmers), although they too sometimes advanced money to the Crown

régie: administrative body, usually for tax purposes, operated directly by the state, not through intermediaries: the tobacco monopoly, for instance, was a *régie*

rentes (sur l'Hôtel de Ville): annuities or interest-bearing bonds issued in return for loan or capital investment; the *Hôtel de Ville* (town hall) in question was that of Paris. It was a way for the Crown to raise money on security of the Paris revenues, first launched in 1522.

rescontre: (financial) clearing or compensation

saison: a field in crop rotation

sapinière: river boat made of deal, usually with a limited life

seigneurie: the feudal domain over which the *seigneur* or lord could claim rights (e.g. *corvée*) even if he did not own the land outright; used in a particular sense of towns gaining independence in the Middle Ages: '*se muer en seigneurie*'

setier: grain capacity measure, varying between 150 and 300 litres

société anonyme: limited-liability company

société en commandite: mixed-liability company, or limited partnership (partners liable only up to share invested) *sol/sou*: currency, the twentieth part of a *livre*

sole: field in crop-rotation system

sous-fermier, sous-traitant: subcontracting tax-farmers

stère: a cubic metre, used to measure timber

subdélégue: administrator of an *élection*, subordinate to an *intendant*

surintendant des finances: early version of the controller-general; it was a powerful post to occupy but usually dangerous for the incumbent

terre vaine: poor land, left untended for years and ploughed only occasionally

toise: measure of length or depth; about six feet or a fathom

tonlieu: duty charged on goods in transit; also fee paid by market stall-holders

traitant: another name for tax-farmer

tramontane: strong north-west wind which blows in Languedoc and Roussillon

Trente Glorieuses: the thirty years after 1945 which saw dramatic economic expansion in France (term coined by the economist Jean Fourastié, on the model of the 'Trois Glorieuses', the three days of the 1830 July Revolution)

turgotines: old name for royal mail-coaches set up in 1775 in Paris, after the minister of the time, Turgot

ustensile: see *étape*

vaine pâture: the right to graze flocks on land temporarily available, e.g. fields of stubble after harvest

vendémiaire: first month in the republican calendar: 21–2 September to 21–2 October

ville franche: medieval town which had emancipated itself from an overlord

visa: the state bankruptcy declared during the minority of Louis XV and the body set up to administer it

Index

cost of living, 179; land usage, 262,
343; grain, 363, 365, 378, 384; grain
riots, 394, 396; social problems, 395;
industry, 455; finance, 456, 483–4,
589, 616, 634, 636, 637, 640, 647,
653, 656, 658; circulation problems,
489, 491; industry, 516, 520, 532,
538; power, 665
Andalusia, 309, 312
Andorra, 254
Andrézieux, 492
Angers, 239, 393, 421, 427, 439, 447
Angoulème, 476
Angoumois, 329
animal farming, 258, 279, 282, 286,
287, 288, 289, 294–315, 358;
shortage of livestock, 278, 371–4;
type of care, 294–9; stabling and
open air, 299–302; buying and
selling, 302–5; transhumance, 305–8;
scientific breeding, 308–12; as
marginal activity, 313–15; see also
animals; grazing; names of animals
animals: prehistoric period, 24, 26, 28,
30, 33, 34, 35, 36, 38, 39, 49, 52;
draught, 49, 52, 142, 247–8, 251,
256–7, 295, 296, 314, 401, 675;
Celtic period, 60; wild, 171, 265–6;
disease, 240, 241; source of manure,
251, 252, 277, 285, 295, 306, 352;
fodder, 277, 367, 520; in towns, 420;
see also animal farming; names of
animals
Anjou, 273
d'Anjou, duc, 571, 645
d'Anjou, Gui, 134
Annales school, 460
Anne of Austria, 665
Annecy, 478, 494, 548
Anse, council of (994), 233
Anthony, St, 99
anti-semitism, 211, 23
Antigua, 578
Antiquités celtiques et antédiluviennes
(Boucher de Perthes), 21–2
Antwerp, 376, 457, 562, 588, 621, 626,
629, 630, 631, 642
Anzin, 523, 524, 594, 655
Anzin Mining Company, 523
Apt, 430
Aquitaine: prehistory, 36, 43, 48;
slaves, 92; Franks, 108, 110;

agriculture, 269, 305, 362, 389;
revolts, 387, 388; trade, 579
Aquitania, 59, 79
Arabia, 123
arable land, 140, 258, 260, 261, 263,
276, 288, 294, 342, 345, 352, 358; see
also names of crops grown on arable
land
Arabs, 119, 357, 560
Arago, Dominique, 527
Arbellot, Guy, 192, 470
Arbois, 330
Arches, 424
architecture, 150, 151, 172, 437
Ardèche, 303, 418
Ardennes, 112, 246, 274, 278, 343, 344
Ardrey, Robert, 35
Argens valley, 351
d'Argenson, marquis, 612, 617, 673;
Mémoires, 383, 428; Journal, 651
Argentan, 287
Argentat, 474
Argenteuil, 316
Arianism, 107
Arica, 573
Ariège, 258, 269, 530
Ariès, Philippe, 195
Ariovistus, 73, 77
Aristotle, 151
Arithmétique (Trenchant), 621
Arles, 79, 111, 122, 232, 233, 421, 433,
490
Armagnac, 590, 593
Armagnac Noir, 287, 405
Armagnacs, 160
Armorica, 62, 110, 358; see also Brittany
Armorican Massif, 358, 388
Arnould, 598
Aron, Raymond, 212
Arques, battle of (1589), 387
Arras, 233, 422, 478
Arroumet, 474
art, prehistoric, 32–3
Arte della Lana, 164, 506
Arthonnay, 366
artificial meadows see forage crops
Artois, 285, 514, 599
Arverni, 62, 75
Ashtor, Elyas, 103, 627
Asia, 95, 119, 283, 562, 672
Asia Minor, 57, 58
Aspre valley, 676

existed from time of Philip Augustus, 634, 637; farms, 636, 643, 663; farmers, 636, 639, 663; Ferme Générale, 635–6, 637, 639, 647, 648, 651, 663; and Louis XIV, 640, 662; problems, 643; Revolution, 652–3
telegraph, 495, 496, 528
Templars, 141
Terra Amata, 29
Terray, Controller-General, 651
Tertry, battle of (687), 112, 114, 117
Tessé, maréchal de, 485
Tetricus, 88
Teutons, 58, 63, 318
textiles/cloth: industry, 331, 332, 433, 452, 453–4, 511, 516, 518–19, 524, 534–5, 544–5, 562, 659; trade, 565, 567; see also names of textiles
Thames valley, 355
Thélusson, house of, 652
Theodosius, 134
Thibaud II, count, 150
Thiérache, 343, 355
Thierry, Augustin, 97
Thiers, Adolphe, 494, 650
Third Republic, 204, 335, 466, 537, 540, 614, 656
Third World, 180, 455
Thirty Years War (1618–48), 169
Thonon, 548
Thorner, Daniel, 223–4, 227
Thracian coast, 564
Three Bishoprics, 278
Thuringia, 108
Thurins, 496
Tiberius, emperor, 78, 80
Tilly, Louise, 386, 395
timber/wood, 140, 232, 474, 479, 480, 520, 522
tin, 47, 50, 53, 60, 62
Tizi Ouzou, 217
tobacco, 258, 261, 267, 576, 578, 583
Tobago, 578, 579
Tolbiac, 107
Tolfa, 567
tolls, 474, 489, 491
tombs see burial
tools: prehistoric, 21, 24, 28, 30, 34, 35, 43, 44, 45, 46, 47, 48, 52, 504; Celtic, 61; see also farm equipment
Tortuga, 577
Toul, 333

Toulon, 311, 351, 384, 424, 428; siege of, 672
Toulouse, 85, 234, 344, 392, 428, 441; and barbarian invasions, 98; three centres, 144; grain trade, 175, 269; riots, 396–7; construction work, 439; failed to industrialize, 456; investment in real estate, 456–7; railway, 494, 499–500; currency, 604, 611
Touraine, 316, 344, 638
Tourcoing, 453, 454
Tournai, 381
Tournon, Cardinal de, 641
Tournus, 234
Tours, 142, 326, 424, 447, 556, 598, 604, 622
Toutain, Jean-Claude, 369, 480, 486–8, 546
towns, 228, 321, 386, 411; Hallstatt period, 53; Celtic period, 61, 62–3, 64, 65, 66; Roman period, 79, 83–6, 227; and barbarian invasions, 88, 98–9; Merovingian period, 109, 111; growth between 950 and 1450, 132, 142–5, 231, 232; peasants sought refuge during the Fronde, 173–4; during Revolution, 201; links with countryside, 235–6, 511; provided labour for harvest, 244; wine consumption, 329; and mills, 362; need for horses, 373; food shortages, 383; and vagrants, 404, 674; detailed discussion, 415–59; urbanization, 415–18, 444–5; growing role, 419–21; and Crown, 421–3; stability of urban network, 423–5; choice of site, 425–31; people, 432–6; and French economy, 436–44, 445–9; example of Lyon, 449–52; example of Lille, 452–5; apportioning responsibility, 455–9; roads, 469; railways, 494; and industry, 511, 531
Toynbee, Arnold, 207
tractus see saltus
Traité de Charente, 491
Transalpine Gaul, 75
transhumance, 38, 231, 305–8
transport: pre-Roman, 61; and vines/wines, 290, 320, 321, 324, 334; and flour/grain, 362, 363; see also name of mode of transport